TALES TO ASTONISH #46

Plot: Stan Lee
Script: H.E. Huntley
Pencils/Inks: Don Heck
Letters: Sam Rosen

TALES TO ASTONISH #47

Plot: Stan Lee
Script: H.E. Huntley
Pencils/Inks: Don Heck
Letters: John Duffy and
Sam Rosen

TALES TO ASTONISH #48

Plot: Stan Lee
Script: H.E. Huntley
Pencils/Inks: Don Heck
Letters: Sam Rosen

TALES TO ASTONISH #49

Writer: Stan Lee
Pencils: Jack Kirby
Inks: Don Heck
Letters: Sam Rosen

TALES TO ASTONISH #50

Writer: Stan Lee
Pencils: Jack Kirby
Inks: Steve Ditko
Letters: Sam Rosen

TALES TO ASTONISH #51

Writer: Stan Lee
Pencils: Jack Kirby
Inks: Dick Ayers
Letters: Art Simek

WASP FEATURE

Writer: Stan Lee
Script/Pencils: Larry Lieber
Inks: George Bell
Letters: Art Simek

TALES TO ASTONISH #52

Writer: Stan Lee
Pencils/Inks: Dick Ayers
Letters: Art Simek

WASP FEATURE

Writer: Stan Lee
Script/Pencils: Larry Lieber
Inks: George Bell
Letters: Art Simek

TALES TO ASTONISH #53

Writer: Stan Lee
Pencils/Inks: Dick Ayers
Letters: Sam Rosen

WASP FEATURE

Writer: Stan Lee
Script/ Pencils: Larry Lieber
Inks: Don Heck
Letters: Ray Holloway

TALES TO ASTONISH #54

Writer: Stan Lee
Pencils/Inks: Don Heck
Letters: Art Simek

WASP FEATURE

Writer: Stan Lee
Script/Pencils: Larry Lieber
Inks: Sal Brodsky
Letters: Art Simek

TALES TO ASTONISH #55

Writer: Stan Lee
Pencils/Inks: Dick Ayers
Letters: Art Simek

WASP FEATURE

Writer: Stan Lee
Script/ Pencils: Larry Lieber
Inks: George Bell
Letters: Sherri Gail

ESSENTIAL
ASTONISHING
ANT-MAN
VOL. 1

TALES TO ASTONISH #65

Writer: Stan Lee
Pencils: Bob Powell
Inks: Don Heck
Letters: Sheri Gail

TALES TO ASTONISH #66

Writer: Stan Lee
Pencils: Bobby Powell
Inks: Frank Ray
Letters: Sheri Gail

TALES TO ASTONISH #67

Writer: Stan Lee
Pencils: Bob Powell
Inks: Chic Stone
Letters: Art Simek

TALES TO ASTONISH #68

Writer: Stan Lee
Pencils: Bob Powell
Inks: Vince Colletta
Letters: Sam Rosen

TALES TO ASTONISH #69

Writer: Al Hartley
Pencils: Bob Powell
Inks: John Giunta
Letters: Sam Rosen

REPRINT CREDITS

PRESIDENT & COO
PUBLISHING,
CONSUMER PRODUCTS
& NEW MEDIA
BILL JEMAS

EDITOR IN CHIEF
JOE QUESADA

DIRECTOR-PUBLISHING
OPERATIONS
BOB GREENBERGER

COLLECTIONS EDITOR
MATTY RYAN

ASSISTANT EDITOR
MIKE FARAH

MANUFACTURING
REPRESENTATIVE
FENTON ENG

PRODUCTION ASSISTANT
CORY SEDLMEIER

COVER & INTERIOR
DESIGN
**JOHN 'JG' ROSHELL
OF COMICRAFT**

COVER ART
JACK KIRBY

COVER COLORS
CHRIS DICKEY

ESSENTIAL ANT-MAN™ VOL 1. Contains material originally published in magazine form as Tales to Astonish #27, 35-69. First printing, February 2002. ISBN# 0-7851-0822-X. Published by MARVEL COMICS, a division of MARVEL ENTERTAINMENT GROUP, INC. OFFICE OF PUBLICATION: 10 EAST 40th STREET, NEW YORK, NY 10016.

10 9 8 7 6 5 4 3 2 1

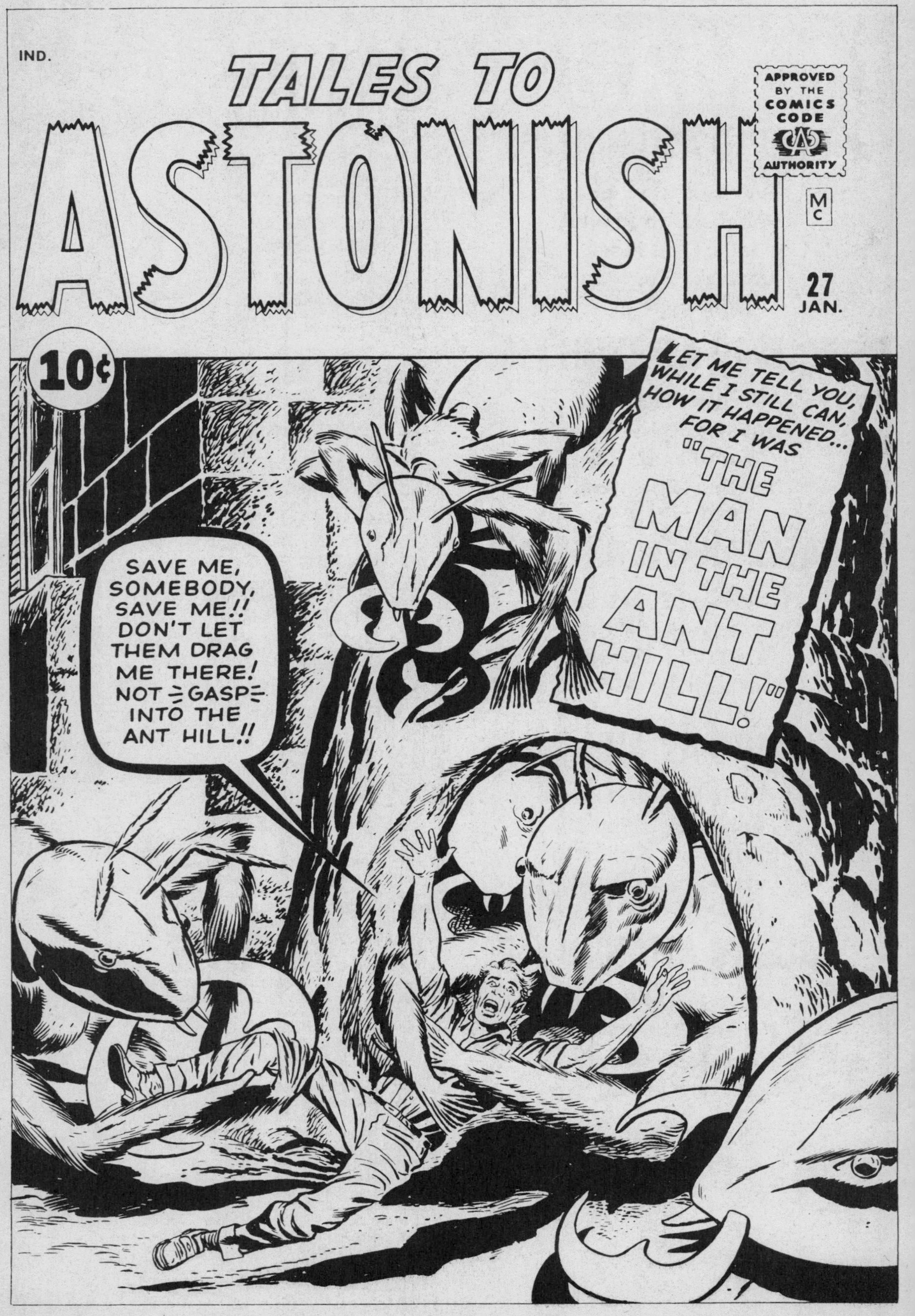

IND.
TALES TO ASTONISH
APPROVED BY THE COMICS CODE AUTHORITY
MC
27
JAN.
10¢
LET ME TELL YOU, WHILE I STILL CAN, HOW IT HAPPENED... FOR I WAS "THE MAN IN THE ANT HILL!"
SAVE ME, SOMEBODY, SAVE ME!! DON'T LET THEM DRAG ME THERE! NOT =GASP= INTO THE ANT HILL!!

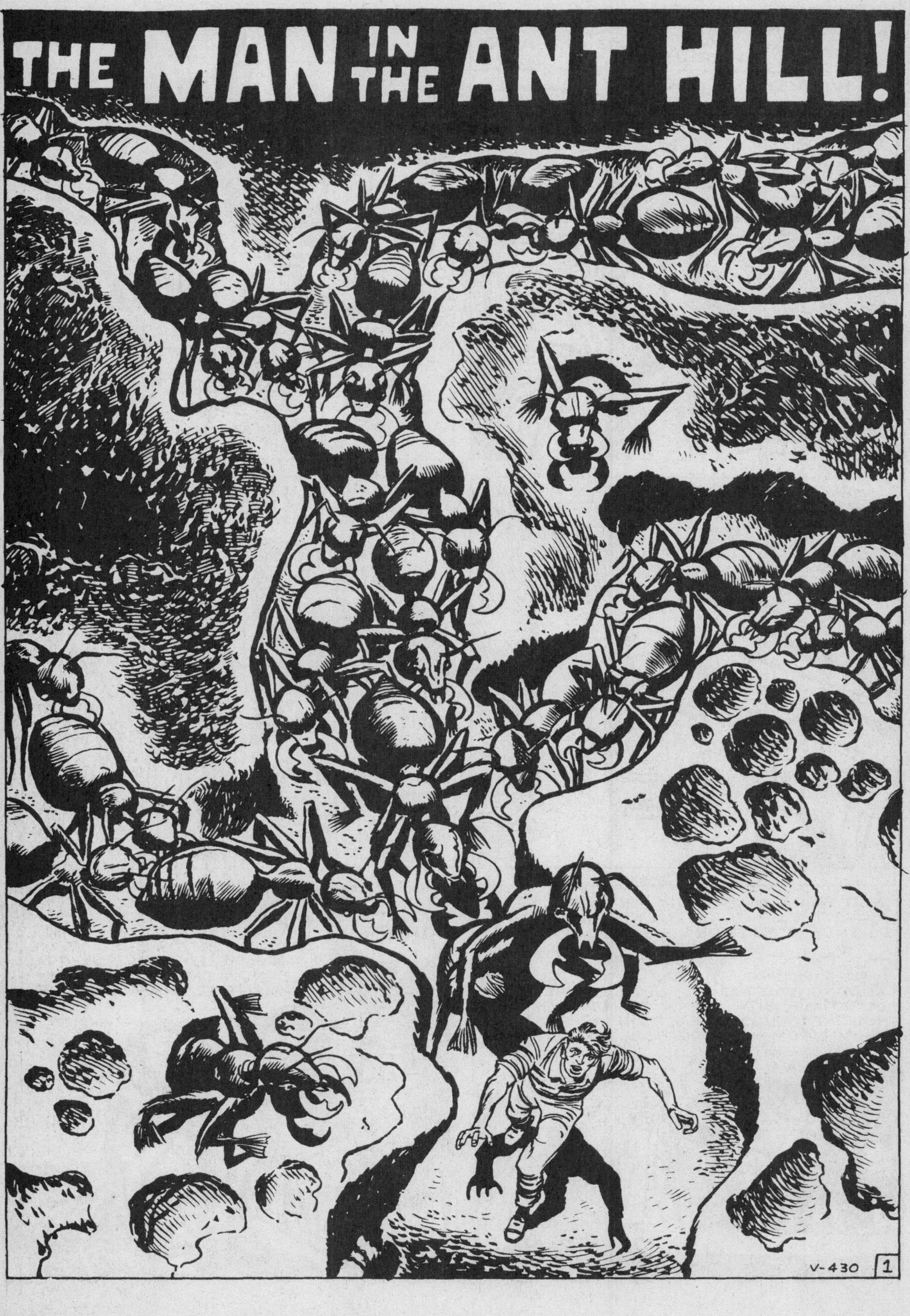
THE MAN IN THE ANT HILL!
V-430

LIVING NIGHTMARES CAN BEGIN IN MANY WAYS! HENRY PYM'S BEGAN WITH A CRY OF TRIUMPH!

IT **WORKS!** I'VE **DONE** IT.!!

I'VE REDUCED THE CHAIR TO DOLL SIZE!

NOW I ONLY HAVE TO APPLY A FEW DROPS OF MY GROWTH POTION...

...AND THE CHAIR RETURNS AGAIN TO ITS NORMAL SIZE!

THIS IS THE GREATEST TRIUMPH I HAVE EVER KNOWN!

AND, WHILE THE CHAIR ENLARGES, HENRY PYM'S THOUGHTS GO BACK... BACK TO A SCIENCE CONVENTION SEVERAL MONTHS AGO...

BAH! YOU'RE ALWAYS WASTING OUR TIME WITH YOUR RIDICULOUS THEORIES! BUT THEY NEVER WORK!

YOU SHOULD STICK TO PRACTICAL PROJECTS!

NO! I'LL WORK ONLY ON THINGS THAT APPEAL TO MY IMAGINATION... LIKE MY LATEST INVENTION!

OH... WHAT'S **THAT?**

I WON'T TELL YOU YET! YOU WOULD ONLY LAUGH AT ME AS YOU'VE DONE BEFORE! BUT WHEN I'VE FINISHED IT, I'LL SHOW YOU! THEN, YOU SHALL KNOW I'M A GREATER SCIENTIST THAN **ANY** OF YOU!

2

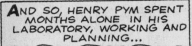
AND SO, HENRY PYM SPENT MONTHS ALONE IN HIS LABORATORY, WORKING AND PLANNING...

SOON I'LL HAVE MY SERUMS PERFECTED! THEN I SHALL BE ABLE TO CHANGE THE SIZE OF ANY OBJECT! WHAT A BOON IT WILL BE FOR MANKIND!

ANYTHING COULD BE REDUCED IN SIZE AND SHIPPED FOR A FRACTION OF THE COST!

AN ENTIRE ARMY COULD BE TRANSPORTED IN ONE AIRPLANE...

BOY! WHAT A WEIRD FEELING!

YEAH, BUT THERE'S NOTHING TO WORRY ABOUT! AS SOON AS WE REACH OUR DESTINATION, THE ENLARGING SERUM WILL RETURN US TO OUR NORMAL SIZE AGAIN!

SO, AT LAST, THE GREAT DAY HAS COME-- MY SERUMS ARE FINISHED! I'VE TESTED THEM ON THE CHAIR-- AND THEY WORK! NOW ALL THAT REMAINS IS TO TEST THEM ON A *LIVING* OBJECT-- ON *MYSELF!!*

FIRST, I'LL TAKE A FEW DROPS OF THE REDUCING POTION!

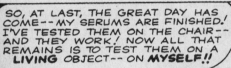

ALMOST AT THE INSTANT OF CONTACT, THE FANTASTIC SERUM STARTS TO ACT!

IT'S SHRINKING ME SO FAST, I CAN *SEE* MYSELF CHANGE!

I'M BECOMING SMALLER AND SMALLER!

IT-- IT'S WORKING FASTER THAN I EXPECTED!...*TOO FAST!*

3

FRANTICALLY, HENRY PYM RACES AROUND THE ROOM, AS FEAR GRIPS HIS HEART! FINALLY, BEFORE HE KNOWS IT, HE HAS STUMBLED THRU THE OPEN DOOR AND--

HOW WILL I EVER GET BACK TO NORMAL?!!

I LEFT THE ANTIDOTE ON THE WINDOW LEDGE! I COULD **NEVER** REACH IT NOW!

NOBODY CAN HELP ME!! NOBODY ≈GASP≈ CAN EVEN **HEAR** MY SMALL, WEAK VOICE NOW!

BUT HENRY PYM IS WRONG! **SOME** EARS **DO** HEAR HIM... UNFORTUNATELY!!

SUDDENLY, THE FRANTIC MAN STOPS SHRINKING! BUT HE IS TOO PANICKY TO NOTICE IT, FOR AT THAT MOMENT, HE SEES A NEARBY **ANT HILL**!

THE ANTS HAVE SPOTTED ME! THEY'RE **ATTACKING**!

CRAWLING SWIFTLY AND SURELY OVER THE GROUND, THE MENACING INSECTS SOON SURROUND THE HAPLESS SCIENTIST!

THEY'RE COMING CLOSER... NO ESCAPE... UNLESS... THE ANT HILL! MAYBE I CAN HIDE IN THERE! IT'S MY ONLY CHANCE!!

THE ANTS BUILD TUNNELS AND CHAMBERS IN THEIR HILLS! IF I CAN JUST HIDE IN ONE OF THEM LONG ENOUGH TO FIGURE A WAY OUT OF THIS NIGHTMARE!

BUT AS LUCK WOULD HAVE IT, THE FRIGHTENED FUGITIVE COMES UPON AN OPEN SHAFT, WHICH HE DOESN'T SEE UNTIL IT'S TOO LATE!!

WHA--?

HELLLLP!!

THE STUFF BELOW! IT'S-- IT'S--

4

...IT'S **HONEY!!**

THE ANTS STORE IT FOR FOOD!

IT'S SO STICKY, I CAN'T GET **FREE** OF IT! THE MORE I **STRUGGLE,** THE TIGHTER IT HOLDS ME!

AND THEN...

AN ANT! HE'S SEEN ME! HE'S CRAWLING TOWARD ME!

IT'S **INCREDIBLE!** HE-- HE'S TRYING TO PULL ME **OUT** OF THE HONEY!!

HE **DID** IT! HE FREED ME! AND NOW HE'S LETTING ME **GO!** HE DOESN'T WANT TO HARM ME!

BUT SUDDENLY THE REMAINDER OF THE ATTACKING HORDE CLOSES IN! AND, AS THE EXHAUSTED HUMAN FALLS BACK IN FEAR, HE SEES...

A **MATCHSTICK!** THEY MUST HAVE BROUGHT IT HERE WHEN THEY BUILT THIS ANT HILL!

IF ONLY IT HASN'T GOTTEN TOO DAMP!

SWIFTLY, NERVOUSLY, THE DESPERATE MAN PICKS UP A PEBBLE, HURLING IT AT THE SULFURIC HEAD OF THE MATCH!

I MUSTN'T **MISS!!** I MUSTN'T!!

5

WITH A SILENT PRAYER OF RELIEF, HE SEES THE PEBBLE STRIKE THE MATCH-HEAD, IGNITING IT!

THE FIRE WILL KEEP THE ANTS AT BAY--LONG ENOUGH FOR ME TO USE THIS MAKE-SHIFT LASSO!

SO FAR, SO GOOD! B-BUT WHAT'S THAT ABOVE ME?

OH NO!!

ANOTHER ANT--WAITING FOR ME!

WITH ALL ITS FURY, THE PREDATORY INSECT ATTACKS THE TINY HUMAN!

UHHH-- STRONG--TOO STRONG FOR ME!

BUT I HAVE ONE ADVANTAGE! A HUMAN BRAIN...

...WHICH HAS LEARNED THE ART OF JUDO!

UP AHEAD... A PATH OUT OF THIS ACCURSED ANT HILL!! IF I CAN ONLY MANAGE TO REACH SAFETY!

LONG, FRENZIED, FEAR-FILLED MINUTES LATER...

MADE IT!! AND NOW... THERE, UP ON THE WINDOW LEDGE IS MY ENLARGING SERUM! THE ONLY THING THAT CAN RETURN ME TO NORMAL SIZE! BUT HOW AM I GOING TO GET TO IT?? I CAN'T CLIMB UP THE WALL!!

IT'S HOPELESS! THEY'RE ALMOST UPON ME!

I--I JUST CAN'T RUN ANY MORE!

6

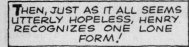

THEN, JUST AS IT ALL SEEMS UTTERLY HOPELESS, HENRY RECOGNIZES ONE LONE FORM!

THE ANT WHO SAVED ME BEFORE! MAYBE--MAYBE HE'LL DO IT AGAIN!!

IF I POINT TO THE WINDOW LEDGE, PERHAPS HE'LL SENSE MY MEANING! IF--IF ONLY HE'LL UNDERSTAND!

AND THE INSECT **DOES** UNDERSTAND! FOR, A MOMENT LATER HE BEGINS THE GRUELING CRAWL UP THE SHEER, STEEP WALL!!

HE'S TAKING ME UP TO THE WINDOW! I'M GOING TO BE SAVED! **SAVED!**

THE SERUM!!

I-I'M **GROWING**!!

I'M GETTING **BIGGER AND BIGGER**!!

I'M **NORMAL** AGAIN!! I'M A **MAN** AGAIN!

AND NOW, THE FIRST THING I MUST DO IS DESTROY THESE GROWTH POTIONS!! THEY'RE FAR TOO DANGEROUS TO EVER BE USED BY ANY HUMAN AGAIN!

AND, AT THE NEXT MONTHLY MEETING OF THE SCIENCE FELLOWSHIP...

SO YOUR EXPERIMENTS FAILED?!

YES! YOU WERE RIGHT! THEY WERE JUST A FOOLISH WASTE OF TIME! FROM NOW ON I'LL STICK TO PRACTICAL PROJECTS!

AND SO, OUR TALE IS ENDED... EXCEPT FOR ONE BRIEF NOTE: NEVER AGAIN DID HENRY PYM KNOWINGLY STEP UPON AN ANT HILL! FOR HE KNEW THAT SOMEWHERE BENEATH HIM, UNKNOWN, AND UNRECOGNIZED, WAS ONE LITTLE INSECT-- ONE SMALL ANT, TO WHOM HE OWED HIS VERY LIFE!

THE END

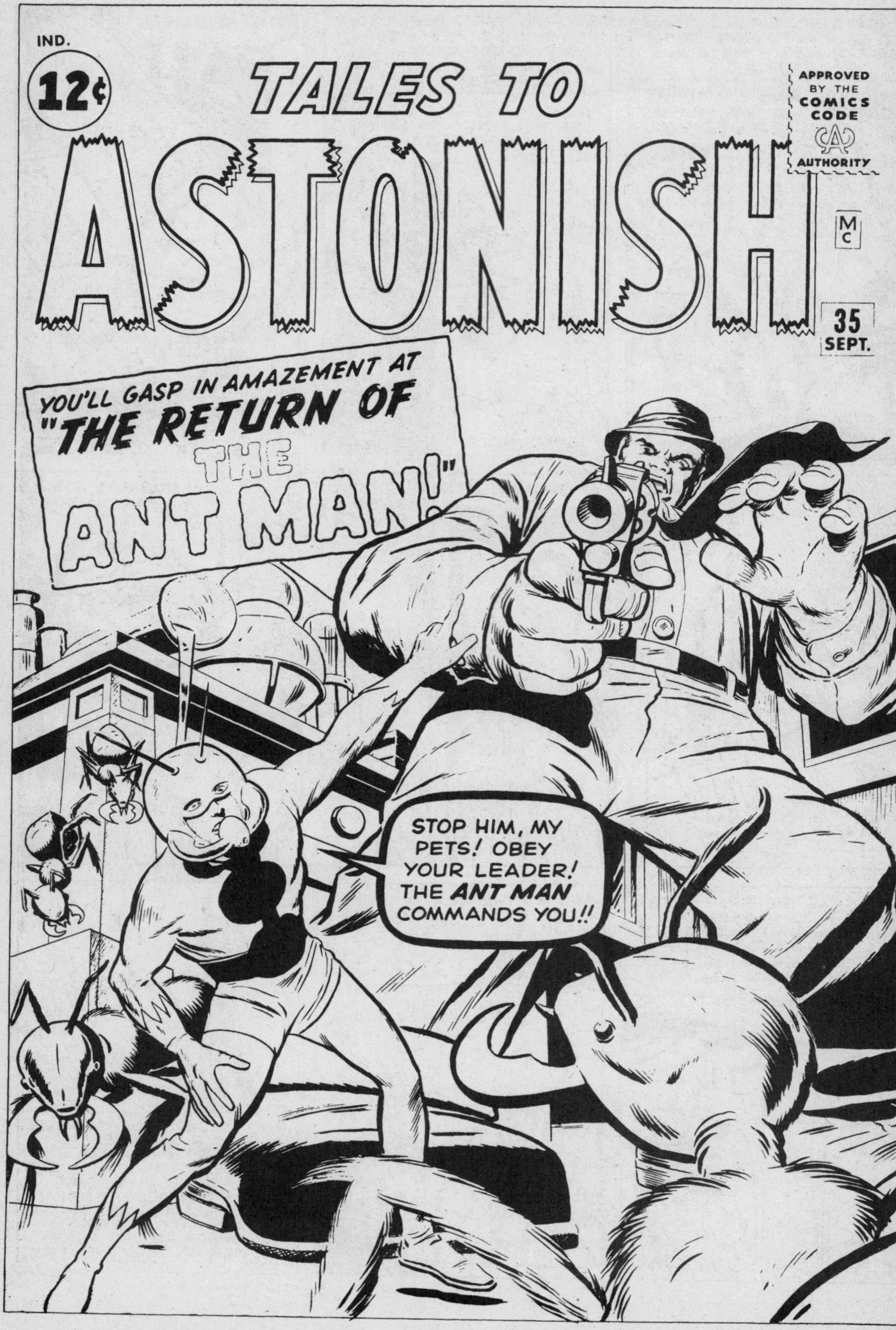
IND.
12¢
TALES TO
ASTONISH
APPROVED BY THE COMICS CODE AUTHORITY
MC
35
SEPT.
YOU'LL GASP IN AMAZEMENT AT
"THE RETURN OF THE ANT MAN!"
STOP HIM, MY PETS! OBEY YOUR LEADER! THE ANT MAN COMMANDS YOU!!

"RETURN OF THE ANT-MAN"

PART 1

In a previous issue of this magazine, we brought you the nightmarish story of Henry Pym, a scientist who invented two incredible serums... one, to reduce objects, and the other to *enlarge* them back to their natural size!

This will be a great boon to mankind! But first, I must make sure it works!

The reducing potion is taking effect! It's working so fast that I can feel myself shrinking!

BUT THE POTION PROVED MORE POWERFUL THAN HENRY PYM HAD ANTICIPATED! IT REDUCED HIM TO THE SIZE OF AN INSECT...AND LED HIM INTO THE MOST FRIGHTENING ENCOUNTER OF HIS LIFE-- *WITHIN A TEEMING ANT-HILL!*

FRANTICALLY, PYM ESCAPED FROM THE ANTS, AND REACHED HIS *ENLARGING* SERUM!

THANK HEAVENS-- IT'S MAKING ME *GROW!*

AFTER HE WAS RESTORED TO NORMAL SIZE, THE SCIENTIST DESTROYED HIS POTIONS, WHICH HE FELT WERE FAR TOO DANGEROUS TO EXIST ON EARTH! HOWEVER, WEEKS LATER...

SO GREAT A DISCOVERY MUST NOT MELT INTO NOTHINGNESS! I MUST CONCOCT THE SERUMS AGAIN!

BUT, THIS TIME...

I WILL HIDE THEM SAFELY AWAY! NO ONE EXCEPT ME WILL EVER KNOW OF THEIR EXISTENCE!

SOMEDAY THE WORLD MAY BE READY FOR THEM ... BUT UNTIL THEN, THEY SHALL REMAIN IN MY SECRET SAFE!

THERE IS ONE OTHER IMPORTANT FACT WORTH NOTING... AFTER HIS EXPERIENCE IN THE ANT-HILL, PYM DEVELOPED A GROWING INTEREST IN ANTS!

IT'S *AMAZING!* THOSE INSECTS ARE ABLE TO LIFT OBJECTS 50 TIMES *HEAVIER* THAN THEMSELVES!

SECRETLY, CONTINUALLY, HE MADE A THOROUGH STUDY OF THE ANT WORLD...

IN EACH COLONY THERE ARE ONLY A FEW *FEMALES** BUT THERE ARE THOUSANDS OF *WORKERS***!

NOTE! * FEMALES ARE CALLED *QUEENS!*
** *WORKERS* ARE SMALLER THAN QUEENS AND ARE *WINGLESS!*

WE KNOW THAT ANTS HAVE SENSE ORGANS AND A NERVOUS SYSTEM! THEY DETECT THINGS BY SIGHT, SMELL AND TOUCH!

BUT NOBODY KNOWS HOW ANTS ARE ACTUALLY ABLE TO *COMMUNICATE* AMONG THEMSELVES!

2

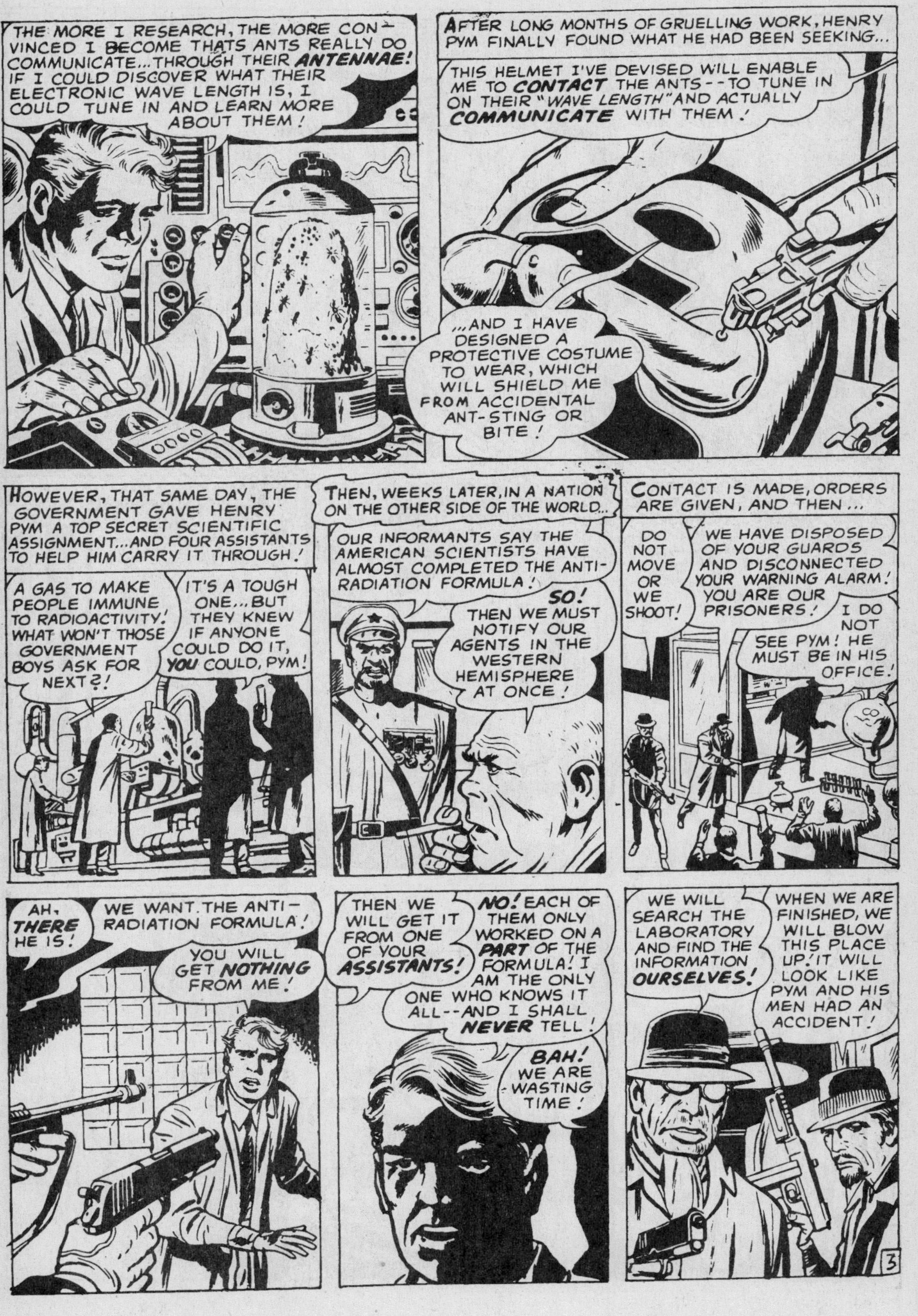
THE MORE I RESEARCH, THE MORE CONVINCED I BECOME THATS ANTS REALLY DO COMMUNICATE... THROUGH THEIR ANTENNAE! IF I COULD DISCOVER WHAT THEIR ELECTRONIC WAVE LENGTH IS, I COULD TUNE IN AND LEARN MORE ABOUT THEM!
AFTER LONG MONTHS OF GRUELLING WORK, HENRY PYM FINALLY FOUND WHAT HE HAD BEEN SEEKING...
THIS HELMET I'VE DEVISED WILL ENABLE ME TO CONTACT THE ANTS--TO TUNE IN ON THEIR "WAVE LENGTH" AND ACTUALLY COMMUNICATE WITH THEM!
...AND I HAVE DESIGNED A PROTECTIVE COSTUME TO WEAR, WHICH WILL SHIELD ME FROM ACCIDENTAL ANT-STING OR BITE!
HOWEVER, THAT SAME DAY, THE GOVERNMENT GAVE HENRY PYM A TOP SECRET SCIENTIFIC ASSIGNMENT... AND FOUR ASSISTANTS TO HELP HIM CARRY IT THROUGH!
A GAS TO MAKE PEOPLE IMMUNE TO RADIOACTIVITY! WHAT WON'T THOSE GOVERNMENT BOYS ASK FOR NEXT?!
IT'S A TOUGH ONE... BUT THEY KNEW IF ANYONE COULD DO IT, YOU COULD, PYM!
THEN, WEEKS LATER, IN A NATION ON THE OTHER SIDE OF THE WORLD...
OUR INFORMANTS SAY THE AMERICAN SCIENTISTS HAVE ALMOST COMPLETED THE ANTI-RADIATION FORMULA!
SO! THEN WE MUST NOTIFY OUR AGENTS IN THE WESTERN HEMISPHERE AT ONCE!
CONTACT IS MADE, ORDERS ARE GIVEN, AND THEN...
DO NOT MOVE OR WE SHOOT!
WE HAVE DISPOSED OF YOUR GUARDS AND DISCONNECTED YOUR WARNING ALARM! YOU ARE OUR PRISONERS!
I DO NOT SEE PYM! HE MUST BE IN HIS OFFICE!
AH, THERE HE IS!
WE WANT THE ANTI-RADIATION FORMULA!
YOU WILL GET NOTHING FROM ME!
THEN WE WILL GET IT FROM ONE OF YOUR ASSISTANTS!
NO! EACH OF THEM ONLY WORKED ON A PART OF THE FORMULA! I AM THE ONLY ONE WHO KNOWS IT ALL--AND I SHALL NEVER TELL!
BAH! WE ARE WASTING TIME!
WE WILL SEARCH THE LABORATORY AND FIND THE INFORMATION OURSELVES!
WHEN WE ARE FINISHED, WE WILL BLOW THIS PLACE UP! IT WILL LOOK LIKE PYM AND HIS MEN HAD AN ACCIDENT!
3

THEY'VE POSTED A GUARD IN FRONT OF MY DOOR AND THERE'S ANOTHER OUTSIDE...SO I CAN'T ESCAPE BY THE WINDOW, EITHER! I'M ISOLATED--TRAPPED IN MY LAB!

BUT WAIT--THERE *IS* A WAY TO STOP THEM! IT'S A FANTASTIC PLAN...

SNAP

...BUT IT *HAS* TO WORK! IF IT FAILS, THE COMMIES WILL HAVE THE ANTI-RADIATION GAS, WHICH WILL PUT THEM MILES AHEAD OF US IN THE COLD WAR!

BUT THEY'LL BE STOPPED...BY A MERE RUBBER BAND AND SOME THREAD, AMONG OTHER THINGS!

I'LL JUST SET THIS ASH TRAY ON THE FLOOR AND STRETCH THE RUBBER BAND ON IT SO...

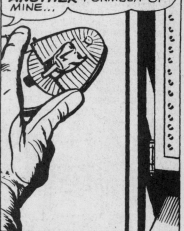

NOW IT IS TIME TO USE *ANOTHER* FORMULA OF MINE...

THE MOST POTENT SERUM EVER DEVELOPED BY MAN!

A SERUM THAT CAN REDUCE A MAN TO THE SIZE OF AN INSECT!

IT'S WORKING!

4

AT LAST! I'M NO BIGGER THAN AN ANT! NOW TO DO WHAT MUST BE DONE!

WHEN I WAS A CHILD, I WENT ON LOTS OF THRILLING RIDES IN THE AMUSEMENT PARK!

BUT *THIS* WILL BEAT ANY OF THEM!

WHOOSHH

MADE IT!

THE CRACK IS SMALL, BUT NOT TOO SMALL FOR AN ANT-SIZE HUMAN TO FIT THROUGH!

I GUESSED RIGHT... THE THREAD REACHES RIGHT DOWN TO THE GROUND!

AND THERE'S MY DESTINATION-- *THE ANT HILL!!*

PART 2

"AN ARMY OF ANTS!"

MUST BE CAREFUL! I DON'T WANT THE ANTS TO SEE ME YET!

WAIT-- I FEEL VIBRATIONS AGAINST MY HELMET!

VIBRATIONS--JUST AS I SUSPECTED! THE ANTS' ANTENNAE **DO** GIVE OFF ELECTRONIC IMPULSES! **THAT'S** HOW THEY COMMUNICATE WITH EACH OTHER!

TWOINNN'GG

BUT, SUDDENLY...

THEY'RE TURNING AROUND! THEY'RE COMING THIS WAY! B-BUT HOW DID THEY ?? OH, NO, I **FORGOT**--

I FORGOT THAT THEY HAVE A HIGHLY DEVELOPED SENSE OF **SMELL**! THEY'RE ABLE TO DETECT ANY ALIEN CREATURE NEAR THEM!

6

THEY HATE INTRUDERS! THEY'LL KILL ME UNLESS--

--UNLESS I SWITCH ON MY HELMET AND GIVE OUT MY *OWN* ELECTRONIC IMPULSES!

THE *CYBERNETIC HELMET*-- BUILT FOR COMMUNICATION BETWEEN MAN AND INSECT...

SHELL HOUSES MINIATURIZED ELECTRONIC EQUIPMENT

ANTENNA

I'VE GOT IT ON FULL POWER! *IT'S WORKING! MY* WAVELENGTH IS STRONGER THAN *THEIRS!* THEY'RE STOPPING! THEY'RE *AFRAID OF ME!*

TRANSMITTER SENDS IMPULSES FROM WEARER ON ANTS' FREQUENCY

DECODER... A MINIATURE COMPUTER THAT CHANGES INCOMING AND OUTGOING SIGNALS INTO INTELLIGIBLE MEANINGS

RECEIVER OPEN TO VIBRATIONS FROM ANTS' ANTENNAE

ALL OF THEM, EXCEPT *HIM!* HE'S THE LARGEST OF THE WORKER ANTS* AND HE'S--*HE'S ATTACKING!!*

*NOTE! IN ANT COLONIES, LARGE WORKERS DO THE FIGHTING, FOOD GATHERING AND EXPLORING! SMALL WORKERS CARRY, FORAGE, BUILD AND TEND THE YOUNG!

AN INSTANT LATER, THE POWERFUL INSECT STRIKES...

BUT, TO HIS SURPRISE, HENRY PYM IS ABLE TO LIFT HIS LARGE ADVERSARY INTO THE AIR...

...AND HURL HIM AWAY WITH EASE!

IT'S INCREDIBLE! BUT THERE'S ONLY *ONE* POSSIBLE EXPLANATION! WHEN I TOOK THE REDUCING SERUM THIS TIME, IT DIMINISHED MY *SIZE,* BUT NOT MY *STRENGTH!* I *STILL* HAVE THE STRENGTH OF A FULL-GROWN MAN!

7

HERE COMES THAT SAME WORKER AGAIN! LOOKS LIKE HE'S GETTING SET TO *BITE* ME!

FAST AS THE *ANT-MAN* IS, THE ENRAGED INSECT IS EVEN FASTER!

OWW!!

BUT THE COLORFUL COSTUME HENRY PYM HAD DESIGNED SERVES ITS PURPOSE WELL! ITS CLOSELY WOVEN FINE STEEL MESH* PROTECTS HIS HUMAN SKIN FROM THE ANT'S RAZOR SHARP MANDIBLES, AND THEN...

NOW!!

*NOTE: THE *ANT-MAN'S* COSTUME IS MADE OF STEEL MESH CONSISTING OF UNSTABLE MOLECULES WHICH STRETCH AND CONTRACT AS HIS OWN BODY DOES!

ONE JUDO BLOW IS ALL IT WILL TAKE TO STOP HIM!

NEXT, I HAVE TO FIND A WAY TO GET THE *REST* OF THESE ANTS OUT OF HERE AND INTO MY LABORATORY!

I'LL TURN UP MY ELECTRONIC IMPULSES AGAIN!

I MUST CONCENTRATE HARD--MY THOUGHTS MUST BE CLEARLY TRANSMITTED TO THIS MIDGET ARMY!

IT'S WORKING! THEY'RE CRAWLING OUT OF ALL THE CHAMBERS!

BUT, NO SOONER DOES HENRY PYM EXIT FROM THE ANT HILL...

A BEETLE! FROM DOWN HERE, HE'S THE SIZE OF A DINOSAUR! HE'S BEEN ATTRACTED BY MY COLORFUL COSTUME!

USING HIS FULL-SIZE STRENGTH, WHICH HE HAS RETAINED, THE TINY HUMAN IS ABLE TO DIG A DEEP HOLE IN MERE SECONDS...

8

WITH HIMSELF AS BAIT, THE ANT-MAN LURES HIS FOE NEAR THE HOLE, WHERE...

HE'S ATTACKING! BUT I'VE MANEUVERED HIM SO THAT THE SUNLIGHT IS GLARING IN HIS EYES!!

NOW TO DUCK AT THE RIGHT SECOND--

I BEAT HIM!

NOW I'LL JUST FILL UP THE HOLE--AND BY THE TIME THE BEETLE CAN DIG HIS WAY OUT, I'LL BE LONG GONE!

CONTINUING WITH HIS FANTASTIC PLAN, HENRY PYM MOUNTS ONE OF THE LARGEST WORKER ANTS...

STEADY-- DO NOT BE AFRAID! I SHALL NOT HURT YOU!

CLIMB! CLIMB UP THE WALL! FOR ME, IT IS MUCH TOO STEEP TO SCALE, BUT YOU CAN DO IT EASILY!

HEED ME, THE REST OF YOU--FOLLOW US!

MY ASSISTANTS ARE STILL HELPLESSLY TIED UP!

WE HAVE ALMOST GATHERED ALL THE NOTES ABOUT THE ANTI-RADIATION GAS!

SOON WE'LL BE READY TO LEAVE! AND WHEN WE DO...

... WE WILL BLOW UP THE LABORATORY BEHIND US! EVERYONE WILL THINK THE AMERICANS HAD AN UNFORTUNATE ACCIDENT!

I MUST UNTIE TOM AND THE OTHERS... AND PUT THE SPIES' GUNS OUT OF ACTION!

9

TOM, IT'S *ME*, HENRY PYM! I'VE COME TO *HELP* YOU!

IT'S *USELESS!* HE—HE CAN'T *HEAR* ME! MY VOICE IS TOO LOW! EVEN IF I *SCREAMED*, IT WOULDN'T BE AUDIBLE TO HIM!

WELL, NO MATTER! I'LL SOON HAVE HIM UNTIED!

BUT, AS THE *ANT-MAN* CLIMBS OVER HIS ASSISTANT'S HAND, THE LARGER MAN REACTS THE WAY ANYONE MIGHT TO THE SENSATION OF A CRAWLING INSECT...

NO! DON'T SHAKE ME OFF—*DON'T*—

FALLING HELPLESSLY, THE *ANT-MAN* FRANTICALLY TURNS ON HIS TRANSMITTER AND SENDS AN URGENT CALL FOR HELP TO HIS INSECT FOLLOWERS! THEY QUICKLY GATHER AND FORM A LIVING NET TO CUSHION HIS FALL...

JUST IN TIME!

AGAIN HENRY PYM ATTEMPTS TO UNTIE HIS ASSISTANT'S BOND...WITH THE HELP OF HIS NEW ALLIES...

AND *THIS* TIME—HE *SUCCEEDS!*

NOW IT'S *OUR* TURN TO STRIKE BACK!

10

PART 3 "The ANT-MAN'S REVENGE!"

ONE BY ONE, HENRY PYM, FREES HIS ASSISTANTS, BUT YET, THE TINY HUMAN'S TASK IS ONLY *HALF DONE!*

MY MEN *STILL* CAN'T ATTACK THE SPIES, WHILE THEY'RE SO WELL-ARMED!

I MUST COMMUNICATE WITH THE ANTS AGAIN! I MUST MAKE THEM UNDERSTAND WHAT THEY ARE TO DO!

MOMENTS LATER, A SWARM OF WORKER ANTS CRAWL OVER TO ONE OF THE SPIES...

AND, AT AN ELECTRONIC SIGNAL FROM THEIR NEW MASTER, THE WORKERS *ATTACK* -- BITING AND STINGING THEIR HUMAN VICTIM!

YIIEEEE

11

THEN, HENRY PYM SIGNALS A SWARM OF HONEY ANTS, TO PLUG UP THE BARREL OF THE FALLEN GUN...

...TO PLUG IT UP WITH--*HONEY!*

MY--MY GUN IS *JAMMED!* IT WILL NOT FIRE!!

SUDDENLY, THERE'S *ANOTHER* SHRIEK...

ANTS! THEY'RE ALL *OVER* ME! *HUNDREDS* OF THEM!!

WHERE DID THEY *COME* FROM? *HOW--?*

HELP!! GET THEM *OFF* ME! I CAN'T *STAND* THEM!

I DON'T KNOW WHAT'S GOING ON, BUT SOMEHOW MY ROPES GOT LOOSE!

MINE, TOO! AND SINCE THOSE MURDEROUS REDS ARE WITHOUT GUNS NOW...

...*LET'S GET 'EM!*

GUESS THE BOYS CAN HANDLE THINGS FROM HERE ON IN! I'D BETTER GET BACK TO MY OFFICE, BEFORE THEY SEARCH FOR ME!

12

THAT'S IT! NOW CARRY ME DOWN TO THE FLOOR!

MOMENTS LATER...

LUCKY I RETAINED MY FULL STRENGTH --OR I MIGHT NOT HAVE BEEN ABLE TO PUSH THIS TEST TUBE OVER!

ALL THAT'S REQUIRED IS ONE DIP IN THE ENLARGING SERUM, AND--

--THERE! I'M MY NORMAL SIZE AGAIN!

I HAD BETTER JOIN THE OTHERS NOW!

HAH! WITHOUT THEIR WEAPONS, THEY WERE A PUSHOVER!

WE NOTIFIED SECURITY! THEY'RE SENDING SOME OFFICERS OVER!

WE'RE FORTUNATE IT TURNED OUT ALL RIGHT! IT COULD HAVE BEEN BIG TROUBLE, NOT ONLY FOR US, BUT FOR THE ENTIRE FREE WORLD!

IT IS OVER! THE DANGER HAS ENDED FOR NOW, AND MY SECRET IS STILL SAFE! BUT I WONDER-- WILL I EVER BE FORCED TO BECOME THE ANT-MAN AGAIN?

YES, HENRY PYM...YOU WILL! SOONER THAN YOU THINK!! BUT WE WILL SAVE THAT STORY FOR THE NEXT ISSUE OF "TALES TO ASTONISH"!

The END

13

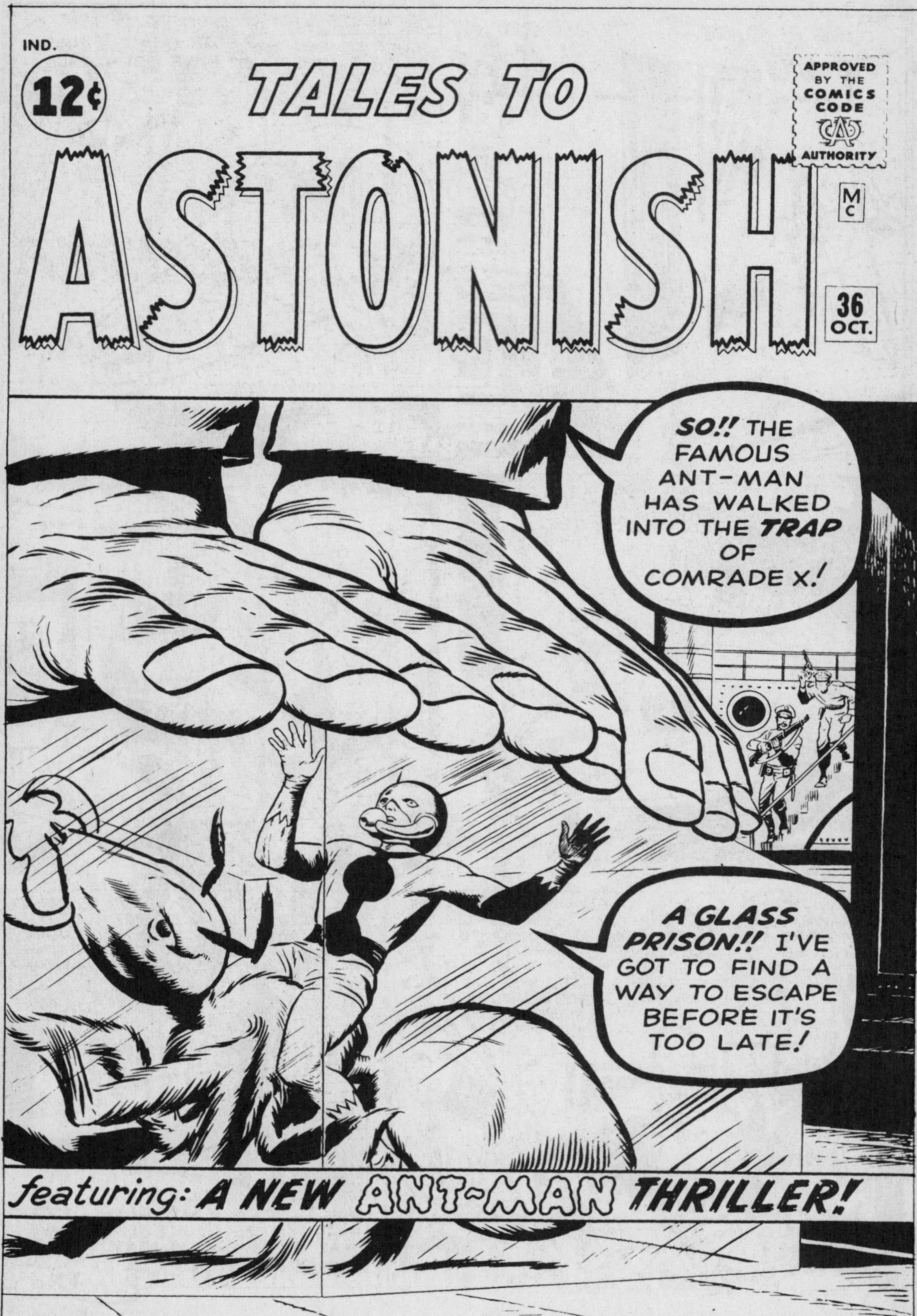
IND.
12¢
TALES TO
ASTONISH
APPROVED BY THE COMICS CODE AUTHORITY
MC
36
OCT.
SO!! THE FAMOUS ANT-MAN HAS WALKED INTO THE TRAP OF COMRADE X!
A GLASS PRISON!! I'VE GOT TO FIND A WAY TO ESCAPE BEFORE IT'S TOO LATE!
featuring: A NEW ANT-MAN THRILLER!

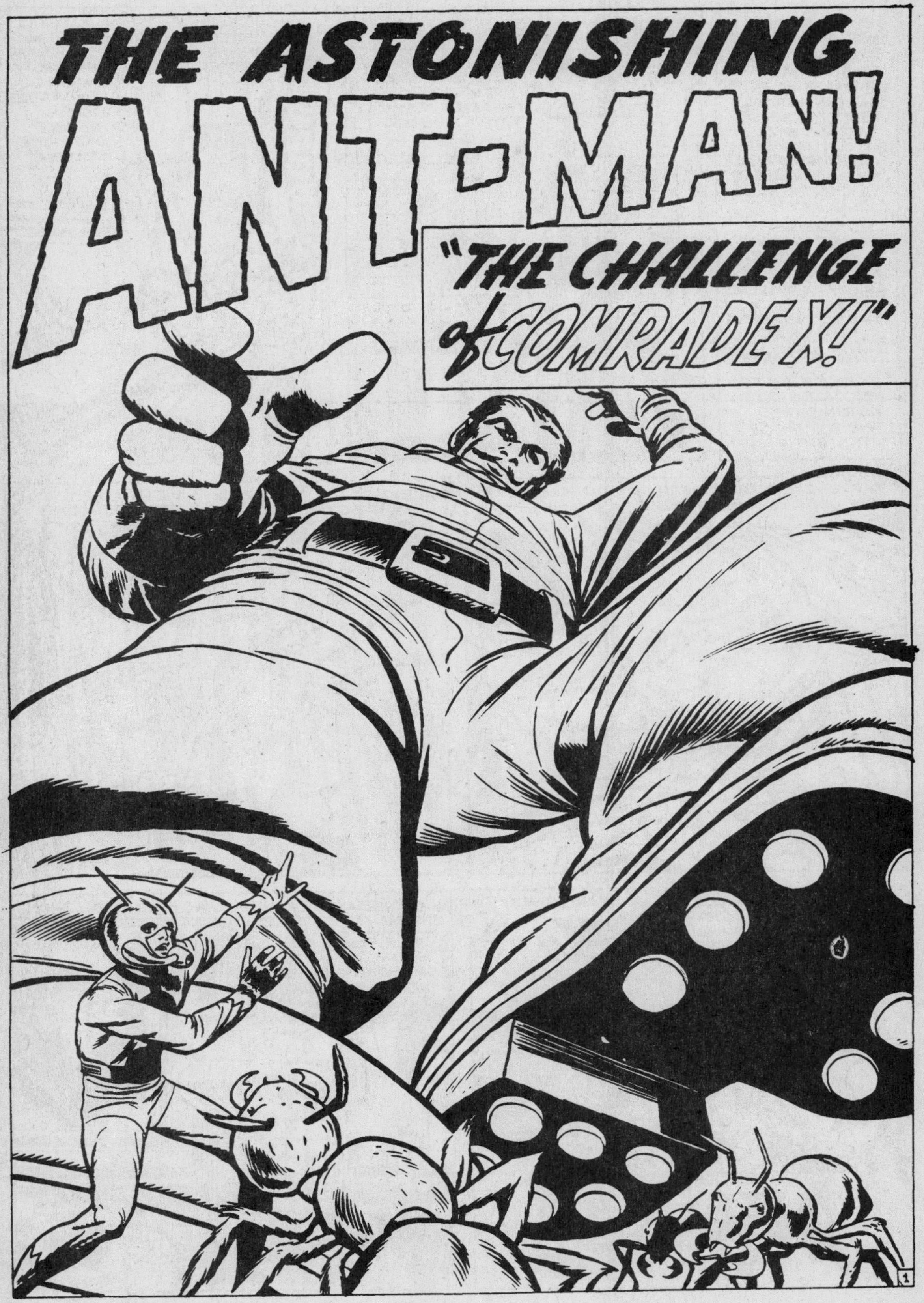
THE ASTONISHING
ANT-MAN!
"THE CHALLENGE
of COMRADE X!"
1

YOU'RE IN FOR ANOTHER GRIPPING ADVENTURE WITH HENRY PYM, THE BRILLIANT SCIENTIST WHO CAN NOT ONLY REDUCE HIMSELF TO ANT SIZE, BUT CAN COMMUNICATE AND CONTROL ANTS BY MEANS OF A CYBERNETIC HELMET*!

USING HIS FANTASTIC POWER TO COMBAT THE FORCES OF EVIL, HENRY HAS ALREADY BECOME THE LIVING LEGEND KNOWN AS

...THE ANT-MAN!

*EDITOR'S NOTE: SEE TALES TO ASTONISH #35 "THE RETURN OF THE ANT-MAN!"

WITHIN THE STEEL CONFINES OF A LOCKED BANK VAULT, THREE MEN WAIT FEARFULLY...

THEIR TIME IS RUNNING OUT!

BLASTED BANK ROBBERS! SERVES THEM RIGHT, GETTING TRAPPED IN A VAULT WITH A TIME LOCK!

THEY'LL SUFFOCATE FOR SURE, UNLESS THE ANT-MAN CAN OPEN THE LOCK IN TIME!

LUCKILY I STILL KEEP MY NORMAL STRENGTH, EVEN WHEN I SHRINK TO ANT-SIZE! OTHERWISE I'D NEVER BE ABLE TO MOVE THESE TUMBLERS!

THERE-- EVERYTHING IS IN POSITION! NOW THE LOCK CAN BE OPENED!

ALRIGHT, BRIGHT BOYS-- COME OUT WITH YOUR HANDS HIGH!

D-DON'T SHOOT! WE'RE COMING!

WE'RE LUCKY TO STILL BE ALIVE!

LOOK! THERE GOES THE ANT-MAN!

HOW DOES HE ALWAYS KNOW WHEN HE'S NEEDED??

SEARCH ME?!

AND THOUSANDS OF MILES AWAY, BEHIND THE IRON CURTAIN!

ONCE AGAIN THE AMERICAN ANT-MAN HAS PERFORMED AN INCREDIBLE FEAT!

THE ANT-MAN! ALWAYS THE ANT-MAN!

...SEND IN COMRADE X!!

2

COMRADE X REPORTING!

COMRADE, YOU ARE OUR BEST ESPIONAGE AGENT! THUS I HAVE SELECTED *YOU* TO CAPTURE THE ANT-MAN AND LEARN HOW HE IS ABLE TO CHANGE HIS SIZE!

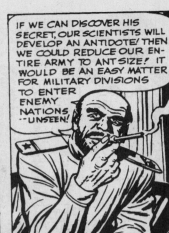

IF WE CAN DISCOVER HIS SECRET, OUR SCIENTISTS WILL DEVELOP AN ANTIDOTE! THEN WE COULD REDUCE OUR ENTIRE ARMY TO ANT SIZE! IT WOULD BE AN EASY MATTER FOR MILITARY DIVISIONS TO ENTER ENEMY NATIONS --UNSEEN!

ONCE BEHIND THE ENEMY LINES, OUR TROOPS WOULD THEN REVERT TO NORMAL SIZE ... AND *STRIKE!* SUCH A SECRET WOULD MAKE US MASTERS OF THE WORLD!

I UNDER-STAND, COMRADE! I WILL LEAVE FOR AMERICA AT ONCE!

SEVERAL DAYS LATER, IN A POLICE STATION IN THE UNITED STATES.

WHAT'S THE TROUBLE, MISS?

YOU MUST PUT ME IN TOUCH WITH THE ANT-MAN AT ONCE! IT'S A MATTER OF LIFE AND DEATH!

IT CAN'T BE DONE!

WE DON'T KNOW HOW TO LOCATE HIM OURSELVES!!

IN SOME MYSTERIOUS WAY, HE JUST APPEARS ON THE SCENE WHENEVER THERE'S TROUBLE!

"JUST APPEARS ON THE SCENE..." YES, THAT'S THE WAY IT SEEMS! BUT, IF THESE OFFICERS WERE TO LOOK IN A NEARBY WASTE BASKET, THEY WOULD SEE SEVERAL *ANTS*...

ANTS WHICH ARE PART OF A VAST NETWORK OF TINY INSECTS, PLANTED IN POLICE STATIONS AND NEWSPAPER OFFICES THRU-OUT THE CITY! THOSE SMALL UNNOTICED AGENTS OF THE ANT-MAN KEEP HIM IN TOUCH WITH EVERY EMERGENCY WHICH OCCURS IN THE VAST METROPOLIS!

CALLING CAR 41---CALLING CAR 41---

GET ME THE F.B.I.!

IF ONLY THE ANT MAN COULD HELP US!

WANTED

3

AS SOON AS THE WORD "ANT-MAN" IS HEARD, THE SILENT INSECT TRANSMITS AN IMPULSE THROUGH ITS ANTENNAE TO ANOTHER NEARBY ANT...

THUS, THE COUNTLESS ANTS UNNOTICED EACH DAY AT THE EDGE OF GUTTERS, IN THE CRACKS OF SIDEWALKS, IN FLOWER POTS, IN VACANT LOTS, AND CITY PARKS--- ALL THESE INSECTS FORM A CITY-WIDE WEB OF *COMMUNICATIONS!*

AND THE NERVE CENTER OF THIS INCREDIBLE NETWORK IS LOCATED IN A SECRET ROOM OF HENRY PYM'S LABORATORY.

AN ELECTRONIC IMPULSE IS COMING IN! IT ORIGINATES FROM PRECINCT FOURTEEN!

PUTTING ON HIS CYBERNETIC HELMET*, THE SCIENTIST SOON TRANSLATES THE INCOMING SIGNAL INTO AN INTELLIGIBLE FORM!

GIRL... IN TROUBLE! SHE MUST... CONTACT ANT-MAN!

THAT MEANS IT'S TIME TO DON MY "WORKING CLOTHES" AGAIN!

* EDITOR'S NOTE: SEE TALES TO ASTONISH #35 FOR DETAILED EXPLANATION OF HELMET'S OPERATION!

I'VE DEVELOPED MY REDUCING AND GROWTH SERUMS IN A GAS FORM! IT MAKES IT A LOT EASIER TO CARRY THEM WITH ME!

ALL I HAVE TO DO NOW IS RELEASE THE REDUCING GAS AND INHALE IT THROUGH MY FILTER...

THERE... IT IS DONE! WITHIN A MOMENT, IT WILL START TO ACT UPON MY CELL TISSUES!

IT'S WORKING! IT'S SHRINKING ME... TO THE SIZE OF ... AN ANT!

EDITOR'S NOTE! AS HENRY PYM SHRINKS, SO DOES HIS COSTUME, WHICH CONSISTS OF UNSTABLE MOLECULES THAT STRETCH AND CONTRACT AS HIS OWN BODY DOES!

4

NOW TO GET TO THE TROUBLE SPOT--- IN MY OWN SPECIAL WAY!

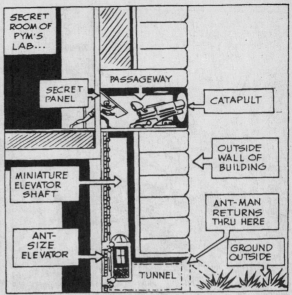

SECRET ROOM OF PYM'S LAB...

SECRET PANEL

PASSAGEWAY

CATAPULT

MINIATURE ELEVATOR SHAFT

OUTSIDE WALL OF BUILDING

ANT-MAN RETURNS THRU HERE

ANT-SIZE ELEVATOR

TUNNEL

GROUND OUTSIDE

ALL I HAVE TO DO IS ADJUST THIS ELECTRONICALLY-CONTROLLED CATAPULT TO ROCKET ME TO AN ALLEY NEAR THE POLICE STATION!

EVERYTHING IS READY! NOW I JUST PRESS THE RELEASE BUTTON---

...AND I'M ON MY WAY!

VOOM

MY CYBERNETIC TRANSMITTER IS SENDING OUT IMPULSES! THE ANTS WILL DETECT THEM WITH THEIR ANTENNAE AND FOLLOW THEM!

THERE THEY ARE— CONVERGING ON THE EXACT SPOT WHERE I'M ABOUT TO LAND!

5.

WELL DONE, MY LITTLE FRIENDS!!

THAT GIRL, GETTING INTO THE CAB---SHE JUST CAME OUT OF THE POLICE STATION! *SHE* MUST BE THE ONE WHO WANTS TO CONTACT ME!

THE DRIVER DOESN'T KNOW IT, BUT HE'S GOING TO BE CARRYING AN EXTRA PASSENGER!

THE DOOR FITS ITS CASING WELL... BUT NOT WELL ENOUGH TO KEEP AN ANT OUT!

CONTROLLING HIS MOUNT WITH ELECTRONIC IMPULSES, THE ANT-MAN REACHES THE TOP OF THE CAR SEAT!

THANKS FOR THE LIFT, LITTLE PAL!

UNNOTICED BY THE GIRL, THE FANTASTIC MINIATURE HUMAN CONCEALS HIMSELF WITHIN HER PURSE---

MINUTES LATER, THE TAXICAB ARRIVES AT ITS DESTINATION!

A MIGHTY NICE-LOOKIN' CHICK!

6.

ONCE INSIDE THE APARTMENT...

AND NOW IT'S TIME FOR HER TO MEET--- THE ANT MAN!

SOMETHING'S ON THE TABLE!

THE ANT-MAN!! BUT... HOW---??

HOW I GOT HERE ISN'T IMPORTANT! FIRST, TELL ME WHY YOU WANTED TO SEE ME!

LAST YEAR IN EUROPE, I FELL IN LOVE WITH A MAN... A MAN I LATER LEARNED WAS THE DEADLY RED MASTER SPY--- COMRADE X!!

BUT I DIDN'T CARE WHO HE WAS! I LOVED HIM--- I LOVED HIM!! THAT IS, UNTIL...

...HE JILTED ME FOR ANOTHER WOMAN!! AND NOW... I WANT REVENGE!! I WANT HIM TO PAY FOR BREAKING MY HEART!

THAT'S WHY I TRIED TO CONTACT YOU! I WANT TO WARN YOU THAT COMRADE X IS IN THE UNITED STATES! HIS MISSION IS TO CAPTURE YOU AND LEARN THE SECRET BEHIND YOUR SIZE!

BUT, YOU CAN BEAT HIM TO THE PUNCH! HE'S HIDING ON A FREIGHTER DOCKED AT PIER 89! IF YOU ACT NOW, YOU CAN SURPRISE HIM BEFORE HE MAKES HIS MOVE!

I'M ON MY WAY!!

I'VE HEARD OF THE MYSTERIOUS COMRADE X, BUT I NEVER THOUGHT I'D HAVE A CHANCE TO CONFRONT HIM, FACE TO FACE!

WELL, THEY SAY THERE'S A FIRST TIME FOR EVERYTHING!!

THE ASTONISHING ANT-MAN!

PART 2

THAT EVENING, THE TINY WARRIOR ARRIVES AT PIER 89...

THERE'S THE FREIGHTER! LET'S BOARD HER!

CONTROLLING THE ANTS BY MEANS OF ELECTRONIC IMPULSES, THEIR HUMAN COMMANDER LEADS THEM UP THE SHIP'S GANG PLANK... AND PAST A HIDDEN ELECTRIC EYE!

AND AT THAT INSTANT, ON BOARD THE VESSEL...

THE LIGHT IS FLASHING!

THE ANT-MAN HAS CUT THE ELECTRIC EYE BEAM! HE IS COMING ABOARD!

GOOD! WE ARE READY FOR HIM!

V-858

HE APPROACHES!

IN A MOMENT, HE WILL BE OUR CAPTIVE!

8

HAH! WE HAVE TRAPPED HIM!

THE PINHOLES IN THE BOX WILL ENABLE HIM TO BREATHE! BUT THEY ARE NOT LARGE ENOUGH FOR EVEN AN ANT TO CRAWL THROUGH!

IN THE MORNING, WE WILL SET SAIL WITH THE GREAT YANKEE ANT-MAN OUR CAPTIVE!

I'M TRAPPED ALRIGHT! THE ONLY THING TO DO IS BRING OUTSIDE ANTS HERE TO HELP ME!

BUT HOW CAN I CONTACT THEM?? THE ELECTRONIC IMPULSES FROM MY HELMET CAN'T PASS THROUGH THE GLASS BOX!

BUT WAIT--THE AIR HOLES! THEY'RE TOO SMALL FOR ME TO PASS THROUGH, BUT NOT TOO SMALL FOR MY SIGNAL TO PASS THROUGH!

AND SO, HENRY PYM ACTIVATES HIS CYBERNETIC TRANSMITTER AND BEAMS IMPULSES IN THE DIRECTION OF THE PINHOLES...

MUST COMMAND THE ANTS TO BOARD THE SHIP, BUT NOT THE WAY I DID!

AND MOMENTS AFTER THEIR ANTENNAE RECEIVE THE SIGNALS, ALL THE ANTS INHABITING THE PIER JOIN IN A COMMON TASK...

THEY MUST CARRY LOOSE BITS OF WOOD TO THE EDGE OF THE PIER...

...AND DROP THEM INTO THE WATER ...HANGING ONTO THEM AS THEY FALL...

THE IMPACT OF THE FALL SHOULD CARRY THE WOOD A LITTLE AWAY FROM THE DOCK... TOWARD THE HULL OF THE SHIP...

...AND THE INSTANT CONTACT IS MADE, THE ANTS WILL CRAWL ONTO THE SHIP!

9

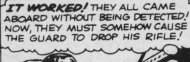

IT WORKED! THEY ALL CAME ABOARD WITHOUT BEING DETECTED! NOW, THEY MUST SOMEHOW CAUSE THE GUARD TO DROP HIS RIFLE!

AGAIN FOLLOWING THE ORDERS OF THEIR HUMAN COMMANDER, THE TINY INSECTS ATTACK THE UNSUSPECTING GUARD!

Y!!!!-- MY LEG.!!

IT SHATTERED THE GLASS.!!

CRASH!

I'M FREE!!

NOW TO SETTLE ACCOUNTS WITH COMRADE X!

HEY, YOU-- COME BACK HERE...

I MISSED!!

CAREFULLY REMAINING OUT OF SIGHT, THE ANT-MAN TRAVELS THROUGHOUT THE SHIP, UNTIL HE COMES TO THE RADIO ROOM!

THAT LAMP HANGING ABOVE THE OPERATOR-- THAT'S ALL THE WEAPON I NEED! C'MON, LITTLE FRIENDS, LET'S GET OVER THERE!

I'D BETTER HOLD ON TIGHT! A FALL FROM THIS HEIGHT COULD *FINISH* ME!

WHEN THEY REACH THE LAMP, THE ANT-MAN ORDERS THE INSECTS TO CHEW AWAY AT THE LAMP CORD!

FORTUNATELY I STILL POSSESS ALL THE STRENGTH OF MY REAL SIZE! I SHOULD BE ABLE TO YANK THIS LOOSE -- IN A FEW SECONDS!

AND WEARING EARPHONES, THE RADIO OPERATOR HEARS NOTHING, UNTIL IT IS... *TOO LATE!*

CLUNK!

10

NOW, IT'S TIME FOR ME TO USE MY **GROWTH GAS!**

THE FUMES ARE ACTING UPON MY CELL TISSUES! THEY'RE RETURNING ME TO NORMAL SIZE!

NOW TO CONTACT THE AUTHORITIES ON SHORE!

AND WHILE HENRY PYM RADIOS FOR HELP, HIS INSECT ARMY CONTINUES TO FOLLOW ITS BATTLE PLAN!

CLICK!

AFTER LOCKING THE DOOR, THE ANTS CRAWL AWAY WITH THE KEY, TEMPORARILY IMPRISONING THE RED SEAMEN...

AS SOON AS HIS MESSAGE IS SENT, THE SCIENTIST-ADVENTURER RETURNS TO ANT-SIZE AND GOES AFTER THE SINISTER COMRADE X!

THERE HE IS! NOW TO TAKE HIM BY SURPRISE!

BUT, IT IS THE ANT-MAN **HIMSELF** WHO IS TAKEN BY SURPRISE!

WELCOME, YANKEE! I HAVE BEEN **EXPECTING** YOU!

THE D.D.T. IN THIS SPRAY GUN HAS BEEN DILUTED! IT WON'T KILL YOU! IT WILL JUST MAKE YOU TOO ILL TO GIVE US ANY FURTHER TROUBLE FOR AWHILE!

11

I *THOUGHT* YOU MIGHT OUT-SMART MY MEN! BUT *NONE* CAN FOOL COMRADE X!

THE ANTS HAVE ALMOST REACHED THE LIGHT! IF THEY CAN COVER IT, BEFORE HE FIRES!

AND AGAIN OBEYING THEIR LEADER'S MENTAL COMMAND, THE TINY ARMY SWARMS OVER THE ENTIRE FLUORESCENT LIGHT, PLUNGING THE ROOM INTO DARKNESS!

WHA--WHAT HAPPENED TO THE LIGHT??

WHERE *ARE* YOU ANT-MAN?? YOU WON'T ESCAPE FROM ME! I'LL *FIND* YOU!!

IT'S TOO DARK FOR HIM TO SEE A TINY FIGURE LIKE ME... BUT NOT TOO DARK FOR *ME* TO SEE A GIANT LIKE *HIM!*

THERE-- I'VE *UNTIED* HIS SHOE-LACE!

BRINGING BOTH SHOELACES BEHIND THE RED SPIES' FEET, THE ANT-MAN AGAIN PREPARES TO USE HIS FULL STRENGTH...

I FEEL LIKE SAMSON, PULLING DOWN THE PILLARS OF THE TEMPLE! HERE GOES...

OHHHH!!

THE INSTANT COMRADE X HITS THE FLOOR, THE ANTS LEAVE THE FLUORESCENT LIGHT AND SWARM DOWN TOWARD HIM...

ANTS!! HUNDREDS OF THEM!

12

THE ANTS ARE SWARMING ALL OVER ME! *EEEKK...*

THEY'RE REMOVING MY *MASK!*

HOW?? DID THE BRAINLESS INSECTS *KNOW??*

THEY LEARNED IT FROM *ME*, COMRADE X! BUT THEN, IT'S *MADAME X*, ISN'T IT.!! JUST AS I *KNEW* IT WAS ALL ALONG!

YOU MADE A MISTAKE, GOING TO THE POLICE STATION! BECAUSE IT GAVE ME A CHANCE TO HIDE IN YOUR POCKETBOOK! AND WHILE IN THERE, I DISCOVERED YOUR RUBBER FACE MASK--COMPLETE WITH THE INSTRUMENT TO MAKE YOUR VOICE MASCULINE!

YOU'RE VERY CLEVER, AREN'T YOU?! WELL, YOU LOATHSOME LITTLE CREATURE--YOU'LL NEVER GET OFF THIS SHIP ALIVE! IF I DON'T KILL YOU, MY *MEN* WILL!

SORRY, LADY, BUT YOU'RE WRONG *AGAIN!*

13

RRRR RRR R

IF YOU LISTEN, YOU'LL HEAR THE SOUND OF SIRENS...I *FIGURED* THE COAST GUARD WOULD ARRIVE BY NOW!

MINUTES LATER, THE REDS ARE TAKEN INTO CUSTODY...

NOW THAT YOU'VE GOT COMRADE X AND HER CREW, YOU WON'T NEED *ME* ANYMORE!

I WONDER WHERE HE GOES...AND WHO HE REALLY IS???

THAT'S *HIS* SECRET... AND IF THAT'S THE WAY HE WANTS IT, THAT'S THE WAY IT'LL REMAIN!

AND SO THE FANTASTIC ANT-MAN DISAPPEARS INTO THE NIGHT! WATCH FOR HIM NEXT MONTH, WHEN HE RETURNS IN ANOTHER TALE... *TO ASTONISH!*

The END

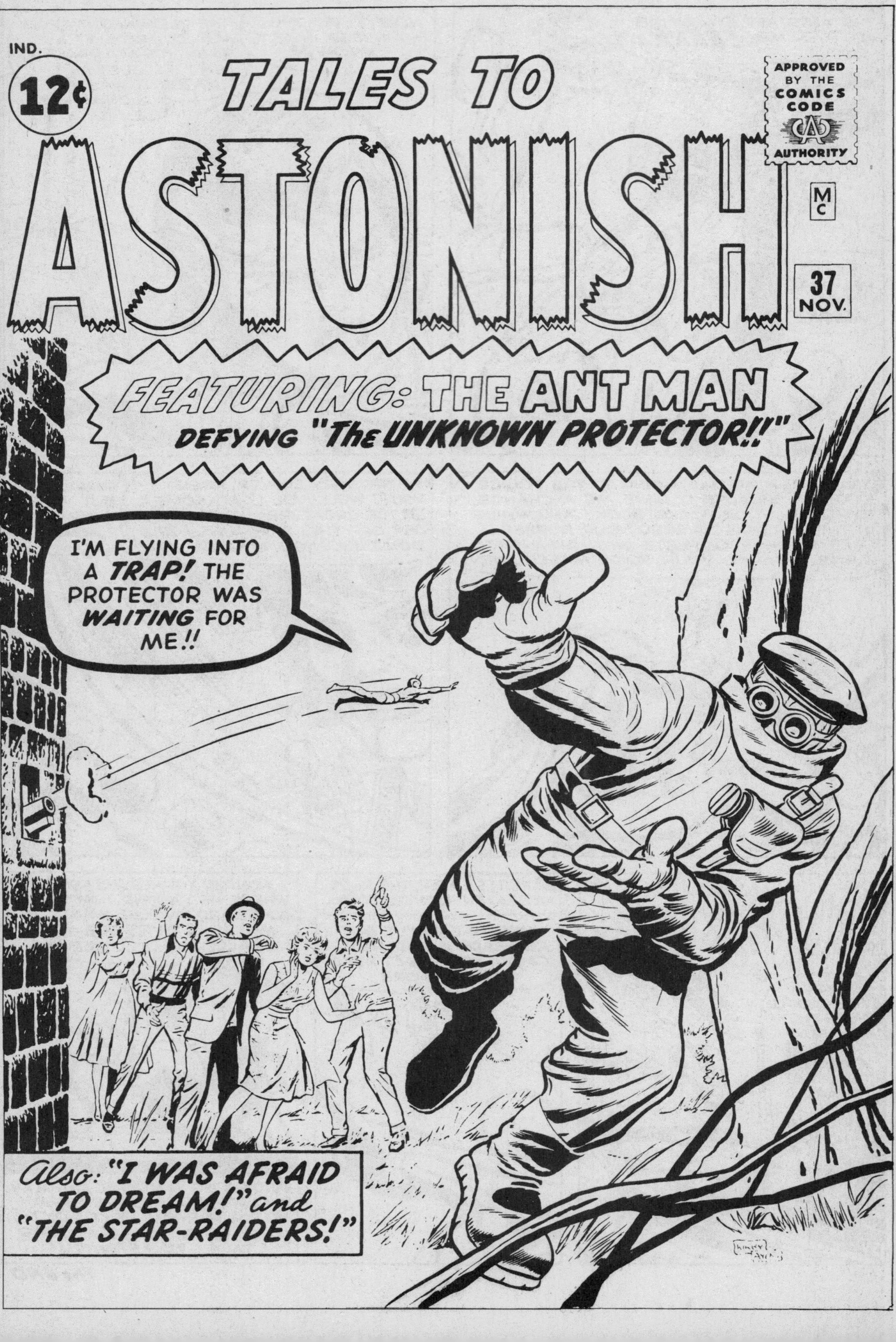
IND.
12¢
TALES TO
ASTONISH
APPROVED BY THE COMICS CODE AUTHORITY
MC
37
NOV.
FEATURING: THE ANT MAN
DEFYING "The UNKNOWN PROTECTOR!!"
I'M FLYING INTO A TRAP! THE PROTECTOR WAS WAITING FOR ME!!
Also: "I WAS AFRAID TO DREAM!" and "THE STAR-RAIDERS!"

THE ASTONISHING ANT-MAN!

"TRAPPED by the PROTECTER!"

EACH DAY A THOUSAND TALES ARE ETCHED IN THE CITY! OURS BEGINS AS A JEWELER, NAMED GERALD MARSH, STAGGERS TO HIS FEET...

OUTSIDE, WE HEAR THE SCREAMING WAIL OF AN APPROACHING POLICE CAR!

ARRRRRRRRRRR

1

BUT THE POLICE SIREN IS HEARD BY OTHER THAN HUMAN EARS! IT IS DETECTED BY THE TINY ANTENNAE OF COUNTLESS CRAWLING **ANTS,** DISPERSED THROUGHOUT THE CITY, FORMING A VAST NET-WORK OF COMMUNICATIONS...

THE ANTS' ELECTRONIC IMPULSES ARE RELAYED TO THE NERVE CENTER OF THIS FANTASTIC NETWORK... THE LABORATORY OF HENRY PYM!

THERE'S TROUBLE AT 523 ELM STREET!

I'D BETTER SEE WHAT'S UP! BUT NOT AS PROFESSOR HENRY PYM...

I'LL JUST RELEASE MY REDUCING GAS...

...AND ALLOW THE VAPOR TO ENGULF ME...TO MAKE ME SMALLER...

AND SMALLER...

AND SMALLER...

...UNTIL AT LAST I CAN GO TO THE TROUBLE SPOT AS **THE ANT-MAN!!**

EDITOR'S NOTE: FOR DETAILED DIAGRAM OF ANT-MAN'S SPECIALLY BUILT EXIT APPARATUS, SEE *TALES TO ASTONISH #36!*

I'LL SET THE CONTROLS OF MY CATAPULT FOR THE GENERAL AREA OF 523 ELM STREET...

2

A MOMENT LATER, THE ANT-MAN TRIGGERS THE CATAPULT, SHOOTING HIMSELF INTO THE AIR!

I'M ON MY WAY!

AS THE TINY WARRIOR FLIES OVER THE CITY, HE USES ELECTRONIC IMPULSES TO CONTACT THE ANTS BELOW! THE INSECTS RECEIVE THE IMPULSES AND FOLLOW THEIR DIRECTION, UNMINDFUL OF ALL OBSTACLES IN THEIR PATH!

...UNTIL AT LAST, THE ANTS CONVERGE AT 523 ELM STREET!

523

Jewelry

GERALD MARS, PROP.

THEY'VE OBEYED MY COMMANDS TO THE LETTER! NOW I HAVE AN ANT HILL TO LAND SAFELY ON!

THE POLICE ARE JUST LEAVING!! SO I CAN QUESTION THE VICTIM WITHOUT BEING DISTURBED!

SECONDS LATER, THE TINY WARRIOR MAKES HIS APPEARANCE KNOWN!

ANT-MAN!! WHAT BRINGS YOU...

THE POLICE HAVE BEEN HERE! AND WHERE THE POLICE GO I GO! TELL ME WHAT HAPPENED HERE!

IT WAS THE PROTECTOR! HE--HE BEAT ME UP!!!

PROTECTOR?? WHO'S HE??

POST NO BILLS

3

THE PROTECTOR IS AN INHUMANLY POWERFUL CRIMINAL WHO HAS BEEN TERRORIZING ALL THE JEWELERS IN TOWN! HE MAKES THEM PAY FOR "PROTECTION"! THEY'RE ALL TOO SCARED TO REFUSE, OR EVEN TO CALL THE POLICE!

TODAY HE CAME INTO *MY* STORE! HE WANTED MONEY! BUT BUSINESS HAS BEEN BAD...

SO YOU CAN'T MAKE YOUR WEEKLY PAYMENT, EH, MARSH?!

HONEST, I DON'T HAVE THE MONEY! YOU MUST BELIEVE ME!

THEN WITH ONE HAND, HE YANKED ME OVER THE COUNTER AS EASILY AS YOU WOULD A TOY...

LET ME SHOW YOU WHAT HAPPENS TO THOSE WHO DON'T BUY MY PROTECTION!

NO!!

YOU SEE THIS GUN? IT FIRES AN ELECTRONIC DISINTEGRATING RAY!

WHOOOSHH!

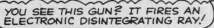

YOU--YOU'VE DISINTEGRATED MY JEWELRY! YOU'VE TURNED IT INTO DUST!

NATURALLY!! BECAUSE YOU WEREN'T *PRO-TECTED* THIS WEEK! NOW, NEXT TIME I COME COLLECTING, YOU'D BETTER PAY UP, OR SOMETHING EVEN *WORSE* WILL HAPPEN!

... AND THEN TO MAKE SURE I'D OBEY HIM, HE-- HE KNOCKED ME UNCONSCIOUS BEFORE LEAVING!

WHEN I RECOVERED, I CALLED THE POLICE, BUT LIKE ALL THE OTHER STORE OWNERS, I WAS TOO SCARED TO SIGN A COMPLAINT!

THANKS, MR. MARSH! YOU'VE GIVEN ME ENOUGH TO GO ON!

4

PERHAPS I MAY HAVE BETTER LUCK THAN THE POLICE IN CATCHING THE PROTECTOR!

IF THERE'S ANY WAY I CAN HELP YOU, JUST LET ME KNOW! I'LL DO ANYTHING TO HELP CATCH THAT FIEND! **ANYTHING!**

AS THE ANT-MAN LEAVES THE SHOP, A LARGE FIGURE FOLLOWS HIM...

WHEN HE REACHES THE CURB, THE INSECT-SIZED WARRIOR TAKES OUT A LASSO OF THREAD AND SKILFULLY TOSSES IT...

THAT CAR'S HEADED IN MY DIRECTION!

THIS BEATS WALKING ANY DAY!

HE GOT AWAY! BUT NEXT TIME, IT'LL BE DIFFERENT....!

LATER, BACK IN HIS LABORATORY...

THE POLICE CAN'T KEEP AN EYE ON EVERY JEWELRY STORE IN TOWN! BUT WITH THE AID OF MY ANTS, I **CAN!**

BY MEANS OF ELECTRONIC WAVE INSTRUCTIONS, HENRY PYM STATIONS ANTS IN FRONT OF ALL THE JEWELRY STORES IN THE CITY! HE THEN CONTROLS THEM SO THEY'LL RESPOND TO SUCH VERBAL STIMULI AS THE WORDS "PROTECTOR" AND "DISINTEGRATING RAY"...

FOR TWO DAYS NOTHING HAPPENS! BUT ON THE THIRD DAY...

I'M GETTING A SIGNAL! IT'S COMING FROM HARLEY AVENUE!

THE ASTONISHING ANT-MAN!

PART 2

"FACE-TO-FACE WITH THE PROTECTOR!"

THE PROTECTOR IS AT 600 HARLEY AVENUE, EXTORTING MONEY FROM A JEWELER! I JUST HOPE HE STAYS PUT LONG ENOUGH FOR ME TO CATAPULT THERE!

OH, OH...THE STREET'S CROWDED! MY PATH TO THE ANT-HILL IS BLOCKED!

I'LL CRASH INTO SOMEONE UNLESS-- WAIT! THAT BABY CARRIAGE--IF I CAN JUST MANEUVER TOWARDS IT!

MADE IT!!

BUT I'M TOO HIGH UP FROM THE GROUND! I'LL HAVE TO TAKE IT IN TWO JUMPS!

FIRST, INTO A NICE SOFT TROUSER CUFF...

THEN, FROM HERE IT'S A CINCH TO LAND SAFELY ON THE CEMENT!

GATHERING TOGETHER A SWARM OF ANTS, THE TINY WARRIOR RUSHES INTO THE JEWELRY STORE...

TWO HUNDRED...TWO FIFTY...THIS WILL BUY YOU PROTECTION TILL NEXT WEEK!

BY MEANS OF ELECTRONIC WAVE IMPULSES, THE ANT-MAN COMMANDS HIS "TROOPS" TO CLIMB UP THE COUNTER! AND WHILE THEY CARRY OUT HIS PLAN...

SO YOU'RE THE PROTECTOR, EH? WELL, YOUR RACKET IS FINISHED!

HUH--WHO SAID THAT??

I DID!

THE ANT-MAN! HAH! YOU IMPUDENT INSECT! I'LL SILENCE YOU FOREVER!!

BUT, AS THE MENACING PROTECTOR COMES TOWARD THE ANT-MAN...

THAT'S *IT*, LITTLE FRIENDS! DROP THE NECKLACE TO THE FLOOR!

THE NECKLACE HITS THE FLOOR--THE STRING BREAKS--AND THE PEARLS SCATTER...

WHA--??

HAPPY LANDING!

NOW, LET'S FINISH OUR FIGHT *OUTSIDE*, WHERE THERE'S MORE ROOM!

AND WHERE I CAN FIND MANY MORE ANTS TO HELP ME!

BUT THE PROTECTOR IS NOT WITHOUT CUNNING HIMSELF! AS HE STEPS FROM THE STORE, HE SEES A BOY WITH A WATER PISTOL...

JUST WHAT I NEED!

HELP!!

HAH! I *GOT* HIM!

I DIDN'T *COUNT* ON THIS! THE WATER WILL CARRY ME OFF THE CURB, INTO THE SEWER!

THAT LOLLIPOP STICK-- IT'S MY ONLY CHANCE!

7

FRANTICALLY, THE ANT-MAN SENDS AN ELECTRONIC COMMAND TO A GROUP OF NEARBY ANTS IN THE GUTTER...

HURRY!! CARRY IT TO THE SEWER-- LAY IT ON THE GRATING!!

≶WHEW!≶ THAT WAS CLOSE!

AND, A MOMENT LATER, WITH THE AID OF STILL MORE ELECTRONIC COMMANDS...

I'M SAFE! BUT I'VE LET THE PROTECTOR ESCAPE!

NOTHING LEFT TO DO NOW BUT RETURN TO THE LAB!

THERE'S ONLY ONE WAY TO DEFEAT THE PROTECTOR, AND THAT'S TO *BAIT* HIM...

...USING *HENRY PYM* AS THE BAIT!

EDITOR'S NOTE: FOR A COMPLETE DIAGRAM OF THE ANT-MAN'S ELEVATOR-TUNNEL EXIT, SEE *TALES TO ASTONISH #36!*

SO, A WEEK LATER, THE AMAZING SCIENTIST RENTS A JEWELRY STORE...

SOONER OR LATER, HE'S BOUND TO COME AROUND SELLING PROTECTION...AND WHEN HE DOES, I'LL BE READY FOR HIM!

THE DAYS PASS SLOWLY-- FUTILELY--UNTIL ONE AFTERNOON...

SOMEBODY JUST CAME IN...

DING-A-LING!

IT'S *HIM!*

MAY I *HELP* YOU?

NO, PAL! BUT *I* CAN HELP *YOU!*

AND AT THAT MOMENT, HENRY PYM PRESSES A HIDDEN BUTTON! WE SHALL LEARN *WHY* LATER!

8

I'M CALLED THE PROTECTOR! THAT'S BECAUSE I PREVENT...

WAIT!

...ACCIDENTS LIKE THIS FROM HAPPENING!

I CAN EVEN PROTECT YOU AGAINST WORSE THINGS -- LIKE HAVING YOUR PRECIOUS MERCHANDISE...

... REDUCED TO DUST!!

NOW THE POINT IS, IF YOU DON'T WANT THESE AWFUL THINGS TO HAPPEN, YOU'D BETTER PAY ME THREE HUNDRED DOLLARS A WEEK! UNDERSTAND...?

Y-YES...

GOOD! AND JUST ONE MORE THING! IF YOU TELL THE COPS ABOUT THIS, I WON'T USE MY DISINTERGRATOR ON YOUR GEMS -- I'LL USE IT ON YOU!!

I'LL SEE YOU NEXT WEEK! HAVE MY MONEY READY!

AS SOON AS THE PROTECTOR LEAVES, HENRY PYM RUSHES TO THE BACK OF THE SHOP AND CHANGES HIS COSTUME! THE HE RELEASES HIS FANTASTIC REDUCING GAS...

OKAY, PROTECTOR, YOU'VE MADE YOUR MOVE! NOW I'LL MAKE MINE!

9

AS THE ANT-MAN RUNS TO THE DOOR, HE PASSES SOMETHING ON THE FLOOR, TOO TINY TO BE NOTED BY A NORMAL-SIZED HUMAN, BUT LARGE ENOUGH FOR *HIS* EYES TO SEE...

DROPS OF MACHINE OIL... RIGHT WHERE THE PROTECTOR WAS STANDING! NOW IT ALL FITS TOGETHER!

"GOOD THING I WAS PREPARED FOR THE PROTECTOR! WHEN HE ENTERED THE SHOP, I PRESSED A BUTTON WHICH SENT ELECTRONIC IMPULSES TO ALL THE ANTS IN THE AREA...

THEN, FOLLOWING PREARRANGED INSTRUCTIONS, A FEW ANTS CLIMBED ONTO HIS BOOT WHEN HE LEFT THE STORE...

AND WHILE THE PROTECTOR DROVE AWAY, THEY EMITTED SIGNALS THROUGH THEIR ANTENNAE, WHICH WERE PICKED UP BY OTHER ANTS IN THE STREET!"

NOW ALL I HAVE TO DO IS FOLLOW THE PROTECTOR'S ELECTRONIC TRAIL, WITH MY CYBERNETIC HELMET!

THE ANTS ARE GIVING OFF STRONG IMPULSES! THE PROTECTOR MUST HAVE DRIVEN *THIS* WAY!

OH, OH, THE WAVES ARE GETTING *WEAKER!*

NOW THEY'RE *STRONG* AGAIN! HE MUST'VE TURNED DOWN THIS STREET!

FINALLY, AN HOUR LATER...

THIS VACANT OLD TENEMENT-- *THAT'S* WHERE HE'S HIDING!

NOW TO SEND OUT ANOTHER ELECTRONIC MESSAGE!

10

As soon as he's sent the message, the tiny warrior gathers together a few ants and enters the old building...

It's so dark in here, I can hardly see! Wait -- I've stepped on something!

What's that *noise*?? It's coming from above me!! I -- I'm being drawn up into the air!!

WHIIRRRRRR

I'm caught inside a *vacuum cleaner*!!

Greetings, Ant-Man! I knew that sooner or later you would find my hide-out... so I prepared this trap for you! Clever, don't you think?! Ha! Ha! Ha!

All I have to do is seal up the opening with glue to prevent you from escaping!

GLUE

There! Now you can't get out -- and *air* can't get in! In a little while, you'll suffocate! Your days of meddling are ended -- forever!!

That's what *he* thinks! I may be no bigger than an ant, but I still have all the strength of my normal size!

And that's more than enough to punch through a paper bag!

We're *free!!*

11

THAT FAN ON THE TABLE GIVES ME AN IDEA!

ONCE AGAIN, ELECTRONIC IMPULSES PASS BETWEEN HUMAN AND ANT...

THAT'S RIGHT! TAKE ME HIGHER! HIGHER!!

AND MOMENTS LATER, WHEN THE PROTECTOR RETURNS...

THERE'S A HOLE IN THE BAG! BUT HOW-- HOW COULD SOMEONE AS TINY AS AN ANT HAVE DONE IT ??!!

HE MUST STILL BE AROUND HERE SOMEWHERE! I'LL FIND HIM! HE WON'T ESCAPE FROM ME!

HE'S REMOVED HIS GOGGLES TO LOOK FOR ME! PERFECT! NOW TO TURN ON THE FAN!

IT WORKED! THE FAN HAS BLOWN ALL THE DUST FROM THE BAG INTO HIS FACE!

MY EYES!! I CAN'T SEE!! AH-- AH--AHH-CHOOO!!

AND, A MOMENT LATER...

DON'T MOVE! WE HAVE YOU COVERED!!

THE POLICE!! B-BUT HOW-- HOW-- AH-- AHH--CHOOO!!

WE GOT YOUR MESSAGE, ANT-MAN!

"WHEN YOU SENT THE ELECTRONIC MESSAGE TO THE ANTS YOU KEEP ALERTED AT OUR POLICE STATION, THEY REACTED PERFECTLY!"..

ANT-MAN PROTECTOR VACANT TENEMENT EVANS ROAD

NOW, THANKS TO YOU, WE'VE CAPTURED HIM!

AND IF YOU REMOVE HIS OUTER CLOTHING, YOU'LL BE IN FOR QUITE A SURPRISE!

12

WELL, I'LL BE--!!

IT'S *MARSH*, THE JEWELER!

RIGHT! HE WORE PLATFORM SHOES AND MECHANICALLY CONTROLLED RODS AND SPRINGS TO PERFORM HIS FEATS OF STRENGTH!

I FIRST SUSPECTED HIM WHEN HE CLAIMED THE PROTECTOR HAD BEATEN HIM UP EVEN THOUGH HIS BUSINESS WAS POOR!

I GUESSED THE PROTECTOR WOULD BE TOO SMART TO TRY TO SHAKE DOWN SOMEONE WHO HADN'T THE MONEY TO PAY!

IT WAS JUST A LIE TO DIVERT SUSPICION FROM MARSH!

...AND LATER, WHEN I FOUND MACHINE OIL WHERE THE PROTECTOR HAD BEEN STANDING, I GUESSED THE SECRET OF HIS GREAT STRENGTH!

BUT WHAT ABOUT THAT DISINTEGRATING GUN OF HIS?

EVEN *THAT* WASN'T REALLY WHAT IT SEEMED!

YOU REMEMBER HOW IT CAUSED A PUFF OF DENSE SMOKE? WELL, UNDER COVER OF THAT SMOKE HE STOLE THE GEMS HIMSELF AND DROPPED SOME GRAINS OF SAND IN THEIR PLACE!

YOU'LL HAVE NO TROUBLE FINDING THE "DISINTEGRATED" GEMS IN MARSH'S SAFE! AND NOW, IT'S TIME FOR ME TO LEAVE!

AND, MOMENTS LATER, HIS MISSION ACCOMPLISHED, THE ASTONISHING ANT-MAN IS LOST IN THE CROWD...

UNTIL-- OUR NEXT SENSATIONAL ISSUE!

THE END

DON'T MISS *ALL* THE AMAZING SUPER HEROES WHICH EVERYONE IS TALKING ABOUT...

THE MIGHTY THOR *APPEARING IN* **"JOURNEY INTO MYSTERY"**

THE HUMAN TORCH *APPEARING IN* **"STRANGE TALES"**

And of Course:

THE FANTASTIC FOUR *and* **THE INCREDIBLE HULK**

AMERICA'S GREATEST FANTASY CHARACTERS!

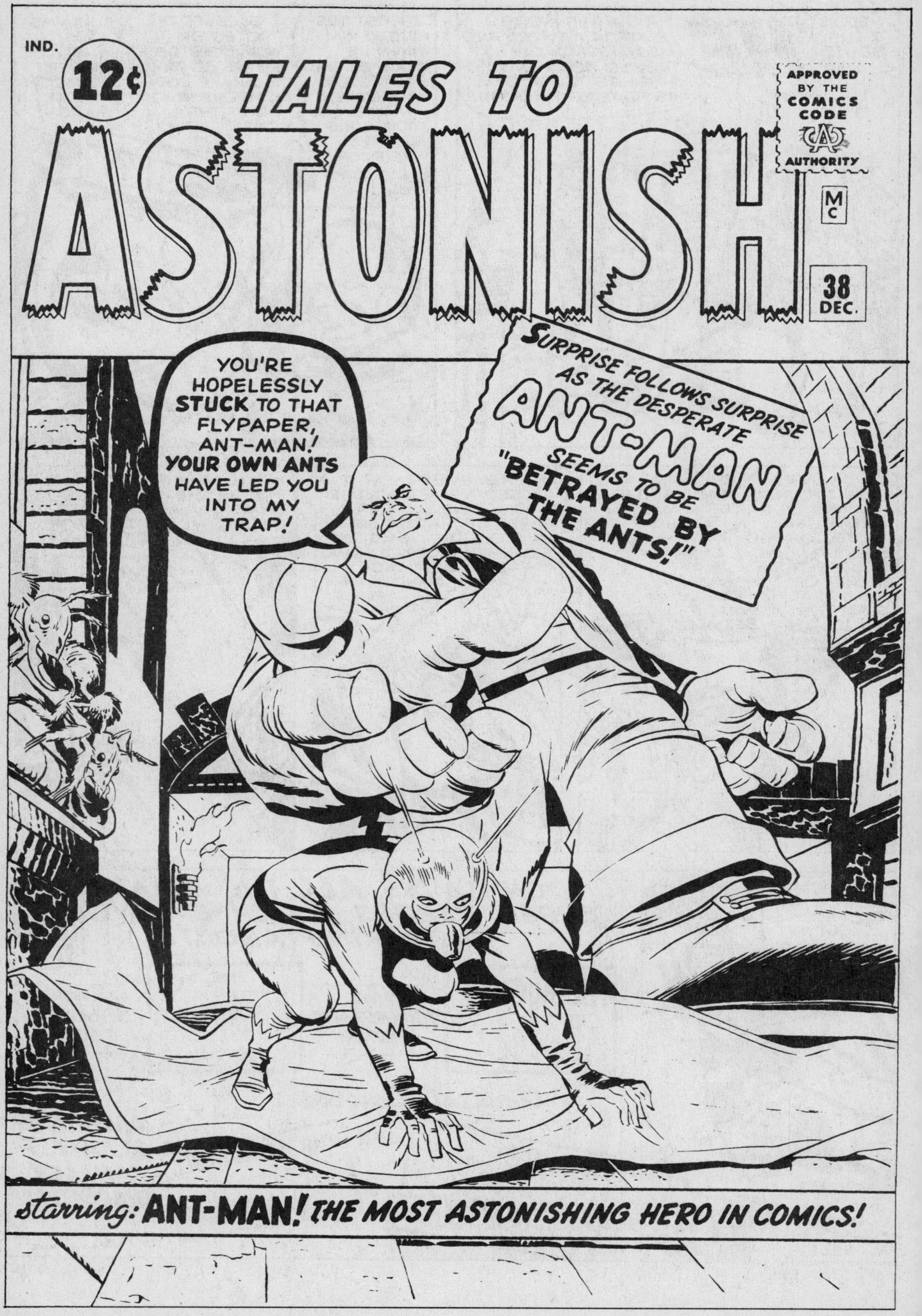

IND.
12¢
TALES TO ASTONISH
APPROVED BY THE COMICS CODE AUTHORITY
MC
38 DEC.
YOU'RE HOPELESSLY STUCK TO THAT FLYPAPER, ANT-MAN! YOUR OWN ANTS HAVE LED YOU INTO MY TRAP!
SURPRISE FOLLOWS SURPRISE AS THE DESPERATE ANT-MAN SEEMS TO BE "BETRAYED BY THE ANTS!"
starring: ANT-MAN! THE MOST ASTONISHING HERO IN COMICS!

THE ASTONISHING ANT-MAN!
"BETRAYED BY THE ANTS!"

PLOT: STAN LEE · SCRIPT: LARRY LIEBER · ART: JACK KIRBY · INKING: DICK AYERS · LETTERING: JOHNNY DEE

SINCE THE APPEARANCE OF THE AMAZING ANT-MAN, THE BUSTLING METROPOLIS HAS OFFERED SLIM PICKINGS FOR THE UNDERWORLD! AND SO...

I TELL YA IF WE DON'T GET RID OF ANT-MAN SOON, WE'LL STARVE TO DEATH!

WE HAVEN'T DARED PULL A ROBBERY IN WEEKS!

WE GOTTA FIND A WAY TO STOP ANT-MAN -- TO MAKE THIS TOWN SAFE FOR CRIME!

STOP HIM, SURE -- BUT HOW?

BRUTE FORCE AIN'T THE ANSWER! EVERY TIME WE'VE TRIED IT, HE'S BEATEN US!

BRAINS! THAT'S THE ANSWER! IT'LL TAKE BRAINS TO LICK THE ANT-MAN!

AND, AT THAT MOMENT, IN WASHINGTON, D.C., FATE PREPARES TO TAKE A HAND IN OUR GRIM DRAMA...

WHO DO THEY HAVE ON THE CARPET IN THERE?

THAT SCIENTIST... THE GUY THEY CALL THE "EGGHEAD"! THEY SUSPECT HIM OF TRYING TO PUT ONE OVER ON UNCLE SAM!

U.S. GOVERNMENT ATOMIC ENERGY BOARD

IT HAS BEEN RUMORED THAT YOU ATTEMPTED TO SELL SECRET ATOMIC INFORMATION TO THE HIGHEST FOREIGN BIDDER!

WHAT HAVE YOU TO SAY FOR YOURSELF?!

NOTHING! TO A GENIUS LIKE ME YOUR INSIPID PATRIOTIC RAMBLINGS ARE LAUGHABLE! I SNEER AT YOU ALL!

ANYWAY, YOU'RE JUST TALKING! YOU'VE GOT NO PROOF, AND YOU KNOW IT!

AS A SCIENTIST, YOU MAY BE BRILLIANT, BUT AS A MAN, YOU'RE BENEATH CONTEMPT!

YOU'RE FIRED! YOU'LL NEVER WORK FOR THE GOVERNMENT AGAIN! GO ON, GET OUT OF HERE!

AND THE FOLLOWING DAY...

SAY -- THIS EGGHEAD CHARACTER -- HE'S OUR ANSWER!

SURE! IF ANYONE CAN OUTFOX THE ANT-MAN, HE CAN! HE'S ALL BRAIN!

BUT WILL HE WORK OUTSIDE THE LAW?

SURE! JUST MAKE THE PRICE RIGHT!

AND SO CONTACT IS MADE, TERMS ARE AGREED UPON, AND AN UNHOLY ALLIANCE IS BORN...

TEN G'S NOW... AND THE REST WHEN YOU'VE DEFEATED THE ANT-MAN!

AGREED!

2

WITH COLD SCIENTIFIC PRECISION, THE MAN CALLED EGGHEAD EMBARKS UPON HIS EVIL TASK...

THESE DOCUMENTARY FILMS SHOW THAT THE ANT-MAN IS CONSTANTLY AIDED BY HIS INSECT ALLIES! WITHOUT THEM, HE WOULD BE FAR LESS DANGEROUS TO HIS FOES!

AND SINCE HE WORKS WITH THE ANTS, HE MUST HAVE SOME METHOD OF COMMUNICATING WITH THEM!

IF I COULD LEARN TO DO THE SAME THING, I MIGHT DEFEAT THE ANT-MAN BY TURNING HIS OWN INSECTS AGAINST HIM!

ALL ABOUT ANTS

ANTS ARE UNABLE TO UTTER SOUNDS AND THEY DON'T USE SIGN LANGUAGE... THE ONLY WAY THAT THEY CAN COMMUNICATE IS BY ELECTRONIC SIGNALS THROUGH THEIR ANTENNAE!

ALL I HAVE TO DO IS DETERMINE WHAT THEIR ELECTRONIC WAVE LENGTH IS, AND I CAN TUNE IN ON THEM, AS THE ANT-MAN DOES!

I THINK I'M GETTING IT...

FINALLY...

THERE! MY MACHINE IS FINISHED! NOW I'M READY TO INVADE THE ANT-MAN'S OWN DOMAIN!

LATER, ON THE OUTSKIRTS OF TOWN...

PERFECT! A LARGE ANT-HILL IN A LONELY FIELD! I'LL BE ABLE TO WORK UNDISTURBED!

ONCE I COMMUNICATE WITH THE INSECTS, THEY'LL RELAY MY MESSAGE ON TO OTHERS! SOON, THERE WON'T BE AN INSECT IN THE COUNTY STILL LOYAL TO THE ANT-MAN!

3

WITH THE MACHINE TRANSLATING HIS WORDS INTO ELECTRONIC WAVE IMPULSES, EGGHEAD SPEAKS TO THE ANT COLONY...

I AM YOUR FRIEND... I HAVE COME TO FREE YOU FROM THE ANT-MAN'S RULE! HELP ME TO CAPTURE HIM AND THEN *YOU* SHALL BE THE MASTERS AND *HE* THE SLAVE!

LISTEN CAREFULLY TO MY INSTRUCTIONS... TELL THE ANT-MAN THAT THIEVES ARE PLANNING TO STEAL THE WENTWORTH NECKLACE FROM THE MUSEUM THURSDAY NIGHT!

THERE WILL BE LOOKOUTS POSTED TO WARN THEM OF THE POLICE! ONLY THE ANT-MAN CAN GET PAST THE LOOKOUTS AND CAPTURE THE THIEVES RED-HANDED!

WHEN THE ANT-MAN FALLS FOR THE BAIT, LEAD HIM TO THE MUSEUM... HAVE HIM ENTER THROUGH AN OPEN WINDOW WHERE I SHALL BE WAITING FOR HIM... WAITING WITH *FLYPAPER!!*

REMEMBER, BETRAY THE ANT-MAN, AND I WILL FREE YOU FROM HIS DOMINATION! THEN YOU WILL BE HIS MASTERS AND HE WILL SERVE YOU FOR THE REST OF HIS DAYS! *YOU* SHALL GIVE THE ORDERS--- FOR YOU ARE HIS SUPERIORS!

THE FIRST PHASE OF MY PLAN IS OVER! THE ANTS WILL NOT BE ABLE TO RESIST THE TEMPTATION I HAVE OFFERED! FOR I HAVE APPEALED TO THEIR GREED, AND THEIR VANITY!

LATER... ...AND WHEN HE ENTERS THE MUSEUM, I'LL BE WAITING WITH *FLY-PAPER!* HE'LL SOON FIND HIMSELF AS HELPLESS AS THOSE INSECTS!

EGGHEAD-- YOU'RE A *GENIUS!* IT CAN'T MISS!

WE'LL SNATCH THE WENT-WORTH NECKLACE AND CAPTURE THE ANT-MAN AT THE SAME TIME!

4

WHEN THURSDAY EVENING ARRIVES, THE SECOND PHASE OF THE MASTER PLAN IS PUT INTO EFFECT...

CAREFUL! DON'T TRIP THE BURGLAR ALARM!

STEADY... STEADY...

A HALF MILLION IN SPARKLERS! WHAT A HAUL!

WENTWORTH NECKLACE

OUTSIDE, A SOUPED-UP GETAWAY CAR STANDS READY...

I HOPE EGGHEAD'S SCHEME WORKS! THE ANT-MAN IS PRETTY SMART HIMSELF!

SUDDENLY, A PLATOON OF TINY FIGURES STEAL ONTO THE SCENE...

EVERYTHING IS READY! THE ANTS ARE LEADING HIM INTO MY TRAP... LIKE A SHEEP GOING TO THE SLAUGHTER...

THE SECONDS PASS SLOWLY -- TENSELY -- AS THE TINY COSTUMED FIGURE COMES CLOSER AND CLOSER TO HIS DATE WITH DESTINY...

HE'LL BE WITHIN RANGE OF MY BELLOWS IN ANOTHER TWO SECONDS---

NOW!

WHOOSHH

5

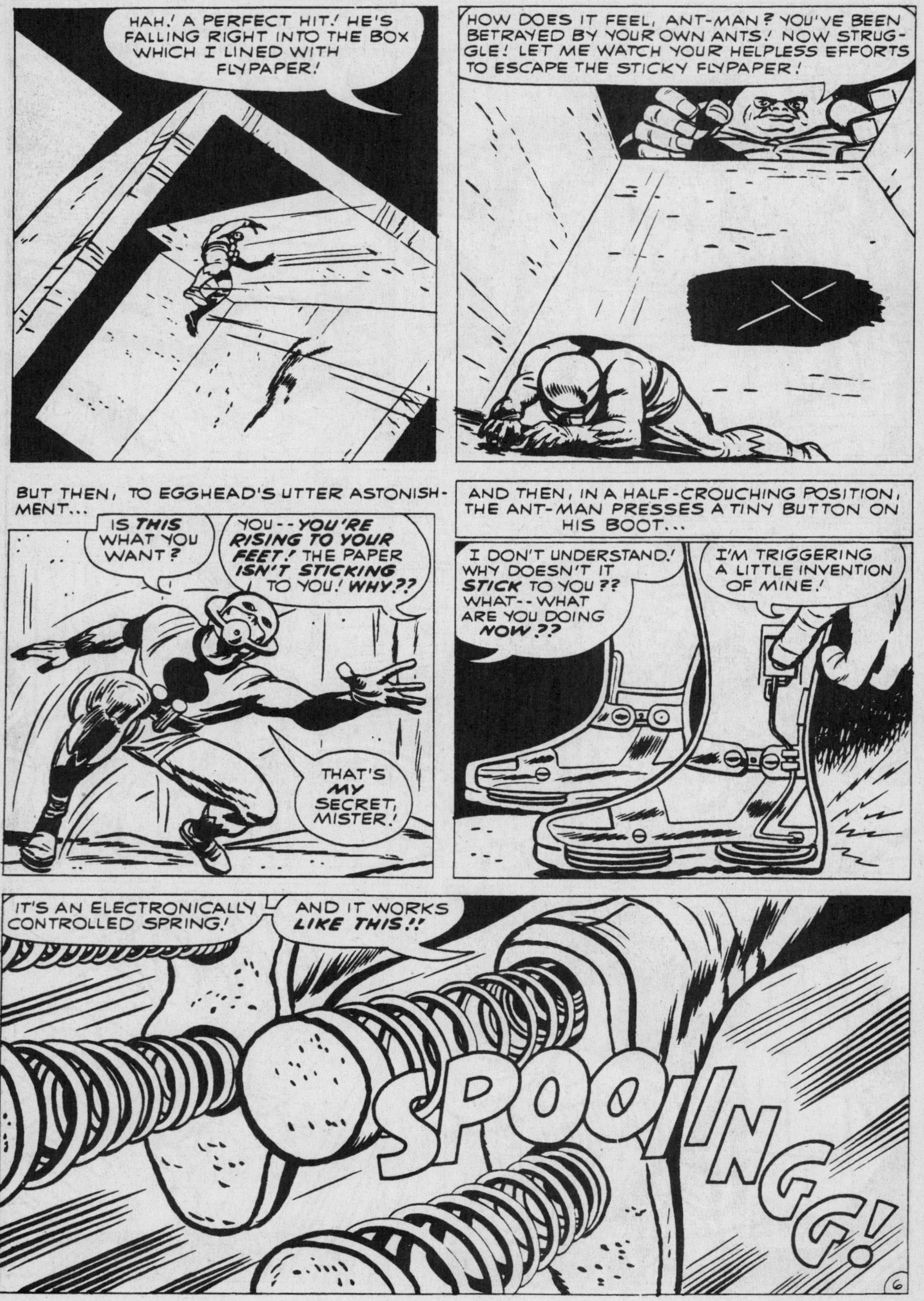
HAH! A PERFECT HIT! HE'S FALLING RIGHT INTO THE BOX WHICH I LINED WITH FLYPAPER!
HOW DOES IT FEEL, ANT-MAN? YOU'VE BEEN BETRAYED BY YOUR OWN ANTS! NOW STRUGGLE! LET ME WATCH YOUR HELPLESS EFFORTS TO ESCAPE THE STICKY FLYPAPER!
BUT THEN, TO EGGHEAD'S UTTER ASTONISHMENT...
IS THIS WHAT YOU WANT?
YOU--YOU'RE RISING TO YOUR FEET! THE PAPER ISN'T STICKING TO YOU! WHY??
THAT'S MY SECRET, MISTER!
AND THEN, IN A HALF-CROUCHING POSITION, THE ANT-MAN PRESSES A TINY BUTTON ON HIS BOOT...
I DON'T UNDERSTAND! WHY DOESN'T IT STICK TO YOU?? WHAT--WHAT ARE YOU DOING NOW??
I'M TRIGGERING A LITTLE INVENTION OF MINE!
IT'S AN ELECTRONICALLY CONTROLLED SPRING!
AND IT WORKS LIKE THIS!!
SPOOIINGG!
6

IS IT OVER? DID YOU CAPTURE THE ANT-MAN??

NO, YOU DOLT! CAN'T YOU *SEE* I FAILED!!! *YOU* TRY TO KEEP HIM HERE UNTIL I CAN THINK OF *ANOTHER* PLAN!

LOOK--*THERE* HE IS!

BLAST IT! I MISSED HIM!

HE'S RACING TOWARDS THAT SUIT OF ARMOR!

I'LL SWAT HIM LIKE A FLY, AND THEN...

ARGHH--MY HAND--

BONG!

PRESSING ANOTHER ELECTRONIC BUTTON, THE ANT-MAN DRAWS THE SPRINGS UP INTO HIS BOOTS AGAIN...AND LOCKS THEM THERE TEMPORARILY...

YOU BLAMED INSECT-- I'LL GRIND YOU TO DUST!

NOT A CHANCE, LOUD-MOUTH! SEE THIS LASSO?

IT'S MADE OF A NYLON FIBER...

...WHICH IS PRACTICALLY *UNBREAKABLE!*

EGGHEAD--*HELP!!* WHERE DID THAT PHONY RUN OFF TO?

7

HOW--HOW COULD *ANY* GUY THAT TINY, BE STRONG ENOUGH TO SPIN A FULL-GROWN MAN AROUND??!

THEY DON'T KNOW THAT EVEN THOUGH I SHRINK DOWN TO ANT-SIZE, I STILL RETAIN ALL THE STRENGTH OF A NORMAL HUMAN!

NEVER MIND HOW ANT-MAN'S STRONG! WE STILL GOTTA SILENCE HIM BEFORE HE CAN GET TO THE COPS!

IT SHOULDN'T BE HARD TO BEAT 'IM NOW THAT HIS ANTS HAVE DESERTED HIM!

BUT, WHILE THE MOBSTERS CONTINUE THEIR FRANTIC SEARCH...

THAT'S RIGHT, MY LITTLE FRIENDS! BRING THE SHEET CLOSER... CLOSER...

NOW! DROP IT *NOW!*

HEY!! LOOK *OUT!*

THE ANTS DROPPED A FLY-PAPER SHEET ON US!

BUT *WHY?* I THOUGHT THEY WERE ON *OUR* SIDE!

CAN'T GET FREE! WE'RE *TRAPPED!*

NOW WE'LL SEE HOW *YOU* JOKERS LIKE THE FEEL OF *FLYPAPER!!*

REALIZING THAT THEIR CAPER HAS FAILED, THE REMAINING GANGSTERS WHO HAD BEEN WAITING OUTSIDE SUDDENLY TURN TAIL AND...

THAT *DOES* IT! I'M LAMMING OUTTA HERE!

WAIT FOR *ME!*

I AIN'T TANGLING WITH ANT-MAN! *NO SIR!*

8

BUT, WHEN THEY FRANTICALLY REACH THEIR CAR...

THE TIRES -- THEY'RE *ALL* FLAT?!

AND SOMEONE SWIPED THE IGNITION KEY! BUT HOW?? I WAS HERE ALL THE TIME!!

SIRENS! IT'S THE *COPS!!*

RUN FOR IT!

ARRRRRRRRR

MOMENTS LATER...

WE ROUNDED UP MOST OF THEM! WE'LL PICK UP THE OTHERS LATER!

EGGHEAD HAD A SHREWD PLAN, BUT HE MADE *ONE* MISTAKE!

HE MISUNDERSTOOD THE PSYCHOLOGY OF ANTS! HE DIDN'T KNOW THAT THE ANTS DO *NOT* CONSIDER THEMSELVES MY *HELPLESS SLAVES!* THEY REGARD THEMSELVES AS MY *FRIENDS*...AND MY *PARTNERS* IN THE WAR AGAINST CRIME!

EGGHEAD TRIED TO APPEAL TO THEIR SENSE OF GREED, OF VANITY! BUT *INSECTS HAVE NO SUCH EMOTIONS!* UNFORTUNATELY, IT IS ONLY *WE HUMANS* WHO POSSESS SUCH PRIMITIVE TRAITS!

MY LITTLE ALLIES TOLD ME EGGHEAD'S ENTIRE PLOT! AND I DECIDED TO TURN THE TABLES ON THE PLOTTER HIMSELF! I WALKED INTO HIS TRAP, BUT UNKNOWN TO HIM, I WAS *PREPARED* FOR IT!

SO *THAT'S* WHAT HAPPENED...

9

"BEFORE I CAME HERE, I COVERED MYSELF WITH A SPECIAL OILY CHEMICAL THAT MADE IT IMPOSSIBLE FOR FLYPAPER TO STICK TO ME...

THEN, WHEN I ARRIVED AT THE MUSEUM, I LET THE AIR OUT OF THE TIRES OF THE GETAWAY CAR...

WHOOOSH!

AND WHILE I WAS INSIDE, BATTLING THE THIEVES, MY SILENT LITTLE PARTNERS TOOK THE KEY FROM THE CAR'S IGNITION...

AND BY THE TIME WE GOT HERE, IT WAS ALL OVER!

THE ONLY THING THAT WENT WRONG WAS THAT EGGHEAD ESCAPED DURING THE BATTLE!

I WOULDN'T WORRY ABOUT HIM! HIS UNDERWORLD PARTNERS WON'T BE HAPPY ABOUT THE WAY THINGS TURNED OUT! IF WE DON'T GET HIM FIRST, THEY WILL!

AND THUS, THE ONCE BRILLIANT ATOMIC SCIENTIST ENDS UP WANTED BY THE POLICE AND HUNTED BY THE UNDERWORLD AS HE HOLES UP IN A DINGY BOWERY FLOPHOUSE...

THE ANTS DEFEATED ME... THEY WERE TOO SMART FOR ME... TOO SMART...

WHO'S HE?

DUNNO! BUT HE'S BEEN MUTTERING TO HIMSELF SINCE HE CAME HERE! SOMETHING ABOUT ANTS...

ANTS? THE GUY MUST BE LOCO!

THAT'S WHAT I FIGGER! HE'S PROBABLY JUST SOME WORTHLESS BUM WITHOUT A BRAIN IN HIS HEAD!

THE END

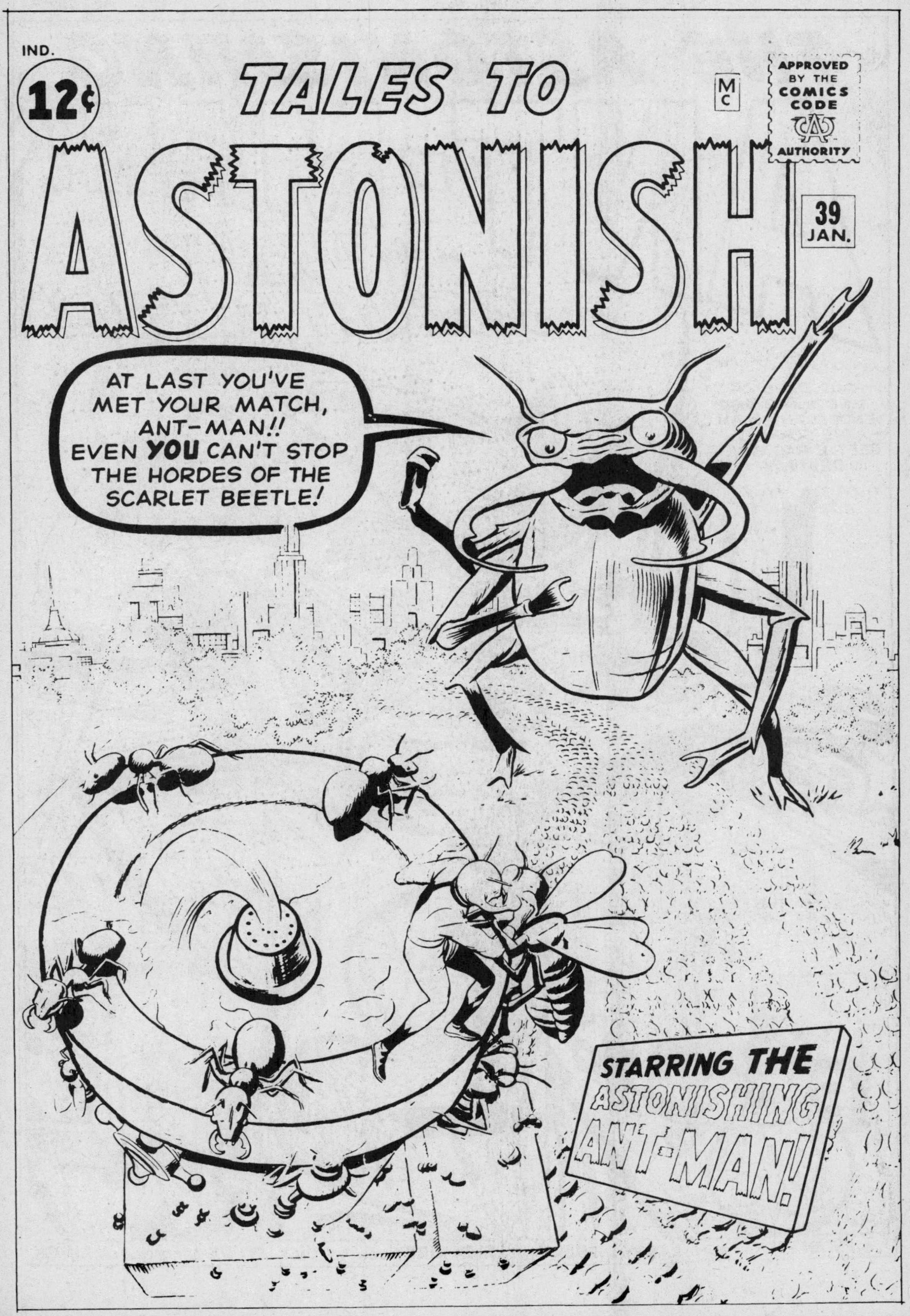
IND.
12¢
TALES TO ASTONISH
MC
APPROVED BY THE COMICS CODE AUTHORITY
39 JAN.
AT LAST YOU'VE MET YOUR MATCH, ANT-MAN!! EVEN YOU CAN'T STOP THE HORDES OF THE SCARLET BEETLE!
STARRING THE ASTONISHING ANT-MAN!

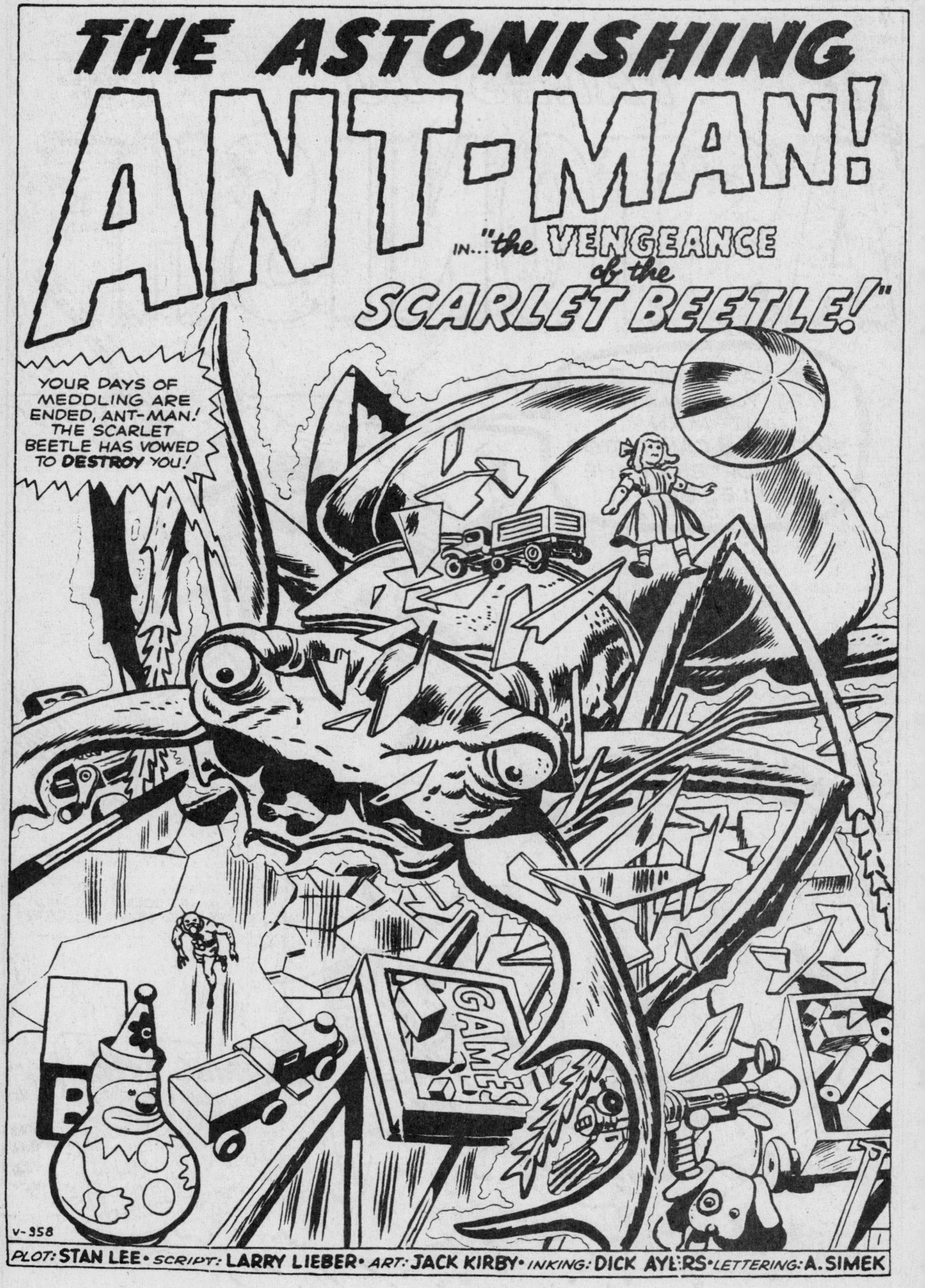
THE ASTONISHING
ANT-MAN!
IN..."the VENGEANCE of the SCARLET BEETLE!"
YOUR DAYS OF MEDDLING ARE ENDED, ANT-MAN! THE SCARLET BEETLE HAS VOWED TO **DESTROY** YOU!
GAMES
V-358

PLOT: STAN LEE • SCRIPT: LARRY LIEBER • ART: JACK KIRBY • INKING: DICK AYERS • LETTERING: A. SIMEK

MOST OF US ARE UNCONCERNED WITH THE INSECT WORLD THAT EXISTS BENEATH OUR FEET...

BUT TO HENRY PYM, THE ACTIVITIES OF THESE TINY CREATURES ARE OF GREAT IMPORTANCE! ESPECIALLY AT THIS MOMENT...

THIS IS THE THIRD SET OF ELECTRONIC WAVES I'VE RECEIVED FROM THE ANTS TODAY! SOMETHING MUST BE BREWING IN THE INSECT WORLD!

JUDGING FROM THE ERRATIC PATTERN OF THE WAVES, I'D SAY IT'S SOMETHING STRANGE -- AND DANGEROUS!

I'D BETTER INVESTIGATE AT ONCE -- AS THE ANT-MAN!!

I'LL RELEASE MY VIAL OF REDUCING GAS... AHHH! IT'S SHRINKING ME TO THE SIZE OF...AN ANT!

MOMENTS LATER, THE TINY WARRIOR CATAPULTS HIMSELF FROM HIS LAB!

NOTE: ALTHOUGH UNNOTICED BY OTHER EYES, THE BUILDING WHICH HOUSES HENRY PYM CONTAINS MANY SECRET DEVICES FOR USE BY AN ANT-SIZED HUMAN!

GUIDED BY SIGNALS FROM THE ANT-MAN'S CYBERNETIC HELMET, A SWARM OF ANTS CONVERGE BENEATH THEIR DESCENDING LEADER...

A NICE SOFT HILL TO LAND SAFELY ON...

OKAY, LITTLE PAL, TAKE ME TO THE SCENE OF THE TROUBLE!

HE'S HEADING INTO THE SEWER! WHAT COULD POSSIBLY BE HAPPENING DOWN THERE??

2

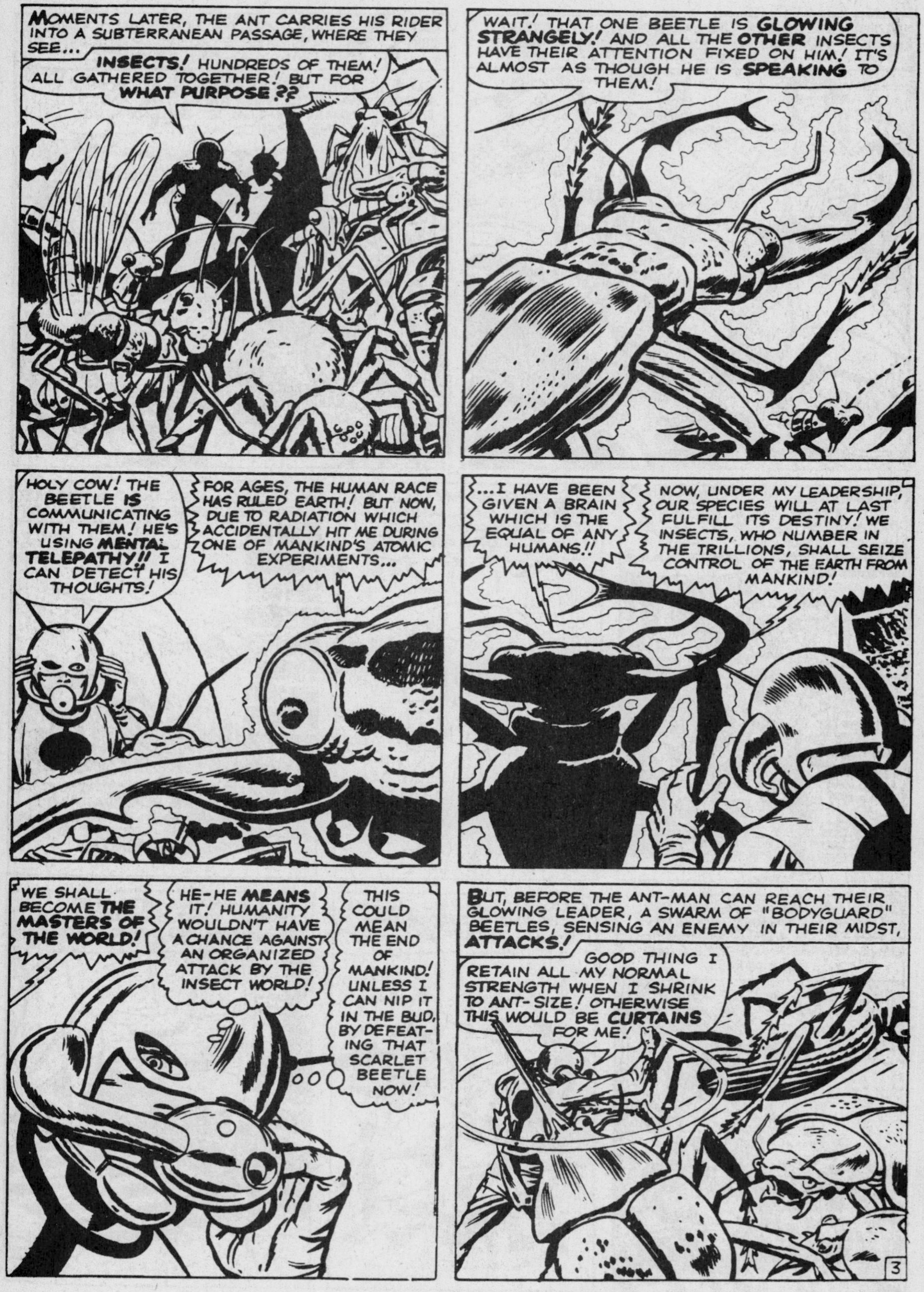
MOMENTS LATER, THE ANT CARRIES HIS RIDER INTO A SUBTERRANEAN PASSAGE, WHERE THEY SEE...
INSECTS! HUNDREDS OF THEM! ALL GATHERED TOGETHER! BUT FOR WHAT PURPOSE??
WAIT! THAT ONE BEETLE IS GLOWING STRANGELY! AND ALL THE OTHER INSECTS HAVE THEIR ATTENTION FIXED ON HIM! IT'S ALMOST AS THOUGH HE IS SPEAKING TO THEM!
HOLY COW! THE BEETLE IS COMMUNICATING WITH THEM! HE'S USING MENTAL TELEPATHY!! I CAN DETECT HIS THOUGHTS!
FOR AGES, THE HUMAN RACE HAS RULED EARTH! BUT NOW, DUE TO RADIATION WHICH ACCIDENTALLY HIT ME DURING ONE OF MANKIND'S ATOMIC EXPERIMENTS...
...I HAVE BEEN GIVEN A BRAIN WHICH IS THE EQUAL OF ANY HUMANS!!
NOW, UNDER MY LEADERSHIP, OUR SPECIES WILL AT LAST FULFILL ITS DESTINY! WE INSECTS, WHO NUMBER IN THE TRILLIONS, SHALL SEIZE CONTROL OF THE EARTH FROM MANKIND!
WE SHALL BECOME THE MASTERS OF THE WORLD!
HE-HE MEANS IT! HUMANITY WOULDN'T HAVE A CHANCE AGAINST AN ORGANIZED ATTACK BY THE INSECT WORLD!
THIS COULD MEAN THE END OF MANKIND! UNLESS I CAN NIP IT IN THE BUD, BY DEFEATING THAT SCARLET BEETLE NOW!
BUT, BEFORE THE ANT-MAN CAN REACH THEIR GLOWING LEADER, A SWARM OF "BODYGUARD" BEETLES, SENSING AN ENEMY IN THEIR MIDST, ATTACKS!
GOOD THING I RETAIN ALL MY NORMAL STRENGTH WHEN I SHRINK TO ANT-SIZE! OTHERWISE THIS WOULD BE CURTAINS FOR ME!
3

BUT EVEN THE ASTONISHING ANT-MAN CANNOT BATTLE HOPELESS ODDS, FOR THE NUMBER OF ATTACKING BEETLES SEEMS ENDLESS! AND THEN, FINALLY...

CAN'T GET AWAY-- UHHH--

CAN'T HOLD OUT ANY LONGER...

YOU HAVE DONE WELL, MY WARRIORS! AND NOW...

I SHALL USE THE GAS VIALS OF OUR FALLEN ENEMY...

BEHOLD HOW THE GROWTH GAS ENLARGES ME! I AM BECOMING AS BIG AS A HUMAN!

NOW, MY PETS, WE SHALL DISPOSE OF THE ANT-MAN! THEN WE SHALL BEGIN THE GREATEST BATTLE THE WORLD HAS EVER KNOWN! THE ENTIRE INSECT SPECIES AGAINST THE HUMAN RACE!

MINUTES LATER, A SEEMINGLY HELPLESS ANT-MAN REGAINS CONSCIOUSNESS, TO FIND...

MY HELMET IS GONE! SO ARE MY GAS CANISTERS!

THE BEETLES PUT ME IN THIS HOLE...AND WITHOUT MY CYBERNETIC HELMET, I CAN'T SUMMON MY ANTS TO RESCUE ME!

I'LL HAVE TO TRY TO CLIMB OUT OF HERE BY MYSELF!

UGH! IT'S TOO STEEP AND SLIPPERY! I CAN'T MAKE IT!

MEANWHILE, FOLLOWED BY COUNTLESS VARIETIES OF INSECTS, THE SCARLET BEETLE LAUNCHES HIS FIRST ATTACK AGAINST MANKIND! *

GO, LITTLE TERMITES--CHEW THROUGH THE TELEPHONE POLES! WE MUST DESTROY THE HUMANS' COMMUNICATION SYSTEM!

CRASH

NOTE: THE ONLY INSECTS WHO DO **NOT** OBEY THE SCARLET BEETLE ARE THE ANTS, LOYAL ONLY TO THEIR HUMAN LEADER!

BUGS, SPIDERS, GRASSHOPPERS... ALL BECOME PART OF THE FANTASTIC PLAN OF CONQUEST!

BRING THE DYNAMITE TO ME! IT WILL PROVE A POWERFUL WEAPON! QUIETLY... QUIETLY!! THAT IS IT...

9th ARMORY NATIONAL GUARD

DYNAMITE

IT'S A SPIDER BITE! HIS HONOR WILL HAVE TO REMAIN IN BED FOR THE NEXT FEW DAYS!

STRANGE! SO MANY PUBLIC OFFICIALS HAVE BEEN STRICKEN BY INSECTS LATELY!

WELL DONE, PET... WELL DONE...

AND THEN, THE MONSTROUS LEADER HIM-SELF STRIKES!

THAT GIANT BEETLE IS WRECKING THE STUDIO!

SHOOT HIM! SHOOT!

I CAN'T! THESE BLAMED BEES WON'T LEAVE ME ALONE LONG ENOUGH TO TAKE AIM!

SOON ALL THEIR TV AND RADIO STATIONS WILL BE DESTROYED!

=GASP= IF WE EVER NEEDED THE **ANT-MAN**, IT'S NOW!

WHERE IN BLAZES **IS** HE??

HE MUST'VE CHICKENED OUT! OR MAYBE HE'S EVEN **IN LEAGUE** WITH THESE INSECTS!

MEANWHILE, AT THAT MOMENT, IN A DARK, ABANDONED PASSAGEWAY BENEATH THE CITY...

I'LL **NEVER** BE ABLE TO CLIMB OUT OF THIS HOLE! WHAT CAN I DO??

5

BUT, UNKNOWN TO THE ANT-MAN, HIS CYBERNETIC HELMET WAS LEFT ON THE GROUND WHERE IT FELL... AND ALL THIS WHILE, ITS TRANSMITTER HAS BEEN SENDING OUT ELECTRIC IMPULSES, WHICH HAVE BEEN PICKED UP BY COUNTLESS ANTS...

REACHING THE HELMET AND FINDING THEIR LEADER GONE, THEY USE THEIR HIGHLY DEVELOPED SENSE OF SMELL TO TRACK HIM DOWN...

...UNTIL...

YOU'VE **FOUND** ME! I'M **SAVED!!**

AND SO, THE ANT-MAN SOON EMERGES AGAIN INTO THE SURFACE WORLD... READY TO MEET THE THREAT OF THE AWESOME SCARLET BEETLE!

HE USED MY **GROWTH GAS** ON HIMSELF! I CAN SEE HIM FROM HERE! BUT IN ORDER TO REACH HIM, WE'LL HAVE TO DEFEAT HIS INSECT ARMY!

LISTEN WELL, MY LITTLE FRIENDS...

HELP! THE SCARLET BEETLE!! **RUN!**

AFTER GIVING HIS ANTS THEIR INSTRUCTIONS, THE TINY AVENGER GOES INTO ACTION...

I'LL TAKE THIS ICE-CREAM POP STICK... IT MAY COME IN HANDY!

LOOK! THE SCARLET BETTLE HAS **SEEN** US! HE'S SENDING A HORDE OF BEETLES TO ATTACK US! NOW-- REMEMBER OUR BATTLE PLAN!

GOOD! THAT IS WHY I ORDERED THE **HONEY** ANTS INTO THE FRONT LINES!

THE BEETLES ARE HELPLESS--THEY'RE TRAPPED IN THE STICKY HONEY!

6

THAT TAKES CARE OF THE BEETLES! NOW THE **GRASSHOPPERS** ARE ATTACKING! I'LL JUST WAIT TILL THEY GET WITHIN RANGE!

I **KNEW** THIS ICE-CREAM POP STICK WOULD COME IN HANDY!

BY PRESSING IT AGAINST THE WATER HOLE, I CAN **MAGNIFY** THE SPRAY!

THEY'RE AFRAID OF THE WATER! THEY'RE **RETREATING!**

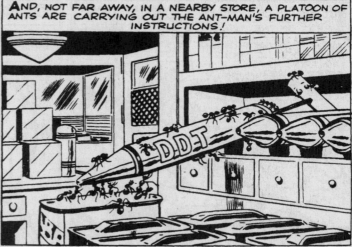

AND, NOT FAR AWAY, IN A NEARBY STORE, A PLATOON OF ANTS ARE CARRYING OUT THE ANT-MAN'S FURTHER INSTRUCTIONS!

DDT

MEANWHILE, THE ANT-MAN AND HIS ARMY ADVANCE CLOSER AND CLOSER TO THE SCARLET BEETLE...

ONLY THING IN OUR WAY NOW IS THAT SWARM OF BEES! OH, OH-- THEY'VE **SEEN** US!

BUT, AS THE BEES DIVE UPON THEIR FOES...

THE DDT! HURRY! BRING IT OVER HERE!

DDT

JUST IN TIME!! NOW STEADY... HOLD THE CAN STEADY! **THAT'S IT!!**

7

RIGHT ON TARGET!

THE **DDT** HAS WEAKENED THEM! THEY'RE FLYING AWAY!

BUT THEN... THE GREATEST DANGER OF ALL APPEARS.!! THE GIANT SCARLET BEETLE!

ANT-MAN! OF ALL THE HUMANS, ONLY **YOU** CAN THWART ME! SO YOU MUST BE MY FIRST VICTIM!

BUT, AS THE SCARLET BEETLE LUNGES AT THE ANT-MAN, THE TINY WARRIOR LEAPS ONTO THE SHOE OF A FLEEING HUMAN!

I'LL NEVER BE ABLE TO DEFEAT THAT MONSTROSITY OUT IN THE OPEN...

AND A MOMENT LATER, JUMPS OFF AGAIN...

...BUT A **TOY STORE** MIGHT BE THE PERFECT PLACE FOR OUR FINAL BATTLE!

I SEE YOU! IT'S FUTILE TO RUN IN THERE! YOU CANNOT ESCAPE FROM ME!

8

CARRY ME TO THE TOP OF THE COUNTER-- SWIFTLY, MY FRIEND!

I'M THRU **RUNNING** NOW!! SO, COME AND GET ME... IF YOU **CAN!**

IF I CAN??! YOU IMPUDENT MIDGET, I'LL SNUFF OUT YOUR LIFE AS I WOULD A CANDLE!

BUT, JUST AS THE GIANT CREATURE STRIKES, THE ANT MAN LEAPS ONTO A TOY CAR...

GR ASH!

YOU DIDN'T THINK I INTENDED TO **WAIT** FOR YOUR BLOW, DID YOU?!

AND, AN INSTANT LATER, THE COLORFUL WARRIOR GRABS A LANCE FROM A TOY KNIGHT...

THIS IS WHERE YOUR DREAM OF CONQUEST COMES TO AN END! IN ANOTHER SECOND, YOU'LL BE **FINISHED!**

FOOL! THAT TINY WEAPON CANNOT HARM THE MIGHTY SCARLET BEETLE!

THAT'S RIGHT! BUT IT **CAN** PUNCTURE THE CONTAINER WHICH HOLDS THE **REDUCING GAS!**

NO!! THE GAS IS ESCAPING! IT'S CAUSING ME TO **SHRINK!!**

AND YOU CAN'T COUNTERACT ITS EFFECT WITH THE ENLARGING GAS BECAUSE YOU'VE ALREADY **USED IT ALL UP!**

9

I'M GROWING SMALLER!! NO--NO!! IT CAN'T BE!! **IT CAN'T!!**

WITH THIS BALLOON PARACHUTE, I'LL BE SAFELY ON THE FLOOR IN NO TIME!

NOW THAT YOU'RE SMALL ENOUGH TO MEET ON EQUAL TERMS, I'LL JUST TAKE HOLD OF YOU...

I ALMOST HAD THE **WORLD** IN MY GRASP...!!

...AND IMPRISON YOU IN THE BALLOON!

NO! NO!!

ALL RIGHT, LITTLE FRIENDS-- BRING HIM TO MY LABORATORY! THE **ANT-MAN** HAS DONE ALL HE CAN! THE REST IS UP TO **HENRY PYM!**

A SHORT TIME LATER...

THERE! I'VE COUNTERACTED THE EFFECTS OF THE RADIATION! THE SCARLET BEETLE HAS LOST HIS INTELLIGENCE AND HIS POWER TO COMMUNICATE! HE'S JUST AN ORDINARY BUG AGAIN!

GO AHEAD, LITTLE FELLA... CRAWL AWAY! YOU'RE FREE TO LIVE OUT YOUR NATURAL LIFE NOW! IT WASN'T **YOUR** FAULT THAT YOU BECAME RADIO-ACTIVE! NOBODY'S TO BLAME --IT WAS JUST A STRANGE QUIRK OF FATE!

WELL, LOOKS LIKE THE NIGHTMARE IS OVER! NO MORE TROUBLE WITH INSECTS LATELY!

GUESS WE'LL **NEVER** REALLY KNOW WHAT HAPPENED! BUT WHAT ABOUT THAT **ANT-MAN!!** I WONDER IF HE WAS **AFRAID** TO TACKLE THE SCARLET BEETLE?

HE WAS NOWHERE AROUND! AND JUST AT THE TIME...

...WHEN WE NEEDED HIM THE MOST!

THE END

10

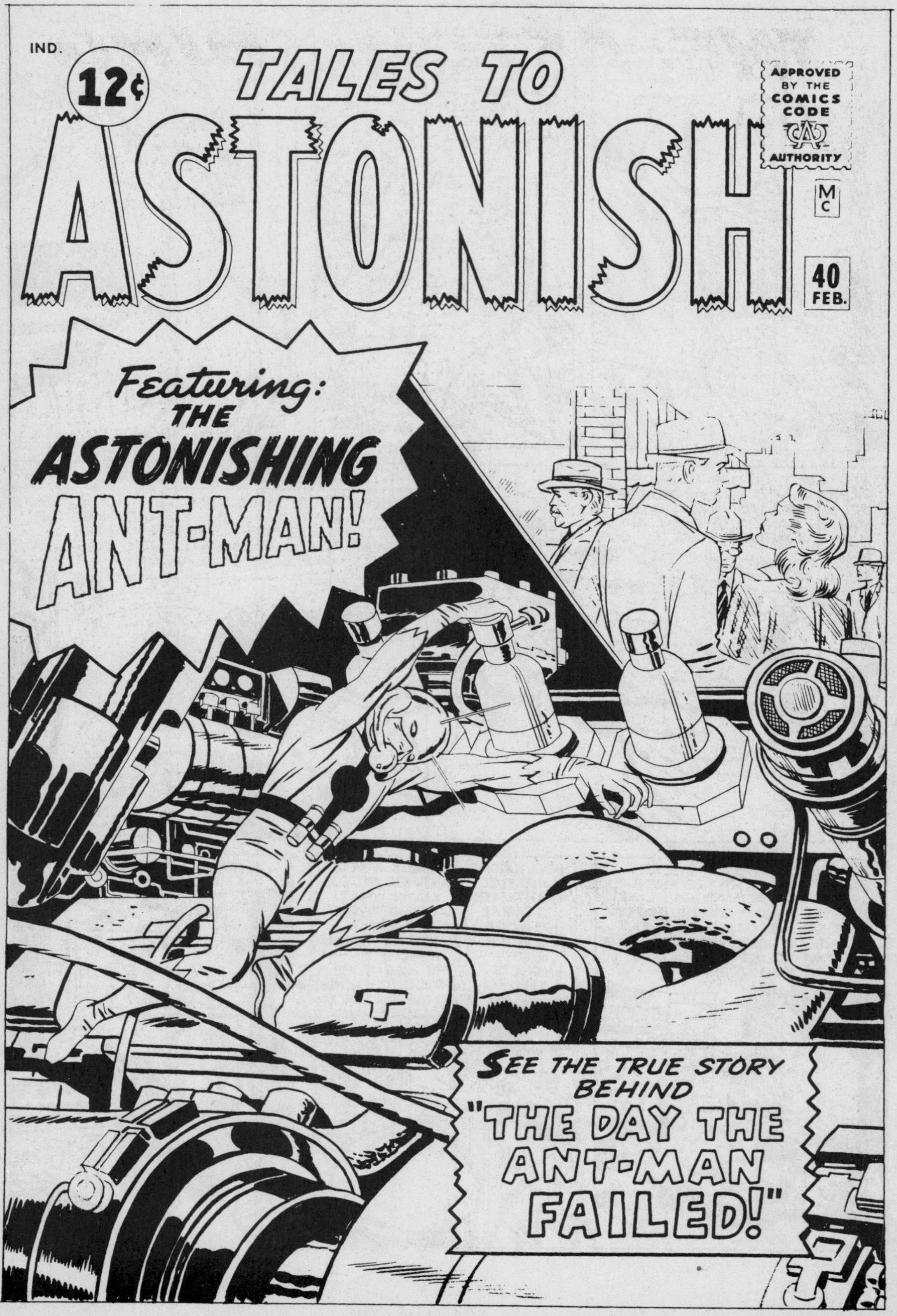
IND.
12¢
TALES TO
ASTONISH
APPROVED BY THE COMICS CODE AUTHORITY
MC
40
FEB.
Featuring:
THE
ASTONISHING
ANT-MAN!
SEE THE TRUE STORY BEHIND
"THE DAY THE ANT-MAN FAILED!"

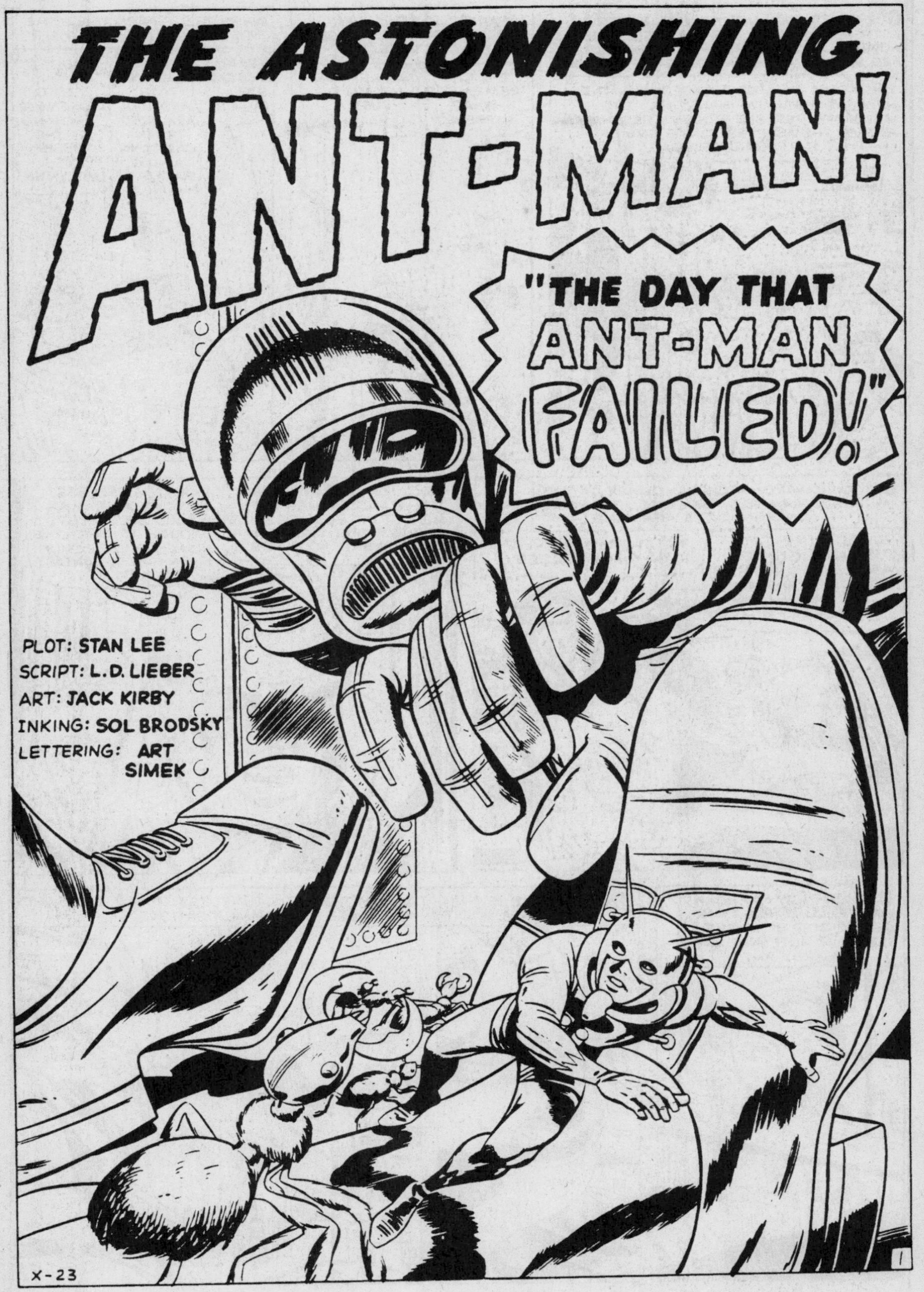
THE ASTONISHING
ANT-MAN!
"THE DAY THAT ANT-MAN FAILED!"
PLOT: STAN LEE
SCRIPT: L.D. LIEBER
ART: JACK KIRBY
INKING: SOL BRODSKY
LETTERING: ART SIMEK
1
X-23

OUR STARTLING ANT-MAN TALE BEGINS WITH HENRY PYM! FOR THE INSECT-SIZED ADVENTURER AND THE BRILLIANT SCIENTIST ARE SECRETLY ONE AND THE SAME PERSON!

THE ARMY WILL BE PLEASED WITH THE NEW GAS MASK I'M INVENTING! IT'S MADE OF UNSTABLE MOLECULES WHICH ADJUST THEMSELVES TO THE SIZE OF THE WEARER'S HEAD!

MEANWHILE, MILES AWAY, TWO DAZED FIGURES STAGGER TOWARD THE CITY...

I-I CAN'T REMEMBER WHAT HAPPENED!

ME NEITHER! MY MIND'S JUST A BLANK!

WHEN THE GUARDS REACH THE CITY, THE NEWS IS MADE PUBLIC...

EXTRA! HIJACKER STRIKES AGAIN!

HE'S MADE OFF WITH ANOTHER ARMORED TRUCK CARRYING A HUGE PAYROLL!

AND THE GUARDS CAN'T REMEMBER ANYTHING OF THE ROBBERY! IT'S UNCANNY!

HIJACKER IN NEW CRIME

BUT TO HOWARD MITCHELL, OWNER OF THE MITCHELL ARMORED TRUCK CO., IT'S MORE THAN UNCANNY! IT'S APALLING!

WHAT KIND OF PRIVATE GUARDS ARE YOU? ANOTHER ROBBERY, AND HAVE YOU CAUGHT THE HIJACKER? NO!!

BUT THERE'S NOTHING TO GO ON! NO CLUES!

NO CLUES! GREAT! WHEN THE HIJACKER HAS PUT ME OUT OF BUSINESS, I'LL TELL MY CREDITORS THAT THERE WERE NO CLUES!

BAH! IT'S USELESS! ONLY THE ANT-MAN WOULD BE CLEVER ENOUGH TO CATCH THE HIJACKER! IF I ONLY KNEW HOW TO CONTACT HIM!

BUT, UNKNOWN TO HOWARD MITCHELL, HIS PLEA HAS BEEN PICKED UP BY THE SENSITIVE ANTENNAE OF A NEARBY ANT...

THE MESSAGE IS THEN TRANSMITTED TO COUNTLESS OTHER ANTS, WHO FORM A CITY-WIDE WEB OF COMMUNICATIONS...

2

...UNTIL FINALLY, THE MESSAGE REACHES THE NERVE CENTER OF THE FANTASTIC NETWORK!

THERE! I'VE FINISHED THE ADJUSTABLE GAS MASK!

OH, OH-- MY ALARM IS BUZZING! THE ANTS MUST BE TRYING TO CONTACT ME!

BZZZZZZ ZZZ

I'D BETTER GO TO THE SECRET COMMUNICATIONS ROOM AND SEE WHAT'S UP!

MOMENTS LATER...

ELECTRONIC IMPULSES COMING IN! THEY ORIGINATE FROM SECTOR 12!

THE ASTONISHING SCIENTIST PUTS ON HIS CYBERNETIC HELMET, WHICH SOON TRANSLATES THE INCOMING SIGNALS INTO AN INTELLIGIBLE FORM!

HOWARD MITCHELL WANTS TO CONTACT ANT-MAN...

SOUNDS LIKE TROUBLE! AND THAT'S MY MIDDLE NAME! I'LL JUST CHANGE INTO MY COSTUME!

NOW I MERELY RELEASE THE REDUCING GAS I DEVELOPED!

THE FUMES ARE ACTING ON MY CELL TISSUES! I'M SHRINKING... SMALLER AND SMALLER!

I'M BECOMING THE TINIEST HUMAN ON EARTH...

--THE ANT-MAN!!

THE INCREDIBLE CRIME-FIGHTER THEN ENTERS HIS SPECIALLY-BUILT CATAPULT!

I'LL ADJUST THE ELECTRONIC CONTROLS TO ROCKET ME TO THE STREET OUTSIDE OF MITCHELL'S OFFICE!

3

THE CONTROLS ARE ADJUSTED, THE RELEASE BUTTON IS TRIGGERED...

...AND I'M ON MY WAY!

VOOOOOOMM

AS HE FLIES ABOVE THE CITY, THE COLORFULLY-CLAD FIGURE USES HIS CYBERNETIC TRANSMITTER TO SEND OUT IMPULSES, WHICH THE ANTS DETECT AND FOLLOW...

MY LITTLE PALS ARE CONVERGING RIGHT ON TARGET! THEY'LL CUSHION MY FALL!

BUT NO MACHINE IS PERFECT! EVEN A CAREFULLY-DESIGNED ELECTRONIC CATAPULT!

I'M OVERSHOOTING THE TARGET! INSTEAD OF LANDING ON THE ANTS, I'LL CRASH INTO THE BUILDING!

HOWEVER, THE TINY INSECTS ARE SWIFT AS THEY ARE LOYAL...

SAVED BY THE ANTS-- AS ALWAYS!

ALRIGHT, LITTLE PAL, YOU'RE BETTER EQUIPPED TO CLIMB WALLS THAN I AM, SO GIVE ME A LIFT UP TO THAT WINDOW! THAT'S IT... STEADY... STEADY...

MITCHELL ARMORED TRUCK CO.

YOU WANTED TO SEE ME, MITCHELL?

ANT-MAN! I DON'T KNOW HOW YOU KNEW TO COME-- BUT THANK HEAVENS YOU'RE HERE!

FOUR OF MY ARMORED TRUCKS CARRYING PAYROLLS WERE STOLEN! AFTER EACH ROBBERY THE GUARDS WERE FOUND DAZED, UNABLE TO REMEMBER WHAT HAPPENED!

MY GUARDS ARE BAFFLED! THEY'VE NO IDEA WHO THE HIJACKER IS, NOR HOW HE MADE OFF WITH THE TRUCKS!

4

YOU MUST **HELP** ME, ANT-MAN! YOU MUST CATCH THE HIJACKER! I CAN'T **AFFORD** ANY MORE ROBBERIES!

EVEN THOUGH THE PAYROLLS WERE INSURED, EACH TIME THEY WERE STOLEN, I LOST A CUSTOMER! IF IT CONTINUES, I'LL SOON BE OUT OF BUSINESS!

THEN YOUR **COMPETITORS** STAND TO BENEFIT BY THESE ROBBERIES! HMMMNN...

ALL RIGHT, MITCHELL, LISTEN! I WANT YOU TO ANNOUNCE THAT ONE OF YOUR ARMORED TRUCKS WILL CARRY A HUGE PAYROLL TOMORROW!

BUT IF THE SHIPMENT IS ANNOUNCED IN ADVANCE, THE HIJACKER WILL BE **CERTAIN** TO STRIKE!

THAT'S WHAT I'M **COUNTING** ON! AND WHEN HE AMBUSHES THE TRUCK, HE'LL FIND **ME** THERE-- WAITING TO TRAP HIM!

BY THE WAY, THAT'S AN INTERESTING COLLECTION OF PRIMITIVE ART! **INCA**, ISN'T IT?

YES! I WAS IN PERU LAST YEAR! I SPENT SOME TIME WITH THE INDIANS IN THE JUNGLE! BUT THAT'S **UNIMPORTANT** NOW! ALL THAT MATTERS IS THAT YOU CATCH THE HIJACKER!

DON'T WORRY! WHOEVER HE IS-- HOWEVER HE OPERATES--THE ANT-MAN WILL DEFEAT HIM! I PROMISE YOU!

AND SO, THE NEXT DAY...

I DON'T LIKE IT! IT'S TOO RISKY! EVERYBODY KNOWS ABOUT THE SHIPMENT, INCLUDING, YOU CAN BET, **THE HIJACKER!**

THAT'S THE IDEA...

WE WANT THAT GUY TO STRIKE AGAIN SO THE ANT-MAN CAN CATCH HIM!

ANT-MAN! I DIDN'T KNOW **YOU'D** BE ALONG!

NOW AT LEAST THE ODDS ARE IN **OUR FAVOR!**

5

BUT SCARCELY HAS ANT-MAN RECEIVED THE VOTE OF CONFIDENCE, WHEN...

OHHH--

WHAT'S THE MATTER??

I'VE GOT A PAIN! UHHH-- IT'S GETTING WORSE! I THINK IT'S... APPENDICITIS!

OH, NO! NOT NOW, OF ALL TIMES!

HOW-- HOW WILL YOU BATTLE THE HIJACKER?

C-CAN'T! I CAN'T WORRY ABOUT HIM NOW! I MUST GET TO A DOCTOR... BEFORE MY APPENDIX RUPTURES!

HURRY, LITTLE FRIEND! UHHH! HURRY...

WHAT DO WE DO NOW?

WITHOUT ANT-MAN'S PROTECTION, THE TRIP WILL BE TOO DANGEROUS! I'M FOR CALLING IT OFF!

BLAST THE LUCK! I'D GIVE ANYTHING TO CALL IT OFF! BUT I'M ALREADY COMMITTED! I'D LOSE ANOTHER CUSTOMER!

AND SO THE ARMORED TRUCK LEAVES, CARRYING A LARGE AMOUNT OF MONEY AND THREE FEARFUL GUARDS!

IT'S THE FIRST TIME THE ANT-MAN'S EVER FAILED ANYONE!

WELL, HE'S ONLY HUMAN! EVEN HE CAN GET SICK SOME TIME!

MITCHELL ARMORED TRUCK CO.

SOON THE TRUCK IS BEYOND THE CITY LIMITS...

I DON'T LIKE THIS ROAD! IT'S TOO LONELY!

AT LEAST WE HAVE PLENTY OF GUNS AND AMMO!

SO HAD THE OTHER GUARDS! AND IT DIDN'T HELP --WAIT!! THERE'S SOMETHING UP AHEAD, BLOCKING THE ROAD!

IT'S A MOVING VAN-- STALLED!

LOOKS LIKE MOTOR TROUBLE! WE'LL HAVE TO HELP THE GUY FIX IT, SO WE CAN GET PAST!

NO! THE HIJACKER MAY BE AROUND! IT'S NOT SAFE FOR US TO LEAVE THE TRUCK!

6

AND THEN, AS THE FRIGHTENED GUARDS PONDER WHAT TO DO...

LOOK! THE BACK OF THE VAN IS SLIDING OPEN!

THERE'S A GIANT MAGNET INSIDE!

IT'S PULLING US INTO THE VAN! BACK UP! QUICKLY!

I--I CAN'T! THE MAGNET IS TOO POWERFUL!

MITCHEL ARMORED TR

THE DOOR OF THE VAN HAS CLOSED AGAIN!

WE'RE TRAPPED IN HERE!

WHAT'LL WE DO??

LOOK! HE MUST BE THE--THE--

THE HI-JACKER!!

EXACTLY! AND AS THE SPIDER SAID TO THE FLY, "WELCOME, SUCKERS!"

NOW TO GET DOWN TO BUSINESS!

GAS!!

IT'S SEEPING INTO THE TRUCK!

I'M DIZZY ...I... I CAN'T STAND...

A FEW MINUTES LATER...

BY NOW THEY MUST BE ALL UNCONSCIOUS! I'LL OPEN THE LOCKED DOOR OF THEIR TRUCK WITH A BLOW-TORCH AND DUMP THE GUARDS OUT ON THE ROAD! BY THE TIME THEY COME TO AGAIN, I'LL BE LONG GONE!

CLEVER PLAN! TOO BAD IT'S GOING TO FAIL!

THE ANT-MAN! B-BUT--HOW??!!

I FIGURED YOU MIGHT NOT STRIKE IF YOU THOUGHT I WAS IN THE TRUCK...SO I FEIGNED ILLNESS AND PRETENDED TO STAY BEHIND!

7

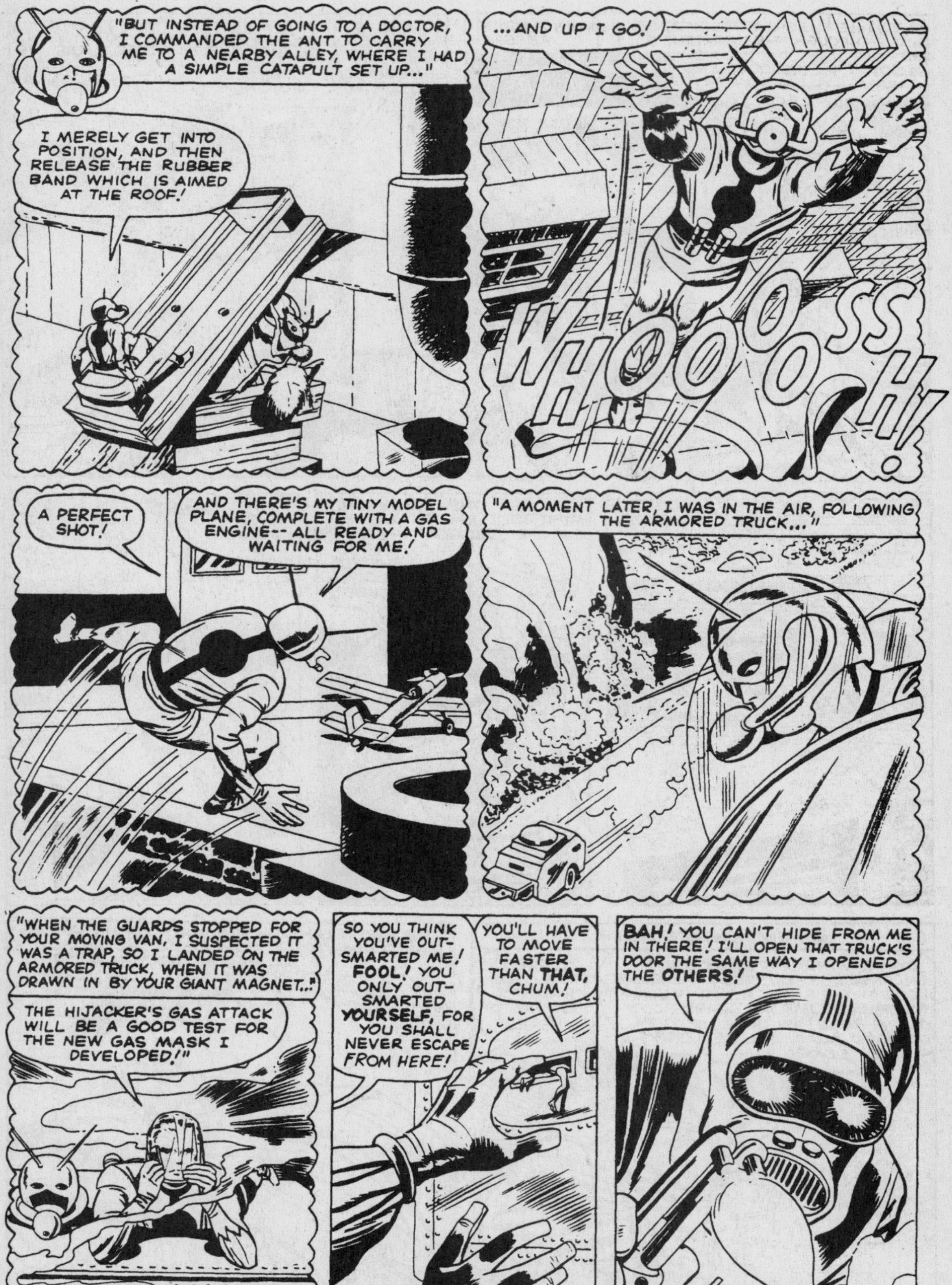
"BUT INSTEAD OF GOING TO A DOCTOR, I COMMANDED THE ANT TO CARRY ME TO A NEARBY ALLEY, WHERE I HAD A SIMPLE CATAPULT SET UP..."
I MERELY GET INTO POSITION, AND THEN RELEASE THE RUBBER BAND WHICH IS AIMED AT THE ROOF!
...AND UP I GO!
WHOOOOOSSH!
A PERFECT SHOT!
AND THERE'S MY TINY MODEL PLANE, COMPLETE WITH A GAS ENGINE-- ALL READY AND WAITING FOR ME!
"A MOMENT LATER, I WAS IN THE AIR, FOLLOWING THE ARMORED TRUCK..."
"WHEN THE GUARDS STOPPED FOR YOUR MOVING VAN, I SUSPECTED IT WAS A TRAP, SO I LANDED ON THE ARMORED TRUCK, WHEN IT WAS DRAWN IN BY YOUR GIANT MAGNET..."
THE HIJACKER'S GAS ATTACK WILL BE A GOOD TEST FOR THE NEW GAS MASK I DEVELOPED!"
SO YOU THINK YOU'VE OUT-SMARTED ME! FOOL! YOU ONLY OUT-SMARTED YOURSELF, FOR YOU SHALL NEVER ESCAPE FROM HERE!
YOU'LL HAVE TO MOVE FASTER THAN THAT, CHUM!
BAH! YOU CAN'T HIDE FROM ME IN THERE! I'LL OPEN THAT TRUCK'S DOOR THE SAME WAY I OPENED THE OTHERS!
8

BUT WHILE THE MENACING HIJACKER BURNS THROUGH THE DOOR, THE ANT-MAN USES THE PRECIOUS SECONDS TO SEND FOR HELP...

MY HELMET'S ELECTRONIC SIGNALS WILL BE PICKED UP BY ALL THE ANTS IN THE AREA!

AND NO SOONER HAS THE MESSAGE BEEN SENT...

I MISSED AGAIN! BUT YOU CAN'T ESCAPE!

I'LL HIDE IN THE IGNITION!

BUT NO SOONER DOES THE ANT-MAN CRAWL INTO THE TINY SPACE THEN THE HIJACKER TURNS THE KEY...

WHEW! IT ALMOST CRUSHED ME!

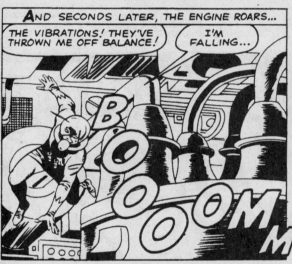

AND SECONDS LATER, THE ENGINE ROARS...

THE VIBRATIONS! THEY'VE THROWN ME OFF BALANCE!

I'M FALLING...

B O O O M M

MADE IT! I'LL BE SAFE HERE ATOP THE ENGINE BLOCK-- AT LEAST FOR A MOMENT!

BUT THAT MOMENT IS SHORT-LIVED, FOR SUDDENLY...

THE NOISE--IT'S SO LOUD! I CAN'T STAND IT!

BEEEEPP BEEEEPP

HAH! HAH! THIS HORN MUST SOUND A THOUSAND TIMES LOUDER TO THE ANT-MAN, THAN IT WOULD TO A NORMAL SIZED PERSON!

BEE EEEEPP

9

I'VE GOT TO REACH THE WIRES THAT CONNECT THE HORN, BEFORE THE NOISE DEAFENS ME!

BEEEE EPP!

THERE! I'VE RIPPED OUT THE WIRES! ANOTHER FEW SECONDS AND MY EARDRUMS WOULD'VE BURST!

EDITOR'S NOTE: EVEN THOUGH THE ANT-MAN IS SMALL AS AN INSECT, HE STILL RETAINS ALL THE STRENGTH OF HIS NORMAL SIZE! OTHERWISE, HE COULDN'T HAVE YANKED OUT THE WIRES!

THE ANT-MAN STOPPED THE HORN! B-BUT WHERE IS HE NOW? I CAN'T FIND HIM!

AH, THERE YOU ARE! YOU'RE VERY AGILE BUT YOU'VE COME TO THE END OF THE LINE!

THE ANTS SHOULD HAVE REACHED THE KNOB BY NOW!

AND, JUST AS THE TINY HUMAN HAS PREDICTED, A SWARM OF FAITHFUL INSECTS TURNS THE WINDSHIELD WIPER CONTROL AS THE ANT-MAN HAD INSTRUCTED THEM...

WELL DONE, FELLAS! THAT'LL GIVE ME JUST THE IMPETUS I NEED!

WHA--?!!

WHISK!

NOW IT'S MY TURN AT BAT!

10

THIS GAS MASK WAS NEVER AS GOOD AS THE ONE I'M WEARING-- THE ONE I INVENTED FOR THE ARMY! BUT NOW I'LL MAKE IT COMPLETELY WORTHLESS!

WITH GAPING HOLES TORN IN HIS MASK, THE HIJACKER SOON BECOMES HELPLESS!

THE GAS IS MAKING ME DIZZY-- I-I'M GOING TO PASS OUT!

QUICKLY, MY LITTLE FRIENDS-- GATHER BELOW ME!

UHHHH... AHHH! LIKE LANDING ON A CLOUD!

AS THE HIJACKER SLUMPS TO THE GROUND, HIS MASK FALLS FROM HIS FACE, TO REVEAL...

JUST AS I SUSPECTED! IT'S MITCHELL, OWNER OF THE ARMORED TRUCK COMPANY!

NOW TO CONTACT THE POLICE, BEFORE HE REGAINS CONSCIOUSNESS!

MINUTES LATER...

I FIRST SUSPECTED MITCHELL WHEN I SAW THE PRIMITIVE STATUES IN HIS OFFICE AND I LEARNED HE'D SPENT TIME IN THE JUNGLES OF PERU!

FOR I KNEW THAT THE INDIANS THERE HAVE AN ANCIENT VAPOR, THE INHALING OF WHICH CAUSES A LAPSE OF MEMORY!

SO YOU FIGURED THAT WAS TIED IN WITH THE HIJACKER! AND THAT'S WHAT MADE YOU DECIDE TO WEAR A GAS MASK!

RIGHT! THEN, THE FACT THAT ONLY MITCHELL KNEW ALL THE ROUTES OF HIS TRUCKS, ADDED TO MY SUSPICION OF HIM!

BUT WHY'D MITCHELL DO IT?

MY COMPANY WAS LOSING MONEY! I THOUGHT I COULD GET IT BACK BY STEALING IT, AND NO ONE WOULD EVER KNOW!

THEN, I THOUGHT IF I MYSELF SENT FOR THE ANT-MAN, HE'D NEVER SUSPECT ME!

AND WE THOUGHT THE ANT-MAN HAD FAILED US BY GETTING SICK!

MISTER, EVEN WHEN THAT GUY FAILS, HE WINS! THAT'S THE ANT-MAN FOR YOU!

THE END

11

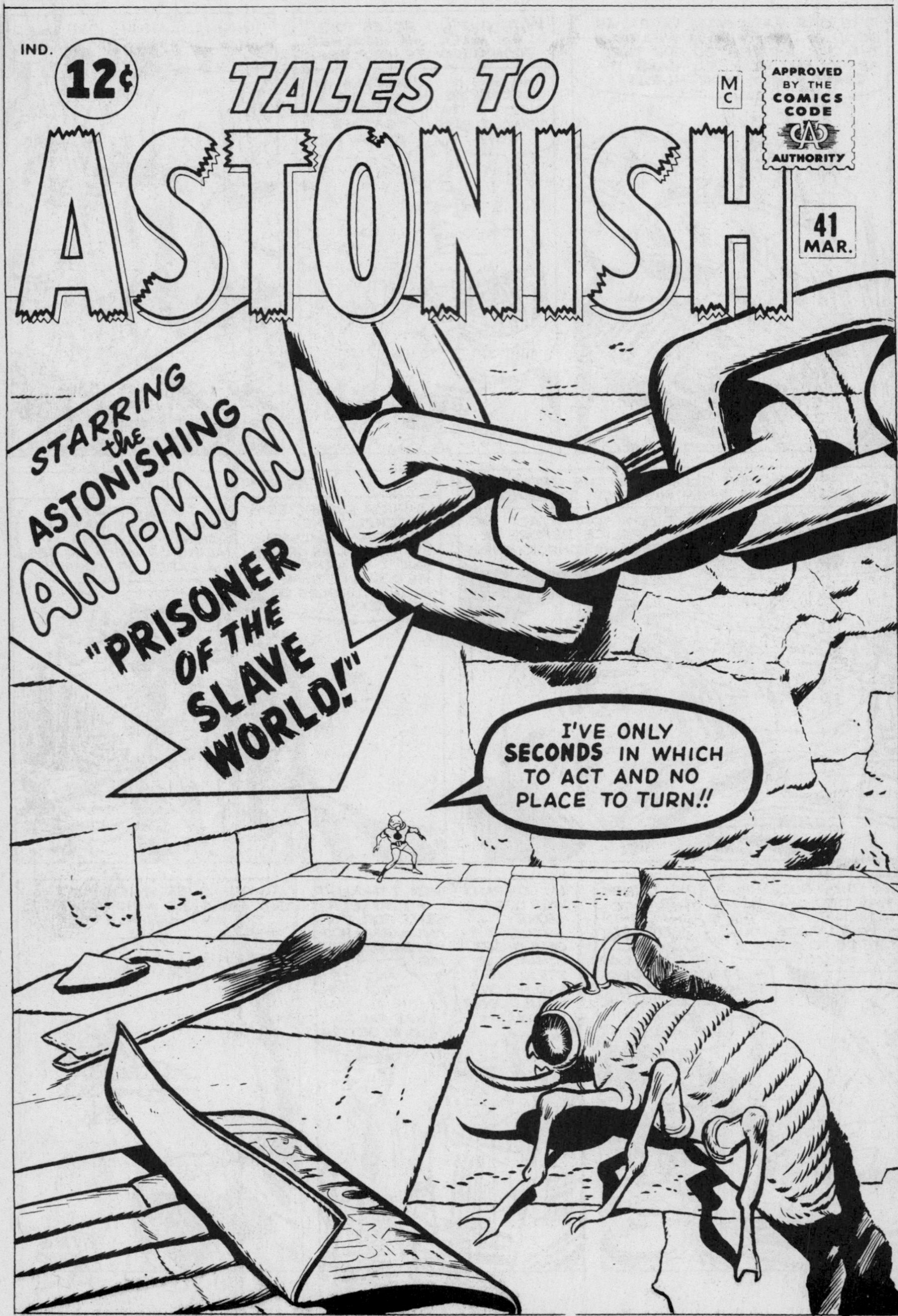
IND.
12¢
TALES TO ASTONISH
MC
APPROVED BY THE COMICS CODE AUTHORITY
41 MAR.
STARRING the ASTONISHING ANT-MAN
"PRISONER OF THE SLAVE WORLD!"
I'VE ONLY SECONDS IN WHICH TO ACT AND NO PLACE TO TURN!!

THE ASTONISHING ANT-MAN!

"PRISONER OF THE SLAVE WORLD!"

IF YOU WERE HENRY PYM, YOU COULD NEVER PREDICT WHEN YOU MIGHT RUN INTO ADVENTURE! IT MIGHT EVEN HAPPEN WHEN YOU UNSUSPECTINGLY VISIT A FELLOW SCIENTIST...

STRANGE... PAUL ASKED ME TO DROP OVER...

...SAID HE HAD A NEW FORMULA TO SHOW ME! YET, HE DOESN'T ANSWER THE BELL!!

...AND SINCE I'VE TAKEN TO WEARING CLOTHES OF UNSTABLE MOLECULES*, I MERELY RELEASE MY REDUCING GAS FROM ITS CONCEALED VIAL, AND...–

THERE! THE GAS IS ALREADY TAKING EFFECT! I'M GROWING SMALLER... SMALLER...

THE DOOR'S LOCKED FROM THE INSIDE! PAUL MUST BE IN THE LAB! MAYBE HE'S ILL! I CAN'T GET IN THERE TO FIND OUT, BUT THE ANT-MAN CAN!

GOOD THING I'VE BEEN CARRYING A SPARE COSTUME WITH ME LATELY!

*EDITOR'S NOTE: CLOTHES COMPOSED OF UNSTABLE MOLECULES ARE ABLE TO STRETCH AND CONTRACT AS THE WEARER'S OWN BODY DOES!

PLOT: STAN LEE
SCRIPT: LARRY LIEBER
ART: DON HECK
LETTERING: ART SIMEK

AND THE FANTASTIC SHRINK-ING PROCESS DOESN'T STOP UNTIL HENRY PYM HAS BEEN REDUCED TO THE SIZE OF --THE ANT MAN!

NOW TO DON MY WORKING SUIT!

NEXT, I'LL SUMMON THE NEAREST ANT IN THE AREA, BY MEANS OF MY CYBERNETIC HELMET!*

*EDITOR'S NOTE: THE ANT-MAN'S HELMET IS DESIGNED TO EMIT ELECTRONIC WAVES, WHICH THE ANTS CAN DETECT THROUGH THEIR SENSITIVE ANTENNAE!

WITHIN A FEW MOMENTS, AN ALLY ARRIVES TO SERVE THE WORLD'S SMALLEST HUMAN!

I'LL GET A BETTER VIEW FROM THE KEYHOLE!

THAT'S RIGHT, FELLA, CARRY ME RIGHT THRU THE LOCK, SO I CAN LOOK INTO THE LAB AND SEE WHAT'S HAPPENED TO PAUL!

BUT, TO THE ANT-MAN'S ASTONISHMENT...

THE LAB'S EMPTY! I DON'T UNDERSTAND --HOW COULD PAUL HAVE LEFT A LOCKED ROOM??

I'D BETTER MAKE A THOROUGH SEARCH OF THE PLACE!

I'VE EXAMINED EVERY NOOK AND CRANNY! THE WINDOWS ARE LOCKED FROM THE INSIDE! THERE ARE NO SECRET EXITS; NO WAY FOR PAUL TO HAVE LEFT! AND YET, HE'S NOT HERE!

AND THAT'S JUST THE BEGINNING! FOR, IN THE DAYS THAT FOLLOW...

...STILL ANOTHER EMINENT SCIENTIST HAS DISAPPEARED! THE POLICE ARE BAFFLED! THE F.B.I. HAS BEEN CALLED INTO THE CASE!

INASMUCH AS I TOO AM A SCIENTIST, WHATEVER HAPPENED TO THEM, IS ALSO LIABLE TO HAPPEN TO ME! BUT, IF IT DOES, I'LL BE PREPARED FOR IT-- AS THE ANT MAN!

2

A FEW DAYS LATER, A WINDOW WASHER COMES TO HENRY PYM'S LABORATORY...

I'M WITH A NEW OUTFIT THAT'S JUST MOVED INTO THE NEIGHBORHOOD! WE'RE GIVING FREE TRIAL WINDOW CLEANINGS THIS WEEK!

FINE! MY WINDOWS CAN USE A GOOD WASHING!

THE BUSY SCIENTIST RETURNS TO HIS EXPERIMENTS, PAYING LITTLE ATTENTION TO THE "WINDOW CLEANER" IN HIS LAB...

IF YOU LIKE OUR WORK, WE HOPE YOU'LL HIRE US REGULAR!

YES... I GUESS SO!

BUT SUDDENLY, WITHOUT THE SLIGHTEST WARNING--

WHAT THE...??!!

I--I CAN'T MOVE! MY LIMBS ARE RIGID! I CAN'T EVEN USE MY VOCAL CORDS... CAN'T SPEAK!!

HAH! THE PARALYZING LIQUID WORKS FAST, DOESN'T IT, PYM? HA! HA! HA!

AND, AT THAT MOMENT, IN ANOTHER DIMENSION OF SPACE AND TIME...

I WONDER WHO THE WINDOW WASHER'S NEXT VICTIM WILL BE?

SILENCE, EARTHLINGS! CONCENTRATE ON YOUR WORK! YOU MUST CONSTRUCT AN INVINCIBLE WEAPON FOR THE MIGHTY WAR LORD, KULLA!

THE PEACE LOVERS OF THIS WORLD THINK TO DEFEAT ME! THEY BESIEGED MY FORTRESS! THEY INTEND TO STARVE ME OUT!

BUT WHEN YOU HAVE BUILT THE ULTIMATE WEAPON FOR ME, AN ELECTRO-DEATH RAY, THEN I SHALL CONQUER THEM ALL!

KULLA, YOU'RE A TYRANT! AND IN THE END, TYRANTS ALWAYS LOSE, NO MATTER WHAT THEIR WEAPON!

YOU DARE SPEAK BACK TO KULLA!?! TO THE DUNGEON WITH HIM!

3

MEANWHILE, BACK IN OUR OWN DIMENSION...

YOU STILL CAN'T MOVE OR SPEAK, AND I'LL BET YOU'RE WONDERING WHY I PUT THESE GADGETS ON OUR HEADS! WELL, YOU'RE GONNA FIND OUT...

THE "WINDOW WASHER" ACTIVATES THE STRANGE HELMETS, AND INSTANTLY BOTH MEN ARE ENGULFED IN A SWIRLING STREAM OF STRANGE IRIDESCENT LIGHT...

WE'RE FADING AWAY!!

AND, AN INFINITY LATER, THE TWO FIGURES AGAIN MATERIALIZE!

AH, YOU'VE BROUGHT ANOTHER TO HELP US BUILD THE ELECTRO-DEATH RAY! EXCELLENT!

YOU WILL BE WELL PAID FOR YOUR WORK!

JUST MAKE SURE YOU PAY ME IN GOLD! YOUR PAPER MONEY WOULDN'T BE WORTH BEANS ON MY WORLD!

SOON, HENRY PYM'S PARALYSIS WEARS OFF, AND HE'S PUT TO WORK WITH THE OTHER CAPTURED SCIENTISTS...

IT'S PYM!

SO THEY KIDNAPPED YOU, TOO!

PAUL! BEN CARTER! WHAT'S THIS ALL ABOUT?

THERE ARE QUESTIONS, EXPLANATIONS, AND FINALLY, WHEN HENRY PYM HAS HEARD ENOUGH...

KULLA IS HOLDING GOOD CARDS! BUT ANT-MAN WILL SOON TRUMP HIM!

NOW I MUST TRANSFORM MYSELF WHERE NOBODY CAN SEE ME! HERE'S ONE WAY TO ACCOMPLISH IT...

DOWN WITH ALL TYRANTS! DOWN WITH KULLA!

DON'T, PYM!

YOU'LL BE PUNISHED!

WHY-- WHY DID HE DO IT!??

4.

A FEW DAYS ALONE IN A DUNGEON, WITHOUT FOOD OR WATER, WILL TEACH THE FOOL A LESSON!

IT WORKED! NOW I CAN RELEASE MY REDUCING GAS WITHOUT BEING SEEN!

ONCE AGAIN I SHRINK INTO THE SMALLEST OF ALL HUMANS! ANT MAN!

OH, OH--I SEE SOME FORMS MOVING IN THE SHADOWS! I'D BETTER GET INTO MY COSTUME FAST!

STRANGE-LOOKING INSECTS! BUT, THEY HAVE ANTENNAE, JUST LIKE ANTS! I'LL TRY TO HOLD THEM AT BAY WITH ELECTRONIC IMPULSES FROM MY HELMET!

THEY'RE NOT STOPPING! THEY MUST RECEIVE ON A DIFFERENT FREQUENCY!

BUT, BEFORE ANT-MAN CAN ALTER THE FREQUENCY OF HIS CYBERNETIC HELMET...

THEY'RE ATTACKING!

...BUT THEY'RE NO MATCH FOR THE STRENGTH OF AN ADULT HUMAN!*

*THOUGH HIS SIZE IS REDUCED, ANT-MAN RETAINS ALL THE STRENGTH OF NORMAL-SIZED HENRY PYM!

THEN, BEFORE THE STARTLED INSECTS CAN REGROUP, ANT-MAN MANAGES TO ALTER THE FREQUENCY OF HIS CYBERNETIC HELMET...

THAT'S IT! NOW I'M TUNED IN ON THE RIGHT FREQUENCY! THEY'RE OBEYING MY MENTAL COMMAND TO FORM A CIRCLE!

NOW I CAN CONTROL THEM JUST AS EASILY AS I DO THE ANTS IN MY OWN DIMENSION!

5

HAVING MASTERED THE INSECTS, THE ANT-MAN HAS NO TROUBLE LEAVING THE DUNGEON...

IRON DOORS DO NOT A PRISON MAKE ...AT LEAST NOT WHILE THE PRISONER IS ANT SIZE!

THE HUMAN SCIENTISTS HAVE COMPLETED THE ELECTRO-DEATH RAY, SIRE!

EXCELLENT! I CAN HARDLY WAIT TO TURN THEM ON THOSE LIBERTY-LOVING FOOLS WHO ATTACK MY FORTRESS!

LOOKS LIKE I ARRIVED JUST IN TIME!

BUT, AS THE TINY COSTUMED FIGURE ENTERS THE ROOM...

OH, OH-- AN ELECTRIC EYE BEAM!

THE WARNING LIGHT IS BLINKING! SOMEONE HAS ENTERED!

LOOK! THERE ON THE GROUND!

IT'S THE ANT-MAN!

HOW IN THE WORLD DID HE EVER GET HERE?

WHAT DOES IT MATTER HOW? JUST SO HE'S HERE! IF ANYONE CAN STOP KULLA, HE CAN!!

WHAT?! THAT PUNY INSECT STOP THE MIGHTY KULLA! HA! HA! HA!

ONE STEP WILL DESTROY HIM FOREVER!

BUT SO TINY IS THE ANT-MAN, THAT HE IS ABLE TO CROUCH SAFELY BETWEEN THE RIDGES OF THE GUARD'S BOOT!

THERE! THAT FINISHES HIM!

THAT'S WHAT YOU THINK, BUSTER!

AND NOW, I'LL JUST TAKE OUT MY MINIATURE, TEMPERED-STEEL PEN KNIFE...

...AND CUT AN OPENING IN THE SOLE, JUST LARGE ENOUGH FOR ME TO CRAWL THROUGH!

6

THE INSECT! HE'S NOT THERE! HE'S DISAPPEARED!!

IMPOSSIBLE! HE COULDN'T JUST VANISH!

HE MUST BE SOMEWHERE NEARBY! LOOK FOR HIM! FIND HIM!

=WHEW!= THIS GUY MUST NEVER WASH HIS SOCKS! BUT, NO MATTER... I'LL SOON BE OUT OF HERE!

NOW, IF I CAN JUST MAKE IT OVER TO THE OTHER PRISONERS BEFORE THE GUARDS CAN CATCH ME!

LOOK! THERE HE IS!

WHERE?

JUMPING DOWN YOUR BOOT! YOU FOOL-- HE WAS HIDING THERE ALL THE TIME!

SEIZE HIM!

DARTING, TWISTING, TURNING, HE MAKES IT!!

HURRY-- CONCEAL ME!!

RIGHT! GATHER 'ROUND, BOYS! SHIELD HIM FROM KULLA!!

ONE OF YOU PICK ME UP! SLIP ME IN YOUR POCKET!

THIS'LL BUY ME A FEW SECONDS! ALL THE TIME I NEED TO TRANSMIT SOME ELECTRONIC SIGNALS!

WHERE IS HE? WHICH ONE OF YOU IS HIDING HIM? SPEAK UP, YOU SWINE!!

HIDING WHO?

YOU'RE SEEING THINGS!

7

GUARDS-- SEARCH THEM ALL! **FIND** THE TINY HUMAN!

KULLA DOESN'T **KNOW** IT, BUT THE INSECTS THAT INHABIT HIS OWN FORTRESS WILL CAUSE HIS DOWNFALL!

THERE! I'M TUNED IN ON THE CORRECT FREQUENCY! NOW TO GIVE THEM THEIR COMMANDS!

HE'S NOT IN **THIS** POCKET!

NOTHING IN HERE!

KEEP LOOKING!

IF I REMAIN HERE, THEY'LL FIND ME! SO...

THAT CRACK IN THE FLOOR! I'LL BE SAFE **THERE**!

I'LL GET HIM!

THERE HE IS!

THEN, WHEN THE TINY FIGURE IS BUT A SPLIT-SECOND FROM SAFETY...

HAH! I GOT HIM!

IT'S THE SAME CHEMICAL WHICH THE WINDOW WASHER PARALYZED ME WITH! **AGAIN** I CAN'T MOVE! I CAN'T EVEN SPEAK!

NOW, MY CLEVER LITTLE FRIEND, YOU HAVE COME TO THE END OF THE ROAD!

HA HA HA HA HA HA

SILENTLY, AS KULLA APPROACHES THE HELP-LESS ANT-MAN, THE ELECTRO-DEATH RAY SLOWLY TURNS...

8

AND, JUST AS THE EVIL WAR LORD IS ABOUT TO STRIKE THE ANT-MAN...

...THE AWESOME WEAPON ZEROES IN ON ITS TARGET-- AND FIRES!!

KULLA IS DEAD!

BUT HOW?? WHO COULD HAVE FIRED THE GUN??

AT LAST! THE CHEMICAL HAS WORN OFF! I CAN MOVE AGAIN!

AND THEN, THE GUARDS DISCOVER WHY THE ANT-MAN IS KNOWN BY THAT NAME-- BECAUSE HE HAS THE FANTASTIC POWER TO MAKE OTHER INSECTS SERVE HIM!

I COULDN'T MOVE OR SPEAK! BUT I COULD THINK! AND MY CYBERNETIC HELMIT TRANSMITTED MY THOUGHTS TO THE INSECTS!

OUR WAR LORD IS GONE! BUT WE CAN STILL CARRY ON!

NO! WITHOUT KULLA WE COULD NEVER CONQUER THE LAND!

YOU'RE THROUGH! EVEN NOW MY INSECTS ARE PULLING THE LEVER WHICH OPENS THE ENTRANCE OF THE FORTRESS!

AND, AS THE MIGHTY GATE SWINGS OPEN, THE ENEMIES OF TYRANNY POUR INTO THE CITADEL...

WHERE THEY HAVE LITTLE TROUBLE IN DEFEATING THEIR LEADERLESS ENEMY...

THE MENACE IS ENDED! THE PEOPLE OF OUR LAND CAN BREATHE EASILY AGAIN!

THANKS TO THE ANT-MAN!

OVER THERE-- LOOK!!

9

IT'S THE WINDOW WASHER WITH **ANOTHER** PRISONER!

HE DOESN'T REALIZE WE'RE **FREE** NOW! HIS GAME IS UP!

NOW'S MY CHANCE TO SNEAK BACK AND ENLARGE MYSELF!

GOT TO BECOME HENRY PYM BEFORE THEY REALIZE I WAS GONE!

C'MON! WE'LL LET PYM OUT OF THE DUNGEON! THE POOR GUY MUST BE STIR CRAZY BY NOW!

JUST IN TIME!

FINALLY...

IT WAS **YOU** WHO TURNED AGAINST YOUR FELLOW HUMANS AND CAUSED US TO BE IMPRISONED HERE!

SO WHAT?! KULLA OFFERED ME A **FORTUNE**! IT WAS **WORTH** THE CHANCE! ANYWAY, YOU CAN'T DO ANYTHING TO ME! YOU AIN'T POLICEMEN!

BUT **WE** CAN DO SOMETHING! WE SHALL KEEP YOU HERE, AS OUR PRISONER, UNTIL YOU HAVE TRULY REFORMED!

MINUTES LATER...

IMAGINE IF KULLA HAD USED HIS SCIENTIFIC KNOWLEDGE FOR GOOD!

EVEN THIS DIMENSION TRANSPORTER, WHICH IS RETURNING US TO OUR OWN WORLD... WHAT A BOON IT COULD HAVE BEEN!

BUT KULLA IS GONE... AND HIS SECRETS ARE LOST WITH HIM!

WE'RE HOME AGAIN!

AHH, TO BREATHE FRESH EARTHLY AIR AGAIN!

BUT **ONE** THING BOTHERS ME! HOW DID THE ANT-MAN REACH THAT OTHER DIMENSION?? AND WHERE IS HE **NOW**??

10

I CAN'T FIGURE THAT ONE OUT **EITHER**! I GUESS WE'LL **NEVER** LEARN THE ANSWER!

PERHAPS IT DOESN'T MATTER **HOW** THE ANT-MAN GETS WHERE HE DOES! JUST SO WE KNOW THAT WHEN-EVER HE'S NEEDED... HE'S ALWAYS **THERE**!

THE END

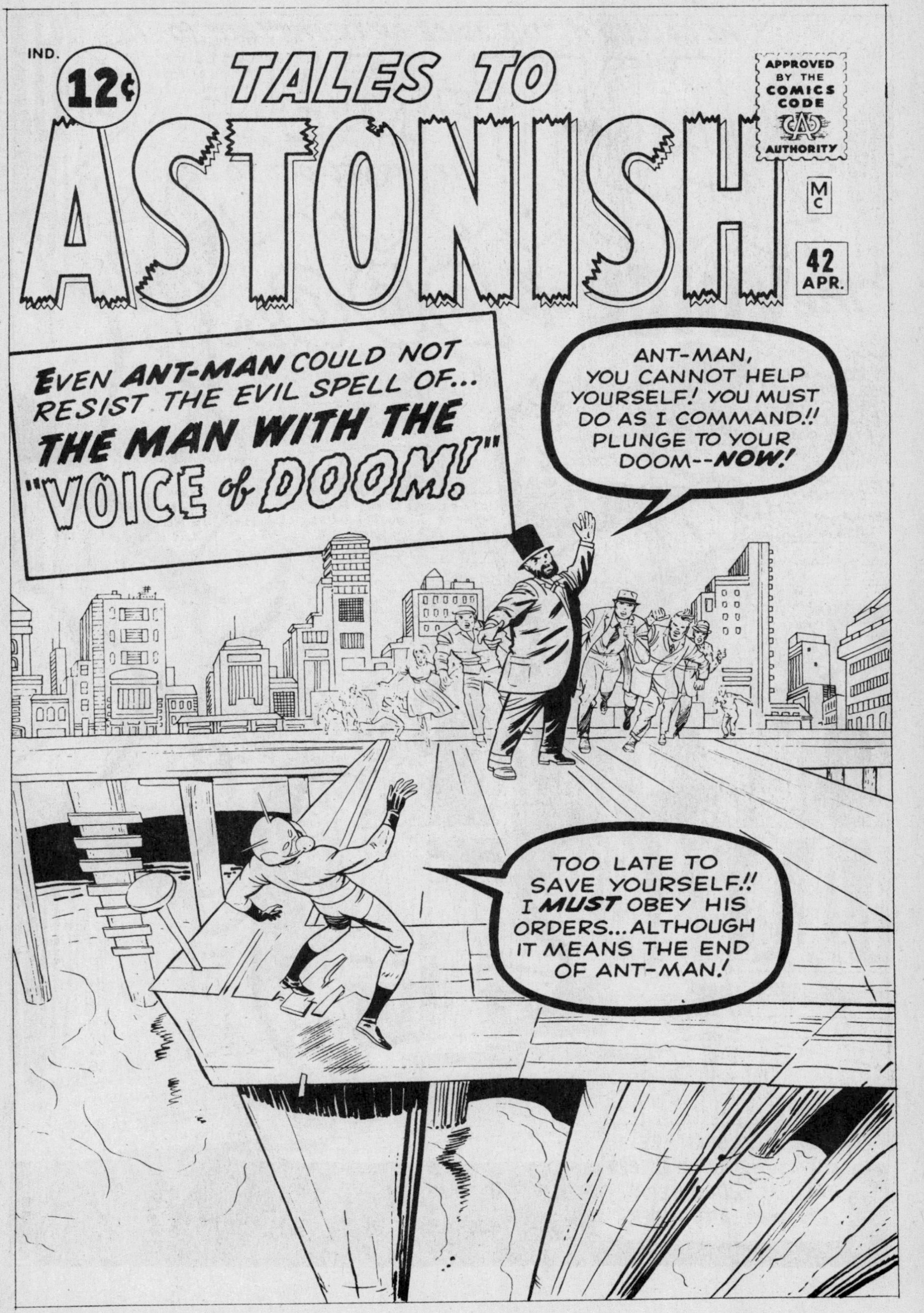
IND.
12¢
TALES TO ASTONISH
APPROVED BY THE COMICS CODE AUTHORITY
MC
42 APR.
EVEN ANT-MAN COULD NOT RESIST THE EVIL SPELL OF... THE MAN WITH THE "VOICE of DOOM!"
ANT-MAN, YOU CANNOT HELP YOURSELF! YOU MUST DO AS I COMMAND!! PLUNGE TO YOUR DOOM--NOW!
TOO LATE TO SAVE YOURSELF!! I MUST OBEY HIS ORDERS...ALTHOUGH IT MEANS THE END OF ANT-MAN!

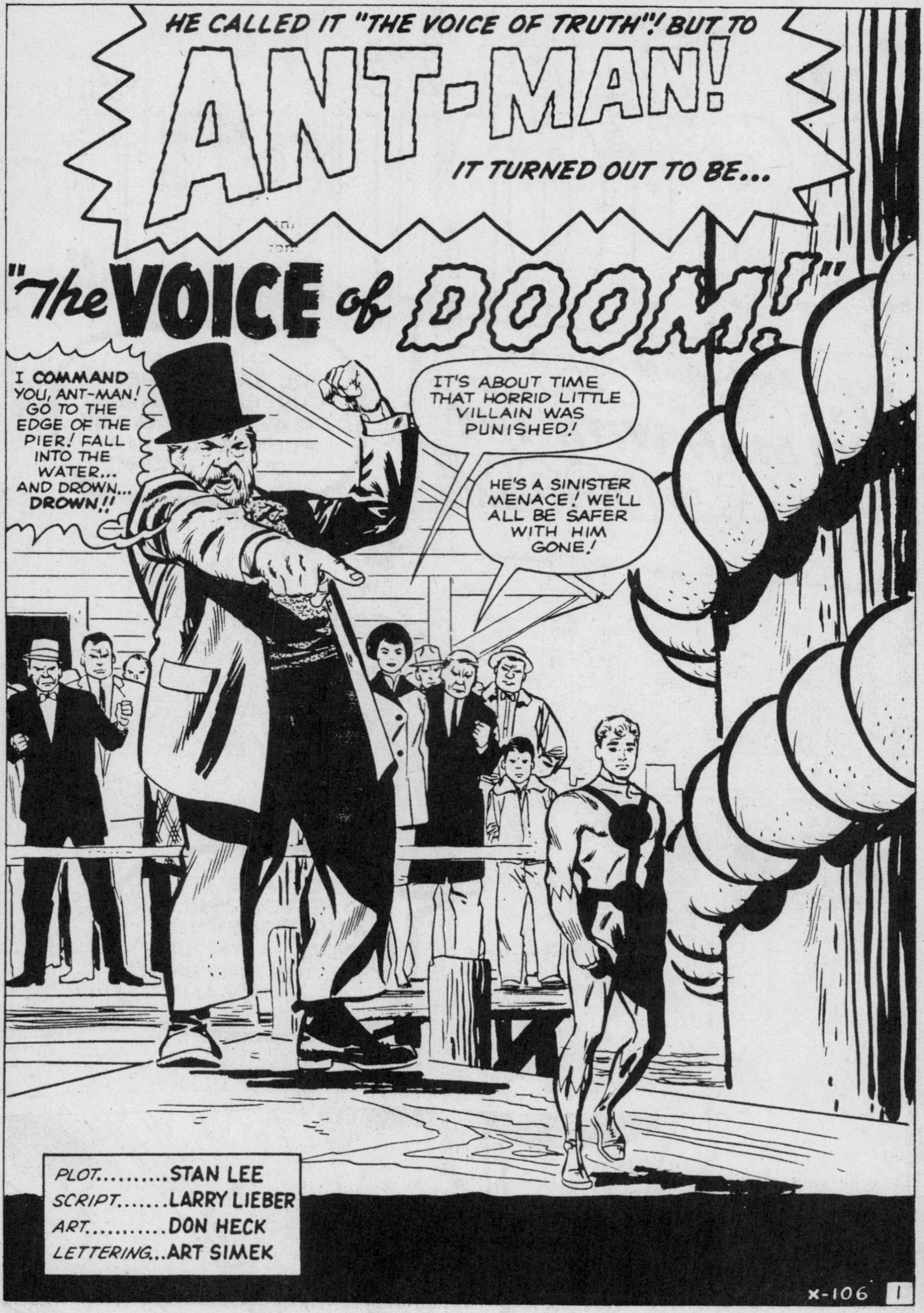

HE CALLED IT "THE VOICE OF TRUTH"! BUT TO
ANT-MAN!
IT TURNED OUT TO BE...
"The VOICE of DOOM!"
I COMMAND YOU, ANT-MAN! GO TO THE EDGE OF THE PIER! FALL INTO THE WATER... AND DROWN... DROWN!!
IT'S ABOUT TIME THAT HORRID LITTLE VILLAIN WAS PUNISHED!
HE'S A SINISTER MENACE! WE'LL ALL BE SAFER WITH HIM GONE!
PLOT.........STAN LEE
SCRIPT.......LARRY LIEBER
ART..........DON HECK
LETTERING...ART SIMEK
X-106
1

TO THOSE SEEING HIM FOR THE FIRST TIME, **JASON CRAGG** SEEMS LIKE JUST A HARMLESS ODDBALL! NO ONE WOULD EVER DREAM THAT HE IS... **THE MOST DANGEROUS MORTAL ON EARTH!**

HEY! GET A LOAD OF THAT KOOK!

HE LOOKS LIKE SOMETHING LEFT OVER FROM THE CIVIL WAR!

HE'S SETTING UP A SOAP BOX! I GUESS HE'S GOING TO MAKE A SPEECH!

WONDER WHAT HE'S SELLING?

IT'S A CINCH IT'S NOT **RAZOR BLADES!**

BUT THE MOMENT THE STRANGER SPEAKS, THE JEERS AND LAUGHTER STOP! FOR HIS IS A **VOICE** BEYOND COMPARE!

GATHER TO ME! HEAR MY WORDS! I, JASON CRAGG, SPEAK TRUTH! **TRUTH!**

NEVER HAVE I HEARD SUCH A **SINCERE** VOICE!

I CAN'T RESIST IT! HE'S ON THE LEVEL! I **KNOW** HE IS!

BUT A TINY FIGURE PASSING NEARBY REMAINS UNAFFECTED...

HE'S ACTUALLY PUT HIS AUDIENCE INTO A TRANCE! YET **I** FEEL NOTHING! MY HELMET MUST IN SOME WAY FILTER OUT THE HYPNOTIC ELEMENT IN HIS VOICE!

AND THEN SUDDENLY, THE AMAZING FEAT TAKES ON A GRIM ASPECT...

HEED ME! THE ANT-MAN IS A SINISTER VILLAIN WHO MUST BE DRIVEN FROM THE CITY!

I HEAR! I BELIEVE!

THE ANT-MAN IS A **MENACE** TO OUR CITY!

JASON CRAGG SPEAKS THE TRUTH!

THE ANT-MAN MUST BE DRIVEN FROM OUR MIDST!

IT'S **FANTASTIC!** WITHOUT LOGIC-- WITHOUT EVIDENCE -- HE'S TURNED THE CROWD **AGAINST** ME! BUT **WHY?** WHAT IS HIS PURPOSE? AND WHO **IS** HE?

WHO, **INDEED** IS THIS SPELL-BINDING ORATOR, WHOSE COMPELLING VOICE CAN BEND A CROWD TO ITS WILL? AND WHY DOES HE VILIFY THE ANT-MAN? FOR THE INCREDIBLE ANSWERS, WE MUST GO BACK A FEW WEEKS...

2.

JASON CRAGG ORIGINALLY CAME FROM THE MIDWEST, WHERE HE WAS A RADIO ANNOUNCER WHO JUST DIDN'T HAVE WHAT IT TAKES!

BUY PEPPO DOG FOOD! THE FOOD FOR DISCRIMINATING DOGS!

HE SOUNDS AS CONVINCING AS A WET SPONGE!

WE'LL HAVE TO DUMP HIM BEFORE WE LOSE ALL OUR LISTENERS!

BUT, THEY NEVER DID FIRE JASON CRAGG, FOR ONE DAY AT A NEARBY ATOMIC EXPERIMENTAL LABORATORY...

CAREFUL! THE RADIOACTIVITY IS GETTING TOO HIGH!

I CAN'T LOWER IT! THE DIAL IS STUCK!

THROW THE EMERGENCY SWITCH! HURRY!

THERE! THE CURRENT IS OFF!

-WHEW!- ANOTHER FEW SECONDS AND THE RADIATION MIGHT HAVE ESCAPED!

BUT, UNKNOWN TO THE SCIENTISTS, BY A MILLION-TO-ONE ACCIDENT, A TINY STREAM OF ELECTRIFIED PARTICLE--IONIZED ATOMS DID ESCAPE, AND WERE PICKED UP BY JASON CRAGG'S MICROPHONE WHERE THEY WERE AMPLIFIED, AND...

I--I FEEL SO STRANGE!

FOR A MOMENT JASON COULDN'T SPEAK! BUT THEN, WHEN HE REGAINED HIS VOICE, IT WAS DIFFERENT! IT HAD AN UNNATURAL TONE...

AND REMEMBER THAT YOUR DOG KNOWS THE DIFFERENCE, SO GIVE IT THE BEST! GIVE IT...

...GIVE IT PEPPO DOG FOOD!

HURRY! LET'S RUN TO THE GROCER'S AND GET SOME!

WE DON'T EVEN HAVE A DOG, BUT WE CAN EAT IT OURSELVES!

NEEDLESS TO SAY, JASON WAS AN OVERNIGHT SUCCESS!

OUR SALES HAVE JUMPED THREE HUNDRED PER CENT!

THANKS TO OUR SILVER-TONGUED SALESMEN! YOU'RE IN FOR A RAISE, M'BOY!

NOT ME! I'M QUITTING!

3

BUT YOU **CAN'T** QUIT! WE **NEED** YOU!

OF **COURSE** YOU DO! BUT **I** DON'T NEED **YOU!** AS A MATTER OF FACT, WITH MY FABULOUS NEW VOCAL POWER, I NEED NEVER WORK AGAIN!

AND JASON CRAGG WAS RIGHT!

TICKET? BUT MY GOOD MAN, TODAY'S THURSDAY, THE DAY WHEN ALL PEOPLE CARRYING HANDKERCHIEFS WITH THE INITIALS "J. C." ARE ALLOWED TO RIDE **FREE!**

FREE? OF COURSE ...YOU'RE **RIGHT,** SIR!

AS HE TRAVELED, HE BECAME BOLDER, MORE DEMANDING! HE EVEN ASSUMED THE FLAMBOYANT APPEARANCE OF AN ORATOR...

I AM HUNGRY! PREPARE ME A STEAK DINNER AT ONCE!

YOUR VOICE... I CANNOT RESIST IT... I MUST OBEY!

AND THEN, WHEN CRAGG HAPPENED TO BE PASSING THROUGH CENTER CITY, HOME OF THE ANT-MAN...

LOOK AT THE **ANT-MAN** TACKLING THOSE **THIEVES!** WOW!

AND HE'S EVEN GOT A BUNCH OF LITTLE ANTS **HELPING** HIM!

YEOOOWW!

ANTS--BITIN' AND STINGIN' ME!

STOP! WE QUIT!

BULLSEYE!

BETWEEN THE ANT-MAN AND THE POLICE, THE CROOKS IN THIS TOWN HAVEN'T GOT A CHANCE!

OKAY, WE'LL TAKE OVER NOW! STEP ASIDE!

YOU DID A SWELL JOB! THANKS, ANT-MAN!

THE WAY HE COMMANDS THOSE ANTS THRU HIS CYBERNETIC HELMET--IT'S TERRIFIC!

HMM... RESPECTED BY THE POLICE...LOVED BY THE PEOPLE ...HE IS INDEED A POWERFUL FIGURE!

BUT, IF I CAN DEFEAT **HIM,** THEN I CAN DEFEAT **ANYONE!** I MUST TEST MY METTLE AGAINST ANT-MAN!

WITH ANT-MAN DISPOSED OF, THIS CITY CAN BE **MINE!**

4

AND SO, IN AN ARROGANT ATTEMPT TO PROVE HIS SUPERIORITY OVER THE ANT-MAN, JASON USES HIS IRRESISTABLE VOICE TO TURN THE PEOPLE AGAINST THEIR HERO...

HE PRETENDS TO BE YOUR FRIEND, BUT HE SECRETLY DESPISES YOU, AS HE DOES **ALL** WHO ARE NORMAL-SIZED!

THE ANT-MAN CATCHES CRIMINALS ONLY TO **DECEIVE** YOU...TO KEEP YOU FROM SUSPECTING THAT **HE HIMSELF** IS THE WORST OF ALL CRIMINALS!

I TELL YOU! HE IS **EVIL**! HE MUST BE DRIVEN FROM THE CITY!

MEANWHILE, AT POLICE HEADQUARTERS...

WE'RE HAPPY TO PRESENT YOU THIS AWARD FOR MERITORIOUS SERVICE!

NO ONE IN THE COMMUNITY DESERVES IT MORE!

GENTLEMEN, I AM **HONORED**!

SUDDENLY...

WHAT MOCKERY--TO HONOR A BASE VILLAIN! INSTEAD, THE ANT-MAN SHOULD BE **ARRESTED**!

THAT VOICE--I CANNOT **RESIST** IT!

ARREST THE ANT-MAN!

B-BUT HE OFFERS NO EVIDENCE--NO **PROOF** TO SUPPORT HIS CHARGE! YOU CAN'T JUST ARREST ME ON HIS SAY-SO!

HE **NEEDS** NO PROOF! HIS IS THE VOICE OF TRUTH! IT MUST BE OBEYED!

YOU'RE TOO **DANGEROUS** TO REMAIN AT LARGE! YOU BELONG IN PRISON!

THEY'RE ALL UNDER CRAGG'S SPELL! THEY WON'T LISTEN! I MUST ESCAPE WHILE I STILL CAN!

AS THE ANT-MAN SNAPS THE RUBBER BAND*, THE TAUTLY ROLLED CERTIFICATE SPRINGS OPEN, HURLING THE TINY FIGURE HIGH INTO THE AIR...

*EDITOR'S NOTE: DESPITE HIS TINY SIZE, ANT-MAN RETAINS THE STRENGTH OF A NORMAL-SIZED HUMAN!

5

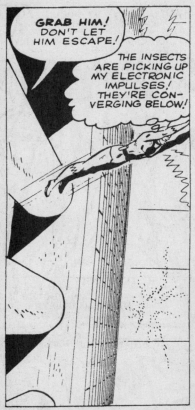

GRAB HIM! DON'T LET HIM ESCAPE!

THE INSECTS ARE PICKING UP MY ELECTRONIC IMPULSES! THEY'RE CONVERGING BELOW!

COULDN'T ASK FOR A SOFTER LANDING SPOT! THANKS, FELLAS!

NOW, I THINK I'D BETTER HITCH A RIDE!

...AND LOSE MYSELF IN THE CROWD!

HE GOT AWAY!

WELL, DON'T JUST STAND THERE! GO AFTER HIM! ALERT THE PEOPLE! CREATE VIGILANTE GROUPS! I, MYSELF, WILL LEAD YOU! WE MUST CAPTURE THE ANT-MAN!

THEIR FREE WILL OVERCOME BY JASON CRAGG'S SPELL-BINDING COMMANDS, SCORES OF CITIZENS JOIN IN A GRIM SEARCH FOR THE TINY HERO WHOM THEY HAD RESPECTED JUST A DAY BEFORE!

WE'VE GOT TO FIND ANT-MAN!

HE MUST BE CAPTURED!

HOW CAN WE DO IT? IT'S LIKE LOOKING FOR A NEEDLE IN A HAYSTACK!

6.

MEANWHILE, THE GALLANT FIGURE WHO HAS BECOME THE HUNTED, MOVES WARILY THROUGH THE CITY...

I MUST RETURN TO MY LAB AND ENLARGE MYSELF-- BECOME HENRY PYM AGAIN!

THEN, I'VE GOT TO FIND A WAY TO STRIP CRAGG OF HIS AWESOME POWER!

BEST TO GO THROUGH THE PARK! IT'S QUICKER!

A MOB! LED BY CRAGG HIMSELF! THEY'RE SEARCHING FOR ME! MY ONLY HOPE NOW IS TO REMAIN HIDDEN IN THIS GRASS!

BUT THEN, THE ANT-MAN SEES THEM... THE MAKESHIFT INSTRUMENTS THAT COULD SPELL HIS DOOM!

IF HE'S HIDING IN THE GRASS, THE MAGNETS WILL DETECT HIS METAL HELMET... AND WE'LL SCOOP HIM UP JUST LIKE THESE PINS AND OTHER BITS OF METAL!

THEY'RE COMING CLOSER! IF I KEEP MY CYBERNETIC HELMET ON, THEY'LL CAPTURE ME!

BUT IF I REMOVE IT, I'LL BE UNABLE TO COMMUNICATE WITH THE ANTS WHEN I NEED THEM!

I'VE GOT NO CHOICE! I MUST GET RID OF THE HELMET AND TAKE MY CHANCES!

I HAD TO DISCARD MY SHRINKING-AND-ENLARGING GAS CONTAINERS, TOO! LUCKY THEY WERE EMPTY... NO ONE CAN USE THEIR CONTENTS!

SECONDS LATER...

LOOK! I'VE PICKED UP HIS HELMET AND GAS PELLET CONTAINERS!

HAH! NOW HE'S AS GOOD AS CAPTURED!

7

BUT HOW CAN WE FIND HIM? IF HE'S WEARING NO METAL, OUR MAGNETS CAN'T ATTRACT HIM!

FOOL! WITHOUT HIS HELMET, HE'S VULNERABLE TO SOMETHING FAR STRONGER THAN MAGNETS! MY VOICE!

ANT-MAN, WHEREVER YOU ARE HIDING, HEED MY WORDS! I, JASON CRAGG, COMMAND YOU TO REVEAL YOURSELF!

OBEY ME, ANT-MAN! COME OUT OF HIDING! YOU CANNOT RESIST MY ENCHANTED VOICE! I AM YOUR MASTER!

IF-- IF ONLY I COULD SHUT OUT THE SOUND!! BUT IT'S TOO POWERFUL!

EVERY WORD HE UTTERS HAS A STRANGE, PERSUASIVE QUALITY THAT FORCES HIS COMMANDS INTO MY BRAIN! IT'S OVERCOMING MY WILL! I CAN'T HOLD OUT MUCH LONGER!

GIVE YOURSELF UP! OBEY ME!

THE TINY FIGURE STRUGGLES COURAGEOUSLY, BUT TO NO AVAIL! FOR NONE CAN DEFY THE ALL-POWERFUL VOICE OF JASON CRAGG!

HERE I AM! I CAN RESIST NO LONGER!

AH, I HAVE WON! BUT MY VICTORY WON'T BE COMPLETE UNTIL I'VE ENDED YOUR VERY EXISTENCE!

I COMMAND YOU TO WALK TO THE PIER... TO DIVE INTO THE RIVER ...AND MAKE NO ATTEMPT TO SWIM! DO NOTHING TO KEEP YOURSELF FROM DROWNING!

MOMENTS LATER, OUTSIDE THE PARK...

GO! WALK TO THE PIER! JUMP TO YOUR DOOM! I HAVE SPOKEN!

8

AND SO, THE HELPLESS ANT-MAN WALKS "*THE LAST MILE*," PAST THE HATE-FILLED EYES OF THOSE WHO ONCE HONORED HIM...

HE PRETENDED TO BE OUR FRIEND, BUT ALL THE WHILE HE WAS A LOATHSOME LITTLE CRIMINAL!

AND HE'D *STILL* BE DECEIVING US, IF NOT FOR JASON CRAGG!

JASON'S GOLDEN VOICE IS THE CLARION CALL OF *TRUTH!*

IT TELLS US TO SHOW THAT VILLAIN NO MERCY-- NO MERCY.

GO, EVIL ONE... TO YOUR RICHLY DESERVED FATE!

MUST WALK TO THE PIER...

BUT THERE ARE **OTHERS** WITNESSING THE GRIM SPECTACLE... TINY CREATURES, SILENTLY WATCHING THEIR HUMAN LEADER MARCH TO HIS DOOM...

YOU HAVE REACHED THE EDGE OF THE PIER! NOW **JUMP**, ANT-MAN... AND MAKE NO ATTEMPT TO SWIM... NO ATTEMPT TO STAY AFLOAT!

I MUST OBEY!

SO POWERFUL IS JASON'S SPELL, THAT IT OVERCOMES EVEN THE ANT-MAN'S BASIC INSTINCT TO SURVIVE...

I MUST NOT SWIM... I MUST DO NOTHING TO SAVE MYSELF!

BUT, AS THE HELPLESS LITTLE FIGURE STARTS TO SINK, IT IS GRIPPED BY A PAIR OF POWERFUL MANDIBLES...

9

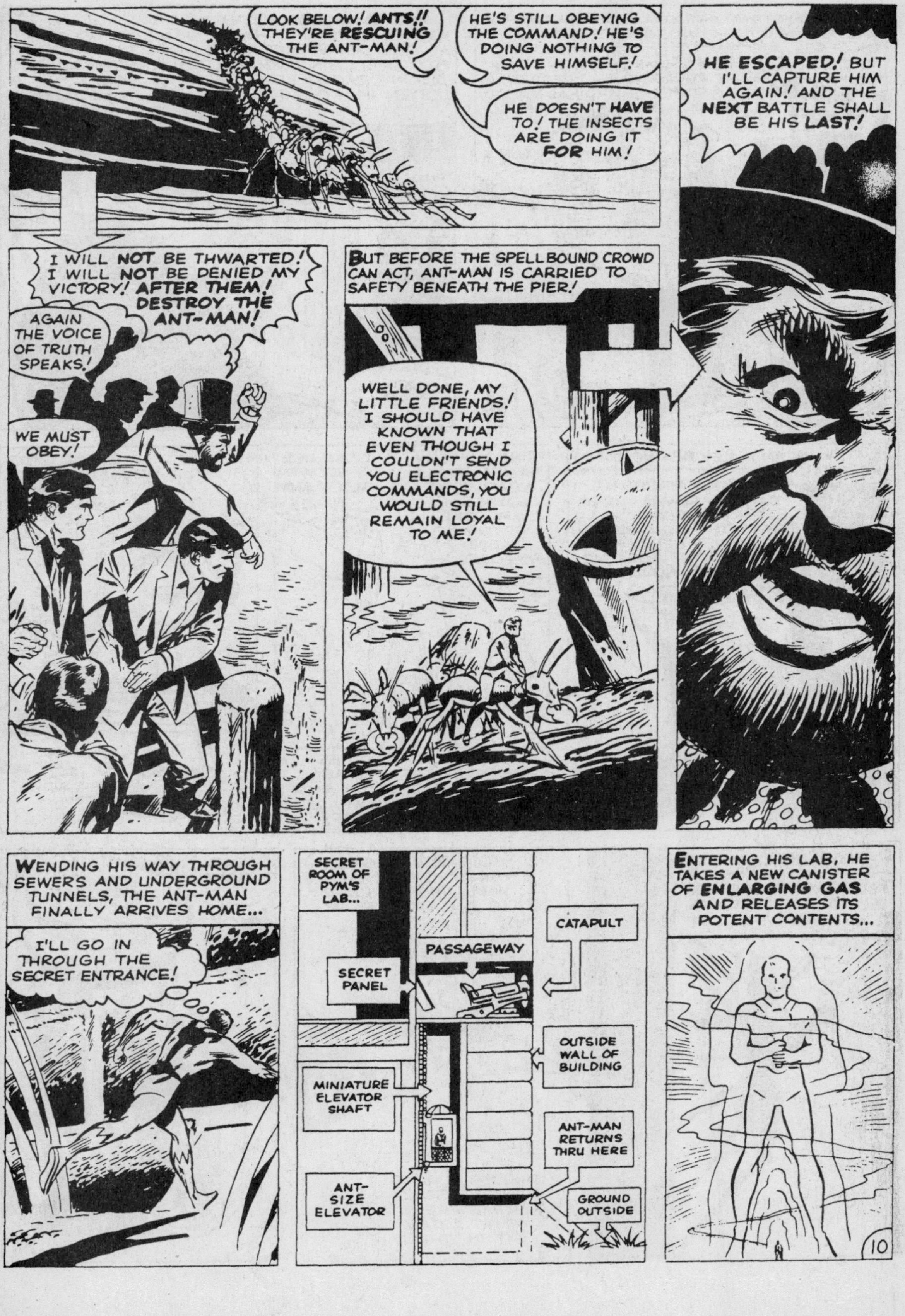
LOOK BELOW! ANTS!! THEY'RE RESCUING THE ANT-MAN!
HE'S STILL OBEYING THE COMMAND! HE'S DOING NOTHING TO SAVE HIMSELF!
HE DOESN'T HAVE TO! THE INSECTS ARE DOING IT FOR HIM!
HE ESCAPED! BUT I'LL CAPTURE HIM AGAIN! AND THE NEXT BATTLE SHALL BE HIS LAST!
I WILL NOT BE THWARTED! I WILL NOT BE DENIED MY VICTORY! AFTER THEM! DESTROY THE ANT-MAN!
AGAIN THE VOICE OF TRUTH SPEAKS!
WE MUST OBEY!
BUT BEFORE THE SPELLBOUND CROWD CAN ACT, ANT-MAN IS CARRIED TO SAFETY BENEATH THE PIER!
WELL DONE, MY LITTLE FRIENDS! I SHOULD HAVE KNOWN THAT EVEN THOUGH I COULDN'T SEND YOU ELECTRONIC COMMANDS, YOU WOULD STILL REMAIN LOYAL TO ME!
WENDING HIS WAY THROUGH SEWERS AND UNDERGROUND TUNNELS, THE ANT-MAN FINALLY ARRIVES HOME...
I'LL GO IN THROUGH THE SECRET ENTRANCE!
SECRET ROOM OF PYM'S LAB...
CATAPULT
PASSAGEWAY
SECRET PANEL
OUTSIDE WALL OF BUILDING
MINIATURE ELEVATOR SHAFT
ANT-MAN RETURNS THRU HERE
ANT-SIZE ELEVATOR
GROUND OUTSIDE
ENTERING HIS LAB, HE TAKES A NEW CANISTER OF ENLARGING GAS AND RELEASES ITS POTENT CONTENTS...
10

IN THE DAYS THAT FOLLOW, THE SEARCH FOR THE ANT-MAN CONTINUES, BUT WITHOUT SUCCESS...

BAH! SOMEONE IN THE CITY MUST BE HIDING HIM! PROTECTING HIM! SOMEONE WHO HAS NOT YET HEARD MY ALL-POWERFUL VOICE!

BUT I'LL SOON FIX THAT!

CITY HALL

...AND TOMORROW NIGHT WE ARE HONORED TO HAVE AS OUR GUEST SPEAKER, THAT SPELLBINDING ORATER, JASON CRAGG! BE SURE TO LISTEN IN, FOLKS!

JUST WHAT I'VE BEEN WAITING FOR! NOW IT'S TIME TO MAKE MY MOVE!

LATER, IN AN ALLEY BEHIND CITY HOSPITAL...

PLENTY OF PEOPLE SAW ME COMING HERE! BUT NONE SUSPECTS THAT THE COLORLESS SCIENTIST, HENRY PYM, IS ALSO THE FUGITIVE ANT-MAN!

I'LL JUST LAY MY COSTUME AND ONE OF MY DUPLICATE HELMETS DOWN HERE FOR A WHILE!

SINCE I'VE TAKEN TO WEARING CLOTHES, COMPOSED OF UN-STABLE MOLECULES...

...I CAN USE MY GROWTH GASES ANY TIME!

EDITOR'S NOTE: CLOTHES COMPOSED OF UNSTABLE MOLECULES STRETCH AND CONTRACT AS THE WEARER'S OWN BODY DOES!

IT'S A LOT EASIER TO DON MY WORKING CLOTHES THIS WAY, THAN IT WOULD BE TO LUG AROUND A LARGE-SIZE COSTUME!

SECONDS LATER...

THAT'S RIGHT... OBEY MY ELECTRONIC COMMANDS ...CLIMB UP THE HOSPITAL WALL...

CLOSED WINDOWS AREN'T EFFECTIVE WHEN THE INTRUDER IS THE SIZE OF AN ANT!

THERE'S ALWAYS A LITTLE CRACK SOMEWHERE THAT I CAN FIT IN THRU!

AND NOW...

11

GOOD THING YOU CRITTERS CAN CARRY UP TO FIFTY TIMES YOUR OWN WEIGHT! CAREFUL! DON'T DROP IT! THE GERMS IN THERE MUSTN'T GET LOOSE-- NOT YET!

NOW I'LL JUST CHANGE TO HENRY PYM AGAIN, ENLARGE MYSELF AND GO OVER TO THE TELEVISION STUDIO!

LATER, AT THE STUDIO THAT JASON CRAGG WILL BROADCAST FROM...

THIS PROP ROOM IS LOADED WITH STUFF, BUT THE ONLY THING THAT INTERESTS ME IS THAT PROP GUN!

AND THE FOLLOWING FATEFUL NIGHT...

WE'RE READY FOR YOU, MISTER CRAGG!

CLAP! CLAP! CLAP! CLAP!

I'LL MAKE MILLION OF VIEWERS HATE THE ANT-MAN! WHEN I'M FINISHED, NO LIVING HUMAN BEING WILL EVER SUPPORT HIM! FOR NONE CAN RESIST MY HYPNOTIC VOICE!

BUT, UN-SEEN BY JASON CRAGG...

HE'S STARTING! CLIMB QUICKLY!

JUST AS THE HATE-MONGER PREPARES TO SPEAK, HE HEARS A TINY WHISPER...

THIS IS THE ANT-MAN, CRAGG! UNLESS YOU SAY EXACTLY WHAT I TELL YOU TO, YOUR LIFE WON'T BE WORTH A DIME!

FOR AT THIS VERY MOMENT, THERE IS A CONCEALED GUN TRAINED ON YOU! ONE SIGNAL FROM ME AND MY ANTS WILL PULL THE TRIGGER! SEE IT?

SO, UNLESS YOU'RE BULLET-PROOF, YOU'D BETTER TELL A MILLION LISTENERS THAT YOU WERE WRONG... THAT ANT-MAN IS AN HONEST, LAW-ABIDING CITIZEN!

FOOL! THAT WON'T HELP YOU! WHAT-EVER I SAY NOW, I CAN CONTRADICT LATER ON!

12

LET **ME** WORRY ABOUT LATER ON!

VERY WELL! LISTEN, MY FRIENDS! I HAVE MADE A SERIOUS ERROR! **I MISJUDGED** THE ANT-MAN! HE'S AN HONEST, LAW ABIDING CITIZEN, WORTHY OF YOUR RESPECT AND ADMIRATION!

AND ONCE AGAIN, THE WORDS OF THE GOLDEN-VOICED ORATOR ARE ACCEPTED WITHOUT QUESTION!

THE ANT-MAN IS **NOT** EVIL!

IF JASON CRAGG SAYS HE IS HONEST, IT **MUST** BE SO!

WE MUST ONCE AGAIN RESPECT HIM! THE VOICE OF TRUTH COMMANDS IT!

WELL DONE, CRAGG! YOU CAN RELAX NOW! THAT GUN THE ANTS ARE HOLDING-- **ISN'T LOADED!**

YOU **TRICKED** ME! BUT I'LL HAVE MY REVENGE! WATCH ME TURN THE ENTIRE CITY **AGAINST** YOU NOW!

EVERYONE, **LISTEN!** LISTEN TO THE GOLDEN VOICE OF-- OF--ARGG---MY VOICE! SOMETHING'S **WRONG**-- IT'S LOST ITS **POWER!** IT SOUNDS **DIFFERENT!** BUT--BUT HOW?

I'LL **TELL** YOU HOW, CRAGG!

BEFORE YOU ARRIVED HERE, I COVERED THAT MIKE WITH MICROBES...MICROBES WHICH CAUSE **LARYNGITIS!!**

LARYNGITIS!! THEN YOU **KNEW** MY VOICE WOULD HOLD OUT JUST LONG ENOUGH TO RECITE YOUR MESSAGE!! BUT, YOU WON'T GET **AWAY** WITH THIS!

HEAR ME! THE ANT-MAN IS **EVIL!** HE MUST BE DESTROYED! YOU MUST --GASP-- BELIEVE ME! MINE IS THE VOICE OF TRUTH!

BUT, WITHOUT THE HYPNOTIC POWER OF HIS ENCHANTED VOICE...

WHAT ARE YOU, SOME KIND OF **NUT,** OR SOMETHING! YOU CAN'T MAKE SPEECHES INCITING PEOPLE TO VIOLENCE HERE!

RUN THE BUM OUT OF TOWN!

WAIT! HEAR ME! HEAR ME!

BUT NONE WILL EVER LISTEN TO CRAGG'S HYPNOTIC COMMANDS AGAIN!

13

LATER...

AND DON'T EVER COME BACK!

THE ANT-MAN... HE DEFEATED ME ...AND EVEN WHEN I **REGAIN** MY VOICE, THE CHANCES ARE A MILLION TO ONE AGAINST IT EVER AGAIN HAVING THE SAME HYPNOTIC QUALITY!!

HE HAD A GREAT POWER! HE MIGHT HAVE DONE SO MUCH **GOOD** WITH IT, BUT INSTEAD, HE MADE THE WRONG CHOICE! AND NOW HIS POWER, HIS VOICE OF DOOM, IS STILLED FOREVER!

THE END

TALES TO ASTONISH

MARVEL COMICS GROUP 12¢

43 MAY

IS THIS THE END OF ANT-MAN?

"THE MAD MASTER OF TIME!" HAD THE ONE POWER WHICH EVEN *ANT-MAN* WAS HELPLESS AGAINST! THE POWER OF *OLD AGE!!* DON'T MISS THIS STARTLING DRAMATIC ANT-MAN SAGA!

WHAT'S HAPPENING TO ME?

I'M GROWING OLDER!

OLDER...

...OLDER!!!

THE ASTONISHING ANT-MAN!

VERSUS "THE MAD MASTER OF TIME!"

PLOT: STAN LEE
SCRIPT: LARRY LIEBER
ART: DON HECK
LETTERING: RAY HOLLOWAY

THOUSANDS OF FOOTSTEPS TREAD DAILY UPON THE SIDEWALKS OF CENTER CITY... AND AT THIS MOMENT, A TINY COSTUMED FIGURE HASTENS AMONG THEM, UNNOTICED...

CAN'T WAIT TO GET BACK TO MY LAB AND BECOME NORMAL-SIZED AGAIN! THE NOISE OF THIS CROWD IS ALMOST DEAFENING TO ANT-MAN'S TINY EARS!

X-125

BUT, ACCIDENTS CAN HAPPEN ANY TIME, INVOLVING ANYONE... EVEN ONE AS SMALL AS AN ANT!

OOPS-- TELEGRAM SLIPPED OUT OF MY HAND!

TELEGRAM

WHA.. WHERE DID THIS FALL FROM??

I'D BETTER PICK IT UP BEFORE IT GETS STEPPED ON! I'LL NEVER GET A TIP, DELIVERING A CRUMPLED TELEGRAM!

1

BUT WHEN THE BOY LIFTS THE TELEGRAM...

HEY! IT'S THE ANT-MAN!

THERE HE IS!

CAREFUL! DON'T STEP ON HIM!

LOOK AT HIS COLORFUL COSTUME, ISN'T HE ADORABLE!

SAY, ANT-MAN, HOW ABOUT YOUR AUTOGRAPH FOR MY KID! YOU'RE HIS NUMBER ONE HERO!

SORRY, PAL... BUT THERE'S NO PEN OR PENCIL SMALL ENOUGH FOR ME TO WRITE WITH!

BESIDES, MAC, EVEN IF HE DID WRITE HIS NAME, YOUR KID WOULD NEED A MICROSCOPE TO READ IT!

AS THE CROWD GROWS LARGER, THE ANT-MAN EMITS AN ELECTRONIC SIGNAL THRU HIS CYBERNETIC HELMET! AND MOMENTS LATER...

LOOK! HE'S SUMMONED ONE OF HIS ANTS TO CARRY HIM AWAY!

OH, DON'T LEAVE YET! I'M A REPORTER FROM THE "WOMAN'S GAZETTE"...

...I WANT TO ASK YOU SOME QUESTIONS!

SORRY, MA'AM-- PERHAPS SOME OTHER TIME!

WHEW! I'D SOONER FACE A MOB OF CRIMINALS THAN A CROWD OF ADMIRERS! GUESS I'M JUST TOO SHY FOR THE ROLE OF PUBLIC CELEBRITY!

THE TINY FIGURE DEPARTS AND THE CROWD DISPERSES! BUT THE SAME TELEGRAM WHICH REVEALED THE ANT-MAN'S PRESENCE IS DESTINED TO SOON LEAD HIM INTO A GRIM AND FANTASTIC ADVENTURE!!

PROFESSOR ELIAS WEEMS?

THAT'S ME, SON!

IT'S FROM MY GRANDSON, TOMMY! NEXT MONTH THE LAD GETS A VACATION FROM SCHOOL AND HE WANTS TO SPEND IT WITH ME! HE'S COMING HERE TO CENTER CITY!

2

GOSH, IT'LL BE GOOD TO SEE TOMMY AGAIN! THE LAD LOVES ME... AND HE'S SO PROUD 'CAUSE I'M A SCIENTIST!

I'LL TAKE HIM TO THE LABORATORY AND SHOW HIM ALL THE INTERESTING THINGS GOING ON! HE'LL BE THRILLED!

BUT, THE FOLLOWING WEEK, DISASTER STRIKES...

FIRED??! BUT WHY?? WHAT HAVE I DONE??

IT'S OUR NEW COMPANY POLICY TO DISCHARGE ALL EMPLOYEES OVER SIXTY-FIVE YEARS OF AGE!

DISTRAUGHT, PANICKY, ELIAS WEEMS GOES ALL THE WAY TO THE TOP TO PLEAD FOR HIS JOB! BUT, TO NO AVAIL!

SORRY, WEEMS, BUT MODERN SCIENTIFIC RESEARCH NEEDS YOUNG, ALERT MINDS! OLD-TIMERS LIKE YOURSELF NO LONGER FIT THE BILL! YOUR IDEAS ARE UNIMAGINATIVE AND OUT-DATED!

TOO OLD... OUT-DATED... AFTER YEARS OF FAITHFUL SERVICE, I'M TOSSED ASIDE LIKE WORTHLESS RUBBISH! IT--IT ISN'T RIGHT!

AND TOMMY, WHO'S SO PROUD OF ME... WHEN HE ARRIVES AND LEARNS I'VE BEEN FIRED, HE'LL NO LONGER RESPECT ME!

I'LL LOSE THE BOY'S LOVE-- HIS ADMIRATION-- EVERYTHING THAT MATTERS TO ME! WELL, I WON'T TAKE THIS LYING DOWN!

A SOCIETY CRUEL ENOUGH TO CONDEMN A MAN SOLELY BECAUSE OF HIS AGE, SHOULD ITSELF BE CONDEMNED!

YES, THAT'S IT! I SHALL MAKE SOCIETY PAY FOR THE WRONG THEY'VE DONE ME! AND I'LL USE THEIR OWN WEAPON --AGE!

IT WILL BE A POETIC REVENGE! THEY SAID I WAS TOO OLD! WELL I SHALL INVENT A MACHINE THAT WILL MAKE OTHERS TOO OLD!! A MACHINE TO AGE ALL LIVING CREATURES!

3

IF I CAN CREATE ELECTROMAGNETIC ENERGY WHICH WILL INCREASE THE MOTION OF THE BODY'S ATOMS... THEN I'LL BE ABLE TO QUICKEN THE ATOMIC ACTIVITY OF ALL LIVING TISSUES... AND THUS CAUSE THEM TO AGE!

LIKE A MAN POSSESSED, ELIAS WEEMS LABORS NIGHT AND DAY ON THE INSTRUMENT OF HIS REVENGE...

I'LL *SHOW* THEM! SOON THEY SHALL KNOW HOW WRONG THEY WERE... ONLY THEN IT WILL BE *TOO LATE!*

FINALLY THE FANTASTIC MACHINE IS COMPLETED!

I'LL EXPERIMENT FIRST ON A PRIMITIVE LIFE FORM!! AHHH... THAT YOUNG SAPLING!

THERE! I'VE SWITCHED ON THE RAY! IT'S BATHING THE ENTIRE YOUNG TREE!

HYPER-ENERGY IS INCREASING THE ATOMIC ACTIVITY WITHIN THE SAPLING'S CELLS...

I'VE DONE IT! WITHIN MERE SECONDS I'VE MADE A YOUNG TREE REACH THE END OF ITS LIFE SPAN! IT'S NOW IN THE TWILIGHT OF ITS LIFE!

MY MACHINE WORKED PERFECTLY! BUT THAT WAS ONLY THE *FIRST* EXPERIMENT! NOW I MUST CONDUCT A MORE AMBITIOUS TEST-- USING AN *ANIMAL* LIFE FORM!

4

AND WHAT BETTER PLACE TO FIND ANIMALS THAN THE LOCAL ZOO?! BUT, FATE IS SPINNING HER GRIM WEB, FOR AMONG THE SPECTATORS IS *HENRY PYM*...

AS THE ANT-MAN, I'M SO CONCERNED WITH TINY INSECTS, THAT I SELDOM THINK ABOUT THE LARGER CREATURES OF EARTH!

"WOULDN'T IT BE IMPRESSIVE IF I COULD CONTROL THOSE HUGE MAMMALS THRU MY CYBERNETIC HELMET AS EASILY AS I CONTROL ANTS!! I COULD MAKE THEM DO ANYTHING..."

BUT HENRY PYM'S DAYDREAM IS SUDDENLY SHATTERED BY A STARTLING SIGHT!

LOOK!

I MUST BE SEEING THINGS!

THE BABY ELEPHANT! IT'S GETTING *BIGGER*!

IT'S GROWING INTO MATURITY, RIGHT BEFORE OUR EYES!

AND, WITHIN A FEW FANTASTIC SECONDS...

IT'S AGED SO MUCH, IT SEEMS OLDER THAN ITS OWN *PARENT* NOW!

ANOTHER SUCCESS! NOW I'LL JUST SWITCH ON THE ANTI-MATTER ENERGY BEAM, AND *REVERSE* THE PROCESS--

NOW THE ELEPHANT'S GROWING *SMALLER*! IT'S GETTING *YOUNGER*!

THERE SEEMS TO BE SOME KIND OF RAY TRAINED ON THE ANIMAL! IT'S COMING FROM THE SHADOWS BACK THERE!

5

THIS WAS THE AREA WHERE THE RAY CAME FROM! BUT IT'S *GONE* NOW!

ONLY ONE REMAINING TEST! THE MOST IMPORTANT ONE OF ALL!

LATER, IN ANOTHER PART OF THE CITY...

HEY, GUYS-- DIG THE LUSCIOUS CHICK!

THERE! I'M FOCUSED ON THAT GIRL! SHE DOESN'T EVEN REALIZE WHAT'S HAPPENING!

GEORGEOUS CHICK? WHO YOU TRYIN' TO KID?

THAT DAME COULD PASS FOR MY *MOTHER!*

B-BUT SHE ...I...I!

AND THEN, AFTER ELIAS WEEMS RESTORES HIS UNSUSPECTING VICTIM TO HER RIGHTFUL AGE AGAIN...

I'VE DONE IT! I'VE PROVEN THAT I CAN AGE HUMANS AS WELL AS ANIMALS! I AM THE MASTER OF AGE! THE MASTER OF *TIME!*

THE FOLLOWING DAY...

THE GUY CALLS HIMSELF THE "TIME-MASTER"! WHAT DO *YOU* THINK?

AWW... MUST BE SOME *NUT!*

BUT SUPPOSE HE'S ON THE LEVEL! SUPPOSE HE REALLY *CAN* DO WHAT HE CLAIMS! REMEMBER THAT WHACKY INCIDENT AT THE *ZOO* YESTERDAY?

6

AS THE OFFICERS SPEAK, THEIR WORDS ARE PICKED UP BY THE TINY ANTENNAE OF SEVERAL ANTS WITHIN THE STATION HOUSE...

THE ANTS THEN SEND OUT ELECTRONIC IMPULSES, WHICH ARE DETECTED AND RELAYED BY COUNTLESS OTHER ANTS DISPERSED THROUGHOUT THE CITY...

HE SAYS THAT UNLESS WE SURRENDER THE CITY TO HIM-- MAKE HIM THE BOSS OF IT-- HE'LL BEGIN TO MAKE PEOPLE OLD BEFORE THEIR TIME!

THE MESSAGE TRAVELS ON AND ON THRU THE VAST INSECT NETWORK, UNTIL IT FINALLY REACHES THE COMMUNICATIONS NERVE CENTER... THE LABORATORY OF HENRY PYM!

CHANGING INTO HIS COSTUME, PYM RELEASES HIS REDUCING GAS...

...AND ENTERS HIS CATAPULT...

THE ELECTRONIC WAVES ARE ORIGINATING FROM STATION HOUSE 86!

THEN, TRAINING THE MINIATURE DEVICE ON AN ALLEY NEAR THE POLICE STATION, THE TINY CRIME-FIGHTER SHOOTS HIMSELF INTO THE AIR!

ZOOOOM!

MY LITTLE PALS ARE CONVERGING IN THE ALLEY! THEY'RE FORMING A LIVING ANT-HILL!

COULDN'T ASK FOR A SOFTER LANDING SPOT!

MINUTES LATER...

...AND WE HAVE NO IDEA WHO THIS "TIME MASTER" REALLY IS!

WE DON'T KNOW IF HE'S JUST A SCREWBALL, OR IF HE REALLY *HAS* SOME MEANS OF SPEEDING UP THE AGING PROCESS!

ONE THING'S FOR SURE... IF HE IS ON THE LEVEL, WE'RE IN *TROUBLE!*

HIS NOTE DIDN'T READ LIKE A TYPICAL CRANK LETTER! IT WAS WELL-WRITTEN-- AND CAREFULLY THOUGHT OUT!

IT'S JUST FANTASTIC ENOUGH TO BE POSSIBLE! I'LL KEEP MY EYES OPEN, FELLAS!

FIRST AN ELEPHANT SUDDENLY AGES... AND NOW *THIS* THREAT! IT ADDS UP, EXCEPT FOR *ONE* THING!

POLICE

WHY WOULD ANYBODY WITH SUCH GREAT SCIENTIFIC ABILITY, TURN IT *AGAINST SOCIETY?*

PLAYING A HUNCH, THE ANT-MAN VISITS VARIOUS LABS AROUND TOWN...

ANGRY OR BITTER? YES... ONE OLD FELLOW, ELIAS WEEMS...

...WE HAD TO LET HIM GO BECAUSE HE WAS TOO OLD, AND I'M AFRAID HE TOOK IT QUITE HARD!

FIRED BECAUSE OF HIS AGE! AND NOW HE THREATENS TO AGE HIS FELLOW MEN!

THIS COULD BE THE LEAD I'M AFTER!

QUICK! LET ME HAVE WEEMS' ADDRESS!

MEANWHILE...

I TOLD THE POLICE TO ANSWER MY ULTIMATUM IN THE NEWSPAPER, BUT THERE'S *NOTHING* HERE! THEY *DEFIED* ME!

ALL RIGHT! I *GAVE* THEM THEIR CHANCE! NOW IT'S *MY* TURN!

SOCIETY HAS WRONGED ME! SOCIETY MUST PAY FOR THAT! AND BY THUNDER, THEY *SHALL* PAY!

NOT IF *I* CAN HELP IT!

I KNOW WHO YOU ARE, WEEMS... BUT YOU CAN'T GO THROUGH WITH YOUR MAD PLAN!

THE ANT-MAN! I DON'T KNOW HOW YOU DISCOVERED ME, BUT IT DOESN'T MATTER! *YOU* CAN'T STOP ME!

8

BEFORE THE ANT-MAN CAN ACT, ELIAS WEEMS GRABS HIS FANTASTIC RAY GUN AND SWITCHES IT ON...

THERE... YOU'RE TRAPPED! AND SOON YOU SHALL BE OLD... JUST AS I AM!

I'M CHANGING... MATURING! BUT HOW... HOW IS IT HAPPENING??

HYPER-ENERGY IS INCREASING THE MOTION OF YOUR ATOMS! EVERY CELL IN YOUR BODY IS MOVING FASTER ... TAKING YOU TO THE END OF YOUR LIFE SPAN!

TIRED -- WEAK -- I'VE AGED YEARS! BUT -- WHY DID YOU STOP THE MACHINE? YOU COULD HAVE FINISHED ME!

I WISH YOU NO HARM! I ONLY WANT TO KEEP YOU FROM INTERFERING WITH MY PLANS!

AND NOW, MY AGED LITTLE FOE...

I CAN'T RUN! MY LEGS ARE NO LONGER LIMBER! MY BODY HAS LOST ITS RESILIENCY!

YOU'RE OLD AND FEEBLE BUT NOT HELPLESS! NOT WHILE YOU STILL HAVE YOUR HELMET!

THERE! NOW YOU WON'T BE ABLE TO ENLIST THE AID OF YOUR ANTS!

IT'S A PITY THAT MY EYESIGHT IS TOO POOR TO OBSERVE YOUR TINY FEATURES CLEARLY! WHEN MY TASK IS DONE, I'LL VIEW YOU MORE CLOSELY THRU A MAGNIFYING GLASS!

UNTIL THEN YOU SHALL REMAIN IMPRISONED IN THIS FLOWER POT!

A FEW MINUTES, AGO, I COULD HAVE CLIMBED UP THESE STONES EASILY! BUT NOW, I'M TOO WEAK... TOO OLD! IS THIS -- THE END OF ANT-MAN?

9

NOW THAT THE ANT-MAN IS TAKEN CARE OF, I SHALL VENT MY WRATH UPON THE ENTIRE CITY! MY FIRST VICTIMS WILL BE THOSE IN THE AREA OF CITY HALL!

I--I JUST *REMEMBERED*... NEITHER WEEMS NOR ANYONE ELSE KNOWS THAT THE ANT-MAN CAN *CHANGE* HIS SIZE... CAN GROW TO *NORMAL SIZE!*

I MAY NOT BE ABLE TO *CLIMB* OUT OF HERE, BUT BY RELEASING MY GROWTH GAS...

THERE! I'M FREE OF *THAT* PRISON... BUT STILL TRAPPED IN AN ELDERLY BODY!

BUT, INFIRM OR NOT, WITH THE CYBERNETIC HELMET AGAIN IN MY POSSESSION, I'M BACK IN BUSINESS!

I WON'T REDUCE MYSELF AGAIN UNTIL I REACH CITY HALL! I'LL MAKE BETTER TIME TRAVELING THIS SIZE! AND WEARING WEEMS' COAT OVER MY COSTUME, I'M NOT APT TO BE RECOGNIZED!

SOMETIME LATER, THE AGED FIGURE OF *HENRY PYM* ARRIVES ON THE SCENE...

THERE HE IS! ON THE ROOF ACROSS FROM CITY HALL! HE'S ABOUT TO AIM HIS AGING RAY AT THE CROWD! I'D BETTER RELEASE MY REDUCING GAS AT ONCE!

10

IN A COUPLE OF SECONDS I'LL BE SMALL ENOUGH TO AGAIN WEAR MY HELMET! THEN I CAN ESTABLISH CONTACT WITH THE ANTS!

BUT, EVEN AS THE ANT-MAN DONS HIS HELMET...

THEY FIRED ME! THEY SAID I WAS OLD AND WORTHLESS! WELL, NOW VENGEANCE SHALL BE MINE!

CLICK!

OH--NO! I'M GROWING OLDER!

WHAT'S HAPPENING??

THAT RAY, IT MUST BE THE RAY--BUT HOW?? HOW??

WE'RE ALL AGING! IT--IT'S IMPOSSIBLE!

IT'S MADNESS! IT CAN'T BE HAPPENING! AND YET--

MY HANDS... MY SKIN... LOOK AT THEM!

I FEEL SO TIRED--SO WEARY!

THEN, AMIDST ALL THE CONFUSION, A YOUNG LAD EMERGES FROM THE NEARBY RAILROAD STATION...

IT'S GRAMPS! --UP ON THE ROOF!

GRAMPS! GRAMPS! WHAT ARE YOU DOING UP THERE? WHAT'S GOING ON?

TOMMY! I DIDN'T EXPECT YOU TODAY! RUN! GET AWAY FROM HERE... FAST!

BUT, BEFORE THE YOUNGSTER CAN FLEE TO SAFETY...

THE RAY IS STRIKING HIM! HE'S GROWING OLDER! NO-- IT MUSTN'T HAPPEN TO TOMMY! NOT TO HIM!

11

ELIAS WEEMS LOOKS ON, HORRIFIED, AS THE ONE PERSON IN THE WORLD HE LOVES MOST-- HIS GRANDSON-- BECOMES ANOTHER HELPLESS VICTIM OF HIS DEADLY AGING RAY! MEANWHILE...

I'VE GATHERED MY ANTS FOR BATTLE! NOW TO COMMAND THEM TO CRAWL UP TO THE ROOF AND ATTACK WEEMS!!

BUT, AT THAT MOMENT...

MUST SWITCH THE AGING BEAM ON TO "REVERSE," SO THAT I CAN MAKE TOMMY YOUNG AGAIN!

IT--IT SLIPPED OUT OF MY HAND!! NO-- NO!!

BUT, OBSERVING WHAT HAS HAPPENED, THE ANT-MAN BARKS A DESPERATE COMMAND...

QUICKLY, MY PETS! FORM AN ANT-HILL! THAT RAY GUN MUST NOT SHATTER ON THE GROUND!

LOOK! THOSE ANTS SAVED THE RAY GUN FROM BEING SMASHED INTO A MILLION PIECES!

SO WHAT! WHO WANTS THE BLASTED THING! LOOK WHAT IT DID TO US!

LISTEN TO ME! BY REVERSING THE INSTRUMENT'S CONTROLS, WE CAN UNDO ALL THE HARM IT HAS DONE!

PICK UP THE RAY GUN AND TRAIN IT ON ME-- ON ALL OF US! THAT'S RIGHT!! IT'S WORKING!

AND SO...

THANK HEAVENS! MY WRINKLES ARE VANISHING! MY MUSCLES ARE BECOMING LIMBER!

IT'S A MIRACLE!

WE'VE RETURNED TO OUR NORMAL AGES!

MOMENTS LATER...

TOMMY-- THANK HEAVENS YOU'RE ALL RIGHT!!

GRAMPS! GRAMPS!

THAT OLD MAN! IT WAS HIM! HE'S TO BLAME!

YEAH! SOMEBODY GRAB 'IM!

12

TOMMY, TOMMY, I WAS SUCH A *FOOL!* I WANTED YOUR LOVE AND RESPECT... AND THEN, IN MY DESPERATION, I ALMOST DID A TERRIBLE THING! CAN YOU *FORGIVE* ME, SON?

DON'T CRY, GRAMPS! I'LL ALWAYS LOVE YOU-- NO MATTER WHAT!

ALRIGHT! BREAK IT UP, FOLKS!

LET'S *GO*, MISTER! YOU GOT A DATE WITH THE JUDGE!

BUT ONCE MORE, FATE TAKES AN IRONIC TURN! FOR, IN COURT, ELIAS WEEMS FINDS A COMPASSION HE DIDN'T SUSPECT EXISTED...

YOUR HONOR, WEEMS *ISN'T* REALLY A CRIMINAL! HE WAS JUST CONFUSED AND AFRAID OF LOSING HIS GRANDSON'S AFFECTION!

HE WAS TORMENTED, AND IN HIS AGONY, HE BLAMED SOCIETY!

IN A SENSE, SOME OF US *WERE* TO BLAME! *I* FIRED HIM FOR HIS AGE! I SAID HE WAS *TOO OLD* AND UNIMAGINATIVE!

WELL, THIS "OLD MAN" INVENTED THE MOST FANTASTIC MACHINE OF OUR TIME! AND I'D BE *HONORED* IF HE'D WORK FOR ME AGAIN!

AND THUS IT COMES TO PASS...

SEE? THIS IS THE LAB WHERE I WORK, TOMMY!

GOLLY, LOOK AT ALL THE GADGETS! THEY'RE TERRIFIC!

FOR A WHILE HE HATED SOCIETY, BUT NOW HE'S ONE OF ITS MOST VALUABLE MEMBERS AGAIN!

AND I'VE LEARNED *MY* LESSON! NEVER AGAIN WILL I JUDGE A MAN'S WORTH SOLELY ON THE BASIS OF HIS AGE!

13

IN A WAY, WE'VE *ALL* LEARNED SOMETHING! WE'VE LEARNED TO *APPRECIATE* OUR YOUTH, AND STRENGTH, AND TO MAKE THE MOST OF THEM WHILE WE CAN, THE BETTER TO SERVE HUMANITY!

The End

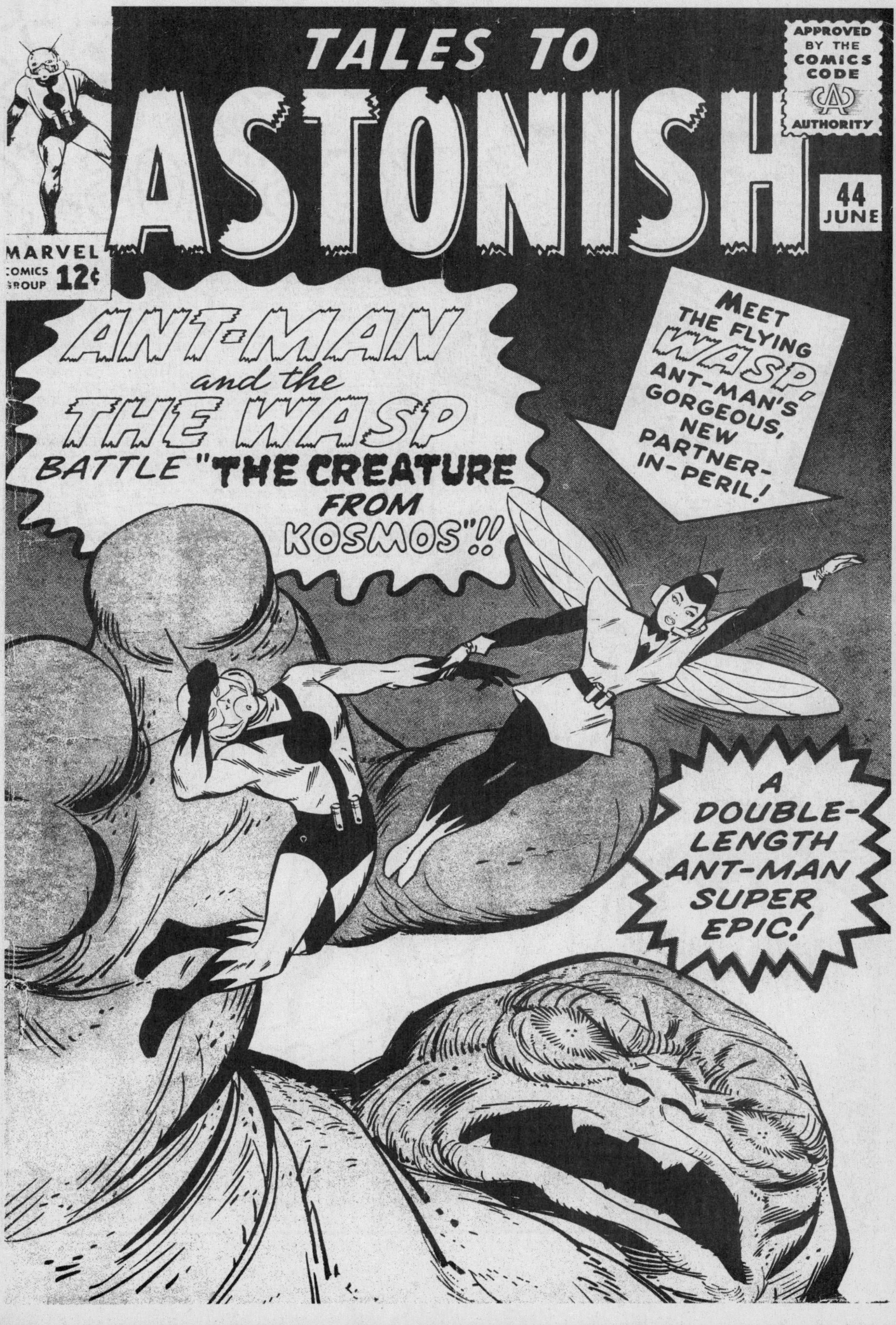
TALES TO ASTONISH
APPROVED BY THE COMICS CODE AUTHORITY
44 JUNE
MARVEL COMICS GROUP 12¢
ANT-MAN and the THE WASP BATTLE "THE CREATURE FROM KOSMOS"!!
MEET THE FLYING WASP, ANT-MAN'S GORGEOUS, NEW PARTNER-IN-PERIL!
A DOUBLE-LENGTH ANT-MAN SUPER EPIC!

ANT-MAN and the WASP! VS. "the CREATURE from KOSMOS!"

THROUGHOUT HISTORY THERE HAVE BEEN MEN WHO HAVE BECOME LEGENDS, MEN WHO HAVE POSSESSED POWERS BEYOND MORTAL KEN, SO THAT, IN TIME, THOSE MEN HAVE BECOME SUPER-HEROES WHO THRILL THE ENTIRE WORLD! WE ARE ABOUT TO TELL YOU OF SUCH A MAN, THE SCIENTIST KNOWN TO THE WORLD AS HENRY PYM, BUT, KNOWN TO **YOU** AS THE ASTONISHING **ANT-MAN!** AND YOU WILL LEARN HERE, FOR THE FIRST TIME, THE REASON THAT HENRY PYM **BECAME** THE ANT-MAN, THE PAST THAT GNAWS LIKE A CANCER AT THE SOUL OF THIS MAN, GIVING HIM NO REST, DRIVING HIM TO THE STRANGEST ADVENTURES ANY HUMAN BEING HAS EVER KNOWN! YOU WILL SEE HIM FIND A COMPANION TO AID IN HIS SOLITARY FIGHT AGAINST INJUSTICE, TYRANNY, AND CRIME, THE COMPANION WHO WILL BECOME KNOWN AS... THE WASP! COME WITH US NOW, AS ANT-MAN AND THE WASP BATTLE THE UN-HUMAN THING FROM BEYOND SPACE AND TIME... *THE CREATURE FROM KOSMOS!*

PLOT.....STAN LEE
SCRIPT..H.E. HUNTLEY
LETTERING...ART SIMEK
ART.......JACK KIRBY
INKING..DON HECK

X-192

1

A HUGE SOLDIER ANT CLACKS ITS MANDIBLES AS THE ANT-MAN DISMOUNTS ON THE WINDOW SILL OF HENRY PYM'S LABORATORY!

THROUGH HIS CYBERNETIC HELMET THE TINY MAN SENDS ELECTRONIC-WAVE COMMANDS TO HIS HYMENOPTERA COMPANIONS...AND THE ANTS FAR AWAY!

YOU MUST LEAVE NOW, MY FRIENDS! I WILL CALL YOU WHEN THERE IS NEED AGAIN!

AND NOW, IT IS TIME TO RESUME MY *OTHER* IDENTITY!

ALONE IN HIS LABORATORY, ANT-MAN RELEASES HIS GROWTH GAS...

AND SO, ANT-MAN BECOMES THE SCIENTIST HENRY PYM, A MAN DRIVEN TO RESTLESSNESS BY BITTER MEMORIES!

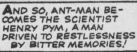

HE IS TIRED... SO VERY TIRED! IF ONLY HE HAD HELP...HUMAN HELP! BUT IT IS HIS DESTINY NEVER TO REVEAL HIS SECRET TO ANY OTHER HUMAN...

I MUST ALWAYS BE ALONE! IT IS MY FATE! IF ONLY *MARIA* WERE HERE BY MY SIDE! TOGETHER WE COULD... BUT... MARIA IS *GONE*...

AND SO HE SITS, THIS MAN OF SCIENCE, OF LEGEND, AS HIS THOUGHTS GO BACK TO THE PAST...

HELLO, MRS. PYM ...MY BEAUTIFUL MARIA, MY LOVELY WIFE!

HELLO, MR. PYM, MY HANDSOME HUSBAND!

DARLING, DO YOU THINK IT WISE FOR US TO COME BACK TO HUNGARY ON OUR HONEYMOON! YOU AND YOUR FATHER WERE POLITICAL PRISONERS AND...

HUSH, MY LOVE! WE ESCAPED TO YOUR WONDERFUL COUNTRY! THEY WILL NOT KNOW ME NOW THAT I AM THE WIFE OF AN AMERICAN! I AM MRS. PYM NOW, NOT MARIA TROVAYA!

2

MY FATHER IS SAFE IN AMERICA, WORKING FOR YOUR WONDERFUL COUNTRY! AND I MERELY WISH TO SEE THE PLACES WHERE I SPENT MY CHILDHOOD!

FASTEN YOUR SEAT BELTS, PLEASE, WE ARE ABOUT TO LAND!

Y'KNOW, DARLING, THIS HONEYMOON IS THE FIRST VACATION I'VE TAKEN IN YEARS! NOW I FEEL AS THOUGH I NEVER WANT TO WORK AGAIN... JUST SPEND EVERY MOMENT OF MY LIFE WITH YOU!

HA! YOU ARE BECOMING A LAZY HUSBAND! MY FATHER ALWAYS USED TO SAY, "GO TO THE ANTS, THOU DULLARD!" BUT YOU ARE NOT AN INDUSTRIOUS ANT, ARE YOU, MY LOVE!

I AM MERELY A MAN IN LOVE, MY DARLING!

HERE'S A TAXI TO TAKE US TO THE HOTEL! AND, PERHAPS YOU ARE RIGHT! NO ONE WILL KNOW YOU WERE ONCE MARIA TROVAYA NOW THAT YOU ARE MRS. HENRY PYM!

BUT, SUDDENLY...

YOU WILL NOT MAKE A SOUND, MARIA TROVAYA, OR YOUR AMERICAN HUSBAND WILL BE SHOT!

HENRY!

WHAT IS THIS?

SILENCE, AMERICAN!

HEY! WAIT! YOU CAN'T... --UGH--

AN HOUR LATER, AT THE AMERICAN EMBASSY!

NEVER MIND MY HEAD! IT'S BEEN AN HOUR NOW...

I KNOW MR. PYM! WE ARE DOING ALL WE CAN TO FIND YOUR WIFE! YOU MUST BE PATIENT!

YES! THIS IS HE! YES? OH! I SEE! YES, I--I'LL TELL HIM!

3

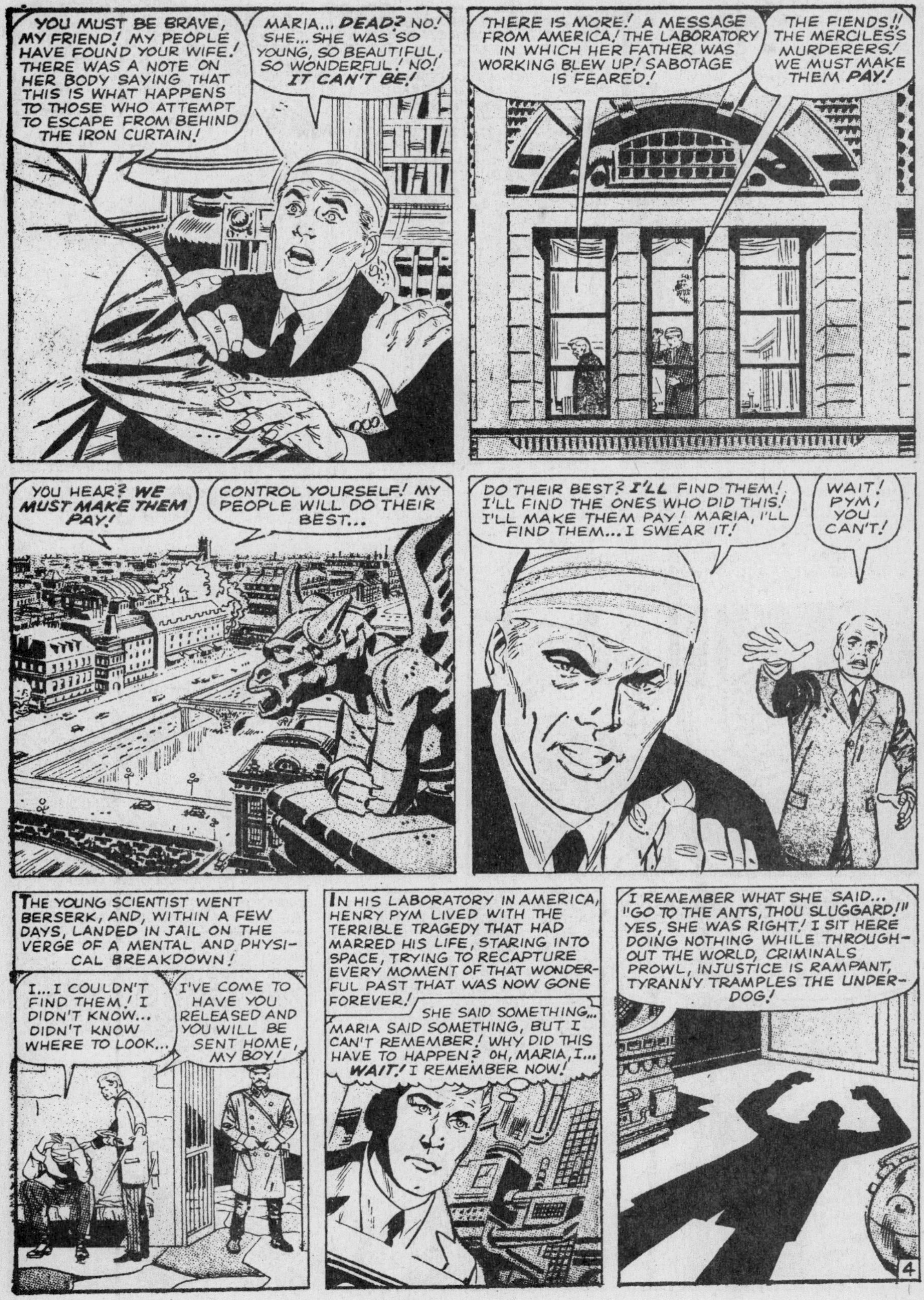
YOU MUST BE BRAVE, MY FRIEND! MY PEOPLE HAVE FOUND YOUR WIFE! THERE WAS A NOTE ON HER BODY SAYING THAT THIS IS WHAT HAPPENS TO THOSE WHO ATTEMPT TO ESCAPE FROM BEHIND THE IRON CURTAIN!
MARIA... DEAD? NO! SHE... SHE WAS SO YOUNG, SO BEAUTIFUL, SO WONDERFUL! NO! IT CAN'T BE!
THERE IS MORE! A MESSAGE FROM AMERICA! THE LABORATORY IN WHICH HER FATHER WAS WORKING BLEW UP! SABOTAGE IS FEARED!
THE FIENDS!! THE MERCILESS MURDERERS! WE MUST MAKE THEM PAY!
YOU HEAR? WE MUST MAKE THEM PAY!
CONTROL YOURSELF! MY PEOPLE WILL DO THEIR BEST...
DO THEIR BEST? I'LL FIND THEM! I'LL FIND THE ONES WHO DID THIS! I'LL MAKE THEM PAY! MARIA, I'LL FIND THEM... I SWEAR IT!
WAIT! PYM, YOU CAN'T!
THE YOUNG SCIENTIST WENT BERSERK, AND, WITHIN A FEW DAYS, LANDED IN JAIL ON THE VERGE OF A MENTAL AND PHYSICAL BREAKDOWN!
I... I COULDN'T FIND THEM! I DIDN'T KNOW... DIDN'T KNOW WHERE TO LOOK...
I'VE COME TO HAVE YOU RELEASED AND YOU WILL BE SENT HOME, MY BOY!
IN HIS LABORATORY IN AMERICA, HENRY PYM LIVED WITH THE TERRIBLE TRAGEDY THAT HAD MARRED HIS LIFE, STARING INTO SPACE, TRYING TO RECAPTURE EVERY MOMENT OF THAT WONDERFUL PAST THAT WAS NOW GONE FOREVER!
SHE SAID SOMETHING... MARIA SAID SOMETHING, BUT I CAN'T REMEMBER! WHY DID THIS HAVE TO HAPPEN? OH, MARIA, I... WAIT! I REMEMBER NOW!
I REMEMBER WHAT SHE SAID... "GO TO THE ANTS, THOU SLUGGARD!" YES, SHE WAS RIGHT! I SIT HERE DOING NOTHING WHILE THROUGHOUT THE WORLD, CRIMINALS PROWL, INJUSTICE IS RAMPANT, TYRANNY TRAMPLES THE UNDERDOG!
4

SO I WILL STRIKE *BACK* AT ALL OF IT, WHEREVER ROTTENNESS EXISTS! I AM A SCIENTIST! I WILL USE MY TALENTS, MY KNOWLEDGE TO FIND A WAY...

AND SO, ALONE, HE THREW HIMSELF INTO HIS WORK, DRIVING ALWAYS TO KEEP THE PAINFUL PAST FROM HIS MIND, A MAN POSSESSED, A MAN PUSHED BEYOND THE LIMITS OF SCIENTIFIC REASON BY MEMORIES...

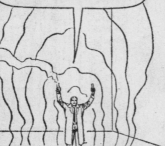

IT WORKS... THE REDUCING GAS WORKS! MY THEORY IS *CORRECT!* LIVING CELLS *CAN* BE REDUCED IN SIZE BY CHEMICAL MEANS... AND MY GROWTH GAS WILL ENLARGE THEM AGAIN...

"GO TO THE ANTS, THOU SLUGGARD!" IT RANG IN HIS BRAIN, OVER AND OVER, UNTIL THAT FATEFUL DAY WHEN HENRY PYM BECAME... *THE ANT-MAN!*

THE SKEIN OF MEMORY BREAKS AND BRINGS OUR HERO BACK TO THE PRESENT!

YES... I BECAME THE ANT-MAN AND DEVELOPED CLOTHING OF UNSTABLE MOLECULES TO WEAR... THE CYBERNETIC HELMET, COMMUNICATION WITH THE ANTS! ALL THIS AND MORE! BUT IT'S *STILL* NOT ENOUGH!

TOO OFTEN HAVE I COME CLOSE TO DEFEAT! I NEED A *PARTNER!* SOMEONE TO STAND BY, TO CARRY ON IF SOMEDAY I MEET DEFEAT AND DEATH! BUT *WHO?* WHO COULD I EVER TRUST TO KNOW THE SECRETS OF THE ANT-MAN... KNOW MY *TRUE IDENTITY?*

I DON'T KNOW! BUT, PERHAPS SOMEDAY, I SHALL FIND THE ONE, AND WHEN I DO I MUST BE READY! WORK! YES, I WILL WORK, FIND THE WAY TO EQUIP THAT PARTNER TO AID ME IN MY WORK...

FOR WEEKS THE SCIENTIST WORKS, TAKING LITTLE NOURISHMENT OR SLEEP... NEVER PAUSING FOR THE MEMORIES TO COME AGAIN!

YES, IT'S TRUE... THE CELLS OF THE WASP CAN BE MADE TO SPECIALIZE, TO GROW AS LEGS, OR WINGS, OR ANTENNAE... BUT ONLY IN A LIFE FORM OF *MINIATURE* SIZE! *WAIT!* WHAT IS THAT NOISE? OH, IT'S THE DOORBELL...

IMPATIENT AT THE INTERRUPTION, HENRY PYM GOES TO THE DOOR!

WHAT IS IT?

AH, YOU ARE HENRY PYM! I AM DR. VERNON VAN DYNE! YOU ARE QUITE FAMOUS, MR. PYM! SO, I HAVE COME TO VISIT, FOR WE ARE *BOTH* SCIENTISTS AND PERHAPS HAVE MUCH IN COMMON!

5

ER...YES, OF COURSE! COME IN!

THIS IS MY DAUGHTER, JANET!

HOW DO YOU DO, DOCTOR PYM?

SHE...SHE LOOKS SOMEWHAT LIKE MARIA! BUT SHE'S MUCH YOUNGER! NOT MUCH MORE THAN A CHILD!

HMMMM, HE'S QUITE HANDSOME! BUT SCIENTISTS ARE SUCH BORES! I PREFER THE ADVENTUROUS TYPE, NOT THOSE DULL, INTELLECTUAL BOOKWORMS!

MR. PYM, I MUST CONFESS THAT MY VISIT IS NOT MERELY SOCIAL! I THINK PERHAPS YOU CAN HELP ME! I HAVE BEEN WORKING ON A GAMMARAY BEAM TO PIERCE SPACE AND DETECT SIGNALS FROM OTHER PLANETS! IF THERE IS LIFE OUT THERE IN THE GALAXY PERHAPS, THROUGH MY BEAM, WE CAN MAKE CONTACT!

I'VE HEARD OF YOUR WORK!

DOCTOR, I'M AFRAID I CAN'T BE OF HELP TO YOU! MY FIELD IS MOLECULAR CELL TRANSITION AND CELL SPECIALIZATION!

I KNOW! BUT I THOUGHT... YOU SEE, THE BEAM NEEDS STRENGTHENING TO REACH ....! AH, BUT I SEE YOU ARE NOT INTERESTED! I UNDERSTAND, MR. PYM! EACH MAN TO HIS OWN FIELD! WELL, IT WAS A PLEASURE MEETING YOU!

LET'S GO, DADDY!

YES, YES OF COURSE! GOODNIGHT, MR. PYM!

SO MUCH LIKE MARIA! IF SHE WERE NOT SUCH A CHILD....!

SO, HENRY PYM RETURNS TO HIS WORK ON SPECIALIZED CELLS, PAUSING ONLY TO TUNE IN WITH HIS FANTASTIC CYBERNETIC MACHINE TO ELECTRONIC IMPULSE MESSAGES FROM THE VAST ARMY OF ANTS THAT ROAM THE CITY!

TROUBLE ON TEMPLE STREET ...BUT THE POLICE HAVE IT WELL IN HAND! NO NEED FOR THE ANT-MAN!

AND DR. VERNON VAN DYNE CONTINUES WITH HIS OWN EXPERIMENT!

I'VE GOT IT! YES, THE BOOSTER IS PUSHING THE RAYS DEEP INTO SPACE...

DADDY, I'M GOING OUT... SOMEPLACE WHERE THERE IS MUSIC AND LAUGHTER AND GAIETY!

BUT, THESE THREE HUMANS DO NOT SUSPECT THAT SOON THEY WILL BE TANGLED TOGETHER IN THE WEB OF FATE, AS THEY CONFRONT THE MOST AWESOME MENACE EVER LET LOOSE UPON OUR UNSUSPECTING WORLD...

6

AH, MY RAYS ARE GOING BEYOND OUR OWN GALAXY...REACHING INTO THE DEPTHS OF SPACE TO OTHER GALAXIES, OTHER WORLDS, STAR WORLDS WE CANNOT EVEN SEE...

WHAT IS THAT? A DARKNESS... A FLUIDITY...FLUX, WHIRLING ...COMING CLOSER! I DON'T UNDERSTAND! SOMETHING, VAST...SHAPELESS, YET WITH FORM! FOLLOWING DOWN THE PATH OF THE RAYS! IT...IT'S...

OHHHHHHHH...

THE DOCTOR LOOKS AT THE THING THAT IS IN THE ROOM WITH HIM! HIS SENSES REEL, HIS FACE TURNS ASHEN AND EVERYTHING HUMAN WITHIN HIM CRIES OUT IN AGONY AGAINST THIS ALIEN THING...A CREATURE SO UNEARTHLY THAT IT IS ALMOST MORE THAN HUMAN EYES CAN BEAR!

WHAT...WHAT ARE YOU?

MALEABLE, A VISCOUS FLOWING, A PRESENCE THAT FILLS THE ROOM, CONSCIENCELESS, HOSTILITY EMANATING FROM IT LIKE A CLOUD OF SNAKES, THE THING ANSWERS IN A SLITHERING VOICE THAT IS NO VOICE, THAT IS A TOUCHING OF THE HUMAN BRAIN WITH WAVES OF MEANING!

I AM FROM THE PLANET KOSMOS, DEEP IN SPACE! WE OF KOSMOS ARE A FLUID FORM OF LIFE! I ESCAPED DOWN THE PATH OF YOUR RAY TO THIS, YOUR PLANET!

E-ESCAPED? YES! I AM A CRIMINAL... THE GREATEST KOSMOS HAS EVER SEEN ...ALONE, I ALMOST SUCCEEDED IN SMASHING KOSMOSIAN SOCIETY, MAKING SLAVES OF THEM ALL! BUT I FAILED! NOW I AM SAFE HERE! HERE I CAN DO WHAT I FAILED TO DO ON KOSMOS! OF COURSE I MUST SMASH YOUR MACHINE TO KEEP ANY FROM FOLLOWING ME, FROM MY OWN PLANET AND... I MUST DISPOSE OF YOU, SO NO ONE KNOWS OF MY PRESENCE HERE! LOOK AT ME, EARTHMAN...LOOK... LOOK...

SILENTLY THE SCIENTIST FIGHTS, KEEPING HIS HEAD TURNED FROM THE MONSTER, KNOWING THAT TO LOOK IS TO DIE! BUT THE ALIEN POWER OF THE CREATURE FROM KOSMOS IS NOT TO BE DENIED! VAN DYNE'S HEAD TURNS...SLOWLY...SLOWLY... UNTIL...

IT IS DONE.!!

7

LATER, JANET RETURNS HOME...

WHAT IS THAT AWFUL MIST!? SEEMS TO BE COMING FROM DADDY'S LAB! DAD... ARE YOU THERE?

DAD!!! OH, NO!!

I... I MUST HAVE HELP! I MUST CALL SOMEBODY! BUT WHO?? I DON'T KNOW ANYONE WHO...! WAIT... PYM! HENRY PYM! HE'S A SCIENTIST, TOO! DAD TRUSTED HIM...

YES, THIS IS HENRY PYM! JANET VAN DYNE! WHAT? YOUR FATHER...! OH, COME NOW!

THOSE BORED SOCIETY PLAYGIRLS ARE ALL ALIKE! BUT IT'S PRETTY GRUESOME FOR HER TO GET HER KICKS BY MAKING UP A HORROR STORY ABOUT HER FATHER!

LIGHTS FLASHING ON THE CYBERNETIC BOARD... IT MEANS A MESSAGE IS COMING FROM THE ANTS! I HAVE NO TIME TO PLAY GAMES WITH A SPOILED BRAT LIKE JANET VAN DYNE!

WHAT? VAN DYNE KILLED....! THEN SHE WASN'T ACTING... IT'S TRUE!

QUICKLY HENRY PYM RELEASES HIS REDUCING GAS...

BUT THIS IS NOT A JOB FOR HENRY PYM...

IT'S A MISSION FOR... ANT-MAN!

8

I'LL SEND ELECTRONIC WAVES THROUGH MY CYBERNETIC HELMET TO SUMMON ALL THE ANTS IN THE VICINITY TO MEET ME AT VAN DYNE'S LABORATORY!

THE CATAPULT WILL GET ME TO MY DESTINATION IN A HURRY! JUST SET THESE DIALS...

ANT-MAN TRIGGERS THE INGENIOUS CATAPULT MECHANISM AND, A MOMENT LATER, SHOOTS SWIFTLY THROUGH THE AIR!

THE ANTS WILL BE WAITING FOR ME TO FORM A SOFT PLATFORM FOR ME TO LAND ON!

GOOD! NOW TO FIND THE GIRL AND SEE WHAT CAUSED DR. VAN DYNE'S DEATH!

THERE SHE IS... UNAWARE OF MY PRESENCE!

HELLO! I'M ANT-MAN! PERHAPS YOU'VE HEARD OF ME! I'VE COME TO HELP YOU!

I HAVE HEARD OF YOU BUT... I THOUGHT YOU WERE ONLY A MYTH! MY FATHER... HE'S DEAD... IN HIS LABORATORY...

THERE WAS A STRANGE MIST... I CAME IN AND FOUND HIM...

HE'S BEEN MURDERED... ALMOST LOOKS LIKE HE DIED OF FRIGHT! THERE'S SOMETHING STRANGE... SOMETHING EERIE HERE! I CAN SENSE IT!

AND THE MACHINE... I SUPPOSE IT WAS HIS RAY MACHINE... IT'S WRECKED! BUT WHAT KIND OF THING COULD TWIST AND SMASH HEAVY METAL THAT WAY?

9

SOMETHING UNEARTHLY, OF AWFUL MENACE AND TERRIBLE POWERS...COMPLETELY *ALIEN*, WAS HERE! BUT *WHAT*...AND HOW DID *IT* GET HERE?

I LOVED MY FATHER! HE WAS THE FINEST MAN ON EARTH! I NEVER SHOWED HIM HOW MUCH I LOVED HIM! I THOUGHT IT WASN'T SOPHISTICATED! NOW I'LL NEVER HAVE THE CHANCE! BUT, THERE IS *ONE* THING I CAN DO...*AVENGE* HIM!

THIS IS SO LIKE MARIA...

CALL IT A WOMAN'S INTUITION IF YOU WISH, BUT I KNOW THAT IT WAS HIS EXPERIMENT TO REACH OUTER SPACE, TO COMMUNICATE WITH OTHER LIFE FORMS ON OTHER PLANETS, THAT WAS THE CAUSE OF HIS DEATH! SOMEHOW I'LL FIND OUT...IF IT TAKES THE REST OF MY LIFE TO DO IT!

SHE'S CHANGED! THE BORED FLIGHTY SHELL SHE WORE IS GONE! SHE HAS DETERMINATION, STRENGTH OF CHARACTER! I WONDER IF *SHE*...?

LISTEN TO ME AND ASK NO QUESTIONS! PHONE THE F.B.I.! ASK FOR LEE KEARNS AND TELL HIM WHAT HAPPENED HERE! THEN GO TO HENRY PYM'S LABORATORY IMMEDIATELY! TRUST ME AND *DO AS* I TELL YOU!

I *DO* TRUST YOU, ANT-MAN!

TEMPLTON 47900

TUV 8

WXY 9

OPERATOR 0

THAT'S STRANGE...THE ANTS HAVE GONE! THEY'RE ALL DOWN BELOW! THIS IS THE FIRST TIME THEY'VE EVER LEFT ME! WELL, GUESS I'LL HAVE TO SHINNY DOWN THE WATER PIPE...

F.B.I.? I WANT TO SPEAK TO LEE KEARNS...

SECONDS LATER...

WHY DID YOU DESERT ME, MY FRIENDS?

SUDDENLY, THERE IS A STRANGE STIRRING AMONG THE ANT HORDE! MANDIBLES CLICK, AND THE OUTER SKELETON ARMOR OF THE INSECTS MOVES WITH SELF-CONSCIOUS MUSCLE PULL! THEN THE HUGE SOLDIER ANT SENDS OUT ITS MESSAGE WAVES...

THE CREATURE THAT WAS IN THERE...THE MIST IT LEFT...IT CONTAINS TRACES OF FORMIC ACID! IT MUST BE KIN TO US, THE ANTS, FOR WE SECRETE FORMIC ACID, TOO! BUT, IT IS ALIEN AND WE ARE AFRAID!

10

WELL THEN, TAKE ME BACK TO MY LABORATORY, QUICKLY! THEN YOU WILL SPREAD OUT, TRY TO FIND SOME TRACE OF THIS CREATURE! AND SOME OF YOU WILL GO TO THE F.B.I. OFFICES AND SEND ME A MESSAGE OF WHAT THEY FIND OUT!

BACK IN HIS LABORATORY, ANT-MAN RELEASES HIS GROWTH GAS...

AND NOW TO WAIT FOR JANET'S ARRIVAL! I MUST GREET HER AS HENRY PYM!

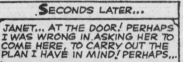

SECONDS LATER...

JANET... AT THE DOOR! PERHAPS I WAS WRONG IN ASKING HER TO COME HERE, TO CARRY OUT THE PLAN I HAVE IN MIND! PERHAPS...

DOCTOR PYM! MY FATHER --HE--

I KNOW! AND I KNOW YOU WANT TO AVENGE HIS DEATH! ARE YOU REALLY SERIOUS? WOULD YOU RISK ANYTHING FOR JUSTICE? I MUST KNOW!

I MEANT WHAT I SAID! I SHALL DEDICATE MY LIFE TO FINDING HIS MURDERER! COMING HERE, I HAD TIME TO THINK! I WISH I COULD HELP TRACK DOWN ALL THE CRIMINALS, THE HUMAN WOLVES WHO PREY ON HONEST PEOPLE! I SUPPOSE YOU THINK I'M JUST A FOOLISH FEMALE, BUT...

COME IN HERE, INTO MY LABORATORY, AND SHUT THE DOOR!

I'M GOING TO TELL YOU WHAT NO ONE ELSE IN THE WORLD KNOWS! IN SO DOING, I PUT MY LIFE IN YOUR HANDS! BUT, I TELL YOU BECAUSE I NEED A PARTNER... AND I HAVE CHOSEN HER! I AM... THE ANT-MAN!

YOU...? BUT, OF COURSE! HOW ELSE COULD YOU HAVE KNOWN ABOUT... BUT YOU SAID YOU HAVE CHOSEN A... PARTNER?

YES! I CAN MAKE YOU SMALL AS ANT-MAN WITH MY SHRINKING GAS! AND, DUE TO MY RESEARCH IN CELL SPECIALIZATION, I CAN GIVE YOU WINGS, ANTENNAE, I CAN MAKE YOU A HUMAN WASP! YES! ANT-MAN AND THE WASP! WE WILL FIND YOUR FATHER'S MURDERER AND BRING JUSTICE TO ALL WHO NEED IT! WHAT IS YOUR ANSWER, JANET VAN DYNE?

YES! I SAY, YES! SHOW ME HOW AND I WILL STAND BESIDE YOU ALWAYS... TO AVENGE MY FATHER'S DEATH! I SWEAR IT!

11

DO YOU SEE THOSE SYNTHETIC CELLS IN THE MICROSCOPIC FIELD? THEY ARE SPECIALIZED CELLS! I CAN IMPLANT THEM BELOW YOUR SKIN TISSUE! IT WILL LEAVE NO SCAR, BUT WHEN YOU ARE REDUCED TO THE SIZE OF A WASP YOU WILL GROW TINY WINGS AND TINY ANTENNAE!

IT...IT ALL SOUNDS SO UNBELIEVABLE... SO WONDERFUL!

ALL I FEEL IS A TINY PIN PRICK! HOW LONG DOES IT TAKE?

JUST *THIS* LONG, JANET! THE SPECIALIZED CELLS ARE NOW IN PLACE!

MEANWHILE, AT THE BUILDING THAT HOUSES DR. VAN DYNE'S LABORATORY...

RUN! IT'S AN EARTHQUAKE!

HELP!!

KEEP BACK! THE BUILDING IS COLLAPSING!

AND, AT THE DOCKS NEARBY, A FEW MINUTES LATER...

HEY, FEEL THAT, JOE? THE WHOLE DOCK'S SHAKIN'!

SEEMS TO BE COMIN' FROM *BEHIND* US!

LOOK! OVER *THERE*...

WHA-- WHAT *IS* IT?

RUN! *RUN*... YELL TO THE OTHERS TO GET OFF THE DOCKS...

AND SO THE WORLD FIRST MEETS THE CREATURE FROM KOSMOS!

WHILE, IN HENRY PYM'S LABORATORY...

ELECTRONIC IMPULSES COMING FROM MY ANT SCOUTS! JANET, IN THE CLOSET IS A COSTUME WOVEN FROM UNSTABLE MOLECULES THAT WILL EXPAND AND SHRINK AS YOU DO! I HAVE A FEELING THIS IS OUR FIRST MISSION!

12

CYBERNETIC UNITS IN THE MACHINE TRANSLATE THE INCOMING SIGNALS INTO HUMAN SPEECH, AS JANET VAN DYNE DONS HER NEW COSTUME...

F.B.I. SAYS VAN DYNE KILLED BY STRANGE ELEMENT AKIN TO FEAR... ENTIRE SYSTEM RUPTURED! F.B.I., POLICE, MILITARY CALLED OUT TO FIGHT ALIEN MENACE! VAN DYNE HOUSE SMASHED AS THOUGH BY GIANT HAND! DOCKS NEARBY UPROOTED, SMASHED!

ALIEN THING ADVANCING TOWARD GEORGE WASHINGTON BRIDGE! POLICE CLEARING MANHATTAN! MILITARY STANDING BY, READY TO FIRE!

THIS IS IT, JANET! THAT IS THE THING THAT KILLED YOUR FATHER! SOMEHOW YOUR FATHER'S SPACE PROBE MACHINE BROUGHT THAT UNEARTHLY MENACE DOWN TO OUR PLANET!

HERE, DON THIS BELT! THE CYLINDERS CONTAIN YOUR REDUCING AND GROWTH GASSES! PRESS THE BOTTOM BUTTON...LIKE THIS!!

I SEE!

THE MIRACULOUS VAPOR ENGULFS THEM AND THEY SHRINK... SMALLER... SMALLER... SMALLER...

OH! IT FEELS SO-- SO *WEIRD!*

YOU'LL GET USED TO IT, JANET!

AND, AS SHE SHRINKS TO MINUTENESS, GOSSAMER, DAINTY WINGS SPROUT FROM JANET'S SHOULDERS AND TINY, DELICATE ANTENNAE ADORN HER FOREHEAD! THE LOVELY GIRL HAS TRULY BECOME... *THE WASP!*

THE SPECIALIZED CELLS... THEY *WORK!!* I CAN HEAR THINGS THROUGH MY ANTENNAE!

THE VOICES OF THE INSECT WORLD... AS I HEAR THEM THROUGH MY CYBERNETIC HELMET! COME, NOW YOU WILL TRY YOUR *WINGS!*

SHOT INTO SPACE BY HIS CATAPULT, ANT-MAN FINDS HIS COMPANION CLOSE BESIDE HIM AS HE FLIES SWIFTLY THROUGH THE AIR!

THIS IS *EXHILIRATING!* WHERE ARE WE GOING?

TO THE GEORGE WASHINGTON BRIDGE! I'VE ORDERED THE ANTS TO GATHER THERE!

ANT-MAN... I THINK YOU'RE *WONDERFUL!* I WANT YOU TO KNOW, IN CASE THIS CREATURE KILLS US, AS IT DID MY FATHER, I-I'M FALLING IN LOVE WITH YOU!

13

NO! YOU MUSTN'T **SAY** THAT, JANET! YOU'RE ONLY A CHILD! LET'S GET THIS STRAIGHT... I CHOSE YOU AS MY PARTNER SIMPLY BECAUSE I THOUGHT YOU HAD A REASON, AS **I** HAVE, TO FIGHT FOR MANKIND!

I NEVER WANT TO LOVE AGAIN! I--I COULDN'T BEAR IT IF I HAD TO LOSE A LOVED ONE-- TWICE!

SO I'M ONLY A **CHILD**, AM I? WELL, MISTER ANT-MAN... WE SHALL **SEE!**

SHE IS SO LIKE MARIA...HER BEAUTY...HER SPIRIT!! I MUST BE CAREFUL LEST I **DO** FALL IN LOVE WITH HER!

THIS IS MY PARTNER, **THE WASP!** YOU WILL BE TO HER AS YOU ARE TO ME! NOW, MY FRIENDS, TOGETHER WE WILL DEFEAT THIS STRANGE MENACE FROM SPACE!

WE **CANNOT** AID YOU THIS TIME, ANT-MAN! THIS CREATURE... THERE IS SOMETHING ABOUT IT THAT PREVENTS US FROM APPROACHING IT! WE CANNOT!

SUDDENLY, THE EARTH SHAKES AS THE MILITARY BATTERIES OPEN FIRE! *THE CREATURE FROM KOSMOS HAS APPEARED!*

NOTHING STOPS IT! SHELLS, BULLETS, MEAN NOTHING TO IT! IT...IT'S TERRIBLE... FORMLESS! I CAN'T **LOOK** AT IT!

DON'T LOOK AT IT, OR YOU'RE LOST! RETREAT! PULL BACK! PASS THE WORD!

THE MOST MODERN WEAPONS WON'T STOP IT! AND WITH- OUT THE ANTS WE HAVE HARDLY A CHANCE!

THAT AWFUL THING KILLED MY FATHER! IF **YOU'RE** AFRAID, I'M NOT!

THE WASP FLIES STRAIGHT TOWARD THE TOWERING, SOULLESS MONSTROSITY...

WASP, COME BACK! YOU FOOL CHILD! **COME BACK!**

I'LL **SHOW** HIM I'M **NOT** A CHILD!

14

ALIEN, MIASMIC TENTACLES LICK OUT AT THE TINY FLYING FIGURE, REACHING FORMLESS FOG-FINGERS, LIKE TRICKLES OF DOOM...BUT STILL SHE FLIES CLOSER--CLOSER--UNTIL HE SEEMS TO DRAW HER TO HIM...

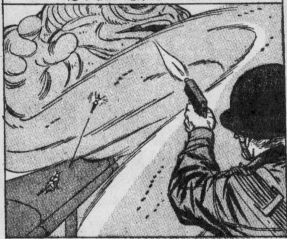

DESPERATELY ANT-MAN CLIMBS ATOP THE STEEL GIRDERS...

DON'T *LOOK* AT THE THING! TURN YOUR HEAD! I'M COMING...

I CAN'T *HELP* MYSELF! I'M BEING DRAWN TOWARDS HIM!

HURLING HIMSELF INTO SPACE, *ANTMAN* SEIZES THE WASP'S HAND, HIS WEIGHT CARRYING HER DOWN, AWAY FROM THE CREATURE FROM KOSMOS...

GOT YOU!

DON'T YOU TRY ANYTHING LIKE THAT AGAIN! I DIDN'T SAY I WAS QUITTING! I'VE JUST GOT TO FIND A *WAY* TO FIGHT THAT THING! AND I THINK I'VE *FOUND* IT NOW!

GOT TO RUSH BACK TO THE LABORATORY! THE MIST...WHAT THE ANTS SAID...IT ALL ADDS UP! THIS CREATURE IS NOT MADE AS WE ARE! IT IS AN ACID SPECIES, COMPOSED MAINLY OF FORMIC ACID...

MINUTES LATER, IN HENRY PYM'S LAB...

ON THE SHELF IN THE CLOSET YOU'LL FIND A 12 GAUGE SHOTGUN AND SOME SHELLS! BRING THEM HERE AND EMPTY OUT THE SHELLS!

YES SIR, BOSS-MAN!

MAN USES FORMIC ACID AS A DYE! MEDIEVAL DOCTORS DISTILLED THE ACID FROM ANTS, BUT MODERN MAN USES AN OXALIC BASE...AND THE ANTIDOTE? YES, HERE IT IS...

15

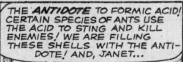

HELP ME FILL THESE SHELLS ...HURRY!

WHAT *IS* THIS STUFF?

THE *ANTIDOTE* TO FORMIC ACID! CERTAIN SPECIES OF ANTS USE THE ACID TO STING AND KILL ENEMIES! WE ARE FILLING THESE SHELLS WITH THE ANTIDOTE! AND, JANET...

YES?

PRAY THAT MY THINKING IS RIGHT! IF IT ISN'T, THIS COULD VERY WELL BE THE END OF OUR WORLD, THE END OF MANKIND AS WE KNOW IT! NOW, WE MUST BECOME *ANT-MAN* AND *THE WASP* AGAIN! ARE YOU READY?

YOU *KNOW* I AM!

AND SO...

BUT NOW, HOW CAN WE CARRY THE RIFLE AND THE SHELLS?

MY FRIENDS, THE ANTS SHALL DO THAT *FOR* US!

ANT-MAN SENDS OUT SIGNALS TO THE ANTS, AND...

CARRY THOSE! WE MUST HURRY! WHERE IS THE ALIEN *NOW*?

WALL STREET! NOTHING STOPS HIM! EVERY WEAPON HAS FAILED!

SO THE STRANGE PROCESSION BEGINS ITS MARCH, AS THE FATE OF MANKIND RESTS ON THE TINY SHOULDERS OF ANT-MAN AND THE WASP!

SHELLS

16

THERE IT *IS*, AHEAD! NOW, MY HEXAPODA FRIENDS, I DO NOT ASK YOU TO FIGHT THIS CREATURE! JUST OBEY MY COMMANDS AND YOU WILL ONLY TAKE A PASSIVE PART IN THIS! UP THE BUILDING HERE TO THE ROOF!

BUT, ANT-MAN, WHAT...?

QUIET, GIRL! I'VE GOT TO THINK THIS OUT!

BUT HOW CAN YOU *LOAD* IT... PULL THE TRIGGER? EVERYTHING IS SO *HUGE*...

YOU WILL FIND, AS I HAVE, THAT THOUGH YOU ARE REDUCED IN SIZE, YOU STILL RETAIN MUCH OF THE STRENGTH OF A FULL-GROWN HUMAN! SEE?

AND NOW, STAND BY WITH OTHER SHELLS READY FOR ME TO LOAD!

HERE IT COMES! OH, THE LOATHSOME THING...

ANT-MAN PULLS THE TRIGGER AS THE ANTS ABSORB THE RECOIL... AND, WITH THE BLAST AND CHARGE GO A FERVENT PRAYER...

BOOOM

NOTHING'S HAPPENED! IT'S *STILL* ADVANCING!

DON'T *LOOK* AT IT!

BOOOMM

17

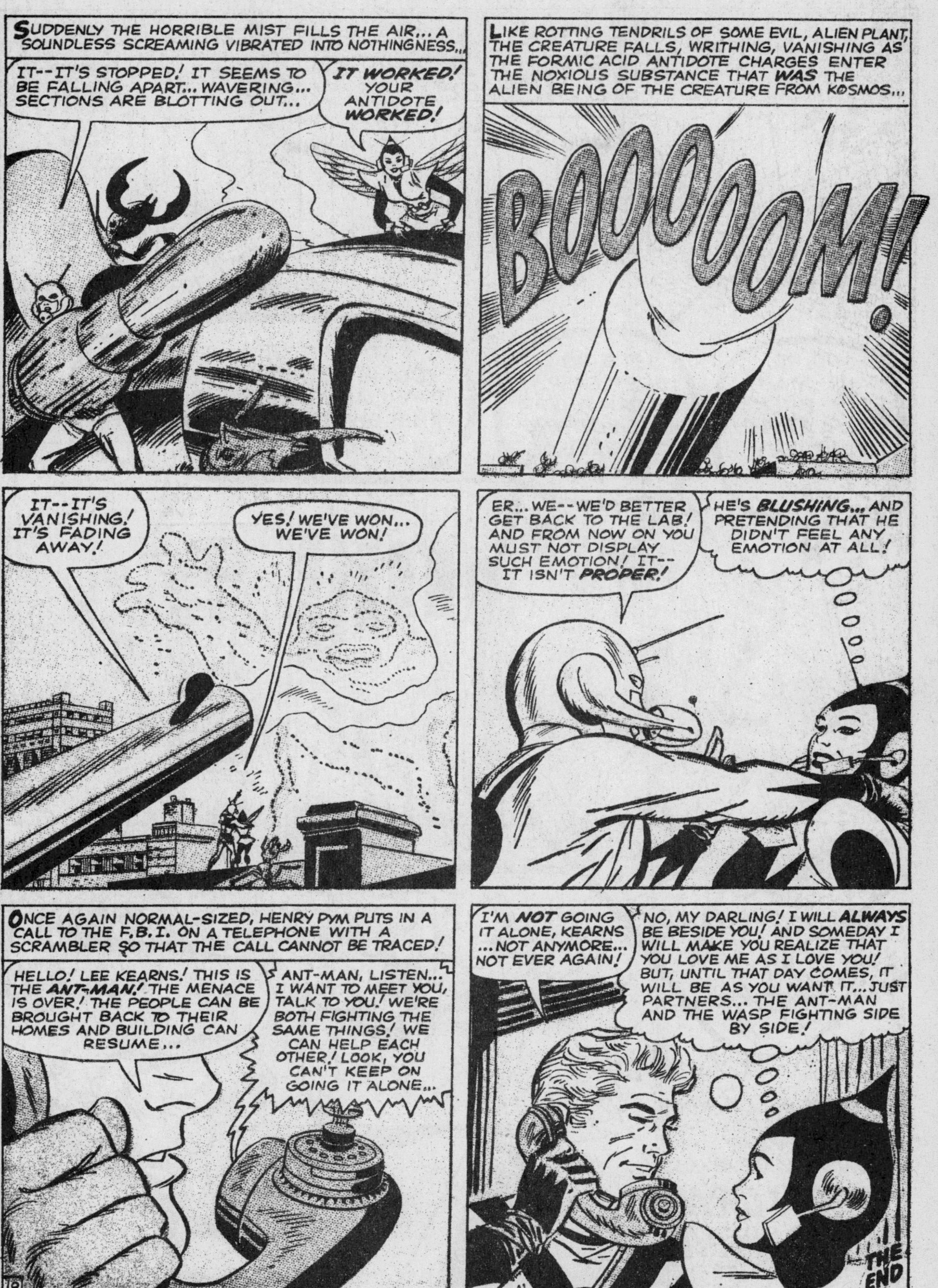
SUDDENLY THE HORRIBLE MIST FILLS THE AIR... A SOUNDLESS SCREAMING VIBRATED INTO NOTHINGNESS...
IT--IT'S STOPPED! IT SEEMS TO BE FALLING APART... WAVERING... SECTIONS ARE BLOTTING OUT...
IT WORKED! YOUR ANTIDOTE WORKED!
LIKE ROTTING TENDRILS OF SOME EVIL, ALIEN PLANT, THE CREATURE FALLS, WRITHING, VANISHING AS THE FORMIC ACID ANTIDOTE CHARGES ENTER THE NOXIOUS SUBSTANCE THAT WAS THE ALIEN BEING OF THE CREATURE FROM KOSMOS...
BOOOOOM!
IT--IT'S VANISHING! IT'S FADING AWAY!
YES! WE'VE WON... WE'VE WON!
ER... WE--WE'D BETTER GET BACK TO THE LAB! AND FROM NOW ON YOU MUST NOT DISPLAY SUCH EMOTION! IT-- IT ISN'T PROPER!
HE'S BLUSHING... AND PRETENDING THAT HE DIDN'T FEEL ANY EMOTION AT ALL!
ONCE AGAIN NORMAL-SIZED, HENRY PYM PUTS IN A CALL TO THE F.B.I. ON A TELEPHONE WITH A SCRAMBLER SO THAT THE CALL CANNOT BE TRACED!
HELLO! LEE KEARNS! THIS IS THE ANT-MAN! THE MENACE IS OVER! THE PEOPLE CAN BE BROUGHT BACK TO THEIR HOMES AND BUILDING CAN RESUME...
ANT-MAN, LISTEN... I WANT TO MEET YOU, TALK TO YOU! WE'RE BOTH FIGHTING THE SAME THINGS! WE CAN HELP EACH OTHER! LOOK, YOU CAN'T KEEP ON GOING IT ALONE...
18
I'M NOT GOING IT ALONE, KEARNS ...NOT ANYMORE... NOT EVER AGAIN!
NO, MY DARLING! I WILL ALWAYS BE BESIDE YOU! AND SOMEDAY I WILL MAKE YOU REALIZE THAT YOU LOVE ME AS I LOVE YOU! BUT, UNTIL THAT DAY COMES, IT WILL BE AS YOU WANT IT... JUST PARTNERS... THE ANT-MAN AND THE WASP FIGHTING SIDE BY SIDE!
THE END

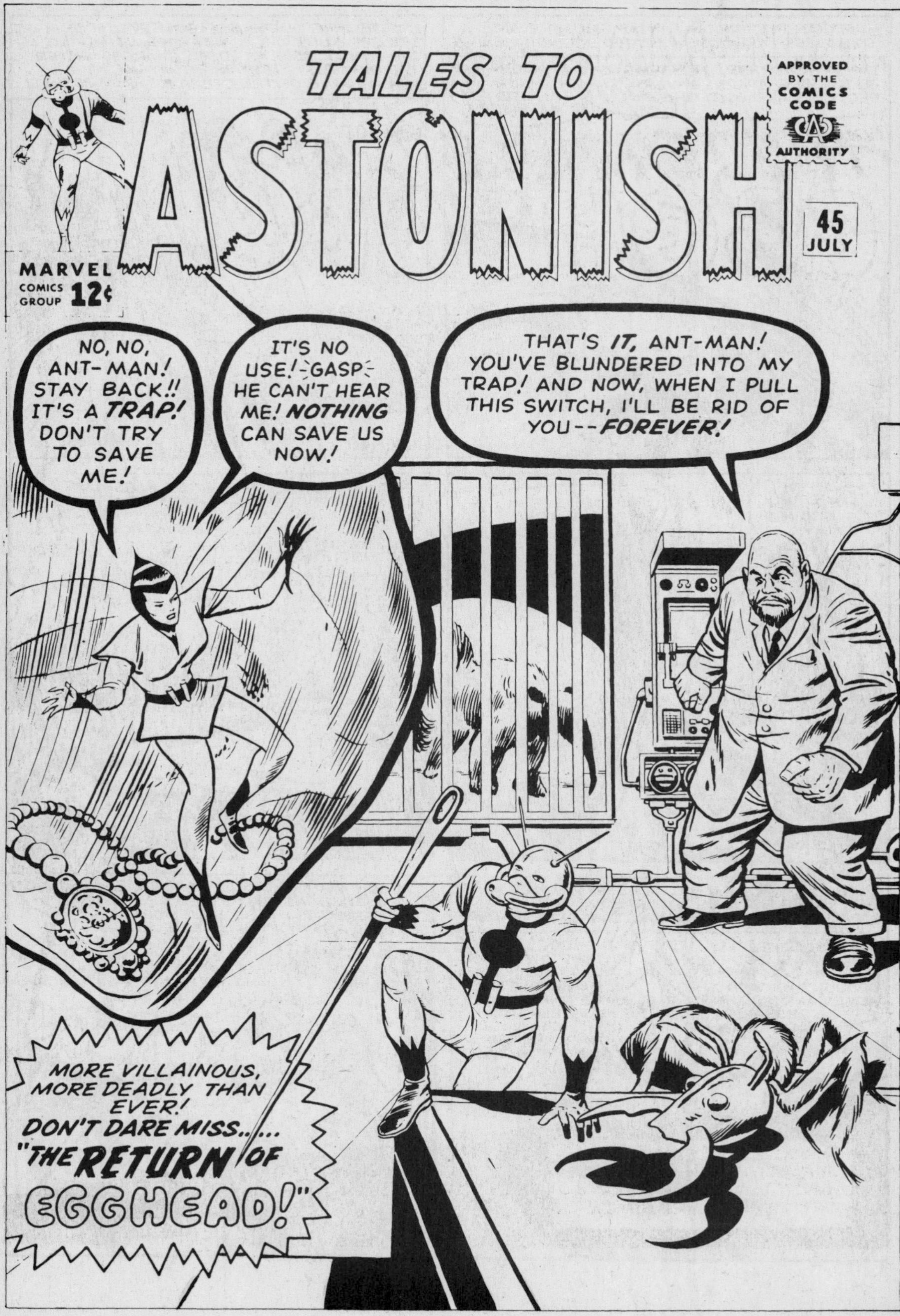
TALES TO ASTONISH
APPROVED BY THE COMICS CODE AUTHORITY
45 JULY
MARVEL COMICS GROUP 12¢
NO, NO, ANT-MAN! STAY BACK!! IT'S A TRAP! DON'T TRY TO SAVE ME!
IT'S NO USE! -GASP- HE CAN'T HEAR ME! NOTHING CAN SAVE US NOW!
THAT'S IT, ANT-MAN! YOU'VE BLUNDERED INTO MY TRAP! AND NOW, WHEN I PULL THIS SWITCH, I'LL BE RID OF YOU--FOREVER!
MORE VILLAINOUS, MORE DEADLY THAN EVER! DON'T DARE MISS..... "THE RETURN OF EGGHEAD!"

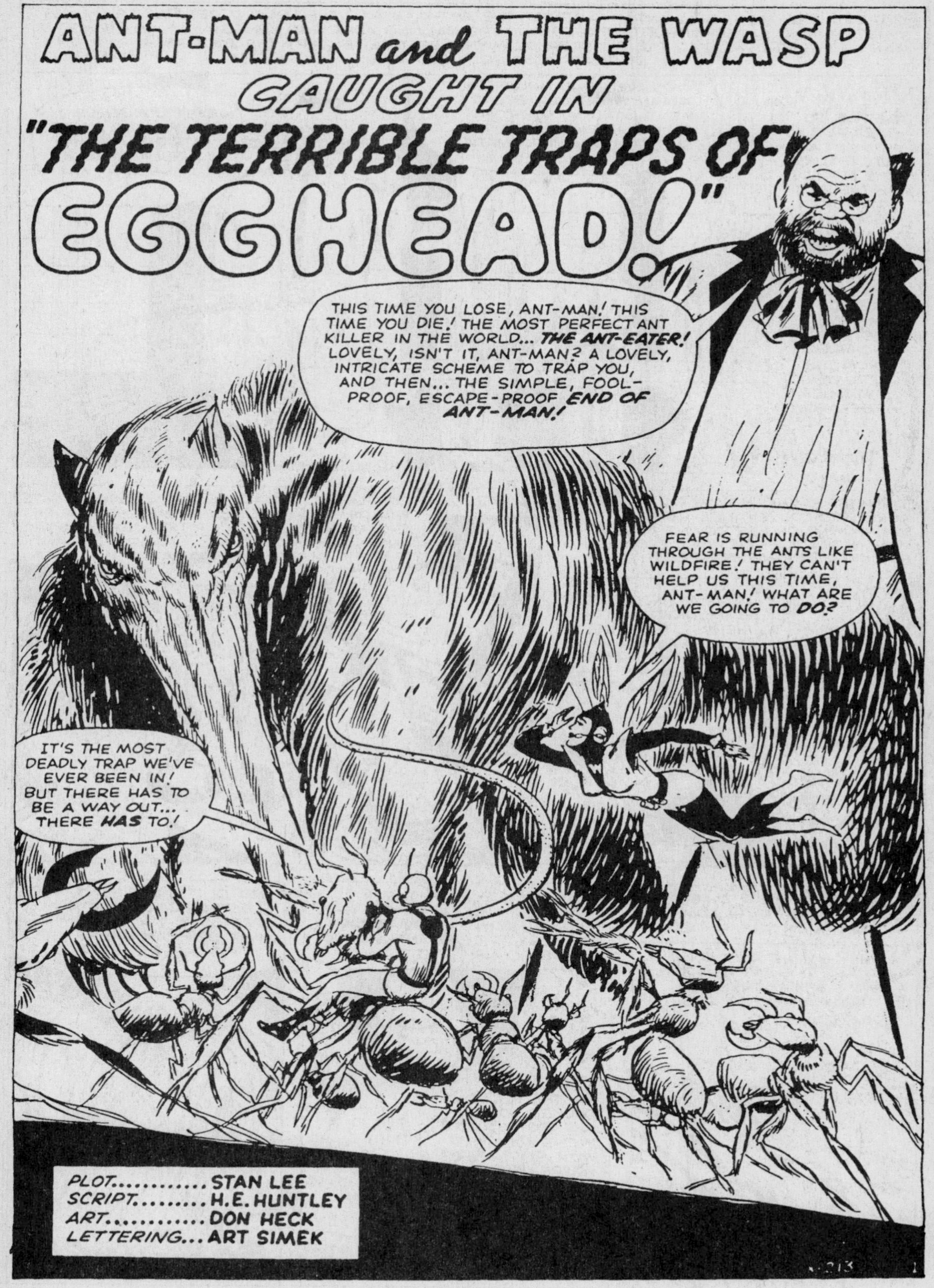
ANT-MAN and THE WASP
CAUGHT IN
"THE TERRIBLE TRAPS OF EGGHEAD!"
THIS TIME YOU LOSE, ANT-MAN! THIS TIME YOU DIE! THE MOST PERFECT ANT KILLER IN THE WORLD... THE ANT-EATER! LOVELY, ISN'T IT, ANT-MAN? A LOVELY, INTRICATE SCHEME TO TRAP YOU, AND THEN... THE SIMPLE, FOOL-PROOF, ESCAPE-PROOF END OF ANT-MAN!
FEAR IS RUNNING THROUGH THE ANTS LIKE WILDFIRE! THEY CAN'T HELP US THIS TIME, ANT-MAN! WHAT ARE WE GOING TO DO?
IT'S THE MOST DEADLY TRAP WE'VE EVER BEEN IN! BUT THERE HAS TO BE A WAY OUT... THERE HAS TO!
PLOT..........STAN LEE
SCRIPT........H.E. HUNTLEY
ART...........DON HECK
LETTERING...ART SIMEK

EGGHEAD, THE MOST BRILLIANT ANTAGONIST THE ANT-MAN HAS EVER FACED, RETURNS AGAIN, HIS TWISTED MIND EATEN WITH BITTERNESS AND THE GALLING ACHE FOR VENGEANCE! NO LIVING MAN HAD EVER DEFEATED THE SINISTER SCIENTIST BEFORE, EXCEPT THE **ANT-MAN**, AND THAT DEFEAT MUST BE WIPED OUT...

LET US GO BACK FOR A MOMENT AND RECAPTURE THE THRILLS OF THE FIRST TIME THAT EGGHEAD AND ANT-MAN CLASHED! REMEMBER, IT BEGAN WHEN THE EVIL MENTAL MASTER WAS DISCHARGED FROM THE GOVERNMENT'S ATOMIC RESEARCH CENTER...

YOU ARE BENEATH CONTEMPT! A MAN WITH YOUR GREAT MENTALITY AND SCIENTIFIC GENIUS, ATTEMPTING TO SELL SECRET ATOMIC INFORMATION...

BAH! TO A GENIUS LIKE ME, YOUR INSIPID PATRIOTIC PHRASES ARE LAUGHABLE! I SNEER AT YOU ALL!

CONTACTED BY THE UNDERWORLD, EGGHEAD AGREED TO CONCENTRATE HIS GREAT BRAINPOWER ON DESTROYING THE ANT-MAN! WITH COLD, SCIENTIFIC PRECISION HE UNDERTOOK HIS DANGEROUS TASK...

ANT-MAN UNDOUBTEDLY COMMUNICATES WITH THE INSECTS HE USES! I MUST FIND A WAY TO DO THE SAME AND TURN HIS OWN ANTS *AGAINST* HIM!

FINALLY...

COMPLETED... A MACHINE THAT CAN TRANSLATE WORDS INTO ELECTRONIC IMPULSES WHICH THE ANTS WILL PICK UP THROUGH THEIR ANTENNAE! NOW I WILL INVADE THE ANT-MAN'S OWN DOMAIN!

EGGHEAD QUICKLY PUT HIS SCHEME TO WORK! HE COMMUNICATED WITH THE ANTS!

OBEY MY INSTRUCTIONS, YOU OF THE ANT KINGDOM, AND I SHALL FREE YOU FROM ANT-MAN'S RULE!

WITH THE HELP OF THE CRIMINALS WHO EMPLOYED HIM, EGGHEAD COMMITTED A COLORFUL ROBBERY TO LURE ANT-MAN TO THE SCENE! AND THEN...

HA, THE BELLOWS SUCKED YOU UP AND DROPPED YOU IN THE BOX LINED WITH *FLYPAPER!* YOU'RE HELPLESS!

NOT QUITE, EGGHEAD! THESE ELECTRONICALLY CONTROLLED SPRINGS IN THE BOTTOM OF MY SHOES CAN BREAK THE FYYPAPER'S HOLD!

SPOIINGG!

2

THEN, AIDED BY HIS ANTS, ANT-MAN USED SOME FLYPAPER OF HIS OWN... A HUGE SHEET THE ANTS DROPPED UPON THE FLEEING CRIMINALS!

EGGHEAD HAD MADE HIS ESCAPE AND, IN HIDING, LISTENED TO ANT-MAN EXPLAIN HOW HE HAD DEFEATED THE UNSCRUPULOUS SCIENTIST...

EGGHEAD TRIED TO APPEAL TO THE ANTS' SENSE OF GREED AND VANITY! BUT INSECTS HAVE NO SUCH EMOTIONS! EGGHEAD MISUNDERSTOOD THE PSYCHOLOGY OF THE ANTS... THEY AREN'T MY SLAVES, THEY ARE MY FRIENDS AND PARTNERS!

DEFEATED, HUNTED, THE ONCE BRILLIANT SCIENTIST, HIS CONFIDENCE SHAKEN, BECAME A BUM IN A BOWERY FLOP-HOUSE!

ALL HE DOES IS MUTTER ABOUT ANTS! MUST BE SOME KINDA NUT!

THE ANTS... THEY WERE TOO SMART FOR ME...THEY DEFEATED ME...THE ANTS DEFEATED ME!

YES, IT ALL HAPPENED MONTHS AGO! BUT LAST NIGHT, IN THAT SAME FLOPHOUSE...

HE GOT ALL THE OTHERS! WE WERE LUCKY TO GET AWAY, TWISTER!

YEAH! I TELL YUH, APE, WITH THE ANT-MAN LOOSE, AN HONEST CRIMINAL DOESN'T STAND A CHANCE! 'SPECIALLY NOW HE'S GOT THE WASP WITH HIM...

WHAT WAS THAT YOU SAID? YOU SPOKE OF THE ANT-MAN!!

LET GO, YUH KOOK! FORGET WHAT I SAID! ME AN' APE AIN'T BEEN HERE IF THE COPS ASK YOU! GET IT?!!

YOU DON'T UNDERSTAND! THE ANT-MAN DEFEATED ME, TOO! LISTEN, WE CAN HELP EACH OTHER!

SHOULD I SQUASH THIS BUM, TWISTER?

HOLD IT, APE! IT WON'T HURT TO LISTEN!

IT HAD BEEN BUILDING UP INSIDE HIM, THE HATE, THE NEED FOR REVENGE, AND SUDDENLY DESPAIR LEFT EGG-HEAD TO BE REPLACED BY A DRIVING, VICIOUS NEED TO ENCOUNTER AGAIN THE MAN WHO DEFEATED HIM!

I'M GOING TO TELL YOU WHO I AM AND THEN YOU'LL UNDERSTAND! A PLAN IS BEGINNING TO FORM IN MY MIND! YOU MENTIONED THE WASP! TELL ME ALL ABOUT HER...

3

"...AND THAT'S THE WHOLE STORY! ANT-MAN AND THE WASP ARE PARTNERS NOW!... LOOK, I REMEMBER HOW YOU ALMOST BEAT THE ANT-MAN! APE AND ME'LL WORK WITH YOU!"

GOOD! FIRST, WE MUST FIND SOME HIDDEN PLACE WHERE I CAN SET UP A LABORATORY... AND I MUST TAKE A NEW IDENTITY! YES, THE PLAN IS BEGINNING TO FORM...

EVERY MAN HAS HIS ACHILLES HEEL! WE WILL STRIKE AT ANT-MAN THROUGH HIS... *THE WASP!* WE WILL CAPTURE HER AND USE HER AS THE BAIT FOR OUR TRAP TO CAPTURE THE ANT-MAN!

NEWS
AMYTER WINS.

AND *THIS* TIME I SHALL NOT FAIL! I KNOW MY ANTAGONIST BETTER, AND I AM MORE FULLY AWARE OF HIS POWERS! THROUGH THE WASP I SHALL CRUSH HIM FOREVER! FIRST, I SHALL NEED SOME SCIENTIFIC EQUIPMENT...

IN THE CELLAR OF A DESERTED BUILDING THE SINISTER TRIO MAKE THEIR HEADQUARTERS AS EGGHEAD SETS UP HIS LAB...

WITH THIS MACHINE, I'LL BE ABLE TO INTERCEPT, EVEN SCRAMBLE, MESSAGES THE ANTS SEND TO ANT-MAN...

OKAY, OKAY! BUT WHEN WE GONNA GET INTO HIGH GEAR?

SOON! FIRST, I MUST COMPLETE MY DISGUISE AND ESTABLISH MYSELF AS PROFESSOR CARL STRIKER, ZOOLOGIST! BE PATIENT... OUR FOE IS POWERFUL... WE MUST NOT FAIL A SECOND TIME!

THUS, EGGHEAD PUTS HIS PLAN INTO ACTION, STEP BY CAUTIOUS STEP!

... SO YOU SEE, DEAR LADIES, INSECTS CAN BE OUR FRIENDS, AS WELL AS OUR ENEMIES! THE PROBLEM IS TO UNDERSTAND THEM, TO STUDY AND APPRECIATE THE INTRICACIES OF THE INSECT WORLD! I THANK YOU!

WONDERFUL! A BRILLIANT LECTURE!

MOST INTERESTING MEETING WE'VE EVER HAD! SUCH A FASCINATING MAN!

CLAP CLAP CLAP
CLAP

4

Among the large audience at one of Professor Striker's lectures, are the famous scientists, Henry Pym and young Janet Van Dyne, daughter of the deceased scientist, Dr. Vernon Van Dyne!

SOMEHOW THAT MAN, PROFESSOR STRIKER, SEEMS FAMILIAR! BUT I CAN'T REMEMBER WHERE OR HOW WE MET!

HE MUST BE A VERY BRILLIANT MAN... HE SOUNDS SO SURE OF HIMSELF!

To those who surround them in the crowd they seem to be just a handsome, serious, intelligent young man and a lovely young girl.! But, in reality, they are—

ANT-MAN and--

--the WASP!

THE TIME HAS COME! I'VE BEEN ASKED TO LECTURE AT THE CITY ZOO! IT'S WHAT I'VE BEEN WAITING FOR! WE WILL BUILD A FASCINATING EXHIBIT ABOUT... WASPS! I DON'T THINK THE REAL WASP... WHOEVER SHE IS... WILL BE ABLE TO RESIST IT.!!

BUT HOW'S THAT GONNA CATCH ANT-MAN?

AND I'VE BEEN THINKIN', EGGHEAD... WHAT'S IN IT FOR US WHEN WE GET ANT-MAN?

FIRST, APE; I WILL USE BAIT TO CATCH THE WASP JUST AS I WILL USE HER AS BAIT TO CATCH ANT-MAN! ONCE THE ANT-MAN IS OUT OF THE WAY, I WILL MASTERMIND A SERIES OF PERFECT CRIMES THAT WILL MAKE US ALL AS RICH AS CROESUS AND COMPLETELY SAFE FROM THE POLICE! THAT SHOULD ANSWER YOUR QUESTIONS.!!

In his laboratory, Egghead and his criminal cohorts begin their work, as the radio blares...

EACH OF THESE EXHIBITS MUST BE PERFECT... POTTER WASP, MUD DAUBER, MASON WASP, PAPER WASP, BALD FACE HORNET...

...AND THE MIDDLETON DIAMOND HAS BEEN PLACED IN THE HANDS OF THE FAMOUS DIAMOND CUTTER, ANTON MYERS, TO CUT INTO A PENDANT FOR THE PRICELESS LADY ELIZABETH NECKLACE!

HEAR THAT? WE SHOULD BE...

YES, APE... AND WE WILL! THAT IS THE BAIT WE WILL USE TO LURE THE WASP INTO OUR CLUTCHES!

Several days later at the zoo...

PLACE THAT ONE OVER THERE!

DON'T KNOW WHY YOU CHOOSE THE REPTILE HOUSE FOR YOUR EXHIBIT AND LECTURE, PROFESSOR!

'CAUSE IT'S WARM! NOW LET'S HAVE LESS LIP, EH?

5

AFTER THE ZOO ATTENDANT LEAVES...

THAT GUY HAD A POINT! ONLY ONE THING IN THE WORLD I'M SCARED OF... *SNAKES!*

WE HAVE NO TIME FOR FEAR OF ANYTHING! LET'S GET BACK TO THE LAB...

AN HOUR LATER...

THIS IS A BLUEPRINT OF ANTON MEYER'S DIAMOND-CUTTING ESTABLISHMENT! THE EMINENT PROFESSOR STRIKER VISITED HIM THE OTHER DAY! HA! YOU SEE WHERE THE BURGLAR ALARM WIRES ARE SITUATED...

WOW! WITH A BLUEPRINT LIKE THAT, WE CAN'T MISS! WHEN DO WE HIT THE JOINT?

TONIGHT! TWISTER, THIS IS AN ELECTRONIC DEWELDING GUN I'VE CREATED! WITH IT, YOU'LL BE ABLE TO BURN THE ALARM WIRES APART WITHOUT SETTING OFF THE ALARM! APE, YOU WILL CARRY MY INSECT MESSAGE INTERCEPTOR!

THAT NIGHT, A SLEEPING-GAS GUN TAKES CARE OF THE WATCHMAN IN THE DIAMOND CUTTER'S BUILDING.

QUICKLY, APE! GIVE ME THE MACHINE...

I'LL GET TO WORK ON THE ALARM WIRES!

I THINK IT WOULDA BEEN EASIER IF WE JUST GRABBED THE ICE, AND...

IT'S BEST IF YOU DON'T TRY TO THINK, APE! YOU HAVEN'T THE EQUIPMENT! NOW I'LL SEND OUT ELECTRICAL IMPULSES THAT WILL JAM AND SCRAMBLE THE MESSAGES THE WATCHDOG ANTS WILL SEND THE ANT-MAN!

AND, IN HENRY PYM'S LABORATORY...

MESSAGE COMING IN FROM ANTS BUT I CAN'T MAKE IT OUT! SOMEONE'S FIGURED OUT HOW ANT-MAN GETS HIS INFORMATION AND IS SCRAMBLING THE IMPULSES!

A FEW MINUTES LATER, IN THE APARTMENT OF THE LOVELY SOCIALITE PLAYGIRL, JANET VAN DYNE...

HELLO! YES, THIS IS SHE! *ANT-MAN??!* I'LL BE RIGHT OVER!

6

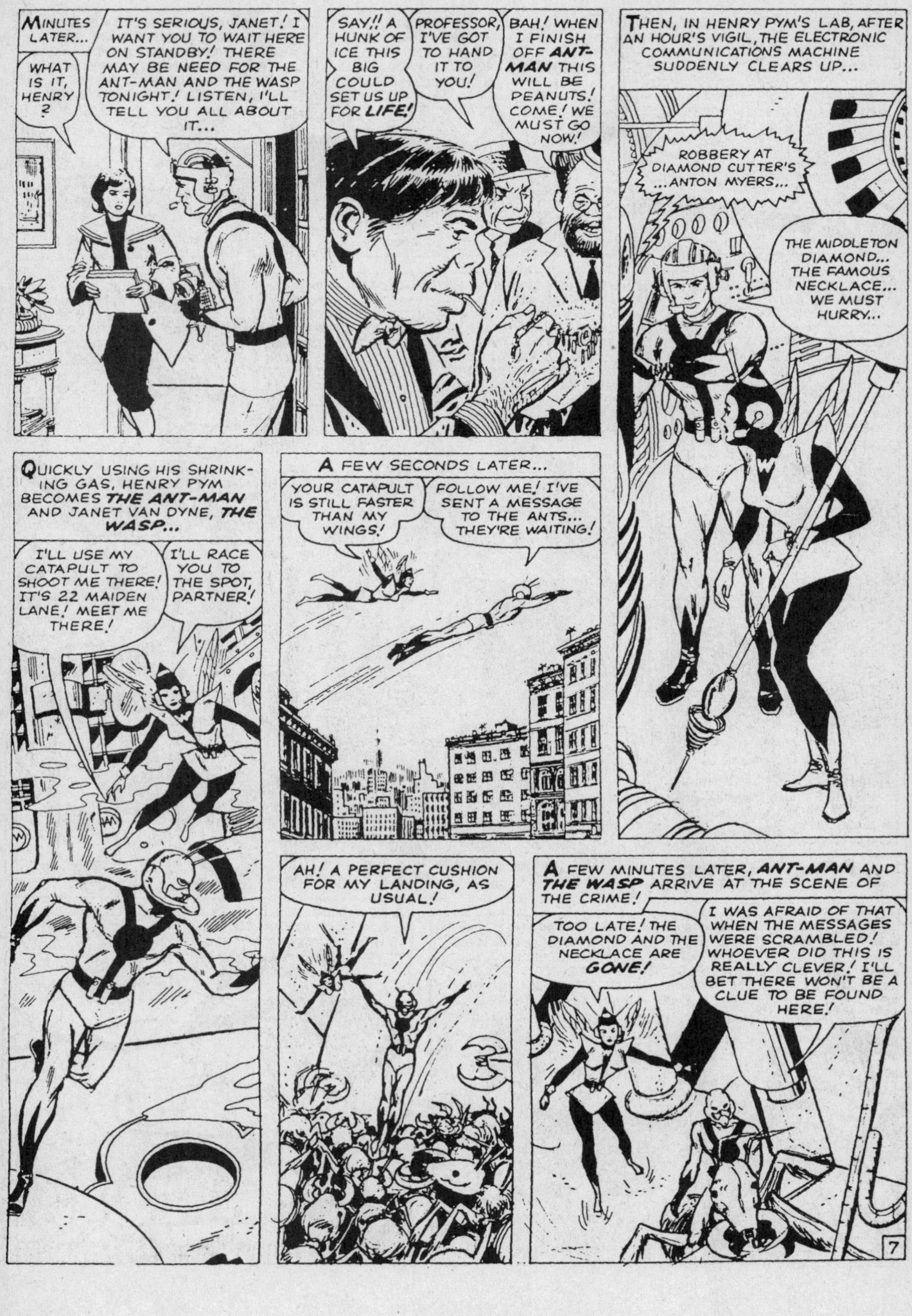
MINUTES LATER...
WHAT IS IT, HENRY?
IT'S SERIOUS, JANET! I WANT YOU TO WAIT HERE ON STANDBY! THERE MAY BE NEED FOR THE ANT-MAN AND THE WASP TONIGHT! LISTEN, I'LL TELL YOU ALL ABOUT IT...
SAY!! A HUNK OF ICE THIS BIG COULD SET US UP FOR LIFE!
PROFESSOR, I'VE GOT TO HAND IT TO YOU!
BAH! WHEN I FINISH OFF ANT-MAN THIS WILL BE PEANUTS! COME! WE MUST GO NOW!
THEN, IN HENRY PYM'S LAB, AFTER AN HOUR'S VIGIL, THE ELECTRONIC COMMUNICATIONS MACHINE SUDDENLY CLEARS UP...
ROBBERY AT DIAMOND CUTTER'S ...ANTON MYERS...
THE MIDDLETON DIAMOND... THE FAMOUS NECKLACE... WE MUST HURRY...
QUICKLY USING HIS SHRINKING GAS, HENRY PYM BECOMES THE ANT-MAN AND JANET VAN DYNE, THE WASP...
I'LL USE MY CATAPULT TO SHOOT ME THERE! IT'S 22 MAIDEN LANE! MEET ME THERE!
I'LL RACE YOU TO THE SPOT, PARTNER!
A FEW SECONDS LATER...
YOUR CATAPULT IS STILL FASTER THAN MY WINGS!
FOLLOW ME! I'VE SENT A MESSAGE TO THE ANTS... THEY'RE WAITING!
AH! A PERFECT CUSHION FOR MY LANDING, AS USUAL!
A FEW MINUTES LATER, ANT-MAN AND THE WASP ARRIVE AT THE SCENE OF THE CRIME!
TOO LATE! THE DIAMOND AND THE NECKLACE ARE GONE!
I WAS AFRAID OF THAT WHEN THE MESSAGES WERE SCRAMBLED! WHOEVER DID THIS IS REALLY CLEVER! I'LL BET THERE WON'T BE A CLUE TO BE FOUND HERE!
7

AFTER AN EXHAUSTIVE SEARCH, ANT-MAN'S WORDS PROVE TO BE PROPHETIC!

YOU WERE RIGHT, ANT-MAN... NOT A CLUE!

WHOEVER IT WAS IS BOUND TO STRIKE AGAIN... AND NEXT TIME WE'LL BE READY FOR HIM! NOW I'VE GOT SOME THINKING TO DO!

AND, AT THE SECRET LAB OF EGGHEAD, ALIAS PROF. CARL STRIKER...

WE DID IT! NOW WE GOTTA FENCE THESE THINGS AND LAY LOW UNTIL...

FOOLS! ALL YOU SEE IS WHAT IS IN FRONT OF YOUR EYES! THESE ARE MERELY THE BAIT TO CATCH THE WASP, AND ANT-MAN!

BAIT? NO YUH DON'T! HAND 'EM BACK, BIG BRAIN OR I'LL PULVERIZE YA!

I'M WITH APE! WE GOT THE LOOT, WORTH MORE DOUGH THAN WE EVER DREAMED OF! WHO CARES ABOUT THE WASP AND ANT-MAN NOW?!

IDIOTS! ANT-MAN WILL EVENTUALLY TRACK YOU DOWN! YOU'LL NEVER BE FREE TO SPEND YOUR MONEY! YOU MUST TRUST ME! HAVEN'T I DONE WELL SO FAR?

...I GUESS SO....! ALL RIGHT, WE'LL STRING ALONG!

GOOD! NOW GET THAT FINE WIRE! WE'VE GOT WORK TO DO AT THE ZOO...

FOR THE REST OF THE NIGHT THE STRANGE TRIO WORK IN THE REPTILE HOUSE OF THE ZOO...

WASP NESTS

WHAT'S IN THIS BOX? IT'S SOMETHIN' ALIVE... AND IT WEIGHS PLENTY!

A SURPRISE FOR ANT-MAN! THERE, THE SWITCH IS IN PLACE! ONCE ANT-MAN ENTERS, I'LL PULL THE LEVER AND SEND ELECTRICAL CURRENT THROUGH THE WIRES WE'VE STRUNG AT EVERY CRACK THAT AN ANT CAN CRAWL THRU!

PUT THAT AQUARIUM UNDER THE NEST! NOW TO WIRE THE LITTLE TRAP DOOR AT THE BOTTOM!

THIS IS A WASTE OF TIME! WHY DON'TCHA JUST STEP ON HIM WHEN HE SHOWS UP?

8

HE'S NOT THAT EASY TO STEP ON, MY FRIEND! BESIDES, IT'S PART OF MY PLAN! THE JEWELS SHALL LURE THE WASP HERE...

HOW DO YOU KNOW THE WASP WILL SHOW UP?

HOW COULD SHE RESIST COMING TO AN EXHIBITION ABOUT WASPS? THEN, SHE'LL SEE THE JEWELS AND RECOGNIZE THEM... AND WHEN SHE TRIES TO RETRIEVE THEM... WE'LL *HAVE* HER!

THE NEXT DAY...

MANY WASPS USE THEIR STING TO RENDER OTHER INSECTS UNCONSCIOUS, THEN DRAG THEM TO THEIR NEST FOR THEIR YOUNG TO FEED UPON! NOW, HERE'S AN INTERESTING OVERSIZED REPLICA OF A WASP'S NEST!

SOMETHING INSIDE THE NEST... SPARKLING! *JEWELS!* THEY LOOK LIKE... THEY *ARE!* THE *STOLEN GEMS!* BUT WHY WERE THEY PUT IN *THERE?*

SHOULD I NOTIFY THE POLICE? *NO!* I'LL TELL HENRY AND WE'LL....! NO, I WON'T DO *THAT*, EITHER! HE TREATS ME LIKE A SCATTERBRAINED LITTLE GIRL, AND I WANT HIM TO THINK OF ME AS A FULL-FLEDGED WOMAN...A WOMAN IN LOVE!

THE WASP IS SOME-WHERE IN THIS CROWD! I CAN *SENSE* IT!

I'LL SHOW HIM I CAN DO A JOB ON MY OWN! FIRST, I'LL GET THE JEWELS AND THEN TRACK DOWN THE THIEVES... FOR THEY CAN'T BE FAR FROM WHERE THE JEWELS ARE HIDDEN!

THAT NIGHT, IN HER APARTMENT, THE LOVELY JANET VAN DYNE, BECOMES... *THE WASP!*

THERE'S THE REPTILE HOUSE JUST AHEAD!

9

WONDER WHAT THIS **WIRE** IS FOR? OH, WELL, IT DOESN'T MATTER!

SO INTENT IS SHE UPON HER PURPOSE THAT SHE FAILS TO SEE THE EYES WATCHING FROM THE SHADOWS!

BE READY TO MOVE FAST NOW...

I'M INSIDE THE WASP'S NEST! BUT... WHAT **IS** THIS? SOME STRANGE SORT OF **MAZE!**

SHE'S **TRAPPED!** TWISTER, GET THE SHOES I'VE WIRED SO THE ANTS CAN'T CRAWL UP ON US! APE, GET THAT IGUANA AND PUT IT IN THE AQUARIUM! IN A FEW MINUTES THE WASP WILL BECOME FRANTIC AND SEND OUT HER SIGNALS TO ANT-MAN! WHEN HE ARRIVES WE'LL INTRODUCE HIM TO THE DEADLY SURPRISE WE'VE ARRANGED FOR HIM!

INSIDE THE NEST, THE WASP KNOWS THAT SHE HAS SOMEHOW BEEN TRAPPED BY THE JEWEL THIEVES, AND, AFTER A FRANTIC EFFORT...

THERE IS NO WAY OUT! I--I DIDN'T WANT TO DO IT, BUT I'LL HAVE TO SEND OUT A CALL FOR HELP TO **ANT-MAN!**

HER DELICATE ANTENNAE VIBRATE TREMULOUSLY AS THE MESSAGE IS SENT... AND...

FOOLISH GIRL! I'VE **WARNED** HER NOT TO TACKLE JOBS ALONE! IF ANY HARM COMES TO HER--!

MINUTES LATER...

PUT ON THE MAGNIFYING GOGGLES SO WE DON'T LOSE ANT-MAN!

SHE'S INSIDE!

AS ANT-MAN STEPS INSIDE THE NEST, THE MASTER CRIMINAL PULLS A SWITCH AND...

10

ANT-MAN, IT IS I, *EGGHEAD!* I HAVE RETURNED TO CONQUER YOU! YOU PLAY THE MODERN KNIGHT, SO I AM GIVING YOU A CHANCE TO PROVE YOUR PROWESS AS DID THE KNIGHTS OF OLD! HERE IS YOUR LANCE AND *THERE IS... YOUR DRAGON!*

I WAS A FOOL! I SHOULD HAVE SUSPECTED! ONLY *YOU* COULD HAVE THOUGHT OF SUCH A DIABOLICAL SCHEME!

BUT THERE IS NO TIME FOR MORE CONVERSATION!

HE USED THE WASP TO BAIT THIS TRAP! FOR THAT ALONE I MUST PAY HIM BACK! BUT FIRST, I MUST DEFEAT THIS IGUANA LIZARD!

ANT-MAN COUCHES HIS LANCE AS DID THE KNIGHTS OF OLD, THEN SIGNALS TO HIS ANT MOUNT...

CHARGE!

HISS-SSS

SWERVING, AVOIDING THE LASHING TONGUE AND SLASHING FEET OF THE LIZARD, ANT-MAN CLOSES IN QUICKLY, HIS LANCE AIMED AT A VULNERABLE SPOT...

I'VE *WON,* EGG-HEAD!

NOT YET!! THIS IS ONLY THE FIRST ROUND! YOU'RE STILL TRAPPED IN THAT GLASS CASE...

THE ANT-SIZED HUMAN CROUCHES LOW, PRESSING A TINY BUTTON IN HIS BOOT, ACTIVATING AN ELECTRONICALLY CONTROLLED SPRING...

BUT NOT FOR *LONG!*

CRASH!

APE, OPEN THE CRATE DOOR! HURRY!

11

WHERE IS THE WASP? **ANSWER ME,** EGGHEAD, IF YOU VALUE YOUR LIFE!

THE WASP MEANS NOTHING TO ME! IT'S **YOU** I WANT, ANT-MAN... AND I'LL GET YOU YET!

HERE I AM, ANT-MAN! I FOUND THE OPENING YOU FELL THROUGH!

THANK, GOODNESS YOU'RE NOT HARMED! NOW, WITH THE AID OF OUR SOLDIER ANTS, WE'LL TACKLE EGGHEAD AND HIS BULLY BOYS!

BUT, WHEN ANT-MAN TURNS AROUND...

THE SECOND TRICK IN MY BAG, ANT-MAN ...AN **ANT-EATER!** THE MOST PERFECT WEAPON AGAINST ANTS EVER DESIGNED! BEAUTIFUL, ISN'T HE, ANT-MAN... THE ULTIMATE WEAPON!

THE CREATURE'S LONG, VISCOUS TONGUE LICKS OUT... THEN FLICKERS BACK, INTO THE SMALL MOUTH OPENING, TAUNTINGLY...

NEITHER YOU NOR YOUR ANTS CAN ESCAPE! I PULL THIS SWITCH AND EVERY CRACK IN THE ROOM HAS A LIVE WIRE ACROSS IT THAT WILL ELECTROCUTE ANY INSECT OR INSECT-SIZED CREATURE THAT ATTEMPTS TO PASS OVER IT! THIS IS YOUR FINISH, ANT-MAN!

THE HUGE ANT-EATER MOVES TOWARDS ANT-MAN, ITS TONGUE DARTING IN ANTICIPATION OF SUCH AN UNUSUAL MORSAL...

ANT-MAN! WHAT CAN WE **DO?**

STAY BACK! I'LL HANDLE THIS!

HIS LASSO, MADE OF TINY STRANDS OF STEEL-STRONG SYNTHETIC FIBER, SNAPS OUT AND LOOPS AROUND THE ELONGATED SNOUT OF THE ANT-DESTROYING CREATURE... THEN, ANT-MAN GIVES A POWERFUL YANK...

WASP, PULL THAT SWITCH TO TURN OFF THE CURRENT AROUND THE CRACKS! **HURRY!**

WILL DO, BOSS MAN!

12

IT'S TIME TO USE OUR LAST WEAPON... THE WATER PISTOLS FILLED WITH LIQUID GAS! THIS IS ONE THING EVEN *ANT-MAN* CANNOT FIGHT! *FIRE.!!*

THE PIN ANT-MAN USED AGAINST THE LIZARD! I'VE *GOT* IT!

AT LAST I'VE FOUND MY *STING*... THE ONE THING, AS THE WASP, THAT I HAD LACKED!

YEEOOOOW

QUICKLY THE WASP FLITS FROM ONE TO THE OTHER, USING HER NEW-FOUND STINGER ON THEIR HANDS TO MAKE THEM DROP THE DEADLY GUNS...

CRASH

IF YOU MOVE, THE SNAKES WILL STRIKE!

I--I AINT MOVIN' A MUSCLE!

EGGHEAD... HE'S *GONE!* GOT AWAY WHILE WE WERE TAKING CARE OF THE OTHER TWO!

THOUGH THEY SEARCH FEVERISHLY, THEY CAN FIND NO TRACE OF THE BRILLIANT ARCH CRIMINAL! THEN, BACK IN THEIR LAB AGAIN...

WELL, THE JEWELS HAVE BEEN RECOVERED AND APE AND TWISTER CAPTURED... BUT EGGHEAD, THE BIGGEST PRIZE OF ALL, IS STILL AT LIBERTY!

13

AS FOR *YOU,* YOUNG LADY, DON'T YOU EVER TRY ANYTHING LIKE THAT AGAIN! WE'RE A *TEAM*-- AND WE'LL WORK AS A *TEAM!* UNDERSTAND?!

OH, ANT-MAN, CAN'T YOU SEE THAT I'M A WOMAN, AND IN LOVE WITH YOU? HOW CAN A MAN SO BRILLIANT BE SO BLIND?!

AND, IN HIS OWN HIDEAWAY...

I'LL BE BACK! EACH TIME I LEARN A LITTLE MORE AND THE NEXT TIME IT WILL BE DIFFERENT! NEXT TIME I'LL SET A TRAP THAT NO HUMAN CAN ESCAPE! NOT EVEN-- *ANT-MAN!*

THE END

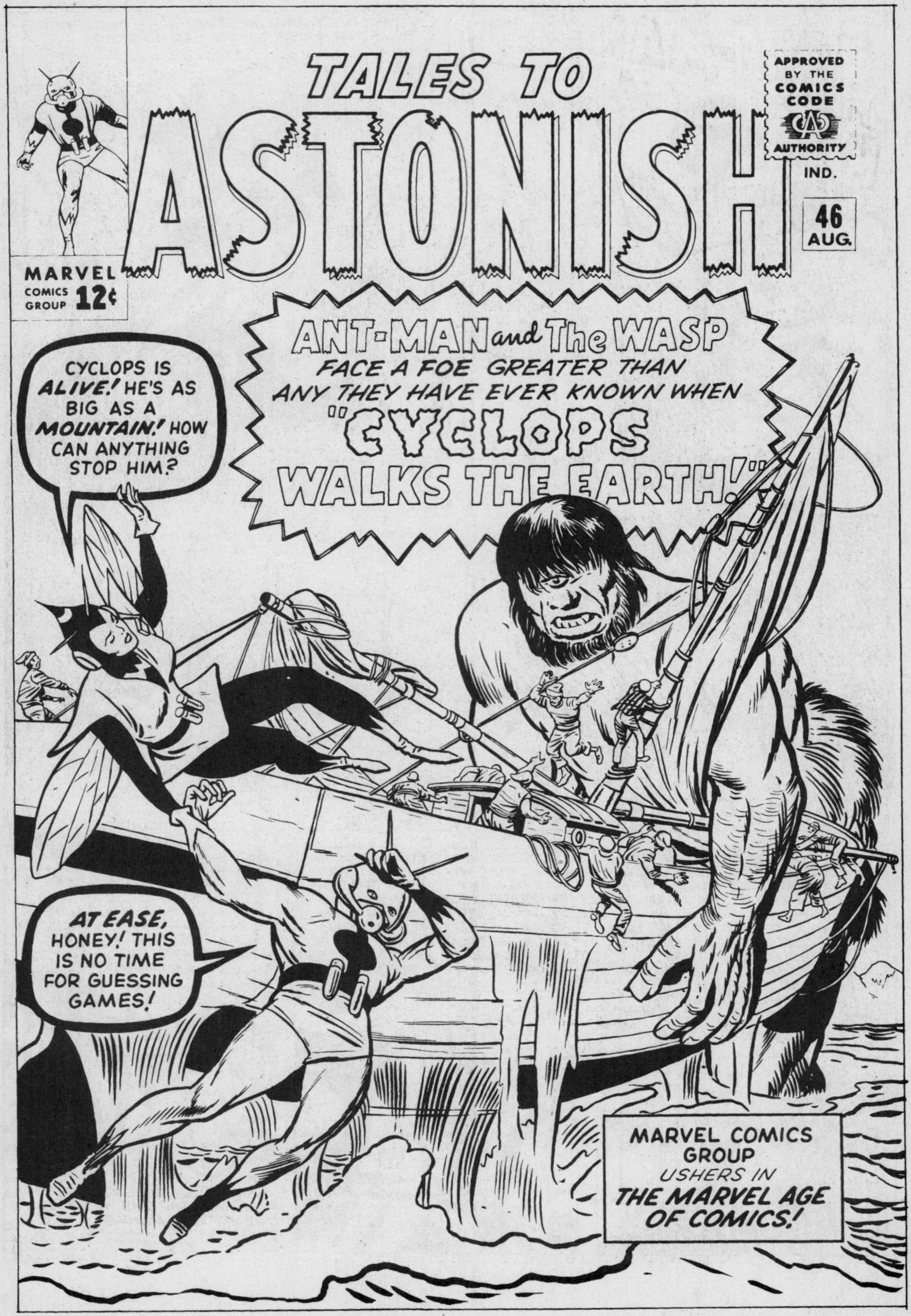

TALES TO ASTONISH
APPROVED BY THE COMICS CODE AUTHORITY
IND.
46 AUG.
MARVEL COMICS GROUP 12¢
ANT-MAN and The WASP FACE A FOE GREATER THAN ANY THEY HAVE EVER KNOWN WHEN "CYCLOPS WALKS THE EARTH!"
CYCLOPS IS ALIVE! HE'S AS BIG AS A MOUNTAIN! HOW CAN ANYTHING STOP HIM?
AT EASE, HONEY! THIS IS NO TIME FOR GUESSING GAMES!
MARVEL COMICS GROUP USHERS IN THE MARVEL AGE OF COMICS!

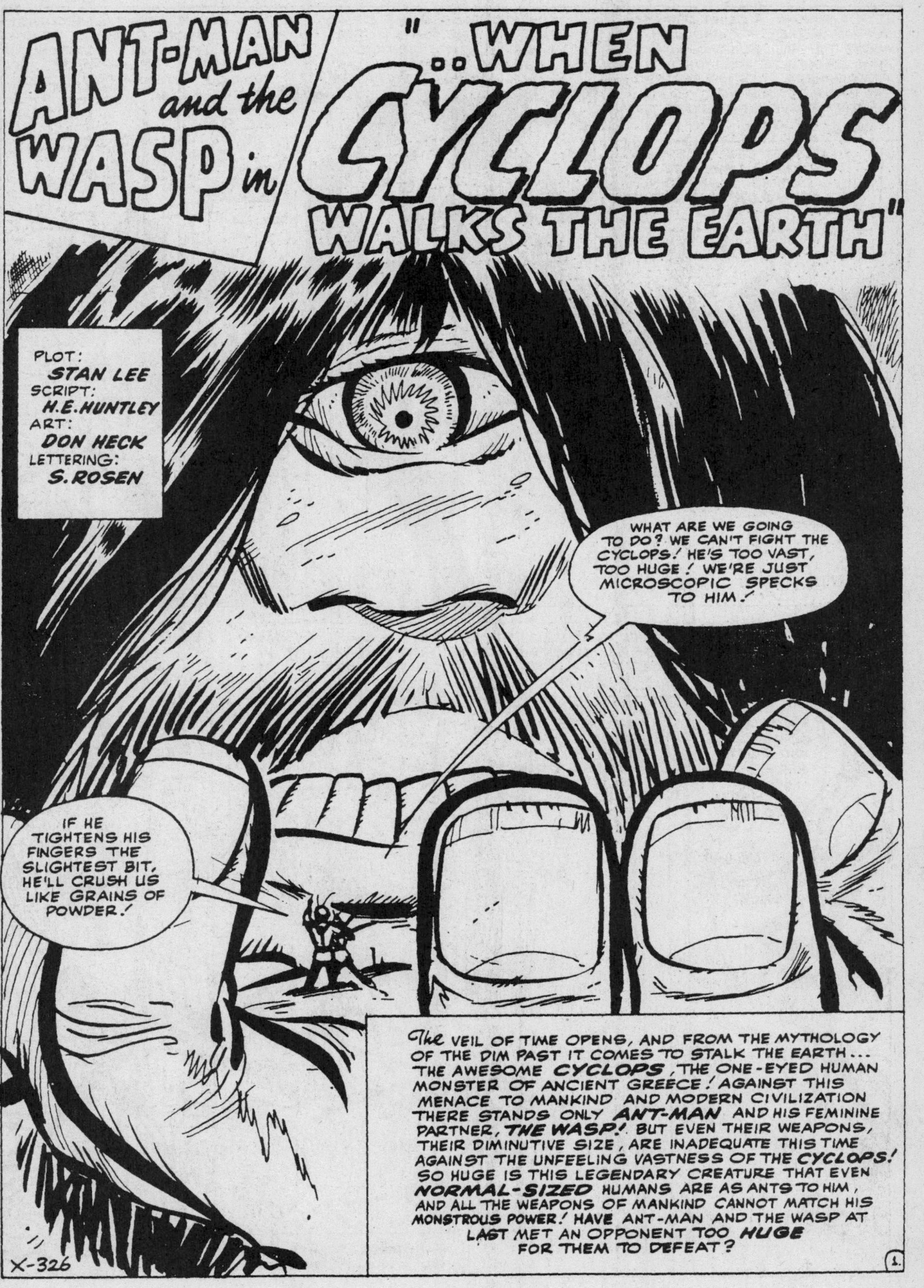

ANT-MAN and the WASP in
"..WHEN CYCLOPS WALKS THE EARTH"
PLOT: STAN LEE SCRIPT: H.E. HUNTLEY ART: DON HECK LETTERING: S. ROSEN
WHAT ARE WE GOING TO DO? WE CAN'T FIGHT THE CYCLOPS! HE'S TOO VAST, TOO HUGE! WE'RE JUST MICROSCOPIC SPECKS TO HIM!
IF HE TIGHTENS HIS FINGERS THE SLIGHTEST BIT, HE'LL CRUSH US LIKE GRAINS OF POWDER!
The VEIL OF TIME OPENS, AND FROM THE MYTHOLOGY OF THE DIM PAST IT COMES TO STALK THE EARTH... THE AWESOME CYCLOPS, THE ONE-EYED HUMAN MONSTER OF ANCIENT GREECE! AGAINST THIS MENACE TO MANKIND AND MODERN CIVILIZATION THERE STANDS ONLY ANT-MAN AND HIS FEMININE PARTNER, THE WASP! BUT EVEN THEIR WEAPONS, THEIR DIMINUTIVE SIZE, ARE INADEQUATE THIS TIME AGAINST THE UNFEELING VASTNESS OF THE CYCLOPS! SO HUGE IS THIS LEGENDARY CREATURE THAT EVEN NORMAL-SIZED HUMANS ARE AS ANTS TO HIM, AND ALL THE WEAPONS OF MANKIND CANNOT MATCH HIS MONSTROUS POWER! HAVE ANT-MAN AND THE WASP AT LAST MET AN OPPONENT TOO HUGE FOR THEM TO DEFEAT?
X-326
1

It's a Sunday, a quiet, drowsy Sunday in the city, and high above the tall buildings, Ant-Man catapults into the atmosphere with his partner, the Wasp, flying next to him, as they survey the streets below...

I DON'T SEE ANY TROUBLE STIRRING! ARE YOU PICKING UP ANYTHING ON *YOUR* ANTENNAE ???

NOTHING! ALL'S QUIET!

I'LL CONTACT SOME OF MY FRIENDS, THE ANTS, IN THE VARIOUS CITY DISTRICTS! SEE IF *THEY* HAVE ANYTHING TO REPORT!

Ant-Man alters the frequency of his cybernetic helmet, sending and receiving electronic impulses...the language, through antenna projection, of the ants!

ALL IS QUIET!

PEACE REIGNS!

THERE IS NO TROUBLE! ALL IS QUIET!

APPARENTLY THERE IS NO TROUBLE ANYWHERE! LET'S RETURN HOME!

ROGER! THOUGH ACTUALLY, IT'S SO PEACEFUL AND QUIET HERE, THAT I FEEL TOO LAZY EVEN TO *FLY!* I'LL MEET YOU IN THE LAB!

Then, the smallest of all humans sends out his call to the ants...

ANT-MAN CALLING! MEET ME AT MY HOUSE, LITTLE FRIENDS! I'M COMING DOWN!

And a group of Hexapoda* hear and... answer!

MESSAGE RECEIVED! ACKNOWLEDGED! WE ARE ON OUR WAY, ANT-MAN!

When Ant-Man descends at his home, a soft, living mattress of ants, awaits to cushion his fall to the ground!

THANK YOU, MY FRIENDS!

DO YOU WISH TRANSPORTATION TO YOUR ROOMS?

*HEXAPODA - FROM THE GREEK HEX (SIX) AND PODA (FEET).

2.

NOT THIS TIME! I WILL ASCEND IN MY ELEVATOR!

AND SO, IN HIS MINIATURE ELEVATOR, ANT-MAN RISES TO THE CATAPULT COMPARTMENT...

THIS IS A GOOD TIME TO CHECK MY CATAPULT... TO MAKE SURE IT'S IN PERFECT WORKING CONDITION!

EVERYTHING SEEMS IN ORDER! WORKS PERFECTLY!

THROUGH A TINY PANEL IN THE CATAPULT ROOM, ANT-MAN ENTERS THE SECRET LAB OF THE SCIENTIST, HENRY PYM, HIS "ALTER EGO"!

WHAT DETAINED YOU? I'VE RETURNED TO MY NORMAL SIZE...BEEN WAITING FOR YOU FOR HOURS!

OH, COME NOW, IT'S NOT BEEN THAT LONG! ONLY A FEW MINUTES!

I'LL RELEASE THE GROWTH GAS AND BE RIGHT WITH YOU UP THERE, JAN!

A FEW SECONDS PASS AS ANT-MAN MIRACULOUSLY ATTAINS HIS NORMAL HUMAN SIZE...

THE TROUBLE WITH YOU, MY DEAR, IS THAT YOU'RE BORED! LET'S TUNE IN THE CYBERNETIC MACHINE AND SEE WHAT'S HAPPENING ON THE OUTSKIRTS OF THE CITY...

YOU'RE PERFECTLY CORRECT! I AM BORED....! NOTHING HAS HAPPENED IN THE LAST TWO WEEKS! WHAT GOOD ARE CRIME-SMASHERS WITH NO CRIME TO SMASH!!

EVERYTHING'S PEACEFUL! NO TROUBLE IN THIS AREA!

SEE WHAT I MEAN? ANT-MAN AND THE WASP HAVE MADE CRIME SO UNPOPULAR AND UNPRODUCTIVE THAT THE CRIMINALS ARE AFRAID TO STIR! PEACE! QUIET! HOW GHASTLY!

3

WHAT YOU NEED... PERHAPS WHAT WE *BOTH* NEED, IS A SHORT *VACATION!* HOW *ABOUT* IT? WHERE WOULD YOU LIKE TO *GO?*

A GREAT IDEA! I'VE ALWAYS WANTED TO GO TO GREECE, THE BIRTHPLACE OF MODERN CIVILIZATION... HELLAS...CRETE.. CYPRUS!

FINE! I THINK IT WILL DO US BOTH GOOD! I'LL MAKE RESERVATIONS IMMEDIATELY ON THE FIRST FLIGHT!

I'LL RUN AND PACK!

TWO DAYS LATER...

THERE IT IS, HENRY... GREECE, THE CRADLE OF MYTHOLOGY! OH, I'M SO EXCITED...

PLEASE FASTEN YOUR SEATBELTS! WE ARE ABOUT TO LAND!

HAPPILY PREPARING TO SEE THE SIGHTS, HENRY PYM AND JANICE ARE UNAWARE THAT THEY ARE ABOUT TO EMBARK ON THEIR MOST DANGEROUS ADVENTURE... AND FACE THE MOST MONSTROUS CREATURE THE WORLD HAS EVER SEEN! AND THEN...

DO YOU *SENSE* SOMETHING... A TENSENESS.. PERHAPS *FEAR,* THAT SEEMS TO EMANATE FROM THESE PEOPLE?

NONSENSE! YOU'RE JUST IMAGINING THINGS! COME ON! LET'S HIRE A BOAT AND CRUISE THE ISLANDS WHERE HOMER SAILED AND HERCULES WALKED!

THAT'S *STRANGE..* THE BOATS ARE ALL *DOCKED!* MOST OF THEM SHOULD BE OUT FISHING, CARRYING CARGO...

WE'D LIKE TO CHARTER A BOAT TO CRUISE THE ISLANDS!

THE *ISLANDS?*

A MURMUR SWEEPS THROUGH THE GROUP OF SEAMEN, AS THOUGH THEY CANNOT BELIEVE THEIR EARS! THEN, HALTINGLY, FEARFULLY, THEY ANSWER...

NO, LADY, WE WILL *NOT* SAIL AMONG THE ISLANDS! NO SEAMAN WILL TAKE HIS VESSEL FROM THE DOCKS! PLEASE ... YOU *GO AWAY* NOW, LADY, EH?

WELL, OF ALL THE NERVE! AND JUST *WHY* WON'T YOU SAIL THE ISLANDS!?

ASK *HIM...* CAPTAIN ANDROPOLUS! HE HAS *SEEN* IT!

SEEN *WHAT?*

THE MONSTER! BIG AS A SIX-STORY BUILDING, COMING AT US AS WE SAILED BY THE ISLAND, BLOCKING OUT THE MOON AND STARS!... WEIRD LIGHTS IN THE ISLAND HILLS!

4.

YOU ACTUALLY SAW A **MONSTER**?

NOT CLEARLY ENOUGH TO KNOW **WHO** OR **WHAT** IT WAS! BUT SO HUGE WAS IT THAT IT CREATED **HIGH WAVES** AS IT CAME TOWARDS US! THEY ROCKED THE SHIP AND MY ARM WAS BROKEN! AND I AM NOT THE **ONLY** ONE WHO SAW IT! ASK **GEORGE** IN THE RADIO SHACK!

RIDICULOUS! NOTHING THAT **LIVES** IS THAT BIG! SILLY SUPERSTITION!

WE'LL SEE! COME ON, WE'LL QUESTION THE RADIO OPERATOR!

NO, THEY DO NOT LIE! **OTHER** MEN ON **OTHER** BOATS HAVE SEEN THE MONSTER, TOO! IN FACT, TWO BOATS HAVE **DISAPPEARED ENTIRELY!** ONE OF THEM RADIOED AN ALARM ABOUT A HUGE MONSTER ATTACKING THE SHIP...THEN THE RADIO WENT DEAD! EXCUSE ME, A **MESSAGE** IS COMING IN!

SOUNDS INTERESTING, DOESN'T IT? TOO BAD WE'RE ON A **VACATION**, OR WE COULD HAVE A MONSTER HUNT, AND...

OH, STOP **TEASING!** WE'VE **GOT** TO FIND A BOAT AND SAIL TO THAT ISLAND!

PERHAPS **YOU** KNOW WHERE WE COULD HIRE A BOAT?

YOU CAN HIRE **MINE!** YOU WILL, OF COURSE, HAVE TO SAIL IT **YOURSELVES!** UNDER THE CIRCUMSTANCES, NO SAILOR COULD BE HIRED TO GO **WITH** YOU!

A PRICE IS AGREED UPON, AND THEN...

THANK YOU! OH, THERE IS ONE THING I FORGOT TO MENTION! THE LAST SOUND I HEARD OVER THE AIR FROM THAT ILL-FATED SHIP, JUST BEFORE THE RADIO WENT DEAD, WAS THE WORD... **"CYCLOPS!"** JUST THAT ONE WORD... AND THEN SILENCE!

*W*ITHIN THE HOUR, THEY'RE ON THEIR WAY...

IN THE KNAPSACK YOU'LL FIND **OUR** COSTUMES AND EQUIPMENT! WE'LL APPROACH THE ISLAND AT DUSK AND, IF THERE **IS** ANYTHING TO THOSE STORIES, WE'LL BE PREPARED! SCARED, JAN?!

WHO, **ME**? YOU'RE TALKING TO THE WRONG GAL, PARTNER! THE ONLY THING **I'M** SCARED OF IS THAT IT'LL BE A FALSE ALARM!

5.

WELL, WE'LL SOON KNOW, MY LITTLE EAGER BEAVER! *CYCLOPS* IS FROM GREEK MYTHOLOGY, *KYLOS* MEANING "CIRCLE" AND *OPS* MEANING "EYE", ONE-EYED, LEGENDARY PEOPLE, SAID TO HAVE MIGRATED FROM THRACE! SHEPHERDS LIVING ON AN ISLAND IN THE WESTERN SEA!

I'LL CHANGE INTO MY COSTUME BEFORE YOU DECIDE TO GIVE ME A *TEST*, PROFESSOR!

LATER... YOU CAN COME IN NOW! TELL ME, HENRY, DO YOU THINK A *CYCLOPS* REALLY MIGHT EXIST??

COULD BE, JAN! AFTER ALL, *STRANGER* THINGS HAVE HAPPENED...

THERE IS AN *ANT-MAN!* AND A *WASP!* CREATURES EVERY BIT AS BIZARRE AS ANY OL' *CYCLOPS,* EH?

DON'T YOU DARE CALL ME A CREATURE! INCIDENTALLY, THERE ARE ANTS IN THE GALLEY... WINGED ONES!

AS THEY CHANGE TO INSECT SIZE, ANT-MAN IMMEDIATELY CONTACTS THE ANTS ON THE SHIP, A SPECIES OF DRIVER ANTS OF WHICH THE MALES ARE WINGED, FLYING HEXAPODA!

GREETINGS, FRIENDS! I WISH TO ASK YOU SOME QUESTIONS!

LOOK! THERE'S AN ISLAND... AND THERE ARE THE STRANGE LIGHTS IN THE HILLS THE SEAMEN SPOKE OF!

WELL, *THAT* PART AT LEAST, WAS TRUE! WE'LL ANCHOR THE BOAT OFF SHORE AND FLY TO THE ISLAND! I'LL USE ONE OF THESE WINGED ANTS AS A PEGASUS * AND... *LOOK!!* THAT HUGE SHADOW!!

*NOTE: PEGASUS, THE WINGED HORSE OF GREEK MYTHOLOGY.

IT..IT'S THE *CYCLOPS!!*

THEY DIDN'T LIE! HE *IS* AT LEAST 50 FEET TALL... HE'S *MONSTROUS!*

HE'S REACHING FOR THE *BOAT!*

GET DOWN ON THE DECK! *FAST!*

6.

MONSTROUS HANDS, UNBELIEVABLY HUGE, GRASP THE SMALL CRAFT AS THOUGH IT WERE A SMALL TOY...

BACK... **BACK!!** HIS THUMB COULD **CRUSH** US!

HE'S LOOKING RIGHT **AT** US! DON'T MOVE A MUSCLE!

WE'RE **TOO** SMALL FOR HIM TO NOTICE... **I HOPE!**

THE GREAT BULK OF THE ONE-EYED GIANT TURNS AND, HOLDING THE BOAT IN ONE HUGE HAND, WADES BACK TOWARDS THE SHORE...

HE LOOKED RIGHT **AT** US! I CAN'T UNDERSTAND WHY HE DIDN'T SEE US! WITH AN EYE THAT LARGE, HIS VISION SHOULD BE EXTREMELY KEEN!

OH, ANT-MAN! WHAT DO WE DO **NEXT?**

CALMLY, ANT-MAN CALLS ONE OF THE WINGED ANTS TO HIM...

THE **FIRST** THING TO DO IS TO GET FREE OF THIS BOAT! I'LL RIDE ONE OF THESE FLYING ANTS! WE'LL KEEP CLOSE TO THE CYCLOPS! YOU FLY NEXT TO ME! LET'S GO!

SO, YOU WERE AFRAID IT WOULD JUST BE A FALSE ALARM, EH? HOW DO YOU FEEL ABOUT IT NOW, YOUNG LADY?

JUST BETWEEN YOU AND ME, PARTNER... I THINK **I** TALK TOO MUCH!

I JUST **THOUGHT** OF SOMETHING, ANT-MAN! ABOUT THOSE EERIE **LIGHTS** IN THE HILLS... ARE THERE **MORE** CYCLOPS HERE? AND... WHERE DID HE, OR THEY, COME FROM?

WE'LL FIND OUT SOON ENOUGH, WASP! JUST WAIT!

7.

FOR A MOMENT, THE MOUNTAINOUS CREATURE STARES DOWN AT THE SHIPS! THEN, HIS ENORMOUS ONE-EYED HEAD LIFTS AS THOUGH LISTENING TO SOME SOUNDLESS SUMMONS AND HE BEGINS TO SHUFFLE TOWARD THE HILLS AND THE STRANGE LIGHTS!

THERE'S SOMETHING *STRANGE* ABOUT THE CYCLOPS! HIS MOVEMENTS... THEY'RE SO AWKWARD!

LISTEN! I HEAR VOICES... HUMAN VOICES!

IT'S THE SAILORS FROM THE MISSING SHIPS! THEY'RE PRISONERS!

WE'VE GOT TO *FREE* THEM!

HOLD IT, WASP! FIRST I WANT TO INVESTIGATE THOSE STRANGE LIGHTS IN THE HILLS! THEY SEEM TO HAVE CYCLOPS *SPELLBOUND!*

THERE ARE *PEOPLE* UP THERE! LOOK! THEY HAVE ONE OF THE SAILORS TIED UP... DOING SOMETHING TO HIM!

THOSE ARE *SPACE SHIPS*, GIRL! THIS IS ALL BEGINNING TO TIE TOGETHER NOW!

THOSE "PEOPLE" ARE ALIENS! THEY SEEM TO BE TESTING THE CAPTIVE SAILOR'S BRAIN IMPULSES!

THEY'RE REMOVING THE WIRES FROM HIS HEAD NOW...

SUDDENLY, THE WASP CRIES OUT IN AGONY AND FALLS WRITHING TO THE GROUND! ANT-MAN GRASPS HIS HELMET, AS HIS WINGED ANT TUMBLES ON ITS SIDE IN A HELPLESS FRENZY!

ELECTRONIC IMPULSES!!

SWIFTLY ANT-MAN'S FINGERS MOVE A TINY DIAL ON HIS HELMET, CHANGING HIS ELECTRONIC WAVE PATTERNS!

I...I COULD REMOVE THE HELMET AND THE ALIEN IMPULSES WOULDN'T BOTHER ME... BUT THE WASP *CAN'T* REMOVE HER ANTENNAE! I'VE GOT TO FIND A WAVE LENGTH TO COUNTER-ACT THEIRS ... GOT..TO.. FIND IT FAST! MY MIND IS BURSTING! THE PAIN ...THE AGONY... IT'S UNBEARABLE!

8.

THERE...I'VE **FOUND** IT, AND NOT A MINUTE TOO SOON! WAIT! I'M GETTING NEW IMPULSES NOW...I'M ON THE ALIENS' WAVELENGTH! THEY CONVERSE THROUGH ELECTRONIC IMPULSES EMANATING FROM THEIR BRAINS! I CAN **UNDERSTAND** THEM!

YOU CAN READILY SEE THE MENTAL PATTERNS OF THESE EARTHMEN FROM THOSE WE HAVE MEASURED UNDER THE MENTALSCOPE! THEY ARE INFERIOR CREATURES AND WOULD BE EASILY CONQUERED!

I CAN **HEAR** THEM NOW, TOO!

YOU ADVISE THEN THAT WE INFORM OUR HOME PLANET, A-CHILTAR III, THAT EARTH SHOULD BE CLASSIFIED AS FIT TO BE CONQUERED AND COLONIZED!?

DEFINITELY! STEP ON THOSE INSECTS, KRAGLIN! I CANNOT **ABIDE** THE THINGS!

I OBEY YOUR COMMAND, CAPTAIN!

INSECTS! HE MEANS **US!!**

USE YOUR **STINGER**, WASP, WHILE I LASSO HIS FOOT!

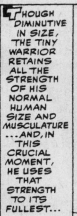

THOUGH DIMINUTIVE IN SIZE, THE TINY WARRIOR RETAINS ALL THE STRENGTH OF HIS NORMAL HUMAN SIZE AND MUSCULATURE ...AND, IN THIS CRUCIAL MOMENT, HE USES THAT STRENGTH TO ITS FULLEST...

PERFECT! YOUR STING MADE HIM LIFT HIS FOOT ENOUGH FOR ME TO GET HIM OFF BALANCE!

WHAT IS THIS **FOOLISHNESS**, KRAGLIN? CAN'T YOU OBEY A SIMPLE COMMAND?

I...I DON'T KNOW WHAT **HAPPENED!** I FELT A STINGING PAIN IN MY SOLE, AND THEN... I FLEW THROUGH THE AIR! IT IS VERY STRANGE!

9.

I DON'T SEE THE INSECTS...

NEVER MIND! YOU WILL ALL JOIN ME IN DIRECTING BRAIN IMPULSES TO THE CYCLOPS! WE WILL DIRECT HIM TO DESTROY THE IMPRISONED EARTHMEN! WE HAVE NO FURTHER USE FOR THEM!

NOW I KNOW WHY THE CYCLOPS DIDN'T SEE US AND WHY HE MOVED SO AWKWARDLY! HE'S JUST A ROBOT, BUILT BY THOSE ALIENS TO FRIGHTEN SHIPS AWAY WHILE THEY INVESTIGATE OUR PLANET! THEY MUST KNOW ALL ABOUT OUR CULTURE TO HAVE KNOWN MYTHOLOGY AND...

WHILE YOU'RE LECTURING AGAIN, I'M GOING TO FREE THOSE SAILORS BEFORE THE CYCLOPS KILLS THEM!

WAIT! WASP, DON'T! SHE DOESN'T HEAR ME... OR PRETENDS SHE DOESN'T!

SLOWLY, THE ONE-EYED MECHANICAL BEHEMOTH WALKS TOWARDS THE STOCKADE!

NO TIME TO GO AFTER THE WASP NOW! I'VE GOT TO FIND THE BRAIN CENTER OF THAT KING-SIZED MECHANICAL MAN AND SHUT IT OFF BEFORE IT OBEYS THE ALIENS!

THE MOUTH...IT KEEPS OPENING AND CLOSING ITS MOUTH! I CAN GET IN THROUGH THERE... IF I'M LUCKY!

THANKS, LITTLE FRIENDS! YOU CAN GO NOW! IT'S UP TO ME ALONE FROM HERE ON IN...

I FEEL LIKE ONE OF THOSE LITTLE CARTOON CHARACTERS IN A T.V. COMMERCIAL, SHOWING HOW PILLS DISSOLVE INSIDE THE BODY! WELL, NOW TO HUNT FOR THE CYCLOPS' "BRAIN"!

10

MEANWHILE, THE WASP REACHES THE PRISONERS' COMPOUND...

GUARDS! I'VE GOT TO GET RID OF THEM QUICKLY! WHAT'S THAT? A WASP'S NEST... HANGING FROM THAT TREE?!

FRIENDS, I NEED YOUR HELP! FOLLOW ME!!

THEN, WITH HER ANGRY WASPS BEHIND HER...

BZZZ BZZZ ZZZ ZZZZZ ZZZ

ATTACK!!

YEEOOOW!

I MUST USE THE GROWTH GAS TO BRING MYSELF TO NORMAL SIZE AGAIN, SO THAT I CAN MORE EASILY COMMUNICATE WITH THE CAPTIVE SAILORS!

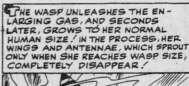

THE WASP UNLEASHES THE ENLARGING GAS, AND SECONDS LATER, GROWS TO HER NORMAL HUMAN SIZE! IN THE PROCESS, HER WINGS AND ANTENNAE, WHICH SPROUT ONLY WHEN SHE REACHES WASP SIZE, COMPLETELY DISAPPEAR!

HURRY! YOU MUST GET AWAY IMMEDIATELY, BEFORE THE...

LOOK!! THE CYCLOPS— HE COMES!

THE TINY GROUP OF HUMANS STAND FROZEN WITH DREAD AS THE MONSTER MOVES DOWN UPON THEM, ITS GIGANTIC FINGERS EXTENDED FATEFULLY!

IT...IT'S TOO LATE! THE CYCLOPS WILL NEVER LET US ESCAPE!

11.

MEANWHILE, INSIDE THE CREATURE'S MECHANICAL BRAIN...

THERE MUST BE *SOMETHING* HERE THAT TRAPS THE MENTAL IMPULSES OF THE ALIENS, SENDS THE MESSAGE THROUGHOUT THE CYCLOPS' FRAME, CONTROLLING ITS MOVEMENTS!

RECKLESSLY, ANT-MAN MOVES AMONG THE WHIRLING WHEELS, THE MOVING COGS AND ARMS, THE VIBRATING DEADLY CHARGED WIRES OF THE CREATURE'S "BRAIN"...

ELECTRODES! *THIS* MUST BE IT! NOW IF ONLY I CAN CHANGE THE FREQUENCY TO ONE THAT I CAN CONTROL THROUGH MY CYBERNETIC HELMET...

IF I DON'T CHANGE THE FREQUENCY IN THE NEXT FEW SECONDS, IT WON'T MATTER... THE *WASP* WILL BE *FINISHED!* AND WITHOUT HER, I...I CAN'T PICTURE MY LIFE!

ANT-MAN! ANT-MAN! WHERE ARE YOU?

SUDDENLY, AS IF IN ANSWER TO THE GIRL'S ANGUISHED CRY, THE MONSTROUS HAND STOPS, THEN GENTLY FREES THE HUMANS, AS THE *ANT-MAN* EXULTS!

I *DID* IT! NOW THE CYCLOPS OBEYS *ONLY* ME! SO THOSE ALIENS WERE GOING TO CONQUER THE EARTH, WERE THEY?

LOOK! THE CYCLOPS RETURNS... THOUGH WE GAVE IT NO MESSAGE TO DO SO! IT'S CRUSHING ONE OF OUR SHIPS!

IT IS UNDER SOME *OTHER* MENTAL CONTROL EVEN STRONGER THAN *OURS!* IT IS COMING TO *DESTROY* US!

THIS MEANS THAT THE EARTHLINGS HAVE EVEN *STRONGER* MENTAL CONTROL THAN WE HAVE UNDERESTIMATED THEM! HURRY TO THE SHIPS! WE MUST ESCAPE THIS ACCURSED PLANET!

12

THE EARTHLINGS DECEIVED US INTO BELIEVING THEY WERE MENTAL WEAKLINGS...

YES! BUT NOW WE *KNOW* THEIR POWERS! THEY CAN EVEN MOVE MATTER WITHOUT TOUCHING IT, AS WITNESS WHAT HAPPENED TO KRAGLIN! REPORT TO OUR HOME PLANET...EARTH IS TOO STRONG FOR US TO CONQUER!

THE SAILORS, NOW FREE, RUSH TOWARD THE COAST! A TOUCH OF REDUCING GAS AND ONCE AGAIN THE WASP FLIES...DIRECTLY TOWARDS THE EYE OF THE CYCLOPS...

SO *THERE* YOU ARE! I *THOUGHT* SO! WHAT NOW?

I'M GOING TO MAKE CYCLOPS RETRIEVE THE SHIPS AND PUT THEM IN THE BAY AGAIN SO THEY CAN SAIL HOME! SORRY I COULDN'T GET CONTROL SOONER, SO YOU WOULDN'T HAVE BEEN FRIGHTENED!

ME, FRIGHTENED?! DON'T *KID* YOURSELF! ALL I HAD TO DO WAS USE THE REDUCING GAS AND SLIDE RIGHT OUT OF THE ROBOT'S BIG PAWS! I WAS JUST WORRIED FOR THE *OTHERS!*

OKAY, JAN...IF YOU *SAY* SO!

UNDER ORDERS FROM ANT-MAN, THE CYCLOPS DEPOSITS THE VESSELS SAFELY IN THE BAY! THEN, THE MECHANICAL BRAIN RECEIVES ITS FINAL DIRECTIVE FROM ITS NEW MASTER!

WALK INTO THE SEA, CYCLOPS! WALK UNTIL THE WATERS COVER YOU! WALK UNTIL THE SEA SEEPS INTO YOUR MECHANICAL BRAIN AND LIMBS AND RUSTS THEM... UNTIL YOU TOPPLE TO THE OCEAN'S FLOOR ...AND NEVER MOVE FROM THERE AGAIN!

THE END OF THE CYCLOPS...AND OF THE ALIENS WHO WANTED TO CONQUER THE EARTH! NOW, LITTLE LADY, IF WE WANT TO HITCH A RIDE BACK TO THE MAINLAND, WE'D BEST HURRY TO THE SHIPS!

A FEW DAY'S LATER, IN HENRY'S LAB...

I THINK I'LL CHECK THE CYBERNETIC CONTROL BOARD AND SEE IF ANYTHING IS STIRRING!

MY DEAR PROFESSOR, DO ME A FAVOR, PLEASE! IN THE FUTURE, LET US HAVE *NO MORE VACATIONS!*

I JUST CAN'T STAND THE EXCITEMENT!

THE END

13

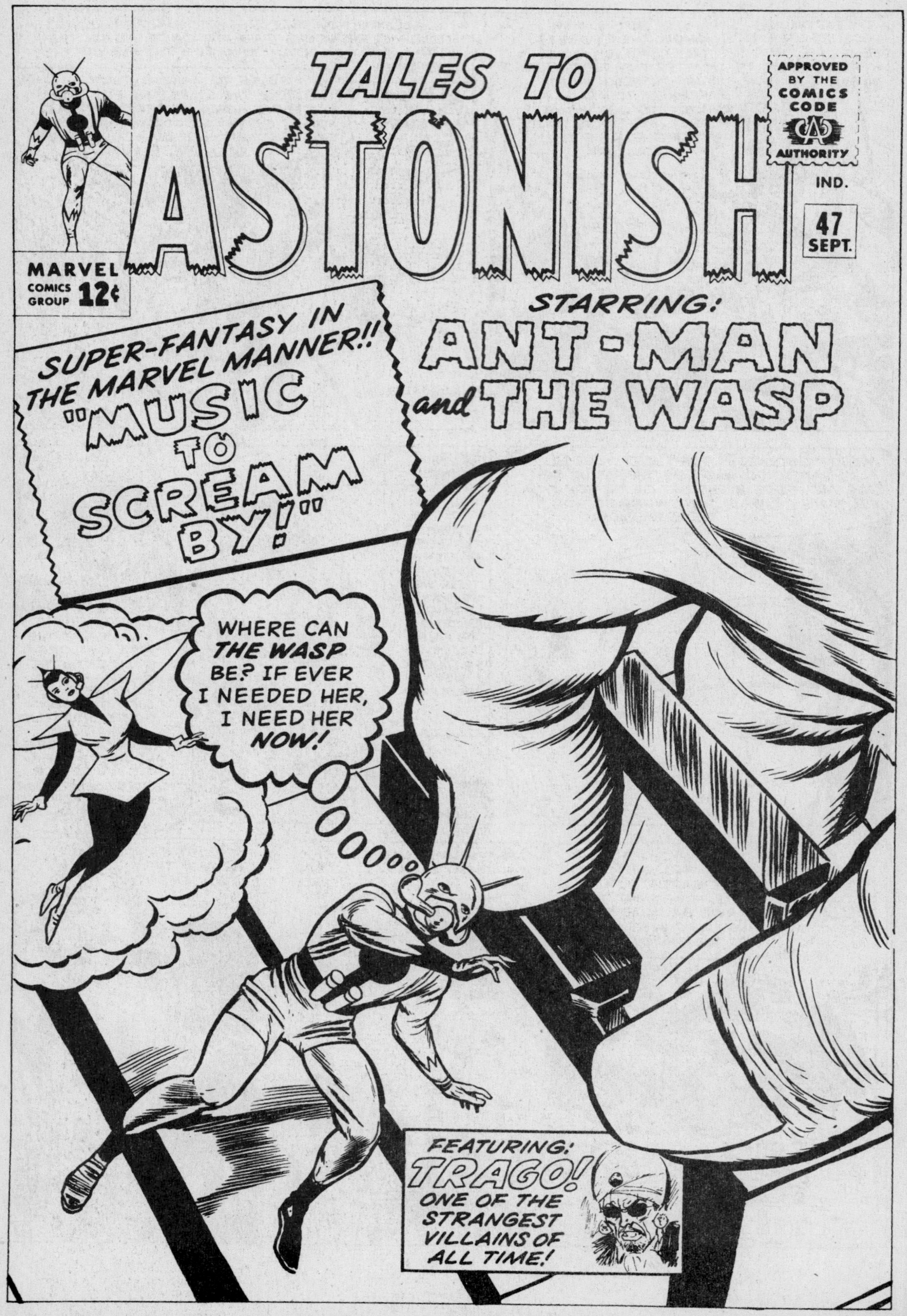
TALES TO ASTONISH
APPROVED BY THE COMICS CODE CA AUTHORITY
IND.
47 SEPT.
MARVEL COMICS GROUP 12¢
STARRING: ANT-MAN and THE WASP
SUPER-FANTASY IN THE MARVEL MANNER!!
"MUSIC TO SCREAM BY!"
WHERE CAN THE WASP BE? IF EVER I NEEDED HER, I NEED HER NOW!
FEATURING: TRAGO! ONE OF THE STRANGEST VILLAINS OF ALL TIME!

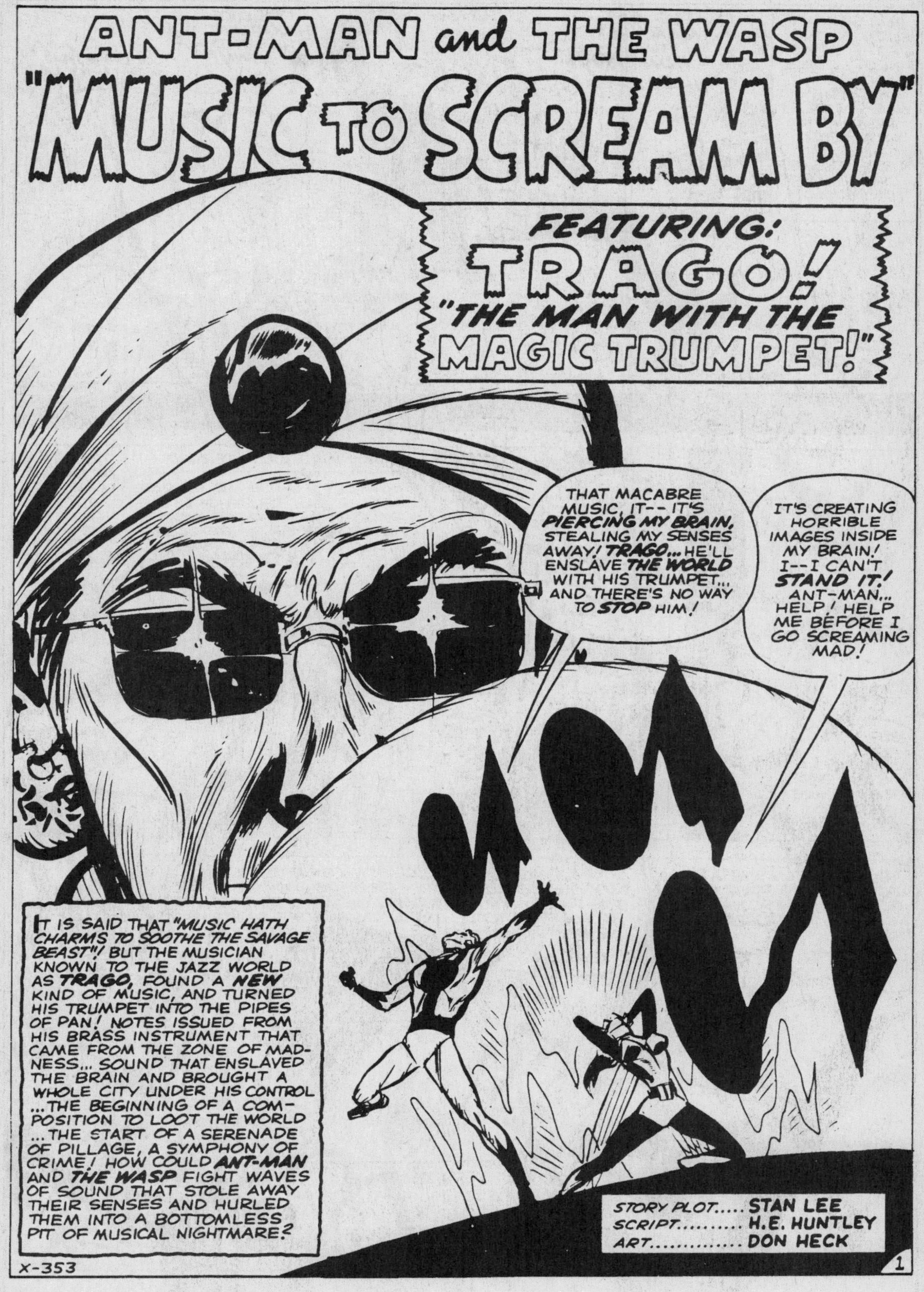

ANT-MAN and THE WASP
"MUSIC TO SCREAM BY"
FEATURING: TRAGO! "THE MAN WITH THE MAGIC TRUMPET!"
THAT MACABRE MUSIC, IT-- IT'S PIERCING MY BRAIN, STEALING MY SENSES AWAY! TRAGO... HE'LL ENSLAVE THE WORLD WITH HIS TRUMPET... AND THERE'S NO WAY TO STOP HIM!
IT'S CREATING HORRIBLE IMAGES INSIDE MY BRAIN! I--I CAN'T STAND IT! ANT-MAN... HELP! HELP ME BEFORE I GO SCREAMING MAD!
IT IS SAID THAT "MUSIC HATH CHARMS TO SOOTHE THE SAVAGE BEAST"! BUT THE MUSICIAN KNOWN TO THE JAZZ WORLD AS TRAGO, FOUND A NEW KIND OF MUSIC, AND TURNED HIS TRUMPET INTO THE PIPES OF PAN! NOTES ISSUED FROM HIS BRASS INSTRUMENT THAT CAME FROM THE ZONE OF MADNESS... SOUND THAT ENSLAVED THE BRAIN AND BROUGHT A WHOLE CITY UNDER HIS CONTROL ...THE BEGINNING OF A COMPOSITION TO LOOT THE WORLD ...THE START OF A SERENADE OF PILLAGE, A SYMPHONY OF CRIME! HOW COULD ANT-MAN AND THE WASP FIGHT WAVES OF SOUND THAT STOLE AWAY THEIR SENSES AND HURLED THEM INTO A BOTTOMLESS PIT OF MUSICAL NIGHTMARE?
STORY PLOT..... STAN LEE
SCRIPT.......... H.E. HUNTLEY
ART............. DON HECK
X-353
1

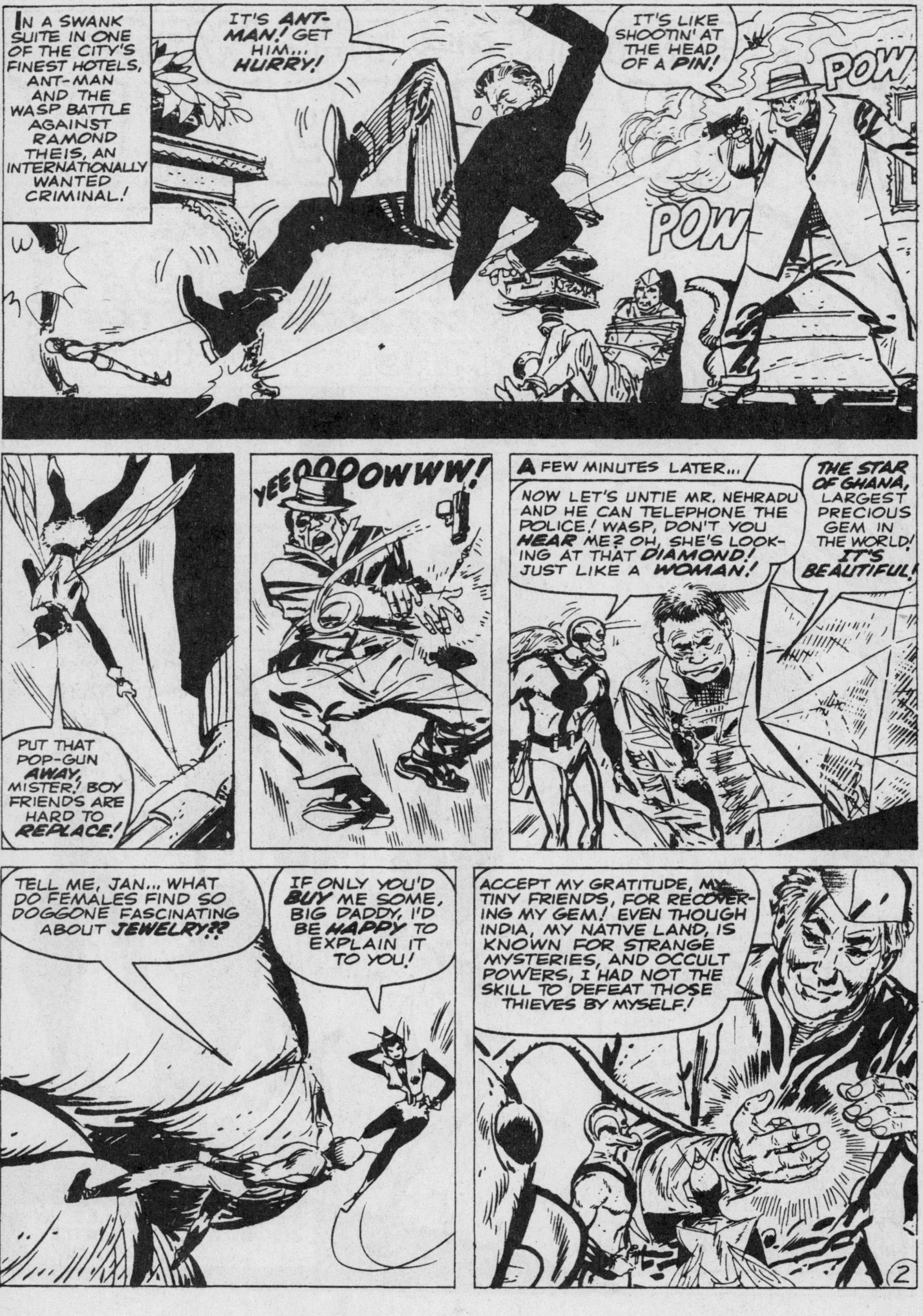
IN A SWANK SUITE IN ONE OF THE CITY'S FINEST HOTELS, ANT-MAN AND THE WASP BATTLE AGAINST RAMOND THEIS, AN INTERNATIONALLY WANTED CRIMINAL!
IT'S ANT-MAN! GET HIM... HURRY!
IT'S LIKE SHOOTIN' AT THE HEAD OF A PIN!
POW
POW
PUT THAT POP-GUN AWAY, MISTER! BOY FRIENDS ARE HARD TO REPLACE!
YEEOOOOOWWW!
A FEW MINUTES LATER...
NOW LET'S UNTIE MR. NEHRADU AND HE CAN TELEPHONE THE POLICE! WASP, DON'T YOU HEAR ME? OH, SHE'S LOOKING AT THAT DIAMOND! JUST LIKE A WOMAN!
THE STAR OF GHANA, LARGEST PRECIOUS GEM IN THE WORLD! IT'S BEAUTIFUL!
TELL ME, JAN... WHAT DO FEMALES FIND SO DOGGONE FASCINATING ABOUT JEWELRY??
IF ONLY YOU'D BUY ME SOME, BIG DADDY, I'D BE HAPPY TO EXPLAIN IT TO YOU!
ACCEPT MY GRATITUDE, MY TINY FRIENDS, FOR RECOVERING MY GEM! EVEN THOUGH INDIA, MY NATIVE LAND, IS KNOWN FOR STRANGE MYSTERIES, AND OCCULT POWERS, I HAD NOT THE SKILL TO DEFEAT THOSE THIEVES BY MYSELF!
2

BUT AREN'T ALL THOSE SO-CALLED INDIAN MAGIC TRICKS, LIKE CLIMBING A ROPE TO NO-WHERE, JUST PHONY STUNTS TO IMPRESS TOURISTS?

PERHAPS **SOME** ARE, MY LITTLE WINGED FRIEND, BUT IN INDIA THERE IS ONE MAN, GHAZANDI, WHOSE MAGIC POWER IS MORE THAN JUST SKILLFUL TRICKERY!

HE CAN TRULY HYPNOTIZE COBRAS WITH HIS MUSIC, AND IT IS SAID THAT HE CAN PLAY NOTES WHICH WILL ALSO HYPNOTIZE **HUMANS!** BUT THIS HE IS **AFRAID** TO DO, FOR IF HE PLAYS THE WRONG NOTE IT WILL **AFFECT** HIM ALSO, AND IT WILL MAKE GHAZANDI LOSE HIS MYSTIC POWER!

WELL, IT'S AN INTERESTING **STORY**, ANYWAY!

NOW I WILL CALL THE POLICE, AND THANK YOU ONCE AGAIN FOR SAVING THE STAR OF GHAMA!

AND IT IS TIME FOR US TO GO!

KORR, TO ME, WINGED KORR!

KORR, THE WINGED ANT, FLIES TO ANT-MAN! A FEW MOMENTS LATER, THE TWO CRIME FIGHTERS WING THEIR WAY THROUGH THE CITY TOWARD HOME!

ANT-MAN! LISTEN TO THAT **HORN!** OHH... DO I **LOVE** GOOD JAZZ!! HOW ABOUT US GOING IN TO LISTEN TO **TRAGO AND HIS MAGIC TRUMPET?**

JAN, I DON'T CARE FOR JAZZ! ANY-WAY, WE'VE GOT **MORE** IMPORTANT THINGS TO DO! FORGET IT, KID!

AH, COME ON, HANK! BREAK DOWN AND BE HUMAN FOR ONCE! THE WORLD WON'T COME TO AN END IF WE RELAX FOR A FEW MINUTES!

OKAY--OKAY! I'M JUST PUTTY IN THE HANDS OF A GIRL! WE'LL GO HOME AND CHANGE, THEN WE'LL COME BACK HERE!

AN HOUR LATER... ANT-MAN AND THE WASP HAVE BECOME HENRY PYM, SCIENTIST, AND JANET VAN DYNE, LOVELY YOUNG SOCIALITE!

HE'S NO **COUNT BASIE**, BUT HE'S **GOOD!** HIS TECHNIQUE IS SIMILAR TO WILD BILL DONOVAN'S!

WHOEVER **THEY** ARE!

THEN, WHEN THE MUSICIANS "TAKE TEN"...

WELL, I'M GLAD **THAT'S** OVER! HAD **ENOUGH?**

OH, SIT DOWN, YOU BIG, HANDSOME SQUARE! THERE'LL BE LOTS **MORE** MUSIC!

3

SAY! WHAT'S THAT? SOUNDS LIKE A *STRUGGLE!* COME ON, JANET!

OH *NO!* NOT ON OUR NIGHT OFF! MAYBE IT'S JUST *MICE!*

MY *CASH BOX!* YOU CROOK, TRAGO, YOU PETTY CROOK! GIVE IT TO ME!

LET GO, YOU FOOL!

HONEY, THOSE AREN'T *MICE!*

HE STOLE MY *CASH BOX!* -- RAN THRU THAT DOOR AND LOCKED IT BEHIND HIM! HE'LL BE OUT THE ALLEY AND AWAY BEFORE WE CAN GET HIM! *HELP!! POLICE!!*

QUICK, JAN! FOLLOW ME INTO THE HALL!

HERE ARE MY *REDUCING* AND *ENLARGING GAS* CYLINDERS! I ALWAYS KEEP THEM WITH ME! YOU STILL HAVE YOUR *WASP UNIFORM* UNDER YOUR CLOTHES, I HOPE?

SURE! I JUST WOULDN'T FEEL *DRESSED* WITHOUT IT!

A SLIGHT HISS AND THE RE-DUCING GAS IS RELEASED... AND HENRY PYM AND JANET VAN DYNE SHRINK RAPIDLY TO... *ANT-MAN* AND *THE WASP!*

ONLY SECONDS HAVE ELAPSED SINCE THE ROBBERY AS ANT-MAN RUSHES UNDER THE JAMB OF THE LOCKED DOOR INTO THE ALLEY...

...WHILE *THE WASP* FLIES SWIFTLY THROUGH THE KEYHOLE!

4

THERE HE IS! STING HIS ANKLE! HURRY, WASP! YOU CAN STOP HIM!

-SIGH- A WOMAN'S WORK IS NEVER DONE!

OWWW!

LISTEN! THE MANAGER IS BREAKING DOWN THE DOOR!

NO NEED TO RUSH! TRAGO WON'T BE GOING ANYWHERE NOW!

AH, THERE YOU ARE! DIDN'T GET AWAY WITH IT, DID YOU, TRAGO? WHY, TRAGO? WHY WOULD YOU DO THIS TO ME?

I-I DON'T KNOW, MISTER COSGROVE! I SAW THE SAFE OPEN -- AND THE MONEY -- AND I DON'T EARN MUCH WITH MY TRUMPET -- SO, IT SEEMED LIKE EASY DOUGH!

YOU MUSICIANS! YOU'RE ALL LUNKHEADS! WELL, THERE IS NO REAL HARM DONE NOW THAT I'VE GOT MY MONEY BACK! COME INTO MY OFFICE...

TRAGO, I'M NOT GOING TO PRESS CHARGES! I'M GOING TO GET YOU A TICKET ON THE FIRST PLANE OUT OF THE COUNTRY... BECAUSE OF OUR FRIENDSHIP! JUST DON'T COME BACK, YOU HEAR? I'LL TAKE THE COST OF THE TICKET OUT OF THE WAGES I OWE YOU!

OKAY BY ME!

HELLO! YOU SAY YOUR NEXT PLANE LEAVES FOR NEW DEHLI, INDIA? THAT'S GOOD ENOUGH! RESERVE ONE SEAT IN THE NAME OF TRAGO! HE'LL BE RIGHT THERE!

WELL, I GUESS THAT'S THE LAST WE'LL HEAR OF THE MAN WITH THE MAGIC TRUMPET! LET'S GO!

AWW... AND HE PLAYED SUCH A MELLOW HORN!

5

NO, ANT-MAN, YOU ARE VERY WRONG! THIS IS BUT THE *BEGINNING!* A PROLOGUE TO THE STORY OF TRAGO, THE MAN WITH THE MAGIC TRUMPET! YOUR LIVES ARE INEXTRICABLY BOUND TOGETHER IN THE WEB OF FATE, AND THE FUTURE WILL BRING ACTION AND DANGER SUCH AS YOU HAVE NEVER DREAMED OF!

WE PICK UP THE TRAIL OF TRAGO AGAIN IN A HUT OUTSIDE OF NEW DELHI, TWO MONTHS LATER!

YOU HAVE BEEN VERY ILL... FEVER, STARVATION! I FOUND YOU ALMOST *DEAD!* MY NAME IS *GHAZANDI,* A MYSTIC, AND SCHOLAR OF ANCIENT PHENOMENA!

THANKS, DAD, FOR HELPING ME! I COULDN'T FIND WORK ...I WAS STARVING!

I PLAY, TOO! SAY! IS IT *TRUE* THAT YOU CATS CAN CHARM SNAKES AND THINGS LIKE THAT, WITH *MUSIC?*

YES, *GHAZANDI* HAS THE POWER! YOU THINK YOU KNOW HOW TO PLAY THAT TRUMPET, MY FRIEND? AH, THERE ARE NOTES, PASSAGES, THAT YOU HAVE NEVER EVEN *IMAGINED!*

IF THAT'S TRUE, THEN *TEACH* ME! MAN, I WANNA SWING! I WANNA BE THE TOP HORN MAN! YOU'RE NOT *KIDDIN'* ABOUT PLAYIN' NOTES NO ONE *ELSE* CAN, ARE YOU?

I KNOW *MANY* THINGS! I KNOW FROM YOUR MIND THAT YOU STOLE' AND THOUGHT YOU SAW TINY HUMAN FIGURES NO BIGGER THAN AN ANT AND A WASP!

YOU *DID* SEE THEM! THERE ARE *MANY* STRANGE THINGS THAT ARE POSSIBLE! I HAVE NEVER BEFORE HAD A STUDENT, BUT IF IT IS WRITTEN IN THE STARS THAT I SHOULD BE YOUR TEACHER, WE WILL BEGIN!

TIME PASSES, AND TRAGO LEARNS MANY THINGS....!

GOOD! YOU HAVE MASTERED THE NOTES THAT HYPNOTIZE THE KING COBRA! I HAVE TAUGHT YOU ALSO THE ART OF HYPNOTISM, USING YOUR *EYES* AS THE POWER MEDIUM!

IF MUSIC CAN HYNOTIZE A *REPTILE,* WHY CAN'T IT HYPNOTIZE *HUMANS?* GHAZANDI, *TELL ME!* I WANT TO KNOW!

THERE IS GREAT *DANGER* INVOLVED! BUT, YOU ARE *MY DISCIPLE!* I WILL *TEACH* YOU!

6

THE MONTHS FLY BY AND THEN, RETURNING FROM HELPING THE POLICE, ANTMAN AND THE WASP ARE REMINDED OF...

REMEMBER *TRAGO*, THE MAN WITH THE MAGIC TRUMPET? WONDER IF HE'S STILL IN *INDIA*?

CERTAINLY I REMEMBER! IT WAS ONE OF THE FEW TIMES I GOT YOU INTO A NIGHT CLUB! HE WAS A COOL BRASS MAN! BUT YOU JUST DIDN'T DIG 'IM!

JAZZ NITE ★ ★ ★ starring The ALL STARS! ★ ★ ★

NO, TRAGO *IS NOT* STILL IN INDIA! FOR, AT THAT MOMENT, IN A SMALL NIGHT CLUB IN CONNECTICUT, OFF THE MERRITT PARKWAY, TRAGO, HIS APPEARANCE ALTERED, IS PLAYING WITH A SMALL COMBO!

GO, MAN, GO!!

NOW IS THE TIME TO TEST MY POWERS! FIRST, I MUST REINFORCE THE HYPNOTIC BONDS WITH WHICH I HOLD MY MUSICIANS ENSLAVED, SO *THEY* WILL NOT BE AFFECTED!!

LOOK DEEP...DEEP! YOU WILL DO ONLY AS MY WILL COMMANDS... YOU WILL HEAR NOTHING BUT THE SOUNDS OF YOUR OWN INSTRUMENTS! NOW... *WE WILL PLAY!!*

THE MUSIC WAILS, SLURRING, JUMPING, SULTRY SOUTHERN JAZZ! THEN, FROM TRAGO'S BLARING TRUMPET, *NEW* NOTES FORM, NOTES NO HUMAN HAS EVER HEARD BEFORE ...

HARRY...I...I FEEL STRANGE! I THINK I'M GOING TO *FAINT!*

MY HEAD! MY BRAIN'S WHIRLING!

THE MUSIC GOES ON AND ON, SOME NOTES UNHEARD BY THE EAR BUT HEARD BY THE *SUB-CONSCIOUS!* THEN, *FANTASY* COMES... MIASMIC IMAGES IN THE MIND, FORMED BY THE MUSICAL HYPNOSIS... AS THE STARTLING STRAINS FILL THE ROOM...

AAIEEEEEE

TRAGO RAISES HIS HAND! THE MUSIC STOPS! THE AUDIENCE IS MOTIONLESS... HELPLESS... COMPLETELY UNDER TRAGO'S SPELL!

NOW! PASS AMONG THE AUDIENCE AND TAKE THEIR VALUABLES! I *COMMAND* YOU!

7.

MOMENTS LATER...

HA! IT WORKED... THE TEST HAS BEEN A COMPLETE SUCCESS! BUT THIS IS NOT WORTH BOTHERING ABOUT... A HANDFUL OF JEWELS AND BILLS! RETURN THOSE BAUBLES, EACH PIECE TO ITS RIGHTFUL OWNER!

NOW, I'LL BREAK THE HYPNOSIS... AND THEY WON'T EVEN KNOW THAT TIME HAS ELAPSED AND ANYTHING HAS HAPPENED! THEN, ON TO NEW YORK, AND THE BIG PRIZE!

I'LL CONTACT A T.V. STATION DIRECTOR, USE MY HYPNOTIC POWERS TO GET MY LITTLE COMBO A BROADCASTING SPOT! THEN, ONCE MY MUSIC IS BEAMED OUT OVER THE AIRWAYS, EVERYONE HEARING IT WILL BE HYPNOTIZED! I'LL HYPNOTIZE AN ENTIRE CITY... AND LOOT IT AT WILL!

A FEW DAYS LATER, IN THE LAB OF HENRY PYM, AS THE SCIENTIST USES HIS FANTASTIC CYBERNETIC MACHINE TO RECEIVE ELECTRONIC IMPULSE MESSAGES FROM THE VAST ARMY OF ANTS WHILE THE WASP LISTENS TO A LOCAL RADIO STATION...

...AND NOW, FRIENDS, WE PRESENT THE MAHARAJAH OF JAZZ ... TRAGO, AND HIS MAGIC TRUMPET!

TRAGO?

THE ANTS REPORT THAT ALL IS QUIET IN THE CITY...

HENRY, COME HERE! LISTEN TO THIS! IT'S TRAGO! REMEMBER HIM?

THEN, SUDDENLY, AS THE MUSIC STARTS...

HENRY!! WHA... WHAT'S HAPPENING?

MY EARS! MY BRAIN! JAN, IT'S THE MUSIC! QUICK! WE MUST REDUCE OUR SIZE... YOU'VE GOT TO TURN OFF THE RADIO... GOT TO!

THE REDUCING GAS SWIRLS AROUND THEM AS THEY SHRINK WITH INCREDIBLE RAPIDITY!

CAN'T DO IT! THAT MUSIC! IT'S TOO POWERFUL! CAN'T RESIST IT!!

NEED HELP... FAST! I'LL CONTACT MY FAITHFUL KORR! KORR... TO ME, KORR!

8.

THE DISCORDANT MUSIC WAILS ON, BRINGING HYPNOSIS, BRINGING NIGHTMARE TO THE MINDS OF THE TWO TINY UNCONSCIOUS FIGURES!

THEN, A TINY FORM APPEARS AT THE WINDOW! IT IS *KORR!* KORR, THE FAITHFUL HAS HEARD THE CALL AND ANSWERED! HE SEES WITH MANY-FACETED EYES...AND HE UNDERSTANDS! HIS ANTENNAE QUIVER AS HE SENDS A CALL FOR HELP!

AND SO THEY COME...*THE ANTS,* SWARMING TO KORR'S SIGNAL...

"AND THEY CARRY THE HELPLESS ANT-SIZE HUMANS AWAY!"

WHILE TRAGO PLAYS...

AND, THROUGHOUT THE CITY, PEOPLE ARE FROZEN IN A HYPNOTIC TRANCE!

BUT TRAGO HAS NOT FORGOTTEN THE TWO TINY HUMANS HE ONCE SAW, WHO FOILED HIS EARLIER ATTEMPT AT ROBBERY...AND HIS HORN SENDS A MESSAGE TO THE REPTILES IN THE GARDENS AND FIELDS... *"FIND ANTMAN, CAPTURE HIM!"*

THEN TRAGO'S EYES SEND THEIR MESSAGE TO HIS HYPNOTIZED MUSICIANS!

HEAR ME! HEAR MY MENTAL COMMANDS! FIND THOSE BANKS IN THE CITY WHERE MY MUSIC HAS REACHED...AND LOOT THEM!! NOW GO!

9.

MEANWHILE, KORR CARRIES HIS ANT-SIZE HUMAN FRIENDS DEEP INTO THE MIDDLE OF A HUGE ANT-HILL, WHERE THE HYPNOTIC BLARE OF TRAGO'S TRUMPET CANNOT REACH!

THEN, ANTMAN STIRS, FREE FROM THE MAD SYMPHONY, BUT STILL NUMBED BY THE TERRIBLE MENTAL PRESSURE! SUDDENLY, THE ANTS BEGIN TO SWAY, TO MOVE BACKWARDS!

WASP, WAKE UP! I...I REMEMBER SOMETHING... SOMETHING NEHRADU ONCE SAID...

SILENTLY, A FORM SLITHERS TOWARDS THEM! ONLY A SMALL GARDEN SNAKE, BUT A GIGANTIC MENACE TO THE TINY HUMANS! ANTMAN AND THE WASP TRY TO RISE TO FIGHT THE DEADLY DANGER, BUT THEY ARE STILL TOO WEAK!

THE ARMY OF ANTS FORM FOR BATTLE! BUT THEY WILL BE TOO LATE TO SAVE ANTMAN AND THE WASP! THIS KORR KNOWS, AS HE ATTACKS FIRST!

I..FORGOT MY GAS CONTAINERS! THE REDUCING GAS...USE IT, WASP!!

THE HISSING SNAKE STRIKES AT KORR, AND IN THAT SECOND THE WASP AIMS AND RELEASES A STREAM OF REDUCING GAS...BUT TOO LATE TO SAVE THE FAITHFUL ANT!

THAT DANGER IS OVER! IT WILL BECOME SMALL AS A WORM AND THE ANTS WILL TAKE CARE OF IT! BUT... POOR KORR...HE IS BEYOND HELP! WELL, COME ON! TIGHTEN YOUR EAR DISCS TO BLOT OUT TRAGO'S NOTES! ONLY USE YOUR ANTENNAE...

YOU SAID SOMETHING ABOUT NEHRADU..!

ASTRIDE THE FLYING ANT, FOSS, BROTHER OF THE FAITHFUL KORR, ANTMAN DEPARTS WITH THE WASP!

WEARING MY CYBERNETIC HELMET CUTS OFF THE EFFECT OF TRAGO'S MUSIC! WHAT STATION WAS THAT YOU TUNED IN ON, JAN? BECAUSE, THAT'S WHERE WE'RE HEADED!

BUT... WHAT WILL WE DO NOW?

10.

REMEMBER, TRAGO WENT TO INDIA?! AND NEHRADU TOLD US ABOUT AN INDIAN MYSTIC WHO COULD HYPNOTIZE *MEN*, AS WELL AS SNAKES WITH HIS MUSIC! TRAGO MUST HAVE LEARNED THE ART FROM *HIM!*

LOOK AT THE PEOPLE ---FROZEN, HYPNOTIZED, AND THEIR FACES MIRRORING THEIR SHOCK!

HERE'S THE BROADCASTING STATION! THOSE THREE MEN EMERGING *AREN'T* HYPNOTIZED! THAT MEANS... *WAIT!!* I'M GETTING A MESSAGE FROM THE ANTS IN THE STUDIO... ABOUT *TRAGO*...

THOSE THREE ARE *TRAGO'S MUSICIANS!* HE HAS THEM UNDER HIS SPELL, AND HAS SENT THEM OUT TO ROB AND LOOT! WASP, *STOP THEM!* DRIVE THEM BACK INTO THE STUDIO!

THE WASP BUZZES RAPIDLY FROM ONE OF THE HYPNOTIZED MUSICIANS TO THE OTHER, STINGING THEM AND, WITH HER STING, HERDING THEM LIKE SHEEP!

YEEOWW!

HALP!

AS ANTMAN ENTERS THE STUDIO...

NOW I'LL USE MY ENLARGING GAS AGAIN! ONCE I GET MY HANDS ON TRAGO, HE'LL NEVER PLAY ANOTHER HYPNOTIC NOTE!

I-I *FORGOT!* I DON'T *HAVE* MY GAS TUBES! I'LL HAVE TO BATTLE TRAGO WHILE I'M *ANT-SIZED* SOMEHOW!

AND, AT THAT INSTANT, TRAGO *SEES* ANT-MAN!

11.

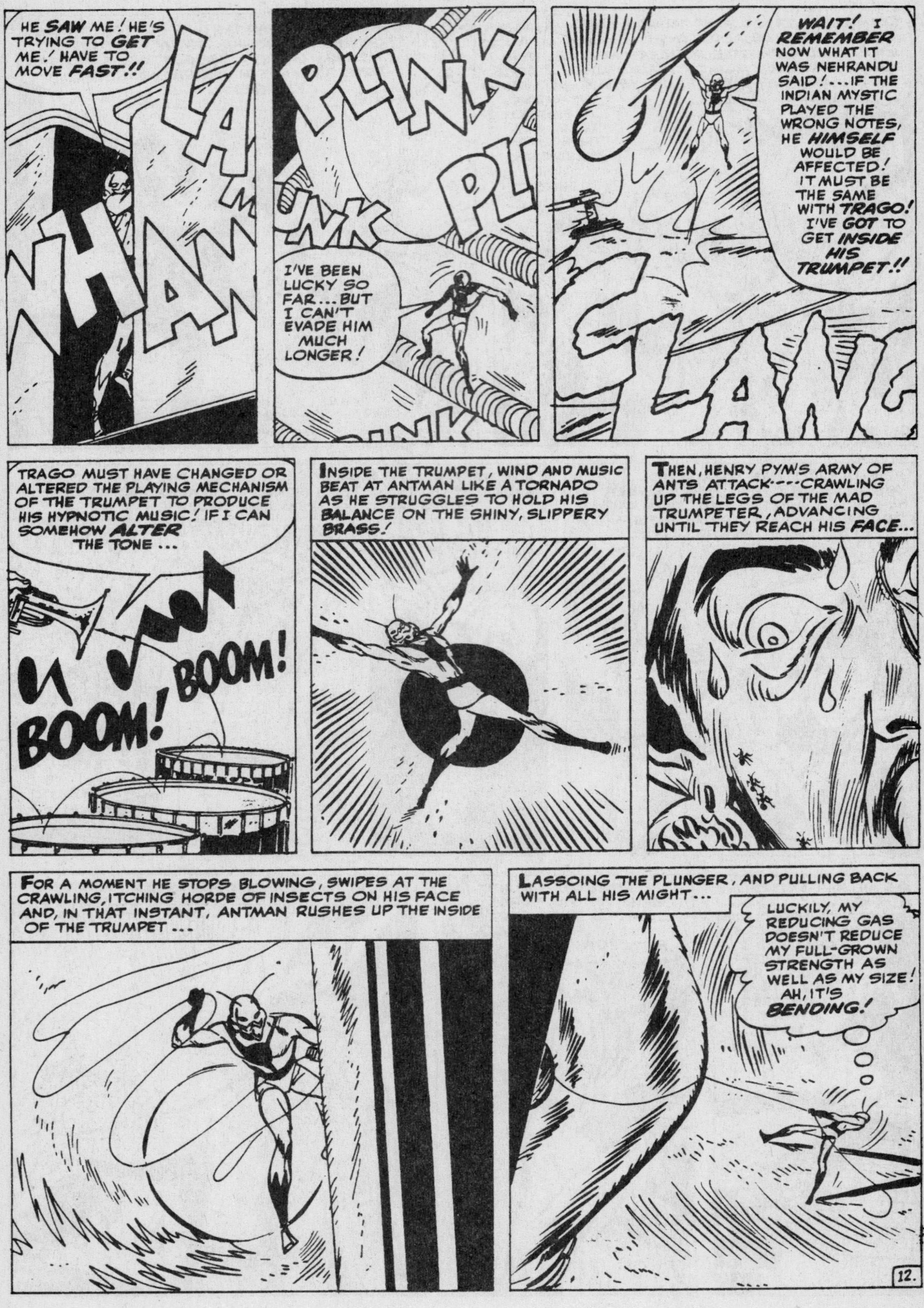
HE SAW ME! HE'S TRYING TO GET ME! HAVE TO MOVE FAST!!
LAM
WHAM
PLINK
UNK
PL
I'VE BEEN LUCKY SO FAR... BUT I CAN'T EVADE HIM MUCH LONGER!
PLINK
WAIT! I REMEMBER NOW WHAT IT WAS NEHRANDU SAID!...IF THE INDIAN MYSTIC PLAYED THE WRONG NOTES, HE HIMSELF WOULD BE AFFECTED! IT MUST BE THE SAME WITH TRAGO! I'VE GOT TO GET INSIDE HIS TRUMPET!!
CLANG
TRAGO MUST HAVE CHANGED OR ALTERED THE PLAYING MECHANISM OF THE TRUMPET TO PRODUCE HIS HYPNOTIC MUSIC! IF I CAN SOMEHOW ALTER THE TONE...
BOOM! BOOM!
INSIDE THE TRUMPET, WIND AND MUSIC BEAT AT ANTMAN LIKE A TORNADO AS HE STRUGGLES TO HOLD HIS BALANCE ON THE SHINY, SLIPPERY BRASS!
THEN, HENRY PYM'S ARMY OF ANTS ATTACK---CRAWLING UP THE LEGS OF THE MAD TRUMPETER, ADVANCING UNTIL THEY REACH HIS FACE...
FOR A MOMENT HE STOPS BLOWING, SWIPES AT THE CRAWLING, ITCHING HORDE OF INSECTS ON HIS FACE AND, IN THAT INSTANT, ANTMAN RUSHES UP THE INSIDE OF THE TRUMPET...
LASSOING THE PLUNGER, AND PULLING BACK WITH ALL HIS MIGHT...
LUCKILY, MY REDUCING GAS DOESN'T REDUCE MY FULL-GROWN STRENGTH AS WELL AS MY SIZE! AH, IT'S BENDING!
12.

SUDDENLY, TRAGO CAN NO LONGER PLAY THE HYPNOTIC NOTES! DISCORD BLARES FROM THE HORN AS TRAGO, IN PANIC, PLAYS A SERIES OF NOTES HE HAS NEVER PLAYED BEFORE...

I HERDED THOSE THREE INTO THE AUDITION BOOTH AND LOCKED THE DOOR!

GOOD WORK, JAN! NOW, KEEP YOUR EYES ON TRAGO!

THOSE NOTES HE HIT BY CHANCE WERE THE ONES GHAZANDI HAD WARNED HIM ABOUT... NOTES THAT AFFECTED THE PLAYER, CHANGING HIS CHARACTER, HIS MENTALITY, STEALING AWAY HIS POWER...

WH...WHAT AM I DOING HERE? I...I FEEL AS THOUGH I'VE BEEN ASLEEP FOR AGES! AND NOW I'VE BEEN REBORN! DON'T REMEMBER ANYTHING SINCE I GOT MY FIRST JOB PLAYING THE HORN!

THROUGHOUT THE CITY PEOPLE STIR, MOVE, CONTINUE ON THEIR VARIOUS WAYS, NOT REMEMBERING THE HYPNOSIS, THE NIGHTMARE THAT HAD DESCENDED ON NEW YORK!

THAT WRAPS THE TRAGO CAPER UP! WE STOPPED HIM BEFORE HE ACTUALLY COMMITTED ANY CRIME! ...AND NO ONE, INCLUDING TRAGO, WILL REMEMBER WHAT HAPPENED! NO ONE, BUT JAN AND I, AND THE ANTS!!

SEVERAL WEEKS LATER, AT A LOCAL BISTRO...

TRAGO'S HAPPY NOW! HE DOESN'T REMEMBER THE PAST, BUT HE'S DOING WHAT HE LOVES BEST... PLAYING THE TRUMPET!

YES, HE'S JUST ANOTHER JAZZ TRUMPETER! YOU HEAR THEM EVERY DAY AND NEVER QUITE REMEMBER THEM!

LEAVING SO SOON? BUT I THOUGHT YOU WERE GETTING TO LIKE JAZZ!

I AM, JAN, BUT I'D LIKE TO GO SOMEPLACE WHERE IT'S QUIET...

I SUPPOSE YOU'LL THINK I'M CORNY... JUST A SENTIMENTAL FOOL, BUT ... I'M THINKING OF KORR! HE WAS ONLY AN ANT, BUT...

I KNOW, HENRY! I KNOW HOW YOU FEEL!

"GREATER LOVE HATH NO ONE THAN THIS, THAT HE LAY DOWN HIS LIFE FOR HIS FRIENDS!"

The End

13.

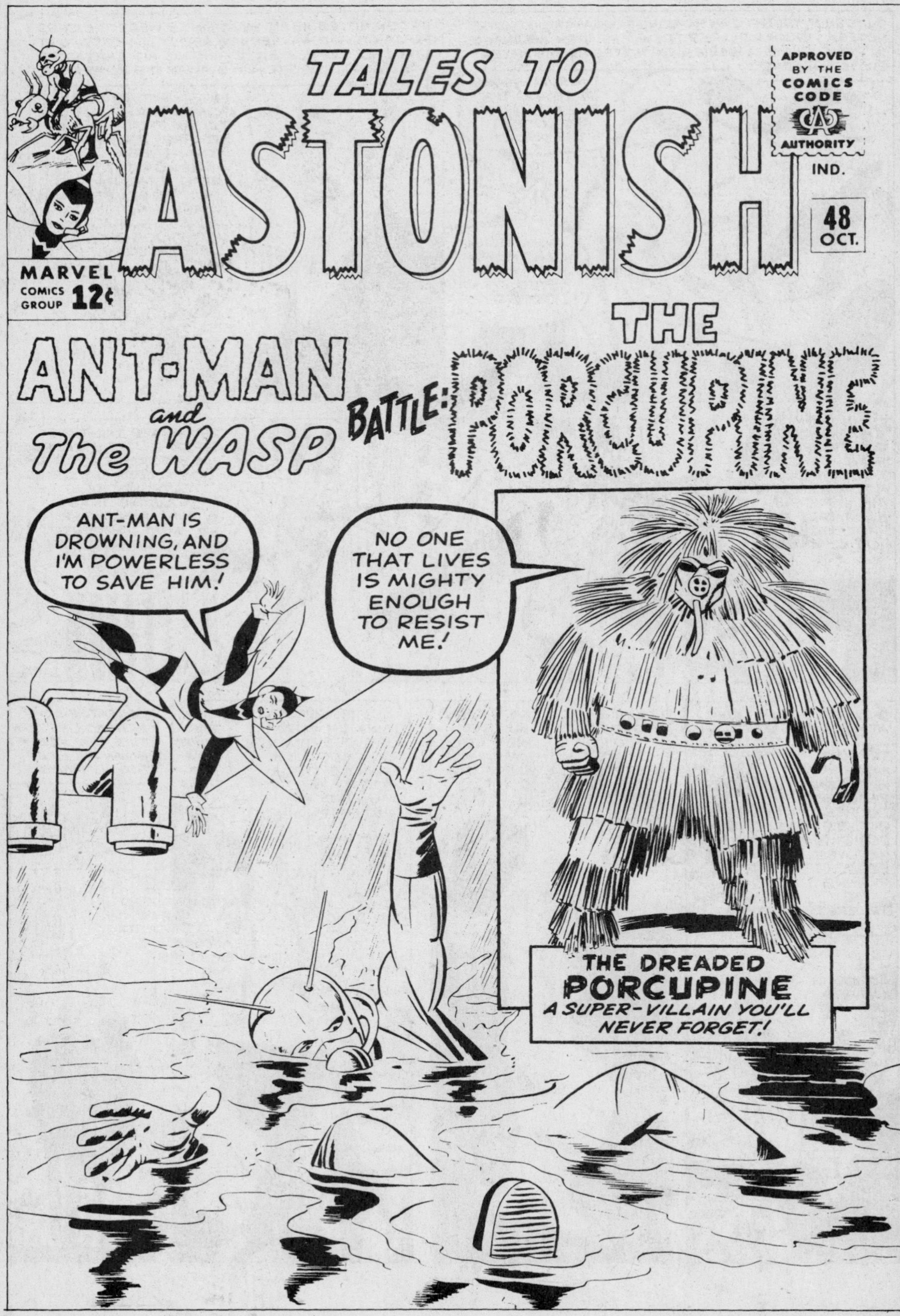

TALES TO ASTONISH
APPROVED BY THE COMICS CODE CA AUTHORITY
IND.
48 OCT.
MARVEL COMICS GROUP 12¢
ANT-MAN and The WASP
BATTLE:
THE PORCUPINE
ANT-MAN IS DROWNING, AND I'M POWERLESS TO SAVE HIM!
NO ONE THAT LIVES IS MIGHTY ENOUGH TO RESIST ME!
THE DREADED PORCUPINE
A SUPER-VILLAIN YOU'LL NEVER FORGET!

ANT-MAN and the WASP DEFY THE PORCUPINE!

STORY PLOT: STAN LEE
SCRIPT: H.E. HUNTLEY
ART: DON HECK
LETTERING: S. ROSEN

THAT'S AN *ARMY ORDNANCE PLANT* BELOW US, JAN! SOME OF THE FINEST INVENTIVE BRAINS IN THE COUNTRY WORK THERE, CONSTANTLY STRIVING TO CREATE NEWER AND BETTER WEAPONS FOR OUR DEFENSE!

YOU WORRY ABOUT THE WEAPONS, ANT-MAN! *I'D* RATHER THINK ABOUT ALL THE GLAMOROUS, ELIGIBLE *MALES* WHO MUST BE WORKING THERE! ≡SIGH≡ I WISH WE HAD SOMETHING TO INVESTIGATE DOWN THERE!

A LIGHT BANTERING CONVERSATION OCCURS AS *ANT-MAN* AND THE *WASP* WING THEIR WAY OVER THE ARMY ORDNANCE CENTER! YET, HOW CAN THEY KNOW THAT WITHIN THOSE WALLS A THREAT IS BEING SPAWNED, A PERIL WITH WHICH THEY WILL SOON COME TO GRIPS...THAT THE MOST DANGEROUS AND DEADLY MENACE THEY HAVE EVER FACED IS EVEN AT THAT MOMENT TAKING SHAPE...

X-387

BUT, JUST AS ANT-MAN AND THE WASP ARE UNAWARE OF WHAT IS HAPPENING BELOW, SO ALEX GENTRY, IN THE LAB AT THE ORDNANCE CENTER, IS UNAWARE OF THEIR FLIGHT *ABOVE* HIM AS HE HOLDS A PICTURE IN HIS HAND AND STUDIES IT...

YES, THE *PORCUPINE* IS NATURE'S PERFECT FIGHTING MACHINE FOR ATTACK OR DEFENSE...A CREATURE THAT *WEARS* ITS WEAPONS, AND THEN SHOOTS THEM AT HIS ENEMY! SO SIMPLE, SO DIRECT...SO FOOLPROOF!

1

USING THE PORCUPINE AS A MODEL, I THINK MY COMBAT SUIT IS THE ULTIMATE IN WEAPONRY! EVERY SOLDIER WEARING IT WILL BECOME A ONE-MAN REGIMENT!

I PERSONALLY SHALL MAKE THE FINAL TEST... BUT WITHOUT LOADING THE QUILL-LIKE TUBES!

AND I MUSTN'T FORGET THE GAS MASK SO THAT THE WEARER WILL NOT BE AFFECTED BY FUMES FROM THE GAS TUBES!

YES, EACH BUTTON CONTROLS A SPECIAL GROUP OF TUBES! ONCE THE QUILLS ARE LOADED... SOME WITH GAS, SOME WITH STUN-PELLETS, AMMONIA, LIQUID FIRE, DETECTOR MINE TUBES AND ALL THE REST... THE MAN WHO WEARS THIS SUIT COULD DEFEAT *ANY* FOE!

A MAN COULD BECOME *ALL-POWERFUL* BY WEARING MY MARVELOUS PORCUPINE SUIT!

AND WHAT WILL BE *MY* REWARD FOR TURNING IT OVER TO THE GOVERNMENT? WILL I BECOME RICH, POWERFUL? NO, THEY'LL SAY, "GOOD JOB, GENTRY! NOW WHIP US UP SOMETHING *ELSE* AND MAYBE IF YOU'RE REALLY SUCCESSFUL IN THE NEXT YEAR OR TWO, WE'LL GIVE YOU A TEN DOLLAR RAISE, IF THE DEFENSE DEPARTMENT *OKAYS* IT!"

NO! NOT THIS TIME! THIS IS MY ONE BIG CHANCE! I COULD BECOME A *KING* USING THIS SUIT...YES..A KING OF CRIMINALS! ME! ALEX GENTRY... NO, NOT ALEX GENTRY... *THE PORCUPINE* ...I SHALL BECOME THE GREATEST CRIMINAL THE WORLD HAS EVER KNOWN!

SLAM!

2

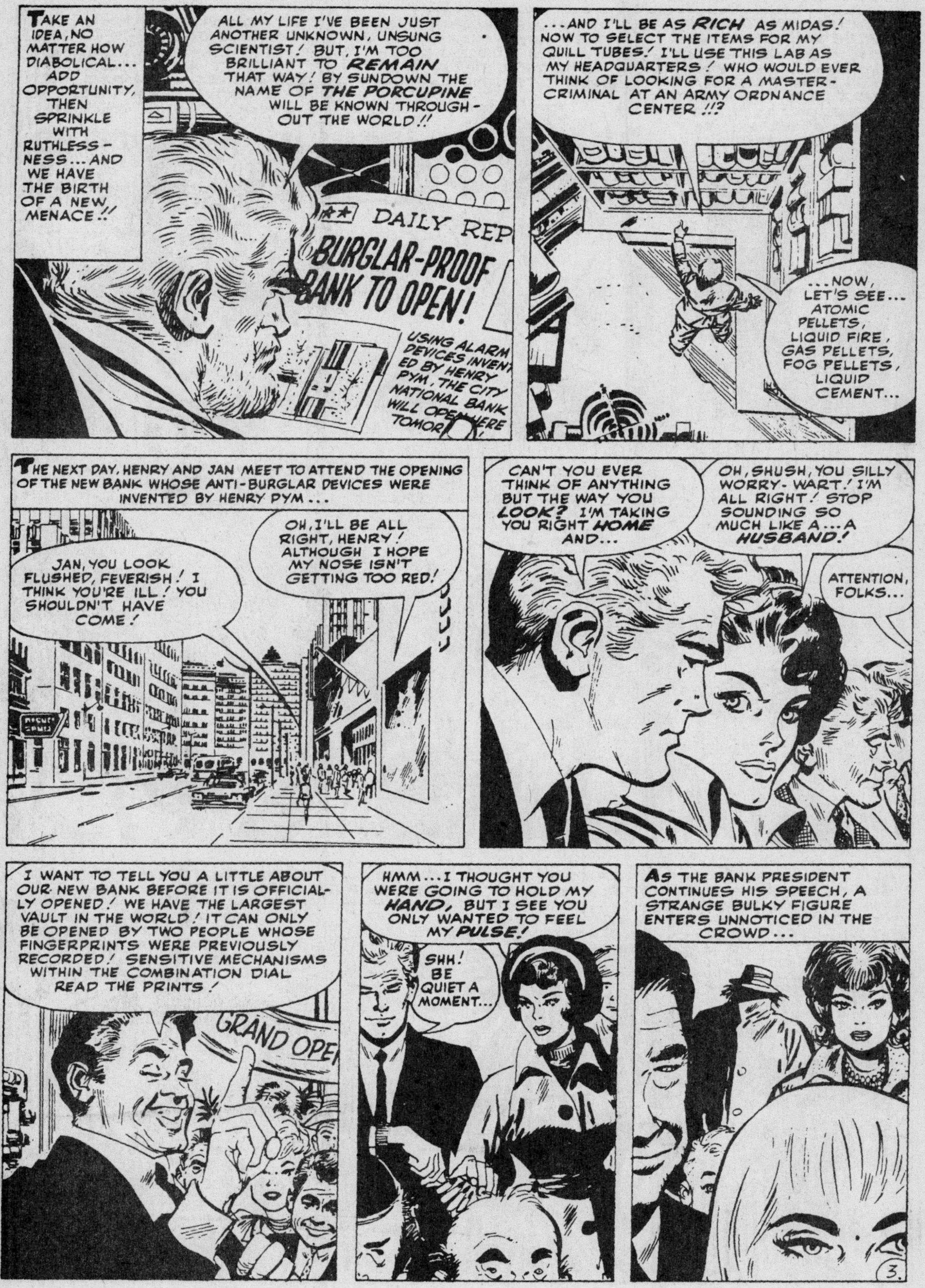
TAKE AN IDEA, NO MATTER HOW DIABOLICAL... ADD OPPORTUNITY, THEN SPRINKLE WITH RUTHLESS-NESS... AND WE HAVE THE BIRTH OF A NEW MENACE!!
ALL MY LIFE I'VE BEEN JUST ANOTHER UNKNOWN, UNSUNG SCIENTIST! BUT, I'M TOO BRILLIANT TO REMAIN THAT WAY! BY SUNDOWN THE NAME OF THE PORCUPINE WILL BE KNOWN THROUGH-OUT THE WORLD!!
DAILY REP
BURGLAR-PROOF BANK TO OPEN!
USING ALARM DEVICES INVENTED BY HENRY PYM, THE CITY NATIONAL BANK WILL OPEN HERE TOMOR
...AND I'LL BE AS RICH AS MIDAS! NOW TO SELECT THE ITEMS FOR MY QUILL TUBES! I'LL USE THIS LAB AS MY HEADQUARTERS! WHO WOULD EVER THINK OF LOOKING FOR A MASTER-CRIMINAL AT AN ARMY ORDNANCE CENTER!!?
...NOW, LET'S SEE... ATOMIC PELLETS, LIQUID FIRE, GAS PELLETS, FOG PELLETS, LIQUID CEMENT...
THE NEXT DAY, HENRY AND JAN MEET TO ATTEND THE OPENING OF THE NEW BANK WHOSE ANTI-BURGLAR DEVICES WERE INVENTED BY HENRY PYM...
JAN, YOU LOOK FLUSHED, FEVERISH! I THINK YOU'RE ILL! YOU SHOULDN'T HAVE COME!
OH, I'LL BE ALL RIGHT, HENRY! ALTHOUGH I HOPE MY NOSE ISN'T GETTING TOO RED!
CAN'T YOU EVER THINK OF ANYTHING BUT THE WAY YOU LOOK? I'M TAKING YOU RIGHT HOME AND...
OH, SHUSH, YOU SILLY WORRY-WART! I'M ALL RIGHT! STOP SOUNDING SO MUCH LIKE A... A HUSBAND!
ATTENTION, FOLKS...
I WANT TO TELL YOU A LITTLE ABOUT OUR NEW BANK BEFORE IT IS OFFICIALLY OPENED! WE HAVE THE LARGEST VAULT IN THE WORLD! IT CAN ONLY BE OPENED BY TWO PEOPLE WHOSE FINGERPRINTS WERE PREVIOUSLY RECORDED! SENSITIVE MECHANISMS WITHIN THE COMBINATION DIAL READ THE PRINTS!
GRAND OPE
HMM... I THOUGHT YOU WERE GOING TO HOLD MY HAND, BUT I SEE YOU ONLY WANTED TO FEEL MY PULSE!
SHH! BE QUIET A MOMENT...
AS THE BANK PRESIDENT CONTINUES HIS SPEECH, A STRANGE BULKY FIGURE ENTERS UNNOTICED IN THE CROWD...
3.

AND THE STEEL COMPOUND OF THE VAULT CANNOT BE AFFECTED BY ANYTHING LESS THAN FLAME SO HOT THAT IT WOULD MELT DIAMONDS! GOOD THING, TOO! FOR INSIDE THAT VAULT, FIVE MILLION DOLLARS ARE SAFELY STORED AWAY!

THE BURGLAR ALARMS THROUGHOUT THE BUILDING ARE A NEW, AND DARINGLY DIFFERENT, DESIGN! AS ADVERTISED, THIS BANK IS ABSOLUTELY BURGLAR-PROOF...

...AND CONTAINS EVERY POSSIBLE SAFEGUARD AGAINST ROBBERY! NOW, I WOULD LIKE TO INTRODUCE YOU TO THE MAN WHO *DESIGNED* OUR BANK'S PROTECTIVE SYSTEM, THE EMINENT SCIENTIST, MR. HENRY...

SUDDENLY, A STRANGE MURMUR RUNS THROUGH THE CROWD... A SHIFTING, AN UNEASY STIRRING...

SOMEBODY BETTER CALL THE ZOO!

WHAT ON EARTH CAN THAT BE?

LOOK, HENRY... THAT FIGURE! WHAT A STRANGE COSTUME! YOU DIDN'T TELL ME THEY WERE GOING TO PULL A GAG LIKE THIS!

I HAVE A SNEAKING SUSPICION THAT THIS *ISN'T* A GAG, JAN!

EEEEE!!

SIR, I DON'T KNOW WHO YOU ARE, BUT THIS IS IN VERY POOR TASTE! I'M SURE YOU DON'T *BELONG* HERE! GUARDS! THROW *THAT*... THAT *CREATURE* OUT!

BUT *OF COURSE*, I, *THE PORCUPINE*, BELONG HERE! WHERE *ELSE* DOES A BANK ROBBER BELONG BUT IN A *BANK?*

As THE GUARDS RUSH FORWARD, THE PORCUPINE PRESSES A STUD IN HIS BELT...

TEAR GAS TO BLIND THEM TEMPORARILY... LIQUID CEMENT TO CLOG THEIR WEAPONS, MAKING THEM USELESS!

4.

AND THEN, PANDEMONIUM BREAKS LOOSE...

HELP!! LET US OUT!

NOT WITHOUT A WHIFF OF SLEEPING GAS FIRST!

PEOPLE JAM AGAINST EACH OTHER, LOOKING FOR ESCAPE! BUT THE DOORS OPEN INWARD AND THE PRESSURE OF THE PANICKY CROWD KEEPS THEM CLOSED, LOCKING EVERYONE IN!

SOME KIND OF SLEEPING GAS! TRY TO BLOCK OUT AS MUCH AS YOU CAN WITH YOUR HANDKERCHIEF...

HENRY, WE'VE GOT TO DO SOMETHING...

WE CAN'T DO ANYTHING IN THIS CROWD! WE CAN SCARCELY MOVE...

I..I'M BEGINNING TO FEEL DROWSY... THE GAS...

NOW, A SMOKE SCREEN TO HIDE MY MOVEMENTS, THEN ACETYLENE FLAME, AS HOT AS ANY YET DEVISED BY MAN TO BURN THROUGH THE VAULT LOCK!

JAN! LIE DOWN FLAT ON YOUR FACE! PUT YOUR NOSE CLOSE TO THE DOOR! THE GAS RISES...JAN, DO YOU HEAR ME? JAN??

5.

WITH THE SLEEPING GAS FUMES SLOWLY DRAINING HIS STRENGTH, HENRY PYM DRAGS THE INERT FORM OF THE LOVELY JAN OVER THE SLEEPING FIGURES ON THE FLOOR...

IF I CAN REACH THE OFFICE... SHUT DOOR... KEEP OUT FUMES... I'VE *GOT* TO MAKE IT!!

PRESIDENT

JUST ANOTHER FEW INCHES...

THE WINDOW! M-MUST GET *AIR*!!

CRASH

MEANWHILE, IN THE MAIN HALL OF THE BANK...

HA, IT WAS EASY... EASIER THAN I ANTICIPATED! AND NOW...

A *FORTUNE*!... MINE!... ALL MINE! AND THIS IS JUST THE BEGINNING! *THE PORCUPINE* WILL LOOT THE TREASURE TROVES OF THE WORLD!

LADEN WITH HIS LOOT, THE PORCUPINE PRESSES ANOTHER BUTTON ON HIS BELT, ACTIVATING A GROUP OF POWER JETS THAT LIFT HIM HIGH OVER THE CITY!

BY THE TIME THEY AWAKE, I'LL BE SAFELY HOME!

CRASH!

WOOSH!

6.

A FEW MINUTES LATER... JAN! WAKE UP! WAKE UP!

OH, HENRY, I WAS HAVING THE NICEST DREAM! I MET THE MOST ROMANTIC BOY AND...

WAIT!! NOW I REMEMBER! THE BANK! THAT PORCUPINE CREATURE... WHAT DO WE DO NOW?

WE DO NOTHING! BUT ANT-MAN AND WASP HAVE A JOB TO DO! CAN'T LET THE PORCUPINE GET AWAY WITH THIS! I GUARANTEED THAT MY DEVICES WOULD MAKE THIS BANK BURGLAR-PROOF...

AND AGAIN GAS SWIRLS! BUT THIS TIME IT IS THE ASTONISHING REDUCING GAS, AND IN SECONDS, HENRY PYM AND JANET VAN DYNE BECOME... ANT-MAN AND THE WASP!

WE'LL JUST WALK UNDER THE DOOR AND...

TOO LATE! HE'S ALREADY LOOTED THE BANK AND DISAPPEARED!

HENRY, MY HEAD IS SPINNING! I ...I FEEL FAINT!

I'D BETTER GET YOU HOME RIGHT AWAY! I KNEW YOU WERE FEELING ILL! HERE COME THE POLICE! NOTHING WE CAN DO HERE NOW, ANYWAY!

ANT-MAN SENDS OUT A CALL TO HIS ANTS THROUGH HIS CYBERNETIC HELMET, AND WITHIN SECONDS, TORNE ARRIVES...

MMM...IT'S WORTH BEING ILL TO HAVE YOU HOLD ME IN YOUR ARMS LIKE THIS, HANK...

POOR KID...THE FEVER'S MADE YOU DELIRIOUS!

7.

I'M NOT THE ONE WHO'S SICK, SICK, SICK! WHAT ARE YOU MADE OF... STONE?

STOP TALKING LIKE A CHILD! THIS IS NO TIME FOR SWEET NOTHINGS... NOT WITH THE PORCUPINE AT LARGE!

LATER, IN THE GUEST ROOM, BEHIND THE LAB...

I'VE SENT FOR THE DOCTOR, DEAR! JUST TAKE IT EASY, LITTLE PARTNER... THE ASPIRIN I GAVE YOU SHOULD REDUCE YOUR FEVER SOON!

FINE THING, WHEN THIS IS THE ONLY WAY I CAN GET YOU TO CALL ME "DEAR"!

REMEMBER, STAY PUT UNTIL YOUR FEVER BREAKS! I'VE GOT TO GO AND CONTACT THE ANTS NOW!

YOU AND YOUR OLD ANTS! I'LL BET IF I HAD SIX LEGS, YOU'D LIKE ME BETTER!

THE NEXT MORNING...

SHE'S STILL ASLEEP! IT WILL DO HER GOOD! I'LL TURN ON THE RADIO AND SEE IF THERE'S ANY MORE NEWS OF THE PORCUPINE!

MEANWHILE, AS A BANK IN THE DOWNTOWN DISTRICT OPENS AND THE DEPOSITORS START FILING IN...

LOOK! IT'S THE PORCUPINE!

PARALYZING PELLETS AND HYPNOTIC WHEELS SHOULD KEEP EVERYBODY UNDER CONTROL!

BAN

THE FEARFUL EYES OF EVERYONE IN THE BANK FOLLOW THE WHIRLING WHEELS AND IN SECONDS, ARE TRAPPED IN A HYPNOTIC TRANCE!

ONE THING IS CERTAIN... ANT-MAN AND THE WASP WILL BE ON MY TRAIL BEFORE VERY LONG... SO I MUST PREPARE FOR THEM AFTER THIS JOB!

BLAM

8.

BUT, UNBLINKING EYES, MANY-FACETED ANT EYES, WATCH THE PORCUPINE'S EVERY MOVE, AS HE LEAVES THROUGH AN ALLEY AFTER HIS SECOND BRAZEN THEFT...

EACH STEP OF THE WAY AN ARMY OF ANTS WATCH...AS HE DIVESTS HIMSELF OF HIS PORCUPINE IDENTITY TO ENTER THE ORDNANCE BUILDING...

SOON, MESSAGES ARE RELAYED TO ANT-MAN'S ELECTRONIC COMMUNICATIONS MACHINE...

ARMY ORDNANCE CENTER? TOP FLOOR LAB? IT..IT DOESN'T SEEM POSSIBLE THAT THE PORCUPINE SHOULD COME FROM THERE! BUT MY ANTS ARE NEVER WRONG!

IN SECONDS, THROUGH THE USE OF HIS REDUCING GAS, HENRY PYM BECOMES ANT-MAN AGAIN...

I'LL LET JAN SLEEP... SHE NEEDS IT! I'LL HANDLE THIS MYSELF!

DOWN A TINY ELEVATOR TO HIS SMALL BUT HIGHLY EFFICIENT CATAPULT, ANT-MAN GOES! HE PRESSES A LEVER AND THE CATAPULT EJECTS HIM HIGH IN THE AIR...

PWWAM

LATER, INSIDE THE CHARGED WIRE THAT SURROUNDS THE ARMY ORDNANCE BUILDING...

OH OH! THE GUARD WOULDN'T HAVE SEEN ME! BUT THE DOG...

GRRRR!

COME ON, ALF, YOU'RE SEEING THINGS! THERE ISN'T ANYTHING THERE!

WHEW!

9

THEN, WITHOUT FURTHER INCIDENT, ANT-MAN CRAWLS UNDER THE DOOR OF THE TOP FLOOR LAB, AND EMERGES IN STYGIAN DARKNESS!

WELCOME, ANT-MAN! I'VE BEEN EXPECTING YOU!

YOUR TINY SIZE WON'T SAVE YOU THIS TIME, ANT-MAN! THESE PHOSPHORESCENT PELLETS ARE ATTRACTED TO THE METAL OF YOUR HELMET AND WILL SPOT-LIGHT YOU NO MATTER WHERE YOU TRY TO HIDE, WHILE I REMAIN IN THE DARK!

THE PORCUPINE CHUCKLES AS HE PRESSES ANOTHER BUTTON ON HIS BELT... AND TINY NETS FLY OUT, ATTRACTED BY A MAGNETIC FIELD SET UP BY THE GLOWING PELLETS!

DON'T STRUGGLE, ANT-MAN! IT'S ALL SO FUTILE!

CAN'T GET LOOSE IN TIME!

NOW, I MERELY REMOVE THE NET, AND THEN I CARE-FULLY TAKE YOUR HELMET, LASSO, AND BELT WITH ITS TINY TUBES! I'M NOT GOING TO LEAVE YOU ANY MEANS OF ESCAPE, MY ANT-SIZED FOE!

I'VE GOT TO CONTACT MY ANTS... FAST!

BUT, BEFORE ANT-MAN CAN SUMMON HIS INSECT FRIENDS, HIS HELMET IS PLUCKED FROM HIS HEAD AND...

COME ALONG, ANT-MAN, YOU'RE GOING FOR A SWIM! BY THE TIME I GET BACK, WE'LL SEE IF YOU WERE ABLE TO REMAIN ABOVE WATER LONG ENOUGH TO SURVIVE!

TREADING WATER FRANTICALLY, ANT-MAN HEARS THE PORCUPINE'S DEPARTING FOOTSTEPS, AND THEN... SILENCE! MOMENTS PASS... HIS ARMS AND LEGS GROW WEARY, AS HE DESPERATELY SEEKS A WAY OUT OF THE SLIPPERY TUB...

10.

MEANWHILE, BACK AT THE LAB, *THE WASP*, HER FEVER NORMAL AGAIN, BEGINS TO WORRY ABOUT ANT-MAN'S PROLONGED ABSENCE...

ONLY *ONE* THING COULD HAVE TAKEN HIM AWAY... HE'S TRACKED DOWN THE PORCUPINE! I'LL CHECK WITH THE *ANTS*! *THEY'LL* KNOW WHERE HE IS!

THE ELECTRONIC COMMUNICATIONS MACHINE, CHANGING THE ANTENNA IMPULSES OF THE ANTS INTO HUMAN LANGUAGE, BRINGS AN OMINOUS MESSAGE TO THE WASP...

ANT-MAN ENTERED THE ARMY ORDNANCE BUILDING, TOP FLOOR LABORATORY, TRAILING THE PORCUPINE! HE'S BEEN GONE OVERLONG, BUT WE CANNOT GO TO HIM UNLESS HE COMMANDS US TO!

YOU MUST *MEET* ME AT THE LAB! I FEAR ANT-MAN IS IN DANGER AND NEEDS OUR HELP!

IN SECONDS, THE NOW FRANTIC GIRL REDUCES HER SIZE AND PREPARES FOR ACTION...

MAYBE IT'S MY WOMEN'S INTUITION, BUT I'M SURE HENRY'S IN TROUBLE! ALTHOUGH HE *WOULDN'T* BE IF HE HADN'T TREATED ME LIKE AN *INVALID*... AND HAD TAKEN ME *WITH* HIM!

LATER...

HENRY, WHERE *ARE* YOU? *HENRY!*

IN *HERE!* HURRY!

I... I CAN'T HOLD OUT MUCH LONGER! ...NEVER BEEN SO GLAD TO SEE ANYONE IN MY *LIFE!*

SOME COMPLIMENT! WHEN YOU'RE *DROWNING* YOU'RE GLAD TO SEE ME!

FOLLOWING THE WASP'S DIRECTION THE ANCHOR ANT GRASPS THE FAUCET WITH FOUR OF HIS LEGS, HOLDING ONTO THE NEXT ANT WITH HIS OTHER TWO! THEN THEY FORM A LIVING CHAIN OF ANT BODIES, REACHING DOWN TO THE WATER.. AND TO THE EXHAUSTED ANT-MAN!

CAREFUL... CAREFUL...

GOT YOU, JAN... YOU *DID* IT!

BUT THE *PORCUPINE* WILL BE BACK ANY MINUTE AND WE MUST BE *READY* FOR HIM! JUST LET ME CATCH MY BREATH... MEANWHILE, JAN, GET ME MY BELT AND HELMET THERE ON THE SINK!

JUST LIKE A MAN...THE MINUTE YOU'RE SAFE, YOU START GIVING ORDERS!

11

WE'VE GOT TO FIND SOME WAY TO PLUG HIS QUILL TUBES! AH, I KNOW! YOU REMEMBER HOW THAT LIQUID CEMENT HE SQUIRTED OUT PLUGGED THE BANK GUARD'S GUNS? WE'LL USE HIS OWN WEAPONS TO DEFEAT HIM!

LIQUID CEMENT

LIQUID CEMENT

LIQ CEM

PULL! *PULL!* GOOD! IT'S TIPPING...!

LIQUID CEMEN

I'VE FOUND SOME PLASTIC BAGS! WILL *THEY* BE OF ANY HELP?

JUST WHAT WE NEED! I'LL PRY THE STOPPER OFF THIS CAN IN A SECOND!

AS WE FILL THEM, WE'LL TWIST THE ENDS CLOSED AND YOU ANTS CARRY THEM UP ON TOP OF THE TABLE! HURRY! THE PORCUPINE WILL BE BACK ANY MINUTE!

FINALLY, ANT-MAN AND HIS TINY INSECT WARRIORS CLIMB TO THE TABLE TOP...

IF THIS WAS AN ADVENTURE STORY, IT WOULD SAY *"THE TENSION MOUNTS"* AT THIS POINT!

QUIET, JAN! I HEAR FOOTSTEPS!

AND THEN...

HA! I *SEE* YOU, *ANT-MAN!* YOU'RE CLEVERER THAN I THOUGHT! BUT *THIS* TIME YOU WILL *NOT ESCAPE!* NEITHER WILL THE *WASP..* OR YOUR HELPLESS ANTS!

THE PORCUPINE'S FINGERS FLY TO HIS BUTTON-STUDDED BELT! BUT, BEFORE HE CAN PRESS THE BUTTON THAT WILL RELEASE A LETHAL RADIATION GAS, *THE WASP STRIKES!*

OW!

GOOD WORK, WASP! NOW QUICKLY, JUMP ATOP ONE OF THE SACKS WITH ME... *HURRY!*

12

BLIPPFT!

His dreaded weapon tubes clogged with cement, the Porcupine presses his control buttons in vain!

I'M *STILL* NOT BEATEN! YOU FORGET...

...MY BACK QUILLS ARE STILL WORKABLE!

BLIPPFFT!

OHHH! I FORGOT ABOUT THOSE ACCURSED *ANTS* BEHIND ME!

MEANWHILE, ANT-MAN LASSOS PORCUPINE'S ARM AND...

CRASH!

But, as the Porcupine plunges toward the ground, he frantically pushes two more studs on his belt... and two tiny jet tubes, untouched by the liquid cement, manage to break his fall!

ANT-MAN WON THE FIRST ROUND... BUT I'LL MAKE MY SUIT MORE PERFECT, AND THEN... I'LL BE *BACK!!*

OH, HENRY... IF.. IF I HADN'T GOTTEN HERE IN TIME... IF ANYTHING HAD *HAPPENED* TO YOU...

THERE, THERE! TAKE IT EASY, JAN! LISTEN, LET'S GET BACK TO THE LAB! I'VE *GOT* SOMETHING FOR YOU...

Later, as Jan eagerly waits...

WHAT CAN IT *BE?* FURS? JEWELRY? OR PERHAPS A *RING??*

HERE, JAN, I GOT THIS FOR YOU! *AUREOMYCIN!* I WANT YOU TO GO BACK HOME AND TAKE THIS ANTIBIOTIC! I DON'T WANT YOU TO HAVE A RELAPSE OF THE FLU!

HENRY PYM... I *HATE* YOU!

LIKE I ALWAYS SAY...

...YOU CAN'T PLEASE A *FEMALE!*

13.

THE END

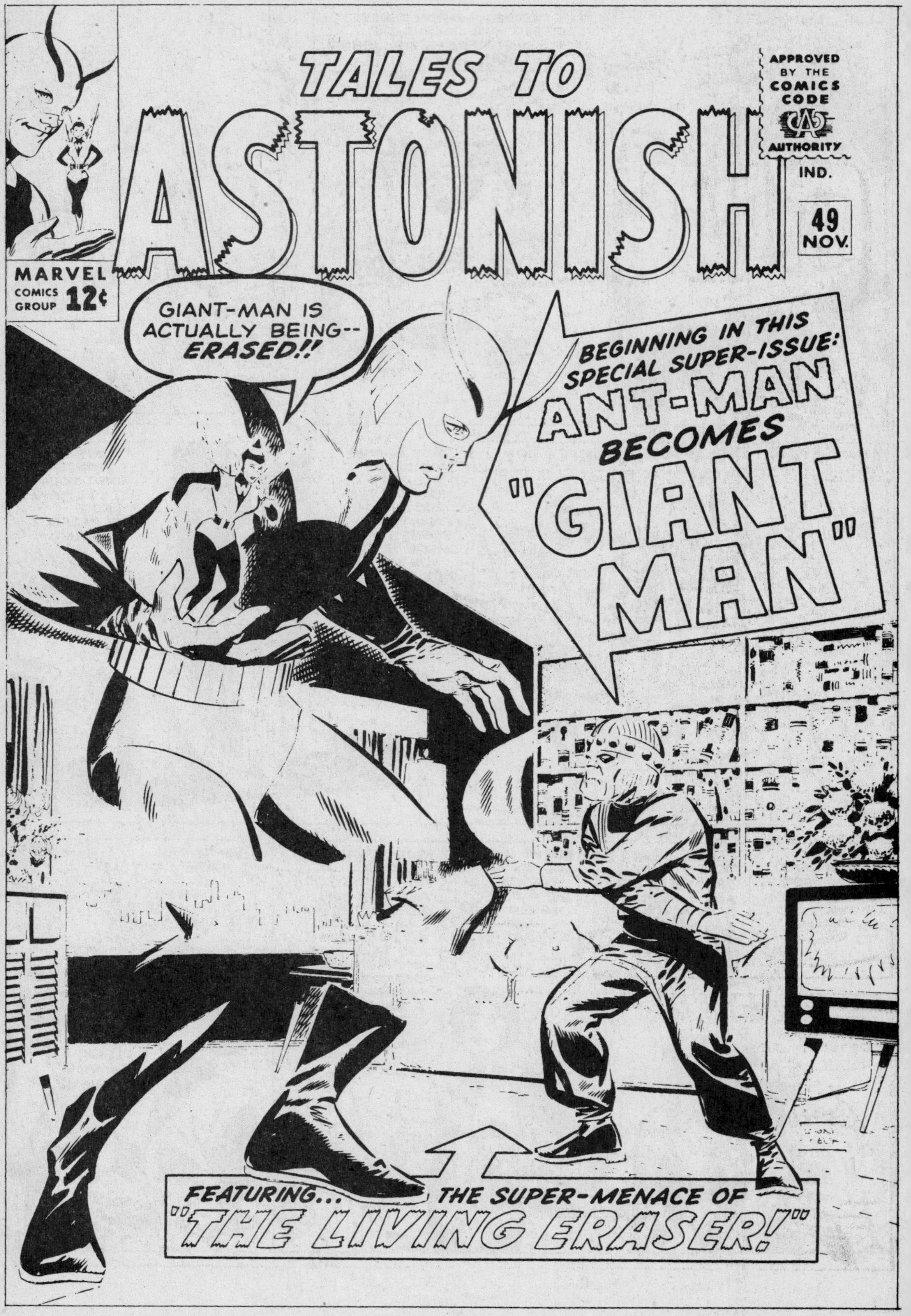
TALES TO ASTONISH
APPROVED BY THE COMICS CODE AUTHORITY
IND.
49
NOV.
MARVEL COMICS GROUP 12¢
GIANT-MAN IS ACTUALLY BEING-- ERASED!!
BEGINNING IN THIS SPECIAL SUPER-ISSUE: ANT-MAN BECOMES "GIANT MAN"
FEATURING... THE SUPER-MENACE OF "THE LIVING ERASER!"

ANT-MAN and THE WASP starring in "THE BIRTH OF GIANT-MAN!"

A MARVEL COMICS GROUP SUPER-SPECTACULAR

WRITTEN BY: STAN LEE
DRAWN BY: JACK KIRBY
INKING: DON HECK
LETTERING: S. ROSEN

AN EAR-SPLITTING EXPLOSION ROCKS A QUIET HOUSE ON THE NEW JERSEY PALISADES OVERLOOKING THE HUDSON RIVER! AND THEN... A GIGANTIC FIGURE EMERGES!

WHA...?? WHAT IN THE NAME OF CREATION... IS THAT??!

JUST MADE IT! ANOTHER MINUTE AND I'D HAVE BEEN CRUSHED INSIDE THOSE WALLS!

IT..IT ISN'T POSSIBLE! I MUST BE GOING MAD! IT'S A GIANT!! A HUGE, COSTUMED GIANT!

PLEASE...DON'T BE AFRAID! I WON'T HURT YOU! I..I NEED HELP!

THE POLICE! I'VE GOT TO GET THE POLICE!

COME BACK! WAIT!

SUDDENLY, ANOTHER BRIGHTLY COSTUMED FIGURE APPEARS! IT IS THE LOVELY JANET VAN DYNE, BETTER KNOWN TO THE WORLD, WHEN SHE ATTAINS HER INSECT SIZE, AS THE WONDERFUL *WASP!*

JAN! MY EXPERIMENT BACKFIRED! I— I MUST HAVE TAKEN TOO BIG A DOSE OF THE NEW *ENLARGING FLUID!*

I'M STILL GROWING! QUICKLY, DROP A REDUCING PELLET IN MY MOUTH!

I HEARD THE EXPLOSION! LUCKILY, I WAS NEARBY! I SAW THE GARDENER RUNNING DOWN THE ROAD IN PANIC, AND GUESSED WHAT MUST HAVE HAPPENED!

HERE, SWALLOW THIS RIGHT AWAY! I ALWAYS *SAID* YOU HAD A BIG HEAD, BUT *THIS* IS RIDICULOUS!

WITHIN SECONDS, THE ASTONISHING CHEMICAL BEGINS TO WORK...

I...I LEARNED AN IMPORTANT LESSON, JAN! WHEN I WAS GIANT-SIZED, I WAS ALMOST TOO WEAK TO MOVE!

I MUST NEVER ALLOW MYSELF TO GROW TALLER THAN *TWELVE FEET*... ANY MORE THAN THAT, AND I BECOME TOO BIG TO SUPPORT MY OWN WEIGHT!

AS FAR AS *I'M* CONCERNED, HENRY PYM, I LIKE YOU JUST THE WAY YOU *ARE!* YOU'RE A PERFECT *HUG-SIZE* NOW!

BE SERIOUS, JAN! THIS IS NO TIME FOR THAT KIND OF TALK!

YOU BIG, UNROMANTIC DREAMBOAT! I *AM* SERIOUS!

LOOK, KID... I'VE WORKED FOR WEEKS TO PUT OUR GROWTH AND SHRINKING VAPORS IN CAPSULE FORM! I'VE EVEN DESIGNED THIS NEW UNIFORM TO WEAR WHEN I GET *LARGER* THAN LIFE SIZE! BUT, THE JOB ISN'T FINISHED! I'VE GOT TO *PERFECT* THEM!

WHY COULDN'T I HAVE FALLEN IN LOVE WITH A NICE SIMPLE BUTCHER OR BAKER?

HONEY, YOU'RE JUST IN LOVE WITH THE IDEA OF *BEING* IN LOVE! NOW BUTTON THOSE RUBY LIPS UNTIL WE FINISH THIS JOB!

EVEN WHEN YOU CALL ME "HONEY" YOU MAKE IT SOUND... *MEDICINAL!*

2

FINALLY, AFTER HOURS OF PAINSTAKING WORK...

NOW, IF WE ESTIMATED EVERYTHING CORRECTLY, SWALLOWING THIS CAPSULE SHOULD INCREASE MY HEIGHT TO EXACTLY TWELVE FEET!

I FEEL LIKE THE INNOCENT ASSISTANT TO A MAD SCIENTIST IN AN OLD-TIME HORROR MOVIE!

EXACTLY ONE MICROSECOND AFTER SWALLOWING THE CAPSULE...

HI, SHORTY! IT WORKED PERFECTLY!

CONGRATULATIONS, BIG MAN!

MEANWHILE, AT A NEARBY NEW JERSEY POLICE STATION...

I TELL YOU, THERE'S A GIANT WRECKING HENRY PYM'S HOUSE!

WAIT! LISTEN TO ME! WHERE'S EVERYONE RUNNING TO?

SO YOU SAW A GIANT, HUH? WELL, WE'RE FOLLOWIN' UP A REPORT ABOUT A LIFE-SIZE PIXIE WHO'S RUNNIN' AROUND ERASING PEOPLE!! THE NEXT NUTTY CALL WILL PROBABLY REPORT A GREMLIN STEALIN' CITY HALL!

B-BUT I DID SEE A GIANT!

FIVE MINUTES LATER, AT A LOCAL PARK...

FAN OUT, YOU GUYS! THIS IS WHERE THE ERASER WAS LAST SIGHTED!

WHAT KIND OF WILD GOOSE CHASE IS THIS? HOW CAN ANYONE ERASE A HUMAN BEING?

BEATS ME, PAT! BUT THE CHIEF SAYS SEARCH, SO WE SEARCH!

3.

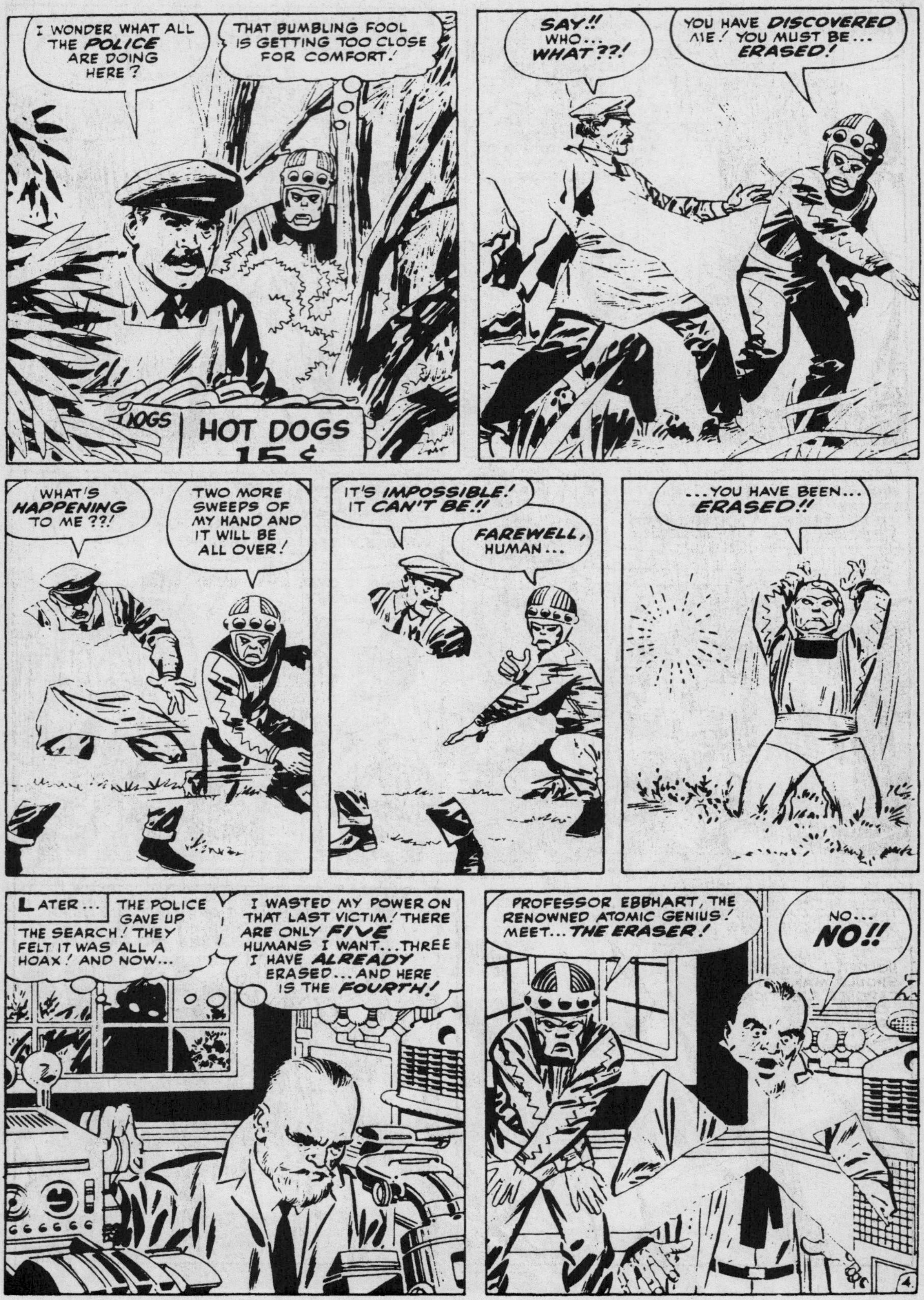
I WONDER WHAT ALL THE POLICE ARE DOING HERE?
THAT BUMBLING FOOL IS GETTING TOO CLOSE FOR COMFORT!
HOT DOGS 15¢
SAY!! WHO... WHAT??!
YOU HAVE DISCOVERED ME! YOU MUST BE... ERASED!
WHAT'S HAPPENING TO ME??!
TWO MORE SWEEPS OF MY HAND AND IT WILL BE ALL OVER!
IT'S IMPOSSIBLE! IT CAN'T BE!!
FAREWELL, HUMAN...
...YOU HAVE BEEN... ERASED!!
LATER... THE POLICE GAVE UP THE SEARCH! THEY FELT IT WAS ALL A HOAX! AND NOW...
I WASTED MY POWER ON THAT LAST VICTIM! THERE ARE ONLY FIVE HUMANS I WANT... THREE I HAVE ALREADY ERASED... AND HERE IS THE FOURTH!
PROFESSOR EBBHART, THE RENOWNED ATOMIC GENIUS! MEET... THE ERASER!
NO... NO!!
4

IT IS *DONE!*

I HAVE ERASED TWO MORE ATOMIC EXPERTS...DOCTOR LEWIS STEMM, AND PROFESSOR EBBHART! AND NOW, I SHALL FINISH MY TASK...

THE *LAST* NAME ON MY LIST IS *HENRY PYM*, THE EXPERIMENTAL WIZARD!

WITH A MERE STROKE OF MY HAND, I SHALL ERASE *HIM* AS EASILY AS THE OTHERS!

MEANWHILE, AT THE HOME OF THE UNSUSPECTING HENRY PYM...

STUDY THESE ENLARGEMENTS OF THE VARIOUS SIZE-CHANGE CAPSULES, JAN!

NOTICE THAT EACH SIZE AND COLOR CORRESPONDS TO A DIFFERENT REACTION IN GROWTH OR SHRINKAGE!

ONE INCH   SIX INCHES   ONE FOOT   TWO FEET   FOUR FEE

AW, HANK... WE'VE BEEN OVER IT SO OFTEN THAT I KNOW THEM BY HEART!

WE CAN'T TAKE CHANCES, GIRL! BEING ABLE TO REACH THE RIGHT CAPSULE INSTANTLY MAY SAVE OUR LIVES SOMEDAY!

THIS CARTRIDGE BELT HOLDER I CONSTRUCTED SHOULD MAKE THE CAPSULE EJECTION COMPLETELY FOOLPROOF!

DOES YOUR BELT FIT ALL RIGHT, JAN?

HENRY, YOU'RE THE LOVE OF MY LIFE AND THE APPLE OF MY EYE... BUT, WHAT YOU DON'T KNOW ABOUT LADIES' FASHIONS....!!!

5.

I NEVER *CLAIMED* TO BE A *CHRISTIAN DIOR,* KID! NOW TEST YOUR SHRINKING CAPSULES... ATTAIN A HEIGHT OF ONE INCH... *IMMEDIATELY!*

YES, B'WANA!

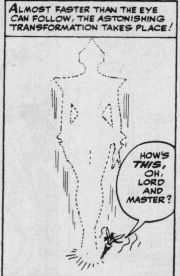

ALMOST FASTER THAN THE EYE CAN FOLLOW, THE ASTONISHING TRANSFORMATION TAKES PLACE!

HOW'S *THIS,* OH, LORD AND MASTER?

PERFECT, WASP! EVEN YOUR *WINGS* SPROUTED AT THE SAME INSTANT THAT YOU SHRUNK!

SO WHERE'S MY *REWARD,* LOVEBUG?

BUT, AT THAT VERY INSTANT, A STRANGE FIGURE ENTERS THE ROOM... MAKES A DRAMATIC GESTURE, AND...

I'VE *COME* FOR YOU, HENRY PYM!

WHA....!!

YOU MOVED *QUICKLY,* HUMAN... BUT FLIGHT IS USELESS! ONE MORE PASS, AND YOU WILL BE *GONE!*

IT CAN'T BE!! I'M ACTUALLY BEING... ERASED!

THEN, A SPLIT-SECOND LATER...

I..I'VE BEEN *TRANSPORTED!* TO ANOTHER WORLD!

NO! TO ANOTHER *DIMENSION!* WELCOME TO DIMENSION "Z", HUMAN!

6.

BUT I DO NOT SEE MY FAITHFUL "ERASER"! AH, HE ARRIVES *NOW*!

MISSION ACCOMPLISHED, YOUR SUPREMACY! THIS IS THE THIRD AND FINAL HUMAN SCIENTIST YOU REQUESTED!

THAT "ERASING"...IT'S REALLY A METHOD OF TRAVELING FROM YOUR DIMENSION TO OURS!

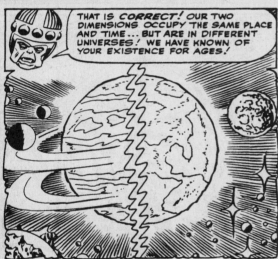

THAT IS *CORRECT*! OUR TWO DIMENSIONS OCCUPY THE SAME PLACE AND TIME...BUT ARE IN DIFFERENT UNIVERSES! WE HAVE KNOWN OF YOUR EXISTENCE FOR AGES!

"ALTHOUGH WE MONITORED YOU FOR CENTURIES, YOU WERE MUCH TOO PRIMITIVE TO BE OF ANY INTEREST TO US! IN FACT, WE WERE *AMUSED* BY YOUR SAVAGE ANTICS!"

"BUT, YEARS LATER, WHEN WE MONITORED THE SAME SPOT, WE WERE OVERWHELMED BY THE *PROGRESS* YOU HAD MADE! FOR WE WITNESSED A TEST OF THE ONE THING WE NEEDED... *ATOMIC POWER*!"

AND SO WE DEVELOPED A METHOD OF TRAVELING FROM OUR DIMENSION TO YOURS...A METHOD KNOWN AS "ERASING"!

ENOUGH TALK! NOW THAT WE HAVE OUR PRISONERS, PUT THEM TO *WORK*! THEY MUST INSTRUCT *OUR* SCIENTISTS ON HOW TO CREATE ATOMIC WEAPONS!

7.

SO THAT YOU CAN INVADE OUR DIMENSION *IN FORCE?!* SO THAT YOU CAN ATTACK US WITH OUR *OWN* WEAPONS? MISTER, YOU GOT YOURSELVES THE *WRONG BOY!!*

THE HUMAN HAS COURAGE...BUT HE IS ALSO FOOLHARDY! SHOW HIM THAT RESISTANCE IS USELESS!

AT ONCE, YOUR SUPREMACY!

ALTHOUGH HENRY PYM STRUGGLES VALIANTLY, HE IS HOPELESSLY OUTNUMBERED AND ATTACKED BY WEAPONS THE LIKE OF WHICH NO HUMAN HAS EVER BEFORE ENCOUNTERED!

NO ONE CAN ELUDE THE CLINGING BANDS!

HANK, OLD BUDDY BOY, IT LOOKS AS THOUGH YOU'RE *REALLY* IN THE SOUP NOW

I--I HEAR *WHISPERING!* WHO *SAID* THAT??

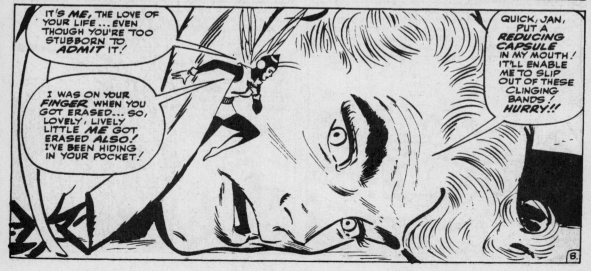

IT'S *ME*, THE LOVE OF YOUR LIFE... EVEN THOUGH YOU'RE TOO STUBBORN TO *ADMIT* IT!

I WAS ON YOUR *FINGER* WHEN YOU GOT ERASED... SO, LOVELY, LIVELY LITTLE *ME* GOT ERASED *ALSO!* I'VE BEEN HIDING IN YOUR POCKET!

QUICK, JAN, PUT A *REDUCING CAPSULE* IN MY MOUTH! IT'LL ENABLE ME TO SLIP OUT OF THESE CLINGING BANDS! *HURRY!!*

8

I THINK THE "TWELVE INCHES TALL" CAPSULE WOULD BE JUST RIGHT FOR YOU, HANK! OR WOULD YOU RATHER BE A *DIFFERENT* SIZE? HOW ABOUT....?

FOR PETE'S SAKE, *DROP* THAT BLAMED THING, AND *STOP* YAPPING!!

HMMPH! NEXT TIME I'LL LET YOU *STAY* TIED UP, YOU BIG OL' *GROUCH!*

ONE BILLION FEMALES IN THE WORLD, AND *I* HAD TO PICK THAT EXQUISITE EMPTY-HEAD FOR A PARTNER!

THE PRISONER IS *GONE!!*

LOOK! HE HAS BECOME ONLY A FOOT TALL!

I TOOK THEM BY *SURPRISE!* SO FAR, SO GOOD!

STOP, HIM!

HE *MUST NOT GET AWAY!!!*

HE MOVES TOO *FAST!!*

GRAB HIM!!

AS THE "DIMENSION Z" MEN CLOSE IN, THE WASP USES HER OWN DIVERSIONARY TACTICS..

NYAH! NYAH! YOU CAN'T CATCH ME!

WHAT IS *THAT?!*

YOUR FLIGHT IS IN VAIN, HUMAN! OUR *HUNTER HOUND* WILL CATCH YOU, NO MATTER *WHERE* YOU RUN!

I'VE GOT TO *SLIP OUT* OF THESE DUDS AND REACH MY *BELT-CAPSULE* CONTAINERS!

9.

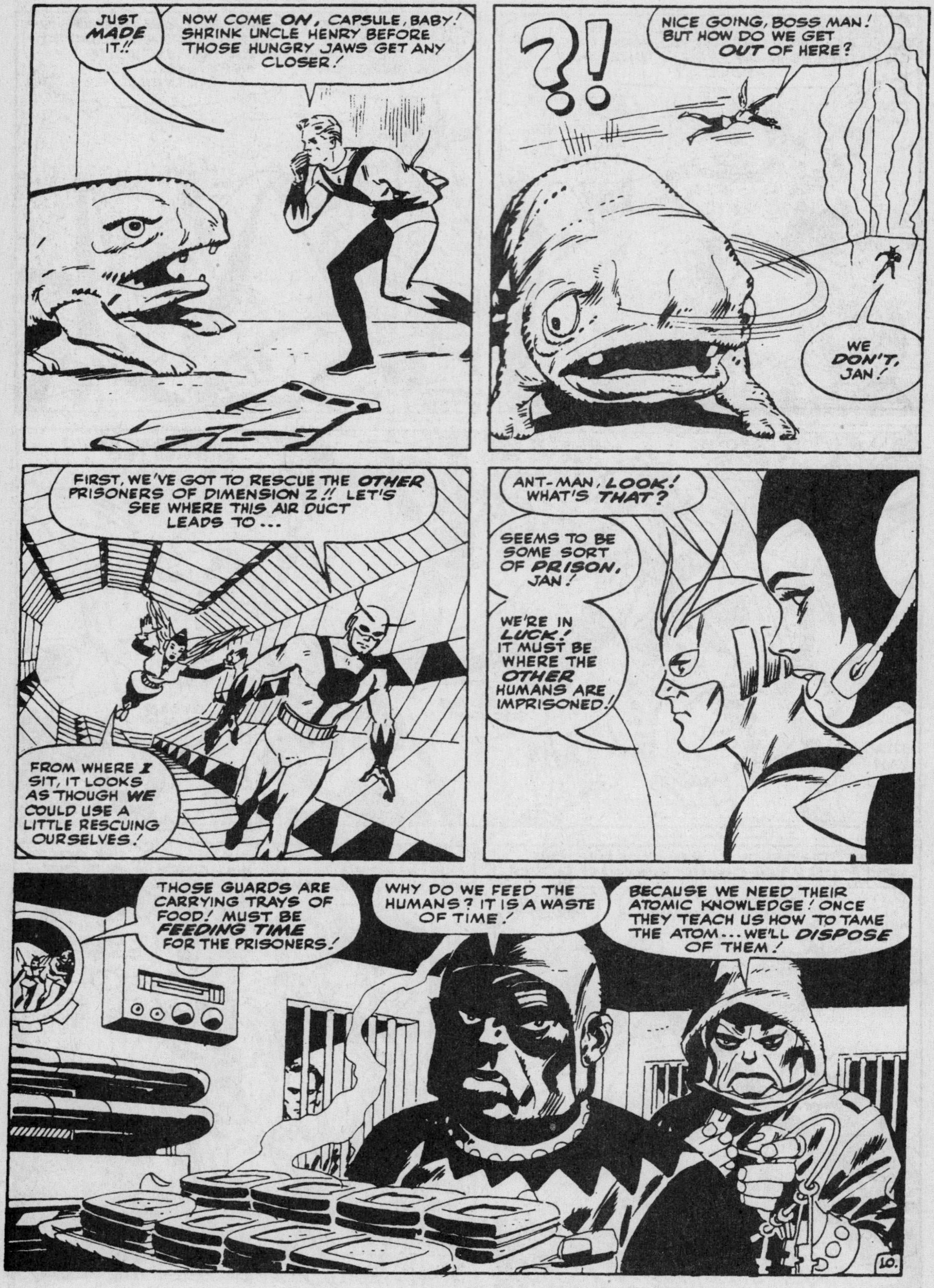

JUST MADE IT!!
NOW COME ON, CAPSULE, BABY! SHRINK UNCLE HENRY BEFORE THOSE HUNGRY JAWS GET ANY CLOSER!
?!
NICE GOING, BOSS MAN! BUT HOW DO WE GET OUT OF HERE?
WE DON'T, JAN!
FIRST, WE'VE GOT TO RESCUE THE OTHER PRISONERS OF DIMENSION Z!! LET'S SEE WHERE THIS AIR DUCT LEADS TO...
FROM WHERE I SIT, IT LOOKS AS THOUGH WE COULD USE A LITTLE RESCUING OURSELVES!
ANT-MAN, LOOK! WHAT'S THAT?
SEEMS TO BE SOME SORT OF PRISON, JAN!
WE'RE IN LUCK! IT MUST BE WHERE THE OTHER HUMANS ARE IMPRISONED!
THOSE GUARDS ARE CARRYING TRAYS OF FOOD! MUST BE FEEDING TIME FOR THE PRISONERS!
WHY DO WE FEED THE HUMANS? IT IS A WASTE OF TIME!
BECAUSE WE NEED THEIR ATOMIC KNOWLEDGE! ONCE THEY TEACH US HOW TO TAME THE ATOM... WE'LL DISPOSE OF THEM!
10.

MINUTES LATER...

DO NOT BE IMPATIENT! SOON YOU WILL BE TAKEN TO OUR SCIENCE LABORATORY!

A LOT OF GOOD I'LL DO YOUR SCIENTISTS!

YOU CAN'T KEEP US HERE THIS WAY!

RELAX, PROFESSOR! THEY CAN AND THEY KNOW IT!

THE GUARDS ARE LEAVING! NOW'S OUR CHANCE!

OUR CHANCE FOR WHAT?

I'LL EXPLAIN AS WE GO! SEE THAT SMALL ELECTRONIC DEVICE ON THE CEILING? DISMANTLE IT!!

WHAT A BOSSY HUSBAND YOU'D MAKE!

IT'S SOME SORT OF SCANNING DEVICE! THEY MUST KEEP TABS ON THEIR PRISONERS THIS WAY!

R-RIP!

BUT NOT ANY LONGER! I DISCONNECTED THE WHOSIS FROM THE WHATCHAMACALLIT!

GOOD GIRL! NOW I'LL TAKE MY GROWTH CAPSULE!

LOOK! WE - WE HAVE A NEW GUEST!

LISTEN, QUICKLY, GENTLEMEN! WE HAVEN'T MUCH TIME...I'M HERE TO HELP YOU!

HE'S GROWING BEFORE OUR EYES!

11

HURRY, HANDSOME! THE *GUARDS* HAVE BEEN ALERTED!

LOOK! I'M GOING TO FIND A WAY *OUT* OF THIS DIMENSION... THEN I'LL RETURN FOR YOU! MEANTIME, STALL THEM ALL YOU CAN!

A TINY FLYING GIRL! I'M GOIN' *NUTS!*

OUR SCANNING DEVICE IS NOT WORKING!

GUARDS! TO THE PRISON! QUICK!!

IF ANY PRISONERS HAVE ESCAPED, THESE SUPER-SENSITIVE SEARCH-BEAM GUNS WILL FIND THEM!

GOOD THING YOU SHRUNK DOWN AGAIN, HANK! WE'RE *TOO SMALL* FOR THEIR SEARCH-BEAMS TO PICK UP!

YOU *STAY* THIS SIZE, JAN! IT'LL BE SAFER FOR YOU! AS FOR *ME*... WHAT MUST BE DONE *NOW* CAN ONLY BE DONE BY *ONE PERSON*...

WHAT DO YOU MEAN?

I MEAN... IT'S TIME FOR OUR LITTLE FRIENDS TO MEET... *GIANT-MAN!!*

LOOK!! ANOTHER HUMAN!

GET HIM!

12.

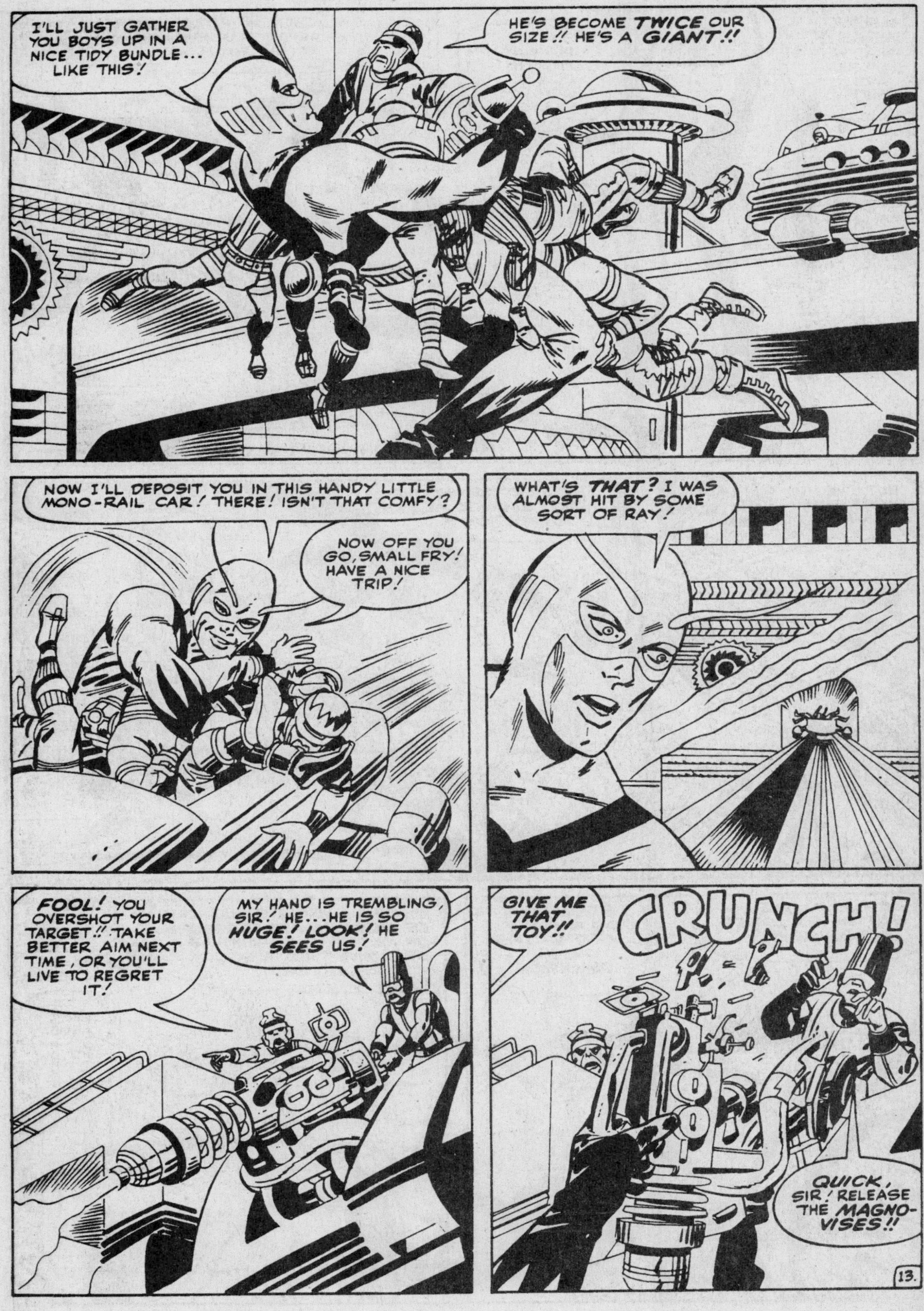

I'LL JUST GATHER YOU BOYS UP IN A NICE TIDY BUNDLE... LIKE THIS!
HE'S BECOME TWICE OUR SIZE!! HE'S A GIANT!!
NOW I'LL DEPOSIT YOU IN THIS HANDY LITTLE MONO-RAIL CAR! THERE! ISN'T THAT COMFY?
NOW OFF YOU GO, SMALL FRY! HAVE A NICE TRIP!
WHAT'S THAT? I WAS ALMOST HIT BY SOME SORT OF RAY!
FOOL! YOU OVERSHOT YOUR TARGET!! TAKE BETTER AIM NEXT TIME, OR YOU'LL LIVE TO REGRET IT!
MY HAND IS TREMBLING, SIR! HE...HE IS SO HUGE! LOOK! HE SEES US!
GIVE ME THAT TOY!!
CRUNCH!
QUICK, SIR! RELEASE THE MAGNO-VISES!!
13.

MAGNO-VISES?? WHAT IN SAM HILL ARE THEY?

UH OH! DOWN BELOW... COMING TOWARDS MY LEGS...!!

LUCKILY, MY REFLEXES ARE SHARPER THAN EVER WHEN I ATTAIN GIANT SIZE!

BUT I'VE NO MORE TIME TO WASTE!

I'VE GOT TO FIND THE WAY BACK TO MY OWN DIMENSION!

LOOK.!! OUTSIDE OUR BALCONY... A GIANT.!!

LET HIM GO! OUR SENTRY PLANES WILL GET HIM WHEN HE REACHES THE ROOF!

SO FAR, ALL I'VE GOTTEN IS A LOT OF EXERCISE!!

I STILL CAN'T FIND A WAY OUT OF THIS ALIEN DIMENSION!

UH OH!! A WHOLE SQUADRON OF PLANES ARE ZEROED IN ON ME! WELL, I MIGHT AS WELL GIVE THEM A GOOD RECEPTION!

14

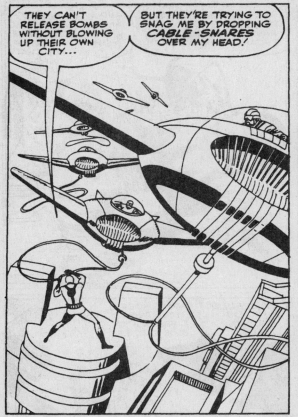

THEY CAN'T RELEASE BOMBS WITHOUT BLOWING UP THEIR OWN CITY...

BUT THEY'RE TRYING TO SNAG ME BY DROPPING *CABLE-SNARES* OVER MY HEAD!

BUT HERE'S WHERE OL' *GIANT-MAN* TURNS THE TABLES ON HIS WEE PLAYMATES!

I'LL BE DARNED IF THIS DOESN'T FEEL LIKE A SCENE RIGHT OUT OF *KING KONG!!*

THERE WE ARE! YOU GUYS HANG AROUND AND TALK THINGS OVER FOR A WHILE! AT LEAST IT'LL KEEP YOU OUT OF THE POOLROOM!

GIANT-MAN! WHILE *YOU'VE* BEEN KIDDING AROUND UP HERE, *I'VE* LOCATED THE CHIEF SCIENTIST OF THIS WHOLE DIMENSION! *HE'S* THE ONE WHO'D KNOW HOW WE CAN ESCAPE!

GOOD GIRL! WHERE *IS* HE?

LOWER YOUR VOICE, BIG MAN!! YOU'LL *DEAFEN* ME!

15.

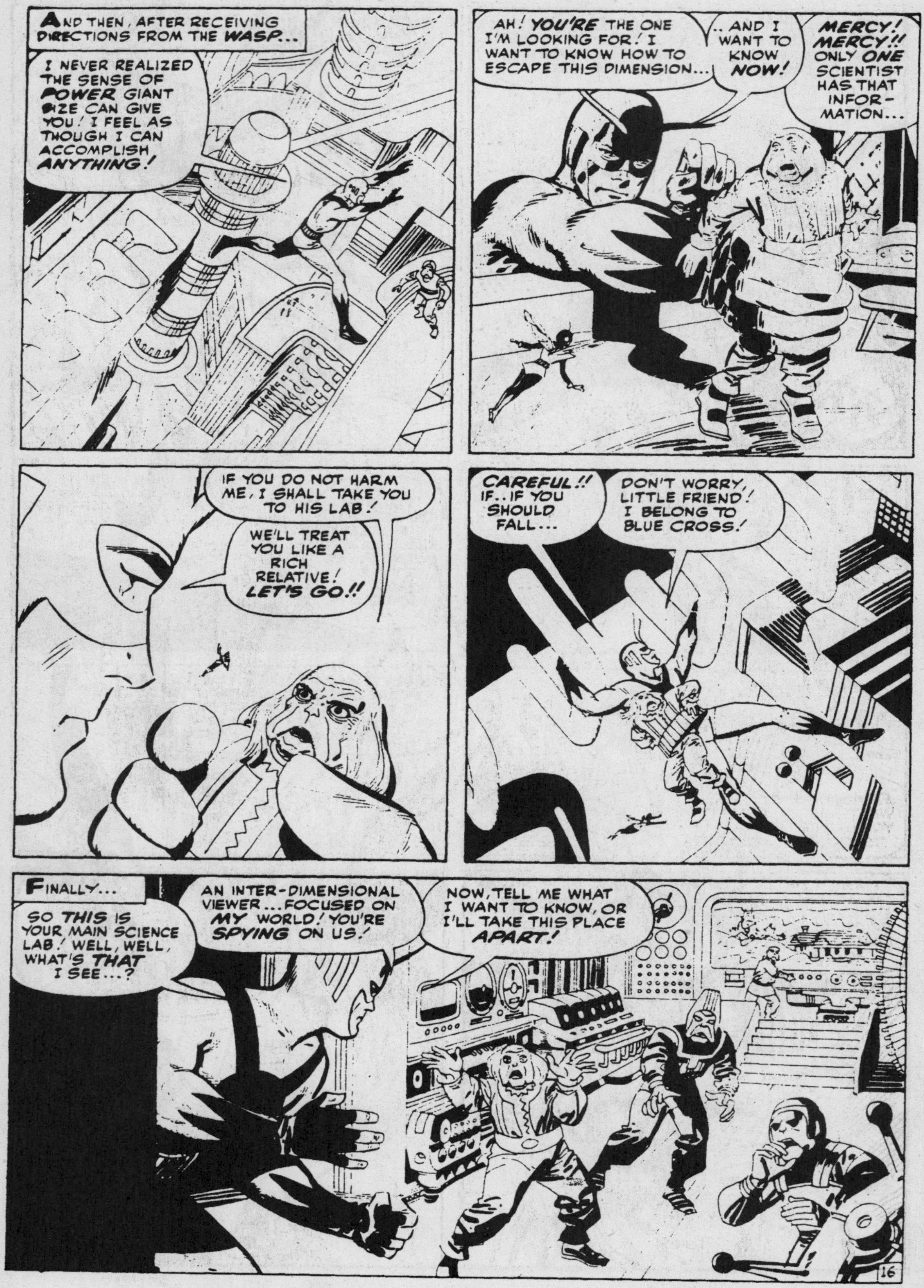
AND THEN, AFTER RECEIVING DIRECTIONS FROM THE WASP...
I NEVER REALIZED THE SENSE OF POWER GIANT SIZE CAN GIVE YOU! I FEEL AS THOUGH I CAN ACCOMPLISH ANYTHING!
AH! YOU'RE THE ONE I'M LOOKING FOR! I WANT TO KNOW HOW TO ESCAPE THIS DIMENSION...
..AND I WANT TO KNOW NOW!
MERCY! MERCY!! ONLY ONE SCIENTIST HAS THAT INFORMATION...
IF YOU DO NOT HARM ME, I SHALL TAKE YOU TO HIS LAB!
WE'LL TREAT YOU LIKE A RICH RELATIVE! LET'S GO!!
CAREFUL!! IF.. IF YOU SHOULD FALL...
DON'T WORRY, LITTLE FRIEND! I BELONG TO BLUE CROSS!
FINALLY...
SO THIS IS YOUR MAIN SCIENCE LAB! WELL, WELL, WHAT'S THAT I SEE...?
AN INTER-DIMENSIONAL VIEWER...FOCUSED ON MY WORLD! YOU'RE SPYING ON US!
NOW, TELL ME WHAT I WANT TO KNOW, OR I'LL TAKE THIS PLACE APART!
16

THE ONE YOU SEEK HAS NOT ARRIVED YET! YOU MUST WAIT... HE WILL BE HERE WITHIN MINUTES!

I DON'T LIKE THAT LOOK IN YOUR EYE! YOU'RE *UP* TO SOMETHING!

NO, NOT *I*! IT IS THE *OTHER*! THE ONE WHO HAS SILENTLY ENTERED *BEHIND* YOU!

AN UNBREAKABLE *GLASS CAGE*! IT DROPPED FROM ABOVE! I WAS TOO OVER-CONFIDENT!

ERASER! YOU ARE JUST IN TIME!

I AM THE ONLY ONE WHO KNOWS HOW TO TRAVEL BETWEEN DIMENSIONS! BUT THAT KNOWLEDGE SHALL *NEVER* BE SHARED WITH ANOTHER!

I MIGHT HAVE KNOWN... IT'S *THE ERASER*!! BUT *HE'S* GOT THE UPPER HAND RIGHT NOW!

ERASER! WHAT ARE YOU GOING TO DO ??

FIRST, I SHALL DISPOSE OF MY WEAKLING FELLOW SCIENTIST! *THIS* IS THE PRICE YOU PAY FOR LEADING GIANT-MAN *HERE*!

AND NOW, HUMAN ...I KNOW NOT HOW *YOU* ENTERED *DIMENSION Z*, BUT YOU SHALL NEVER *LEAVE* IT ALIVE!

ONLY THE ONE WHO WEARS THIS ATOMICALLY-PRINTED CIRCUIT ON THE PALM OF HIS HAND CAN TRAVEL BACK TO YOUR DIMENSION! IT IS THE ONLY ONE IN EXISTENCE, AND NONE BUT *I* EVER WEAR IT!

17.

DON'T **BET** ON THAT, LAUGHING BOY! AS SOON AS I GET THAT GLASS CAGE RAISED, THERE'LL BE A FEW **CHANGES** MADE AROUND HERE!

THE WASP!! AT LAST!

ALL RIGHT, MISTER... HERE'S WHERE WE SEPARATE THE MEN FROM THE BOYS!

OOOF!!

I'LL JUST BORROW THIS LITTLE CIRCUIT OF YOURS BEFORE I PUT YOU INTO DREAMLAND!

BETTER TURN **ANT-SIZED** AGAIN! IT'LL BE EASIER TO TRAVEL UNSEEN!

AND SO...

YOU WERE **RIGHT**, JAN! NONE OF THE GUARDS EVEN **SAW** US!

THIS IS THE PART I DON'T LIKE! I **MISS** IT WHEN MEN DON'T WHISTLE AT ME!

HOLD STILL, GENTS! THIS'LL ONLY TAKE A MINUTE!

LOOK! WE'RE BEING **ERASED** AGAIN!

WE'RE RETURNING TO OUR OWN DIMENSION! WE'RE **SAVED!!**

AND NOW FOR **US**, JAN! HERE, I'VE LEARNED HOW TO DO TWO AT A TIME!

THIS IS SILLY... AT A DRAMATIC MOMENT LIKE THIS, ALL I CAN THINK OF IS... IT **TICKLES!**

AND, FINALLY...

Y'KNOW, DREAMBOAT, THERE'S ALWAYS **SO** MUCH TO READ IN THE PAPERS WHEN **YOU'RE** AROUND!

NOW THAT **GIANT-MAN** HAS COME INTO BEING, THEY'D BETTER START PRINTING MORE EDITIONS, MY PRETTY LITTLE PEST!

WAIT TILL YOU SEE **GIANT-MAN** NEXT ISSUE!!

Nation Wonders: "WHO IS GIANT-MAN?"

DAILY NEWS

MISSING SCIENTISTS FOUND!

13.

The End

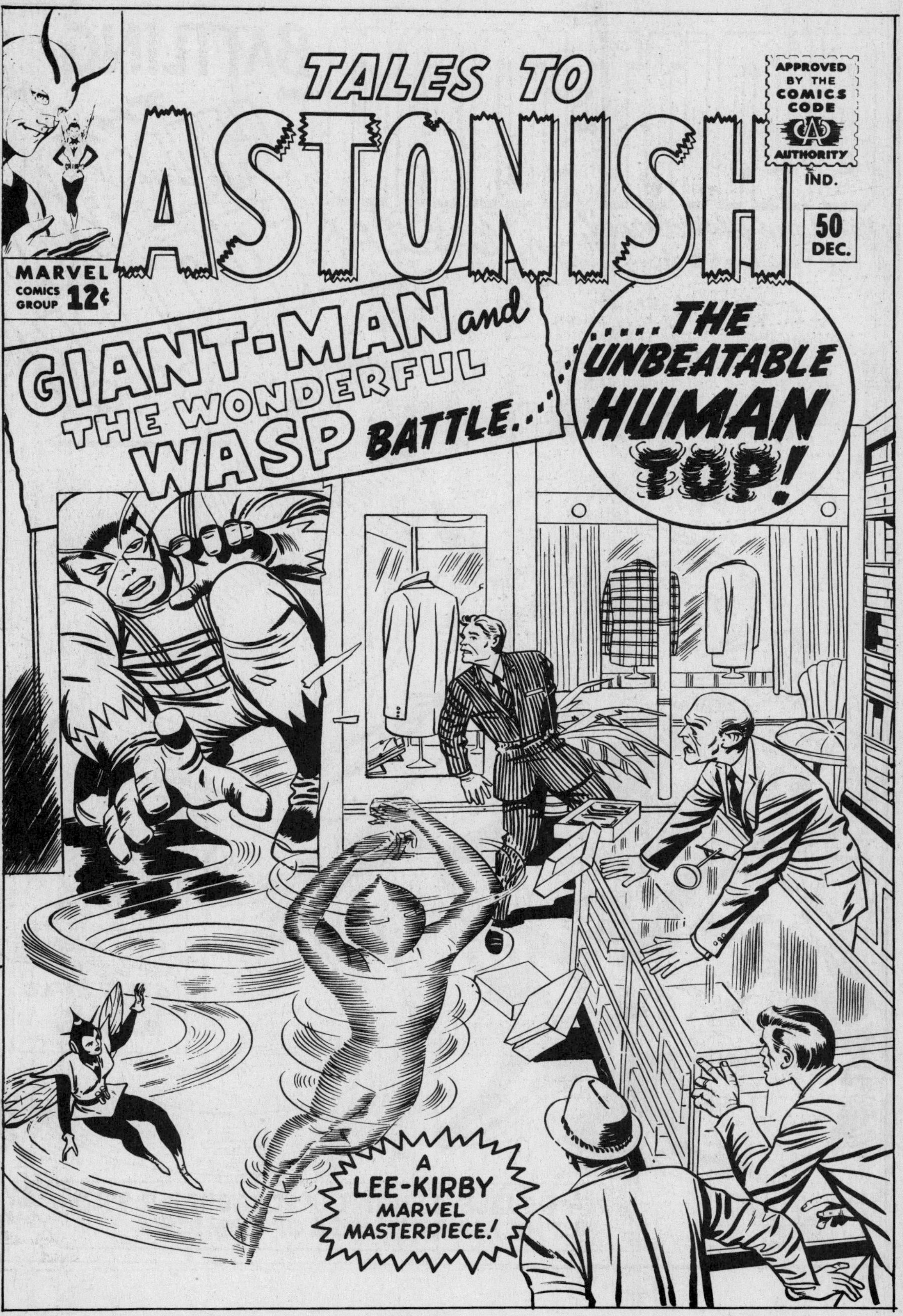
TALES TO ASTONISH
APPROVED BY THE COMICS CODE AUTHORITY
IND.
50 DEC.
MARVEL COMICS GROUP 12¢
GIANT-MAN and THE WONDERFUL WASP BATTLE...
.....THE UNBEATABLE HUMAN TOP!
A LEE-KIRBY MARVEL MASTERPIECE!

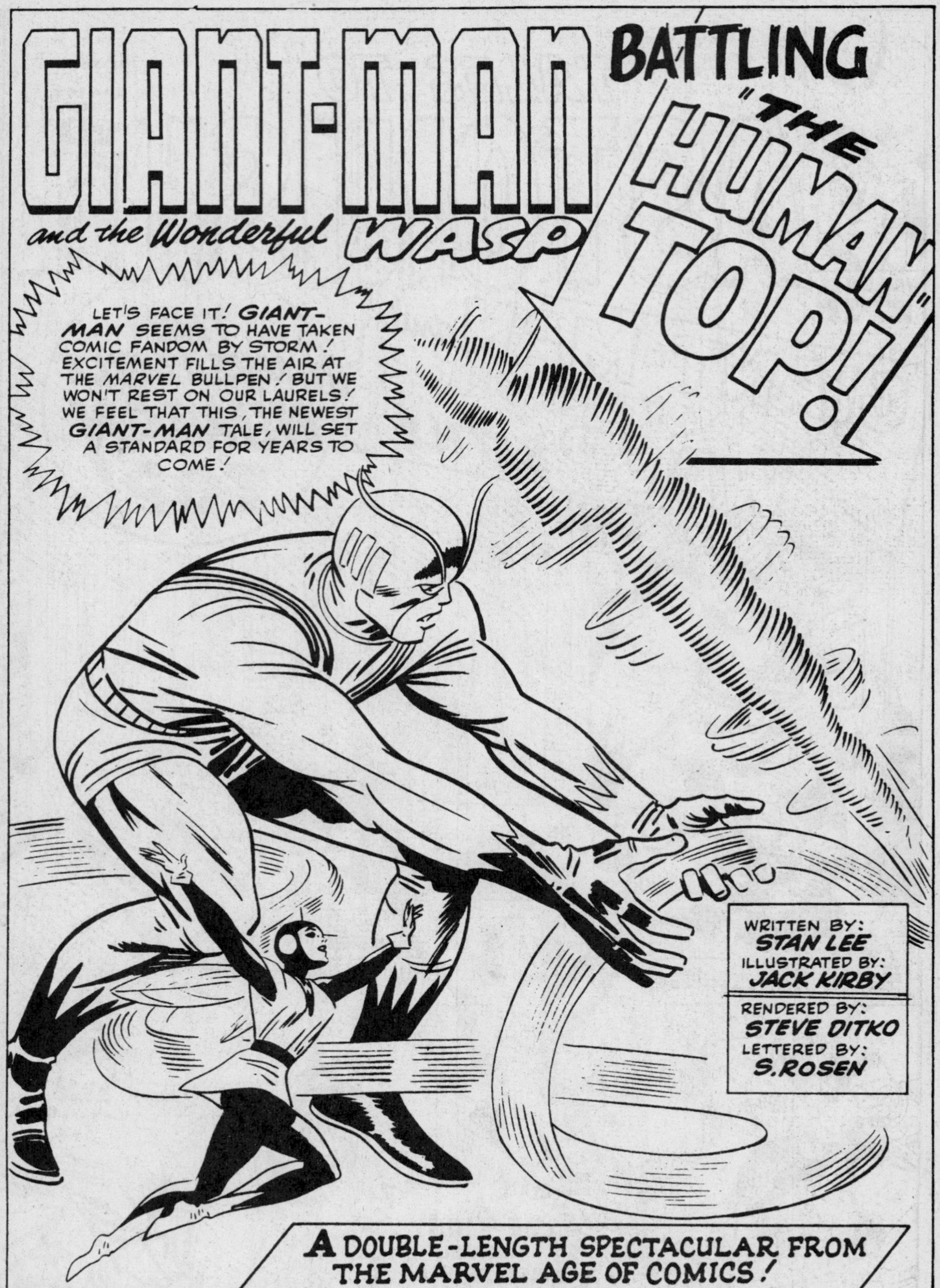
GIANT-MAN
and the Wonderful WASP
BATTLING
"THE HUMAN TOP!"
LET'S FACE IT! GIANT-MAN SEEMS TO HAVE TAKEN COMIC FANDOM BY STORM! EXCITEMENT FILLS THE AIR AT THE MARVEL BULLPEN! BUT WE WON'T REST ON OUR LAURELS! WE FEEL THAT THIS, THE NEWEST GIANT-MAN TALE, WILL SET A STANDARD FOR YEARS TO COME!
WRITTEN BY: STAN LEE
ILLUSTRATED BY: JACK KIRBY
RENDERED BY: STEVE DITKO
LETTERED BY: S.ROSEN
A DOUBLE-LENGTH SPECTACULAR FROM THE MARVEL AGE OF COMICS!

IN EVERY CENTURY, SOME HUMANS ARE BORN WITH FANTASTIC TALENTS! ONE PRIME EXAMPLE IS *DAVE CANNON*, WHOSE AMAZING ABILITY TO WHIRL AROUND AT GREAT SPEED IS THE BASIS FOR OUR ASTONISHING TALE *!*

WOWIE! NOBODY CAN DO WHAT *DAVEY* CAN!

YEAH! TOO BAD A GUY WITH HIS TALENT HAS TO BE SUCH A ROTTEN *BULLY*!

THOUGHT I COULDN'T *HEAR* YA WHILE I WAS SPINNIN' AROUND, HEH? JUST FOR THAT, I'M CHARGIN' YOU *DOUBLE* FOR THE SHOW!

SURE, DAVEY... SURE! I'LL PAY! HONEST!

DAVEY'S SO *FAST* NOBODY *DARES* TO FIGHT HIM!

ALAS, UNFORTUNATELY FOR THE NEIGHBORHOOD KIDS, AND FOR THE WORLD AT LARGE, FATE HAD SEEN FIT TO BESTOW A RARE GIFT ON ONE WHO WAS NOT DESERVING OF IT!

GET HIM! HE SWIPED MY FRUIT!

NO ONE CAN CATCH ME!

BUT, ALTHOUGH HE ACHIEVED INCREDIBLE SPEED BY WHIRLING LIKE A TOP, DAVE CANNON WAS STILL YOUNG, AND NO MATCH FOR THE FORCES OF LAW!

WE WERE *READY* FOR YOU THIS TIME, SON!

OKAY, YOU WIN! I'LL *PAY* FOR THE FRUIT!

AS THE YEARS ROLLED BY, DAVE CANNON USED HIS SUPER-HUMAN SPINNING ABILITY IN EVERY WAY HE COULD! HE BECAME A CIRCUS PERFORMER, PROFESSIONAL WRESTLER, AND THEN HE FOUND A MORE LUCRATIVE SOURCE OF INCOME...

BAM!

...GET SET... GO!!

HEY! WHAT GIVES?? LOOK AT THAT GUY CANNON *MOVE*! NOBODY CAN SKATE *THAT* FAST!

HE CAME IN *LAST* DURING ALL THE *OTHER* RACES, JUST TO BRING THE BETTING ODDS UP!

THE BETTING SYNDICATE WILL PAY ME A REAL *BUNDLE* FOR THIS CAPER!

2.

AND, AFTER THE RACE...

NICE WORK, CANNON! HERE'S YOUR CUT! NOW YOU BETTER LEAVE TOWN BEFORE THEY START INVESTIGATIN' YOU!

WHAT FOR? I'M NOT SCARED OF ANY—THING!

SUIT YOURSELF, SONNY! BUT, REMEMBER, GOOD AS YOU ARE, THE COPS ARE A LOT BETTER!

GOOD AS I AM, EH? THE FOOLS! THEY HAVE NO IDEA HOW GOOD I *REALLY* AM!

WELL, I REALIZE NOW THAT I DON'T *NEED* THEM ANYMORE! I DON'T NEED *ANYONE!* I'VE GOT THE TALENT TO DO WHATEVER I WANT TO DO... *ALONE!*

AND, UNFORTUNATELY FOR THE GOOD OF MANKIND, THE THINGS DAVE CANNON "WANTED" TO DO WITH HIS GREAT TALENT WERE THESE...

1959 BURGLAR SPINS WAY TO FREEDOM! AMAZING ACCOUNT OF NEW!!!!

1961 POLICE DRAGNET FAILS TO STOP SPINNING ROBBER!

1960 SPINNING CRIMINAL IN NEW FANTASTIC ROBBERY

1962 WHIRLING FELON STRIKES AGAIN! STILL AT LARGE!

THE ENTIRE CITY FOLLOWED CANNON'S CRIME CAREER WITH INTEREST, INCLUDING ONE *HENRY PYM!*

"HUMAN TOP," EH? WONDER WHO HE REALLY IS!?

JUST A CHEAP CROOK! NO NEED FOR GIANT-MAN TO TACKLE HIM!

STAR-BULLETIN

HUMAN TOP

NAMED AS PUBLIC ENEMY NUMBER ONE BY AUTHORITIES!

NO ONE KNOWS HIS TRUE IDENTITY!

EVEN HENRY PYM DOESN'T REALIZE HOW DANGEROUS THE HUMAN TOP WILL BE, AS HE MAKES A ROUTINE CALL...

HELLO, JAN! JUST WANT TO REMIND YOU WE HAVE A BRIEFING SESSION IN AN HOUR!

REMIND ME?? SILLY BOY! I'VE BEEN AT THE BEAUTY PARLOR ALL DAY, PREPARING FOR THE EVENT!

FOR PETE'S SAKE, GIRL! HOW MANY TIMES MUST I TELL YOU OUR MEETINGS ARE STRICTLY *BUSINESS?!* YOU DON'T HAVE TO GET PRETTIED-UP FIRST!

OH, *DON'T I?* IF HE THINKS I BECAME THE *WASP* BECAUSE I LIKE TO CHASE CRIMINALS, HE'S *MAAAD!!*

HE MAY GO FOR ALL THAT ADVENTURE JAZZ, BUT *I* GO FOR BIG, WONDERFUL, DREAMY *HIM!*

3.

IF ONLY HANK COULD SEE ME AS A *GIRL*, INSTEAD OF A COSTUMED CRIME-FIGHTER!

WHAT'S *HE* LOOKING AT?? *OMIGOSH!* I FORGOT TO SHRINK TO WASP SIZE!!

BETTER TAKE MY REDUCING CAPSULE *NOW!* BEFORE HIS EYES BUG RIGHT OUT OF HIS HEAD!

IS SOMETHING WRONG, SIR?

ULP! THIS IS NO TIME FOR QUESTIONS! WHERE'S THE NEAREST *EYE DOCTOR?*

HERE I *AM*, HANDSOME! WHERE'S THE BRASS BAND? AND YOU'D BETTER NOTICE THE NEW *PERFUME* I'M WEARING!

DARN! I JUST REMEMBERED! HE CAN HARDLY *HEAR* ME WHEN I'M WASP-SIZED! TIME FOR MY *ENLARGING* CAPSULE AGAIN!... I'M BEGINNING TO FEEL LIKE AN *ELEVATOR!*

HAVE NO FEAR, *DREAMBOAT!* THE *WASP* IS HERE!

JUST IN TIME, JAN! I WAS JUST ABOUT TO BECOME *GIANT-MAN!*

WHEN ARE YOU GOING TO REALIZE THAT THOSE SILLY SIZE-PILLS ARE NO SUBSTITUTE FOR MOONLIGHT AND ROSES, HANK?

AS SOON AS *YOU* REALIZE THERE'S A TIME AND PLACE FOR EVERYTHING, YOUNG LADY!

OH, SO YOU *DO* KNOW THAT I'M A YOUNG LADY! THEN THINGS AREN'T COMPLETELY HOPELESS!!

YOU'LL HAVE TO TALK *LOUDER*, SHORTY!

Y'KNOW, SCATTER-BRAIN, YOU *ARE* KIND OF CUTE AT THAT! FOR A MIDGET, THAT IS!

HENRY PYM, YOU PUT ME DOWN THIS *MINUTE!* YOU...YOU *SHOW-OFF* YOU *!!*

HOLD IT, KID! A MESSAGE IS COMING THROUGH FROM THE *ANTS*, ON OUR THOUGHT-WAVE COMMUNICATOR! LET'S SEE IF WE CAN INTERPRET IT!

IF ONLY THOSE SILLY ANTS COULD *SPEAK*, YOU WOULDN'T HAVE TO TRY READING THEIR THOUGHTS!

QUIET, JAN! LOOK...A SPINNING TOP, WITH HUMAN FEATURES!

THE CITY'S LARGEST DEPARTMENT STORE...WITH AN ACCENT ON MONEY!

Danly's DEPARTMENT STORE

NOW I GET IT! SOMEHOW, ONE OF OUR SNOOPER ANTS SENSED THE *HUMAN TOP* PLANNING TO ROB DANLY'S TOMORROW MORNING AT TEN A.M.! BUT WHY WOULD THEY NOTIFY *ME* OF SUCH A ROUTINE CRIME?

AUG. 4.

A.M.

I THINK I LIKE YOU BETTER AS *ANT-MAN!* SINCE YOU BECAME GIANT-SIZE, YOU THINK YOU'RE TOO GOOD FOR ANYONE OR ANY-THING *!!*

MAYBE YOU'RE RIGHT, JAN! WAIT! I'LL GET BACK TO NORMAL AND WE'LL TALK IT OVER *!!*

IF I SEEM TO BE GETTING TOO SWELL-HEADED, I'M SORRY, HONEY! AND I'M GRATEFUL TO YOU FOR BRINGING ME BACK TO EARTH!

YOU MAY BE BACK TO EARTH...BUT WHEN YOU CALL ME "HONEY" LIKE THAT, *I'M* ON CLOUD NINE!

5.

MEANWHILE, DAVE CANNON REHEARSES FOR THE OPENING OF THE NEW ICE SHOW, WITH NO ONE SUSPECTING THAT HE IS THE NOTORIOUS *HUMAN TOP!*

MUSTN'T SPIN *TOO* FAST! DON'T WANT ANYONE PUTTING TWO AND TWO TOGETHER AND GUESSING MY LITTLE SECRET!

ALL RIGHT, CANNON! YOU LOOKED PRETTY SHARP THERE! YOU CAN KNOCK OFF TILL NEXT REHEARSAL!

I SURE WILL! I'LL KNOCK OFF DANLY'S DEPARTMENT STORE!

EARLY THE NEXT MORNING, AT HIS LAVISH MIDTOWN APARTMENT...

I CAN'T AFFORD AN EXPENSIVE PAD LIKE THIS ON AN ICE SKATER'S CRUMMY SALARY!

BUT, LUCKILY, I HAVE ANOTHER, MORE UNUSUAL SOURCE OF INCOME!

IT'S ALMOST TIME FOR THE PAYROLL TO BE DELIVERED TO DANLY'S!

BUT *THIS* TIME THE *HUMAN TOP* WILL BE ON HAND, TO HELP THEM WITH HIS OWN LITTLE PROFIT-SHARING PLAN!

AND, ON DANLY'S MAIN FLOOR, A NEW "SALES CLERK" GOES THROUGH HIS PACES...

WHEN THE *HUMAN TOP* SHOWS UP, THE WASP AND I WILL BE READY FOR HIM!

AND THEN, AT THE ENTRANCE TO THE SPRAWLING STORE...

HURRY IT UP, SAM! I'VE GOT A DATE TONIGHT!

RELAX! WE'LL BE OUTTA HERE IN NO TIME!

THAT'S RIGHT! NO ONE'S GONNA MESS AROUND WITH THREE ARMED PAYROLL GUARDS!

6.

BUT THEN, LIKE A BOLT FROM THE BLUE...

HOLY COW! WHAT'S *THAT*?

IT..IT'S THE *HUMAN TOP*!!

THAT PAYROLL BAG LOOKS AWFULLY HEAVY FOR YOU THREE GUYS! LET ME GIVE YOU A HAND WITH IT...OR SHOULD I SAY, A *FOOT*?

HELP!! THE STORE IS *HAUNTED*!

REALLY? THEN I'D BETTER GET OUT OF HERE, FAST! I'M *TERRIFIED* OF GHOSTS!

SO *THAT'S* THE BIG, BAD HUMAN TOP! WELL, I'VE TACKLED LOTS WORSE THAN *HIM* IN MY TIME!

S-SOMEBODY *DO* SOMETHING!

I HEAR YA TALKIN'! SO STEP ASIDE, LITTLE FRIEND!

YIPE!! AND TO THINK I BECAME A FLOOR-WALKER BECAUSE I THOUGHT IT WAS A NICE, QUIET, SAFE OCCUPATION!

OH, *NO*!! STILL *ANOTHER* ONE! IT'S LIKE CONTEST TIME AT THE MARDI GRAS!

WAIT FOR *ME*, LOVER BOY!

WELL, WELL! IT SEEMS THAT I'VE GOT COMPANY! *GIANT-MAN*! AND THE *WASP*! I'VE *HEARD* OF THEM!

BUT I'LL MAKE THEM WISH THAT THEY HAD NEVER HEARD OF *ME*!

7.

GIANT-MAN! LOOK OUT FOR THE TRAFFIC!

HAH! YOUR HUGE UNGAINLY SIZE IS NOTHING BUT A HANDICAP TO YOU!

STAY BACK!

HEY! WATCH WHERE YOU'RE GOING, MAC!!

YEAH! GET BACK TO THE FREAK SHOW WHERE YOU BELONG!

CAREFUL! YOU'LL CAUSE A TRAFFIC ACCIDENT IF YOU DON'T WATCH OUT!

I'M NO HELP TO HIM THIS WAY! I'VE GOT TO SHRINK TO WASP-SIZE!

IF I CAN BEAT GIANT-MAN, I CAN BEAT ANYBODY! AND HE HASN'T A CHANCE AGAINST ME!

I'VE GOT TO HELP HANK CATCH HIM! WAIT! I CAN CONTACT HIS LOYAL ANTS THROUGH MY SPECIAL HELMET! IT'S WORTH A TRY!

A FEW SECONDS LATER...

ATTENTION, LITTLE FRIENDS! YOU MUST QUICKLY CHEW THROUGH THE PAVEMENT, SOFTENING IT! THE ANT-MAN COMMANDS!!

I'LL REST HERE FOR A WHILE AND TAUNT GIANT-MAN!

WELL, LOOKY HERE! YOU FINALLY CAUGHT UP TO ME! NOW I KNOW YOUR STRATEGY... YOU'RE WAITING FOR ME TO DIE OF OLD AGE!

I'LL GET YOU YET, LITTLE MAN!

SOME JOKE! YOU COULDN'T EVEN CATCH A COLD! IN FACT...

HEY! WHAT HAPPENED TO THIS PAVEMENT? I'VE LOST MY BALANCE!!

S'MATTER, BIG BRAIN? YOU NEVER SUSPECTED THAT ENOUGH OBEDIENT ANTS COULD SOFTEN A CONCRETE SIDEWALK'S CRUST??

8.

OBEDIENT *ANTS?* NEXT YOU'LL BE SAYIN' YOU'VE GOT *GREMLINS* WORKING FOR YOU, *TOO!*

BAH! I'LL *STILL* BE GONE BEFORE *YOU* CAN REACH ME!

GUESS AGAIN, LOUD-MOUTH! I'VE GOT YOU NOW... YEEOPP!!

S'MATTER, BIG BRAIN? YOU NEVER SUSPECTED THAT A GUY WHO CAN SPIN AS FAST AS I, CAN ALSO *ROLL* OUT OF DANGER *JUST* AS FAST??!

I'LL *GET* YOU IF IT'S THE *LAST*... OWW!!

AREN'T YOU *EMBARRASSED,* YOU CLUMSY APE?? YOU'RE MAKING A FOOL OF YOURSELF IN FRONT OF THE WHOLE *CITY!*

HE'S *RIGHT!* IF I DON'T *GET* HIM, I'LL BE A *LAUGHING STOCK!* GOT TO TRY AGAIN!!

HOLY SMOKE! I CAN STAND HOWLING ALLEY CATS, OR NOISY GARBAGE COLLECTORS, BUT *THIS* IS TOO MUCH!

YOU'RE A ONE-MAN *WRECKING CREW,* BIG BOY! THE REPAIRMEN'S UNION WILL *LOVE* YA FOR THIS!

9

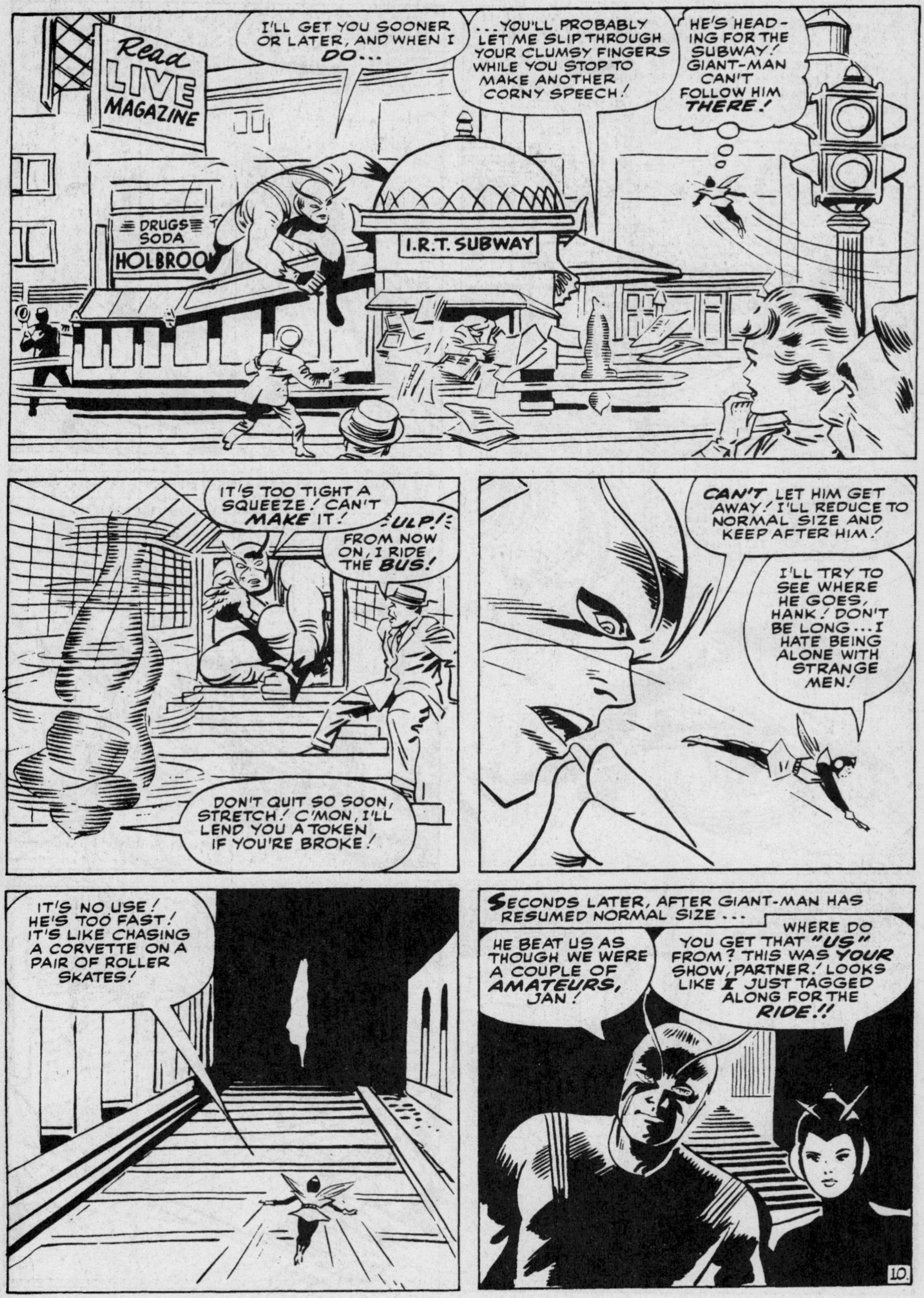
Read LIVE MAGAZINE
DRUGS SODA
HOLBROO
I.R.T. SUBWAY
I'LL GET YOU SOONER OR LATER, AND WHEN I DO...
...YOU'LL PROBABLY LET ME SLIP THROUGH YOUR CLUMSY FINGERS WHILE YOU STOP TO MAKE ANOTHER CORNY SPEECH!
HE'S HEADING FOR THE SUBWAY! GIANT-MAN CAN'T FOLLOW HIM THERE!
IT'S TOO TIGHT A SQUEEZE! CAN'T MAKE IT!
GULP!! FROM NOW ON, I RIDE THE BUS!
DON'T QUIT SO SOON, STRETCH! C'MON, I'LL LEND YOU A TOKEN IF YOU'RE BROKE!
CAN'T LET HIM GET AWAY! I'LL REDUCE TO NORMAL SIZE AND KEEP AFTER HIM!
I'LL TRY TO SEE WHERE HE GOES, HANK! DON'T BE LONG... I HATE BEING ALONE WITH STRANGE MEN!
IT'S NO USE! HE'S TOO FAST! IT'S LIKE CHASING A CORVETTE ON A PAIR OF ROLLER SKATES!
SECONDS LATER, AFTER GIANT-MAN HAS RESUMED NORMAL SIZE...
HE BEAT US AS THOUGH WE WERE A COUPLE OF AMATEURS, JAN!
WHERE DO YOU GET THAT "US" FROM? THIS WAS YOUR SHOW, PARTNER! LOOKS LIKE I JUST TAGGED ALONG FOR THE RIDE!!
10.

The next morning, a highly satisfied Dave Cannon gloats as he reads the headlines...

HMM, NOT *BAD* FOR A BEGINNER! I MADE ALL THE FRONT PAGES!

AND THE *BEAUTY* OF IT IS THAT THE PUBLIC WILL END UP SYMPATHIZING WITH *ME* BECAUSE I'M THE LITTLE GUY! NO ONE LIKES A *BIG* FELLA TO WIN A FIGHT!

STAR-BULLETIN
GIANT-MAN DEFEATED BY HUMAN TOP IN DRAMATIC CHASE!
TOP MAKES OFF WIT LARGE PAYROLL!

Daily Chronicle
HUMAN TOP VICTOR IN CLASH...

HUMAN TOP WINS BATTLE...

BUT I BETTER NOT KID MYSELF! GIANT-MAN ISN'T THE TYPE TO GIVE UP! HE'LL HOUND ME *FOREVER!*

AND EVEN A *GENIUS* LIKE ME CAN MAKE A MISTAKE SOMETIME! THAT'LL BE ALL HE NEEDS TO *POUNCE* ON ME!

THERE'S ONLY *ONE* WAY FOR ME TO BE REALLY SAFE... I'VE GOT TO GET *HIM* BEFORE HE CAN GET ME! I'VE GOT TO FINISH HIM FOR *GOOD!*

Meanwhile, a determined Henry Pym has some plans of his *own!*

HI, HANDSOME! WHY THE MAD SCIENTIST BIT?

I'VE DECIDED THE ONLY WAY TO BEAT THE HUMAN TOP IS FOR ME TO INCREASE MY OWN *SPEED* AND MY *REFLEXES!*

SO I'VE RIGGED UP SOME APPARATI TO HELP ME DO THAT LITTLE THING!

LIKE THIS BOUNCING BALL EXERCISE! IT KEEPS GOING FASTER AND FASTER...

...AND THE MORE I WORK AT IT, THE CLOSER I COME TO CATCHING IT!

11

NOW *THIS* IS THE MOST IMPORTANT DEVICE OF ALL... AN ELECTRONIC GYRO-TOP, OPERATED BY REMOTE CONTROL!

FOR HEAVENS SAKE! ARE YOU SURE YOU HAVEN'T BEEN READING TOO MANY ADVENTURES OF *MR. FANTASTIC!*

NEVER MIND THE ADOLESCENT HUMOR, LITTLE ONE! HERE! I'LL SHOW YOU HOW TO OPERATE THE GYRO-TOP...

HMMM, I SHOULD HAVE KNOWN YOU DIDN'T INVITE ME BECAUSE THE MOON WAS FULL AND YOU WANTED TO WHISPER SWEET NOTHINGS! OKAY, TALL, DARK AND DISAPPOINTING, BRIEF ME!

*T*HEN, AFTER EXPLAINING THE MACHINE'S OPERATION...

THIS IS A CHEMICAL ENERGIZER I'VE DEVELOPED! IT WILL INCREASE MY *SPEED*, AS WELL AS MY SIZE, WHEN I BECOME *GIANT-MAN!* TO HELP ME KEEP PACE WITH THE *TOP!*

AS SOON AS I DRINK THIS, RELEASE THE GYRO-TOP AND THEN STAND BACK!

AS YOU COMMAND, SAHIB!

THERE! OH! I..I NEVER DREAMED IT WOULD BE SO *FAST!*

THAT'S THE *PURPOSE* OF IT, KID! IT'S THE ONLY WAY I'LL TRAIN MYSELF TO OUTSPEED THE *HUMAN TOP!*

TRY TO *OUTGUESS ME!* MAKE IT CHANGE DIRECTION SUDDENLY!

12.

HE CAN'T REALIZE IT HIMSELF, BUT I CAN TELL FROM HERE HE'S NOT *NEARLY* FAST ENOUGH! IT..IT'S *HOPELESS!* HE'LL *NEVER* BE ABLE TO BEAT THE *HUMAN TOP!*

I'VE GOT TO KEEP *AT* IT! I *MUST* LEARN TO MATCH HIS SPEED...TO BE ABLE TO TWIST AND DART AS EASILY AS HE!

HAH! I GOT IT! I GOT IT!!

IF I COULD CATCH MY *GYRO-TOP*, I OUGHT TO BE ABLE TO CATCH THE *HUMAN* ONE!

BUT THEN, BEFORE GIANT-MAN CAN TIGHTEN HIS GRIP...

IT SPUN OUT OF MY FINGERS! IT WHIRLS TOO FAST... IT'S TOO SLIPPERY... I'M *STILL* NOT GOOD ENOUGH FOR IT!

BUT I *ALMOST* HAD IT! I *FEEL* MY SPEED INCREASING! I NEED JUST A FEW MORE WEEKS OF INTENSIVE TRAINING...

I HAVEN'T THE HEART TO TELL HIM I ONLY HAD THE GYRO-TOP OPERATING AT *HALF-SPEED!* AS FOR THE FEW WEEKS HE SAYS HE NEEDS... WHAT IF THE *HUMAN TOP* STRIKES *BEFORE* THEN?

AND AS THOUGH IN ANSWER TO THE *WASP'S* TORTUROUS THOUGHT, THE SINISTER FORM OF THE *TOP* SLINKS THROUGH THE DARKENED STREETS, ABOUT TO MENACE MANKIND AGAIN!

BUT THIS TALE IS TOO BIG, TOO FILLED WITH SURPRISES YET TO COME, TO SQUEEZE INTO ONE ISSUE! AND SO THE FINAL HALF WILL APPEAR *NEXT ISSUE*, AS *GIANT-MAN* AND THE *HUMAN TOP* FIGHT TO THE FINISH!!

DON'T MISS ASTONISH #51!

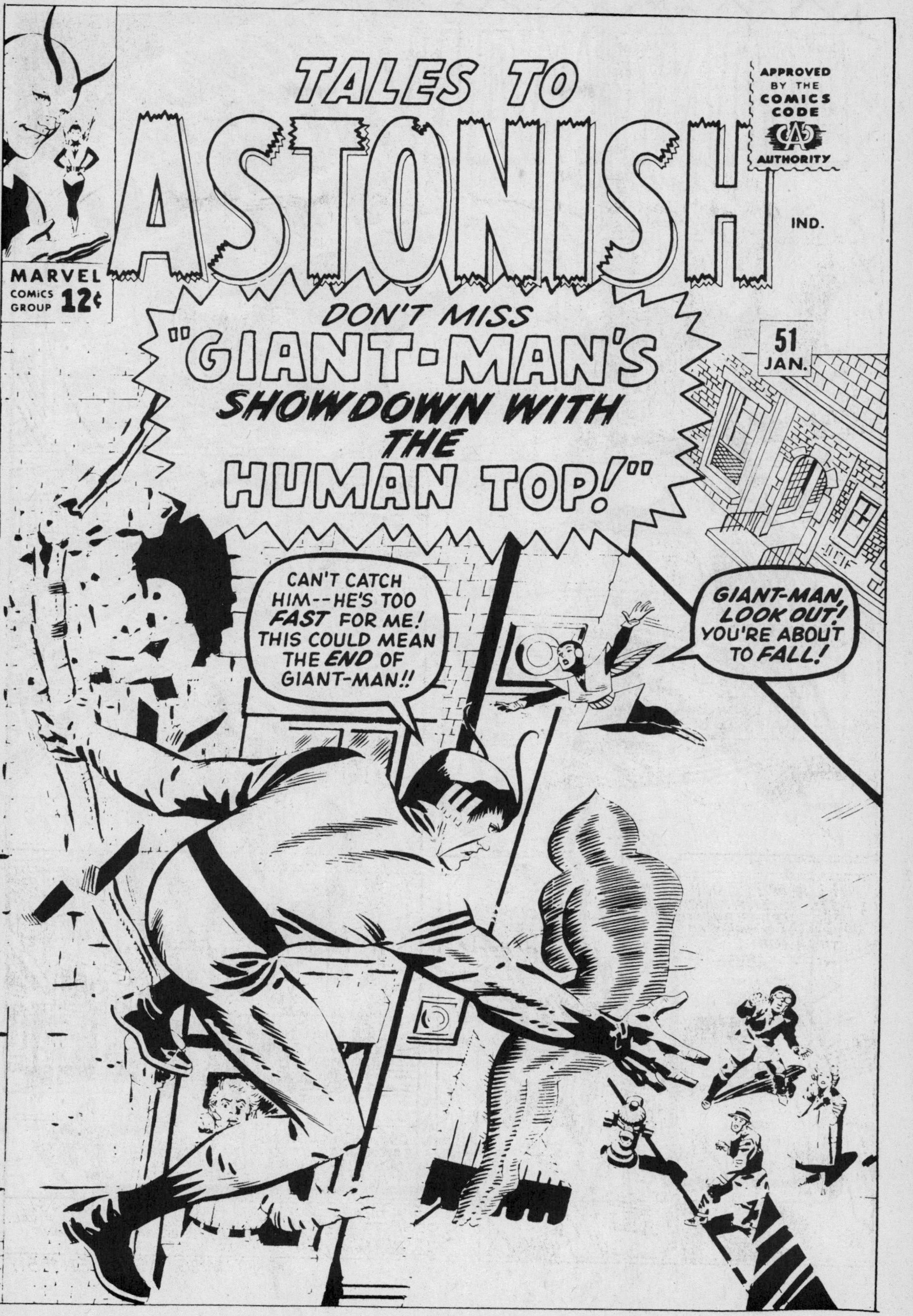

TALES TO ASTONISH
APPROVED BY THE COMICS CODE AUTHORITY
IND.
MARVEL COMICS GROUP 12¢
51 JAN.
DON'T MISS "GIANT-MAN'S SHOWDOWN WITH THE HUMAN TOP!"
CAN'T CATCH HIM--HE'S TOO FAST FOR ME! THIS COULD MEAN THE END OF GIANT-MAN!!
GIANT-MAN, LOOK OUT! YOU'RE ABOUT TO FALL!

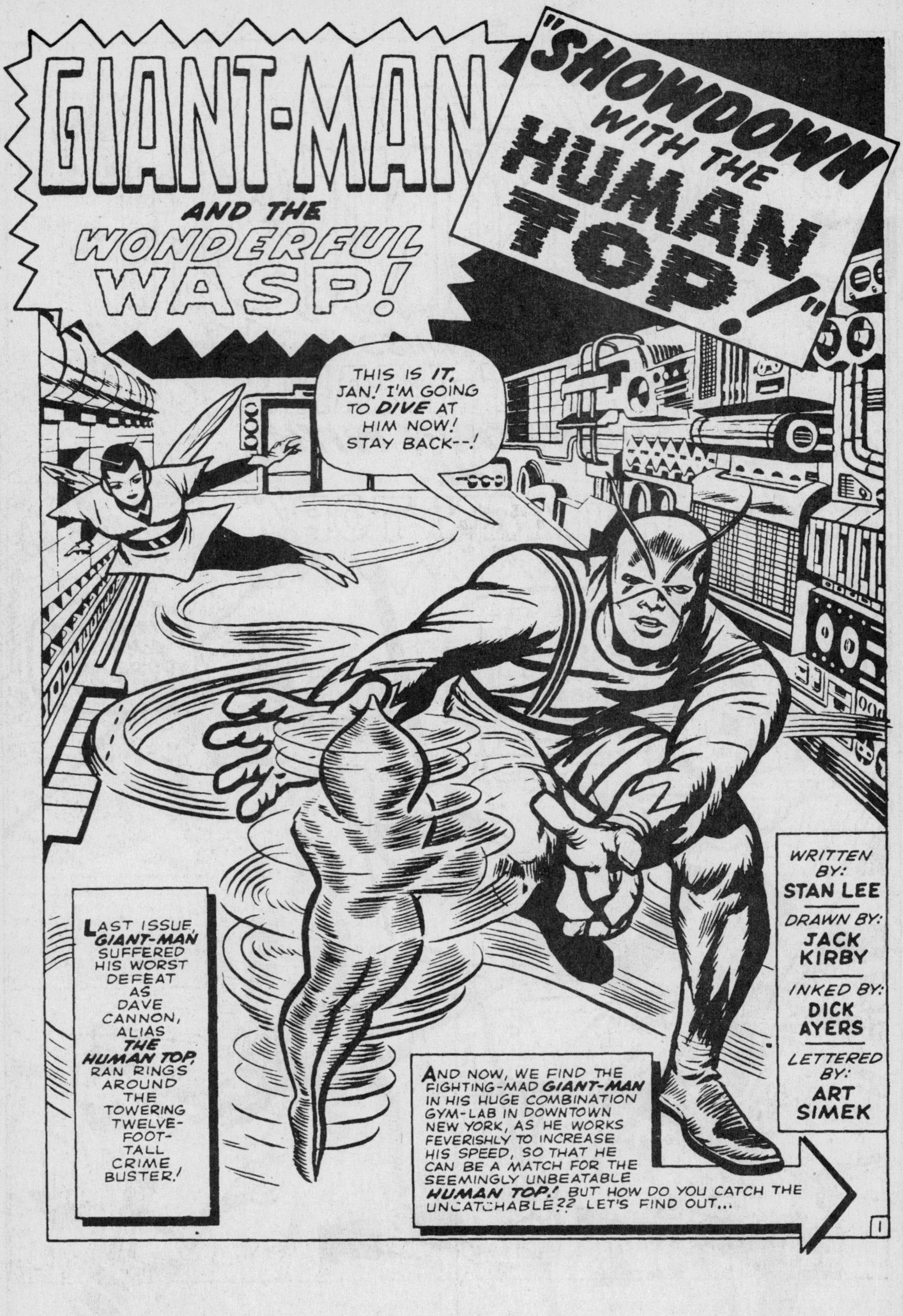
GIANT-MAN
AND THE WONDERFUL WASP!
"SHOWDOWN WITH THE HUMAN TOP!"
THIS IS IT, JAN! I'M GOING TO DIVE AT HIM NOW! STAY BACK--!
WRITTEN BY: STAN LEE
DRAWN BY: JACK KIRBY
INKED BY: DICK AYERS
LETTERED BY: ART SIMEK
LAST ISSUE, GIANT-MAN SUFFERED HIS WORST DEFEAT AS DAVE CANNON, ALIAS THE HUMAN TOP, RAN RINGS AROUND THE TOWERING TWELVE-FOOT-TALL CRIME BUSTER!
AND NOW, WE FIND THE FIGHTING-MAD GIANT-MAN IN HIS HUGE COMBINATION GYM-LAB IN DOWNTOWN NEW YORK, AS HE WORKS FEVERISHLY TO INCREASE HIS SPEED, SO THAT HE CAN BE A MATCH FOR THE SEEMINGLY UNBEATABLE HUMAN TOP! BUT HOW DO YOU CATCH THE UNCATCHABLE?? LET'S FIND OUT...
1

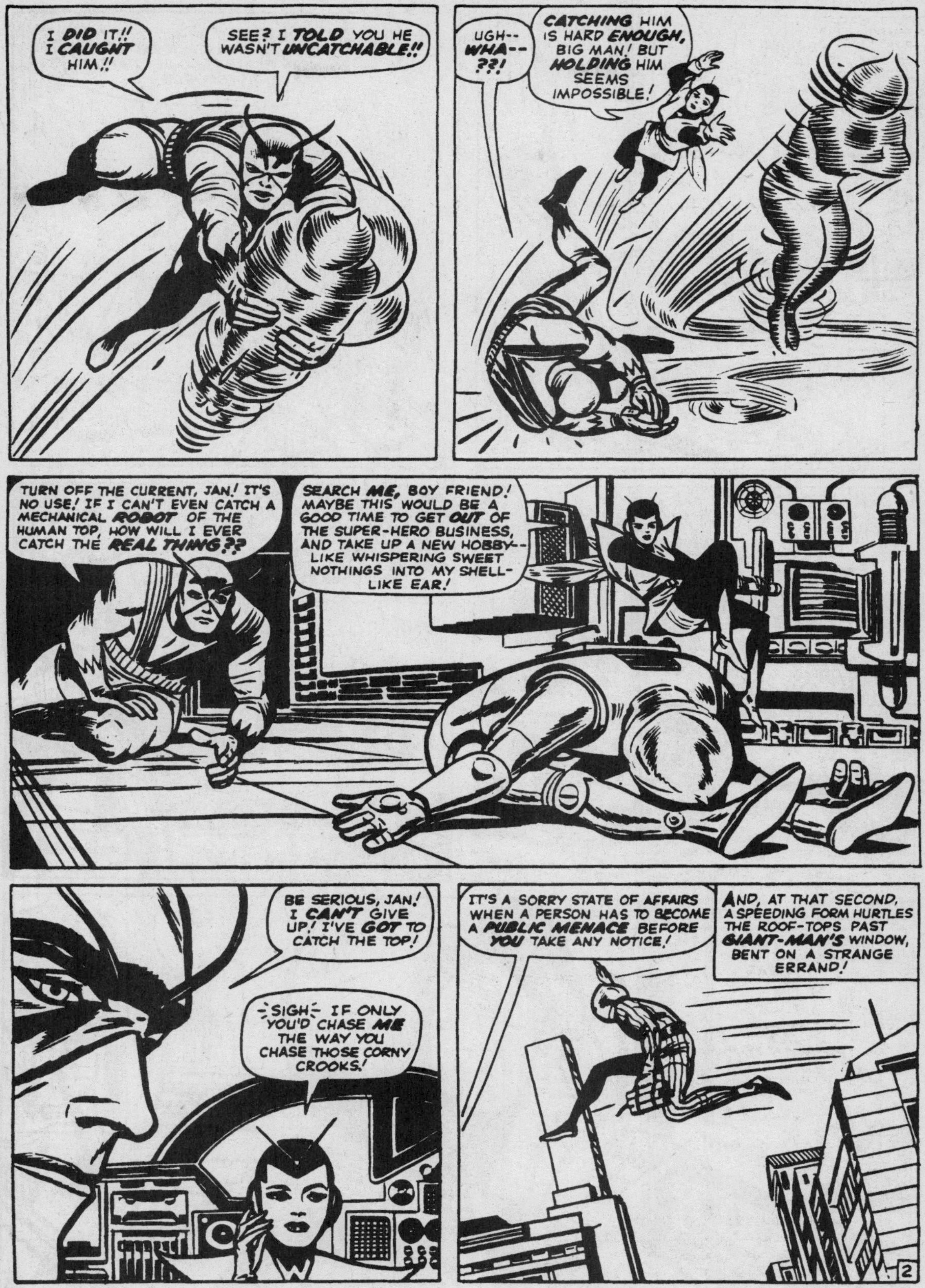

I DID IT!! I CAUGHT HIM!!
SEE? I TOLD YOU HE WASN'T UNCATCHABLE!!
UGH-- WHA-- ??!
CATCHING HIM IS HARD ENOUGH, BIG MAN! BUT HOLDING HIM SEEMS IMPOSSIBLE!
TURN OFF THE CURRENT, JAN! IT'S NO USE! IF I CAN'T EVEN CATCH A MECHANICAL ROBOT OF THE HUMAN TOP, HOW WILL I EVER CATCH THE REAL THING??
SEARCH ME, BOY FRIEND! MAYBE THIS WOULD BE A GOOD TIME TO GET OUT OF THE SUPER-HERO BUSINESS, AND TAKE UP A NEW HOBBY-- LIKE WHISPERING SWEET NOTHINGS INTO MY SHELL-LIKE EAR!
BE SERIOUS, JAN! I CAN'T GIVE UP! I'VE GOT TO CATCH THE TOP!
-SIGH- IF ONLY YOU'D CHASE ME THE WAY YOU CHASE THOSE CORNY CROOKS!
IT'S A SORRY STATE OF AFFAIRS WHEN A PERSON HAS TO BECOME A PUBLIC MENACE BEFORE YOU TAKE ANY NOTICE!
AND, AT THAT SECOND, A SPEEDING FORM HURTLES THE ROOF-TOPS PAST GIANT-MAN'S WINDOW, BENT ON A STRANGE ERRAND!
2

THAT'S JUST WHAT I'VE BEEN SEEKING! AN ABANDONED OLD SCOW, ROTTING AWAY IN THE HARBOR!

IT'S JUST WHAT I NEED TO HELP ME COMMIT THE CRIME OF THE CENTURY!

ALL I HAVE TO DO IS HIT IT WITH THIS SPECIALLY CONSTRUCTED INCENDIARY BOMB, AND LET NATURE TAKE ITS COURSE!

BULLS EYE! FROM FAR AWAY, IT WILL LOOK AND SOUND LIKE A MAJOR DISASTER! NOBODY WILL SUSPECT THAT NOTHING MORE THAN AN OLD, HALF-SUNK TUG BOAT WAS DAMAGED!

EVERYTHING IS WORKING *PERFECTLY!* THEY'RE RUSHING TO THE DOCKS AT THE EAST SIDE OF TOWN TO INVESTIGATE! AND NOW IT'S TIME FOR THE *SECOND* PHASE OF THE *HUMAN TOP'S* MASTER PLAN!

RREEEEEE

MEANWHILE, IN GIANT-MAN'S GYM-LAB...

LOOK, HANK! SOMETHING HAPPENED IN THE EAST RIVER!

A TV NEWS BULLETIN! MUST BE SOMETHING *BIG!*

3

THAT'S NO **ACCIDENT!** AND YET, WHY WOULD ANYONE BOTHER TO CAUSE AN EXPLOSION ON A WORTHLESS OLD TUGBOAT HULK?

UNLESS--IT'S A **DIVERSIONARY** TACTIC! TO LURE THE POLICE FROM THE **OTHER** SIDE OF TOWN! I SMELL A **RAT!**

YOU **BEAST!** I'M WEARING TWENTY-DOLLAR-AN-OUNCE PERFUME!

GET READY, WASP! I'M BECOMING **GIANT-MAN** AGAIN, AND WE'RE GONNA COVER THE **WEST** SIDE OF TOWN!

HOLD IT, CASANOVA! SOMEONE'S AT THE DOOR!

IT'S **GIANT-MAN!** WE **FOUND** HIM!

AND THERE'S THE **WASP!**

GIANT-MAN FAN CLUB

WE NEED PICTURES FOR OUR SCHOOL MAG!

WE'RE PUTTING YOU ON THE **COVER,** DOLL!

GO, GO, GIANT-MAN!

LOOK, FELLAS! WE HAVEN'T **TIME** FOR PICTURES NOW!

HEY! I SAID--

RELAX, HIGH POCKETS! IT WON'T TAKE LONG!

A LITTLE MORE SMILE, BEAUTIFUL! THAT'S IT! **HOLD IT!**

IS THIS **REALLY** FOR THE **COVER** OF YOUR SCHOOL MAGAZINE?

WELL, IT'S NOT FOR THE WALL STREET JOURNAL!! NOW SMILE!

LISTEN, YOU GUYS--

STAND BACK! YOU'RE SHAKIN' OUR CAMERAS!

WE'LL GET TO **YOU,** LATER, STRETCH!

4

SOME FAN CLUB! ALL THEY'RE INTERESTED IN ARE PIN-UP PIX OF THE *WASP!* WELL, THERE'S *ONE* WAY TO FINISH THIS OFF FAST--

NOW HEAR THIS!

WH-WHAT WAS *THAT?*

A *SONIC BOOM!!* WHAT *ELSE!*

GIANT-MAN, YOU'RE AN OLD MEANIE! THIS MIGHT HAVE BEEN THE START OF A NEW *CAREER* FOR ME!

OH WELL... THAT'S SHOW BIZ!

WHILE YOU WERE POSING FOR THOSE TEEN-AGE WOLVES, THE HUMAN TOP MIGHT HAVE STOLEN HALF OF NEW YORK!

HENRY PYM!! IF IT WASN'T FOR THE FACT THAT YOU HAVE AN *ICE CUBE* FOR A HEART, I'D SAY YOU SOUNDED *JEALOUS!*

WE'LL DISCUSS MY HEART *LATER,* PEST! RIGHT NOW-- *LOOK!* MY HUNCH WAS *RIGHT!* HE'S COMING FROM THE DIRECTION OF THE FEDERAL BUILDING!

IT'S THE *HUMAN TOP!!*

GIANT-MAN! BE *CAREFUL!* YOU KNOW HOW *DANGEROUS* HE IS!!

THE BIG *GOOP!* HE DOESN'T EVEN *HEAR* ME!

I'LL *GET* YOU *THIS* TIME, TOP!

YOU SHOULD *LIVE* SO LONG, LOUDMOUTH!

5

C'MON!! IF YOU'RE GONNA CATCH ME, THEN *CATCH* ME! IT GETS *DRAFTY* SPINNING AROUND THIS WAY!

I'M NOT TRYIN' TO CALL YOU A *SLOW-POKE*...

...BUT ARE YOU *SURE* YOU'RE NOT WALKIN' IN YOUR *SLEEP*, CHUM??

YOU *LITTLE WEASEL!* WHEN I GET MY HANDS ON YOU--

THAT, AS THEY SAY IN TV, WILL BE THE *DAY!*

SPEED IT UP, WILL YA?? YOU'RE NOT THE *ONLY* GUY I WANNA MAKE A *FOOL* OF TODAY!

HE'S GETTING OVER-CONFIDENT! GOOD! JUST WHAT I *HOPED* FOR!

NOW TO PUT INTO EFFECT WHAT I'VE BEEN PRACTICING! I'LL TRY TO *ANTICIPATE* HIS NEXT MOVE!

I'LL PRETEND TO HEAD FOR THE *LEFT*, AND THEN...

Y'KNOW, YOU RUN PRETTY GOOD FOR A GUY WITH TWO LEFT FEET!

IT *WORKED!* YOU WERE SO BUSY *TALKING*, THAT I OUT-GUESSED YOU!

SO A BIG MAN CAN'T CATCH A SPEEDY *LITTLE* MAN, EH? WELL, WHAT DO YOU SAY ABOUT *THIS?*

I'LL LET MY SPINNING *BODY* TALK FOR ME! I NEVER *THOUGHT* I COULD INCREASE MY WHIRLING SPEED, DID YOU??

C-CAN'T HOLD ON! HE'S SPINNING TOO FAST! MY HANDS --BEGIN-NING TO *ACHE!*

THERE! I'M SPINNING AT CLOSE TO TOP SPEED NOW! FEELS A LITTLE LIKE A TALKING *BUZZ SAW*, DOESN'T IT?

6

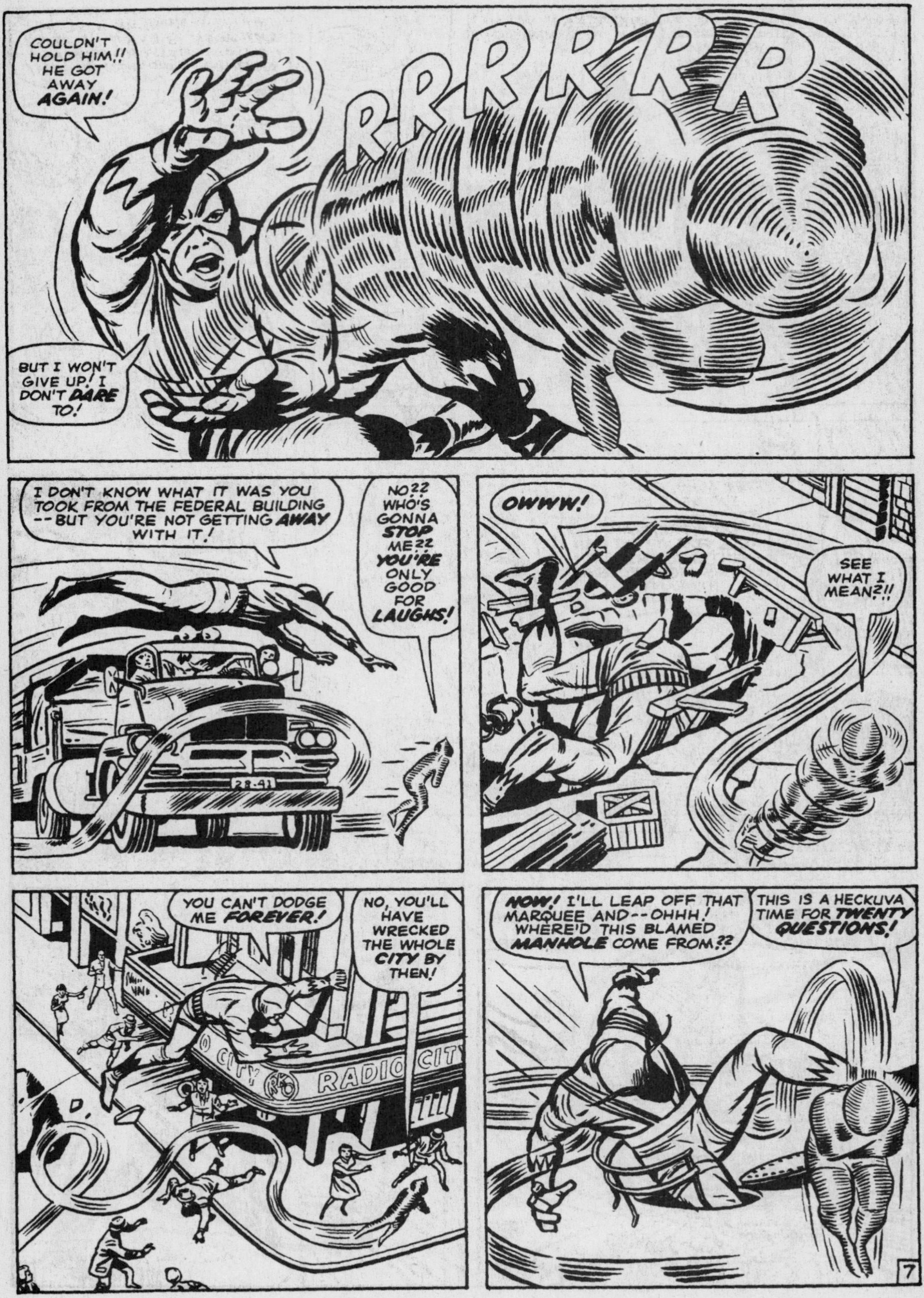
COULDN'T HOLD HIM!! HE GOT AWAY AGAIN!
RRRRRRR
BUT I WON'T GIVE UP! I DON'T DARE TO!
I DON'T KNOW WHAT IT WAS YOU TOOK FROM THE FEDERAL BUILDING --BUT YOU'RE NOT GETTING AWAY WITH IT!
NO?? WHO'S GONNA STOP ME?? YOU'RE ONLY GOOD FOR LAUGHS!
28-41
OWWW!
SEE WHAT I MEAN?!!
YOU CAN'T DODGE ME FOREVER!
NO, YOU'LL HAVE WRECKED THE WHOLE CITY BY THEN!
RADIO CITY
NOW! I'LL LEAP OFF THAT MARQUEE AND--OHHH! WHERE'D THIS BLAMED MANHOLE COME FROM??
THIS IS A HECKUVA TIME FOR TWENTY QUESTIONS!
7

A FEW MINUTES LATER...

LOOK OUT! THE TOP'S COMING **BACK** AGAIN!

WE'LL HAVE YOU OUT OF THERE IN **NO** TIME, GIANT-MAN!

DISPERSE, MEN! TRY TO **SURROUND** HIM!

IT'S LIKE TRYING TO SURROUND A **CYCLONE!**

I JUST WANTED TO BE SURE THAT **GIANT-MAN** IS OKAY! I'D **MISS** MY CLUMSY SPARRING PARTNER IF ANYTHING HAPPENED TO HIM!

NEVER MIND, GIANT-MAN! HOW ABOUT **ME?** I'M HERE WAITING FOR YOU!!

GOOD WORK, WASP! HE FELL FOR IT! HE RAN RIGHT INTO THE PATH OF THIS HIGH-PRESSURE HYDRANT!

I'LL GRAB HIM BEFORE HE CAN REGAIN HIS BALANCE! JUST A LITTLE FURTHER--!!

NOTHING I LIKE **BETTER** THAN BEING CHASED BY A BEAUTIFUL BABE!

STAND ASIDE, WASP! HE'S **STILL** DANGEROUS!

WE'LL TAKE OVER NOW, MISS!

DON'T **LISTEN** TO THOSE KILL-JOYS, BABY! HANG AROUND! I **LIKE** IT!

8

BUT THEN, ONCE OUT OF THE PATH OF THE HIGH-PRESSURE WATER STREAM--

THREE'S A CROWD, SO *I'M* CUTTIN' OUT!

♪ FARE THEE WELL FOR I MUST LEAVE THEE! DO NOT LET THE PARTING GRIEVE THEE! ♪

HE--HE'S *SPINNING* AGAIN!

THIS IS *AWFUL!* THERE JUST *HAS* TO BE A WAY TO STOP HIM!

DON'T WORRY, LADY! WE'VE GOT A NICE, COZY CELL WAITING FOR HIM! AND SOONER OR LATER...

HOW ABOUT *YOU,* GIANT-MAN? YOU OKAY NOW?

LIKE THEY SAY-- THE BIGGER THEY ARE, THE HARDER THEY FALL, EH?

DON'T WORRY ABOUT *ME,* BOYS! MY *PRIDE'S* THE ONLY THING THAT'S REALLY HURT!

BUT I REALIZE WE'VE BEEN ON THE WRONG TRACK!

SPELL IT OUT FOR US, BIG DADDY!

HE'S FASTER THAN WE ARE, BUT WE'VE BEEN TRYING TO MATCH HIS SPEED! IT'S A WASTE OF TIME! THERE'S A *BETTER* WAY!

NOW YOU TELL ME-- AFTER I GOT A RUN IN MY BEST LEOTARD!

AND, AS *GIANT-MAN* AND THE POLICE PLAN A NEW TRAP FOR THE *HUMAN TOP,* THE OBJECT OF THEIR ATTENTION UNMASKS IN HIS APARTMENT IN MIDTOWN...

SO FAR, SO GOOD!

I SPUN IN HERE SO FAST THAT NO ONE *SAW* ME!

IT WAS SIMPLE FOR ME TO TAKE THESE CIVIL DEFENSE PLANS FROM THE FEDERAL BUILDING!

THE COMMIES ARE SURE TO OFFER A BIG PRICE FOR THIS SCRAP OF PAPER-- AND I'M JUST THE BOY TO *COLLECT* IT FROM THEM!

9

LATER, AT A TOP-LEVEL MEETING...

THE **HUMAN TOP** IS A **FOOL!** THOSE CIVIL DEFENSE PLANS HE STOLE ARE **OBSOLETE!** WE'VE ALREADY DRAWN UP **NEW** ONES!

BUT HE WON'T **KNOW** THAT! HE'S SURE TO TRY TO CONTACT THE TOP RED AGENT IN THIS CITY! AND WE'VE HAD THAT COMMIE UNDER SURVEILLANCE FOR MONTHS!

IT ALL FITS IN WITH OUR MASTER PLAN! AS SOON AS THE TOP CONTACTS THE RED AGENT, WE LAUNCH OPERATION **CLAMPDOWN!**

AND, WITH YOUR HELP, GENTLEMEN, I PROMISE TO DELIVER THE **TOP** TO YOU WITHIN TWENTY-FOUR HOURS!

MMMM, IF THERE'S ONE THING I LIKE, IT'S BEING IN A ROOM FULL OF **MEN!**

LET'S RECHECK OUR PLAN AGAIN! WE'LL SET UP OUR TRAPS IN THESE AREAS!

IT'S A CLEVER SCHEME, GIANT-MAN...

IT **HAS** TO BE, SIR! WE'RE UP AGAINST AN ENEMY WHO IS AS CUNNING AS HE IS RUTH-LESS! BUT HE MUST BE TAUGHT THAT THE **LAW** CAN BE EVEN **MORE** CUNNING!

HOURS LATER, AT THE APARTMENT OF THE TOP RED AGENT IN THE METROPOLITAN AREA...

DA! I WILL MEET YOU AT THE CORNER OF ELEVENTH STREET -- JUST WEST OF THE RIVER! BRING THE PLANS! EIGHT SHARP! THAT IS ALL!

AND, AT THE OTHER SIDE OF THE APARTMENT WALL...

THAT'S YOUR CUE, GIANT-MAN! WE HAVE THE TIME AND THE PLACE!

GOOD WORK! THE REST IS UP TO **ME!**

10

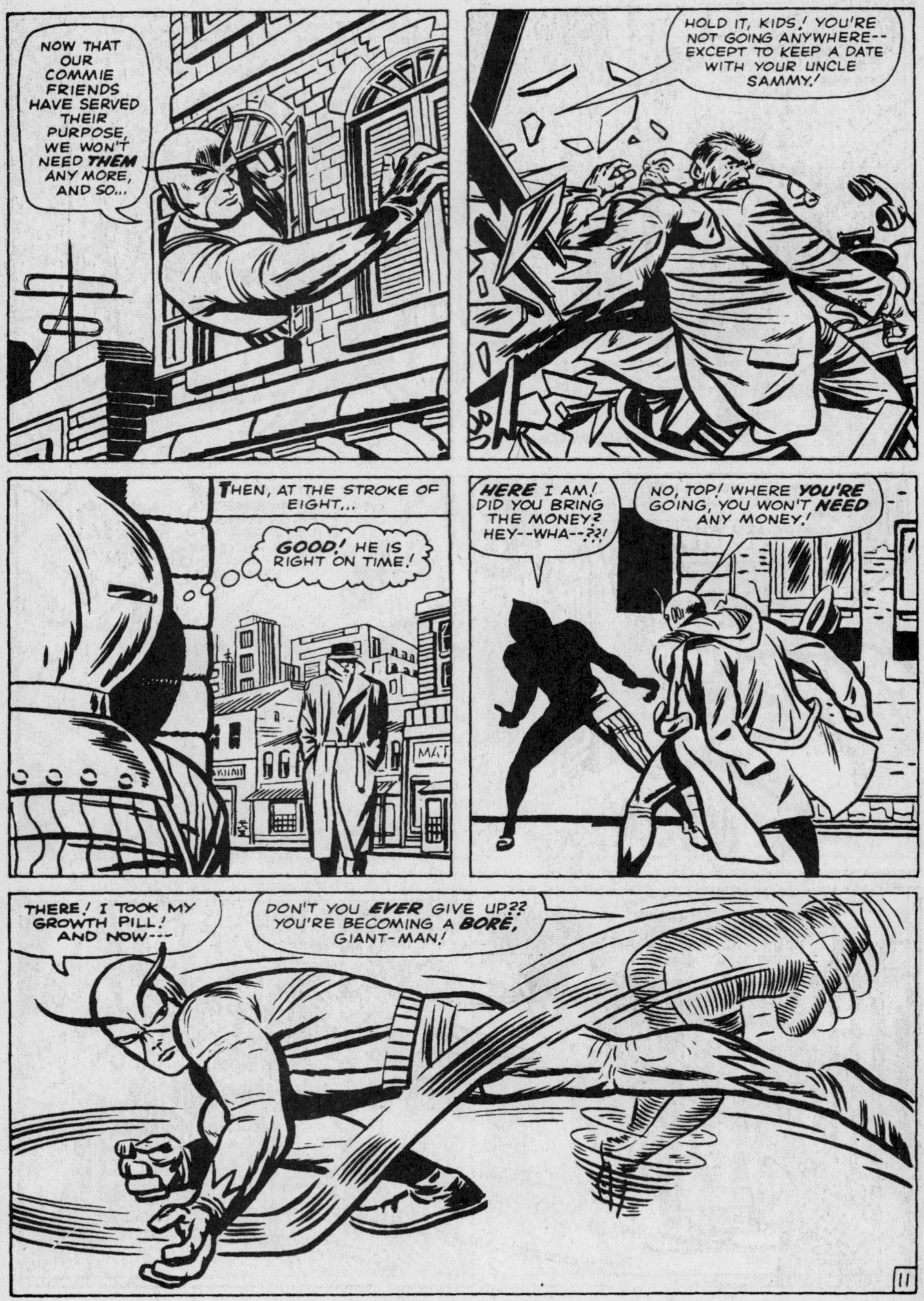
NOW THAT OUR COMMIE FRIENDS HAVE SERVED THEIR PURPOSE, WE WON'T NEED THEM ANY MORE, AND SO...
HOLD IT, KIDS! YOU'RE NOT GOING ANYWHERE-- EXCEPT TO KEEP A DATE WITH YOUR UNCLE SAMMY!
THEN, AT THE STROKE OF EIGHT...
GOOD! HE IS RIGHT ON TIME!
HERE I AM! DID YOU BRING THE MONEY? HEY--WHA--??!
NO, TOP! WHERE YOU'RE GOING, YOU WON'T NEED ANY MONEY!
THERE! I TOOK MY GROWTH PILL! AND NOW---
DON'T YOU EVER GIVE UP?? YOU'RE BECOMING A BORE, GIANT-MAN!
11

DON'T WORRY, WISE-GUY! *THIS* TIME YOU WON'T BE BORED FOR TOO LONG!

YOU'RE NOT *KIDDING!* I'M THROUGH WASTIN' TIME WITH YOU! IT'S GOODBYE FOREVER, PLAYMATE!

I'LL JUST SPIN DOWN THIS STREET AND--

HEY! WHAT'S *THIS??* WHERE'D THIS *FENCE* COME FROM??

WELL, WHO *CARES!* THERE ARE PLENTY OF *OTHER* STREETS!

SONNY, ARE *YOU* LIVING IN A FOOL'S PARADISE!

ANOTHER FENCE-- HERE *TOO!* ALMOST AS THOUGH THEY *KNEW* I'D BE HERE!

RUN ALL YOU *WANT* TO, TOP! *EVERY* SIDE STREET IS FENCED OFF THAT WAY!

PRETTY CLEVER, OF YOU, BIG MAN! BUT THIS IS A LONG AVENUE! I'LL LOSE YOU ANY TIME I *WANT* TO!

12

WHILE HE KNOCKS HIMSELF OUT DOWN THERE...

--I'LL JUST TAKE A LITTLE SHORT CUT!

TH-THE LANDLORD *WARNED* ME TO PAY MY RENT ON TIME--B-BUT I NEVER THOUGHT HE'D RESORT TO *THIS!*

FOR *DAYS* THE HUMAN TOP HAS SNEERED AT MY SIZE-- CALLING ME A CLUMSY CLOD!

WELL, MY SIZE HAS *SOME* ADVANTAGES... SUCH AS LETTING ME LEAP FROM ROOF TO ROOF LIKE AN OVER-SIZED *TARZAN!*

SURPRISED TO *SEE* ME, LITTLE MAN?? YOU'RE NOT SO FULL OF WISE-CRACKS NOW, ARE YOU?

IT NEVER OCCURRED TO YOU THAT THE POLICE MIGHT CORDON OFF AN ENTIRE NEIGHBORHOOD, AND THEN LEAVE YOU TRAPPED WITHIN ITS BORDERS--ALONE WITH *ME!*

EVEN *YOU* CAN'T KEEP SPINNING FOREVER! YOU'RE GROWING TIRED! YOU'RE SLOWING DOWN!

I'LL ESCAPE YOU *YET!*

NOT *THIS* TIME, LITTLE MAN! NOT WHEN IT'S SO *EASY* TO STOP A TOP FROM SPINNING, ONCE YOU'VE *CAUGHT* IT!!

WHAP!

NO NEED TO RUSH, GENTLE-MEN! OUR FAST-MOVING FRIEND ISN'T GOING ANYWHERE! AND HE'S EAGER TO RETURN EVERY-THING HE'S STOLEN--*AREN'T* YOU, PEE WEE?

YES! YES! *ANYTHING!* I'LL DO ANYTHING-- JUST GET YOUR UGLY PAWS OFF ME! I CAN'T *BEAR* TO BE MANHANDLED!

13

DON'T WORRY, PLAY-MATE! WE'LL TREAT YOU NICE AND GENTLE DOWN AT HEAD-QUARTERS! LET'S *GO!*

BUT I DON'T *UNDERSTAND!* HE SLIPPED OUT OF YOUR GRASP SO EASILY *BEFORE*-- WHY COULDN'T HE DO IT *NOW?*

BECAUSE *THIS* TIME, MY INQUISITIVE LITTLE IMP, I TOOK THE PRECAUTION OF APPLYING A STRONG COATING OF *GLUE* TO MY GLOVES! YOU'LL NOTICE *YOU* CAN'T GET AWAY NOW, EITHER!

HMMM, BUT *I'M* NOT STRUG-GLING! I *LIKE* IT THIS WAY!

NEXT ISSUE *GIANT-MAN* IS EVEN GREATER THAN EVER! BE SURE TO SEE HIM IN *TALES TO ASTONISH* #52! WE'LL BE *LOOKING* FOR YOU!

the END

THE WONDERFUL WASP TELLS A TALE

When she's not on a case with Giant-Man, Janet Van Dyne devotes a great deal of time visiting veterans' hospitals and orphans' homes, entertaining the shut-ins with imaginative tales of fantasy as only she can tell them! Such a tale is this one! How about listening in...?

"SOMEWHERE WAITS A WOBBOW!"

HOW ARE YOU FEELING TODAY, BOYS?

GREAT, WASP! NOW THAT YOU'RE HERE!

GOT ANOTHER THRILLER FOR US, BEAUTIFUL?

STORY PLOT... STAN LEE
SCRIPT AND ART }.. LARRY LIEBER
INKING......... G. BELL
LETTERING.... ART SIMEK

X-502

YOU BET! THIS IS A NEW ONE! IT TAKES PLACE IN THE YEAR TWO THOUSAND! I CALL IT...

"SOMEWHERE WAITS A WOBBOW!"

"PICTURE A MERCENARY SPACE PILOT! HIS NAME IS RACK MORGAN, AND FOR MONEY HE WOULD DO ANYTHING... OR ANYONE!

TAKING AN ILLEGAL SHORT-CUT THRU ANOTHER COMPANY'S SPACE LANE IS RISKY BUSINESS! BUT IF I DELIVER MY CARGO EARLY, I'LL GET A BIG BONUS!

OH, OH! THERE'S AN X-32 SAUCER DEAD AHEAD!

1

"VEERING SWIFTLY, THE TWO SHIPS NARROWLY MISS COLLIDING.!"

—WHEW!— A FOOT CLOSER AND WE'D HAVE *HAD* IT!

I *RECOGNIZE* THAT SHIP! IT BELONGS TO RACK MORGAN!

THAT BLASTED FOOL DOESN'T CARE *HOW MANY* RULES HE BREAKS, JUST SO IT GIVES HIM AN EDGE OVER EVERYONE ELSE!

"YES, MORGAN WAS TOTALLY WITHOUT SCRUPLES..."

I WAS VERY LUCKY TO GET THE BLAKE ORDER, MORGAN!

YOU SURE WERE! LET'S DRINK TO YOUR GOOD LUCK, SAM!

"...BUT, NO SOONER DOES THE OTHER PILOT DOWN HIS DRINK, WHEN..."

M-MY HEAD! SO DIZZY! I-I-UHHH--

THOSE KNOCKOUT DROPS I SLIPPED IN HIS DRINK WORKED LIKE A CHARM!

NOW, WHILE HE'S SLEEPING IT OFF, I'LL GO TO THE SPACEPORT AND FLY THE BLAKE CARGO *MYSELF!*

2

"BUT, ALL EVIL PEOPLE SOONER OR LATER OUTSMART THEMSELVES! IN RACK MORGAN'S CASE IT HAPPENS DURING AN INTERGALACTIC HOP..."

THERE'S THE PLANET DRACONIUS! EARTHMEN ARE FORBIDDEN TO LAND THERE BECAUSE IT'S SUPPOSED TO BE INHABITED BY DANGEROUS CREATURES CALLED *WOBBOWS!*

"SUDDENLY, ONE OF THE COUNTLESS COSMIC PERILS APPEARS ON THE SCENE!"

A METEOR SHOWER... HEADING THIS WAY! I'VE GOT TO SWERVE OUT OF ITS PATH!

"BUT, VEERING HIS SHIP TO SAFETY BRINGS MORGAN CLOSER TO DRACONIUS..."

I'VE NEVER SEEN THE PLANET CLOSE UP BEFORE! IT HAS A ROCKY TERRAIN-- *WAIT!!* THAT LOOKS LIKE--

...IT *IS!* IT'S *GOLD!!* HUGE *CHUNKS* OF IT JUST LAYING OUT THERE IN THE OPEN! *WHAT A FIND!*

BUT THE WOBBOWS--I'D BETTER EXPLORE THE AREA AND SEE IF ANY DANGEROUS CREATURES ARE AROUND BEFORE I LAND!

3

THERE'S NO SIGN OF ANY LIFE FOR MILES AROUND! I'LL BET THE WOBBOWS DON'T EVEN *EXIST!* THE BIG BRASS BACK ON EARTH JUST *MADE UP* THAT STORY TO KEEP PEOPLE FROM LANDING HERE!

SURE! OTHERWISE THOUSANDS OF EARTHMEN WOULD COME AND STEAL THE GOLD, THEREBY FLOODING THE MARKET AND REDUCING THE VALUE OF GOLD!

BUT, IF I *ALONE* LAND, I CAN TAKE JUST ENOUGH GOLD FOR *ME* TO BECOME RICH, AND NO ONE WILL EVER KNOW WHERE IT CAME FROM!

"SO, IN DEFIANCE OF SPACE REGULATIONS, RACK MORGAN LANDS ON THE FORBIDDEN PLANET!"

THOSE LARGE CHUNKS OVER THERE! ANY *ONE* OF THEM WOULD BE WORTH *MILLIONS* BACK ON EARTH!

UHH -- IT'S SURE HEAVY! BUT I'M NOT COMPLAINING! THIS BABY WILL KEEP ME LIVING IN LUXURY THE REST OF MY LIFE!

"MOMENTS LATER, THE EARTHMAN IS AGAIN SPACE BORNE!"

YES SIR, ONLY *FOOLS* OBEY RULES! ME, I'VE ALWAYS BROKEN THEM AND NOW I'M RICH! *RICH!!*

"BUT THE EARTHMAN'S JUBILATION IS SUDDENLY SHATTERED AS HE HEARS A NOISE... AND THEN TURNS TO FIND..."

THAT *SOUND!* IT'S THE *GOLD!* NO! IT CAN'T BE!!

4

THE GOLD IS *CHANGING*! IT'S COMING TO *LIFE*!!

NOW I UNDERSTAND! THE WOBBOWS *DO* EXIST... BUT THEY *DISGUISE* THEMSELVES!

YES! WE TURN OURSELVES INTO WHATEVER *BAIT* IS MOST ATTRACTIVE TO OUR ENEMIES!

AND, TO A GREEDY, SELFISH HUMAN *NOTHING* IS MORE TEMPTING THAN *GOLD*!

NO! STAY BACK! KEEP AWAY!!

AND THAT WAS THE *LAST* ANYONE EVER HEARD OF RACK MORGAN!

HECK! IS THE STORY *OVER* SO SOON?

HOW ABOUT TELLING IT *AGAIN?* WE, EH, MAY HAVE *MISSED* SOME IMPORTANT PARTS!

SORRY, FELLAS! JUST LIKE THE WOBBOW, IT'S TIME FOR *ME* TO CHANGE NOW... LIKE *THIS*!

AS SOON AS I GET ONE OF MY REDUCING CAPSULES!

HEY! SH-SHE'S *GONE!!*

IT HAPPENS EVERY *TIME!*

OH WELL, MAYBE SHE'LL COME *BACK* SOME TIME! HOW'D YOU LIKE HER *STORY*, JOE?

WHAT STORY? WITH A DOLL LIKE *THAT* IN FRONT OF YOU, WHO CAN *LISTEN?!!*

...*WE* CAN, THAT'S WHO! AND WE'LL LISTEN AGAIN *NEXT* ISSUE, WHEN THE WASP TELLS ANOTHER TALE! *THE END*

5

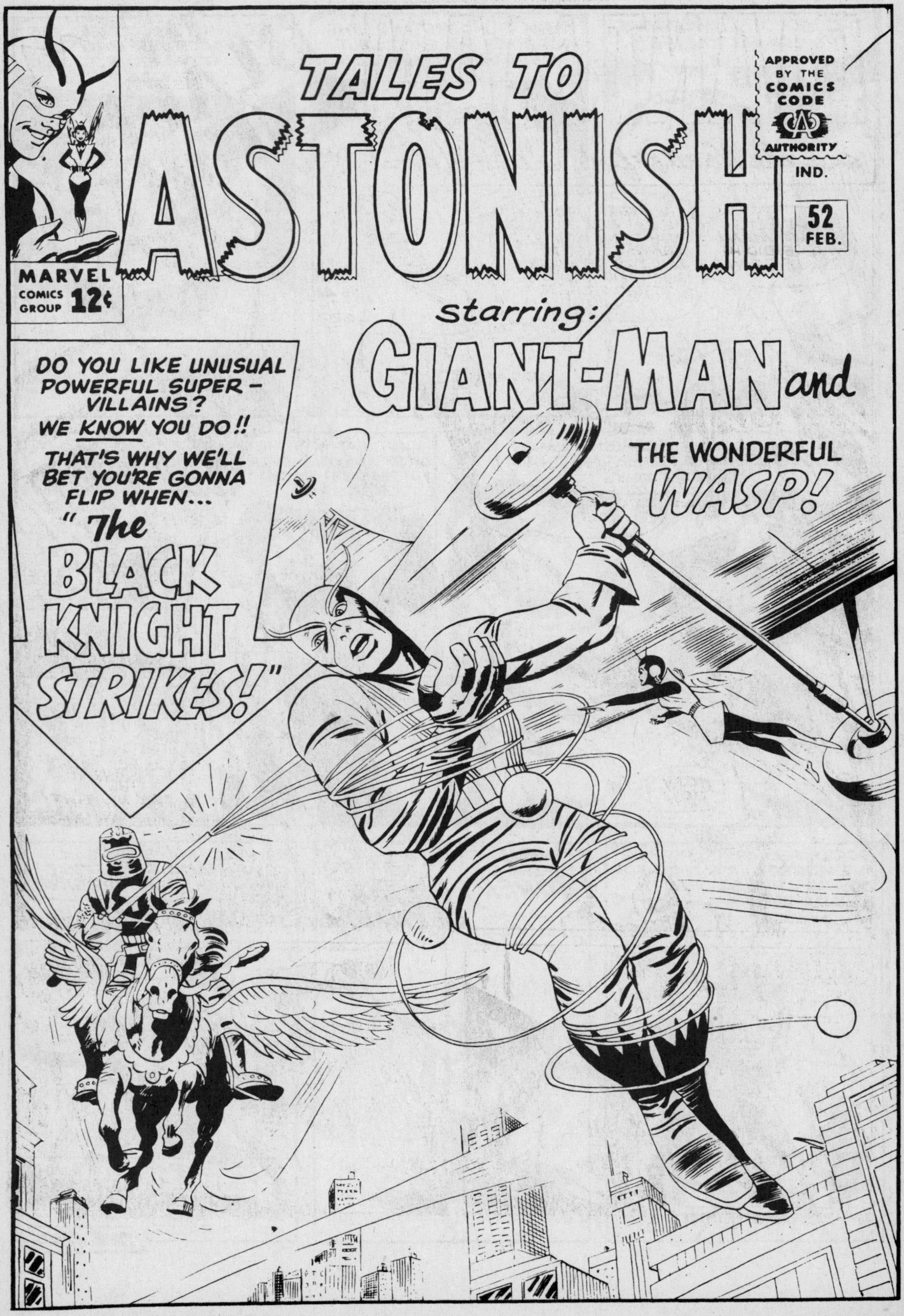
TALES TO ASTONISH
APPROVED BY THE COMICS CODE CA AUTHORITY
IND.
52 FEB.
MARVEL COMICS GROUP 12¢
starring: GIANT-MAN and THE WONDERFUL WASP!
DO YOU LIKE UNUSUAL POWERFUL SUPER-VILLAINS? WE KNOW YOU DO!! THAT'S WHY WE'LL BET YOU'RE GONNA FLIP WHEN... "The BLACK KNIGHT STRIKES!"

GIANT-MAN
and the Wonderful WASP!

"THE BLACK KNIGHT STRIKES!"

LOOK!! IT'S GIANT-MAN! WHERE DID HE COME FROM?

THE STORK BROUGHT ME, GARRETT! BUT THE MAIN THING IS WHERE YOU'RE GOING...TO JAIL, FOR DELIVERING SCIENTIFIC SECRETS TO RED CHINESE SPIES!!

THEY DON'T REALIZE I SPIED ON THEM UNSEEN AS ANT-MAN, AND THEN TOOK A GROWTH CAPSULE TO SHOOT UP INTO GIANT-MAN!

THOUGH HE IS TWICE NORMAL SIZE HE CANNOT CATCH ALL OF US!

RUSH HIM!

WE THINK YOU'LL AGREE THAT GIANT-MAN'S LATEST FOE WILL RANK WITH THE WORLD'S GREATEST SUPER-VILLAINS, AND SO WE PRESENT THE ORIGIN OF-- THE BLACK KNIGHT!

WRITTEN BY: STAN LEE
ILLUSTRATED BY: DICK AYERS
LETTERED BY: ART SIMEK

X-553

BIG AS HE IS, BULLETS WILL STILL STOP HIM!

YES, IF YOU GET A CHANCE TO FIRE THEM!!

BUT THEY FORGET HOW LONG MY REACH IS!

HE REACHED OUT AND GRABBED THEM BEFORE THEY COULD FIRE! BUT I'LL STILL GET AWAY!

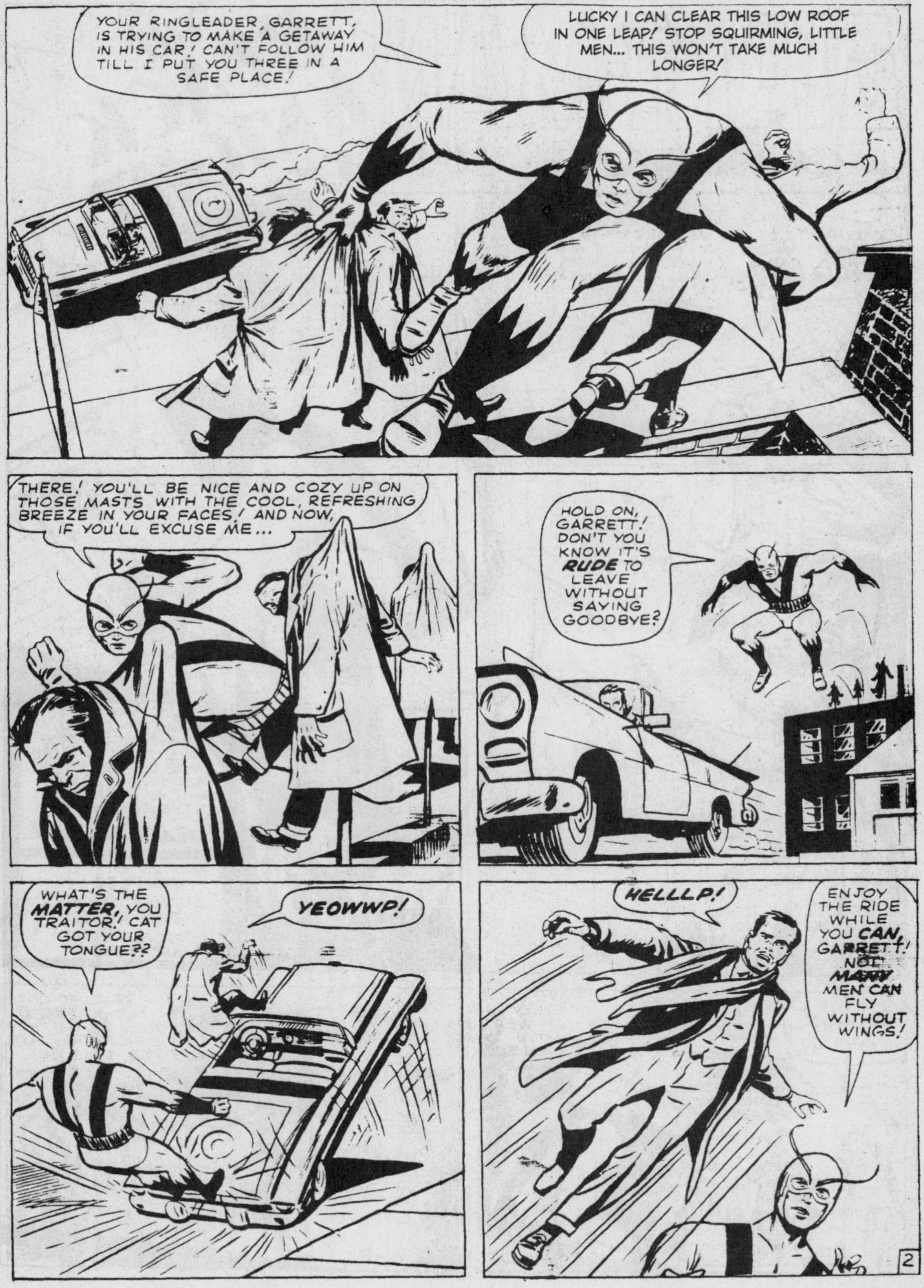

YOUR RINGLEADER, GARRETT, IS TRYING TO MAKE A GETAWAY IN HIS CAR! CAN'T FOLLOW HIM TILL I PUT YOU THREE IN A SAFE PLACE!
LUCKY I CAN CLEAR THIS LOW ROOF IN ONE LEAP! STOP SQUIRMING, LITTLE MEN... THIS WON'T TAKE MUCH LONGER!
THERE! YOU'LL BE NICE AND COZY UP ON THOSE MASTS WITH THE COOL, REFRESHING BREEZE IN YOUR FACES! AND NOW, IF YOU'LL EXCUSE ME...
HOLD ON, GARRETT! DON'T YOU KNOW IT'S RUDE TO LEAVE WITHOUT SAYING GOODBYE?
WHAT'S THE MATTER, YOU TRAITOR! CAT GOT YOUR TONGUE??
YEOWWP!
HELLLP!
ENJOY THE RIDE WHILE YOU CAN, GARRETT! NOT MANY MEN CAN FLY WITHOUT WINGS!
2

TWANNG!

HOPE YOU *ENJOYED* YOUR LITTLE RIDE, MISTER, BECAUSE WHERE *YOU'RE* GOING, THERE WON'T BE ENOUGH *ROOM* FOR SO MUCH FUN AND GAMES!

THINK YOU'RE PRETTY CLEVER, HUH, GIANT-MAN?? WELL, IF *I* EVER HAD A SUPER-POWER TO MATCH YOURS, THINGS WOULD BE A LOT DIFFERENT.!

SURE, GARRETT! AND IF THREATS COULD KILL, I'D HAVE BEEN *KAPUT* LONG AGO!

PROFESSOR GARRETT, THE FACT THAT YOU ARE A FAMOUS RESEARCH SCIENTIST WHO HAS BEEN GIVEN HIGH HONORS BY THIS COUNTRY MAKES YOUR CRIME OF TREASON MORE REPREHENSIBLE THAN EVER! AND SO, I AM FIXING YOUR BAIL AT *ONE HUNDRED THOUSAND DOLLARS!*

I SHOULD WORRY! THE REDS WILL PAY IT RATHER THEN TAKE A CHANCE OF ME *TALKING* AT MY TRIAL!

THE TRAITOROUS PROFESSOR GARRETT'S PREDICTION COMES TRUE! AND, ONE HOUR AFTER HIS BAIL HAS BEEN PAID, THE RENE-GADE SCIENTIST FLEES THE COUNTRY BY MEANS OF A COUN-TERFEIT PASSPORT!

I'LL LOSE MYSELF IN SOME SMALL NATION IN EUROPE WHERE THEY'LL *NEVER* FIND ME!

A FEW DAYS LATER, IN A REMOTE BALKAN KINGDOM NESTLED IN THE ALPS, A GRIM-FACED MAN STARES AT A STATUE IN THE VILLAGE SQUARE...

FOR AGES THERE HAVE BEEN LEGENDS OF FLYING HORSES...AND MEN HAVE CONSIDERED THEM MERELY FABLES! BUT WHAT IF IT WERE *POSSIBLE*?? WHAT IF THERE ONCE *HAD* BEEN SUCH CREATURES??

3

INTRIGUED BY THE NOTION OF A FLYING HORSE, AND HAVING UNLIMITED TIME ON HIS HANDS, THE BRILLIANT, UNSCRUPULOUS SCIENTIST RENTS A DESERTED CASTLE, LOCKING HIMSELF INSIDE AS HE BEGINS ONE OF THE STRANGEST EXPERIMENTS OF ALL TIME!

I HAVE ALWAYS BELIEVED THAT ANYTHING IS POSSIBLE-- *ANYTHING*, SO LONG AS A MAN HAS ENOUGH *TALENT!*

THE DAYS TURN TO WEEKS, TO MONTHS. AND STILL GARRETT WORKS, CONDUCTING COUNTLESS GENETIC EXPERIMENTS, UNTIL...

I *KNEW* IT COULD BE DONE, ONCE I FOUND THE *KEY!* BY INJECTING JUST THE RIGHT PROPORTION OF AN EAGLE'S BLOOD CELLS INTO A STALLION... I'VE ACHIEVED THE *IMPOSSIBLE!*

WEEKS LATER, HALF-WAY AROUND THE GLOBE, *ANOTHER* SCIENTIST IS AT WORK IN HIS LAB, AS A LOVELY MINIATURE-SIZED FLYING GIRL ENTERS EXCITEDLY...

IT'S ABOUT *TIME* YOU SHOWED UP, WASP! YOU WERE SUPPOSED TO BE HERE TO HELP WITH THIS EXPERIMENT AT *SEVEN!* WHAT DELAYED YOU?

NOW DON'T LOSE YOUR TEMPER, BOSS MAN, UNTIL I TELL YOU WHAT HAPPENED! IT WAS THE MOST *UNBELIEVABLE* THING...!

FOR THE LOVE OF PETE, JAN! CAN'T YOU EVER JUST ADMIT YOU FORGOT INSTEAD OF MAKING UP SOME RIDICULOUS *EXCUSE* ALL THE TIME??

"DON'T YOU *DARE* SHOUT AT ME, HENRY PYM! IT SO HAPPENS I WAS IN A TAXI, COMING ACROSS THE WASHINGTON BRIDGE, WHEN WE GOT CAUGHT IN A TRAFFIC JAM..."

OH DEAR! I'LL *NEVER* GET TO HENRY'S LAB BY SEVEN!

"KNOWING WHAT A GRUMPY OL' GROUCH YOU ARE ABOUT PEOPLE BEING LATE, I CHANGED INTO THE *WASP* AND STARTED TO *FLY* TOWARDS THE LAB, THINKING I COULD MAKE BETTER TIME!"

KEEP THE CHANGE, DRIVER!

HOLY MACKEREL! THE JALOPY'S *HAUNTED!*

4

"AND THEN I **SAW** IT! AT FIRST, ALL I HEARD WAS THE **SOUND**, A THUNDEROUS RUSTLING OF WINGS! I LOOKED AROUND, AND..."

OH **NO!** NO! IT JUST ISN'T **POSSIBLE!**

"IT WAS A KNIGHT IN BLACK ARMOR, RIDING A MIGHTY **FLYING HORSE!** I THANKED MY LUCKY STARS I WAS **WASP-SIZED**, AND TOO SMALL TO ATTRACT HIS ATTENTION!"

"AS I WATCHED, INCREDULOUSLY, HE SWOOPED DOWN TO AN ARMORED CAR, AND THEN, PRESSING A BUTTON ON HIS STRANGE LANCE, HE MELTED A HOLE RIGHT THROUGH THE STEEL SIDE!"

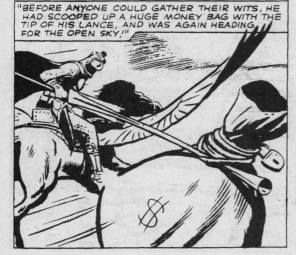

"BEFORE ANYONE COULD GATHER THEIR WITS, HE HAD SCOOPED UP A HUGE MONEY BAG WITH THE TIP OF HIS LANCE, AND WAS AGAIN HEADING FOR THE OPEN SKY!"

"I'D HAVE GIVEN **ANYTHING** TO BE ABLE TO FOLLOW HIM...BUT HIS FLYING HORSE WAS FAR TOO FAST, AND HE REACHED A HEIGHT WHICH I COULD NEVER HOPE TO REACH!"

CAN'T FOLLOW HIM-- BUT I'VE GOT TO TELL GIANT-MAN!

5

JAN, YOU'RE WASTING YOUR TIME BEING MY PARTNER! YOU COULD MAKE A **FORTUNE** WRITING COMICS! NOW, HOW ABOUT BEING **SERIOUS** FOR A WHILE? WE'VE STILL GOT A LOT OF WORK TO DO!

HENRY PYM, YOU ARE THE MOST EXASPERATING, FRUSTRATING, AGGRAVATING MAN I'VE EVER **KNOWN!**

SURE, SURE! I LOVE YOU **TOO**, KID! NOW SUPPOSE YOU SWITCH ON THE RADIO! IT'S ABOUT TIME FOR THE NEWS!

IT WILL BE A **PLEASURE** TO HEAR SOMETHING BESIDES THE SOUND OF YOU RATTLING YOUR TEST TUBES!

BULLETIN! THREE GUARDS WERE TAKEN INTO CUSTODY TONIGHT AFTER THEIR ARMORED CAR WAS ROBBED! THEY INSIST THE CRIMINAL ATTACKED THEM ON A FLYING HORSE!

I'M READY FOR YOUR ABJECT **APOLOGY** NOW, MY DEAR MR. KNOW-IT-ALL!

HOLD IT, JAN! LET ME TUNE IN TO MY CYBERNETIC ANT-COMMUNICATOR!

IF A MYSTERIOUS FLYING HORSE WAS SEEN IN THE CITY, SOME OF MY ANTS SOMEWHERE ARE SURE TO HAVE WITNESSED THE SIGHT! A MENTAL IMPULSE PICTURE WILL FORM IN SECONDS...

THERE IT **IS!** YOU-- YOU WERE **RIGHT**, JAN! IT **IS** A FLYING HORSE... AND IT APPEARS HE'S ATTACKING A **HELICOPTER** RIGHT **NOW!**

VERY WELL, BIG BOY! I KNOW YOU'RE WONDERING HOW TO APOLOGIZE TO ME, SO I'LL MAKE IT **EASY** FOR YOU! A PIECE OF **JEWELRY** WOULD BE NICE-- AND PERHAPS TWO TICKETS TO A BROADWAY SHOW, AND THEN DINNER AND DANCING, AND...

WHOA, MY GORGEOUS LITTLE GOLD-DIGGER! SUPPOSE YOU SETTLE FOR A **REDUCING CAPSULE** RIGHT NOW, BECAUSE WE'VE GOT A **JOB** ON OUR HANDS!

I'M TURNING INTO **GIANT-MAN** AND GOING UP AFTER THAT FLYING MENACE! YOU FOLLOW AS BEST YOU CAN-- BUT BE CAREFUL! I DON'T WANT YOU WITHIN RANGE UNTIL WE KNOW WHAT HIS **POWERS** ARE!

6

AND SO... FILL ME IN ABOUT THAT RIDER ON THE WINGED HORSE, CHIEF! PERHAPS I CAN HELP!

NOT MUCH TO TELL, GIANT-MAN! HE'S ATTACKING A NEW, JET-ASSISTED WHIRLY-BIRD! WE CAN'T FIRE AT HIM -- FOR FEAR OF HITTING THE PLANE OR ITS PASSENGERS!

HE'S TRYING TO CAPTURE THE PLANE; USE IT FOR HIS OWN! IT'S PIRACY IN THE AIR!

MINUTES LATER, A HUGE AIR FORCE CARGO PLANE HEADS FOR THE SPOT WHERE THE AIR BATTLE IS TAKING PLACE...

SO FAR SO GOOD! NOW FLY DIRECTLY ABOVE THE HELICOPTER!

DON'T MISS, BIG FELLA! IT'S A LONG WAY DOWN -- AND WE HAVEN'T A PARACHUTE THAT CAN HOLD YOU!

IF I DO MISS, MAJOR, TELL THE WASP THAT-- AW, FORGET IT! SHE MUST KNOW HOW I REALLY FEEL ABOUT HER!

SEE YOU AROUND, PAL! HERE GOES!

BIG AS HE IS, HIS SIZE WILL NEVER MATCH HIS COURAGE!

WHEW! MADE IT!

7

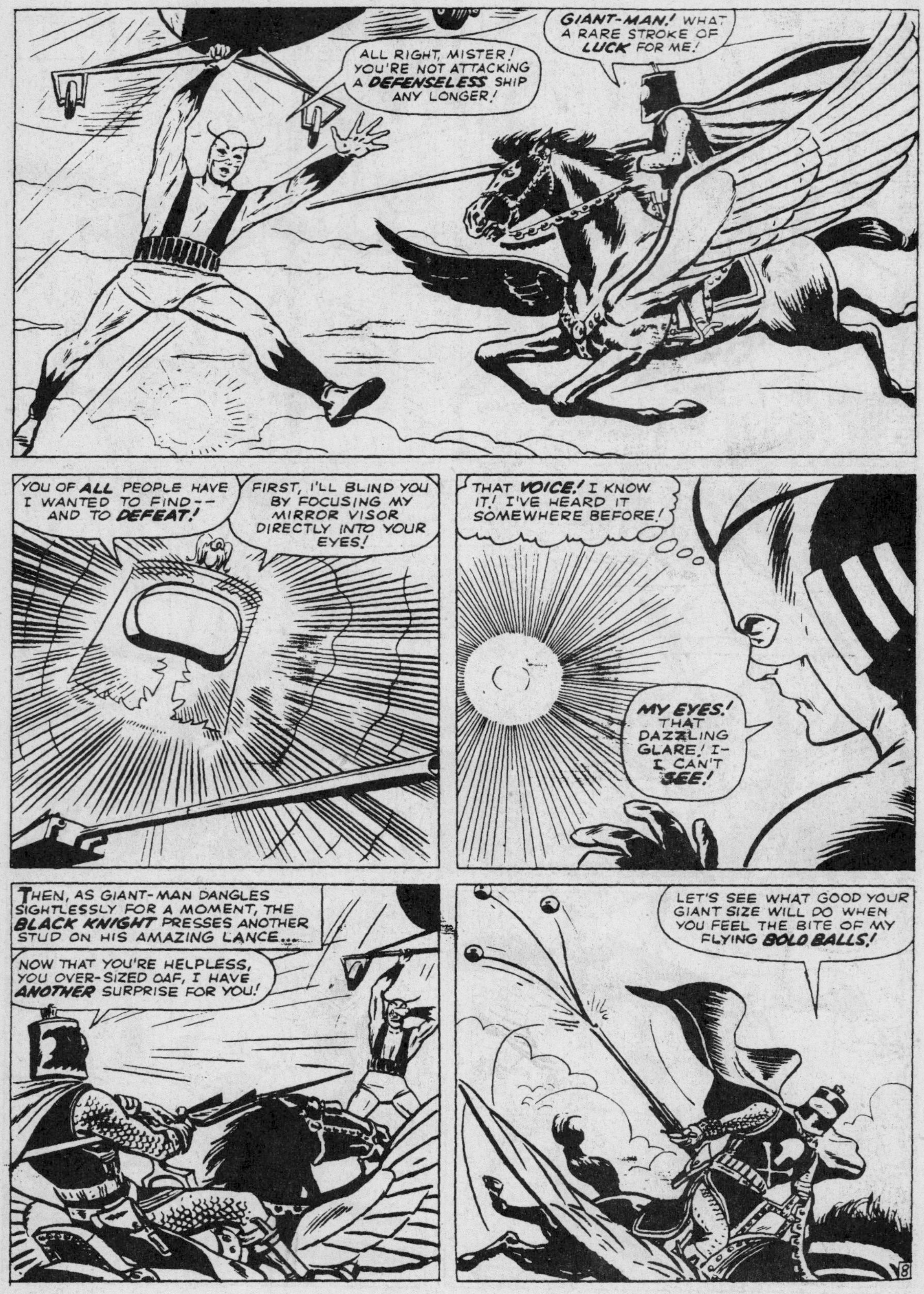
ALL RIGHT, MISTER! YOU'RE NOT ATTACKING A DEFENSELESS SHIP ANY LONGER!
GIANT-MAN! WHAT A RARE STROKE OF LUCK FOR ME!
YOU OF ALL PEOPLE HAVE I WANTED TO FIND-- AND TO DEFEAT!
FIRST, I'LL BLIND YOU BY FOCUSING MY MIRROR VISOR DIRECTLY INTO YOUR EYES!
THAT VOICE! I KNOW IT! I'VE HEARD IT SOMEWHERE BEFORE!
MY EYES! THAT DAZZLING GLARE! I-- I CAN'T SEE!
THEN, AS GIANT-MAN DANGLES SIGHTLESSLY FOR A MOMENT, THE BLACK KNIGHT PRESSES ANOTHER STUD ON HIS AMAZING LANCE...
NOW THAT YOU'RE HELPLESS, YOU OVER-SIZED OAF, I HAVE ANOTHER SURPRISE FOR YOU!
LET'S SEE WHAT GOOD YOUR GIANT SIZE WILL DO WHEN YOU FEEL THE BITE OF MY FLYING BOLO BALLS!
8

I PURPOSELY ATTACKED THE HELICOPTER, HOPING IT WOULD BRING YOU OUT IN THE OPEN WHERE I COULD *STRIKE* AT YOU!

FOR I *KNEW* I'D HAVE TO GET YOU IN THE *AIR*, IN ORDER TO SMASH YOU FOREVER!

THERE! MY SUPER-STRONG STEEL CABLE HAS YOU IN A GRIP WHICH EVEN YOUR OVER-SIZED MUSCLES CAN'T SHATTER! ALL YOU CAN DO IS EVENTUALLY LOOSEN YOUR HOLD AND FALL TO YOUR DOOM BELOW!

YOU'VE GONE TO A LOT OF *TROUBLE* PREPARING FOR THIS MEETING! *WHY?*

BECAUSE I ONCE TOLD YOU THAT IF *I* HAD A SUPER POWER TO MATCH YOURS, THINGS WOULD HAVE TURNED OUT DIFFERENTLY-- REMEMBER??

OF *COURSE!* NOW I KNOW-- YOU'RE PROFESSOR *GARRETT*, THE TRAITOR! BUT-- *HOW--??*

I WAS *HOPING* YOU'D ASK! IT WILL MAKE MY REVENGE *COMPLETE* TO TELL YOU THE WHOLE STORY-- BEFORE I MAKE MY FINAL *CHARGE!*

HIS ONE VULNERABLE POINT IS HIS *COLOSSAL* *VANITY!* I'VE GOT TO *GOAD* HIM INTO BOASTING ABOUT HIM-SELF UNTIL I CAN THINK OF A COUNTER-PLAN!

9

HERE, GIANT-MAN... TAKE A GOOD LOOK AT THE MAN YOU **THOUGHT** YOU HAD DEFEATED!

THE MAN WHO WILL SOON **DESTROY** YOU!

"REMEMBER HOW I JUMPED BAIL AND FLED TO EUROPE? WELL, I DIDN'T REMAIN FEARFULLY IN HIDING--**NO!** I WORKED! OH, HOW I WORKED ON A SCHEME TO SMASH YOU!"

I'VE GOT TO DEVELOP ENOUGH WEAPONS TO MAKE ME THE MASTER OF GIANT-MAN IN ANY SITUATION!

"MY SUPREME ACHIEVEMENT, IN REGARD TO WEAPONS, IS MY MULTI-STUDDED **LANCE**, WHICH CONTAINS EVERY TYPE OF BATTLE DEVICE I MIGHT EVER NEED!"

NO ONE WOULD EVER SUSPECT THAT A .45 CALIBER **MACHINE GUN** IS MOUNTED IN THE CONTROL HANDLE OF MY LANCE!

TAC

TAC TAC TAC TAC

"YES, I USED THE SOUND-PROOF CASTLE DUNGEON AS A TESTING AREA FOR EVERY WEAPON I CREATED-- AND ALWAYS I WAS SPURRED ON BY HATRED FOR **YOU!**"

IMAGINE GIANT-MAN'S SHOCK WHEN HE SEES AN **ACETYLENE TORCH** FLAME SHOOT OUT OF MY LANCE, CAPABLE OF BURNING THROUGH A TWO FOOT STEEL WALL!

BUT NOT **ALL** MY WEAPONS ARE WITHIN MY LANCE! I'LL KEEP THIS SMALL **PARALYZER PISTOL** SEPARATE, ALWAYS CLOSE AT HAND!

ZAP!

THERE! I "FROZE" THAT CAT IN MID-RUN, AND I "FROZE" THE MOUSE IT WAS CHAS- ING, TOO! THEY'LL REMAIN MOTIONLESS FOR A FULL HOUR!

AND PERHAPS YOU'RE WONDERING WHAT **THIS** LITTLE GADGET IS, GIANT-MAN? I KEEP IT STRAPPED TO MY LEG, WHERE I CAN REACH IT IN A SPLIT- SECOND! I CALL IT THE **ITCH- RAY**--AND HERE'S **WHY**--

10

OHHH! IT'S LIKE PLAIN ITCHING POWDER-- ONLY A THOUSAND TIMES *WORSE!* IT-- IT'S MAKING ME ITCH ALL OVER!!!

C-CAN'T HOLD ON ANY LONGER!! BETWEEN THE STRAIN ON MY MUSCLES-- AND THE TERRIBLE ITCHING-- IT-- IT'S *TOO MUCH!!*

SO LONG I HAVE ONE HAND FREE, I *STILL* HAVE AN ACE UP MY SLEEVE WHICH THE BLACK KNIGHT DOESN'T SUSPECT!!

HE'S FOLLOWING ME DOWN! *GOOD!* IT'S JUST WHAT I *HOPED* HE'D DO!

NOW I'VE JUST GOT TO USE MY FREE HAND TO TAKE A *SHRINK- ING CAPSULE* FROM MY BELT!

THE **WASP** SHOULD BE CLOSE AT HAND BY NOW! I **TOLD** HER TO FOLLOW ME!

IF SHE STOPPED TO BUY A NEW HAT-- OR GET A NEW HAIRDO, THEY'RE SURE GOING TO **MISS** ME FROM NOW ON.!!

WELL, HERE GOES **NOTHING!** AT LEAST I'M FREE OF THE BOLO CABLES!!

IT- IT'S **IMPOSSIBLE.!!** HE DISAPPEARED RIGHT BEFORE MY EYES!! B-BUT **HOW???**

LOOKING FOR SOMEONE, DREAM-BOAT?

NOT ANY **MORE,** HONEY! I'VE **FOUND** HER!

C-CAN'T HOLD YOU MUCH LONGER, HANK-- --MY **WINGS** AREN'T STRONG ENOUGH!

DON'T GIVE IT A THOUGHT, JAN! WE'RE GETTING A **LIFT** RIGHT NOW!

TERRIFIC, JAN! I COULD **KISS** YOU FOR THIS!

WELL? WHO'S **STOPPING** YOU?

12

LITTLE PARTNER, WHEN ARE YOU GOING TO LEARN THAT THERE'S A TIME AND PLACE FOR EVERYTHING?

THIS LOOKS LIKE AS GOOD A PLACE AS ANY, BOSS MAN! AND I'VE GOT NOTHING BUT TIME!

I HATE TO BE A PARTY POOP, JAN, BUT THERE'S STILL THE LITTLE MATTER OF DEFEATING THE BLACK KNIGHT TO ATTEND TO!

AW, YOU CAN DO IT WITH ONE HAND TIED BEHIND YOU!

MY HANDS WERE TIED JUST A FEW MINUTES AGO, AND YOU NEVER SAW A SADDER-LOOKING CRIME-FIGHTER IN YOUR LIFE, KID!

NOW, FIND A PLACE TO GET A GOOD GRIP ON HIS SADDLE, BECAUSE I'M GONNA MAKE THINGS START SHAKING AROUND HERE!

WHY, WHY COULDN'T YOU HAVE BEEN A DISC JOCKEY, OR SOMETHING REALLY GLAMOROUS, INSTEAD OF A HERO-TYPE KOOK??!

I'LL JUST TAKE A NORMAL-SIZE CAPSULE! IF I BECOME GIANT-MAN AGAIN, HIS HORSE WON'T BE ABLE TO SUPPORT MY WEIGHT!

CAN'T WAIT TO SEE THE BLACK KNIGHT WHEN HE LEARNS HE'S GOT A HITCH-HIKER ABOARD!

PARDON ME, PAL-- GOT A MATCH?

GIANT-MAN!! IT-IT ISN'T POSSIBLE!!

ANYTHING'S POSSIBLE, LITTLE FRIEND! DON'T YOU EVER READ SCIENCE FICTION STORIES???

MY LANCE!

13

DON'T **WORRY** ABOUT IT, BUSTER! WHERE **YOU'RE** GOING, THAT OVERGROWN TOOTHPICK WOULD ONLY GET IN THE WAY!

GET **OFF**-- YOUR WEIGHT IS MAKING MY WINGED STEED LOSE ALTITUDE--!! WE'LL **CRASH!**

HE'S **RIGHT!** CAN'T TAKE THE CHANCE-- NOT WITH THE **WASP** HANGING ON! I'LL HAVE TO DIVE OFF! WE'RE LOW ENOUGH NOW!

WAITING UNTIL THE LAST SPLIT-SECOND-- TRYING DESPERATELY TO PICK JUST THE RIGHT SPOT-- THE INTREPID MASKED ADVENTURER FINALLY HURLS HIMSELF FROM THE FLYING HORSE, MUTTERING A SILENT PRAYER AS HE FALLS!

HE PANICKED-- AS I **HOPED** HE WOULD! THIS WILL BE THE **END** OF HIM!!

BUT THE COSTUMED CRUSADER IS NOT SO EASILY DISPOSED OF--!

GOT ROOM FOR A KIBITZER, FOLKS?

PARACHUTE

THANKS FOR THE LIFT, KIDS! NEXT TIME WE MEET, THE RIDE'LL BE ON **ME!**

BOY! YOU MEET ALL **KINDS** IN A PLACE LIKE THIS!

14

MEANTIME, THE WASP DECIDES IT'S TIME THAT *SHE* TOOK A HAND...

HENRY'S *SAFE.!!* NOW, THE SOONER WE TAKE CARE OF THE BLACK KNIGHT, THE SOONER I'LL HAVE MY BASHFUL BOY-FRIEND ALL TO *MYSELF* AGAIN!

SO, THE *FIRST* THING TO DO IS SEPARATE THIS ARMORED CORNBALL FROM HIS FLYING HORSE...

...AND A *SIMPLE* FEMININE TRICK LIKE A SHARP *PINCH* OUGHT TO DO THAT LITTLE THING!

WHEEE! THE WASP STRIKES *AGAIN!!*

BUT, THE BLACK KNIGHT *ALSO* POSSESSES GREAT AGILITY, AND HE MANAGES TO MANEUVER HIMSELF IN MID-AIR AS HE FALLS, SO THAT HE LANDS SAFELY ATOP A ROLLER COASTER CAR...

SOMETHING MUST HAVE SHOCKED MY HORSE! BUT, NO MATTER-- HE'LL FLY BACK TO ME IN A MATTER OF SECONDS!!

AND THEN, ONCE I AM ASTRIDE HIM AGAIN, I'LL-- *WHA--?* OH NO-- NO!

OH *YES*, SHORTY! YOU DIDN'T THINK YOU'D SEEN THE *LAST* OF ME, DID YOU??!

15

STOP SQUIRMING, GARRETT! IT'LL ONLY HURT A MINUTE!

MEANTIME, IN AN EFFORT TO GAIN CONTROL OF THE WILD FLYING STEED, THE WASP TAKES A GROWTH CAPSULE, RETURNING TO NORMAL SIZE!

EASY, BOY!! WHOA!

WON'T HANK BE IMPRESSED IF I CAN GENTLE THIS FLY-BABY!

BUT, BEFORE THE STARTLED GIRL CAN SECURE HERSELF FIRMLY IN THE SADDLE, THE WINGED HORSE EXECUTES A ROLLING LOOP IN MID-AIR, UNSEATING HER!!

OHHH-- HELP!!

AND GIANT-MAN'S SUPER-SENSITIVE CYBERNETIC ANTENNAE PICK UP THE WASP'S FAINT CALL...

HELP!

IT'S JAN! SHE'S IN TROUBLE!

SEIZING HIS OPPORTUNITY, THE BLACK KNIGHT USES THAT SPLIT-SECOND TO WREST HIMSELF FREE OF HIS GIANT CAPTOR'S GRASP!

NOW'S MY CHANCE!

16

THE 'COPTER IS TRYING TO REACH HER, BUT IT'LL NEVER *MAKE* IT! I'VE ONLY TIME FOR *ONE* LEAP--!!

CAN'T AFFORD TO MISS! JUST *CAN'T*!!

GIANT-MAN-- *NO*!! EVEN IF YOU CATCH ME, WE'LL *BOTH* FALL TO OUR DEATHS!

NOT IF I TIMED THIS JUST AS I *TRIED* TO! MY ARM SHOULD BE JUST LONG ENOUGH...

...TO REACH THE COPTER, AND BREAK OUR FALL!!

MADE IT!

I-I COULDN'T SAVE MYSELF BY BECOMING THE *WASP*, BECAUSE MY SHRINKING PILLS WERE USED UP! IF NOT FOR *YOU*...!

FORGET IT, LADY! YOU'RE SAFE NOW!

WOW! THEY SURE PUT ON GREAT SHOWS AT THIS PARK!

AND NOW, IT'S TIME TO SETTLE OUR SCORE WITH THE *BLACK KNIGHT!*

BUT WHERE *IS* HE?

17

LOOK SHARP, WASP! I HAVE A FEELING HE ISN'T FAR AWAY!

FOOL! I'M CLOSER THAN YOU THINK! AND ONE BLAST FROM MY PARALYSIS RAY WILL FINISH YOU OFF FOREVER!

BUT, AIDED AGAIN BY HIS SUPER-SENSITIVE CYBERNETIC ANTENNAE, GIANT-MAN HEARS THE FAINT CLICK OF THE BLACK KNIGHT'S GUN HAMMER, AND...

SOMEONE BEHIND ME!! CAN'T AFFORD TO TAKE CHANCES, I'LL TAKE A SHRINKING CAPSULE--FAST!!

I MUST BE LOSING MY MIND.!! HE CHANGED SIZE RIGHT BEFORE MY EYES!!!

JUST IN TIME!! I FELT SOMETHING WHIZZ OVER MY HEAD!!

EITHER YOU'RE NOT HUMAN, OR I'M GOING MAD--MAD--MAD!!!

GARRETT! LOOK OUT! YOU'RE FALLING THROUGH THE GUARD RAIL!!

HIS WINGED STEED FLEW UNDER HIM, SAVING HIM JUST IN TIME!!!

YOU'VE BEATEN ME THIS TIME, GIANT-MAN--BUT I'LL BE BACK! SOONER OR LATER--I'LL BE BACK!!

CAN'T ANY OF THE ENEMIES YOU BEAT EVER JUST LOSE GRACEFULLY AND JOIN THE FOREIGN LEGION? DO THEY ALL HAVE TO MAKE THOSE CORNY EXIT SPEECHES??

SOMETHING TELLS ME THAT WAS NO IDLE BOAST, HONEYCHILE! IF YOU EVER HEAR THE RUSTLE OF WINGS ABOVE YOU IN THE FUTURE, HEAD FOR COVER! IT'S LIABLE TO BE MORE THAN JUST SOME PIGEONS!

AND THERE YOU HAVE IT! ANOTHER REASON WHY GIANT-MAN AND THE WONDERFUL WASP ARE BECOMING TWO OF FANDOM'S MOST TALKED-ABOUT NEW CHARACTERS! BE WITH US AGAIN NEXT ISSUE WHEN THE MIGHTY MARVEL GROUP COMBINES TALENTS TO PRESENT THE GREATEST GIANT-MAN TALE OF ALL! SEE YOU THEN!

THE END

18

THE WONDERFUL **WASP** TELLS A TALE!

"NOT WHAT THEY SEEM!"

Story Plot: **STAN LEE**
Script and Art: **LARRY LIEBER**
Inking: **G. BELL**
Lettering: **ART SIMEK**

X-521

SHE SHOULD'VE **BEEN** HERE BY NOW!

I'LL BET SHE DOESN'T EVEN SHOW UP!

YEAH! WHY WOULD SUCH A FAMOUS GIRL WASTE HER TIME COMING TO VISIT **US?**

THROUGH THE WINDOW OF A LOCAL ORPHANAGE FLIES A BEAUTIFUL FEMALE FIGURE, TOO TINY TO BE NOTICED BY UNSUSPECTING EYES! THOUGH HER NAME IS JANET VAN DYNE, SHE'S BETTER KNOWN TO HER COUNTLESS ADMIRERS THROUGHOUT THE FREE WORLD AS-- THE WONDERFUL **WASP!**

PERHAPS IT'S BECAUSE SHE LIKES TO ENTERTAIN HER YOUNG FRIENDS!

LOOK! IT'S **THE WASP!** SHE'S **HERE!!**

WOW! SHE JUST TOOK A **GROWTH** CAPSULE!! SHE'S GETTING **BIGGER!**

OKAY, FELLAS-- FASTEN YOUR SEAT BELTS! WE'RE TAKING AN IMAGINARY JOURNEY INTO THE FUTURE... TO THE YEAR **3,000!**

OH BOY!

"IMAGINE A LONELY PRISON PLANET IN OUTER SPACE! SUDDENLY, THE SILENCE IS SHATTERED BY A BLARING ALARM....!"

FIVE PRISONERS ARE MISSING!

AFTER THEM! THEY MUSTN'T ESCAPE!

FASTER! RUN FASTER!

"BUT, THE JAILBREAK IS WELL PLANNED, AND BEFORE THE GUARDS CAN RECAPTURE THE FUGITIVES...."

THERE THEY GO! ALERT THE SPACE PATROL!

THEY HAD A SHIP WAITING!

WELL, WE'RE OUTA STIR, BUT WE'RE NOT SAFE YET!

THE LAW WILL BE AFTER US! WE'LL HAVE TO HIDE OUT ON SOME ISOLATED WORLD TILL THE HEAT'S OFF!

YES, WE MUST CHOOSE OUR PLANET CAREFULLY!

I USED TO BE A SPACE PIRATE, AND I KNOW HOW DECEPTIVE ALIEN WORLDS CAN BE!

"ON SOME WORLDS, LIFELIKE MANIKINS GIVE THE APPEARANCE OF A PEACEFUL POPULATION!'"

2

"WHILE BENEATH THE SURFACE, THE **REAL** WARLIKE INHABITANTS STAND POISED TO AMBUSH ANY STRANGERS WHO VISIT THE INNOCENT-LOOKING PLANET!"

"ON **OTHER** PLANETS, THE ANIMALS WHICH **SEEM** TAME, ARE **NOT**!"

"THEY ARE REALLY VICIOUS CARNIVORES THAT PURSUE AND SLAY FIERCE-LOOKING, BUT HARMLESS VEGETARIANS!"

"AND THERE ARE STILL **OTHER** PLACES WHICH SEEM LIKE OUR NATIVE EARTH, BUT WHERE THE BIOLOGICAL BALANCE OF POWER IS DRASTICALLY DIFFERENT..."

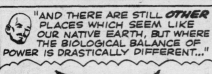

"FOR, ON **THOSE** WORLDS, **PLANTS** HAVE THE GREATEST INTELLIGENCE AND THEREFORE DOMINATE ALL THE OTHER LIFE FORMS...INCLUDING THE HUMAN RACE, WHICH THEY ENSLAVE BY HYPNOSIS!"

3

SO YOU SEE, WE'VE GOT TO BE **CAREFUL** SELECTING A SAFE HIDEOUT IN THE GALAXY!

HEY! THERE'S A **SPACE PATROL SHIP** ON OUR TAIL!

TRY TO **LOSE** 'EM IN THAT STAR CLUSTER UP AHEAD!

LATER, AFTER MUCH MANEUVERING...

WE'RE IN THE CLEAR!

YEAH, BUT NOT FOR **LONG!** WE'D BETTER LAND AND **HIDE** SOMEWHERE!

WHAT ABOUT THAT OXYGEN WORLD BELOW?

THERE SEEMS TO BE A BATTLE GOING ON BETWEEN THE SEXES!

HMMN-- LET'S LOOK THE SITUATION OVER!

THE MEN ARE STRONGER THAN THE WOMEN! THEY'RE WINNING THE FIGHT!

IF WE LAND AND HELP THOSE GUYS WRAP IT UP, THEY'RE SURE TO BE **GRATEFUL** AND HIDE US FROM THE LAW!

SO, AFTER CAREFUL CONSIDERATION, THE FUGITIVES ENTER THE BATTLE!

LOOK! **STRANGERS!**

HELP US! PLEASE-- YOU **MUST** HELP US!

NOT ON YOUR LIFE, SISTER!

WE'RE TEAMING UP WITH THE **MALES!**

BUT YOU MUSTN'T SIDE WITH **THEM!** THEY'RE IN THE **WRONG!**

SO WHAT? WE AINT EXACTLY BOY SCOUTS, OURSELVES!

AND SOON...

THE BATTLE IS OVER! WE'VE WON!

AND DON'T FORGET THAT **WE** HELPED YOU! NOW WE'VE A LITTLE FAVOR TO ASK!

FAVOR? SURELY YOU MUST BE JESTING!

4

WHAT DO YOU MEAN "JESTING"?

WE MEAN THAT YOU'RE GOING TO BE LOCKED UP!

SEIZE THE STRANGERS!

HEY, LEGGO!

IT'S USELESS TO RESIST! YOU'RE HOPELESSLY OUTNUMBERED!

FOOLS! DON'T YOU KNOW WHY WE WERE BATTLING THE FEMALES??

WE SAW YOU THROUGH OUR TELESCOPES!

IT'S OUR CUSTOM TO CAPTURE SPACE TRAVELERS AND KEEP THEM ON EXHIBITION!

BUT OUR WOMEN DON'T APPROVE OF THE CUSTOM AND THEY WERE TRYING TO STOP US!

BUT NOW WE'VE WON AND WE SHALL DO AS WE PLEASE!

THE EARTHMEN LOOK NICE IN THEIR NEW CAGE!

WE WALKED RIGHT INTO IT!

IT WAS ANOTHER SPACE TRAP!

IT'S AMUSING TO WATCH THEM!

AND SO THE FUGITIVES DIDN'T REALLY ESCAPE JUSTICE AFTER ALL! NO CRIMINAL EVER DOES! ALWAYS REMEMBER THAT!

WE SURE WILL, WASP!

NOW IT'S TIME FOR ME TO SPROUT WINGS AND BUZZ OFF!

AW, MUST YOU LEAVE SO SOON? DON'T YOU HAVE ANY MORE TALES FOR US?

SURE, BUT AS GIANT-MAN WOULD SAY, THERE'S ALWAYS TOMORROW! KEEP WELL, FRIENDS, AND WATCH FOR-- THE WASP!

ANOTHER VISIT WITH THE WONDERFUL WASP NEXT ISSUE! YOU WON'T WANT TO MISS IT!

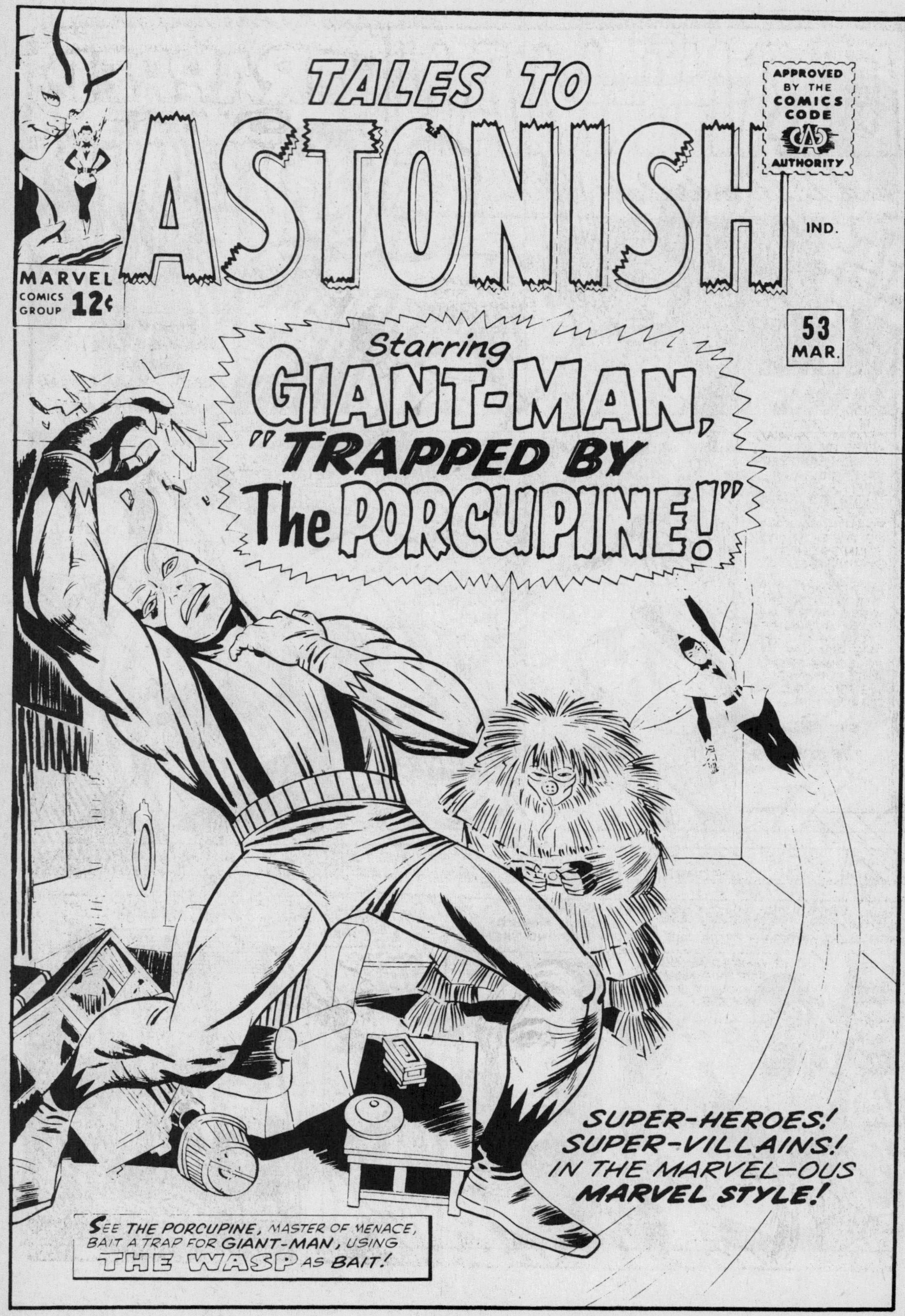
TALES TO ASTONISH
IND.
APPROVED BY THE COMICS CODE CA AUTHORITY
MARVEL COMICS GROUP 12¢
53 MAR.
Starring GIANT-MAN, "TRAPPED BY The PORCUPINE!"
SUPER-HEROES! SUPER-VILLAINS! IN THE MARVEL-OUS MARVEL STYLE!
SEE THE PORCUPINE, MASTER OF MENACE, BAIT A TRAP FOR GIANT-MAN, USING THE WASP AS BAIT!

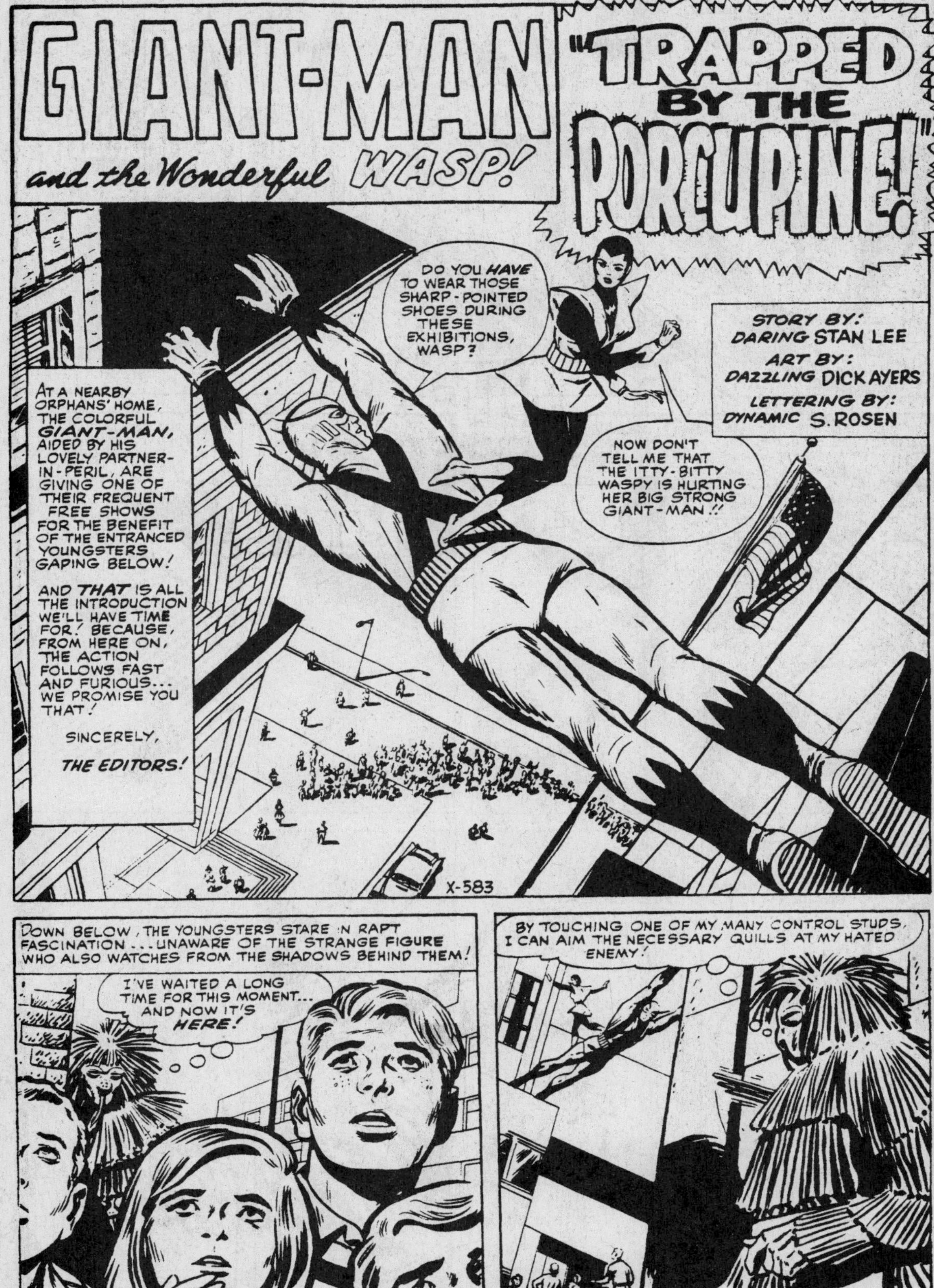
GIANT-MAN
and the Wonderful WASP!
"TRAPPED BY THE PORCUPINE!"
DO YOU HAVE TO WEAR THOSE SHARP-POINTED SHOES DURING THESE EXHIBITIONS, WASP?
STORY BY: DARING STAN LEE
ART BY: DAZZLING DICK AYERS
LETTERING BY: DYNAMIC S. ROSEN
AT A NEARBY ORPHANS' HOME, THE COLORFUL GIANT-MAN, AIDED BY HIS LOVELY PARTNER-IN-PERIL, ARE GIVING ONE OF THEIR FREQUENT FREE SHOWS FOR THE BENEFIT OF THE ENTRANCED YOUNGSTERS GAPING BELOW!
AND THAT IS ALL THE INTRODUCTION WE'LL HAVE TIME FOR! BECAUSE, FROM HERE ON, THE ACTION FOLLOWS FAST AND FURIOUS... WE PROMISE YOU THAT!
SINCERELY,
THE EDITORS!
NOW DON'T TELL ME THAT THE ITTY-BITTY WASPY IS HURTING HER BIG STRONG GIANT-MAN!!
X-583
DOWN BELOW, THE YOUNGSTERS STARE IN RAPT FASCINATION... UNAWARE OF THE STRANGE FIGURE WHO ALSO WATCHES FROM THE SHADOWS BEHIND THEM!
I'VE WAITED A LONG TIME FOR THIS MOMENT... AND NOW IT'S HERE!
BY TOUCHING ONE OF MY MANY CONTROL STUDS, I CAN AIM THE NECESSARY QUILLS AT MY HATED ENEMY!

A PERFECT SHOT!!

WASP! SOMETHING *HIT* ME! I LOST MY GRIP!

I'M *FALLING!*

QUICK, JAN...TAKE A REDUCING PILL BEFORE YOU HIT BOTTOM! *MOVE*, GIRL!

B-BUT WHAT GOOD WILL *THAT* DO?

IF YOU TURN INTO THE *WASP* IN TIME, YOU CAN *FLY* TO SAFETY! DON'T WORRY ABOUT *ME*...I'LL BE ALL RIGHT! NOW QUICK... *SWALLOW* IT!

I'LL NEVER KNOW HOW YOU THINK SO *FAST*...EVEN IN EMERGENCIES!

THERE! I *DID* IT! NOW...IF ONLY IT WILL *WORK* IN TIME!

GOOD GIRL! YOU SAVED YOURSELF! NOW FLY OUT FROM UNDER ME, BEFORE I *FALL* ON YOU!

I'M OUT OF HARM'S WAY NOW...BUT WHAT ABOUT *YOU*, HANK?? HOW CAN YOU BREAK YOUR FALL?

IT WON'T HELP *ME* TO TURN ANT-SIZE...I SPROUT NO *WINGS* WHEN I DO! MY BEST BET IS TO *REMAIN* LARGE!

MY MUSCLES, BEING TWICE THEIR NORMAL SIZE AND STRENGTH, ENABLE ME TO DO A FULL FLIP BEFORE STRIKING THE GROUND, SLOWING MY SPEED AND LETTING MY *LEGS* ABSORB THE FULL FORCE OF THE LANDING!

UGHH! ALTHOUGH I ROLLED WITH THE IMPACT...MY ANKLE *STILL* HAD TO BEAR THE WEIGHT OF 360 POUNDS ON IT!

BAH! HE ESCAPED WITH NOTHING WORSE THAN A FRACTURED ANKLE! I'LL HAVE TO DO *BETTER* NEXT TIME!

2

I'LL MAKE MY ESCAPE NOW, WHILE I CAN! THEN I'LL RETURN TO MY LAB TO FIND A *FOOLPROOF* METHOD OF DESTROYING GIANT-MAN! ...I *OWE* HIM THAT!

"I STILL REMEMBER HOW SUCCESSFULLY MY CRIME CAREER BEGAN! MY POWER QUILLS COULD DO ALMOST ANYTHING... STALL MOTORS...OPEN BANK VAULTS... EVEN FLY ME TO SAFETY!"

"EVERYTHING WENT MY WAY, THANKS TO THE INGENIOUS PORCUPINE SUIT I HAD INVENTED WHILE I WAS STILL WORKING AS AN INDUSTRIAL DESIGNER! EACH QUILL WAS A DIFFERENT WEAPON... UNTIL I MET *GIANT-MAN* AND THE *WASP!*"*

BLIPPFT!

*SEE *TALES TO ASTONISH* #48 "DEFYING THE PORCUPINE" —ED.

"JUST WHEN I THOUGHT I WAS UNBEATABLE, THEY SQUIRTED LIQUID CEMENT AT MY PORCUPINE SUIT, COVERING UP ALMOST ALL THE QUILLS! THE CEMENT HARDENED INSTANTLY, RENDERING ME *HELPLESS!*"

ALL MY OFFENSIVE WEAPON QUILLS... COVERED WITH QUICK-DRYING CEMENT!

CAN'T USE ANY OF THEM! GIANT-MAN OUT-SMARTED ME!

"LUCKILY, I WAS ABLE TO ESCAPE BY HURTLING THROUGH THE WINDOW AND PROPELLING MYSELF TO SAFETY WITH MY POWERFUL ROCKET JET QUILLS! GIANT-MAN AND THE WASP HAD BEATEN ME...EXCEPT, HE WAS KNOWN AS *ANT-MAN* AT THAT TIME!"

IF THAT LIQUID CEMENT HAD NOT BEEN NEARBY, I WOULD HAVE DESTROYED ANT-MAN AND HIS FEMALE PARTNER! BUT *NEXT* TIME WE MEET THEY WILL NOT BE SO LUCKY!

RETURNING TO HIS LAB, THE PORCUPINE REMOVES HIS PROTECTIVE SUIT, REVERTING BACK TO THE IDENTITY OF ALEX GENTRY...INVENTIVE GENIUS!

THIS NEW CONCOCTION OF MINE WILL FINISH GIANT-MAN FOREVER!

3.

IT'S A NEW TYPE OF **SLEEPING GAS**, POTENT ENOUGH TO KNOCK OUT A PAIR OF LUNGS AS STRONG AS GIANT-MAN'S! BUT, I'VE GOT TO THINK OF A WAY TO GET CLOSE ENOUGH TO **ADMINISTER** IT TO HIM!

WAIT!! I THINK I KNOW THE ANSWER! ALMOST EVERY BIG CITY HAS A **GIANT-MAN** AND **WASP FAN CLUB!** NEW YORK WILL BE NO EXCEPTION! IF I CAN JUST FIND THE PHONE NUMBER...

A SHORT TIME LATER, AT A MEETING OF THE MIDTOWN CHAPTER OF ONE OF THE MANY **GIANT-MAN, WASP** FAN CLUBS...

OKAY, MEMBERS! LET'S ALL PUT ON OUR GIANT-MAN VILLAINS COSTUMES!

I'VE GOT **MINE** ALL READY!

HEY! THAT'S **TERRIFIC!** YOU'RE SUPPOSED TO BE THE **BLACK KNIGHT!**

LOOK AT **ME!**

I'M THE HUMAN TOP!

YOU LOOK MORE LIKE THE HUMAN **TURNIP,** CHARLIE!

HOLD IT, FELLAS! THERE'S A KNOCK AT THE DOOR! LET OL' **EGG-HEAD** GET IT! I'M ANXIOUS TO SHOW OFF MY OUTFIT ANYWAY!

I'M A, EH, **FAN** OF GIANT-MAN'S! MAY I COME IN, EGG-HEAD?

SAY! IF YOU RECOGNIZE WHO MY COSTUME IS SUPPOSED TO BE, YOU **MUST** BE A FAN! SURE, COME IN, SIR!

GIANT-MAN FAN CLUB IN SESSION KEEP OUT!

4.

I REALIZE I'M CONSIDERABLY *OLDER* THAN YOU LADS! I HOPE YOU HAVE NO AGE LIMIT FOR YOUR MEMBERS!

GEE. WE NEVER EVEN *THOUGHT* ABOUT THAT! NO, IF YOU'RE A FAN, YOU'RE A *FAN!* AND I GUESS THAT'S IT!!

YOU'RE VERY KIND! AND NOW I HAVE AN IDEA FOR YOU! I HEARD GIANT-MAN IS LAID UP WITH AN INJURED ANKLE! DON'T YOU THINK HE'D ENJOY HAVING US *VISIT* HIM... WEARING THESE COSTUMES OF HIS OLD VILLAINS!

SAY! THAT'S A *GREAT* IDEA! IT OUGHTTA *REALLY* CHEER HIM UP!

YES, IT'S A GREAT IDEA, ALL RIGHT! AND I KNOW JUST THE COSTUME *I'LL* BE WEARING... ONLY *MINE* WILL BE THE *REAL THING!*

LATER, IN THE DOWNTOWN FULL-FLOOR LOFT WHICH GIANT-MAN RENTS AS A COMBINATION GYM AND LAB, WE FIND HIM RESTING WITH HIS ANKLE IN A CAST...

I CAN'T WAIT TILL THIS HEALS, JAN. I CAN'T CHANGE MY SIZE UNTIL THE BONE SETS, UNLESS I WANT TO SHATTER IT COMPLETELY

I CAN'T WAIT TILL YOU RECOVER, EITHER! I'M GETTING WEARY OF BEING A NURSEMAID TO BIG, BOLD HELPLESS YOU!

LISTEN, HANDSOME! WHAT'S ALL THAT RUCKUS IN THE STREET?

SOUNDS LIKE A PARADE OF SOME SORT!

GIANT-MAN FAN CLUB

OH, *NO!* IT'S A WHOLE KABOODLE OF YOUR *FANS* IN *COSTUME*... AND HEADING THIS WAY!

5.

WELL, WELL! COME IN, LITTLE FRIENDS! YOU'RE ALL JUST WHAT THE DOCTOR ORDERED!

NOW, DON'T GET TOO WILD, OR GET GIANT-MAN TOO TIRED! HE'S SUPPOSED TO BE RESTING!

GIANT-MAN! GIANT-MAN! RAH-RAH-RAH! GIANT-MAN! GIANT-MAN! SIS-BOOM-BAH!

YAY... GIANT MAN

HOW DO YOU LIKE OUR COSTUMES, GIANT-MAN? CAN YOU TELL WHO WE ARE?

OF COURSE I CAN! YOU'RE THE BLACK KNIGHT... STANDING NEXT TO DOCTOR DOOM!

BUT YOURS IS THE MOST REALISTIC COSTUME, PORCUPINE!

YAY, WASP

HE CAN SAY THAT AGAIN! MY COSTUME SHOULD LOOK REALISTIC... LITTLE DOES THE UNSUSPECTING FOOL REALIZE THAT I'M THE REAL PORCUPINE!

OH, I JUST REMEMBERED... I LEFT A PRESENT FOR GIANT-MAN DOWNSTAIRS IN MY CAR! WOULD YOU GET IT, WASP? IT'S THE GREEN SEDAN ON THE CORNER!

CERTAINLY! I WOULDN'T DREAM OF TEARING ONE OF MY BLUE-EYED PARTNER'S FANS AWAY FROM HIM! YOU WAIT HERE!

I'LL JUST REDUCE DOWN TO WASP SIZE BY TAKING A LITTLE CAPSULE! IT MAKES TRAVELING SO MUCH EASIER FOR ME!

IT WORKED! SHE DOESN'T SUSPECT A THING!!

I'LL BE A PLEASURE TO GET A BREATH OF AIR!

NOW, WITH HER OUT OF THE WAY, I CAN EXECUTE "PHASE TWO" OF MY PLAN!

ALL RIGHT, KIDS! NOW IT'S TIME FOR US ALL TO TAKE OUR MASKS OFF AND SHOW GIANT-MAN WHO WE REALLY *ARE!*

I CAN'T GET OVER THE *PORCUPINE'S* COSTUME! IT'S SO *AUTHENTIC-LOOKING*...DOESN'T SEEM AS HOME-MADE AS ALL THE OTHERS!

NOW! WHILE THE FOOL KIDS ARE BUSY FUMBLING WITH THEIR MASKS...

WITHIN *SECONDS*, I SHALL BE THE ONLY ONE STILL AWAKE IN THIS ENTIRE ROOM!

BEFORE ANYONE CAN MAKE A MOVE, THE ENTIRE AREA IS FILLED WITH THICK, ODORLESS GAS FUMES...

AND THEN, AS THE MISTS BEGIN TO CLEAR...

WHAT HAPPENED?? WH-WHY AM I SO...TIRED??

CAN'T KEEP MY EYES OPEN! TIRED...TIRED...

I *KNEW* THE KIDS WOULD FEEL THE EFFECTS FIRST! THEY'LL BE ASLEEP WITHIN FIVE MORE SECONDS!

HAVE TO LIE DOWN...SHUT MY EYES...CAN'T STAY AWAKE ANY LONGER!

CAN'T FIGHT IT...TOO TIRED...HAVE TO SLEEP...SLEEP...

THE EFFECTS ON THEM WILL LAST FOR A FULL HALF-HOUR! BUT NOW *GIANT-MAN* IS FALLING UNDER...AND I'LL ARRANGE IT SO THAT HE *NEVER* AWAKENS!

7.

BUT THEN, GIANT-MAN MOVES WITH UNEXPECTED SPEED...

YOU THOUGHT MY ANKLE WOULD STOP ME FROM GRABBING YOU, EH?

I'M NOT WORRIED! YOU'LL BE ASLEEP WITHIN SECONDS!

NOT IF I CAN HELP IT! ALTHOUGH IT'S PAINFUL TO PUT WEIGHT ON MY ANKLE, I CAN USE THIS RING FOR SUPPORT, LIKE A CANE!

AND NOW, SUPPOSE THE TWO OF US TAKE A LITTLE RIDE! BEING TWICE AS LARGE AS ANYBODY ELSE, IT TAKES SUCH THINGS AS SLEEPING GAS TWICE AS LONG TO AFFECT ME!

AND NOW, BY SPINNING AROUND ON THE RING, AT BREAKNECK SPEED, I CAN BLOW EVERY LAST TRACE OF SLEEP GAS OUT OF THE ROOM... MAKING YOUR PLAN A TOTAL FAILURE!

I'VE HAD ENOUGH! SEE HOW EASILY I CAN ESCAPE YOU... I MERELY MAKE MY QUILLS BEAT AGAINST YOUR ARM, LIKE A THOUSAND PNEUMATIC DRILLS!

HAH! I KNEW IT! YOU HAD TO LET GO!

8

AND NOW, I'LL LEAVE YOU! I'D ADVISE YOU NOT TO FOLLOW ME! REMEMBER, THE WASP IS NOW *MY PRISONER!*

THE WASP?!

THE OVERSIZED FOOL DIDN'T REALIZE WHEN I SENT HER DOWN TO MY CAR THAT I HAD THE CAR *BOOBY TRAPPED!* ONCE SHE OPENS THE DOOR TO GET IN, IT WILL SHUT TIGHT BEHIND HER, TRAPPING HER INSIDE!

I'VE FLOWN FAR ENOUGH! IT'S TIME TO SHOOT MY *SUCTION TIP QUILL!*

MY JETS PROPEL ME IN SHORT SPURTS... BUT I HAVE TO USE MY INGENUITY IN ORDER TO *STOP,* WHICH IS WHAT I'M DOING *NOW!*

PLIP!

ONCE MY SUCTION CUP QUILL, AT THE END OF AN UNBREAKABLE STEEL CABLE, CATCHES ON TO A BUILDING OR SIMILAR OBJECT, I CAN THEN REEL MYSELF IN, THUS STOPPING MY JET-POWERED ESCAPE FLIGHT!

PLOP!

PERFECT!! I CALCULATED THE DISTANCE PERFECTLY! THIS WILL BRING ME RIGHT TO THE SPOT WHERE I PARKED MY CAR!

IF *GIANT-MAN* IS WATCHING, HE MUST FINALLY REALIZE THAT HE'D *NEVER* HAVE A CHANCE AGAINST THE UNBEATABLE *PORCUPINE!*

HE'S FAR MORE DANGEROUS... FAR MORE POWERFUL THAN HE WAS WHEN I *FIRST* FOUGHT HIM!

9.

...WHICH IS ALL THE MORE REASON I MUST GO AFTER HIM NOW... I MUST *STOP* HIM !! NO MATTER *WHAT* THE COST!

THE DOCTOR TOLD ME NOT TO USE MY ANKLE, BUT I *MUST!* THERE'S TOO MUCH AT STAKE NOW!

IF THE *WASP* IS THE PORCUPINE'S PRISONER, NO POWER ON EARTH WILL KEEP ME FROM FINDING HIM !!

"I WAS A *FOOL* TO LET HER GO ON THAT ERRAND FOR HIM! I SHOULD HAVE SUSPECTED FROM THE START THAT IT WAS A TRAP!"

"I CAN *VISUALIZE* HIS ENTIRE PLAN! HE HAD A PACKAGE ON THE BACK SEAT... THE WASP FLEW IN AND LANDED ON IT..."

SLAM!

"INSTANTLY, A SHIELD OF UNBREAKABLE GLASS SHOT UP FROM BEHIND THE DRIVER'S SEAT, IMPRISONING JAN IN THE BACK!"

"I CAN ALMOST IMAGINE HOW SHE MUST HAVE *CRIED* OUT IN ALARM WHEN SHE DISCOVERED..."

NO HANDLES ON THE DOORS! NO WAY FOR ME TO REACH THE DRIVER... OR THE STREET OUTSIDE! AND THERE'S NO POINT IN WASTING A GROWTH PILL... WHAT *GOOD* WOULD IT DO ME ??

BY THE TIME HE HAS RELIVED ALMOST THE WHOLE TABLEAU IN HIS MIND'S EYE, THE GRIM-VISAGED GIANT-MAN REACHES THE STREET... ONLY TO FIND...

I'M TOO LATE! MY ANKLE SLOWED ME DOWN TOO MUCH! CAN'T REACH THEM! HE'S GETTING AWAY SCOT FREE... AND WITH *JAN!*

10.

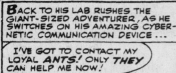
BACK TO HIS LAB RUSHES THE GIANT-SIZED ADVENTURER, AS HE SWITCHES ON HIS AMAZING CYBERNETIC COMMUNICATION DEVICE...

I'VE GOT TO CONTACT MY LOYAL *ANTS!* ONLY *THEY* CAN HELP ME NOW!

WITH THE AID OF THE BUILT-IN CYBERNETIC AMPLIFIER IN HIS HEAD COWL, THE GENIUS OF HENRY PYM IS ABLE TO MAKE HIS THOUGHTS KNOWN TO HIS EVER-PRESENT ARMY OF ANTS...

YOU MUST COMB THE CITY! DO NOT STOP UNTIL YOU HAVE FOUND THE WASP! THESE ORDERS CANNOT BE COUNTER-MANDED!

BUT MINUTES LATER HE IS SHOCKED TO SEE...

IT'S HOPELESS! THE PORCUPINE ANTICIPATED THE MOVE! HIS CAR IS EMITTING CLOUDS OF DDT... THE ANTS WHO LOCATE HIM CANNOT REPORT BACK TO ME!

FINALLY, THE PORCUPINE BRINGS HIS LOVELY CAPTIVE TO A SPECIALLY-PREPARED BUILDING AT THE EDGE OF TOWN...

NO HARM SHALL COME TO YOU! BUT YOU WILL REMAIN A PRISONER HERE UNTIL YOU REVEAL GIANT-MAN'S *TRUE* IDENTITY TO ME!

YOU WILL BE LOCKED IN THAT ROOM... A ROOM WHICH IS AS ESCAPE-PROOF AS HUMAN INGENUITY CAN MAKE IT! SOONER OR LATER YOU WILL TELL ME WHAT I *MUST* KNOW!

NEVER! I'LL NEVER BETRAY GIANT-MAN! NOT IF I STAY THERE FOR-EVER!

THOSE ARE BRAVE WORDS, MY DEAR! BUT WE'LL SEE WHAT YOU SAY AFTER A FEW DAYS OF SOLITUDE HAVE BROUGHT YOU TO THE BRINK OF MADNESS!

YOU'RE THE ONE WHO'S MAD! GIANT-MAN WILL FIND ME, SOONER OR LATER! AND WHEN HE DOES, THERE'LL BE NO PLACE ON EARTH WHERE YOU CAN HIDE!

MEANTIME, THE TOWERING AVENGER FEELS THE ANGER IN HIS BREAST BURST INTO A PAROXYSM OF WHITE HOT *FURY!!*

I *CAN'T* JUST REMAIN HERE DOING *NOTHING!* I'LL FIND THE WASP IF I HAVE TO TEAR THE ENTIRE *CITY* APART!

AND, ONCE I GET MY HANDS ON THE *PORCUPINE*, I'LL MAKE SURE HE NEVER RETURNS TO MENACE ANYONE AGAIN! NOTHING SHORT OF *DEATH* ITSELF WILL STOP ME!

I'VE WORN THIS BANDAGE LONG ENOUGH! NO INJURY... NO PAIN... CAN STOP ME NOW FROM WHAT I HAVE TO DO!

MEANWHILE, AT THE OUTSKIRTS OF TOWN, IN HIS HIDDEN LABORATORY THE PORCUPINE PREPARES FOR PHASE TWO OF HIS SUBTLE PLAN TO DESTROY GIANT MAN!

THE GIRL BELIEVED MY STORY! SHE DOESN'T SUSPECT MY *REAL* MOTIVE!

SHE DOESN'T KNOW THAT HER ROOM IS *NOT* ESCAPE-PROOF!...THAT I REALLY *WANT* HER TO ESCAPE!

...FOR WHEN SHE *DOES*, SHE WILL HEAD FOR GIANT-MAN'S SECRET HEADQUARTERS... AND THIS TINY ELECTRONIC RADAR QUILL, ATTRACTED BY HER BODY HEAT, WILL *FOLLOW* HER!

ALL IS IN READINESS NOW! I HAVE BUT TO REMOVE THIS TINY PLUG, AND LET THE WASP THINK SHE HAS FOUND AN ESCAPE ROUTE!

MINUTES LATER...

WHAT A STROKE OF LUCK! THIS TINY KNOT-HOLE WAS PROBABLY TOO SMALL FOR THE PORCUPINE TO NOTICE... BUT NOT TOO SMALL FOR THE WASP TO ESCAPE THROUGH!

IT IS ALMOST TOO EASY! THERE GOES THE WASP... AND HERE GOES MY INGENIOUS LITTLE QUILL...WHICH WILL RADIO BACK HER LOCATION TO ME DURING EVERY SECOND OF FLIGHT!

IT'S WORKING LIKE A CHARM! SHE'S HEADING UP THE WEST SIDE OF MANHATTAN... HER SPEED IS SLOW....SHE'S RESTING AT EVERY THIRD BLOCK! IT'S A LONG JOURNEY FOR ONE SO SMALL!

NOW SHE'S HEADING FOR THE GEORGE WASHINGTON BRIDGE! GIANT-MAN'S HOME MUST BE IN *NEW JERSEY*!

12.

AND, A SHORT TIME LATER, A SMALL FLYING FIGURE WINGS HER WAY INTO THE WINDOW OF A QUIET HOME OVERLOOKING THE HUDSON PALISADES!

YOU CAN LEAVE THOSE TEST-TUBES NOW, DR. JEKYLL! YOUR EVER-LOVIN' LITTLE PARTNER IS BACK AGAIN!

WASP! YOU ESCAPED! I WAS JUST WORKING ON A NEW FORMULA TO LOCATE YOU BY THE ENERGY IMPRINT OF YOUR HEARTBEAT!

I NEVER REALIZED I COULD MISS ANYONE SO MUCH... WORRY ABOUT ANYONE SO MUCH... NEED ANYONE SO MUCH! WITH YOU GONE, I FELT AS THOUGH...

WHOA, BIG BOY! HOLD IT! WAIT TILL I GET LIFE-SIZED AGAIN, SO YOU CAN PUT YOUR ARMS AROUND ME WHILE YOU SAY THAT!

THE SIGNALS HAVE STOPPED! IT MEANS JUST ONE THING! I'VE FOUND GIANT-MAN! AND NOW TO FINISH HIM OFF, FOR GOOD!

I NOW KNOW THE EXTENT OF HIS POWERS... BUT WITH MY PORCUPINE COSTUME ON, I AM HIS MASTER!

AND EVEN IF HE ESCAPES ME, I SHALL KNOW HIS REAL IDENTITY... HE'LL NEVER BE ABLE TO HIDE FROM ME!

THEN, WHEN THE UNDERWORLD LEARNS THAT THE PORCUPINE IS THE ONE WHO HAS DEFEATED GIANT-MAN, I SHALL BE ABLE TO WRITE MY OWN TICKET... I SHALL BECOME THE KING OF CRIME!

BUT, THE PORCUPINE IS NOT DEALING WITH A CHILD!

WASP! SOMETHING IS HOVERING IN THE AIR ABOVE YOU! I DON'T LIKE IT!

WITH ONE MOVEMENT OF HIS GIGANTIC HAND, THE MIGHTY ADVENTURER SMASHES THE RADAR QUILL TO SMITHEREENS! BUT, THE DAMAGE IS ALREADY DONE... FOR THE PORCUPINE IS ON HIS WAY!

IT'S A MINIATURE DETECTION DEVICE! I THINK YOU'VE BEEN TRICKED, LITTLE PARTNER! PREPARE FOR ACTION!!

13.

SO CONFIDENT IS THE PORCUPINE, THAT HE NEGLECTS HIS D.D.T. DEFENSE VAPOR AS HE DRIVES ACROSS THE WASHINGTON BRIDGE...

LOOK, JAN! A MESSAGE FROM THE ANTS! THE PORCUPINE IS ON HIS WAY! HE'S ALMOST HERE!

CORRECTION, GIANT-MAN! I AM HERE... THANKS TO MY CONCUSSION RAY QUILL SMASHING DOWN YOUR DOOR!

IT'S HIM! QUICKLY, WASP! FLY TO SAFETY!

THERE IS NO SAFE PLACE WHEN YOU FIGHT THE PORCUPINE! WATCH MY FLY-PAPER PELLET BRING HER DOWN!

OH, NO! IF ONE OF THOSE LARGE STICKY SHEETS TOUCH ME, I'LL BE NO USE TO GIANT-MAN!

GIANT-MAN! I CAN'T MOVE! I'M TRAPPED! DON'T COUNT ON ME FOR HELP! YOU'VE GOT TO BEAT HIM ALONE!

I'M ACTUALLY GLAD JAN IS OUT OF IT. PORCUPINE'S TOO DANGEROUS! I WANT TO TACKLE HIM ALONE!

HIS LEFT LEG MUST STILL BE WEAK! IF I CAN AIM THIS TABLE ACCURATELY...

UHHH! HE HIT MY FRACTURED ANKLE! IT'S AGONY! BUT... CAN'T LET IT STOP ME!

NOW THAT I'VE WEAKENED YOU, GIANT-MAN, I'LL FINISH THE JOB... AS ONLY THE PORCUPINE CAN!

YOUR COSTUME IS A HEROIC ONE... BUT IT'S TOO BAD YOU NEGLECTED TO INCLUDE A GAS MASK, AS I HAVE... SO THAT YOU COULD NOT BE STOPPED BY ONE OF MY SLEEPING GAS QUILLS!

SHOULD HAVE PREPARED FOR THIS! CAN'T LET IT AFFECT ME!

IT'S SO POWERFUL, SO FAST-ACTING... I'VE GOT TO FIGHT IT... MUSTN'T GO UNDER... MUSTN'T...

I'VE WON! I'VE BEATEN HIM!

BUT, WITH ONE VALIANT, ALMOST-SUPERHUMAN EFFORT, THE GIANT CRUSADER GRASPS THE EDGE OF THE RUG BENEATH HIS FEET AND SHAKES, FAST AND FURIOUS...

THIS OUGHT TO DISPEL THE GAS... IT'LL BLOW IT THROUGH THE WINDOW!

I NEVER THOUGHT HE'D BOUNCE BACK SO QUICKLY! NOW HE'S COMING FOR ME! I'LL HAVE TO HIDE... IN SOME SMALL SPACE, WHERE HE CAN'T REACH ME!

I SHOULD BE SAFE HERE!... AT LEAST LONG ENOUGH FOR ME TO THINK OF ANOTHER PLAN OF ATTACK!

BUT THERE CAN BE NO SAFETY WHEN YOU FIGHT A FOE WHO CAN ALTER HIS SIZE BY THE MERE SWALLOWING OF A CAPSULE! AND SO...

THERE'S NO PLACE YOU CAN HIDE, PORCUPINE, WHERE ANT-MAN CANNOT REACH YOU!

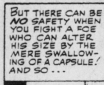

15.

YOU *OUT-SMARTED* YOURSELF THIS TIME, FOOL! YOU MADE YOURSELF *TOO* SMALL! I'LL CRUSH YOU LIKE A FLEA!

EVER TRY TO CATCH A FLEA... IT'S TOUGHER THAN YOU THINK!

HE'S LOST ALL HIS CAUTION! *GOOD!* NOW FOR ANOTHER *GROWTH* CAPSULE!

AND *NOW*, PORCUPINE, WE'LL FINISH THIS OFF...UNDER *GIANT-MAN'S* TERMS!

HE CAUGHT ME NAPPING! BUT I *STILL* HAVE A CHANCE!

I'LL LET HIM GRAB ME! HE'S SURE TO PICK ME UP! THAT'S WHAT I *WANT!* I'VE GOT TO BE ABLE TO REACH HIS BELT CAPSULES!

SO YOU DECIDED TO STOP RUNNING! ALL RIGHT, LITTLE MAN, THAT SAVES US *BOTH* A LOT OF UNNECESSARY TROUBLE!

SO FAR, SO GOOD! I'VE GOT TO BE SURE HE DOESN'T FEEL ME REACHING FOR HIS CAPSULE POUCHES!

I'M A LITTLE *SURPRISED* AT YOU, PORCUPINE! I EXPECTED YOU TO PUT UP A BETTER FIGHT THAN *THIS!* OR ARE YOU *STILL* PLANNING SOMETHING TRICKY??

16

BUT, AS GIANT-MAN SPEAKS...HOLDING THE PORCUPINE UP OFF THE GROUND AS EFFORTLESSLY AS THOUGH HE WERE WEIGHTLESS, ONE QUILL-COVERED ARM SILENTLY MOVES FORWARD, AND...

YOU SEEM STRANGELY SILENT! IF I DIDN'T KNOW BETTER, I'D THINK... WAIT! MY..MY CAPSULE POUCH!

TOO LATE, YOU OVERSIZED BUFFOON! I'VE TAKEN A HANDFUL OF YOUR GROWTH CAPSULES! THIS SNEEZING GAS QUILL WILL HOLD YOU OFF WHILE I SWALLOW THEM!

STOP! COME BACK! YOU DON'T KNOW WHAT YOU'RE... AHH CHOOO!!!

GESUNDHEIT!! DON'T WORRY, I KNOW WHAT I'M DOING ALL RIGHT!

IF ONE CAPSULE MAKES YOU TWELVE FEET TALL, IMAGINE HOW BIG I'LL BECOME WHEN I TAKE ALL OF YOUR GROWTH PILLS! YOU WON'T HAVE A CHANCE AGAINST ME!

YOU'RE MAD! YOU MUSTN'T TAKE ALL THOSE CAPSULES! LET ME EXPLAIN! WAIT!!

HAH! YOU CAN'T KEEP THE TERROR OUT OF YOUR VOICE! YOU KNOW YOU'RE FINISHED NOW! TOO LATE! I'VE TAKEN THEM!

I CAN FEEL THEM TAKING EFFECT ALREADY! WITHIN SECONDS I'LL BE ABLE TO SMASH YOU AT WILL! YOU'RE FINISHED, GIANT-MAN...THE PORCUPINE HAS WON!

17

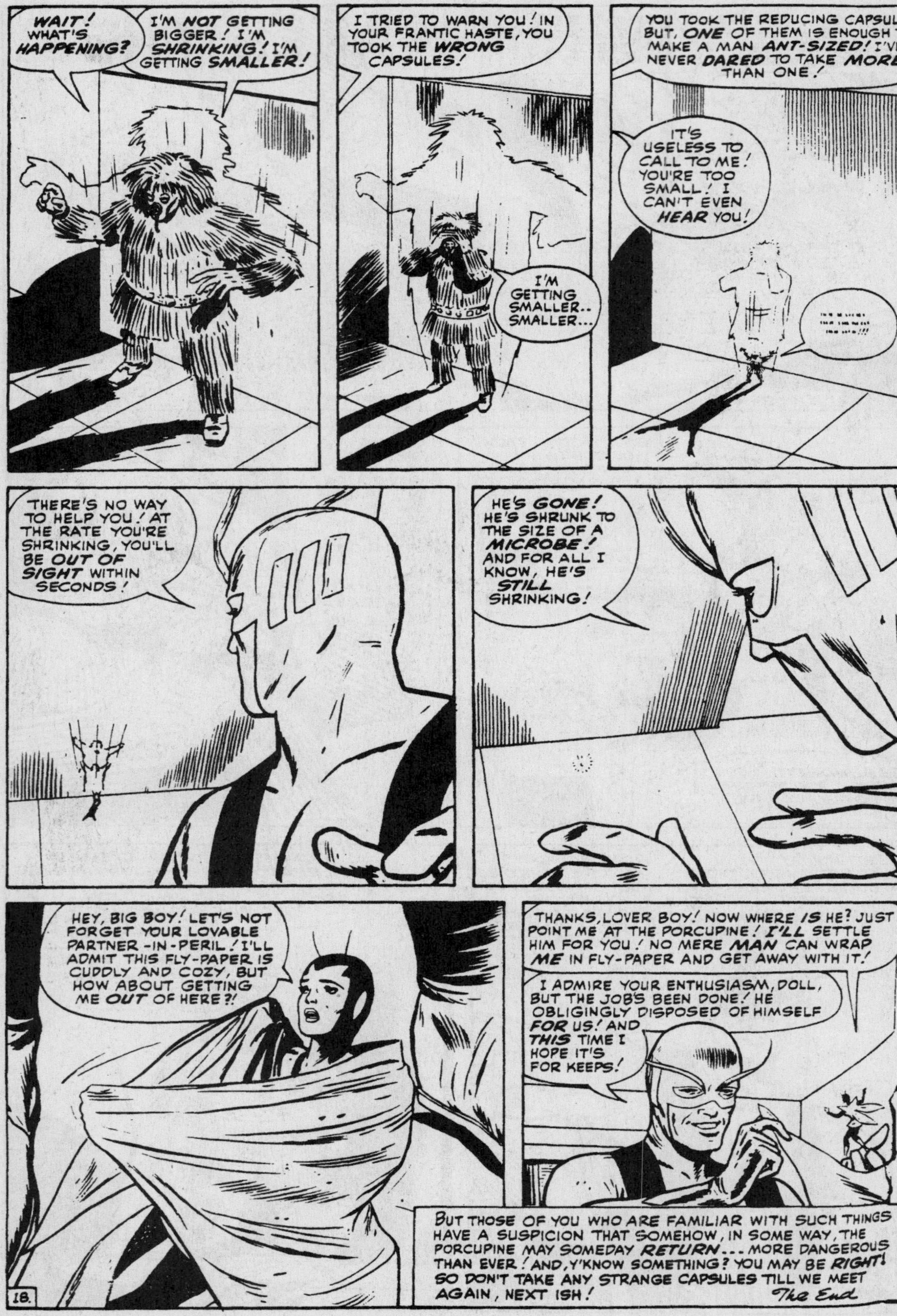
WAIT! WHAT'S HAPPENING?
I'M NOT GETTING BIGGER! I'M SHRINKING! I'M GETTING SMALLER!
I TRIED TO WARN YOU! IN YOUR FRANTIC HASTE, YOU TOOK THE WRONG CAPSULES!
I'M GETTING SMALLER.. SMALLER...
YOU TOOK THE REDUCING CAPSULES! BUT, ONE OF THEM IS ENOUGH TO MAKE A MAN ANT-SIZED! I'VE NEVER DARED TO TAKE MORE THAN ONE!
IT'S USELESS TO CALL TO ME! YOU'RE TOO SMALL! I CAN'T EVEN HEAR YOU!
THERE'S NO WAY TO HELP YOU! AT THE RATE YOU'RE SHRINKING, YOU'LL BE OUT OF SIGHT WITHIN SECONDS!
HE'S GONE! HE'S SHRUNK TO THE SIZE OF A MICROBE! AND FOR ALL I KNOW, HE'S STILL SHRINKING!
HEY, BIG BOY! LET'S NOT FORGET YOUR LOVABLE PARTNER-IN-PERIL! I'LL ADMIT THIS FLY-PAPER IS CUDDLY AND COZY, BUT HOW ABOUT GETTING ME OUT OF HERE?!
THANKS, LOVER BOY! NOW WHERE IS HE? JUST POINT ME AT THE PORCUPINE! I'LL SETTLE HIM FOR YOU! NO MERE MAN CAN WRAP ME IN FLY-PAPER AND GET AWAY WITH IT!
I ADMIRE YOUR ENTHUSIASM, DOLL, BUT THE JOB'S BEEN DONE! HE OBLIGINGLY DISPOSED OF HIMSELF FOR US! AND THIS TIME I HOPE IT'S FOR KEEPS!
BUT THOSE OF YOU WHO ARE FAMILIAR WITH SUCH THINGS HAVE A SUSPICION THAT SOMEHOW, IN SOME WAY, THE PORCUPINE MAY SOMEDAY RETURN... MORE DANGEROUS THAN EVER! AND, Y'KNOW SOMETHING? YOU MAY BE RIGHT! SO DON'T TAKE ANY STRANGE CAPSULES TILL WE MEET AGAIN, NEXT ISH!
The End
18.

THE WONDERFUL WASP TELLS A TALE

"WHEN WAKES THE COLOSSUS!"

I THOUGHT YOU WERE GOING TO THE *VETERANS HOSPITAL*, JAN, TO ENTERTAIN THE FELLAS WITH SOME FANTASY TALES!

I *AM*, HANK! BUT FIRST I HAVE TO PUT ON MY FACE! I WOULDN'T WANT THOSE HANDSOME EX-G.I.'S TO SEE ME NOT LOOKING MY BEST!

STORY PLOT: STAN LEE
SCRIPT & ART: L. D. LIEBER
INKING: D. HECK
LETTERING: R. HOLLOWAY

WANT ME TO GIVE YOU A *PREVIEW* OF ONE OF THE STORIES I'LL TELL?

I KNOW BETTER THAN TO TRY TO *STOP* YOU, KID! SHOOT!

"IT TAKES PLACE ON AN ALIEN WORLD FAR OUT IN SPACE! THERE, AN EVIL WARLORD NAMED MINGO AND HIS RUTHLESS HORDE PREY ON THE PLANET'S MORE PRIMITIVE RACES...."

SILENCE! MINGO SPEAKS.

HEAR ME! EVEN THOUGH THE PRIMITIVES FAR OUTNUMBER US WE CAN CONQUER THEM EASILY BY PLAYING UPON THEIR FEARS AND SUPERSTITIONS!

THUS, WE SHALL ATTACK THE ASIKII TRIBE AT NIGHT, FOR THEY WILL OFFER NO RESISTANCE THEN! THEY BELIEVE IF THEY'RE SLAIN AT NIGHT, THEIR GODS WILL BE UNABLE TO FIND THEIR SOULS IN THE DARK TO CARRY THEM TO HEAVEN... AND THEY WILL REMAIN IN LIMBO FOREVER!

AND SO, MINGO AND HIS WARRIORS LAUNCH THEIR ATTACK IN THE DEAD OF NIGHT!

SPARE US! WE SURRENDER!

WE'RE DROPPING OUR ARMS! DON'T SLAY US!

THE FOOLS! TAKE THEM ALL PRISONER!

PLAYING UPON HIS VICTIMS' PAGAN FEARS, MONGO VANQUISHES ONE RACE AFTER ANOTHER...

THE DELTONIANS WORSHIP ANIMALS! THEY WON'T DARE FIGHT THEM! AND SO...

ATTACK!!

THEY'RE WEARING THE GUISE OF OUR SACRED CREATURES! WE DARE NOT STRIKE BACK!

WE MUST SURRENDER!

AGAIN WE WIN, WITHOUT THE LOSS OF A SINGLE WARRIOR! HOW EASY IT IS TO DEFEAT THE PRIMITIVES THROUGH THEIR OWN FOOLISH SUPERSTITIONS!

BUT A TYRANT'S PROBLEMS DON'T END WITH CONQUEST...

I'VE VANQUISHED AND SUBJUGATED ALL THE INFERIOR RACES! BUT NOW I MUST MAKE CERTAIN THAT THEY DON'T REBEL AGAINST MY RULE! BUT HOW?

WAIT-- I HAVE IT! I'LL KEEP THEM FROM REVOLTING WITH THE SAME WEAPON THAT I USED TO CONQUER THEM-- THEIR OWN SUPERSTITIOUS FEAR!

2

SO, THE CUNNING WARLORD PUTS A SINISTER PLAN INTO OPERATION...

YOU WANT THE STATUE TO BE 200 FEET HIGH, SIRE!!

YES! IT MUST BE HUGE AND AWESOME... TO STRIKE FEAR INTO THE HEARTS OF ALL THE SUPERSTITIOUS FOOLS WHO WILL BEHOLD IT!

AND, WHEN THE STONE COLOSSUS IS FINALLY COMPLETED, MINGO ADDRESSES THE CAPTIVE PRIMITIVES...

SEE HOW THE GIANT'S EYES ARE CLOSED IN SLUMBER! BUT, EVEN WHILE THE GIANT SLEEPS, HE STANDS GUARD OVER MY LAND! AND IF EVER YOU SHOULD OPPOSE MY RULE-- IF EVER YOU SHOULD REVOLT AGAINST MY AUTHORITY--THEN, MY STONE GIANT SHALL AWAKEN AND WREAK HIS TERRIBLE VENGEANCE UPON YOU!

AND, THE INCREDIBLE THREAT HITS HOME!

THE STONE GIANT DOES INDEED LOOK CRUEL!

IF WE ANGERED THE COLOSSUS IT WOULD SHOW US NO MERCY! IT WOULD DESTROY US ALL!

WHILE THE GREAT STATUE STANDS, WE MUST OBEY MINGO WITHOUT QUESTION-- FOR DEFIANCE WOULD MEAN OUR DOOM!

THUS, THE CAPTIVE RACES ACCEPT THE TYRANNY OF MINGO WITHOUT PROTEST...

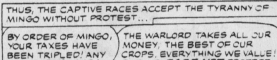

BY ORDER OF MINGO, YOUR TAXES HAVE BEEN TRIPLED! ANY COMPLAINTS!

THE WARLORD TAKES ALL OUR MONEY, THE BEST OF OUR CROPS, EVERYTHING WE VALUE! BUT WE DARE NOT PROTEST... NOT WHILE THE GIANT EXISTS!

COME! ALL MALES OVER THIRTEEN ARE ORDERED TO WORK IN THE MINES!

THEY'RE TAKING OUR SON! (SOB!)

AND WE DARE NOT STOP THEM--LEST WE AWAKEN THE SLEEPING COLOSSUS!

WE'RE HELPLESS! HELPLESS!

HA! HA! NEVER HAS AN OPPRESSOR BEEN SO SAFE FROM THOSE WHOM HE TYRANNIZES!

AND ALL BECAUSE I'VE CONVINCED THE GULLIBLE FOOLS OF THE IMPOSSIBLE--THAT THEIR DEFIANCE WOULD BRING A STONE STATUE TO LIFE!

3

BUT AS MINGO'S ABUSES INCREASE, THE ENSLAVED PEOPLE GROW MORE DESPERATE... AND SOON BOLD VOICES ARE HEARD... AND THE TIDE BEGINS TO TURN!

LET US REVOLT! WE FAR OUTNUMBER THE OPPRESSORS AND CAN DEFEAT THEM EASILY! I TELL YOU WE HAVE NOTHING TO FEAR BUT OUR OWN COWARDICE!

VIKOR IS RIGHT! THE TIME HAS COME TO FIGHT FOR FREEDOM!

EVEN IF THE STONE COLOSSUS AWAKENS AND DESTROYS US, WE WOULD BE BETTER OFF THAN LIVING IN BONDAGE!

SO, LED BY VIKOR, THE SUBJUGATED PRIMITIVES REVOLT AGAINST THEIR TYRANNICAL MASTERS!

ATTACK! SEIZE THEIR WEAPONS!

ONWARD! FOR LIBERTY!

BUT, SUDDENLY...

BEHOLD THE GREAT STATUE! ITS EYE IS... OPENING!

THE STONE GIANT IS AWAKENING!

IT'S HAPPENING JUST AS MINGO WARNED IT WOULD!

THE COLOSSUS HAS COME TO LIFE!

HE SEES US! HE'S COMING TOWARDS US!

YOU, VIKOR... THIS IS ALL YOUR FAULT! YOU TOLD US WE HAD NOTHING TO FEAR! AND NOW WE'RE DOOMED! WE'LL MAKE YOU PAY FOR THIS!

WAIT! LOOK! THE STATUE IS PASSING US BY! IT'S LUMBERING TOWARD MINGO'S PALACE!

4

AND MOMENTS LATER, WHEN THE INCREDIBLE TITAN HAS REACHED ITS OBJECTIVE, IT *STRIKES!*

NO! *IT CAN'T BE!* THE STONE FIGURE HAS ACTUALLY COME TO *LIFE!!*

AS SAVAGELY— AS MERCILESSLY— AS A WRATHFUL GOD OF VENGEANCE, THE STONE GIANT DEMOLISHES MINGO'S CITADEL OF EVIL!

ALL IS LOST!

FLEE! FLEE FOR YOUR LIVES!

AND, WHEN THE HOLOCAUST IS ENDED, THE TOWERING STATUE RETURNS AGAIN TO ITS MOTIONLESS STATE!

THE TYRANTS HAVE BEEN ROUTED! WE'RE FREE! *FREE!*

YOU WERE *RIGHT,* VIKOR! YOU SAID WE HAD NOTHING TO FEAR BUT OUR OWN *COWARDICE!*

YES, FOR I FELT THAT WHATEVER SUPERNATURAL POWER CONTROLLED THE COLOSSUS WOULD NOT GUIDE IT AGAINST MEN SEEKING ONLY THEIR LIBERTY! *MORTALS* MAY BE EVIL, BUT THE *SUPERNATURAL POWERS ARE NOT!*

AS FOR THE ONCE-MIGHTY MINGO, IT IS RUMORED THAT FROM THAT DAY ON, HE WANDERED AIMLESSLY ABOUT THE COUNTRY-SIDE, MUTTERING INCOHERENTLY LIKE A WITLESS FOOL...

THE STATUE *LIVED!!* NOT POSSIBLE... NO... NOT POSSIBLE!

WELL, THAT'S MY TALE, HANK! HOW DID YOU LIKE...? WHY, YOU'VE HAD YOUR NOSE BURIED IN THOSE *TEST TUBES* ALL THE TIME I'VE BEEN TALKING! YOU DIDN'T HEAR A *THING!*

HUH? WHAT DID YOU SAY, JAN, DEAR?

I SAID I'M *LEAVING!* YOU -- YOU *BRUTE!*

GOSH! I WONDER WHAT MAKES THAT GAL SO *EXCITABLE?*

5

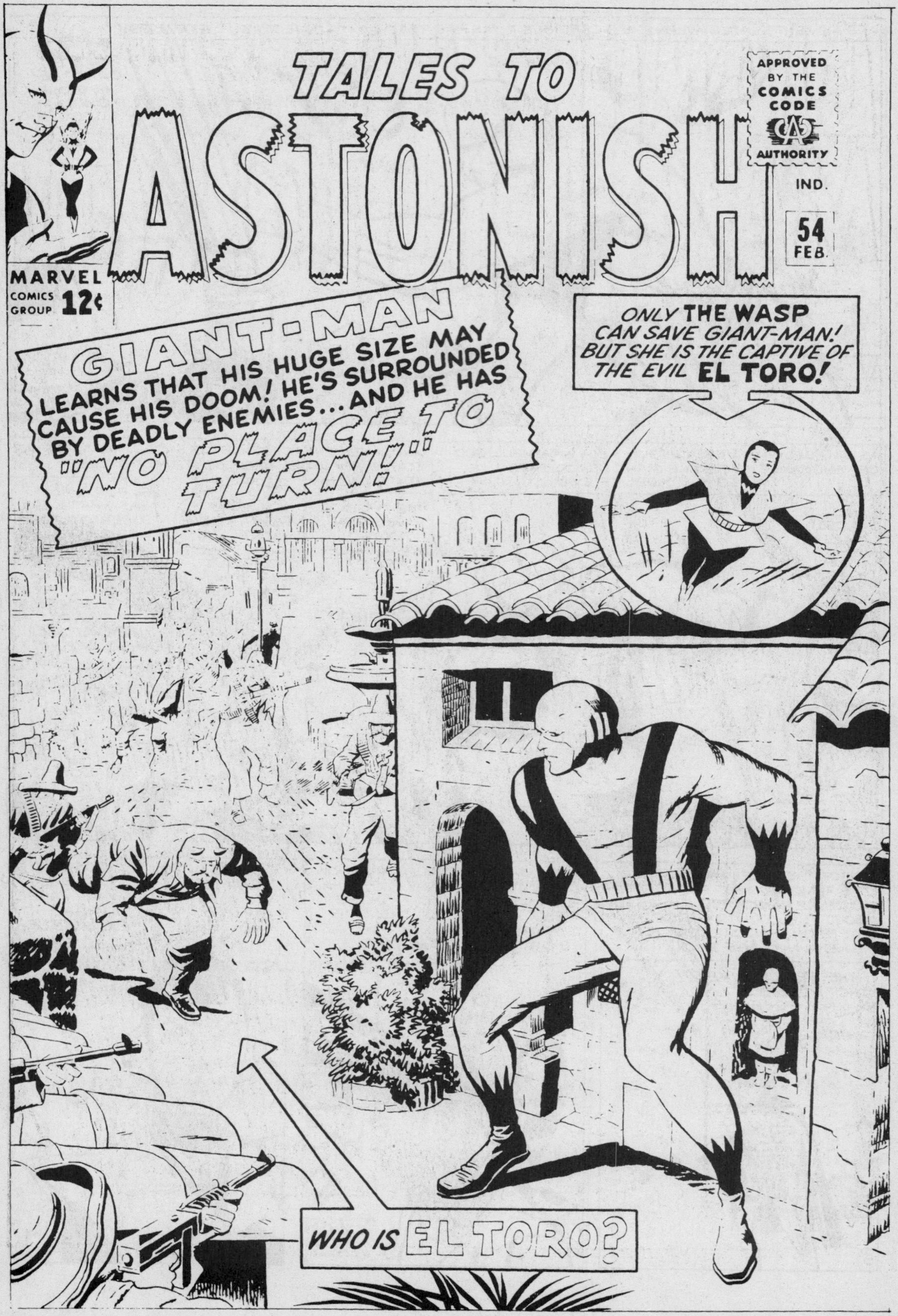

TALES TO ASTONISH
APPROVED BY THE COMICS CODE CA AUTHORITY
IND.
54 FEB.
MARVEL COMICS GROUP 12¢
GIANT-MAN LEARNS THAT HIS HUGE SIZE MAY CAUSE HIS DOOM! HE'S SURROUNDED BY DEADLY ENEMIES... AND HE HAS "NO PLACE TO TURN!"
ONLY THE WASP CAN SAVE GIANT-MAN! BUT SHE IS THE CAPTIVE OF THE EVIL EL TORO!
WHO IS EL TORO?

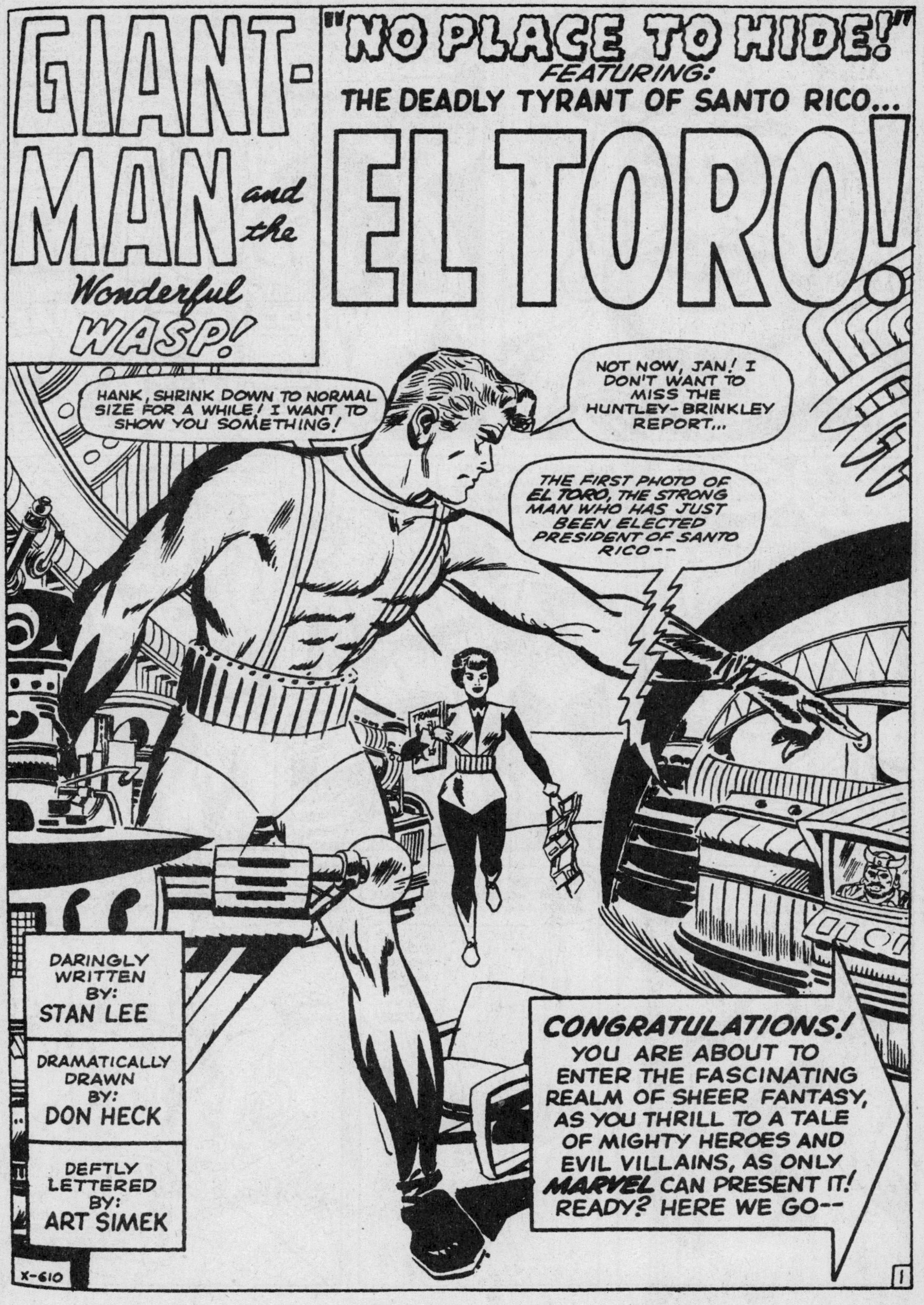
GIANT-MAN and the Wonderful WASP!
"NO PLACE TO HIDE!"
FEATURING:
THE DEADLY TYRANT OF SANTO RICO...
EL TORO!
HANK, SHRINK DOWN TO NORMAL SIZE FOR A WHILE! I WANT TO SHOW YOU SOMETHING!
NOT NOW, JAN! I DON'T WANT TO MISS THE HUNTLEY-BRINKLEY REPORT...
THE FIRST PHOTO OF EL TORO, THE STRONG MAN WHO HAS JUST BEEN ELECTED PRESIDENT OF SANTO RICO--
DARINGLY WRITTEN BY: STAN LEE
DRAMATICALLY DRAWN BY: DON HECK
DEFTLY LETTERED BY: ART SIMEK
CONGRATULATIONS! YOU ARE ABOUT TO ENTER THE FASCINATING REALM OF SHEER FANTASY, AS YOU THRILL TO A TALE OF MIGHTY HEROES AND EVIL VILLAINS, AS ONLY MARVEL CAN PRESENT IT! READY? HERE WE GO--
X-610
1

--HIS ELECTION IS ONE OF THE YEAR'S BIG POLITICAL UPSETS! NO ONE EXPECTED EL TORO TO WIN--

--- THOUGH SANTO RICO HAS LONG BEEN A DEMOCRATIC REPUBLIC, THIS COMMUNIST-SUPPORTED CANDIDATE WON BY THE LARGEST VOTE EVER--

IT DOESN'T MAKE *SENSE!* WHY DID THEY ELECT A *RED??!*

HENRY PYM! DON'T YOU *DARE* TURN YOUR BACK ON ME WHEN I WANT TO TALK TO YOU!

SORRY, JAN! I WAS DEEP IN THOUGHT, I GUESS!

WELL, NOW THAT I'VE GOT YOUR EAR--

I'LL TURN *THIS* RIGHT OFF! I HAVE SOME *VACATION* PLANS TO DISCUSS WITH YOU!

GOOD NIGHT, DAV--

CLICK!

VACATION PLANS?? I *TOLD* YOU WE HAVEN'T TIME FOR A VACATION!

OKAY THEN, I'LL *MAKE* TIME! I'LL SMASH A FEW OF YOUR SILLY OL' TEST TUBES...

GIVE ME THOSE, YOU LITTLE IMP! JAN! COME BACK HERE!

SORRY, BIG BOY! WE WASPS CAN BE *VERY* STUBBORN!

NICE TRY, PESTY-- BUT *GIANT-MAN* CAN BECOME *ANT-MAN* JUST AS EASILY!

OH, GO COMB YOUR HAIR WITH FLY-PAPER!

I'LL DO BETTER THAN THAT, YOUNG LADY! A *RUBBER-BAND* IS ALL I'LL NEED TO CATCH YOU--

TWANG

UH OH! SHE JUST TOOK ANOTHER *GROWTH* CAPSULE!

2

HI, SHORTY! I OUT-FOXED YOU *THIS* TIME!

ONLY BECAUSE YOU'VE HAD A GOOD *TEACHER*, DOLL!

JUST LIKE A MAN TO TRY TO TAKE CREDIT FOR *EVERYTHING!*

NOW TAKE YOUR GROWTH PILL LIKE A GOOD BOY AND WE'LL HAVE OUR LITTLE TALK!

YOU *ASKED* FOR IT, LADY!

OHNN! HENRY PYM-- HOW *COULD* YOU??!

THERE'S ONLY ROOM FOR *ONE* BOSS IN THIS COMBO, JAN BABY!

NOW, I'LL JUST KEEP YOUR SIZE-CAPSULES TILL YOU RETURN MY TEST TUBE!

ALL RIGHT, YOU BIG GROUCH! I DIDN'T *WANT* THE SILLY THING ANYWAY!

C'MON, GORGEOUS, DON'T SULK! WHAT SAY WE KISS AND MAKE UP?

BITE YOUR TONGUE, MISTER!

THEN AFTER TAKING ANOTHER GROWTH PILL...

I WOULDN'T KISS *YOU* IF YOU WERE THE LAST MAN ON EARTH, YOU BIG *BULLY*, YOU!!

FOR THE LOVE OF *PETE!* THE MORE I KNOW ABOUT FEMALES, THE LESS I KNOW ABOUT THEM!

THERE! NOW I'VE GOT HIM SO MIXED-UP THAT THE *NEXT* TIME I SUGGEST A VACATION HE'LL *AGREE* BEFORE HE KNOWS WHAT HE'S DOING!

A SHORT TIME LATER...

MUST BE JAN, COMING BACK TO MAKE UP!

KNOCK! KNOCK!

3

OH *NO!!* IT'S ONE OF MY *FAN CLUBS!!*

HI, HERO MINE! THE WASP CALLED AND TOLD US YOU WERE *FREE* TODAY, AND WOULD *LOVE* TO HAVE COMPANY!

SO WE CAME TO *INTERVIEW* YOU! WE'VE GOT A *ZILLION* QUESTIONS TO ASK--!!

JAN BABY, HOW COULD YOU *DO* THIS TO ME??!

ENJOYING YOURSELF, LOVER BOY? I FIGURE *THIS* MAKES US EVEN!

I'LL SPEAK TO *YOU* LATER!!

WOULD YOU SHOW US HOW YOU CHANGE SIZE AGAIN, GIANT-MAN??

HOLD IT, KIDS! THERE'S THE PHONE!

MY! LOOK AT THAT *REACH!*

I SURE WOULDN'T WANNA EAT AT THE SAME BOARDING HOUSE TABLE WITH *HIM!*

R-ING-G-G!

SECONDS LATER...

SORRY, YOUNGSTERS! IT'S AN OFFICIAL CALL--FROM *WASHINGTON!* YOU'LL HAVE TO LEAVE NOW!

AND THEN, AFTER THE LAST RELUCTANT FAN HAS LEFT...

YOU SHOULD BE *ASHAMED* OF YOURSELF, TELLING A FIB TO GET RID OF YOUR FANS!

IT WASN'T A FIB, GORGEOUS!

GRAB YOUR TOOTHBRUSH! WE'RE OFF TO WASHINGTON!

4

BUT *WHY*, HANK? WHAT'S GOING ON?

WE'LL FIND OUT WHEN WE *GET* THERE! NOW CLOSE THOSE RUBY LIPS WHILE I CALL MY FLYING ANT!

MEANWHILE, OUTSIDE PYM'S DOOR--

WE'LL WAIT FOR HIM HERE, AND THEN *FOLLOW* HIM! HE MUST BE OFF ON A BIG CASE!

GOOD THING WE CHANGED TO ANT-SIZE, OR WE'D NEVER SHAKE OUR FAITHFUL FANS!

FINALLY, AFTER WAITING ANOTHER FIFTEEN MINUTES...

THE DOOR'S UN-LOCKED!

HECK! THEY GOT AWAY! I WONDER WHERE THEY'RE OFF TO??

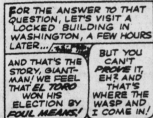

FOR THE ANSWER TO THAT QUESTION, LET'S VISIT A LOCKED BUILDING IN WASHINGTON, A FEW HOURS LATER...

AND THAT'S THE STORY, GIANT-MAN! WE FEEL THAT *EL TORO* WON HIS ELECTION BY *FOUL MEANS!*

BUT YOU CAN'T *PROVE* IT, EH? AND THAT'S WHERE THE WASP AND I COME IN!

WE WANT YOU TO *GO* TO SANTO RICO, AS TOURISTS, AND SEE IF YOU CAN UNEARTH ANY EVIDENCE OF A COMMUNIST PLOT! THEN, REPORT BACK TO THE ORGANIZATION OF AMERICAN STATES--

AND SO, BEFORE DAY'S END, A SPEEDY JET LANDS IN SANTO RICO WITH TWO "TOURISTS" ABOARD...

I FEEL LIKE A CHARACTER IN AN IAN FLEMING NOVEL!

YOU *LOOK* LIKE ONE TOO, GORGEOUS! WELL, HERE WE ARE--

EVERYTHING'S *CHANGED* HERE SINCE THE ELECTION! IT LOOKS LIKE A REAL *POLICE STATE!*

ARMED TROOPS EVERYWHERE! EL TORO MEANS TO RULE WITH AN IRON HAND!

HERE, JAN--*YOU* HOLD OUR SIZE CAPSULES! IN CASE I'M SEARCHED, I WOULDN'T WANT THEM TO BE FOUND ON ME!

I'LL KEEP THEM IN MY HANDBAG-- WITH MY COSMETICS!

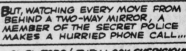

BUT, WATCHING EVERY MOVE FROM BEHIND A TWO-WAY MIRROR, A MEMBER OF THE SECRET POLICE MAKES A HURRIED PHONE CALL...

SI, EL TORO! THEY LOOK *SUSPICIOUS!* THEY MUST BE QUESTIONED!

5

AMERICANS!! HERE?? THEY MUST BE *SPIES!* SEIZE THEM!

HANK--HELP! THEY'RE TRYING TO *ARREST* ME!

TAKE YOUR HANDS OFF THAT GIRL! SHE'S DONE NOTHING!

WE SHALL TAKE *YOU* TOO, GRINGO!

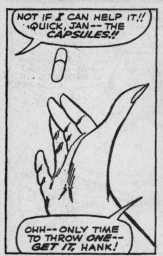

NOT IF I CAN HELP IT!! QUICK, JAN-- THE *CAPSULES!!*

OHH-- ONLY TIME TO THROW *ONE*-- GET IT, HANK!

CATCHING THE ONE CAPSULE, HENRY PYM RACES AROUND A NEARBY BUILDING, DROPPING HIS OUTER CLOTHES AS HE SWALLOWS THE POTENT PILL, UNTIL...

HANG ON, JAN HONEY! HERE COMES *GIANT-MAN!!*

I'LL TAKE A SHORT-CUT THRU THAT BUILDING AND--AH! THERE THEY ARE!

A COSTUMED *GIANT!!* EL TORO-- HELP!

CRASH!

BAH! NO ONE CAN RESIST THE BATTERING ATTACK OF *EL TORO*-- NO MATTER *WHAT* HIS SIZE!!

OHHH--

6

SECONDS LATER, AS GIANT-MAN PAINFULLY STRUGGLES TO HIS FEET...

MY ACHIN' BACK!! SO *THAT'S* WHY HE CALLS HIMSELF *EL TORO*... MEANING "THE BULL"! THAT HEADGEAR HE WEARS ISN'T JUST FOR *SHOW*-- IT'S ACTUALLY A *WEAPON!!*

BUT THEY'RE *GONE* NOW-- AND THEY TOOK JAN *WITH* THEM!

HOLY SMOKE!! JAN HAD ALL THE SIZE-CAPSULES WITH HER! THAT MEANS I'VE GOT TO *REMAIN* AS GIANT-MAN UNTIL I CAN *FIND* HER! NO WONDER THEY WERE WILLING TO JUST *LEAVE* ME HERE--

CONSIDERING MY SIZE, THEY CAN FIND ME WHENEVER THEY *WANT* TO! HOW CAN A TWELVE-FOOT TALL MAN *HIDE* HIMSELF??

AND, IN HIS HEAVILY-GUARDED HEADQUARTERS, *EL TORO* SEEMS TO HAVE ARRIVED AT THAT SAME CONCLUSION...

NOW THAT THE GIRL IS SAFELY HIDDEN AWAY, WE CAN CONCENTRATE ON DESTROYING THE GRINGO *GIANT-MAN!*

DO NOT LET HIS SIZE FRIGHTEN YOU! A BULLET CAN *STILL* SLAY HIM! SO *FIND* GIANT-MAN --AND SEE THAT HE BOTHERS US NO MORE! NOW GO!

ONCE THE ORDER HAS BEEN GIVEN, THE SMALL CITY IS COMBED UNTIL--

THERE HE IS!

GET HIM!

YOUR LITTLE RECEPTION ISN'T GONNA HELP THE *TOURIST TRADE*, BOYS! BUT, IF YOU WANT ME, YOU'LL HAVE TO COME AND CATCH ME!

WE CANNOT MATCH THE SPEED OF HIS *HUGE* LEGS! YOUR GUNS-- USE YOUR *GUNS!*

7

I'LL OUT-DISTANCE THEM EASILY, AND-- UH OH! DIDN'T NOTICE THESE TELEPHONE WIRES!!

--OOOF!-- LUCKY THEY HURLED ME BACK!! THERE WERE MORE SOLDIERS WAITING AROUND THE CORNER-- FULLY ARMED!!

SO FAR I'M ONE JUMP AHEAD OF THEM-- BUT HOW LONG CAN I STAY THAT WAY!??

IF ONLY I HAD MY SHRINKING CAPSULES--!!

BLAST IT!! I DIDN'T EVEN NOTICE THAT FRUIT STAND!!

TEMPORARILY BLINDED BY THE FALLING CANVAS COVER, GIANT-MAN STUMBLES INTO THE PATH OF AN ONRUSHING CAR, AND...

CARREMBA!!!

BY THE TIME HE HAS SHAKEN OFF THE CANVAS, HE'S COVERED WITH BRUISES AND RACKED WITH PAIN...

THUMP!

8

LATER, IN A DARK ALLEY...

--WHEW!! I NEVER SUSPECTED THAT BEING DOUBLE-SIZE COULD BE SUCH A HANDICAP!! WHAT DO I DO NOW??

BUT BEFORE THE TRAPPED ADVENTURER CAN REACH A DECISION--

IT'S HIM! THE ONE EL TORO'S MEN ARE SEEKING!

MUCH AS I HATE THE TYRANT EL TORO--IT WOULD MEAN DEATH TO ANY CITIZEN WHO DOES NOT REPORT THE GIANT ONE!

HELP! POLICE! HE IS HERE! I HAVE FOUND HIM!

RAT-TAT-TAT!

CAN'T KEEP RUNNING MUCH LONGER! IF ONLY I COULD LEARN WHERE THEY'VE TAKEN JAN!!

NOTHING'S GOING MY WAY! THE BRIDGE ISN'T STURDY ENOUGH TO SUPPORT MY WEIGHT!!

CRASH

MAYBE IT'S JUST AS WELL! I'LL RUN ALONG THESE TRACKS--AT LEAST THERE'LL BE NO OBSTACLES TO SLOW ME DOWN!

THERE HE GOES! STOP HIM!

9

HE'S TOO BIG-- TOO FAST!! WE'LL NEVER CATCH HIM!

NO MATTER! HE WILL DEFEAT *HIMSELF!* THERE CAN BE NO ESCAPE FOR THE GIANT ONE *THAT* WAY!

IF I CAN FOLLOW THESE TRACKS TO OPEN COUNTRY BEFORE THEY STOP ME, I MIGHT HAVE A CHANCE TO HIDE MYSELF IN THE HILLS- TO THINK UP A NEW PLAN OF ATTACK!

I DO NOT UNDERSTAND! WHY CAN THE HUGE ONE NOT ESCAPE THAT WAY??

FOOL! DO YOU FORGET WHAT *TIME* IT IS?? LISTEN--

WHEEEE

IT IS ALMOST THE HOUR OF THREE -- TIME FOR THE RIO EXPRESS -- AND THERE IT IS *NOW!*

A *TRAIN!!* COMING TOWARDS ME THRU THE TUNNEL!! NO TIME TO TURN BACK NOW!!

THAT'S WHY THEY GAVE UP THE CHASE! THEY FIGURED THE *TRAIN* WOULD FINISH ME OFF!!

WHEEEE

I'VE ONLY *ONE* CHANCE-- IF THERE'S ENOUGH CLEARANCE BETWEEN THE CARS AND THE TOP OF THE TUNNEL!!

10

MINUTES LATER, THE FAST EXPRESS HURTLES THRU THE COUNTRYSIDE WITH A FANTASTIC PASSENGER RIDING ABOVE...

LOOKS AS THOUGH MY LUCK IS FINALLY CHANGING! I WAS ABLE TO MAKE IT TO THE TOP OF THE TRAIN -- AND WE WENT BY THE TROOPS SO FAST THAT THEY COULDN'T STOP ME!!

THE ONLY THING IS -- WE'RE COMING TO THE CAPITOL CITY!! BUT THIS TIME NIGHT IS FALLING -- PERHAPS I CAN FIND A HIDING PLACE IN THE DARK, BIG AS I AM!

TWENTY MINUTES LATER...

THIS IS A BIG CHANCE, BUT I'VE GOT TO TAKE IT! IF I CAN JUST REACH MY BAGGAGE IN THE ROOM WHERE THEY'VE LOCKED IT, I'LL BE ABLE TO CONTACT THE ANTS!!

NEXT, WE FIND THE DESPERATE CRIME-FIGHTER HIDING IN THE SHADOWS ON THE ROOF OF THE BUILDING, AS HE TEARS HIS BAGGAGE OPEN AND REMOVES HIS AMAZING PORTABLE CYBERNETIC COMMUNICATOR --

SO FAR, SO GOOD -- THANKS TO THE DARKNESS! NOW TO CONTACT THE NEAREST ANTS...

INASMUCH AS MY DEVICE OPERATES ON THOUGHT IMPULSES, LANGUAGE IS NO BARRIER!!

AH! I'VE REACHED ONE NOW! HE'LL CONTACT THE OTHERS...

WITHIN MINUTES, A VAST NETWORK OF ANTS HAS ONLY ONE THOUGHT IN MIND -- LOCATE THE WASP! AND FINALLY...

CAPTIVE GIRL IN SHIP -- ANCHORED OFF COAST -- INFORM ANT-MAN -- INFORM ANT-MAN --

AND SO, BEFORE DAWN BREAKS OVER THE HORIZON...

THAT MUST BE THE SHIP!

I'M TOO BIG TO FIT IN ANY OF THESE SPEED BOATS...

-- BUT, WHERE THERE'S A WILL THERE'S A WAY! THIS BEATS WATER-SKIING ALL HOLLOW!!

11

FINALLY... WELL! IT'S ABOUT *TIME* YOU FOUND ME!

SAVE THE TEMPER TANTRUM FOR *LATER*, JAN! WHERE ARE THE CAPSULES I GAVE YOU??

IN MY PURSE! THE WAY THEY TIED ME, I COULDN'T *REACH* THEM!

REACHING THRU THE PORTHOLE, IT'S ONLY A MATTER OF SECONDS BEFORE GIANT-MAN GETS THE CAPSULES, TAKING ONE -- AND THEN--

OKAY, DOLL! NOW HERE'S ONE FOR *YOU*--

AND, A SHORT TIME LATER...

EL TORO SAYS THE GIRL MUST BE A DEMOCRATIC *SPY*! SHE IS TO BE EXECUTED BEFORE THE GIANT ONE CAN FIND HER!

WHAT A PITY! SUCH A BEAUTIFUL SENORITA! HOW COULD SUCH A LOVELY ONE BE ANY THREAT TO THE REIGN OF EL TORO??

BUT, WE MUST OBEY EL TORO'S ORDERS! SO-- CARREMBA!! WHAT IS *WRONG*??

THE *GIRL*! SHE HAS *VANISHED*! THE CABIN IS EMPTY!!

WE MUST INFORM EL TORO! SHE MUST NOT ESCAPE!

OUR LIVES WILL BE *WORTHLESS* IF SHE IS NOT RECAPTURED! FASTER, YOU FOOL!!

WOULDN'T THEY BE SURPRISED TO KNOW WE WERE RIDING ON THEIR SHOULDERS?!!

END OF THE LINE, JAN! WE'VE REACHED EL TORO! I'M TAKING A *GROWTH PILL* AGAIN!

AND SO...

I HEAR YOU'VE BEEN *LOOKING* FOR ME, CHUBBINS!

THE *GIANT ONE*!!

I BATTERED YOU *ONCE* WITH MY IRRESISTIBLE CHARGE, AND I'LL DO IT *AGAIN*--

GUESS AGAIN, PLAYMATE! *THIS* TIME YOU'RE NOT TAKING ME BY *SURPRISE*!

12

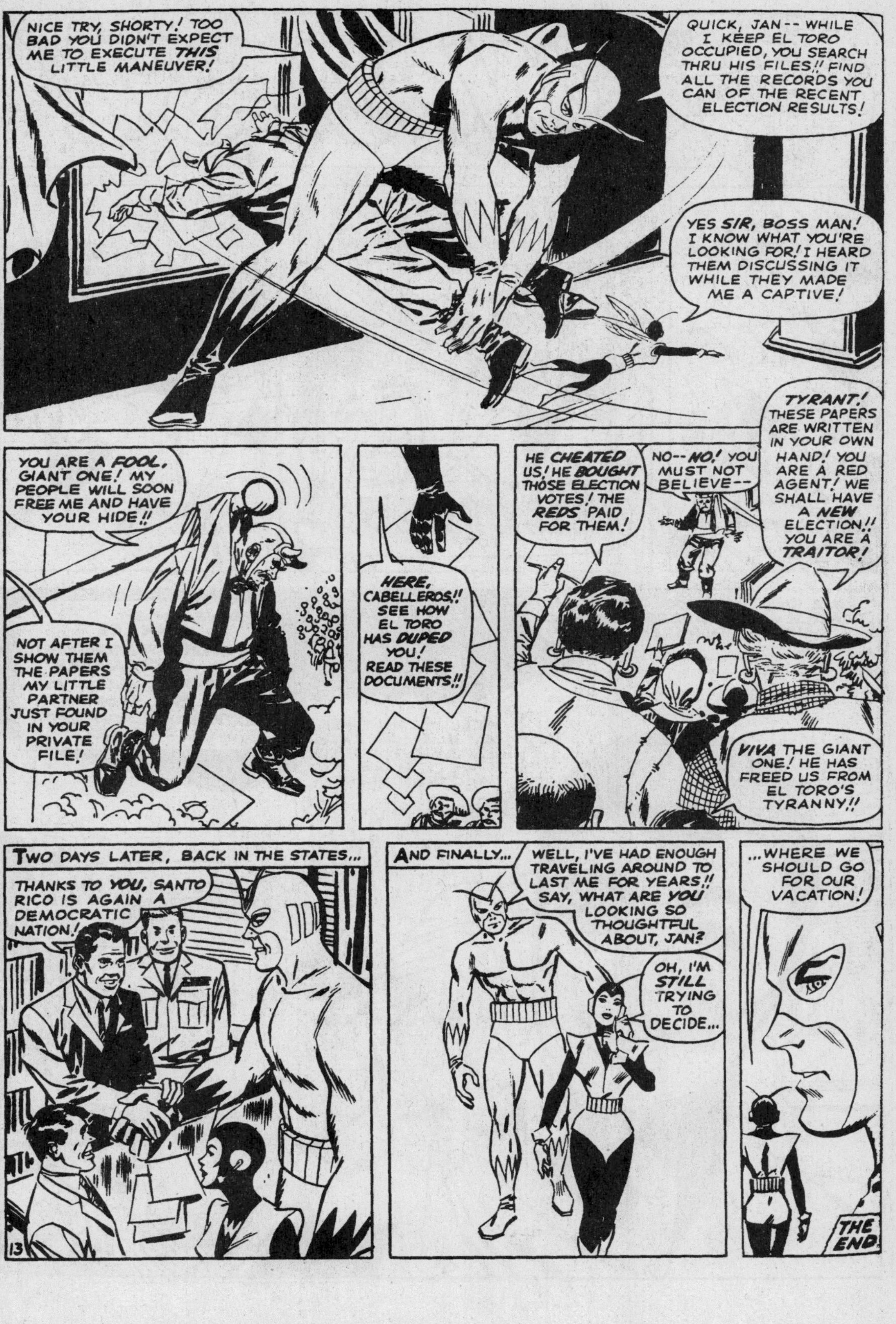
NICE TRY, SHORTY! TOO BAD YOU DIDN'T EXPECT ME TO EXECUTE THIS LITTLE MANEUVER!
QUICK, JAN-- WHILE I KEEP EL TORO OCCUPIED, YOU SEARCH THRU HIS FILES!! FIND ALL THE RECORDS YOU CAN OF THE RECENT ELECTION RESULTS!
YES SIR, BOSS MAN! I KNOW WHAT YOU'RE LOOKING FOR! I HEARD THEM DISCUSSING IT WHILE THEY MADE ME A CAPTIVE!
YOU ARE A FOOL, GIANT ONE! MY PEOPLE WILL SOON FREE ME AND HAVE YOUR HIDE!!
NOT AFTER I SHOW THEM THE PAPERS MY LITTLE PARTNER JUST FOUND IN YOUR PRIVATE FILE!
HERE, CABELLEROS!! SEE HOW EL TORO HAS DUPED YOU! READ THESE DOCUMENTS!!
HE CHEATED US! HE BOUGHT THOSE ELECTION VOTES! THE REDS PAID FOR THEM!
NO-- NO! YOU MUST NOT BELIEVE--
TYRANT! THESE PAPERS ARE WRITTEN IN YOUR OWN HAND! YOU ARE A RED AGENT! WE SHALL HAVE A NEW ELECTION!! YOU ARE A TRAITOR!
VIVA THE GIANT ONE! HE HAS FREED US FROM EL TORO'S TYRANNY!!
TWO DAYS LATER, BACK IN THE STATES...
THANKS TO YOU, SANTO RICO IS AGAIN A DEMOCRATIC NATION!
AND FINALLY...
WELL, I'VE HAD ENOUGH TRAVELING AROUND TO LAST ME FOR YEARS!! SAY, WHAT ARE YOU LOOKING SO THOUGHTFUL ABOUT, JAN?
OH, I'M STILL TRYING TO DECIDE...
...WHERE WE SHOULD GO FOR OUR VACATION!
THE END
13

The WONDERFUL WASP TELLS A TALE!

"CONQUEST!"

AH! A PHONE CALL! MUSIC TO THE EARS OF ANY FEMALE!

BRIINNG

HI, JAN! THIS IS HANK! I'VE JUST FINISHED MY LAB EXPERIMENTS AND I'M FREE FOR AWHILE! HOW ABOUT DINNER AND DANCING?

HENRY PYM...LOVE OF MY LIFE... WHY DID YOU HAVE TO PICK TONIGHT TO FINALLY ASK ME OUT?

WHY? WHAT'S UP?

WELL, MY GIRL FRIEND IS IN THE HOSPITAL, AND, AS A FAVOR I'M BABY SITTING WITH HER SON!

SOME FINE WAY FOR A SNAZZY FEMALE ADVENTURESS TO SPEND HER EVENING, EH?!!

WELL, IT CAN'T ALL BE GLAMOR AND EXCITEMENT, HONEY! WE'LL MAKE IT ANOTHER NIGHT!

DREAMED UP BY: STAN LEE
SCRIBBLED & SKETCHED BY: LARRY LIEBER
FINISHED IN INDIA INK BY: SOL BRODSKY
LETTERED & BORDERED BY: ART SIMEK

C'MON, AUNT JAN... YOU PROMISED TO TELL ME A BEDTIME STORY!

X-570   1

OKAY, TOMMY! PREPARE YOURSELF FOR A FAR-OUT TALE ABOUT A MIGHTY MONARCH NAMED--*SHANN!*

"ON A PLANET FAR AWAY IN TIME AND SPACE, A LONELY, BROODING RULER GAZES OUT OF HIS PALACE WINDOW...'"

MY DOMAIN IS SERENE! MY SUBJECTS ARE PROSPEROUS AND HAPPY! AND ALAS, *THAT* IS THE *TROUBLE!*

THINGS RUN SO SMOOTHLY--THE PEOPLE ARE SO CONTENTED--THAT THEY TAKE ME FOR GRANTED! THEY ARE NO LONGER AWED BY THE GREATNESS OF KING SHANN!

THAT IS WHY I MUST WIN THEIR RESPECT AND ADMIRATION ANEW!

I MUST PERFORM SOME KIND OF ENORMOUS FEAT! BUT *WHAT?* WAIT-- I KNOW! THE CONQUEST OF ANOTHER PLANET! I WILL LEAD MY ARMY IN BATTLE-- LEAD THEM TO VICTORY--AND DOWN THRU THE AGES I WILL BE REMEMBERED AS *SHANN, THE CONQUEROR!*

"SO, AT KING SHANN'S COMMAND, A ONCE-PEACEFUL CIVILIZATION PREPARES FOR WAR!'"

SHANN SAYS WE ARE TOO SOFT AND COMPLACENT! THE RIGORS OF BATTLE WILL STRENGTHEN US!

THE INVASION OF AN ALIEN WORLD! IT IS THE GREATEST UNDERTAKING IN OUR HISTORY!

AND WHEN VICTORY IS OURS, WE WILL HAVE FAME AND GLORY SUCH AS FEW MORTALS HAVE EVER KNOWN!

2

"AFTER MONTHS OF PREPARATION, SHANN'S BATTLE-READY ARMY BLASTS OFF AND SCOURS THE GALAXY IN SEARCH OF A PLANET TO VICTIMIZE.!"

THE SPECTRO-SCOPE SHOWS THAT WORLD UP AHEAD--ANDROMIA --TO BE INHABITED!

THE ANDROMIANS' ARE WEAK! THEY WILL BE UNABLE TO WITHSTAND OUR SUPERIOR ARMED MIGHT!

WHAT SAY YOU, SIRE?

I, SHANN, SAY... ATTACK!

"SO, WITHOUT WARNING, THE ARMADA FROM OUTER SPACE STRIKES.!"

THE INVADERS HAVE CAUGHT US UNAWARE!

THEY DESTROY OUR SPACESHIPS BEFORE WE CAN EVEN GET THEM OFF THE GROUND!

"RALLYING THEIR FORCES, THE ANDROMIANS DEFEND THEIR HOMELAND VALIANTLY! BUT IT'S USELESS! THE SUPERIOR ALIEN FOE LEVELS THEIR CITIES ...!"

"AND LAYS WASTE TO THEIR FERTILE LAND..."

"UNTIL FINALLY ALL RESISTANCE IS CRUSHED.!"

WE SURRENDER!

I HAVE DONE IT! I HAVE VANQUISHED AN ENTIRE PLANET! THIS IS THE PROUDEST MOMENT OF MY LIFE!

3

"HIS MISSION FULFILLED, SHANN, GREATEST OF CONQUERORS, RETURNS HOME STEEPED IN GLORY!"

NOW THE CROWDS CHEER ME! FROM THIS DAY ON MY SUBJECTS WILL BE IN AWE OF ME,...UNBORN GENERATIONS WILL HONOR MY NAME!

LONG LIVE HIS HIGHNESS!!

HOORAY!!

"BUT SHANN SOON LEARNS THAT THERE IS *MORE* TO CONQUEST THAN GLORY! THERE IS ALSO -- *RESPONSIBILITY!*"

WE DEMOLISHED THE ANDROMIANS' CITIES AND RAVAGED THEIR LAND! NOW THEY ARE DESTITUTE AND HUNGRY!

AS A CONQUERED PEOPLE, THEY ARE UNDER OUR DOMAIN! WE CANNOT LET THEM STARVE!

TRUE! WE MUST FEED THEM AND HELP THEM TO REBUILD THEIR CIVILIZATION, UNTIL THEY ARE AGAIN SELF-SUFFICIENT!

"AND SO, MAMMOTH OPERATIONS ARE PUT INTO EFFECT FOR THE SURVIVAL OF A VANQUISHED WORLD!"

LAST TIME, OUR SHIPS CARRIED WARRIORS AND WEAPONS TO ANDROMIA!

NOW THEY TRANSPORT FOOD, FARM EQUIPMENT, AND TECHNICIANS TO HELP RE-BUILD THE RUINED CITIES!

"BUT SUCH A MASSIVE REHABILITATION PROGRAM TAKES MUCH MONEY AND EFFORT... AND SOON, SHANN'S SUBJECTS ARE HEARD TO COMPLAIN..!"

EVER SINCE WE CONQUERED ANDROMIA, OUR TAXES HAVE GONE UP!

AND WE HAVE TO WORK LONGER HOURS TO MANU-FACTURE GOODS FOR THE CAPTIVE PEOPLE, AS WELL AS FOR OURSELVES!

"THE RESENTMENT GROWS..."

WE DIDN'T PROFIT AT *ALL* BY DEFEATING THE ANDROMIANS!

WE WERE MUCH BETTER OFF *BEFORE* WE INVADED THEM!

IT'S ALL SHANN'S FAULT! HE MADE US WAGE WAR ONLY TO ENHANCE HIS OWN PRESTIGE!

4

"AND THUS, IT COMES TO PASS..."

MY SUBJECTS DO NOT WAVE, OR CHEER! THEY ALL *LOATHE* ME, FOR THEY BLAME THEIR PRESENT HARDSHIPS ON ME! I-I NEVER DREAMT IT WOULD TURN OUT THIS WAY!

IT'S ALL SO IRONIC! I IN-VADED ANDROMIA TO WIN *MORE* RESPECT AND ADMIRA-TION FROM MY PEOPLE...

AND NOW, THEY HAVE *NONE* FOR ME! I AM A RULER DESPISED THRUOUT HIS REALM!

SUCH IS THE PRICE OF VANITY --I HAVE CONQUERED A WORLD-- BUT LOST THE RESPECT OF MY OWN PEOPLE!

AND THAT'S IT, TOMMY! SAY, I THOUGHT YOU'D HAVE FALLEN *ASLEEP* BY NOW! DID YOU LIKE THE STORY?

SURE... BUT CAN YOU *EXPLAIN* SOMETHING TO ME?

HE HAS A QUESTION! GOOD! IT MEANS THE TALE *INTERESTED* HIM!

HOW COME YOU DON'T HAVE YOUR *WASP'S WINGS* WHEN YOU'RE NORMAL-SIZED?

KIDS! I'LL *NEVER* FIGURE THEM OUT!

5

THE END

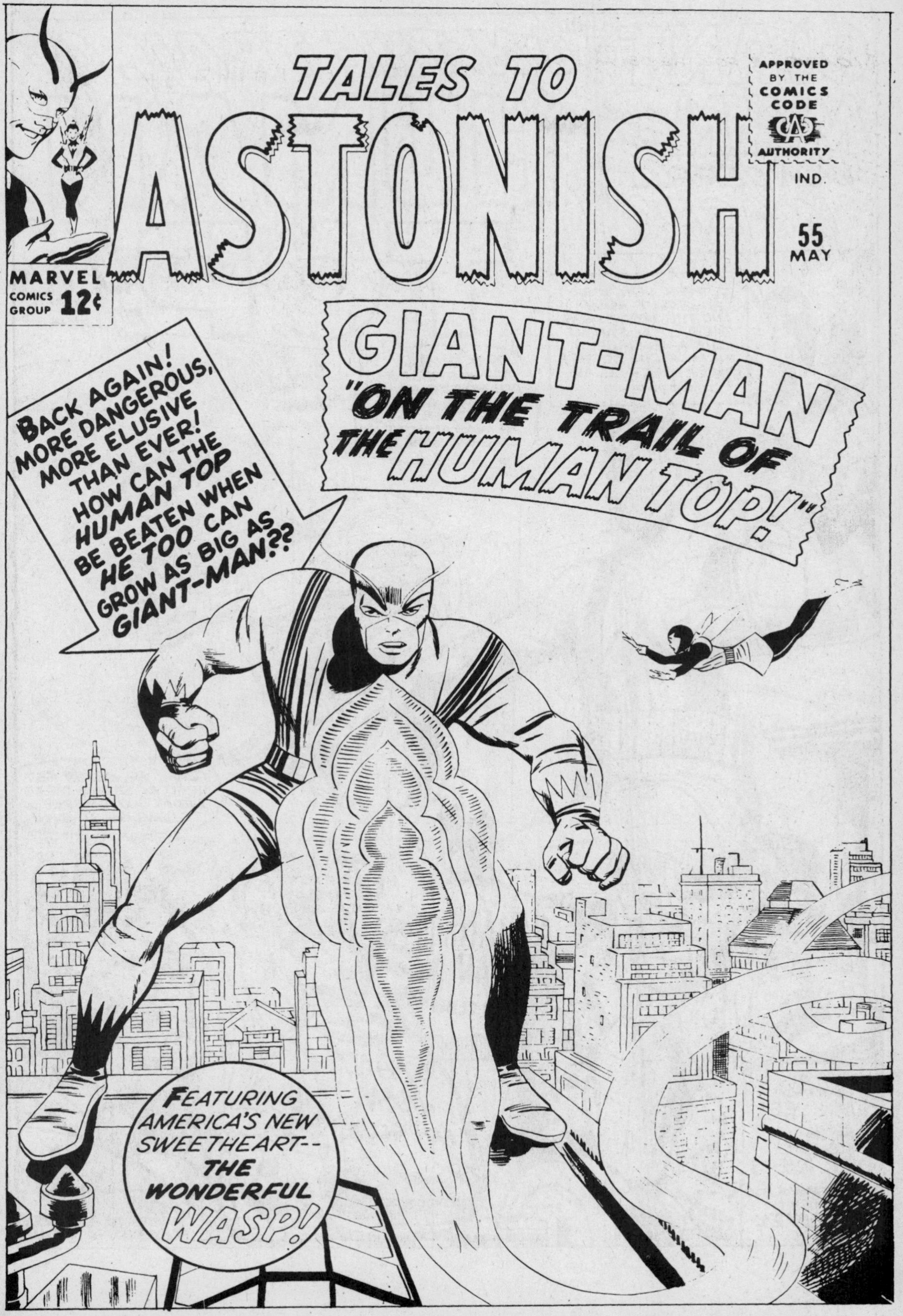

TALES TO ASTONISH
APPROVED BY THE COMICS CODE AUTHORITY
IND.
55 MAY
MARVEL COMICS GROUP 12¢
GIANT-MAN "ON THE TRAIL OF THE HUMAN TOP!"
BACK AGAIN! MORE DANGEROUS, MORE ELUSIVE THAN EVER! HOW CAN THE HUMAN TOP BE BEATEN WHEN HE TOO CAN GROW AS BIG AS GIANT-MAN??
FEATURING AMERICA'S NEW SWEETHEART-- THE WONDERFUL WASP!

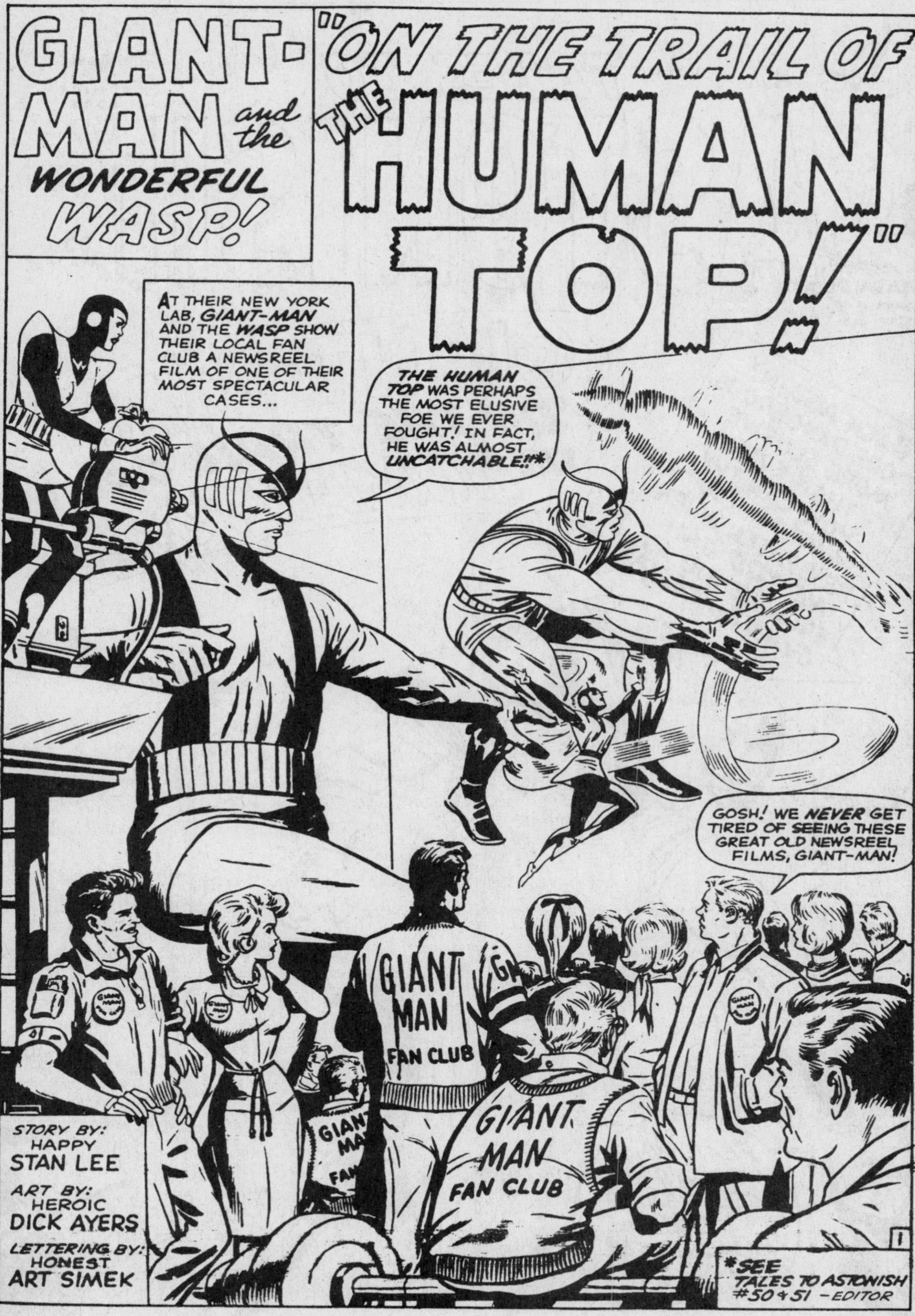
GIANT-MAN and the WONDERFUL WASP!
"ON THE TRAIL OF THE HUMAN TOP!"
AT THEIR NEW YORK LAB, GIANT-MAN AND THE WASP SHOW THEIR LOCAL FAN CLUB A NEWSREEL FILM OF ONE OF THEIR MOST SPECTACULAR CASES...
THE HUMAN TOP WAS PERHAPS THE MOST ELUSIVE FOE WE EVER FOUGHT! IN FACT, HE WAS ALMOST UNCATCHABLE!!*
GOSH! WE NEVER GET TIRED OF SEEING THESE GREAT OLD NEWSREEL FILMS, GIANT-MAN!
GIANT MAN FAN CLUB
GIANT MAN FAN CLUB
STORY BY: HAPPY STAN LEE
ART BY: HEROIC DICK AYERS
LETTERING BY: HONEST ART SIMEK
1
*SEE TALES TO ASTONISH #50 & 51 -EDITOR

REMEMBER HOW IT SEEMED AS THOUGH THE HUMAN TOP WOULD *NEVER* BE CAUGHT??

DO I? I STILL HAVE NIGHTMARES ABOUT THAT GUY!

I DON'T THINK *ANY* FOE EVER MADE ME LOOK AS CLUMSY-- OR *FEEL* AS FOOLISH AS *HE* DID! OF COURSE, I HADN'T HAD MY GIANT POWERS VERY LONG, AND STILL WASN'T TOO *USED* TO THEM!

I'LL BET IF YOU HAD TO CATCH HIM *NOW*, IT WOULD BE LOTS *EASIER* FOR YOU, GIANT-MAN!

I APPRECIATE YOUR CONFIDENCE, LITTLE FRIEND-- AND I WISH I *SHARED* IT!

ACTUALLY, I NEVER *DID* MANAGE TO MATCH HIS SPEED! I ONLY SUCCEEDED IN DEFEATING HIM BY A *TRICK!*

THIS ENDS THE FILM! GEE, WASN'T HE *HAND-SOME* -- FOR A CRIMINAL, THAT IS!

DON'T LET HIS LOOKS *FOOL* YOU, YOUNG LADY! BEHIND THOSE MOVIE STAR FEATURES IS A DANGEROUS AND UNPREDICTABLE MENACE!! IT'S LUCKY FOR *ALL* OF US THAT HE'S SAFELY IN JAIL!

IMAGINE IF HE EVER *ESCAPED!!* IT'S A FRIGHTENING THOUGHT!

2

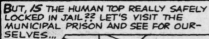

BUT, *IS* THE HUMAN TOP REALLY SAFELY LOCKED IN JAIL?? LET'S VISIT THE MUNICIPAL PRISON AND SEE FOR OUR-SELVES...

IT'S ALMOST TIME FOR CELL CHECK! THIS IS *IT!*

THEY KEPT A TWENTY-FOUR HOUR GUARD AT MY CELL FOR THE FIRST FEW MONTHS, BUT THEN, WHEN THEY SAW I WAS A MODEL PRISONER, THEY DISMISSED HIM! THAT WAS THEIR FIRST MISTAKE!

FOR NOW IT'S TIME FOR *THE HUMAN TOP* TO BREAK OUT OF THIS PLACE--AS ONLY THE TOP CAN DO IT.!!

THAT'S STRANGE! THE HUMAN TOP'S CELL LOOKS *EMPTY!!* BUT--HOW CAN THAT BE??

SPINNING SO FAST THAT HE IS VIRTUALLY INVISIBLE, THE HUMAN TOP CANNOT BE SEEN BY THE MYSTIFIED GUARD, IN THE DIM LIGHT OF THE TINY CELL--

THE CELL DOOR WAS *LOCKED*--BUT HE'S *GONE!* THE GUY MUST BE A *MAGICIAN!!*

THINKING THE TOP HAS ESCAPED, THE GUARD RACES FROM THE CELL, LEAVING THE IRON DOOR OPEN BEHIND HIM!

NOT A MINUTE TO LOSE! I'VE GOT TO GIVE THE ALARM!!

HA! I'LL BE OVER THE WALL AND OUT OF HERE BEFORE ANY-ONE CAN FIGURE OUT HOW IT WAS DONE!

3

A FEW HOURS LATER, AT A NEARBY DRIVE-IN BANK...

NOW THAT I'M FREE, I'LL NEED A STAKE SO I CAN LIVE IN THE MANNER I DESERVE!! AND THE BEST PLACE TO GET WHAT I WANT IS A BANK!

WHERE'D THAT WIND COME FROM?? LOOK-- UP THERE! IT'S THE HUMAN TOP!!

I HEARD HE COULD SPIN SO FAST THAT HE ACTUALLY COULD RISE IN INTO THE AIR, DEFYING GRAVITY! BUT I NEVER THOUGHT I'D SEE IT! WH-WHERE'D HE GO??

SPINNING INTO THE BANK, THE TOP CONTINUES TO WHIRL ABOUT AT BREATH-TAKING SPEED, CAUSING A MINIATURE TORNADO WHICH SCATTERS BILLS, BANK NOTES, DEPOSIT SLIPS, AND EVERY LOOSE BIT OF PAPER -- CAUSING A VIRTUAL PAPER BLIZZARD!

WHILE BACK AT GIANT-MAN'S LAB, AFTER THE YOUNG FANS HAVE LEFT...

PUT ON THE TV, BLUE EYES! THERE ARE SOME GOOD TEAR-JERKERS AT THIS HOUR!

YOU CAN HAVE THEM, JAN! I JUST WANT TO CATCH THE MID-AFTERNOON NEWS FIRST!

HENRY-- LOOK!! IS--IS IT A GAG?? IT CAN'T BE TRUE!!

I'M AFRAID IT IS, JAN! IT'S WHAT I'VE BEEN DREADING FOR MONTHS! HE'S ESCAPED!!

4

IT'S LUCKY THERE WAS A MOBILE TV NEWS UNIT IN THE AREA, OR WE MIGHT NOT HAVE BEEN ALERTED IN TIME! LET'S GO, GAL--EVERY SECOND COUNTS!!

I'LL TAKE A SHRINKING CAPSULE, HANK, SO THAT I CAN FLY TO THE BANK AS THE WASP! IT'LL BE THE FASTEST WAY FOR ME!

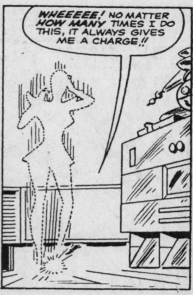

WHEEEEE! NO MATTER HOW MANY TIMES I DO THIS, IT ALWAYS GIVES ME A CHARGE!!

SAY! WHAT ARE YOU WAITING FOR? AREN'T YOU GOING TO BECOME ANT-SIZED, AND CALL ONE OF YOUR FLYING ANTS FOR A LIFT?

NOT THIS TIME, JAN! I'VE GOT ANOTHER METHOD OF GOING INTO ACTION THAT I WANT TO TRY!

I'LL TURN INTO GIANT-MAN INSTEAD--LIKE THIS!!

WAIT! STOP! YOU-- YOU'LL KILL YOURSELF, HANK!! WHAT ARE YOU DOING.??

RELAX, LITTLE PARTNER! I'M JUST TAKING THE FAST WAY DOWN!

5

I HAD THIS SPECIAL RIG INSTALLED AT THE SIDE OF OUR BUILDING WEEKS AGO! FROM THE STREET IT LOOKS LIKE AN ORDINARY FLAGPOLE!

--BUT IT'S REALLY A POWERFUL TENSION-CABLE DEVICE WITH JUST THE RIGHT AMOUNT OF RESILIENCY TO LOWER ME TO THE GROUND!

HOLY SMOKE!! FIRST SNOW-- THEN SLEET-- NOW IT'S RAININ' GIANTS!!!

WELL, IT'S ABOUT TIME, LITTLE LADY! I THOUGHT YOU'D NEVER GET HERE!

HEY, MISTER! SIT SOMEWHERE ELSE, HUH? I GOT A SCHEDULE TO MAKE!!

HENRY PYM!! DON'T YOU EVER GIVE ME A SCARE LIKE THAT AGAIN, HEAR?? YOU--YOU BIG SHOW-OFF, YOU!!

SORRY, JAN! GUESS I SHOULD HAVE EXPLAINED FIRST! WELL, NEVER MIND! WE'VE A JOB TO DO NOW!

MIND TAKING A HITCH-HIKER, BIG BOY?

6

COVERING THE MANY BLOCKS WITH HUGE, DISTANCE-SWALLOWING STRIDES, GIANT-MAN SOON REACHES THE DRIVE-IN BANK, WITH HIS LITTLE PASSENGER STILL ATOP HIS SHOULDER, ONLY TO FIND...

I'LL NEVER GET THRU THIS CROWD WITHOUT STEPPING ON SOMEONE!!

STAND ASIDE, FOLKS!! I'M TRYING TO GET IN THERE! STEP TO ONE SIDE!!

IT'S NO USE, GIANT-MAN! EVERYONE IS SO EXCITED, THEY'RE SCRAMBLING AROUND IN HOPELESS CONFUSION!

WELL, I DON'T WANT TO TRAMPLE ON ANY INNOCENT PEOPLE, SO THERE'S ONLY ONE THING TO DO!

A SPLIT SECOND LATER, COMPLETELY UNNOTICED BY THE MILLING CROWD, TWO ANT-SIZED FIGURES DASH THRU THE SEA OF LEGS INTO THE BANK...

THIS MAY NOT LOOK AS DRAMATIC, BUT IT'LL GET US INSIDE!!

BUT, ONCE INSIDE, THE PAPERS AND DEBRIS WHICH THE HUMAN TOP HAS SCATTERED, FORM AN ALMOST-IMPENETRABLE BARRIER TO THE INSECT-SIZED ADVENTURERS!

WE'LL NEVER GET THRU ALL THAT WHILE ANT-SIZED! BETTER ATTAIN OUR NORMAL SIZE NOW!

AND SO...

I APPRECIATE YOUR RUSHING HERE, GIANT-MAN AND WASP, BUT I'M AFRAID YOU'RE TOO LATE! THE TOP HAS GONE -- WITH A SMALL FORTUNE OF OUR MONEY!

WELL, ONE THING IS FOR SURE-- WE'LL NEVER CATCH HIM BY CHASING HIM! GETTING THAT MONEY BACK IS GOING TO TAKE SOME MIGHTY CAREFUL PLANNING!

7

MEANWHILE, A SHORT DISTANCE FROM THE BANK, AN AVERAGE-LOOKING MAN CARRYING A PLAIN-LOOKING VALISE, WALKS BRISKLY DOWN THE STREET, HIS KEEN EYES OBSERVING EVERYTHING AROUND HIM FROM BEHIND HIS DARK GLASSES...

IT WORKED LIKE A CHARM! THE WHOLE THING WENT OFF WITHOUT A HITCH! AND THAT'S ONLY THE *BEGINNING!* *NOBODY* CAN EVER CATCH ANY-ONE AS FAST AS *I* AM!

THEN, AT THE FIRST SHADOWY ALLEY, THE MASTER CRIMINAL SHEDS HIS STREET CLOTHES AND BE-GINS TO SPIN...

FROM NOW ON, I'LL TRAVEL *MY* WAY-- THE *BEST* WAY!

WHILE BACK AT THE BANK, GIANT-MAN MAKES A SOLEMN PLEDGE...

I PROMISE YOU THIS--NO MATTER HOW LONG IT TAKES--NO MATTER HOW HOPELESS IT SEEMS--I'LL NEVER REST UNTIL THE TOP IS BEATEN!

AND THEN...

NO NEED FOR HASTE NOW, JAN! I'LL HAIL A CAB!

OH NO! LET'S *WALK*, HANK! IT'S SUCH A LOVELY DAY-- AND I LIKE TO SHOW YOU OFF!

OKAY, HONEY! BUT I FEEL LIKE A GOOF PARADING AROUND THE STREET IN A COSTUME LIKE THIS!

BUT SUCH A *HANDSOME* GOOF!! :SIGH:

WELL WELL! THIS IS MY LUCKY DAY! LOOK WHO'S THERE!!

IT'S *GIANT-MAN*, AND THAT GORGEOUS GAL FRIEND OF HIS! HE *BEAT* ME LAST TIME WE MET-- BUT *NOW* THE STORY WILL END *DIFFERENTLY!!!*

8

LATER, UNAWARE THAT THEY HAVE BEEN FOLLOWED BY THE VERY FOE THEY'VE BEEN SEEKING, GIANT-MAN AND THE WASP ENTER THEIR COMBINATION LAB-WORKSHOP...

OKAY, JAN, FUN-TIME'S OVER! NOW WE'VE GOT TO REALLY GET DOWN TO WORK--TO FIGURE OUT A PLAN TO CATCH THE TOP!

I'LL LEAVE THE BRAINWORK TO YOU, HERO MINE! I'M BETTER IN THE MOONLIGHT AND ROSES DEPARTMENT!

I HATE TO SOUND LIKE A STUFFED SHIRT, JAN-- BUT I WISH YOU'D START TAKING YOURSELF SERIOUSLY!

YOU'RE EASILY THE BRAINIEST, CLEVEREST GIRL I'VE EVER MET--AS WELL AS THE MOST BEAUTIFUL AND COURAGEOUS! AND YET, YOU TRY TO SOUND LIKE AN EMPTY-HEADED, FLIGHTY COQUETTE! BUT I KNOW THE REAL YOU, HONEY--AND I LIKE WHAT I KNOW!

HENRY PYM!! THIS IS THE NEAREST THING TO A GENUINE, FOURTEEN-CAROT COMPLIMENT YOU'VE EVER GIVEN ME! IF--IF I WASN'T AFRAID OF RUNNING MY MASCARA, I THINK I'D SIT DOWN AND CRY!

VERY TOUCHING! IT'S MOST HEART-WARMING TO SEE TWO PEOPLE WHO ARE DEEPLY IN LOVE THAT WAY! WHAT A PITY THE HUMAN TOP IS ABOUT TO BREAK UP THEIR LITTLE ROMANCE--FOREVER!

THE FIRST THING TO DO IS CONTACT OUR LEGION OF ANTS THRUOUT THE CITY, AND SEE IF ANY OF THEM HAVE SEEN THE TOP!

I'LL SAVE YOU THE TROUBLE, YOU COSTUMED CLOD! JUST TURN AROUND!!

WHA--??? WHO SAID--?? MY CAPSULE BELT!! SOMETHING RIPPED IT OFF!!

9

CORRECTION, MISTER! NOT "SOMETHING" --SOMEONE!!

THE HUMAN TOP!!

YOU'RE MIGHTY OBLIGING TO SAVE US THE TROUBLE OF FINDING YOU!

YOU KNOW ME, PAL O' MINE! I'M ALL HEART!

AND NOW I'LL TAKE ONE OF YOUR OWN GROWTH PILLS--!!

HE GREW TO DOUBLE-SIZE!! NOW WHEN HE SPINS AROUND, IT--IT'S LIKE A TORNADO!!

THE WIND IS BLOWING ME INTO THE EMPTY CLOSET-- LIKE A HURRICANE!! CAN'T STOP MYSELF!!

SO MUCH FOR MY HELPLESS FOE! NOW, I'LL BLOW THE DOOR SHUT BEHIND HIM, LIKE THIS!

AND WITH ONE TURN OF THE KEY, HE IS TRAPPED INSIDE THE WINDOWLESS CLOSET, POWERLESS WITHOUT HIS SIZE CAPSULE BELT!!

AND NOW--!

MUSTN'T PANIC! MUST REMEMBER GIANT-MAN'S TRAINING!!

10

I'VE GOT TO SWALLOW A *SHRINKING PILL* BEFORE HE CAN GET ME!

CHANGING YOUR SIZE WON'T SAVE YOU FROM *ME!*

OH *NO??* IT'S NOT EASY TO CATCH A *WASP!*

STRANGE! HE RAN RIGHT *PAST* ME! AND YET, I'M *SURE* HE SAW ME SHRINK DOWN.!!

HE'S STILL GOING! I'D BETTER STAY CLOSE BEHIND AND SEE WHAT HE'S *UP* TO!

IN CASE YOU WERE *WONDERING,* MY DIMINUTIVE LITTLE DOLL, I WAS MERELY LOOKING FOR A SMALL JAR IN WHICH TO *IMPRISON* YOU!

HE TOOK ME BY *SURPRISE!* HOW COULD I HAVE BEEN SO *CARELESS.!!*

YOU FORGOT THAT I LOST NONE OF MY *SPEED* OR AGILITY WHEN I INCREASED MY SIZE! AND YOU WILL *PAY* FOR THAT OVERSIGHT BY BECOMING MY *PRISONER!*

AS LONG AS I HAVE *YOU* FOR A HOSTAGE, GIANT-MAN WON'T DARE TO ATTACK ME AGAIN EVEN IF HE MANAGES TO FREE HIMSELF FROM THAT LOCKED CLOSET.!

HE THINKS HE'S BEATEN US! BUT HE'LL SOON LEARN THAT THE FIGHT'S JUST *BEGUN!*

11

FAREWELL, GIANT-MAN! THANKS FOR YOUR SIZE-CAPSULE BELT! I PROMISE YOU THAT I'LL GET A *LOT* OF USE OUT OF IT! AND DON'T FEEL TOO LONELY-- AT LEAST I LEFT YOU WITH YOUR *LIFE!*

MY SIZE-CAPSULES IN *HIS* HANDS WILL BE A MENACE TO ALL MANKIND! I'VE *GOT* TO CATCH HIM SOON!

HE THINKS I'M HELPLESS IN THIS EMPTY CLOSET! HE DOESN'T KNOW ABOUT MY CYBERNETIC HELMET, THRU WHICH I CAN CONTACT MY LOYAL ANTS IN AN EMERGENCY, AS I'M *NOW* DOING BY CONCENTRATING MY THOUGHTS....!

THE BRILLIANT SCIENTIST'S ASTONISHING HELMET SERVES HIM WELL, FOR THE POWERFUL CYBERNETIC IMPULSES SOON REACH THE SENSITIVE ANTENNAE OF EVERY ANT IN THE AREA...

ANT-MAN CALLING

ANT-MAN CALLING

ANT-MAN CALLING

WITHIN MINUTES, A SILENTLY MOVING ARMY OF OBEDIENT ANTS CRAWLS OVER THE WINDOW-SILL INTO HENRY PYM'S LABORATORY...

THEY'RE COMING! NOW FOR MY NEXT COMMAND!

REACH MY SPARE CAPSULE BELT ON LAB SHELF... TAKE CAPSULE OUT OF CENTER POCKET...

BRING IT TO ME UNDER DOOR... STEADY... STEADY...

12

THEY **DID** IT! THEY BROUGHT ME A **SHRINKING CAPSULE!!**

I **KNEW** I COULD COUNT ON YOU, MY **LOYAL LITTLE FRIENDS!!**

AND NOW, SHRINKING DOWN TO ANT SIZE, I'LL HAVE NO TROUBLE GETTING **OUT OF** HERE!

FOLLOW ME, MY LITTLE ALLIES! OUR JOB IS JUST **BEGINNING!** I SUSPECT I'LL HAVE MUCH **MORE** NEED OF YOUR SPECIAL TALENTS BEFORE THE HUMAN TOP IS DEFEATED AND THE WASP IS RESCUED!

NOW THAT I'M **FREE** AGAIN, I NEED **TWO** THINGS! FIRST, I'LL SUMMON MY **FLYING ANTS!**

AND NEXT, I'VE GOT TO SPILL SOME **FABRIC REDUCER** ON MY SPARE CAPSULE BELT...

THERE! NOW THAT I'VE REDUCED THE ENTIRE BELT, IT FITS PERFECTLY AROUND ME WHILE I OPERATE AS **ANT-MAN!**

AND HERE ARE MY FLYING ANTS, JUST IN TIME! I'LL HARNESS THEM TO MY CELLOPHANE AIR CHARIOT WITHIN SECONDS!

FABRIC REDUCER

LET'S **GO**, MY SPEEDY LITTLE WINGED STEEDS! EVERY SECOND COUNTS!!

13

AT THAT MOMENT, NOT FAR AWAY, THE HUMAN TOP LUX-URIATES IN HIS FEELING OF NEW-FOUND POWER!

WHAT A SENSE OF *SUPERIORITY* IT GIVES ME TO BE *TWICE* THE SIZE OF EVERY-ONE ELSE--TO BE A *GIANT* AMONG MERE HUMANS!!

MY SIZE, AND SKILL NOW MAKE ME THE MOST FORMIDIBLE BEING OF ALL!

DO NOT FRET, MY TINY *CAPTIVE!* YOU WILL SOON *FORGET* GIANT-MAN! I'LL SEE TO THAT!

BUT, SO CONFIDENT IS THE HUMAN TOP, THAT HE DISREGARDS HIS OWN NATURAL CAUTION, NOT NOTICING THE TINY WINGED FORMS WHO BUZZ TO A LANDING AT HIS FEET! BUT THEN HE HEARS--FAINTLY--AS THOUGH FROM FAR AWAY--!!

I'VE *FOUND* YOU, TOP! THIS IS *IT!*

ANT-MAN!! YOU DARE CHALLENGE ME! I'LL PUT YOU OUT OF ACTION WITH ONE SIMPLE MOTION....!

I TIMED IT *PERFECTLY!* NOW TO SWALLOW MY QUICK-ACTING *ENLARGING CAPSULE!!*

STILL THINK YOU'LL FINISH ME SO EASILY?? THIS TIME YOU'RE FACING *GIANT-MAN!!*

B-BUT *HOW--??!*

14

WELL, IT DOESN'T MATTER *HOW* YOU PERFORM YOUR *HOPELESS* LITTLE STUNTS! I'M STILL AS LARGE AS YOU--AND ONCE I START *SPINNING*, YOU'RE *THRU!*

NOT WHILE I HOLD ONTO YOUR *WRISTS* THIS WAY! YOU WON'T ESCAPE ME BY SPINNING *THIS* TIME!

OH *NO??* HERE'S A SMALL SAMPLE-- SEE HOW LONG YOU CAN KEEP YOUR GRIP!!

HE'S *RIGHT!* I CAN'T TAKE IT! GETTING DIZZY! CAN'T HOLD ON MUCH LONGER!!

MY ONLY CHANCE-- CONTACT *WASP* THRU HELMET-- IT'S UP TO *HER* NOW!

WASP! NOW... WHILE HE CAN'T STOP YOU... FREE YOUR- SELF...

I HEAR YOU TALKING, BIG MAN!

I HEAR HIM CONTACTING THE *TERMITES* IN THE CELLAR NOW! WHAT CAN HIS PLAN BE??

CAN'T HOLD ON ANY LONGER-- BUT I'LL TAKE A *SHRINKING PILL* BEFORE I LET GO! *THERE!!*

HAH! I *KNEW* I'D SHAKE YOU OFF!

15

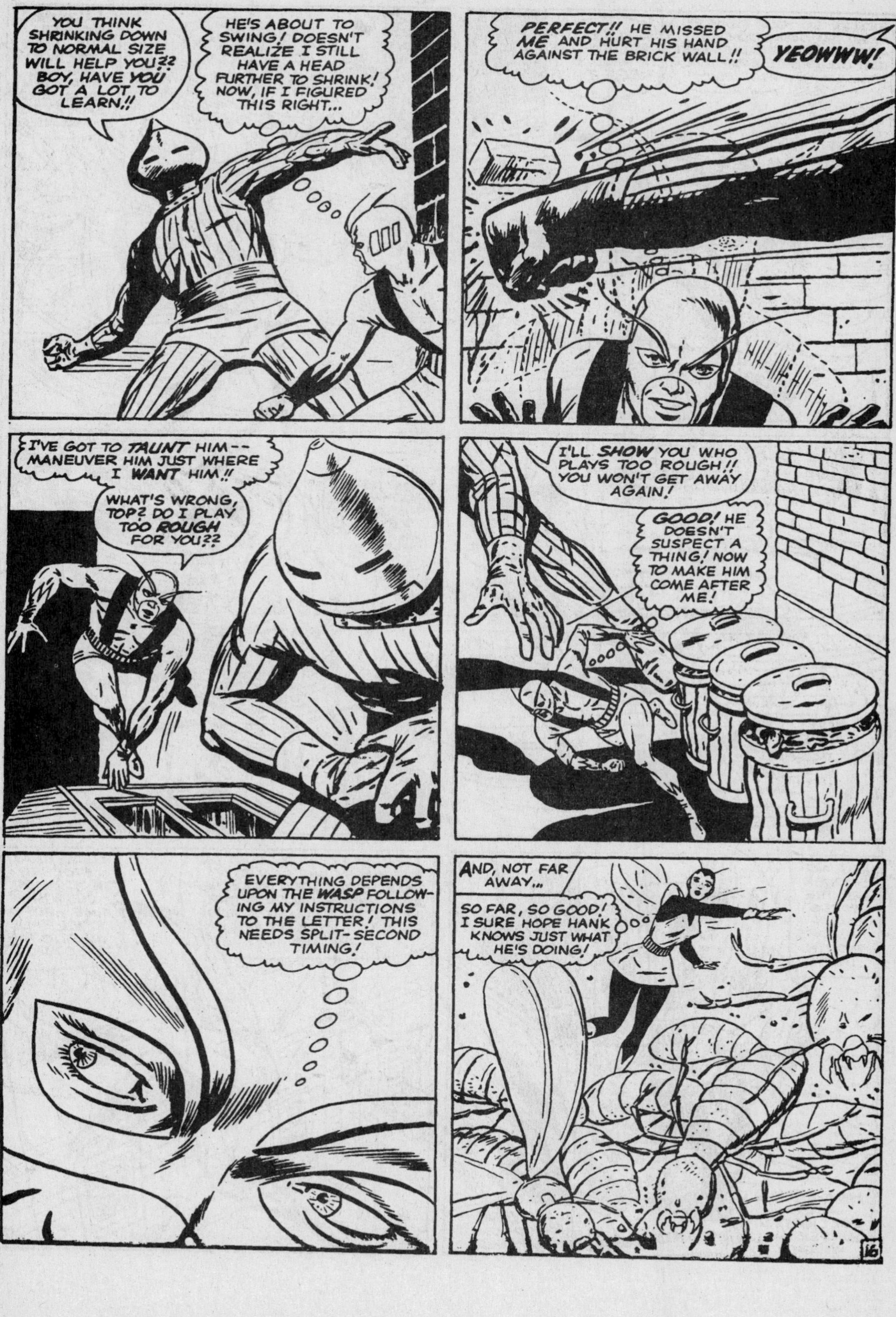
YOU THINK SHRINKING DOWN TO NORMAL SIZE WILL HELP YOU?? BOY, HAVE YOU GOT A LOT TO LEARN!!
HE'S ABOUT TO SWING! DOESN'T REALIZE I STILL HAVE A HEAD FURTHER TO SHRINK! NOW, IF I FIGURED THIS RIGHT...
PERFECT!! HE MISSED ME AND HURT HIS HAND AGAINST THE BRICK WALL!!
YEOWWW!
I'VE GOT TO TAUNT HIM-- MANEUVER HIM JUST WHERE I WANT HIM!!
WHAT'S WRONG, TOP? DO I PLAY TOO ROUGH FOR YOU??
I'LL SHOW YOU WHO PLAYS TOO ROUGH!! YOU WON'T GET AWAY AGAIN!
GOOD! HE DOESN'T SUSPECT A THING! NOW TO MAKE HIM COME AFTER ME!
EVERYTHING DEPENDS UPON THE WASP FOLLOWING MY INSTRUCTIONS TO THE LETTER! THIS NEEDS SPLIT-SECOND TIMING!
AND, NOT FAR AWAY...
SO FAR, SO GOOD! I SURE HOPE HANK KNOWS JUST WHAT HE'S DOING!
16

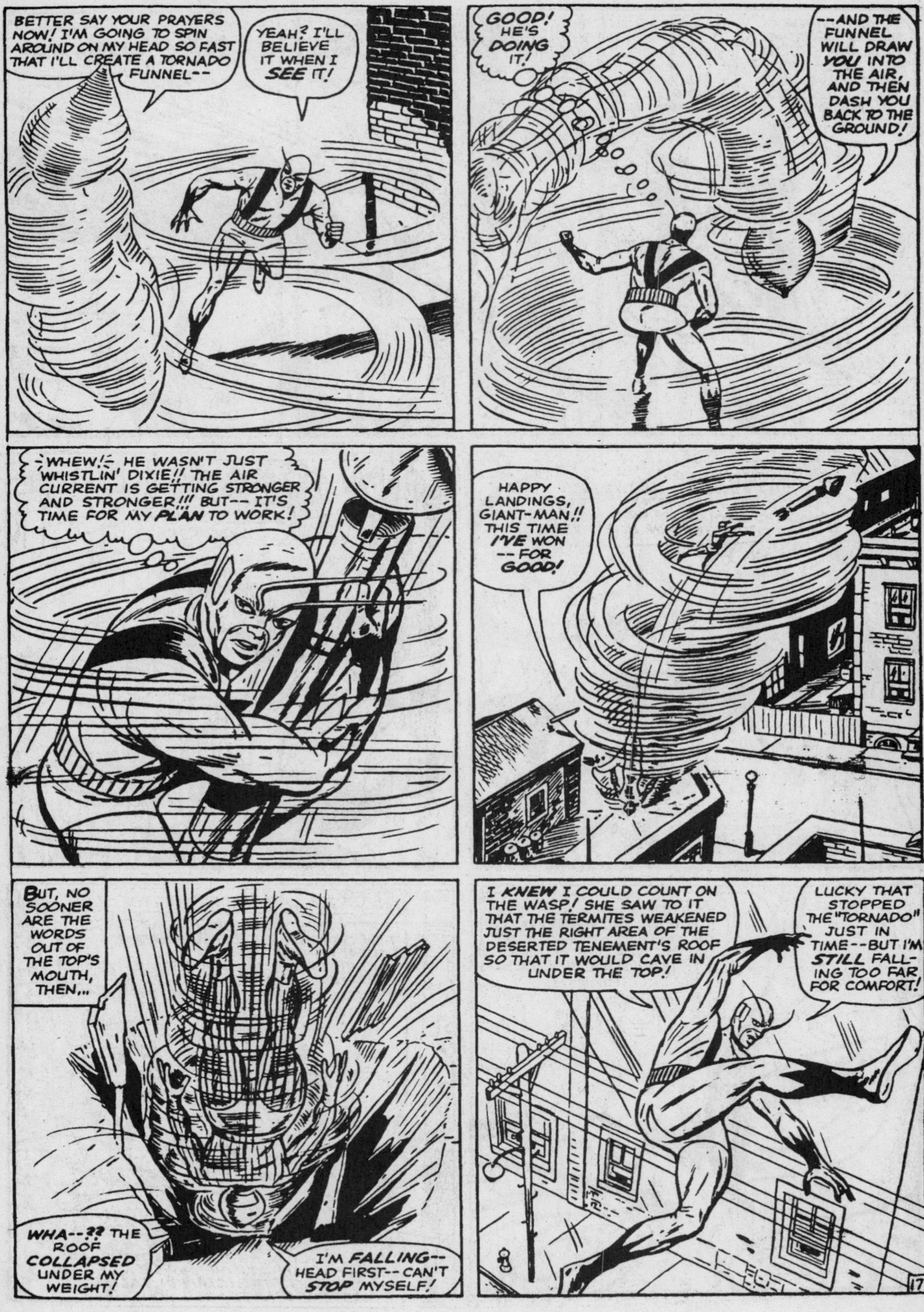

BETTER SAY YOUR PRAYERS NOW! I'M GOING TO SPIN AROUND ON MY HEAD SO FAST THAT I'LL CREATE A TORNADO FUNNEL--
YEAH? I'LL BELIEVE IT WHEN I SEE IT!
GOOD! HE'S DOING IT!
--AND THE FUNNEL WILL DRAW YOU INTO THE AIR, AND THEN DASH YOU BACK TO THE GROUND!
WHEW!-- HE WASN'T JUST WHISTLIN' DIXIE!! THE AIR CURRENT IS GETTING STRONGER AND STRONGER!!! BUT-- IT'S TIME FOR MY PLAN TO WORK!
HAPPY LANDINGS, GIANT-MAN!! THIS TIME I'VE WON --FOR GOOD!
BUT, NO SOONER ARE THE WORDS OUT OF THE TOP'S MOUTH, THEN...
WHA--?? THE ROOF COLLAPSED UNDER MY WEIGHT!
I'M FALLING-- HEAD FIRST-- CAN'T STOP MYSELF!
I KNEW I COULD COUNT ON THE WASP! SHE SAW TO IT THAT THE TERMITES WEAKENED JUST THE RIGHT AREA OF THE DESERTED TENEMENT'S ROOF SO THAT IT WOULD CAVE IN UNDER THE TOP!
LUCKY THAT STOPPED THE "TORNADO" JUST IN TIME--BUT I'M STILL FALLING TOO FAR FOR COMFORT!
17

HERE'S WHERE MY LONG HOURS OF TUMBLING PRACTICE PAY OFF!! I'VE GOT TO TWIST MYSELF SO THAT I HIT THOSE PHONE WIRES--AT JUST THE RIGHT ANGLE--LIKE --THIS!!

AHHHH! IT MAKES A PERFECT SPRINGBOARD! AND NOW, IF I FIGURED THE TRAJECTORY CORRECTLY--

TWANG!

--WHEW!!--NOT BAD FOR A L'IL FELLA! HOPE JAN WAS WATCHING!!

THE TOP FELL THRU THE WEAKENED ROOF JUST AS YOU PLANNED, HANK! AND I POPPED A SHRINKING CAPSULE IN HIS MOUTH WHILE HE WAS UNCONSCIOUS TO MAKE HIM NORMAL-SIZED!

GOOD WORK, HONEY!

BAH! BEING BIG IS FOR THE BIRDS! I WOULDN'T HAVE CRASHED THRU THE ROOF IF I HADN'T BEEN GIANT-SIZED! NEXT TIME'LL BE DIFFERENT!

THERE WON'T BE ANY NEXT TIME, TOP!

THE NEXT DAY...

GOSH, GIANT-MAN, HOW DID YOU BEAT THE HUMAN TOP A SECOND TIME-- EVEN AFTER HE BECAME AS LARGE AS YOU??

SIZE ISN'T EVERYTHING, KIDS! SOMETIMES, EVEN A TERMITE CAN TOPPLE A GIANT!

AND, AS THE LATE EDITIONS HIT THE STANDS...

PRETTY NICE WRITE-UP THEY GAVE US, LITTLE PARTNER! HOW DOES IT FEEL TO SEE YOUR NAME IN PRINT?

WONDERFUL, DREAM MAN! ALTHOUGH I'D MUCH RATHER SEE IT ON A WEDDING LICENSE, YOU BIG, BLIND, WONDERFUL GOOF!

the END

JANET VAN DYNE ALMOST GETS HER WISH NEXT ISH-- DON'T MISS THE SURPRISES WHEN GIANT-MAN AND THE WASP MEET THE MYSTIFYING MAGICIAN IN TALES TO ASTONISH #56! SEE YOU THEN!

The Wonderful **WASP** tells a **TALE**

"THE GYPSY'S SECRET!"

WE OPEN WITH A TYPICALLY PEACEFUL, HARMONIOUS SCENE IN GIANT MAN'S LABORATORY...

DON'T *BOTHER* ME NOW, JAN! I'M BUSY CONDUCTING AN EXPERIMENT! GO ON, *SHOO!* BUZZ OFF!

DON'T YOU DARE "BUZZ OFF" ME, HENRY PYM! I'M A *WOMAN,* NOT A BUMBLE BEE! AND I DON'T GIVE A HOOT FOR YOUR SILLY OLD EXPERIMENT!

STORY PLOT: STAN LEE
SCRIPT AND ART:
L.D. LIEBER
INKING: GEORGE BELL
LETTERING: SHERIGAIL

X601

BESIDES, IT'S *DISGRACEFUL* THE WAY YOU KEEP YOUR NOSE TO THE TEST TUBE! DON'T YOU REALIZE THAT EVEN IF YOU *FIND* WHAT YOU'RE LOOKING FOR, YOU MIGHT NOT BE *SATISFIED!*

HUH? WHAT DO YOU MEAN?

YOU'LL *KNOW* WHAT I MEAN WHEN YOU HEAR MY TALE! IT'S CALLED "THE GYPSY'S SECRET" AND I WANT YOU TO LISTEN TO IT *ATTENTIVELY,* UNDERSTAND?

HMMN... LOOKS LIKE I'M A CAPTIVE AUDIENCE! OKAY, YOU GORGEOUS LITTLE PEST! GUESS I CAN USE A BREAK!

0

EVEN IN THIS MODERN ERA, THERE ARE *STILL* MANY GYPSIES WANDERING ABOUT THE COUNTRYSIDE OF SMALL EUROPEAN NATIONS! BUT THERE IS ONLY *ONE* GYPSY NAMED *GORKO*...AND IT IS ONLY *GORKO* WHO HAS A FANTASTIC POWER!

IN ALL THE WORLD, ONLY *I* KNOW THE SECRET OF TRUE *ALCHEMY!*

ONLY I CAN TAKE A BASE METAL SUCH AS THIS WORTHLESS CHUNK OF LEAD...

...AND, BY IMMERSING IT IN A SECRET SOLUTION OF MIXED CHEMICALS...

...THEN HEATING IT IN THE GLOWING, PURIFYING FLAME OF MYSTERIOUS ANCIENT POWDERS...

... I CAN TRANSFORM IT INTO THE MOST PRECIOUS OF ALL EARTHLY METALS... *SOLID GOLD!*

BUT, THOUGH I COULD CREATE ENOUGH GOLD TO LIVE LIKE A MONARCH, I CONTENT MYSELF WITH JUST ENOUGH TO BUY FOOD AND OTHER BARE NECESSITIES! FOR I DESIRE ONLY TO SUSTAIN MYSELF WHILE I CARRY OUT MY FATEFUL TASK... WHILE I JOURNEY THROUGHOUT THE LAND SEARCHING... SEARCHING FOR THE ONLY THING OF IMPORTANCE TO ME!

AND, POSSESSED WITH A STRANGE INNER VISION, THE AGED GYPSY CONTINUES TO EXPLORE THE COUNTRYSIDE, STOPPING ONLY FOR FOOD AND DRINK...

WILL THIS PAY FOR THE MEAT AND WINE?

A GOLD NUGGET! IT... IT IS MUCH *MORE* THAN ENOUGH!

YOU ARE VERY GENEROUS! BLESS YOU, OLD MAN!

2

MY FATEFUL QUEST GOES ON! BUT I CAN SENSE THAT I AM NEAR THE END! SOON I WILL DISCOVER THAT WHICH I SEEK!

THEN, A FEW DAYS LATER, GORKO HAS AN ACCIDENT, AND GOES TO A NEARBY CASTLE FOR ASSISTANCE!

WHO IS *THERE?* WHO DARES INTRUDE UPON THE PRIVACY OF *BARON RADZIK?*

MY WAGON IS STUCK IN THE MUD A FEW MILES FROM HERE! I NEED SOMEONE TO HELP ME FREE IT! I WILL PAY WELL FOR THE SERVICE!

IT IS A *GYPSY* IN NEED OF HELP, BARON!

A GYPSY? THROW THE FILTHY BEGGAR OUT! TELL HIM IF HE'S NOT OFF MY PROPERTY IN TEN MINUTES, I'LL SET MY *HOUNDS* ON HIM!

BUT, BARON, HE IS NOT A BEGGAR! HE HAS GOLD TO *PAY* FOR OUR AID!

GOLD? NO GYPSY CAN COME BY GOLD HONESTLY! HE MUST BE A THIEF... AND THIEVES DO NOT KEEP THEIR ILL-GOTTEN GAINS WHILE *I* AM AROUND!

SPEAK, YOU OLD ROGUE! HOW MUCH GOLD HAVE YOU STOLEN? WHERE IS THE *REST* OF IT? I DEMAND IT FOR MYSELF!

I HAVE STOLEN *NOTHING!* I CREATED THE GOLD OUT OF LEAD!

WHAT? YOU CLAIM YOU CAN TRANSFORM BASE METAL INTO *GOLD?*

YES! I KNOW THE ANCIENT ART OF ALCHEMY!

THEN YOU MUST TELL ME THE SECRET! I, TOO, SHALL CREATE GOLD! I SHALL BECOME AS RICH AS MIDAS!

NO! THE SECRET IS MINE ALONE! YOU ARE TOO CRUEL AND SELFISH TO BE WORTHY OF IT!

WHY, YOU MISERABLE OLD FOOL! I'LL SOON LOOSEN YOUR TONGUE!

STOP! UNHAND ME!

③

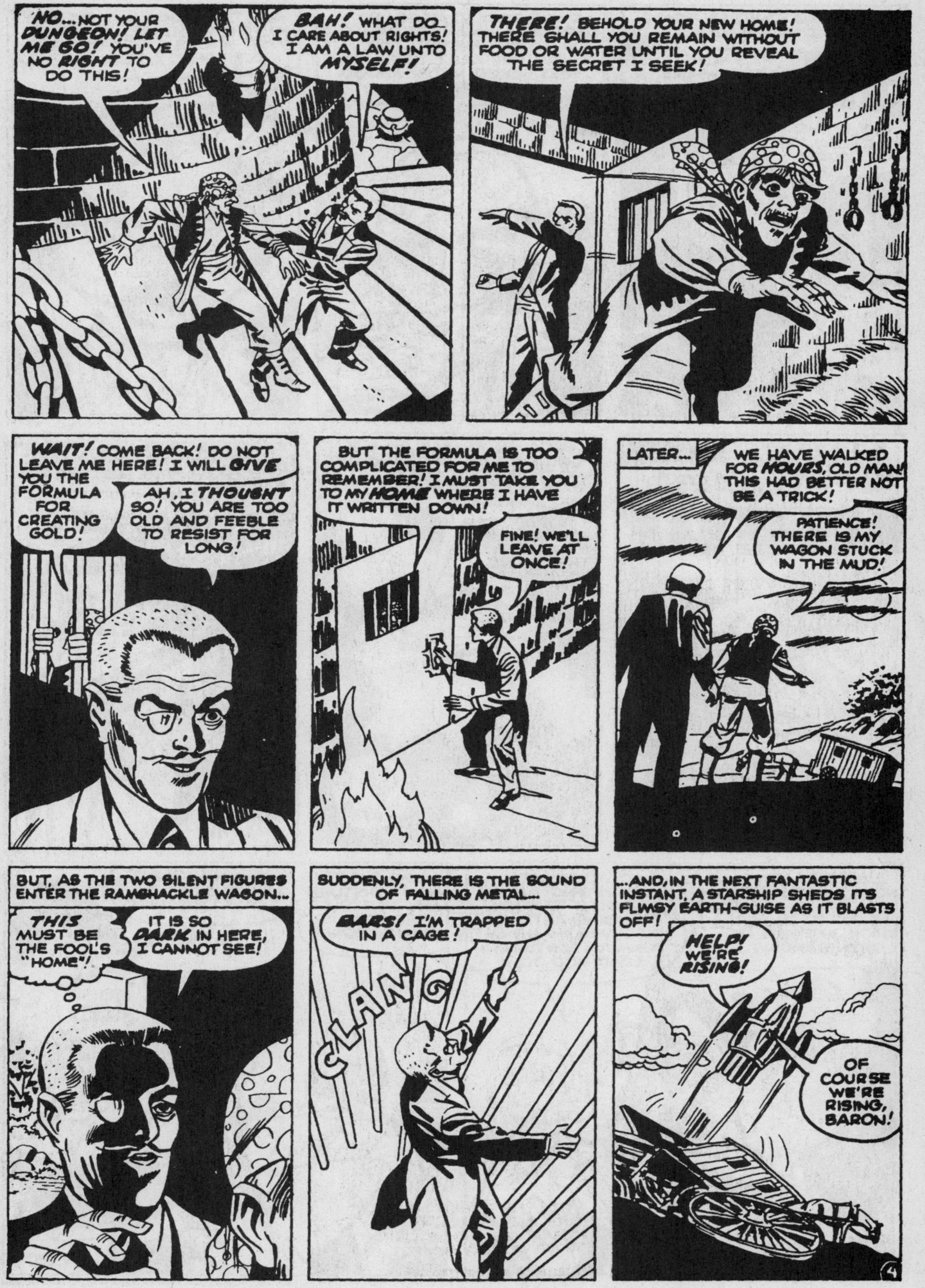
NO...NOT YOUR DUNGEON! LET ME GO! YOU'VE NO RIGHT TO DO THIS!
BAH! WHAT DO I CARE ABOUT RIGHTS! I AM A LAW UNTO MYSELF!
THERE! BEHOLD YOUR NEW HOME! THERE SHALL YOU REMAIN WITHOUT FOOD OR WATER UNTIL YOU REVEAL THE SECRET I SEEK!
WAIT! COME BACK! DO NOT LEAVE ME HERE! I WILL GIVE YOU THE FORMULA FOR CREATING GOLD!
AH, I THOUGHT SO! YOU ARE TOO OLD AND FEEBLE TO RESIST FOR LONG!
BUT THE FORMULA IS TOO COMPLICATED FOR ME TO REMEMBER! I MUST TAKE YOU TO MY HOME WHERE I HAVE IT WRITTEN DOWN!
FINE! WE'LL LEAVE AT ONCE!
LATER...
WE HAVE WALKED FOR HOURS, OLD MAN! THIS HAD BETTER NOT BE A TRICK!
PATIENCE! THERE IS MY WAGON STUCK IN THE MUD!
BUT, AS THE TWO SILENT FIGURES ENTER THE RAMSHACKLE WAGON...
THIS MUST BE THE FOOL'S "HOME"!
IT IS SO DARK IN HERE, I CANNOT SEE!
SUDDENLY, THERE IS THE SOUND OF FALLING METAL...
BARS! I'M TRAPPED IN A CAGE!
CLANG
...AND, IN THE NEXT FANTASTIC INSTANT, A STARSHIP SHEDS ITS FLIMSY EARTH-GUISE AS IT BLASTS OFF!
HELP! WE'RE RISING!
OF COURSE WE'RE RISING, BARON!
4

I'M TAKING YOU TO MY *HOME*, JUST AS I PROMISED!

YOUR HOME? WHERE... WHERE *IS* IT?

WHY, IN THE NINTH GALAXY, OF COURSE!

I WAS SENT TO EARTH TO CAPTURE A HUMAN SPECIMEN FOR OUR INTERPLANETARY ZOO! BUT IT WAS DIFFICULT TO FIND ONE WHO WOULD NOT BE MISSED ON EARTH!

AND THEN, LUCKILY, I MET *YOU!* A MORTAL OVER WHOSE LOSS NONE WILL EVER SHED A TEAR!

BUT DON'T WORRY... I'LL GIVE YOU THE ALCHEMIST'S FORMULA AS I PROMISED... ALTHOUGH IT WON'T DO YOU MUCH GOOD!

... BECAUSE, YOU SEE, ON *MY* WORLD, GOLD IS THE COMMONEST, AND THEREFORE *MOST WORTHLESS* OF ALL METALS!

SO YOU SEE, BOSS MAN, A PERSON CAN GET WHAT HE'S AFTER AND *STILL* BE UNHAPPY, JUST LIKE THE BARON!

YOU'VE SOLD ME, JAN! I'M *QUITTING* MY EXPERIMENT! YOUR TALE GAVE ME A *BETTER* IDEA!

I *HOPED* IT WOULD! NOW, SINCE I'M FREE TONIGHT, YOU CAN TAKE ME OUT TO DINNER! A THICK JUICY STEAK... THEN DANCING...

NO, YOU DON'T UNDERSTAND! I MUST GET RIGHT TO WORK! I'M GOING TO TRY TO DISCOVER THE ANCIENT FORMULA FOR TURNING LEAD INTO GOLD!

NOW, *SCAT!* DON'T DISTURB ME, JAN! I'LL SEE YOU *TOMORROW!*

THEY *WARNED* ME THERE'D BE DAYS LIKE THIS!

THE END

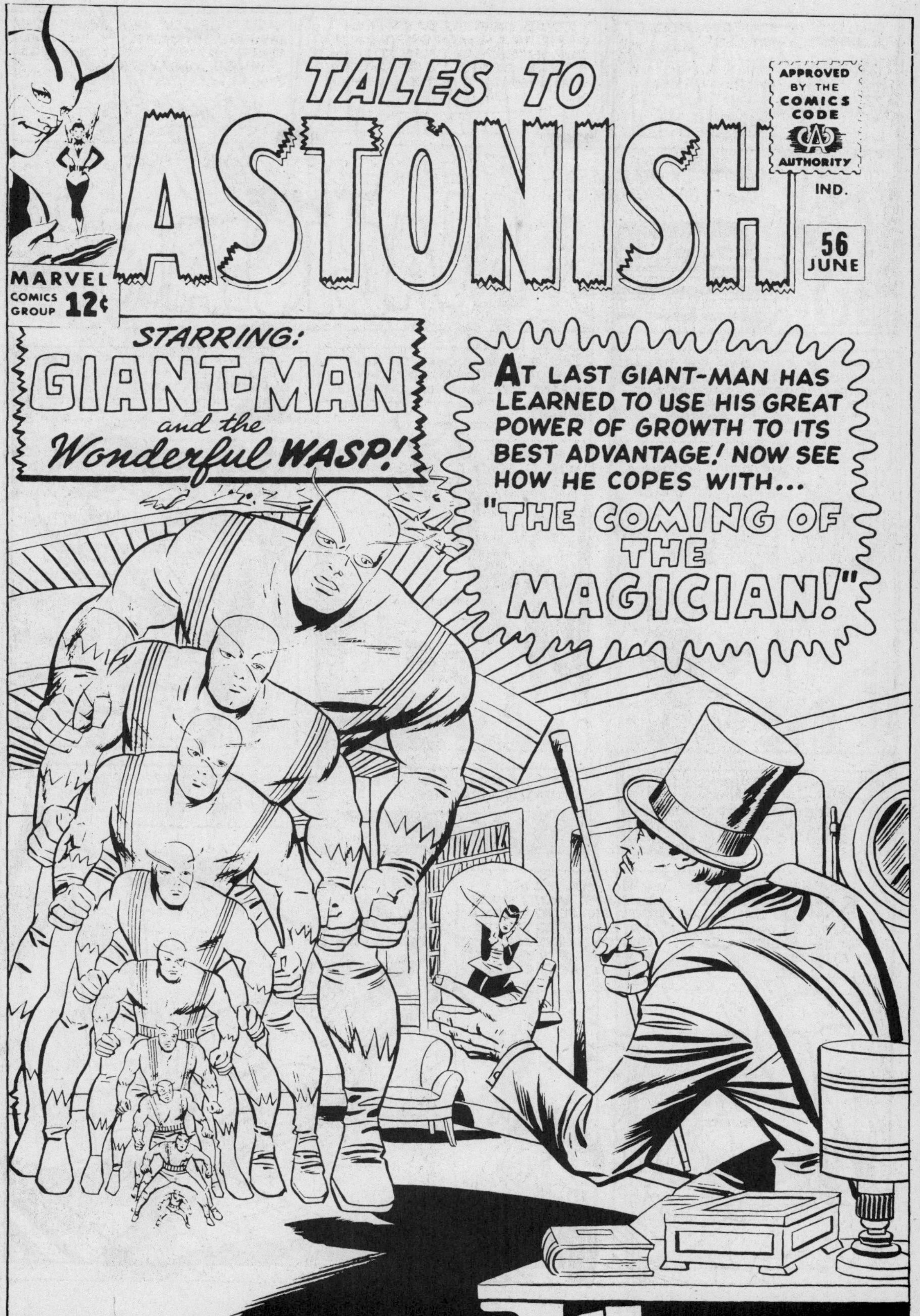
TALES TO ASTONISH
APPROVED BY THE COMICS CODE AUTHORITY
IND.
56
JUNE
MARVEL COMICS GROUP 12¢
STARRING:
GIANT-MAN
and the
Wonderful WASP!
AT LAST GIANT-MAN HAS LEARNED TO USE HIS GREAT POWER OF GROWTH TO ITS BEST ADVANTAGE! NOW SEE HOW HE COPES WITH...
"THE COMING OF THE MAGICIAN!"

Starring GIANT-MAN *and the Wonderful WASP!*

WRITTEN BY: STAN LEE
DRAWN BY: DICK AYERS

"The Coming of THE MAGICIAN!"

PASSERS-BY IN MIDTOWN NEW YORK ARE SUDDENLY STARTLED TO NOTICE A 12-FOOT TALL COSTUMED FIGURE ACTIVATE A SKYHOOK AT THE SIDE OF A BUILDING BY REMOTE CONTROL!

THEN, BEFORE ANYONE REALIZES WHAT IS HAPPENING, THE GIGANTIC ADVENTURER LEAPS UP, CATCHING THE DESCENDING RING...

...WHICH PULLS HIM ALOFT TO THE UPPER STORIES AS HE SWINGS TOWARDS THE WALL...

AND THEN...

IT WORKS LIKE A CHARM! FASTEST METHOD OF REACHING MY OVERSIZED LAB THAT I'VE EVER CREATED!

I'M GLAD I REACHED HERE BEFORE THE *WASP!* I HAVE A REAL *SURPRISE* FOR HER, AND I WANT TO GET IT ALL PREPARED PERFECTLY BEFORE SHE ARRIVES!!

X-659

FIRST THING TO DO NOW IS TAKE A *SHRINKING* CAPSULE!

WHAT I HAVE TO DO NOW CAN BE DONE BETTER WHILE I'M *ANT-SIZED*!

THERE IT IS, JUST WHERE I LEFT IT! IT'S TAKEN ME *MONTHS* TO GET UP THE COURAGE, BUT I'M FINALLY GOING TO OFFER JAN AN *ENGAGEMENT RING* AND ASK HER TO *MARRY ME*!

THE JEWELER LETTERED THE INSCRIPTION PERFECTLY, JUST AS I ASKED HIM TO!

WHILE I'M *ANT-SIZED* I CAN EXAMINE THE STONE MORE PERFECTLY THAN ANY DIAMOND EXPERT! IT HAS A FULL *58* FACETS, AND EVERY ONE IS FLAWLESS! IT'S A PERFECT, PURE WHITE GEM!

EVERYTHING IS READY FOR HER! I JUST HAVE TO PRAY THAT SHE SAYS "YES"! AND NOW...

MY *ANTENNAE* ARE TINGLING! IT MEANS SHE'S APPROACHING!! I'LL HIDE THE RING.. FAST!

HI, HANK! LIKE MY NEW HAIRDO AND HEADPIECE?

YOU'D LOOK GORGEOUS IN A FRIGHT WIG, JAN DARLING!

2

WHAT SAY WE SWITCH BACK TO NORMAL SIZE, BOSS MAN?

STRANGE... I'VE NEVER SEEN HIM LOOK SO *NERVOUS* BEFORE!

SURE, JAN! THE BIGGER YOU ARE, THE MORE OF YOU THERE IS FOR ME TO ENJOY LOOKING AT!

HANK IS GREAT WITH THE COMPLIMENTS, BUT HE NEVER THINKS OF MARRIAGE! THIS IS AS GOOD A TIME AS ANY TO TRY TO MAKE HIM JEALOUS!

OH, I JUST REMEMBERED, HANK! I HAVE TO BE RUNNING NOW! I'M INVITED TO A PARTY!

A *PARTY!?* BUT I..I WANTED TO... I MEAN...

I'M SORRY, BLUE EYES! IT'S BEING THROWN BY STERLING STUYVESANT, OF THE SOCIAL REGISTER STUYVESANTS! WE'VE KNOWN EACH OTHER FOR YEARS, AND TONIGHT I SUSPECT HE'S GOING TO *PROPOSE!*

THERE! IF HANK HAS ANY FEELING FOR ME AT ALL IN THAT SCIENTIFIC HEART OF HIS, *THAT* OUGHT TO STIR HIM INTO SOME ACTION! AND IF *THIS* DOESN'T WORK, I'LL JUST HAVE TO GIVE UP!

WHAT A *FOOL* I WAS... THINKING SHE CARED FOR *ME!* I EVEN BOUGHT THE *RING!* SHE'D PROBABLY HAVE LAUGHED IN MY FACE IF I OFFERED IT TO HER!

I SHOULD HAVE *KNOWN!* AN EX-DEBUTANTE... A BLUE-BLOOD, THE CREAM OF SOCIETY! SHE GETS HER KICKS BEING MY PARTNER IN PERIL... BUT WHEN IT COMES TO *ROMANCE,* SHE WANTS SOMEONE AS WEALTHY AS SHE!!

THAT'S WHAT I GET FOR OUT-CLASSING MYSELF! FOR TRYING TO GET OUT OF MY LEAGUE! I'M JUST A SCIENTIFIC ADVENTURER... I WAS NEVER CUT OUT TO BE A *DON JUAN!*

SO UPSET, SO FRUSTRATED IS HENRY PYM, THAT HE DOESN'T NOTICE ONE OF HIS OBSERVER ANTS, TRYING DESPERATELY TO SIGNAL HIM VIA HIS CYBERNETIC COMMUNICATOR...

BUT I'LL NEVER STOP LOVING HER... EVEN THOUGH SHE NEVER SUSPECTS IT!

3.

I GUESS THERE'S NO PLACE FOR MARRIAGE IN MY LIFE ANYWAY! BETWEEN MY EXPERIMENTS, AND MY CRIME-FIGHTING...

AND SO LONG AS I REMAIN A MEMBER OF THE AVENGERS, I MUST BE ON CALL 24 HOURS A DAY! SO, PERHAPS IT'S ALL FOR THE BEST!

AND THEN, FINALLY...

MY COMMUNICATOR!! I'M BEING SUMMONED!! SOMETHING IMPORTANT MUST BE HAPPENING!

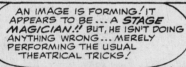

AN IMAGE IS FORMING! IT APPEARS TO BE...A STAGE MAGICIAN!! BUT, HE ISN'T DOING ANYTHING WRONG... MERELY PERFORMING THE USUAL THEATRICAL TRICKS!

AND YET...HIS EYES LOOK SINISTER...MERCILESS! THE ANTS MUST HAVE A REASON FOR PROJECTING THIS IMAGE!

NOW THEY'RE SHOWING ME THE BUILDING WHERE I CAN FIND HIM! WAIT... THAT'S THE BUILDING WHERE STERLING STUYVESANT LIVES!

CAN THERE BE SOME CONNECTION BETWEEN THAT EVIL-LOOKING MAGICIAN AND THE PARTY JAN IS ATTENDING?? I'D BETTER BECOME ANT-SIZED FAST AND NOT WASTE A SECOND!

LET'S GO, MY LOYAL WINGED STEEDS!! I HAVE A FEELING WE'RE HEADING INTO A GREAT ADVENTURE!

BUT LET US GO BACK JUST A FEW MINUTES, TO THE SCENE OF STERLING STUYVESANT'S PARTY...

I HAVE AN IMPORTANT QUESTION TO ASK YOU TONIGHT, JAN DEAR!

IF IT'S WHAT I *THINK* IT IS, STUY, I...I WISH YOU WOULDN'T....!

NONSENSE, DARLING! THERE'S A TIME AND PLACE FOR EVERYTHING! AND I CAN'T THINK OF A BETTER TIME AND PLACE THAN THIS!

JAN, WE'VE KNOWN EACH OTHER SINCE WE WERE YOUNGSTERS IN SOUTHHAMPTON! YOU *KNOW* HOW I FEEL ABOUT YOU!

STUY...PLEASE! LET'S SAVE IT TILL *LATER*...TILL *AFTER* THE PARTY!

OKAY, THEN, WE'LL GET THE PARTY *OVER* WITH AS SOON AS POSSIBLE! MAY I HAVE YOUR *ATTENTION,* FRIENDS?

I WANT TO ANNOUNCE OUR *ENTERTAINMENT* FOR TONIGHT!

HERE HE *IS*...ONE OF THE MOST AMAZING ACTS I'VE EVER SEEN! HE'S KNOWN ONLY AS...*THE MAGICIAN!!* AND I WAS LUCKY TO BE ABLE TO HIRE HIM FOR TONIGHT!

5.

DON'T MOVE!! REMAIN AS YOU ARE... WHERE YOU ARE!! YOU ARE ABOUT TO WITNESS THE INCREDIBLE!!! THE *IMPOSSIBLE!!*

MODEST, ISN'T HE?!

ABRA KADABRA!! ALLA KAZAAM!!

HOW DOES HE *DO* IT? IT SEEMS LIKE *REAL* MAGIC!!

I'VE SEEN ALL SORTS OF STAGE MAGICIANS... BUT *HE'S* GOT THEM BEAT BY A MILE!!

HE CERTAINLY IS *SENSATIONAL,* STUY! WHERE DID YOU EVER *FIND* HIM ??

HE FOUND ME, JAN! HE HEARD OF MY PARTY, AND OFFERED TO PERFORM HERE TONIGHT!

NO *WONDER* YOU ARE SO WEALTHY, MR. *STUYVESANT!* I SEE YOU CAN EVEN MAKE COINS COME OUT OF YOUR *EAR!*

6.

FOR YOU, MY LOVELY... A BOUQUET!

AND NOW, THE GRAND FINALE TO MY ACT!!

WHERE DID THAT HUGE CANVAS COME FROM? WHAT'S HE GOING TO DO NOW??

DOES THIS ANSWER YOUR QUESTIONS, YOU UNSUSPECTING FOOLS?!

HOW SIMPLE FOR A SLIGHT-OF-HAND MASTER LIKE ME TO TAKE THEIR VALUABLES WHILE THEY FLOUNDER BENEATH THAT CANVAS!

BUT THERE IS ONE WHO IS NOT "FLOUNDERING"!!

GOOD THING I BROUGHT MY WASP COSTUME WITH ME! IT'S SO TINY I WAS ABLE TO STUFF IT INSIDE THE SPECIAL HOLLOW SECTION OF MY BRACELET!

A SPLIT-SECOND LATER, AFTER QUICKLY TAKING A SHRINKING CAPSULE...

AND NOW, MR. MAGICIAN! WHATEVER YOUR LITTLE GAME IS, WE'LL SEE IF THE WASP CAN PUT A STOP TO IT!!

7.

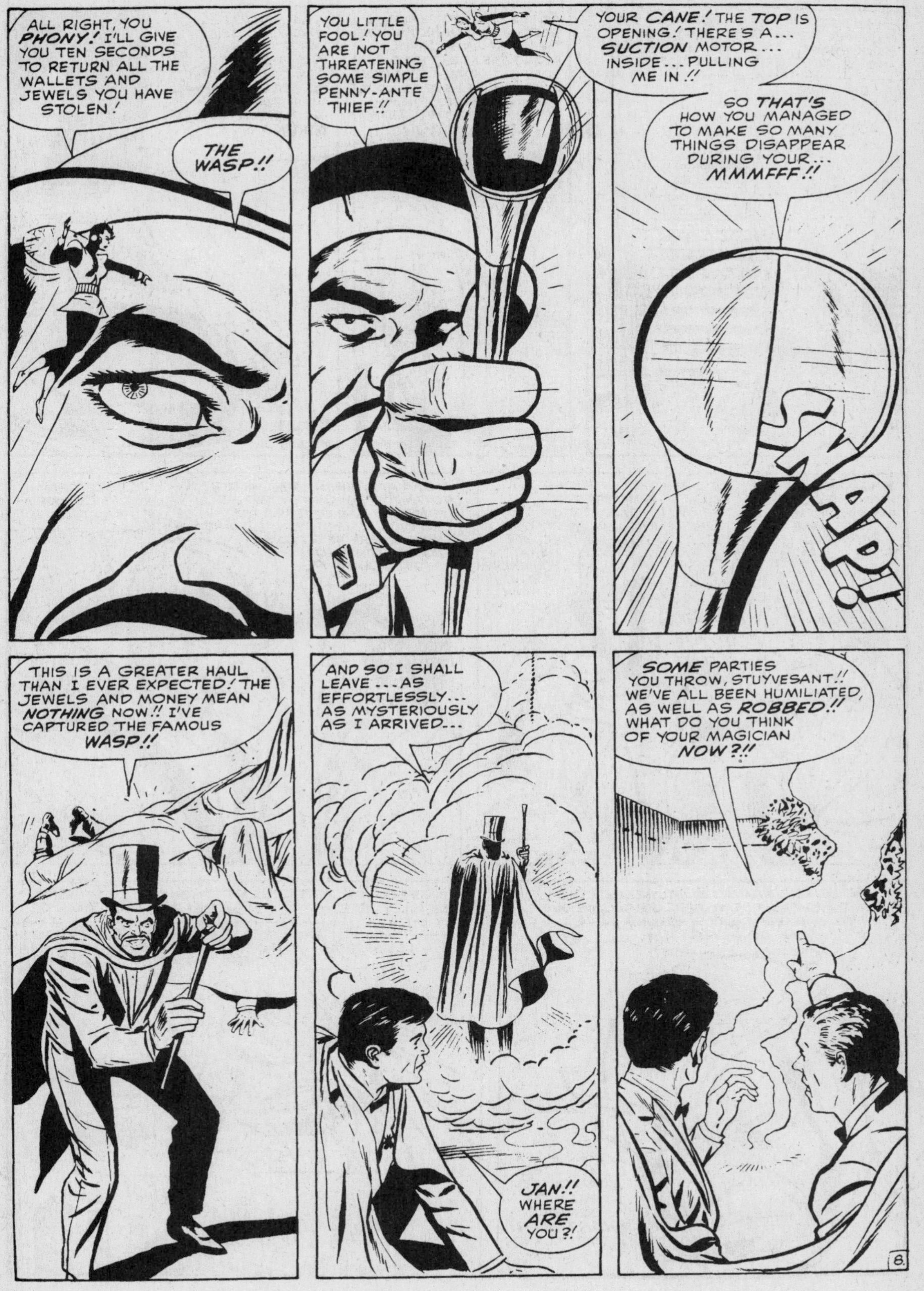
ALL RIGHT, YOU PHONY! I'LL GIVE YOU TEN SECONDS TO RETURN ALL THE WALLETS AND JEWELS YOU HAVE STOLEN!
THE WASP!!
YOU LITTLE FOOL! YOU ARE NOT THREATENING SOME SIMPLE PENNY-ANTE THIEF!!
YOUR CANE! THE TOP IS OPENING! THERE'S A... SUCTION MOTOR... INSIDE... PULLING ME IN!!
SO THAT'S HOW YOU MANAGED TO MAKE SO MANY THINGS DISAPPEAR DURING YOUR... MMMFFF!!
SNAP!
THIS IS A GREATER HAUL THAN I EVER EXPECTED! THE JEWELS AND MONEY MEAN NOTHING NOW!! I'VE CAPTURED THE FAMOUS WASP!!
AND SO I SHALL LEAVE ...AS EFFORTLESSLY... AS MYSTERIOUSLY AS I ARRIVED...
JAN!! WHERE ARE YOU?!
SOME PARTIES YOU THROW, STUYVESANT!! WE'VE ALL BEEN HUMILIATED, AS WELL AS ROBBED!! WHAT DO YOU THINK OF YOUR MAGICIAN NOW?!!
8

SECONDS LATER, ALL IS QUIET ATOP THE POSH PENTHOUSE SUITE OF STERLING STUYVESANT... WITH THE *MAGICIAN* AND HIS PRISONER NOWHERE IN SIGHT!!

HE'S *GONE!!* BUT WHERE...?? HOW...??

AS THE BAFFLED PLAYBOY SPEAKS, HE DOESN'T NOTICE THE THREE ANTS CRAWLING ALONG THE LEDGE BELOW HIM! BUT, *ARE* THEY THREE ANTS?? IF HE WERE TO LOOK DOWN AND STUDY THEM, HE WOULD SEE *TWO* ANTS ...PLUS... *ANT-MAN!!*

I'M ALMOST READY TO BELIEVE HE *IS* A MAGICIAN!

I'VE HEARD *ENOUGH!* THE MAGICIAN IS GONE, AND HE'S CAPTURED JAN, TOO! I'VE GOT TO BECOME NORMAL-SIZE *QUICKLY* AND SPEAK TO STUYVESANT!!

WHO ARE *YOU?* HOW'D YOU *GET* HERE? THIS ISN'T A *COSTUME PARTY!!*

I'LL ASK THE QUESTIONS, *FELLA!* I WANT TO FIND THE *MAGICIAN!* AND I WANT TO FIND HIM *FAST!* NOW TELL ME WHAT YOU *KNOW* ABOUT HIM!

I CAN ANSWER IN *ONE* WORD... *NOTHING!* HE CONTACTED ME YESTERDAY AND OFFERED TO PERFORM AT MY PARTY! I DON'T KNOW WHERE HE'S FROM... I DON'T EVEN KNOW HIS *NAME!!*

YOU'RE ONE SMART COOKIE, AREN'T YOU?!

I'M BEING *UNFAIR* TO STUYVESANT! THIS ISN'T *HIS* FAULT! I'M JUST *JEALOUS* DUE TO JAN! BUT THERE'S NOTHING MORE I CAN DO *HERE!*

IF YOU HEAR ANYTHING MORE, CALL THE POLICE! TELL THEM TO CONTACT *GIANT-MAN!* THEY'LL KNOW HOW!

WITHIN SECONDS, AFTER THE ASTONISHING COSTUMED ADVENTURER *SEEMS* TO VANISH BEFORE STUYVESANT'S VERY EYES...

BACK TO THE LAB, MY WINGED FRIENDS! I'LL NEED ALL MY SCIENTIFIC APPARATUS FOR THIS CASE! WE'RE UP AGAINST A MYSTERIOUS, POWERFUL FOE!!

9.

AT HIS COMPLETELY-EQUIPPED LAB ONCE MORE, HENRY PYM CONTACTS HIS OBSERVER ANTS, ALERTING THEM AT THEIR POSTS THROUGHOUT THE ENTIRE SURFACE OF EARTH...

THIS SPECIALLY-ADAPTED MIKE WILL CONVERT MY VERBAL COMMANDS INTO CYBERNETIC THOUGHT IMPULSES WHICH CAN BE THOROUGHLY UNDERSTOOD BY MY LEGION OF ANTS!

BUT, THE REPORTS WHICH ARE TRANSMITTED BACK FROM EVERY SECTION OF THE GLOBE ARE ALL IDENTICAL...

IT'S THE SAME ALL OVER...NO TRACE OF THE MAGICIAN! NO SIGN OF THE WASP! BUT HE MUST BE SOMEWHERE!

IF HE REALLY WERE MAGIC, I'D SUSPECT HIM OF TAKING JAN TO A DIFFERENT DIMENSION, A DIFFERENT AGE OR GALAXY! BUT I'M CONVINCED HE'S AS HUMAN AS I AM!

HE MUST BE OUT THERE SOMEWHERE... HIDING! HIDING SO WELL, MY ARMY OF ANTS CAN FIND NO TRACE OF HIM!

BUT, I CAN'T AFFORD TO WAIT ANY LONGER! I'VE GOT TO TAKE THE OFFENSIVE! I'VE GOT TO MAKE HIM COME TO ME!

AND SO, THE QUICK-THINKING ADVENTURER DECIDES UPON A SUBTLE PLAN...

HELLO, "TIMES" SOCIETY EDITOR? I WANT TO ANNOUNCE A PARTY WHICH I'M THROWING...

IF HE SPECIALIZES IN ROBBING SOCIETY PARTIES, I'LL GIVE HIM BAIT HE CAN'T RESIST!

YOU ARE INVITED TO A FULL-DRESS BALL ABOARD THE LUXURY YACHT "NEPTUNE"

THIS GALA EVENT WILL BE FOR THE BENEFIT OF CHARITY.

Henry Pym
Sutton Place
N.Y.

Mr. & Mrs. J.D. Van Carton
10065
Park Ave.
New York

THEN, WHEN ALL THE GUESTS ARE ASSEMBLED AT THE DOCK...

I'LL HAVE MY RENTED LAUNCH TAKE THEM TO A DIFFERENT YACHT! THE "NEPTUNE" WILL REMAIN DESERTED...EXCEPT FOR ME... AND THE MAGICIAN, WHEN HE ARRIVES!

10.

FINALLY, WHEN ALL THE GUESTS HAVE BEEN PUT ABOARD THE OTHER YACHT...

ALL RIGHT, CHARLIE! NOW TAKE ME TO THE "NEPTUNE"! AND THEN, GET BACK TO YOUR JOB, AND FORGET WHAT YOU'VE SEEN TONIGHT!

I DON'T GET IT! I THOUGHT THE PARTY WOULD BE ON THE "NEPTUNE"! IT WAS IN ALL THE PAPERS!

THERE *WILL* BE A PARTY ON THE "NEPTUNE"! BUT, NOT QUITE THE SORT YOU'D EXPECT!

MISTER, YOU'RE PAYING THE RENT FOR THESE SHIPS, SO YOU'RE THE BOSS! BUT IT SURE SEEMS LIKE A NUTTY WAY TO BURN UP MONEY!

MINUTES LATER, ABOARD THE PALATIAL YACHT "NEPTUNE"...

EVERYTHING'S ALL SET! I'VE GOT THE "NEPTUNE" LIT UP LIKE A CHRISTMAS TREE, AND LOUDSPEAKERS PLAYING DANCE MUSIC WHICH CAN BE HEARD FOR A MILE!

NEPTUNE

I EVEN SPACED CARDBOARD CUTOUTS IN THE SHAPE OF PEOPLE AROUND THE TURN-TABLE, SO THE MAGICIAN WILL THINK THERE REALLY *IS* A PARTY GOING ON!

AND NOW, AS *ANT-MAN* I'LL WAIT AND HOPE HE SNAPS AT THE BAIT! IF HE *DOES*, HE'LL LEARN THAT *I* HAVE A FEW TRICKS OF MY *OWN*!

11.

SUDDENLY, HEARING A SOUND BEHIND HIM, *ANT-MAN* SPINS AROUND, TO FIND...

THE MAGICIAN!! HE SEEMS TO HAVE APPEARED OUT OF *NOWHERE!* HE'S CRAFTIER THAN I *THOUGHT!*

WHAT'S GOING *ON??* MUSIC IS PLAYING... THE SHIP IS ALL LIT UP... BUT WHERE ARE MY INTENDED *VICTIMS??*

I'VE BEEN *TRICKED!!* THE BOAT IS EMPTY! THERE IS NO ORCHESTRA...MERELY A PHONOGRAPH!

AND A FLASHLIGHT BEHIND THOSE SPINNING CARDBOARD FIGURES MAKES IT LOOK LIKE PEOPLE DANCING FROM OUTSIDE!! BUT WHO COULD HAVE *DONE* IT??

I'LL GIVE YOU THREE GUESSES, *MAGICIAN!*

A *VOICE!* FROM *NO-WHERE!* I'VE GOT TO *ESCAPE!*

WHAT'S YOUR *HURRY*, MY OVERDRESSED FRIEND?? DON'T YOU *LIKE* PARTIES??

GIANT-MAN!! WHERE DID YOU *COME* FROM? WELL, NO MATTER!! NOW THAT I KNOW WHO MY ENEMY IS, I'LL KNOW HOW TO *FIGHT* YOU!

12.

AT A GESTURE FROM THE *MAGICIAN*, A LARGE SQUARE OF SILK CLOTH APPEARS FROM OUT OF HIS SLEEVE FLOATING SWIFTLY UPWARDS TOWARDS *GIANT-MAN!*

FIRST, I'LL *BLINDFOLD* YOU...!

CAN'T *SEE!* THE CLOTH WRAPPED ITSELF AROUND MY EYES!! GOT TO RIP IT OFF!

AND NOW FOR MY FAMOUS *INDIAN ROPE TRICK!*

SO! YOU CAN *SEE* AGAIN! BUT I'LL BE SAFELY ABOARD AGAIN BEFORE YOU CAN REACH ME!

SO *THAT'S* HOW HE APPEARS AND VANISHES! A BLIMP... PAINTED BLUE SO IT CAN'T BE SEEN AGAINST THE SKY!

THEN, AS GIANT-MAN ATTEMPTS TO HALT HIS FOES' ESCAPE...

HELP! OUR BOAT'S *CAPSIZING!* WE'LL *DROWN!* HELP!!

OF ALL THE TIMES FOR *THAT* TO HAPPEN!

I'LL HAVE TO LEAVE THE MAGICIAN FOR NOW!

CAN'T STAND BY AND LET TWO INNOCENT PEOPLE DROWN!

LUCKY I'M TALL ENOUGH TO PLACE MY FEET ON THE RIVER BED, GIVING ME ENOUGH LEVERAGE TO EASILY RIGHT THE SAILBOAT!

THANK HEAVENS!! WE'RE SAVED!! IT..IT SEEMS LIKE A *MIRACLE!*

AND LOOK WHO IT *IS*... IT'S *GIANT-MAN!* THIS IS SOMETHING WE'LL TELL OUR *GRANDCHILDREN* ABOUT!

13.

MEANTIME, ABOARD THE MAGICIAN'S BLIMP...

NOW THAT I'VE REELED IN MY TOW LINE, THERE'S NO WAY FOR GIANT-MAN TO REACH ME! I'M COMPLETELY SAFE!

AND WITH YOU AS A HOSTAGE, WASP, GIANT-MAN WOULDN'T DARE ATTACK ME AGAIN, ANYWAY!

BUT, THE MAGICIAN HAS UNDER-ESTIMATED THE POWERS OF THE WASP AND HER WORLD-FAMOUS PARTNER! FOR, EVEN AS HE SPEAKS TO HER...

I'M GETTING A MESSAGE FROM JAN! A CYBERNETIC THOUGHT TRANSFERENCE, VIA MY SENSITIVE ANTENNAE!

SHE'S SAFELY ABOARD THE BLIMP! GOOD!

I'LL JUST BORROW THIS RIGGING ROPE FROM YOU! I CAN USE IT!

GIANT-MAN, YOU CAN HAVE ANYTHING! WE OWE YOU OUR LIVES!

IT WORKED! PROBABLY THE FIRST TIME IN HISTORY THAT A MAN LASSOED A BLIMP!

BUT I'M TOO HEAVY! MY WEIGHT IS FORCING IT OUT OF CONTROL! IT'LL CRASH!!

ONLY ONE THING TO DO!! LUCKY I HAVE A FULL SUPPLY OF SHRINKING CAPSULES!

NOW, AS ANT-MAN, I CAN EASILY CLIMB ABOARD WITHOUT AFFECTING THE BLIMP'S FLIGHT!

THAT ROPE, SWAYING PAST THE WINDOW! THERE'S SOMETHING ON IT! IS IT A BUG... OR...NO! IT CAN'T BE!

OF COURSE NOT! NOBODY CAN OUTSMART YOU, EH ??

14.

IF YOU'RE WHAT I *THINK* YOU ARE, I'LL STEP ON YOU AND... *MISSED!!*

YOU'LL HAVE TO BE FASTER THAN *THAT*, BIG MAN!

ANT-MAN!! HURRY! GET ME OUT OF HERE!

IT'LL BE A *PLEASURE*, JAN! LUCKY I KEEP MY NORMAL STRENGTH EVEN THOUGH I'M REDUCED TO ANT SIZE!

BE *CAREFUL*, HANK! THE MAGICIAN IS *DANGEROUS!* HE'S *TRICKIER* THAN YOU THINK!

JAN, HONEY... *I'M* NOT EXACTLY A PUSHOVER MYSELF! NOW STAND BACK AND WATCH THE FIREWORKS!

YOU *WANT* ME, MAGICIAN? WHY DIDN'T YOU JUST *SAY* SO!

BUT YOU'VE GOT TO BE ABLE TO *HOLD* ME!

IT'S *IMPOSSIBLE!* I'M BEING THROWN OFF-BALANCE BY.. BY A HUMAN *ANT!!!*

YOU HAVEN'T SEEN THE *HALF* OF IT, FELLA!!

QUICK, JAN! WHILE I'M FIGHTING THAT WALKING BAG OF TRICKS, HERE'S WHAT I WANT *YOU* TO DO...

15.

BUT, AS ANT-MAN HURRIEDLY WHISPERS TO THE WASP...

ONLY THE *MAGICIAN* COULD HAVE TRAINED A RABBIT TO BE AN OBEDIENT BEAST OF PREY!

GO, MY PET... CATCH THOSE TWO FOOLS FOR YOUR *MASTER!*

GOOD! GOOD! NOTHING CAN OUTRUN A HIGHLY-TRAINED RABBIT!!

DO AS I TOLD YOU, WASP! I'LL HOLD HIM OFF!

LUCKY I MADE MY GROWTH CAPSULES SO FAST-ACTING!

LOOKS LIKE YOUR "BEAST OF PREY" IS STILL A SCARED RABBIT AT HEART MAGICIAN!

GIANT-MAN! HOW DID *YOU* GET HERE!?

I DON'T ASK HOW YOU DO *YOUR* TRICKS, DO I? NOW JUST STAY WHERE YOU ARE, FELLA! THIS'LL ONLY TAKE A MINUTE!

HOPE JAN IS CARRYING OUT MY ORDERS!

I'LL *STILL* TRIUMPH OVER YOU! BECAUSE OF YOUR HUGE SIZE, YOU'RE MORE VULNERABLE THAN ANYONE TO MY GREATEST POWER... *HYPNOTISM!!*

MEANWHILE, THE WONDERFUL *WASP* FLIES TO THE TOP OF THE BLIMP...

THERE'S THE RELEASE VALVE... JUST WHERE HANK *SAID* IT WOULD BE!

YOUR EYES ARE SO LARGE, THAT I CAN HYPNOTIZE YOU IN *HALF* THE NORMAL TIME!

YOU ARE IN MY POWER! YOUR WILL IS *MY* WILL! I AM YOUR MASTER! YOU MUST OBEY ME!

IT'S WORKING! HE'S GOING UNDER!

16.

BUT, AT THAT VERY SPLIT SECOND...

I OPENED THE AIR RELEASE VALVE AS HANK ORDERED! BUT NOW THE BLIMP WILL CRASH INSTANTLY!! MY *WINGS* WILL SAVE *ME*, BUT...

AS I FLEW UP HERE, THE MAGICIAN WAS HYPNOTIZING HANK! IF HE FALLS TO THE WATER, HEAVY AS HE IS, THE IMPACT COULD *KILL* HIM!

WE'RE GOING TO *HIT!* BUT... I DON'T SEE HANK!

HANK! HANK! WHERE *ARE* YOU? WHAT HAVE I DONE TO YOU, MY DARLING??!

HANK!

17.

No sooner does the blimp sink out of sight, than a police grappling hook writes *FINIS* to the magician's latest crime exploit...

GOOD THING THAT COUPLE ON THE SAIL-BOAT CONTACTED US! WE WERE JUST IN TIME!

DON'T PLAN TO GIVE ANY MORE MAGIC SHOWS FOR THE NEXT FEW YEARS, MAGICIAN! I HAVE A FEELING YOU'RE GOING TO DO ALL YOUR PERFORMING BEHIND *BARS* FROM NOW ON!

WE'LL CRUISE AROUND AND SEARCH FOR ANY OTHER SURVIVORS... BUT IT LOOKS PRETTY HOPE-LESS TO ME!

Meanwhile, on a small buoy, float-ing nearby, Janet Van Dyne becomes normal-sized again, after flying to safety unnoticed, in the identity of the *WASP!*

HANK! HANK! IT'S ALL MY FAULT! I SHOULDN'T HAVE OPENED THAT VALVE!

I-I'VE KILLED THE ONLY MAN I'VE EVER LOVED!!

JAN, HONEY! IT WAS WORTH *EVERYTHING* JUST TO HEAR YOU *SAY* THAT!

HIS *VOICE!!* BUT WHERE?? HOW??

THE MAGICIAN DIDN'T REALIZE THAT MY CYBERNETIC HELMET FILTERED THE EFFECT OF HIS HYPNOTIC POWER, ENABLING ME TO RESIST IT!

HANK! YOU'RE *ALIVE!* YOU'RE *SAFE!*

SURE, HONEY! WHILE WE WERE FALLING, I FOLDED A PAPER AIRPLANE, TOOK A REDUCING CAPSULE, AND GLIDED TO SAFETY, FREE AS THE BREEZE!

HANK, MY DARLING! I'LL NEVER FORGET HOW I FELT WHEN I THOUGHT I HAD LOST YOU! NOW I KNOW THERE CAN *NEVER* BE ANYONE ELSE FOR ME!

THERE NEVER *WILL* BE, JAN! I PROMISE YOU THAT!

Later, at a signal from Henry Pym, the motor launch which had brought him to the "Neptune" picks him up again, and heads for shore!

SAY, WEREN'T YOU *ALONE* WHEN I BROUGHT YOU OUT HERE?? HOW COME..? AW, WHAT AM I TALKING FOR? THEY HAVEN'T HEARD A WORD I SAID!

THIS IS ONLY THE *BEGINNING*, FRIENDS! STAN AND DICK HAVE MANY MORE THRILLING ARCH-VILLAINS FOR GIANT-MAN TO BATTLE, AND MANY MORE OFF-BEAT PLOTS AND ADVENTURES! SO, BE WITH US AGAIN NEXT ISH, AND TILL THEN, BE KIND TO LITTLE BUGS ... ONE OF THEM MIGHT BE A FRIEND!

The End.

18.

THE WASP TELLS A TALE

"BEWARE THE BOG BEAST!"

ARE YOU SCRAWNY? DO GIRLS RIDICULE YOU? DO BULLIES ON THE BEACH KICK SAND IN YOUR FACE? WELL, CHEER UP, PAL! *EVERYONE'S* GOT PROBLEMS-- EVEN *GIANT-MAN!!*

IT'S HUMILIATING! I'M *TWICE* THE SIZE OF *THE HULK,* AND YET HE'S STRONGER THAN I !! BUT, MAYBE IF I CONTINUE WITH THESE OVERSIZED BARBELLS--

SAY, I'VE GOT A PEACHY *RIDDLE* FOR YOU! SEE IF YOU CAN FIGURE IT OUT!

NOT NOW, JAN! CAN'T YOU SEE I'M BUSY! GET OFF MY NOSE! YOU'RE TICKLING ME! YOU'LL MAKE ME--AHHH-- AHHHH--

DON'T BREAK A BICEP, BIG BOY! I LIKE YOU AS YOU ARE!

STORY PLOT..... STAN LEE
SCRIPT & ART.... LARRY LIEBER
INKING.......... PAUL REINMAN
LETTERING...... ART SIMEK

X-646

CHOO!

PUH-*LEESE!!* THINK OF MY LITTLE SHELL- LIKE EARS!

NOW C'MON, HANK! BE A SPORT! LISTEN TO MY RIDDLE AND TRY TO WORK IT OUT!

ALRIGHT, PEST! ANYTHING YOU SAY-- IF YOU'LL PROMISE TO LEAVE ME ALONE AFTERWARDS!

I PROMISE, I PROMISE!! NOW HEAR THIS...

"ON A FAR-OFF PLANET, A ZILLION MILES FROM US, THERE'S A BEAUTIFUL PRINCESS--NO JANET VAN DYNE, MIND YOU, BUT AN ATTRACTIVE DAMSEL NONETHELESS! ANYHOW, AS FATE WOULD HAVE IT, LITTLE MISS ROYALTY HAS LOST HER HEART TO A LAZY PEASANT NAMED LORENZO!"

YOU'RE THE LOVE OF MY LIFE! I WANT TO MARRY YOU! BUT YOU'LL HAVE TO ACCEPT ME AS I AM--WITHOUT ANY DESIRE FOR FAME, OR WEALTH, OR ANYTHING ELSE!

I KNOW YOU'RE UNAMBI-TIOUS, DARLING, BUT I DON'T CARE! ALL THAT MATTERS TO ME IS BEING IN YOUR ARMS!

"HOWEVER, THE COURSE OF TRUE LOVE SELDOM RUNS SMOOTH..."

SO YOU'RE BACK HERE AGAIN, YOU LAZY LOUT! UNHAND MY SISTER AND BEGONE FROM THE PALACE OR I'LL HAVE YOU SLAPPED IN IRONS!

AS YOUR MAJESTY COMMANDS...

BUT, MAXIMUS, I LOVE HIM!

BAH! YOU'RE TOO GOOD FOR THAT IDLER! IN FACT, YOU'RE TOO GOOD FOR MOST MEN! THAT IS WHY I'VE ARRANGED A TEST!

THE MAN WHO WINS YOUR HAND IN MARRIAGE MUST FIRST PROVE HIS COURAGE AND SKILL BY PITTING HIMSELF AGAINST THE MIGHTIEST OF WILD CREATURES -- THE BOG BEAST!

"AND THUS THE KING TAKES HIS SISTER TO THE TINY ISLE OF PERILICA, WHERE DWELLS THE DREADED BOG BEAST!"

FOR MONTHS WE LET THE ANIMAL SMELL YOUR PERFUME AND GAZE AT YOUR PORTRAIT UNTIL HE GREW TO LOVE YOU!

NOW YOU SAY HE WILL GUARD ME JEALOUSLY AND ATTACK ANYONE WHO TRIES TO COME NEAR ME?

EXACTLY! AND ONLY THE MAN WHO CAN FREE YOU FROM THE BOG BEAST WILL BE WORTHY TO BECOME YOUR HUSBAND!

2

"UPON LEARNING OF THE ROYAL CONTEST, SCORES OF SUITORS ARRIVE! BUT, WHEN THEY GLIMPSE THE MONSTROUS *BOG BEAST*, MOST OF THEM LOSE HEART!"

I ADORE THE PRINCESS, BUT I WOULD NOT STAND A CHANCE AGAINST THE CREATURE THAT GUARDS HER!

TO SET FOOT UPON THAT ISLE WOULD SPELL MY DOOM!

FORTUNATELY, THE BOG BEAST IS TOO HEAVY FOR THE BRIDGE TO WITHSTAND HIS WEIGHT! ELSE WE WOULD NOT BE SAFE FROM HIM EVEN *HERE!*

"OF ALL THE SUITORS, ONLY LAZY LORENZO AND TWO OTHERS REMAIN TO FACE THE GRIM CHALLENGE!"

I HAVE THE MIGHT OF A DOZEN GIANTS! ONLY *I* CAN VANQUISH THE BOG BEAST!

I AM THE GREATEST WARRIOR IN THE KINGDOM. THE PRINCESS WILL SOON BE *MINE!*

AND *I* AM IN NO HURRY! I WILL LET YOU GENTLEMEN GO *FIRST!*

HAH! JUST *LET* ME GO FIRST AND THERE WILL BE NO NEED FOR A *SECOND* CONTEST! NOTHING THAT *LIVES* CAN WITHSTAND MY STRENGTH!

I HAVE MERELY TO SEIZE THE CREATURE IN MY UNBREAKABLE GRIP -- AND WITHIN A FEW SECONDS, HE'LL BE UTTERLY HELPLESS!

"BUT, WITH A SUDDEN TWIST OF HIS POWERFUL NECK MUSCLES, THE HUGE BOG BEAST HURLS HIS HUMAN FOE AWAY!"

THE MONSTER TOSSED ME OFF LIKE AN INSIGNIFICANT INSECT! FOR *THAT* AFFRONT HE WILL PAY...

...WITH HIS VERY LIFE!

3

WITH ONE MIGHTY THRUST, I SHALL DESTROY THE BEAST AND WIN THE HAND OF THE PRINCESS!

"BUT, TO THE STRONGMAN'S ASTONISHMENT..."

IT'S *IMPOSSIBLE!* THE CREATURE STILL STANDS-- *UNHARMED!!*

CRACK!

IF HE CAN WITHSTAND SO TREMEN- DOUS A BLOW, HE CAN ENDURE *ANY- THING!* I MUST ESCAPE WHILE THERE'S STILL TIME!

THANK HEAVENS THE STRONGMAN WAS DEFEATED! ELSE I WOULD HAVE HAD TO FORSAKE MY TRUE LOVE FOR HIM!

BAH! A MUSCLEBOUND OAF COULD NOT VANQUISH THE BOG BEAST! BUT I, A SKILLED BATTLE- HARDENED WARRIOR, WILL BE VICTORIOUS!

PERHAPS, BUT TRY TO BATTLE QUIETLY, FOR I FEEL A BIT FATIGUED AND WOULD LIKE TO TAKE A NAP!

SLEEP ALL YOU WANT, SLUGGARD! YOUR TURN WILL *NEVER* COME! FOR WHEN YOU AWAKE, THE GREAT BEAST WILL HAVE ALREADY BEEN SLAIN BY MY DEADLY CROSS- BOW!

"BUT THO' THE GREAT CROSS- BOW IS FIRED WITH UNERRING ACCURACY..."

HIS HIDE IS A THICK AND TOUGH AS IRON! MY ARROWS ARE *USELESS* AGAINST IT!

BUT I DO NOT DESPAIR! I NEED NOT *DESTROY* THE LOATHSOME CREATURE TO DEFEAT HIM! I CAN SIMPLY ENTANGLE HIM IN MY NET!

THERE! I HAVE RENDERED HIM HELPLESS! MIGHTY AS HE IS, HE CANNOT MOVE! NOW I SHALL TAKE THE PRINCESS FROM THIS ISLE AND CLAIM HER HAND IN MARRIAGE!

4

"BUT, BEFORE THE WARRIOR CAN REACH HIS ROYAL PRIZE..."

THE BEAST IS SO ENRAGED THAT HIS BODY IS *SMOLDERING!* HE'S MELTING THE NET!

HE'S ATTACKING! I MUST FLEE ACROSS THE BRIDGE TO SAFETY! I'VE FAILED! *FAILED!*

ONCE AGAIN THE FATES WERE WITH ME! NOW IT IS MY *BELOVED'S* TURN TO FREE ME FROM THE DREAD BOG BEAST!

WELL, WHAT *HAPPENED?* DID LORENZO PULL IT OFF?

OF COURSE! UNARMED, AND WITHOUT EXPENDING ANY EFFORT WHATSOEVER, THE LAZY SUITOR FREED THE PRINCESS FROM HER CAPTIVITY AND THEREBY EARNED THE RIGHT TO MARRY HER! THUS ENDED THEIR ROMANTIC TALE!

ENDED?? WAIT A MINUTE! HOW DID LORENZO GET PAST THE BOG BEAST?? WHAT IN SAM HILL IS THE *ANSWER* TO THE RIDDLE?

THE *ANSWER?* GEE, I GUESS YOU'RE TOO BUSY LIFTING WEIGHTS NOW TO BE INTERESTED IN RIDDLES! BUT PERHAPS IF YOU TAKE ME OUT TO *DINNER* TONIGHT--?

DINNER?! SO *THAT'S* IT! OKAY, LITTLE MISS BLACKMAILER, YOU WIN!

AND THAT EVENING, HENRY PYM, CONSUMED WITH CURIOSITY, PLEADS WITH HIS LOVELY TORMENTOR...

COME ON, JAN! TELL ME THE ANSWER BEFORE I GO *BATTY!*

ALRIGHT, HANDSOME! NOW HEAR THIS-- LAZY LORENZO DIDN'T EVEN *BOTHER* TO CROSS OVER TO THE ISLE! YOU SEE, HE *KNEW* THAT THE BOG BEAST WOULDN'T HARM THE PRINCESS BECAUSE IT *LOVED* HER, SO LORENZO SHOUTED TO THE PRINCESS, TELLING *HER* TO CROSS OVER THE BRIDGE TO *HIM!* AND, OF COURSE, THE JEALOUS BEAST COULDN'T *FOLLOW* BECAUSE HE WAS TOO HEAVY FOR THE BRIDGE TO HOLD!

SO *THAT'S* HOW THEY GOT TOGETHER! HMMN... THIS STEAK IS *DELICIOUS!*

BRO-*THER!* I'LL TAKE BATTLING A SUPER-VILLAIN *ANY* TIME TO MATCHING WITS WITH A GORGEOUS FEMALE!!

THE END

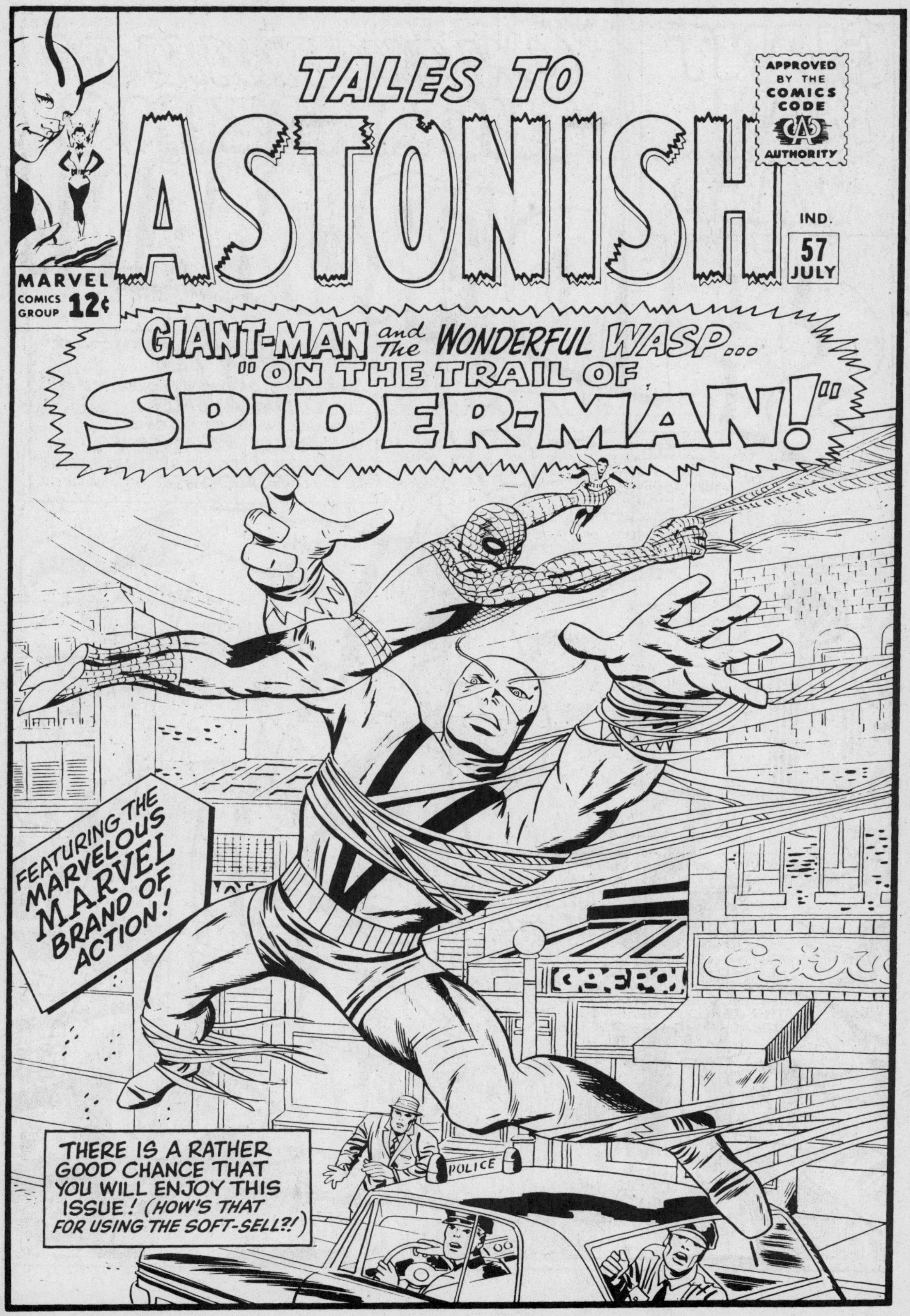
TALES TO ASTONISH
APPROVED BY THE COMICS CODE CA AUTHORITY
IND.
57
JULY
MARVEL COMICS GROUP 12¢
GIANT-MAN and the WONDERFUL WASP...
"ON THE TRAIL OF SPIDER-MAN!"
FEATURING THE MARVELOUS MARVEL BRAND OF ACTION!
OBERON
POLICE
THERE IS A RATHER GOOD CHANCE THAT YOU WILL ENJOY THIS ISSUE! (HOW'S THAT FOR USING THE SOFT-SELL?!)

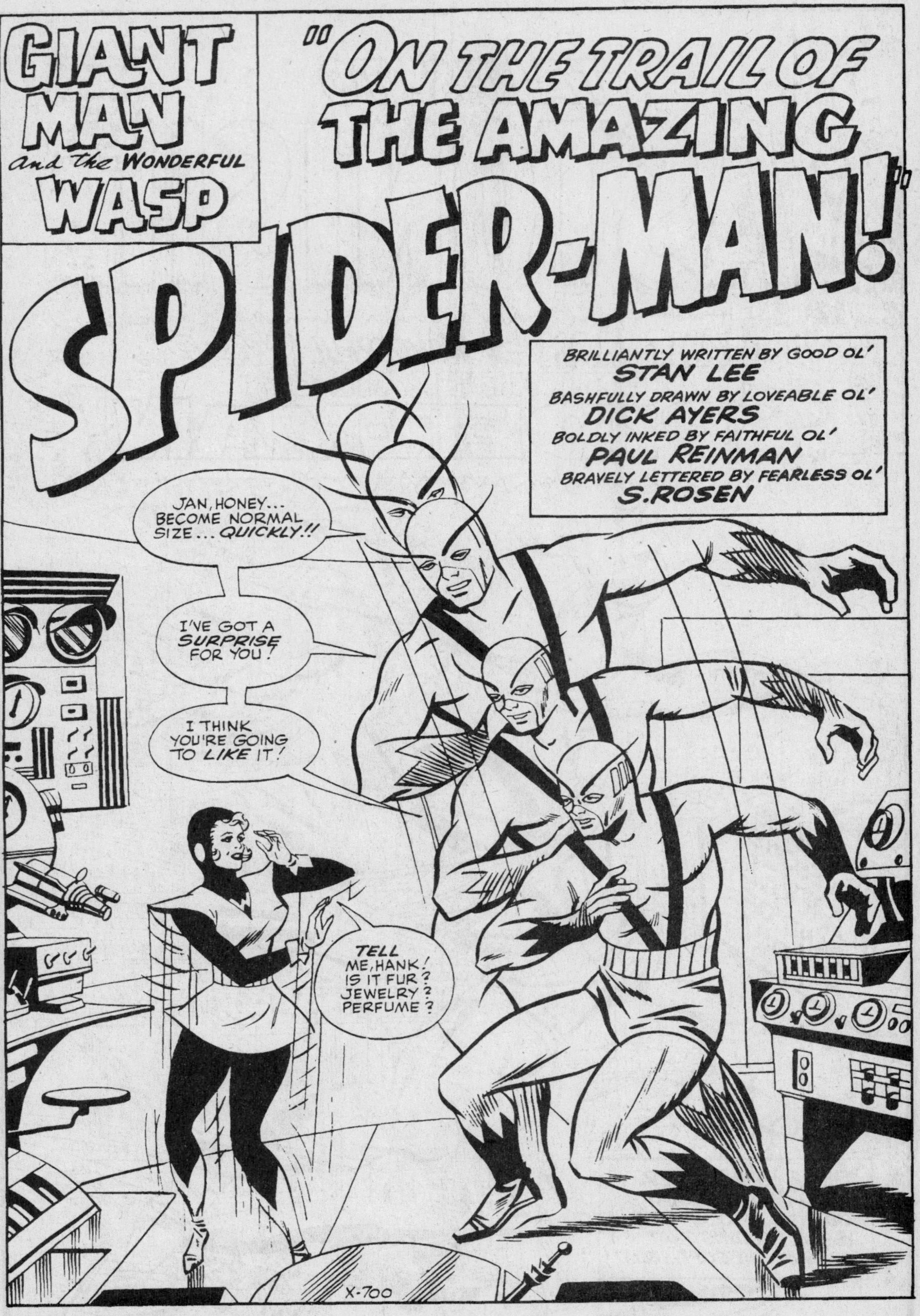
GIANT MAN and the WONDERFUL WASP
"ON THE TRAIL OF THE AMAZING SPIDER-MAN!"
BRILLIANTLY WRITTEN BY GOOD OL' STAN LEE
BASHFULLY DRAWN BY LOVEABLE OL' DICK AYERS
BOLDLY INKED BY FAITHFUL OL' PAUL REINMAN
BRAVELY LETTERED BY FEARLESS OL' S.ROSEN
JAN, HONEY... BECOME NORMAL SIZE... QUICKLY!!
I'VE GOT A SURPRISE FOR YOU!
I THINK YOU'RE GOING TO LIKE IT!
TELL ME, HANK! IS IT FUR? JEWELRY? PERFUME?
X-700

NOT ANYTHING LIKE *THAT*, JAN! I'VE CREATED A NEW *WEAPON* FOR YOU!

HOW ROMANTIC! THERE'S A MOON OUTSIDE... SOFT BREEZES AND THE SCENT OF HONEYSUCKLE IN THE AIR! AND WHAT DO *YOU* HAVE FOR ME?? A *WEAPON*!!

OH, WELL... I SUPPOSE THAT'S WHAT I *GET* FOR TEAMING UP WITH A HANDSOME, BLUE-EYED ADVENTURER INSTEAD OF DATING CARY GRANT!

I'D LIKE TO SEE CARY GRANT.. PERIOD!

JUST WAIT TILL YOU *SEE* THIS WEAPON, LITTLE FRIEND! I'D LIKE TO SEE *CARY GRANT* DREAM UP A DEVICE LIKE *THIS!*

LOOK, HONEY... FOR MONTHS YOU'VE HAD ONLY YOUR SMALL SIZE TO HELP YOU IN ANY TIGHT SPOT! WELL, NOW YOU'RE GOING TO HAVE SOMETHING *ELSE* TO USE IN A PINCH!

WHO NEEDS *THAT?* NO-BODY GOES AROUND PINCHING WASPS!

BE SERIOUS, JAN! THIS IS A HIGHLY POTENT COMPRESSED AIR GUN!

NOW STRAP IT TO YOUR ARM... MAKE SURE IT FITS REAL SNUG, BECAUSE ANY LOOSE-NESS WILL AFFECT YOUR AIM!

I HOPE NOBODY SAYS: "DIG THE CRAZY CHARM BRACELET!"

NOW PUT YOUR FINGER THROUGH THAT LITTLE RING... THAT'S IT! OKAY, AIM IT AT A TARGET, HONEY! STEADY, NOW!

I GET IT, BIG DADDY! ALL I DO IS BEND MY FINGER TO PULL THE CORD WHICH THE RING IS ATTACHED TO, EH?

RIGHT! IT WILL FIRE ONE CONTINUOUS BURST OF COM-PRESSED AIR, OR SHORT SUDDEN ONES, DEPENDING ON HOW LONG YOU HOLD YOUR FINGER DOWN!

AND NOTICE HOW POWERFUL THE BURSTS ARE!

MY, MY! IT'S SOMETHING NO BACHELOR GIRL SHOULD EVER BE WITHOUT!

2.

HANDLE IT, CAREFULLY, DOLL! IT'S VERY FRAGILE! I MADE IT OF THE SAME MOLECULAR SUBSTANCES AS OUR COSTUMES ARE MADE OF... SO THAT IT WILL SHRINK WHEN *YOU* SHRINK, WITHOUT LOSING ANY OF ITS STRENGTH!

DON'T WORRY, HANK! I'LL GIVE IT THE SAME TENDER LOVING CARE THAT I WISH A CERTAIN BLUE-EYED AVENGER WOULD GIVE TO HIS LITTLE WASP!

BUT, PERHAPS THE WASP WOULD NOT BE QUITE SO FLIPPANT IF SHE KNEW OF THE DEVIOUS SCHEME BEING FORMULATED IN THE BRAIN OF ONE OF GIANT-MAN'S MOST DANGEROUS ENEMIES... THE BRILLIANT, EVIL *EGG-HEAD!*

I'VE REMAINED IN HIDING LONG ENOUGH! GIANT-MAN HAS PROBABLY FORGOTTEN ALL ABOUT ME BY NOW!

WHICH MEANS... THE TIME HAS COME FOR ME TO *STRIKE!*

FOR MONTHS I HAVE WORKED ON MY OWN ELECTRONIC IMPULSE COMMUNICATOR THROUGH WHICH I CAN COMMUNICATE WITH THE ANTS ALMOST AS WELL AS *HE* CAN!*

* FOR MORE DETAILS, SEE *TALES TO ASTONISH #45,* "TERRIBLE TRAPS OF EGGHEAD!"

I'VE SET UP MY OWN "RECEIVING STATION" ON A NEARBY ANT-HILL! AND NOW FOR MY PLAN!

I'LL BROADCAST A *FALSE* REPORT TO THE ANTS... WHICH THEY ARE SURE TO TRANSMIT TO MY ARCH-ENEMY! *HE* WON'T SUSPECT THE REPORT IS A TRAP... HE'LL *BELIEVE* HIS ANTS!

AND SO, THE EVIL GENIUS SETS THE STAGE FOR HIS MASTER PLAN! WHILE BACK AT *GIANT MAN'S* LAB, A SHORT TIME LATER...

QUIET, JAN! AN EMERGENCY ALARM IS COMING IN FROM MY ANT SCOUTS! ALTHOUGH... IT'S SOMETHING I'D NEVER HAVE SUSPECTED! IT'S ALMOST UNBELIEVABLE!

URGENT!! SPIDER-MAN HAS BEEN SIGHTED SEARCHING FOR OUR MASTER! HE INTENDS TO ATTACK AND DEFEAT *GIANT-MAN!!*

THEN, AFTER RELAYING THE STARTLING REPORT TO HIS PARTNER IN PERIL, HENRY PYM PREPARES FOR IMMEDIATE ACTION !!

NO TIME TO LOSE, JAN! TAKE A SHRINKING CAPSULE FAST, AND SEARCH THE CITY AS THE *WASP!* SOON AS YOU FIND SPIDER-MAN, REPORT BACK TO ME!

BUT DON'T TRY TO TACKLE HIM *YOURSELF,* HEAR?

ROGER, BOSS! I'M ON MY WAY!

3.

USING THE ARTIFICIAL ANTENNAE WHICH APPEAR WITH HER WINGS WHEN SHE BECOMES WASP-SIZE, THE FABULOUS FLYING FEMALE KEEPS IN CLOSE TOUCH WITH GIANT MAN...

STILL NO SIGN OF HIM, HANK!

KEEP SEARCHING, WASP! AND REMEMBER, NO HEROICS! WHEN YOU FIND HIM, I'LL TAKE OVER!

BUT I'M DYING TO USE MY NEW WASP'S "STING"!

SECONDS LATER...

THERE HE IS! I'VE FOUND HIM!

HE SWINGS FROM ROOF-TOP TO ROOF-TOP LIKE A SILENT, SINISTER GHOST! HE MAY BE SAFELY GONE BEFORE GIANT-MAN CAN REACH THE SPOT!

I'VE GOT TO SLOW HIM DOWN SOMEHOW - EVEN I CAN'T KEEP UP WITH HIM!

THIS IS THE ONLY WAY!

OH, NO! IN MY EAGERNESS, I MADE THE AIR BLAST TOO STRONG! I'VE CAUGHT HIM BY SURPRISE... MADE HIM LOSE HIS BALANCE!!

4.

BUT, THE AMAZING *SPIDER-MAN* HAS THE LIGHTNING-FAST REFLEXES OF THE POWERFUL ARACHNID FOR WHOM HE IS NAMED...

SOMETHING *HIT* ME... SENT ME *TOPPLING!* AN UNSEEN ENEMY! BUT, I'LL STRIKE BACK LATER... FIRST I'VE GOT TO *SAVE* MYSELF!

WHOEVER IS RESPONSIBLE WILL LEARN THAT IT TAKES MORE THAN A SNEAK ATTACK TO DEFEAT *SPIDER-MAN!!*

I'LL SHOOT OUT MY WEB-STRANDS WHILE I'M FALLING... AND, IF I'VE AIMED THEM CORRECTLY...

...THEY'LL WRAP THEMSELVES AROUND THAT IRON LAMP POST.. LIKE *THIS!*

AND *NOW...* I'LL FIND OUT WHO'S RESPONSIBLE FOR ATTACKING ME.. AND MAKE HIM WISH HE'D NEVER *HEARD* OF SPIDER-MAN!

THANK HEAVENS HE *SAVED* HIMSELF!

THEN, THE MYSTERIOUS ADVENTURER USES HIS AMAZING "SPIDER-SENSE"...ONLY TO FIND...

MY SPIDER-SENSE IS RECEIVING A TINY, ALMOST INVISIBLE IMPRESSION! I'M BEING ATTACKED BY SOMETHING THE SIZE OF AN *INSECT!*

5.

HE'S SHOOTING OUT THAT WEB OF HIS...IN MY DIRECTION!

HANK!! I'M *TRAPPED!* HE CAUGHT ME IN HIS *WEB!*

THE LITTLE *FOOL!* I *WARNED* HER NOT TO TACKLE HIM ALONE!

KEEP TRANSMITTING, HONEY! I'LL FOLLOW YOUR BEAM AND BE THERE IN SECONDS!

INSTANTLY BECOMING *GIANT-MAN,* THE DOUBLE-SIZED AVENGER HURLS HIMSELF FROM HIS WINDOW, SEIZING THE SPECIALLY-BUILT TENSION-RING WHICH HANGS OUTSIDE...

LUCKILY, THEY'RE ONLY A FEW BLOCKS FROM HERE...THIS IS THE QUICKEST WAY TO GET THERE!

IF HE'S HARMED A HAIR OF HER HEAD; HE'LL *PAY* FOR IT...NO MATTER *HOW* POWERFUL HE IS!

RELEASE HER, SPIDER-MAN! LET'S SEE HOW BRAVE YOU ARE AGAINST SOMEONE LIKE *ME!!*

GIANT-MAN!! I DON'T KNOW WHAT'S GOING ON HERE, BUT IF IT'S A *FIGHT* YOU WANT, YOU'VE COME TO THE RIGHT GUY!

MEANTIME, WATCHING THE ENTIRE SCENE THROUGH A CYBERNETICALLY-ACTIVATED VIEWER, WE FIND...

THE TWO OF THEM ARE SURE TO DESTROY EACH OTHER ...NEVER DREAMING THAT *I'M* THE REAL ENEMY!

6.

TRIUMPHANTLY, THE MAN CALLED *EGG-HEAD* ADDRESSES AN ASSORTMENT OF UNDERWORLD CHARACTERS WHOM HE HAS ASSEMBLED IN HIS HIDDEN LAB..

NOW FOR PHASE *TWO* OF MY PLAN! WHILE GIANT-MAN IS OCCUPIED WITH HIS WEB-SLINGING ENEMY, *WE* HAVE THINGS TO DO!

YOU'VE SURE GOT EVERY-THING FIGURED OUT TO A "T," BOSS!

NATURALLY! NOW I WANT YOU BOYS TO TAKE THE STATIONS I ASSIGNED YOU TO WHILE I CALL THE POLICE!! WE'RE GONNA PULL THE CRIME OF THE CENTURY... WITH GIANT-MAN'S HELP!!

EGGHEAD, YOU'RE A *GENIUS!*

HELLO, POLICE HEADQUARTERS! I'M A PUBLIC SPIRITED CITIZEN AND I WANT TO REPORT A DANGEROUS FIGHT! SPIDER-MAN AND GIANT-MAN ARE BATTLING IN THE STREET...

YOU'D BETTER SEND A *RIOT SQUAD* OVER BEFORE SOME INNOCENT BYSTAND-ERS GET HURT! IT'S *SHAMEFUL* THE WAY THOSE MASKED MENACES THINK THEY CAN DO WHAT THEY PLEASE IN OUR CITY!

MEANTIME...

BIG AS YOU *ARE*, GIANT-MAN, I'LL BOWL YOU OVER LIKE A TEN-PIN!

MISSED HIM! BUT HOW...??

HE'S *FAST!* BUT SO LONG AS I CAN KEEP CHANGING SIZE IN TIME, I'LL GET HIM, SOONER OR LATER!

HE'S ATTACKING AGAIN! NOW TO *ENLARGE* QUICKLY, AND *GRAB* HIM...!

UH-OH! THE *POLICE* ARE HERE!

SURROUND THEM, MEN! THEN CLOSE IN...ON THE DOUBLE!

POLICE

7

SPIDER-MAN IS TRICKY... HE'S FASTER THAN MY DOUBLE-SIZED DREAM-BOAT! BUT MAYBE THE *WASP* CAN SLOW HIM DOWN!

BULL'S EYE! GOOD OLD HANK! HIS "WASP'S STING" INVENTION REALLY *WORKS*!!

EASY, BOYS! NO SHOOTING UNLESS YOU HAVE TO!

DIDN'T EXPECT ME TO CATCH YOU BY GRABBING YOUR *WEB*, DID YOU?

CORRECTION, HIGH-POCKETS! YOU DIDN'T GRAB *ME*!... I'VE GOT *YOU*... TANGLED IN MY *WEB*!!

I WOULDN'T *BET* ON IT!!

HECK! HE FLEXED THOSE OVERSIZED MUSCLES OF HIS BEFORE MY WEBBING COULD *HARDEN* ENOUGH TO HOLD HIM!

CAPTAIN! KEEP YOUR MEN BACK! *I'LL* GET SPIDER-MAN FOR YOU! ...WITHOUT ANYONE GETTING HURT!

HE SWUNG BACK TO THE ROOF!

SURE, CAPTAIN... HOLD OFF YOUR MEN SO THEY CAN SIT BACK AND ENJOY THE SIGHT! THEY CAN WATCH ME WHITTLE GIANT-MAN DOWN TO MY SIZE!! I'LL TEACH THAT HUMAN STEPLADDER TO TANGLE WITH ME!

8.

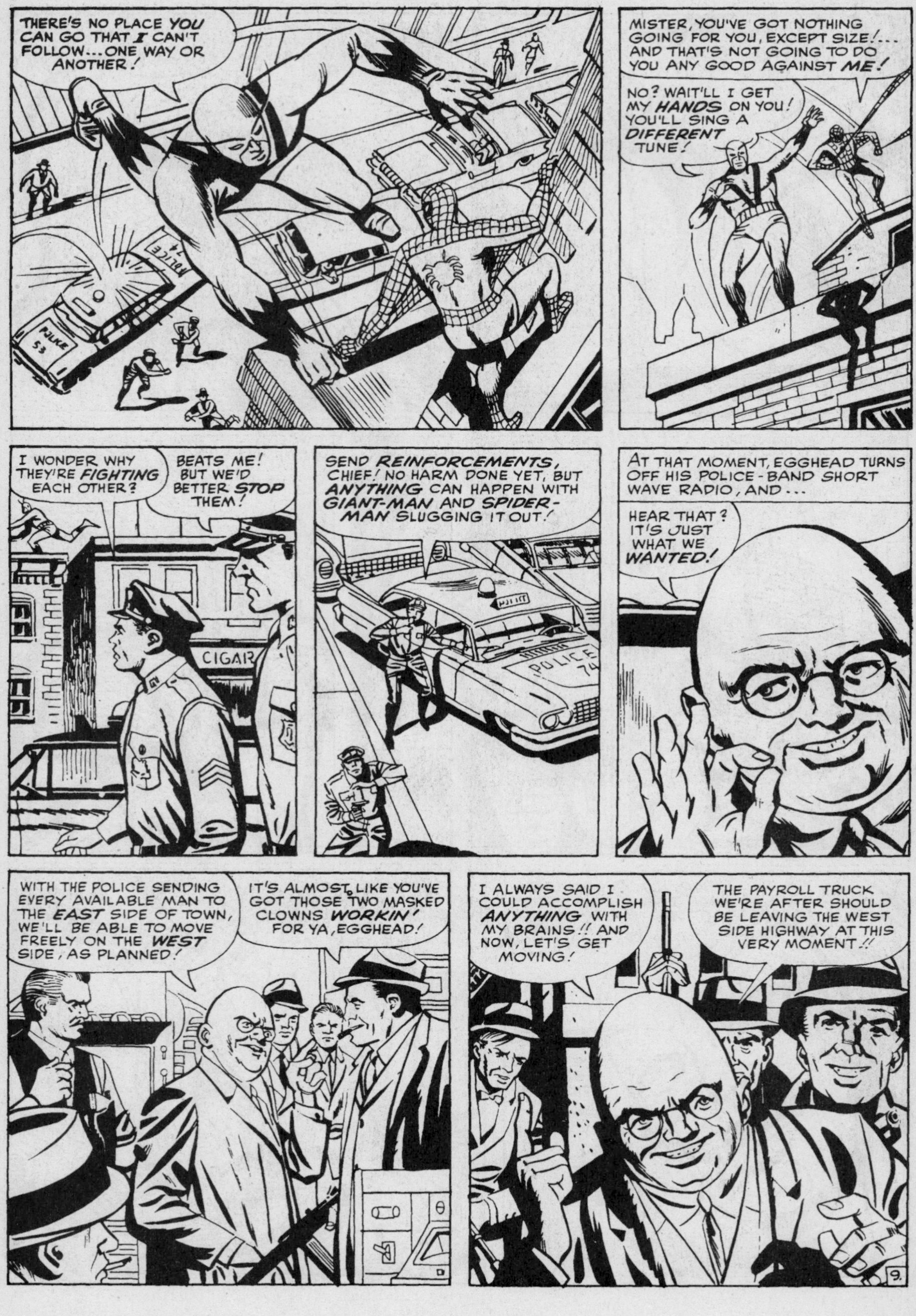
THERE'S NO PLACE YOU CAN GO THAT I CAN'T FOLLOW...ONE WAY OR ANOTHER!
POLICE 74
POLICE 53
MISTER, YOU'VE GOT NOTHING GOING FOR YOU, EXCEPT SIZE!...AND THAT'S NOT GOING TO DO YOU ANY GOOD AGAINST ME!
NO? WAIT'LL I GET MY HANDS ON YOU! YOU'LL SING A DIFFERENT TUNE!
I WONDER WHY THEY'RE FIGHTING EACH OTHER?
BEATS ME! BUT WE'D BETTER STOP THEM!
CIGAR
SEND REINFORCEMENTS, CHIEF! NO HARM DONE YET, BUT ANYTHING CAN HAPPEN WITH GIANT-MAN AND SPIDER-MAN SLUGGING IT OUT!
POLICE 74
AT THAT MOMENT, EGGHEAD TURNS OFF HIS POLICE-BAND SHORT WAVE RADIO, AND...
HEAR THAT? IT'S JUST WHAT WE WANTED!
WITH THE POLICE SENDING EVERY AVAILABLE MAN TO THE EAST SIDE OF TOWN, WE'LL BE ABLE TO MOVE FREELY ON THE WEST SIDE, AS PLANNED!
IT'S ALMOST LIKE YOU'VE GOT THOSE TWO MASKED CLOWNS WORKIN' FOR YA, EGGHEAD!
I ALWAYS SAID I COULD ACCOMPLISH ANYTHING WITH MY BRAINS!! AND NOW, LET'S GET MOVING!
THE PAYROLL TRUCK WE'RE AFTER SHOULD BE LEAVING THE WEST SIDE HIGHWAY AT THIS VERY MOMENT!!
9.

TAKE YOUR POSITIONS IN THE TRUCK WE HIRED FOR JUST THIS PURPOSE! COME ON... MOVE.!!

WITH A GENIUS LIKE EGGHEAD LEADING US, THIS'LL BE THE ROBBERY OF THE CENTURY!

SAY, BOSS... THE FURTHER WEST WE GO, THE EMPTIER THE STREETS BECOME!

NATURALLY! IT'S THE WAY I PLANNED IT! EVERYONE HAS RUSHED TO THE EAST SIDE TO WITNESS THE SPECTACLE OF TWO SUPER-HEROES FIGHTING IN PUBLIC!

CAREFUL, NOW! WE'RE COMING TO OUR DESTINATION! KEEP YOUR EYES OPEN! YOU ALL KNOW THE PENALTY FOR A SINGLE SLIP-UP!!

LOOK! THERE'S THE ARMORED PAYROLL TRUCK NOW... RIGHT ON SCHEDULE!

FINE! FOLLOW PLAN "A" EXACTLY AS I OUTLINED IT!

WAIT TILL THEY REACH THE NEXT CORNER! IT'S WHERE THE POLICE HAVE SET UP A BLOCKADE TO KEEP THE CROWDS FROM GETTING TOO CLOSE TO GIANT-MAN'S BATTLE!

THIS IS THE SPOT! PULL ALONGSIDE THE PAYROLL TRUCK! NOSE HER TO THE CURB! THAT'S IT! NOW JAM ON YOUR BRAKES!

HEY!! WHAT'S GOIN' ON?!

10.

SAY, JOE... LOOK! OVER THERE!

EGGHEAD! THE COPS *SEE* US!!

I *EXPECTED* THAT! JUST KEEP HAULING THE CAR INTO OUR TRUCK WITH YOUR HYDRAULIC GRAPPLING HOOK!

WE'RE BEING PULLED INTO THAT BIG TRAILER VAN!

THEY'RE GETTING *AWAY!* WE CAN'T FOLLOW BY CAR BECAUSE OF THE TRAFFIC JAM!

THEY MUST HAVE *PLANNED* IT THIS WAY! I WONDER IF *GIANT-MAN* AND *SPIDER-MAN* WERE A *PART* OF THE PLAN??!

QUICK! RADIO HEADQUARTERS! WE'VE GOT TO SET UP ROADBLOCKS!

MEANWHILE, HIGH ABOVE THE CITY, WE FIND...

I *TOLD* YOU YOU CAN'T ESCAPE FROM ME!!

ESCAPE?? YOU'VE GOT IT *BACKWARDS*, BIG MAN! I'M JUST GETTIN' YOU INTO POSITION FOR MY KNOCKOUT PUNCH!!

I NEVER REALIZED HANK *CARED* SO MUCH FOR ME! HE'S NEVER BEEN SO FIGHTING MAD BEFORE!

OKAY, GIANT-MAN! HERE'S WHERE YOU LEARN WHAT HAPPENS TO ANYONE WHO TACKLES ME WITHOUT ANY REASON!!

WHO ARE YOU *KIDDING??* WE *KNOW* YOU WERE ABOUT TO ATTACK *US!!*

HOLD IT! WHAT IF YOU ARE *BOTH* WRONG??

11.

AT THAT CRITICAL MOMENT, AN ALERT ANT SENSES THE PRESENCE OF THE ONE WHO SENT THE ORIGINAL MESSAGE A SHORT TIME BEFORE!

WE *MADE* IT, EGGHEAD!

SHUT UP AND KEEP DRIVING!

INSTANTLY, ANOTHER MESSAGE IS TRANSMITTED TO THE LEADER OF THE ANT WORLD, UNSUSPECTED BY EGGHEAD OR HIS MEN...

INTO THE HIDEOUT... *QUICK!* NOBODY WILL EVER FIND US HERE!

BUT EGGHEAD HAS NOT COUNTED ON ONE THING...

SPIDER-MAN... *WAIT!* MY ANTS ARE CONTACTING ME! LOOKS LIKE WE WERE *BOTH* DECEIVED!

WHAT *IS* IT, BLUE EYES??

I'VE GOT TO TAKE A *SHRINKING CAPSULE!* NO TIME TO EXPLAIN ... JUST FOLLOW ME!

IF THIS IS A *TRICK* OF YOURS, IT WON'T *WORK!!*

IT'S NO TRICK, FELLA! YOU'RE WELCOME TO FOLLOW, IF YOU CAN! BUT YOU'LL BE FOLLOWING *ANT-MAN* THIS TIME!

HERE COMES ONE OF MY FLYING ANTS, IN ANSWER TO MY CYBERNETIC SUMMONS!!

WELL, WELL! YOU'RE A REGULAR BAG OF TRICKS!! BUT WHERE *YOU GO, I* GO, BUSTER... NO MATTER *WHAT* SIZE YOU ARE!!

BE MY *GUEST!* I'M HEADING FOR THE DOCKS!

I MAY NOT HAVE A FLYING ANT TO RIDE, BUT MY LI'L OL' *WEB* WILL GET ME THERE EVEN FASTER!

12.

AND, LITTLE DREAMING THAT HE'S "ON-TARGET" FOR TWO OF THE WORLD'S GREATEST SUPER-HEROES, EGGHEAD CONTINUES WITH HIS MASTER PLAN...

KEEP THE GUARDS LOCKED INSIDE THEIR TRUCK AND START UNLOADING THE LOOT!

SO INTENT ARE THEY ON WHAT THEY'RE DOING, THAT EGGHEAD'S MEN FAIL TO NOTICE TWO SILENT STRANDS OF WEBBING SLOWLY DESCENDING...

SOMETHING YANKED THE STRONGBOX RIGHT OUT OF OUR HANDS.!!

THE JOINT MUST BE HAUNTED!

IT'S SPIDER-MAN! GET HIM, YOU FOOLS! WE'VE COME TOO FAR TO BE STOPPED NOW.!!

YOU BOYS MUST HAVE READ ENOUGH STORIES AND SEEN ENOUGH MOVIES TO KNOW THAT CRIME DOESN'T PAY.!!

LUCKY MY SPIDER-SENSE GUIDED ME RIGHT TO THE SPOT WHERE THIS STOLEN STRONG-BOX WAS TAKEN!

UH-OH! EVEN SPIDER-MAN CAN'T LAUGH OFF STEEL BULLETS.!!

COME DOWN FROM THERE... OR ELSE.!!

OR ELSE YOU BOYS WILL FEEL THE WASP'S STING.! IS THAT WHAT YOU MEAN??

HMM...I GUESS IT IS.!!

YEOW!

13.

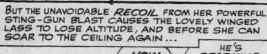

BUT THE UNAVOIDABLE *RECOIL* FROM HER POWERFUL STING-GUN BLAST CAUSES THE LOVELY WINGED LASS TO LOSE ALTITUDE, AND BEFORE SHE CAN SOAR TO THE CEILING AGAIN...

NOW I'VE GOT YOU!!

HE'S *REACHING* FOR ME! MY ONLY CHANCE ...GLIDE TO THE FLOOR!

THERE SHE IS...UNDER YOUR FOOT!! DON'T LET HER GET AWAY!!

I'VE ONLY GOT TWO MORE CHARGES LEFT IN MY STINGER! HAVE TO MAKE THEM BOTH COUNT!

WHERE'S YOUR *MANNERS,* BIG BOY? IT ISN'T *POLITE* TO STEP ON A LADY!!

BOY! THEY PLAY *ROUGH* IN THIS LEAGUE!!

LET *ME* HAVE 'ER, EGGHEAD!

YOU FRESH THING!! WE HAVEN'T EVEN BEEN FORMALLY *INTRODUCED!*

UH-OH! THAT WAS MY *LAST* STING CHARGE! NOW, I'M A MIGHTY WORRIED LITTLE WASP!

GIANT-MAN! WHEREVER YOU ARE, DON'T BE BASHFUL... *SHOW* YOURSELF!!

14.

THEN, IN THE TIME IT TAKES TO SWALLOW ONE ENLARGING CAPSULE...

GIANT-MAN!! HOW'D YOU GET HERE??

IT WASN'T EASY, EGGHEAD! I RAN OUT OF SUBWAY TOKENS AND HAD TO WAIT HOURS FOR A TAXI!

LOOK AT THE SIZE OF 'IM! HE CAN AFFORD TO MAKE WITH THE WISE-CRACKS!!

LOOK OUT WITH THAT PEA SHOOTER, EGGHEAD! YOU MIGHT HIT US!

CAN'T HOLD 'IM! HE'S SWINGIN' US AROUND LIKE YO-YO'S!

YOU AND YOUR CRUMMY PLANS! SO THEY'D FINISH EACH OTHER OFF WHILE WE ROBBED THE ARMORED TRUCK, EH??

SO THAT'S THE EXPLANATION!

MY PLAN STILL HASN'T FAILED! FIRST I'LL FINISH OFF GIANT-MAN, AND THEN WE'LL SEARCH FOR SPIDER-MAN!

YOU WON'T HAVE TO SEARCH VERY FAR, CURLY!

FIRST OF ALL, GIVE ME THAT TOY BEFORE YOU HURT YOUR TUBBY LITTLE SELF!

HE'S HERE! GET HIM!

SORRY, EGGHEAD! YOUR PISTOL-PACKIN' PUNKS ARE BUSY AT THE MOMENT!

WE'VE WON! IT'S OVER! BUT, WHY DO I STILL FEEL SO HOSTILE TOWARDS SPIDER-MAN?? I GUESS IT'S BECAUSE WASPS AND SPIDERS ARE SUCH NATURAL ENEMIES!

15.

WE HAD NO REASON TO FIGHT! EGGHEAD TRIED TO TRICK US! BUT KEEP THE WASP AWAY FROM ME... SHE MAKES ME SEE RED!

HONEY, YOU HEARD THE MAN! HE CAN'T HELP IT... IT'S HIS NATURAL SPIDER INSTINCT!

L-LOOK, GIANT-MAN! THERE'S NO NEED FOR US TO BE ENEMIES! THERE'S ENOUGH STOLEN LOOT HERE FOR ALL OF US TO DIVIDE!

FOR SHAME, EGGHEAD! YOU KNOW THAT MONEY IS THE ROOT OF ALL EVIL!

WELL, HOW ABOUT YOU, SPIDER-MAN? IF YOU BEAT GIANT-MAN FOR ME, I'LL...

FORGET IT! WHY DON'T YOU ASK ME TO DO SOMETHING EASY?? LIKE BRING YOU FORT KNOX!!

OKAY, BOYS! THE PARTY'S OVER! THE POLICE SHOULD BE OUTSIDE BY NOW, SO START WALKING!

WITH PLEASURE! ANYTHING'S BETTER THAN FIGHTIN' YOU, AND THAT WEB-SPINNER, AND THAT NUTTY FLYIN' FEMALE!

DID YOU HEAR WHAT HE CALLED ME? DON'T JUST STAND THERE... DO SOMETHING!

I AM! I'M MAKING MYSELF NORMAL-SIZE!

WELL, I GUESS YOU DON'T NEED ME HERE ANYMORE!

I'VE GOT NEWS FOR YOU, SON! WE NEVER DID!

I WASN'T TALKING TO YOU, LADY! I WOULDN'T WASTE MY BREATH!

OH, GO ON BACK TO YOUR SLIMY OL' SPIDERS... AND GOOD RIDDANCE!!

I'LL TAKE SPIDERS OVER THOSE USELESS FLYING WASPS ANY DAY!

THANK GOODNESS HE'S GONE! OH!! OF ALL THE NASTY, HATEFUL, UNPLEASANT PEOPLE I'VE EVER MET...!!

HE'S A HANDY LAD TO HAVE AROUND IN A PINCH, HONEY! IT'S UNFORTUNATE THAT SPIDERS AND WASPS ARE NATURAL ENEMIES!

AND SO WE LEAVE OUR TWO PARTNERS-IN-PERIL WATCHING THE DEPARTURE OF THE AMAZING SPIDER-MAN... LITTLE DREAMING THAT FATE HAS A STILL STRANGER ADVENTURE IN STORE FOR THEM... AND FOR YOU... NEXT ISSUE!! SEE YOU THEN...!

THE END

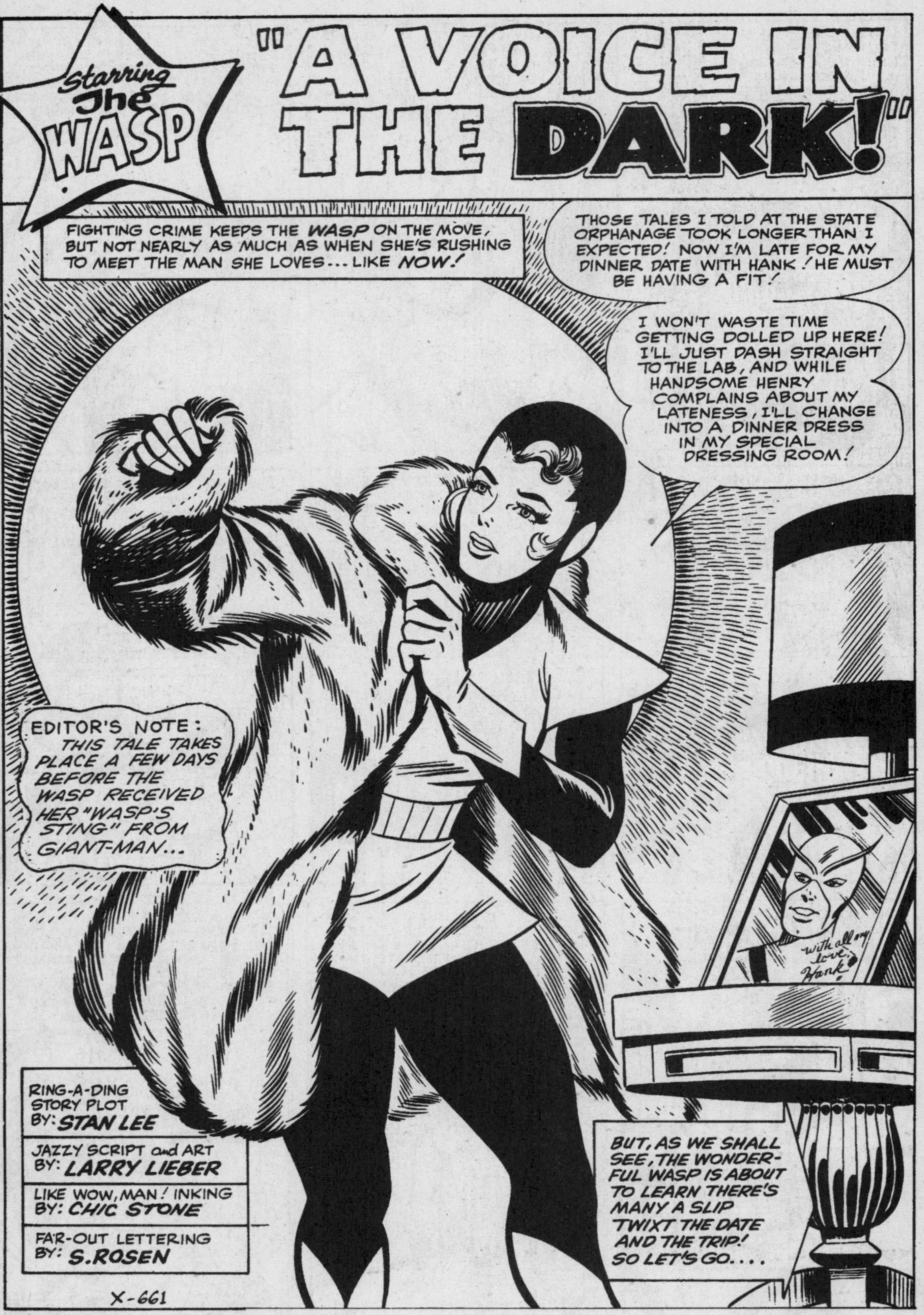
Starring The WASP
"A VOICE IN THE DARK!"
FIGHTING CRIME KEEPS THE WASP ON THE MOVE, BUT NOT NEARLY AS MUCH AS WHEN SHE'S RUSHING TO MEET THE MAN SHE LOVES... LIKE NOW!
THOSE TALES I TOLD AT THE STATE ORPHANAGE TOOK LONGER THAN I EXPECTED! NOW I'M LATE FOR MY DINNER DATE WITH HANK! HE MUST BE HAVING A FIT!
I WON'T WASTE TIME GETTING DOLLED UP HERE! I'LL JUST DASH STRAIGHT TO THE LAB, AND WHILE HANDSOME HENRY COMPLAINS ABOUT MY LATENESS, I'LL CHANGE INTO A DINNER DRESS IN MY SPECIAL DRESSING ROOM!
EDITOR'S NOTE: THIS TALE TAKES PLACE A FEW DAYS BEFORE THE WASP RECEIVED HER "WASP'S STING" FROM GIANT-MAN...
With all my love, Hank
RING-A-DING STORY PLOT BY: STAN LEE
JAZZY SCRIPT and ART BY: LARRY LIEBER
LIKE WOW, MAN! INKING BY: CHIC STONE
FAR-OUT LETTERING BY: S. ROSEN
BUT, AS WE SHALL SEE, THE WONDERFUL WASP IS ABOUT TO LEARN THERE'S MANY A SLIP TWIXT THE DATE AND THE TRIP! SO LET'S GO....
X-661

I DON'T NEED THIS COAT AND HAT TO KEEP ME WARM! MY INSULATED COSTUME TAKES CARE OF THAT! BUT THESE CLOTHES WILL KEEP ME FROM BEING RECOGNIZED AND SLOWED DOWN BY AUTOGRAPH HOUNDS!

IMAGINE ANY GAL CELEBRITY DELIBERATELY TRYING TO AVOID HER ADORING PUBLIC! BOY, THE SACRIFICES I MAKE FOR HANK PYM!

BUT OUR FUN-LOVING HEROINE'S EYE SUDDENLY CATCHES AN UNUSUAL SIGHT...

THAT MAN OPENING THE MANHOLE! STRANGE!! HE'S NOT DRESSED LIKE A CITY WORKER! I WONDER WHAT HE'S UP TO?

HE'S CLIMBING DOWN THE MANHOLE! OF COURSE, HE COULD BE SOME KIND OF NUT WHO FIGURES TRAVELING UNDERGROUND IS A WAY TO BEAT THE HEAVY CROSSTOWN TRAFFIC!

OH, WELL, HE DIDN'T BREAK ANY LAW! IF HE WANTS TO MAKE LIKE A MOLE, THAT'S HIS BUSINESS, NOT MINE!

BUT, WHEN THE WASP TURNS THE CORNER, SHE DISCOVERS SOMETHING THAT IS HER BUSINESS!

THE DOOR OF THIS JEWELRY STORE HAS BEEN FORCED OPEN ... AND THE BURGLAR ALARM WIRES ARE CUT!

NOW IT ALL FITS TOGETHER! THAT JOKER WHO CLIMBED DOWN THE MANHOLE WAS CARRYING A VALISE! I'LL BET IT CONTAINED STOLEN JEWELRY!

2.

I'M **ALREADY** LATE FOR MY DATE WITH HANK, AND IF I KNOW HIM, HE'S PROBABLY WAITING FOR ME, ABOUT AS CALM AS A RAGING TIGER!! BUT THERE'S NO TIME TO CALL THE POLICE, AND IF **I** DON'T CAPTURE THAT THIEF MYSELF, HE'LL ESCAPE!

I'LL JUST LEAVE THIS CUMBERSOME COAT AND HAT IN HERE TILL THE JOB IS DONE!

PRETTY SNEAKY OF THAT CROOK TO TRY A GETAWAY, THROUGH THE CITY'S VAST NETWORK OF UNDERGROUND TUNNELS!

BUT HE DIDN'T RECKON WITH THE **WASP**... DAUNTLESS, BEAUTIFUL, AND...OH, BUT WHY GO ON??

⸺OOOF!!⸺ THIS HUNK OF IRON IS MUCH TOO HEAVY! NO MERE FEMALE COULD LIFT IT UNLESS SHE WERE A FEMALE **HULK**!

FORTUNATELY, THERE'S **ANOTHER** WAY FOR THIS DELICATE DOLL TO GET UNDERGROUND!

I SIMPLY TAKE ONE OF HAPPY HANK'S REDUCING PILLS! AND I DO MEAN **REDUCING**!!

THERE! I'VE EVEN SPROUTED MY "TINKER BELL" WINGS! WHAT MORE DOES ANY GAL NEED FOR SUBTERRANEAN FUN AND GAMES?

3.

WHEW! THE AIR SURE IS STUFFY IN THIS OLD TUNNEL! BUT, WITH LUCK I WON'T BE DOWN HERE FOR LONG!

AH, THERE'S MY BOY...THINKING HE'S IN THE CLEAR, NO DOUBT! WELL, HIS BUBBLE IS ABOUT TO BURST!!

FIRST, I'LL SEPARATE BRIGHT-EYES FROM HIS ILL-GOTTEN GAINS!

HMM...THIS PIN SHOULD PROVE A MOST EFFECTIVE WEAPON!

IT MAY BE TOO DARK IN THE TUNNEL FOR HIM TO SEE THE WASP, BUT HE'S SURE GOING TO FEEL HER STING!

BUT, TO OUR TINY HEROINE'S SURPRISE ...

I MISSED HIS HAND! IT MUST BE BECAUSE OF THE DENSE CHOKING AIR IN THE TUNNEL! IT'S THROWN MY SENSE OF BALANCE OFF!

SNAP!

ODD...THE STIFLING SUB-TERRANEAN AIR DOESN'T SEEM TO BOTHER HIM, BUT IT'S AFFECTING ME WORSE BY THE MINUTE! I'M GETTING SO DIZZY...

I CAN'T REMEMBER WHICH TUNNEL IT WAS! THIS ONE...OR THAT ??

I'VE GOT TO WORK FAST AND CAPTURE HIM BEFORE I PASS OUT!

I'VE AN IDEA! I'LL UNTIE HIS SHOELACES AND FASHION THEM INTO A BOOBY TRAP!

4.

THERE! I'VE UNLACED BOTH OF THEM! NOW I'LL JUST KNOT THEM TOGETHER, AND WHEN MR. JEWEL THIEF STARTS WALKING AGAIN, HE'LL FALL SMACK ON HIS KISSER! AFTER THAT, HE'LL BE EASY TO HANDLE!

BUT, BEFORE THE WASP CAN ATTACH THE LACES, THE TOWERING FUGITIVE STEPS FORWARD, CATCHING THE INSECT-SIZED GIRL OFF BALANCE!

OH!

NOTHING HURT EXCEPT MY PRIDE! WELL, I'M *STILL* NOT GIVING UP! BUT I'D BETTER ACT QUICKLY BEFORE I SUCCUMB TO THIS DENSE AIR! EVEN *NOW* I FEEL LIKE I'M CHOKING!

WAIT! HE'S WALKING THROUGH THAT *DOOR!*

HE CLOSED THE DOOR BEHIND HIM ... BUT THAT CAN'T KEEP A *WASP-SIZED* SWEETIE OUT!

I'LL STASH THE JEWELS HERE TILL THE HEAT IS OFF! NO ONE WILL EVER THINK OF LOOKING FOR THEM IN AN ABANDONED SUBWAY CONTROL ROOM!

THE ROBBERY WENT OFF REAL SMOOTH AND I'M IN THE CLEAR NOW! IN A FEW WEEKS I'LL RETURN FOR MY LOOT AND LIVE ON EASY STREET FOR YEARS TO COME!

HE'S LEAVING! IF I CAN REACH THE DOOR *FIRST*, I'LL CAPTURE HIM! BUT I DON'T KNOW IF I CAN *MAKE* IT! THE AIR IS SO THICK! I'M GETTING DIZZIER AND WEAKER ALL THE TIME! BUT I MUST TRY! I *MUST!*

AH! I BEAT HIM TO THE DOOR! NOW, ALL I HAVE TO DO IS LOCK HIM IN FROM THE OUTSIDE AND BRING THE POLICE!

BUT I'M FIGHTING AGAINST TIME! I'M GROWING FAINT! IF I DON'T GET OUT OF THIS TUNNEL SOON, I'LL PASS OUT!

5.

OH, *NO!* THE STIFLING AIR...THE LACK OF OXYGEN...HAS MADE ME TOO WEAK TO EVEN LOCK THE DOOR! I'M STRAINING AS HARD AS POSSIBLE, BUT I *CAN'T TURN THE KEY!*

HE..HE'S LEAVING THE ROOM! I TRIED TO CAPTURE HIM, AND I *FAILED!* BUT, WAIT...I'VE *ANOTHER* IDEA! THERE'S STILL A CHANCE!

I'LL ROLL A SMALL SCRAP OF PAPER INTO A *MEGAPHONE* TO AMPLIFY MY VOICE...TO MAKE IT LOUD ENOUGH FOR HIM TO HEAR!

AND THEN, UTILIZING ALL HER RAPIDLY WANING STRENGTH THE COURAGEOUS GAL CRIMEFIGHTER TRIES A DESPERATE DECEPTION!

DON'T MOVE, CHUM! THIS IS SUE STORM, *THE INVISIBLE GIRL*, SPEAKING...TELLING YOU TO GIVE YOURSELF UP!

HUH?!

I..I DON'T *SEE* ANYONE! BUT THAT FEMALE VOICE...IT *CAN'T* JUST BE COMING OUT OF EMPTY AIR! IT *MUST* BELONG TO THE INVISIBLE GIRL! THERE'S NO OTHER EXPLANATION!

RIGHT! I'VE BEEN FOLLOWING YOU EVER SINCE I SAW YOU BREAK INTO THE JEWELRY SHOP! I'VE CALLED THE *OTHER* MEMBERS OF THE *FANTASTIC FOUR!* THEY'RE ON THEIR WAY HERE *NOW* TO CAPTURE YOU!

6.

Panel 1: THE FANTASTIC FOUR! *THE THING* COULD PULVERIZE ME! AND I SURE WOULDN'T STAND A BETTER CHANCE AGAINST *THE TORCH* OR *MR. FANTASTIC!* I'M NOT GONNA TANGLE WITH *THEM!* ANYTHING'S BETTER THAN *THAT!*

Panel 2: AND SO... I COMMITTED A ROBBERY TONIGHT! HERE'S THE LOOT! *BOOK ME!* LOCK ME UP! JUST DON'T LET ANY COSTUMED DO-GOODERS WITH SUPER-POWERS GET THEIR *HANDS* ON ME!

≡ WHEW!≡ MY LITTLE TRICK WORKED! THAT WRAPS IT UP! NOW TO BUZZ OFF FOR MY DATE WITH HANK!

5th AVE.

Panel 3: FINALLY... WELL, IF IT ISN'T OL' LIGHTNING HERSELF! WHAT HAPPENED? WHY SO LATE? DO YOU REALIZE HOW *LONG* YOU'VE KEPT ME WAITING?!!

SORRY, HANDSOME! IT COULDN'T BE HELPED! I PASSED A JEWELRY STORE THAT WAS ROBBED AND I CHASED THE THIEF THROUGH AN UNDERGROUND TUNNEL TILL I FINALLY CAUGHT HIM!

Panel 4: IT WON'T WORK, JAN! I *HEARD* ABOUT THAT CAPTURE OVER THE RADIO AND IT WAS THE *INVISIBLE GIRL* WHO PULLED IT OFF!

NO! IT *WASN'T* HER! IT WAS ME, *PRETENDING* TO BE THE INVISIBLE GIRL!

AWW, WHAT'S THE DIFF?!! ARE YOU READY FOR DINNER? I'M *STARVING!*

Panel 5: DINNER? WHAT DO YOU MEAN? *WE* DIDN'T HAVE A DATE FOR THIS EVENING?!!

WHY, HENRY PYM! *OF COURSE* WE HAD A DATE!

UH-UH! IT WASN'T *ME* YOU HAD A DATE WITH! IT WAS REALLY *MR. FANTASTIC,* PRETENDING TO BE ME!

Panel 6: MAYBE *NEXT* TIME SHE'LL THINK TWICE BEFORE SHE HANDS ME A PHONY EXCUSE LIKE *THAT!!*

I ALWAYS *KNEW* THERE'D BE DAYS LIKE THIS! I WONDER WHERE A GAL CAN SELL A SECOND-HAND WASP COSTUME REAL CHEAP?!

7.

The END.

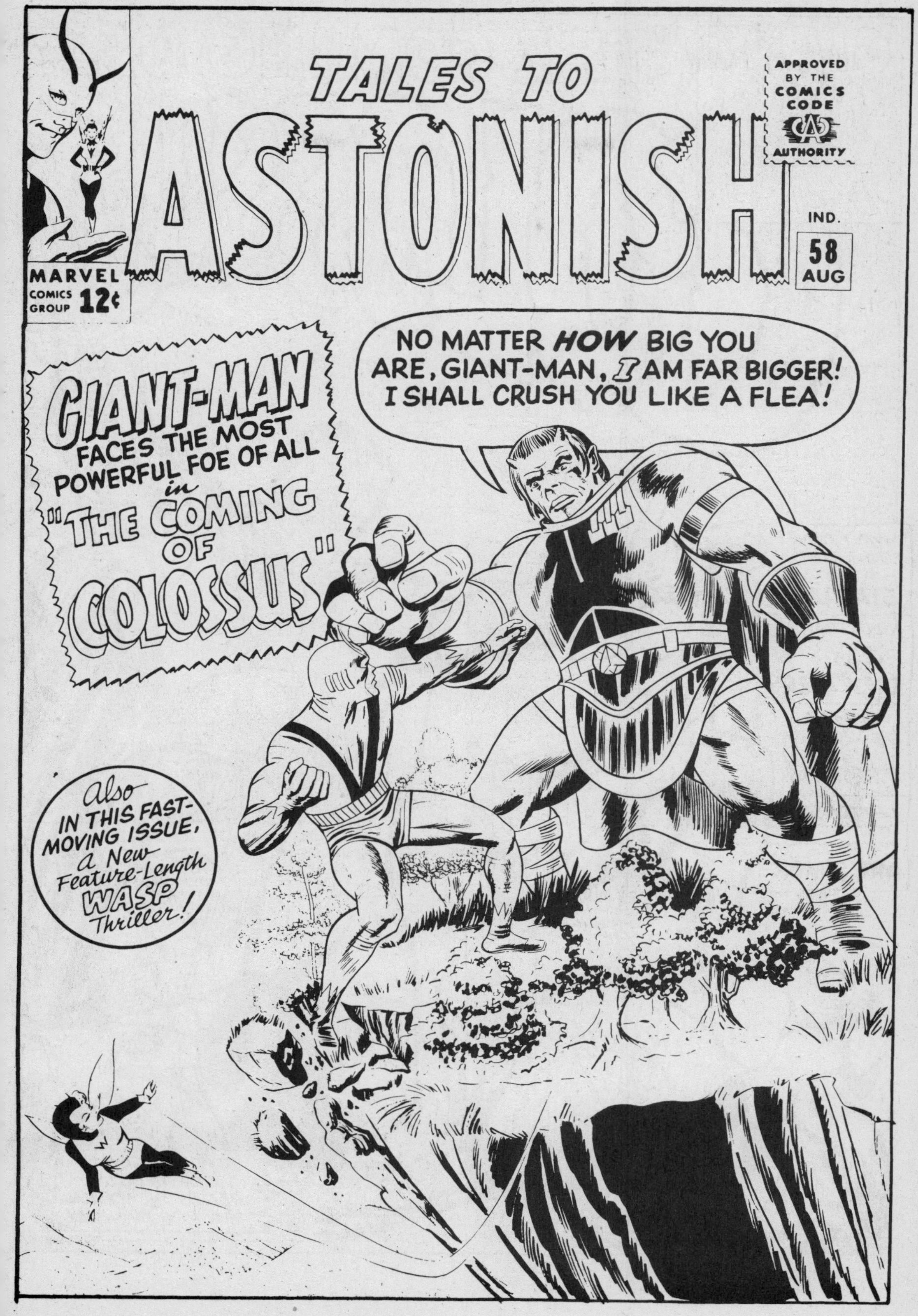
TALES TO ASTONISH
APPROVED BY THE COMICS CODE AUTHORITY
IND.
58
AUG
MARVEL COMICS GROUP 12¢
GIANT-MAN FACES THE MOST POWERFUL FOE OF ALL in "THE COMING OF COLOSSUS"
NO MATTER HOW BIG YOU ARE, GIANT-MAN, I AM FAR BIGGER! I SHALL CRUSH YOU LIKE A FLEA!
Also IN THIS FAST-MOVING ISSUE, a New Feature-Length WASP Thriller!

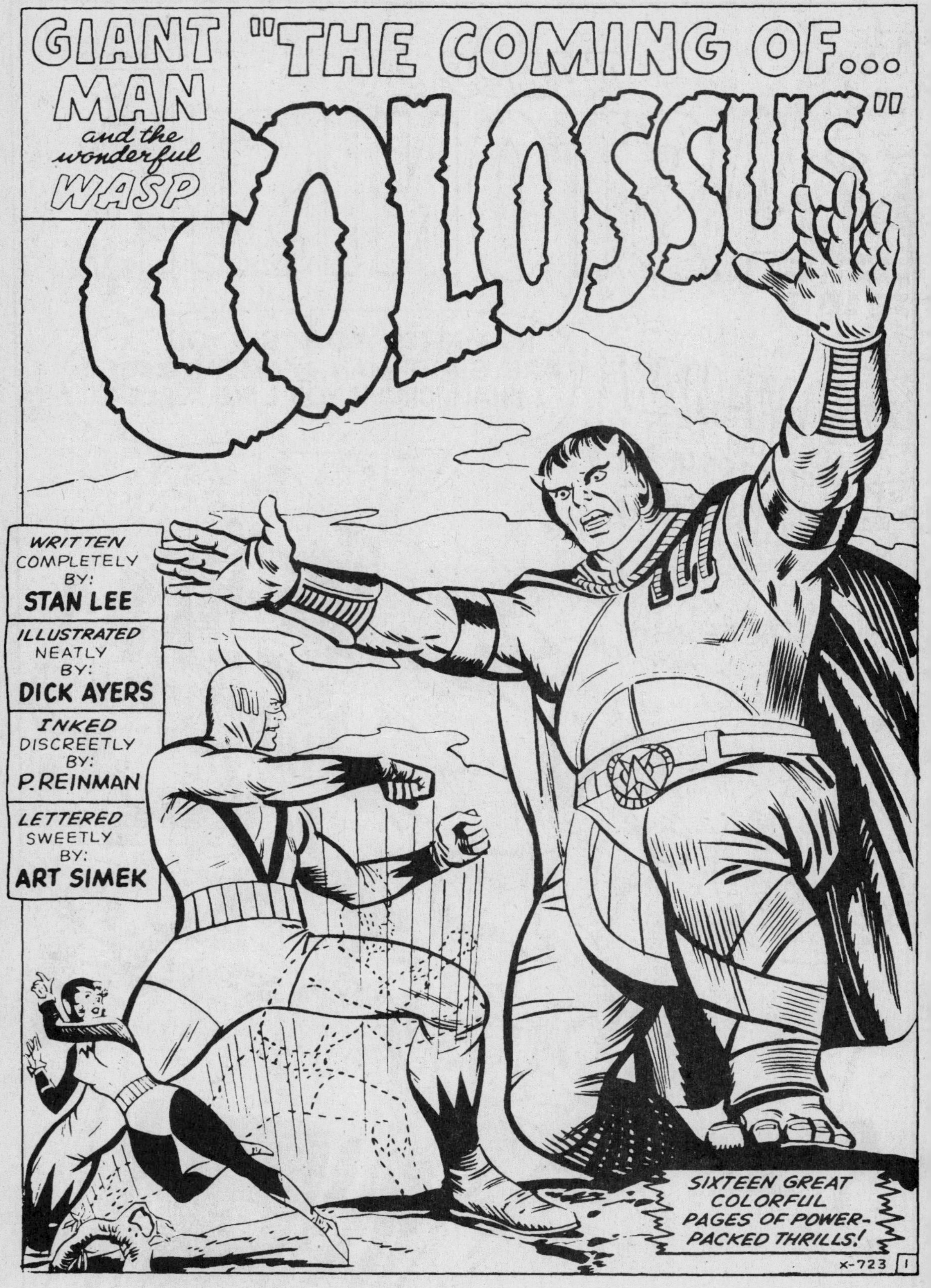
GIANT MAN
and the wonderful
WASP
"THE COMING OF... COLOSSUS"
WRITTEN COMPLETELY BY: STAN LEE
ILLUSTRATED NEATLY BY: DICK AYERS
INKED DISCREETLY BY: P. REINMAN
LETTERED SWEETLY BY: ART SIMEK
SIXTEEN GREAT COLORFUL PAGES OF POWER-PACKED THRILLS!
X-723
1

SOMEWHERE IN THE CANYONS OF NEW YORK IS THE HIGH-CEILINGED PENTHOUSE LAB OF HENRY PYM, BETTER KNOWN TO THE WORLD OUTSIDE AS -- *GIANT-MAN!*

BOSS-MAN, I'VE GOT SOMETHING TO *SHOW* YOU!

NOT NOW, JAN! I'M WORKING ON A NEW PROJECT! TRY ME LATER ON!

BUT THIS WON'T *WAIT*, HANK! THE SKIING SEASON WON'T LAST MUCH LONGER!

THERE'LL BE *OTHER* SEASONS, GAL! BUT I THINK I'VE FOUND A WAY TO CHANGE SIZE WITHOUT HAVING TO SWALLOW ANY MORE GROWTH CAPSULES!

WHAT'S THE *USE*?? MY EVER-LOVIN' BLUE-EYED DREAMBOAT HAS A *TEST TUBE* INSTEAD OF A HEART!

WHILE I'M WEARING MY CYBERNETIC HELMET, WHY SHOULDN'T I BE ABLE TO ALTER MY SIZE MERELY BY USING *MENTAL ENERGY*??

IT WOULD MEAN I'D NO LONGER HAVE TO DEPEND ON BEING ABLE TO REACH MY CAPSULES! I'VE GOT TO *TRY* IT!

WHILE *YOU'RE* MAKING LIKE A MAD SCIENTIST, *I'M* GOING TO REDESIGN MY COSTUME! AFTER ALL, EVEN A *WASP* LIKES TO WEAR SOMETHING *NEW* NOW AND THEN!

HMMM? OH, SURE-- OF COURSE --GOOD IDEA, JAN...

THE BIG GOOP! HE'S NOT EVEN *LISTENING* TO A WORD I SAY!

MINUTES LATER...

THERE! I'VE MADE ALL THE NECESSARY MODIFICATIONS! NOW TO MENTALLY ACTIVATE THE CYBERNETIC IMPULSES--

LET ME GROW LARGER-- *LARGER*--

WOW!!

WHOOM

IT WORKS EVEN BETTER THAN I *EXPECTED*!

OHH, MY ACHIN' BACK!

2

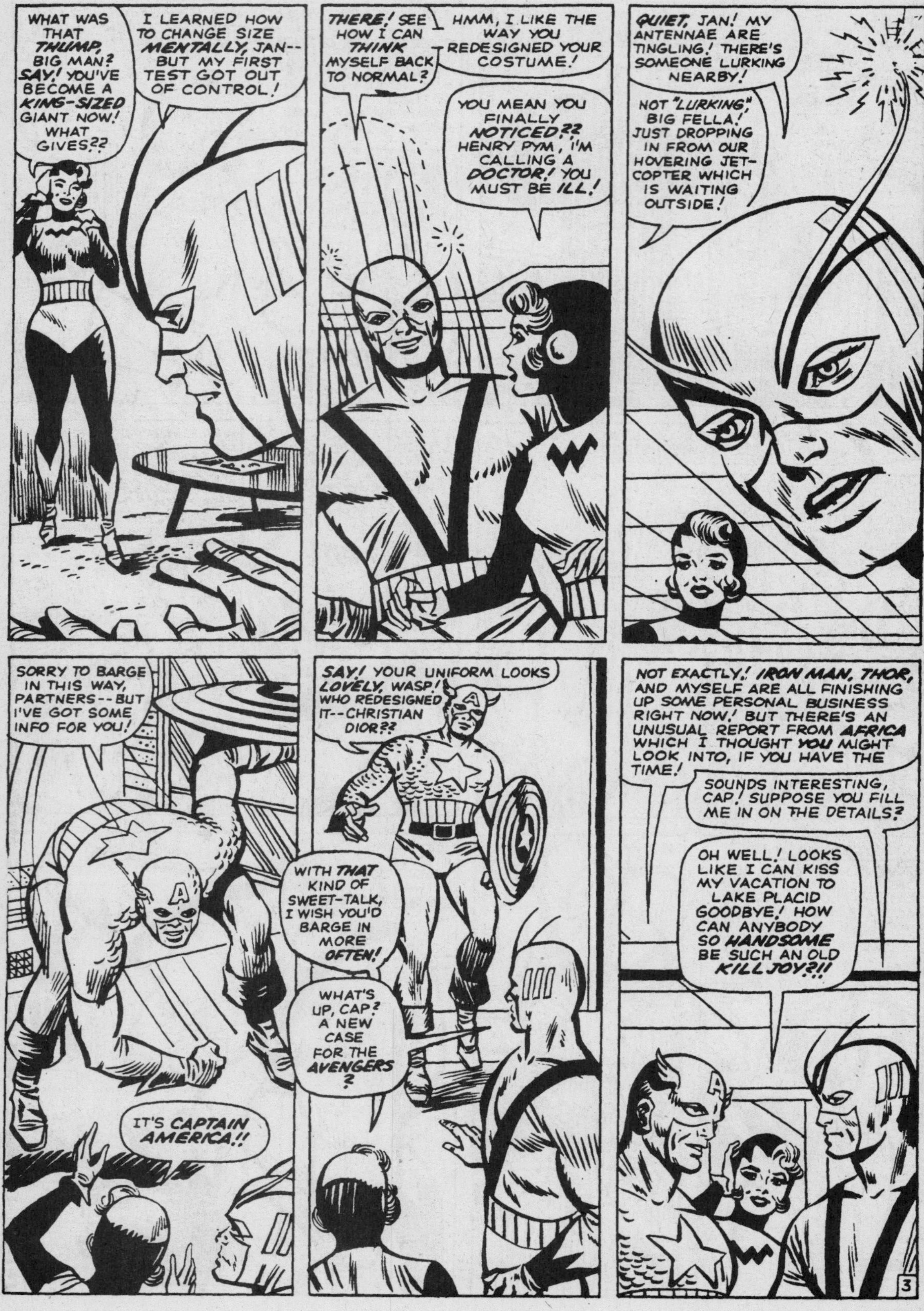

WHAT WAS THAT THUMP, BIG MAN? SAY! YOU'VE BECOME A KING-SIZED GIANT NOW! WHAT GIVES??
I LEARNED HOW TO CHANGE SIZE MENTALLY, JAN-- BUT MY FIRST TEST GOT OUT OF CONTROL!
THERE! SEE HOW I CAN THINK MYSELF BACK TO NORMAL?
HMM, I LIKE THE WAY YOU REDESIGNED YOUR COSTUME!
YOU MEAN YOU FINALLY NOTICED?? HENRY PYM, I'M CALLING A DOCTOR! YOU MUST BE ILL!
QUIET, JAN! MY ANTENNAE ARE TINGLING! THERE'S SOMEONE LURKING NEARBY!
NOT "LURKING", BIG FELLA! JUST DROPPING IN FROM OUR HOVERING JET-COPTER WHICH IS WAITING OUTSIDE!
SORRY TO BARGE IN THIS WAY, PARTNERS-- BUT I'VE GOT SOME INFO FOR YOU!
IT'S CAPTAIN AMERICA!!
SAY! YOUR UNIFORM LOOKS LOVELY, WASP! WHO REDESIGNED IT--CHRISTIAN DIOR??
WITH THAT KIND OF SWEET-TALK, I WISH YOU'D BARGE IN MORE OFTEN!
WHAT'S UP, CAP? A NEW CASE FOR THE AVENGERS?
NOT EXACTLY! IRON MAN, THOR, AND MYSELF ARE ALL FINISHING UP SOME PERSONAL BUSINESS RIGHT NOW! BUT THERE'S AN UNUSUAL REPORT FROM AFRICA WHICH I THOUGHT YOU MIGHT LOOK INTO, IF YOU HAVE THE TIME!
SOUNDS INTERESTING, CAP! SUPPOSE YOU FILL ME IN ON THE DETAILS?
OH WELL! LOOKS LIKE I CAN KISS MY VACATION TO LAKE PLACID GOODBYE! HOW CAN ANYBODY SO HANDSOME BE SUCH AN OLD KILL JOY?!!
3

I CAN'T VOUCH FOR THE **ACCURACY** OF THE REPORTS, BUT FOR DAYS NOW WE'VE BEEN HEARING REPORTS OF A GIGANTIC MAN WHOM THE NATIVES CALL **COLOSSUS!!** THEY SAY HE'S **TWICE** AS BIG AS GIANT-MAN--ABOUT **THIRTY FEET** TALL!

"HE LIVES ATOP A TOWERING PEAK IN THE BORA-BURU REGION-- A PEAK SO STEEP THAT HE IS UNABLE TO DESCEND INTO THE VALLEY!'"

"THE NATIVES BELOW CALL HIM A GOD-- AND LIVE IN DREAD FEAR OF HIM!! HE IS SAID TO BE THE MOST POWERFUL LIVING CREATURE ON EARTH TODAY!"

"**WE** WERE NOTIFIED BECAUSE **COLOSSUS** IS NOW DEMANDING A **HUMAN SACRIFICE**, AND THE NATIVES DON'T KNOW WHERE TO TURN FOR HELP!'"

SAY NO MORE, CAP! THE WASP WAS JUST PESTERING ME FOR A VACATION-- SO I CAN KILL TWO BIRDS WITH ONE STONE!

WE KNEW WE COULD COUNT ON YOU, GIANT-MAN! GOOD LUCK!

SOME VACATION! I WANT TO GO UP NORTH TO LAKE PLACID-- SO WE END UP HEADING FOR DARKEST AFRICA! THANKS A **HEAP!**

WIPE OFF THE FROWN, HONEY! YOU KNOW YOU WOULDN'T MISS IT FOR THE WORLD!

SO WHAT DOES **THAT** PROVE?? I'M NUTTIER THAN **YOU!**

4

SOMETIME LATER, A SPEEDY TWO-MAN JET APPROACHES THE BORA-BURU REGION OF EQUATORIAL AFRICA...

WE'RE ALMOST THERE, JAN! I WANT TO BUZZ THE AREA AND SEE IF WE CAN FIND--JAN!! LOOK!!

I SEE HIM! THEN THE REPORTS WERE TRUE! HE'S GIGANTIC!!

HE'S EASILY THIRTY FEET TALL! THAT'S TWICE AS BIG AS MY FIGHTING SIZE OF TWELVE FEET!

BUT YOU CAN MAKE YOURSELF GROW EVEN LARGER, CAN'T YOU, HANK?

SURE, BUT I GROW PROPORTIONATELY WEAKER, THE LARGER I GET! SAY-- WHAT'S THAT HUGE, SHELL-LIKE THING NEAR COLOSSUS??

I DON'T KNOW, BLUE EYES-- BUT I SURE DON'T LIKE THE WAY HE'S LOOKING AT US! DON'T GET TOO CLOSE!

BLAST IT!! THE CONTROLS ARE JAMMED! CAN'T TURN--!!

HANK-- HANK!! HE CAUGHT US!! LIKE GRABBING A TOY!!

SIT TIGHT! WE'LL SEE WHAT HE DOES!

ATTACK COLOSSUS, WILL YOU??!

HE SPEAKS OUR LANGUAGE!!

HE TOSSED US AWAY-- WE'RE OUT OF CONTROL! HANK-- WE'LL CRASH!

KEEP COOL, JAN! PRESS THAT RED BUTTON AT THE SIDE OF YOUR SEAT--NOW!

EJECTOR SEATS! DREAMBOAT, YOU THINK OF EVERYTHING!

ONE OF US HAS TO, MY LITTLE SCATTER-BRAIN!

5

DON'T GO 'WAY, BIG BOY! YOU HAVEN'T SEEN THE LAST OF US!

THEN, AFTER GIANT-MAN AND THE WASP HAVE SAFELY LANDED...

JAN, THE EASIEST WAY FOR US TO SCALE THAT SHEER PEAK IS TO SHRINK! AS ANT-MAN AND THE WASP, WE CAN EASILY REACH THE TOP!

BESIDES, I'VE BEEN ANXIOUS TO TEST MY MENTAL SHRINKING POWER UNDER BATTLE CONDITIONS! DON'T FAIL ME, LITTLE CYBERNETIC HEADPIECE!! HERE GOES--!

IT'S GOING TO WORK! I CAN FEEL MY ANTENNAE TINGLE AS I CONCENTRATE ON REACHING ANT-SIZE!

TERRIF, HANDSOME! BUT YOU'LL HAVE TO WAIT FOR ME TO JOIN YOU THE SLOW, OLD-FASHIONED WAY! I'LL TAKE MY TRUSTY LITTLE CAPSULE--!

HOW ABOUT THAT, HONEY??

NO! DON'T DO IT!

I SAVED THIS AS A SURPRISE FOR YOU! AS LONG AS I'M WEARING MY CYBERNETIC HEADPIECE, I CAN MENTALLY CHANGE YOUR HEIGHT, ALSO! SEE?

OHHH! IT'S POSITIVELY EERIE!

NOW, WITH OUR INSECT POWERS, IT'S AN EASY MATTER TO DASH UP THE SIDE OF THE PEAK! IT SHOULDN'T TAKE MORE THAN A COUPLE OF HOURS IF WE DON'T STOP!

IT'S A LONG WAY UP! I'LL FOLLOW THIS WAY, TO SAVE MY FLYING ENERGY FOR LATER!

WITH COLOSSUS BEING THIRTY FEET TALL, AND US ONLY INSECT-SIZED, HE'LL NEVER NOTICE US! BUT WHAT DO WE DO WHEN WE REACH HIM??

6

WE'LL WORRY ABOUT THAT *LATER!* HOLD IT, JAN!

Y'KNOW, THIS IS GOING TO TAKE LONGER THAN I THOUGHT!

YOU'RE NOT *KIDDING!* THIS PEAK MIGHT AS WELL BE *MT. EVEREST* WHEN WE'RE INSECT-SIZED!

I KNOW--THAT'S WHY I TUCKED *THIS* LITTLE GADGET IN MY ACCESSORY BELT! IT'LL SPEED THINGS UP FOR US!

WHAT *IS* IT, HANK? I NEVER *SAW* IT BEFORE!

NATURALLY! YOU'RE TOO BUSY READING TRAVEL MAGAZINES WHILE YOUR HARD-WORKING PARTNER-IN-PERIL SLAVES OVER HIS HOT TEST-TUBES!

SEE HOW THOSE TINY PODS ADHERE TO ANY SURFACE THEY TOUCH? AND NOW, WRAP THAT LOOP SECURELY AROUND YOUR WRIST, WHILE I RELEASE THE TENSION SPRING BY A MENTAL CYBERNETIC COMMAND!

IT'S REELING US IN-- LIKE FISH ON A FISHING LINE!!

IT'S A LOT FASTER THAN *CLIMBING* ALL THIS DISTANCE!

AND A LOT MORE *DANGEROUS*, TOO! *NEXT* TIME I'LL BRING A *PARACHUTE*, THANK YOU!

YOU WOULDN'T BE HAPPY UNLESS YOU WERE COMPLAINING ABOUT SOME--*HOLD IT!* LOOK THERE!!

WE'VE REACHED THE *TOP!* FROM HERE ON, BE CAREFUL-- FOR THE DANGER WILL INCREASE!

IT WASN'T EXACTLY A FUN-FILLED HOOTENANNY *UNTIL* NOW, BLUE EYES!

HANK! HE'S WALKING *TOWARDS* US! LOOK AT THE *SIZE* OF HIM!

NO NEED TO WHISPER! HE CAN'T HEAR US 'WAY UP THERE!

7

HE MERELY WALKED TO THE EDGE TO *LOOK* FOR US! HE CAN'T POSSIBLY KNOW WE'RE *HERE*, DOWN AT HIS FEET!

BUT NOW THAT YOU'VE *REACHED* HIM, WHAT CAN YOU DO?? EVEN AS *GIANT-MAN* YOU'LL ONLY BE *HALF* HIS SIZE!

AND I JUST REALIZED SOMETHING *ELSE*! AT THIS HIGH ALTITUDE, THE AIR IS TOO THIN FOR MY WINGS! THE *WASP* WON'T BE ABLE TO FLY AND HELP YOU!

THAT'S OKAY, JAN! I'M GOING TO BECOME *GIANT-MAN* NOW, AND HERE'S WHAT I WANT *YOU* TO DO--

SOMETHING AT MY FEET-- MOVING-- GROWING! WHA--??

I HEAR YOU'VE BEEN DEMANDING A HUMAN SACRIFICE TO BE SENT UP TO YOU BY THE NATIVES! HOW ABOUT *ME*, COLOSSUS?? WILL I DO??

I'VE GOT TO TIME THIS JUST RIGHT, ACCORDING TO HANK'S INSTRUCTIONS! WHEN COLOSSUS BENDS OVER TO SEIZE HIM-- I *STRIKE*!

8

I'VE SET MY **WASP'S STING** AT HIGHEST POWER!! IF I AIM IT JUST RIGHT, WHEN IT HITS COLOSSUS' TOE IT MIGHT MAKE HIM LOSE HIS BALANCE FOR A MOMENT...

...JUST LONG ENOUGH FOR HANK TO **WALLOP** HIM WHEN HIS CHIN IS WITHIN RANGE! **NOW!!**

I **KNEW** I COULD COUNT ON JAN! COLOSSUS IS WONDERING WHAT STUNG HIM IN THE TOE! THIS IS MY CHANCE--MUST MAKE THE **MOST** OF IT!

WHAM!

:WHEW!:-- SCRATCH ONE BRIGHT IDEA! ALL I SUCCEEDED IN DOING WAS NEARLY FRACTURING EVERY KNUCKLE I'VE GOT!

IF THERE **IS** A WAY TO BEAT HIM, IT ISN'T BY A PUNCH IN THE JAW!

YOU ARROGANT FOOL!! DID YOU THINK YOU COULD ELUDE SOMEONE **TWICE** YOUR SIZE??

SAY! I OUGHT TO **REMEMBER** THAT LINE! IT'S A GOOD ONE FOR **ME** TO USE WHEN I GET HOME!

YOU'LL **NEVER** RETURN HOME! **NO ONE** ESCAPES **COLOSSUS!**

OKAY, LITTLE PARTNER --TIME FOR **PLAN B!** AND DON'T TAKE TIME OUT TO POWDER YOUR NOSE!

9

ARE YOU SURE *YOU'LL* BE ALRIGHT WHILE I GO INTO ACTION, HANK?

WELL, I DON'T THINK ANY INSURANCE COMPANY WOULD CALL ME A *GOOD RISK* RIGHT NOW, BUT I'LL KEEP COLOSSUS BUSY WHILE YOU STRUT YOUR STUFF, HONEY!

HERE *GOES!* I HOPE I CAN HANDLE THIS LITTLE GADGET AS WELL AS *YOU* DID, HANDSOME!

BULLS EYE!! IT CAUGHT RIGHT ONTO THE TIP OF COLOSSUS' NOSE! NOW, IF THE TENSION SPRING WILL JUST PULL ME UP FAST ENOUGH--!

MADE IT! NOW, ANOTHER AIR GUN BLAST WHILE I CAN--!!

IT *WORKED!!* SHE CAUSED HIM TO REDUCE THE PRESSURE ON *ME* FOR AN INSTANT--ALL THE TIME I NEED TO BECOME *ANT-MAN* AGAIN!!

MY CAPTIVE! HE *VANISHED!* BUT-- *HOW??*

10

JAN IS SAFE AS LONG AS SHE REMAINS QUIET ATOP COLOSSUS' HEAD!

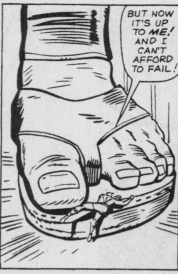

BUT NOW IT'S UP TO ME! AND I CAN'T AFFORD TO FAIL!

MY ANTENNAE ARE TINGLING! HANK IS MENTALLY CONTACTING ME! HE'S TELLING ME TO STAY PUT-- TAKE NO CHANCES! THAT MEANS HE'S GOING TO BATTLE COLOSSUS ALONE!

DON'T DO IT, HANK! HE'S TOO BIG! LET'S JUST ESCAPE WHILE WE CAN!

I HAVE TO, JAN! IT'S THE ONLY WAY! WAIT FOR FURTHER ORDERS!

I'VE GOT TO REACH HIS SIZE! I'VE NEVER DONE IT BEFORE-- BUT I MUST! EVEN THOUGH IT WILL WEAKEN ME!

YOU-- AGAIN???!

COULDN'T MAKE IT IN ONE STAGE! TOO MUCH STRAIN! BUT I'LL TRY AGAIN-- CAN'T QUIT NOW!

THOUGH YOU ARE LARGER THAN ANY OF THE SAVAGES BELOW, YOU ARE STILL A PYGMY TO COLOSSUS! SEE HOW I CAN BOWL YOU OVER BY THE MERE FORCE OF MY HANDCLAP!

MUST KEEP CONCENTRATING-- CAN'T LET ANYTHING STOP ME --HERE GOES!!

STILL CONSIDER ME A PYGMY, COLOSSUS??

YOU'RE GROWING!! BEFORE MY VERY EYES!! WHAT MANNER OF BEING ARE YOU???

OHHHHH... I WAS AFRAID OF THIS! MY HEAD'S SPINNING! FEEL WEAK --GROGGY! GREW TOO BIG--TOO FAST--

11

MEANWHILE, IN THE JUNGLE BELOW, THE MYSTIFIED NATIVES CAN HARDLY BELIEVE THEIR EYES...

BEHOLD!! NOW THERE ARE TWO GIANT DEVIL GODS!

IT IS ALL BEYOND BELIEF!

WITHIN MINUTES, THE INCREDIBLE REPORT IS SPREAD THRUOUT THE JUNGLE--VIA THE OLDEST METHOD OF COMMUNICATION KNOWN TO MAN...

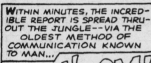

BOOM! BOOM! BOOM!

TWO GIANTS NOW ARE BATTLING IN BORA-BURU REGION!!

WE MUST SEND WARRIORS TO WITNESS SUCH A SIGHT!

TRULY THE GODS MUST BE WRATHFUL! WE ARE DOOMED!

FROM EVERY CORNER OF THE SEETHING DARK CONTINENT THEY COME --INCREDULOUS TRIBESMEN, TO WITNESS THE WONDER OF THE AGES!

WHILE, ON THE MESA ABOVE, THE BATTLE OF TITANS CONTINUES...

THOUGH YOU HAVE MIRACULOUSLY GROWN TO MY SIZE, YOU HAVE ALSO GROWN WEAK! SEE HOW YOU TOTTER--!!

HE'S RIGHT!! EVERYTHING'S SPINNING AROUND--

12

BAH! YOU FELL BY YOURSELF! YOU ARE FINISHED!

I'VE GOT TO SHRINK **DOWN** AGAIN -- BACK TO MY NORMAL GIANT-MAN HEIGHT!

IF I REMAIN **THIS** SIZE, I'M HELPLESS! I MUST NEVER GROW TALLER THAN TWELVE FEET AGAIN!

"IT'S LIKE A **SCULPTOR** ROLLING THE **CLAY** FIGURE OF A MAN BETWEEN HIS HANDS UNTIL IT GROWS LONGER AND LONGER! **BUT,** THE LONGER IT GROWS, THE **WEAKER** IT BECOMES, UNTIL IT FINALLY **SNAPS!**"

REALIZING THAT EVERY SECOND IS VITAL, GIANT-MAN QUICKLY RELAYS A MENTAL COMMAND TO THE WAITING WASP -- VIA HIS CYBERNETIC THOUGHT PROJECTOR!

I **READ** YOU LOUD AND CLEAR, BLUE EYES! HERE I **GO** --!

LUCKY FOR ME THAT COLOSSUS IS SO **BIG!** TO HIM, I'M NO MORE WORTHY OF NOTICE THAN A FLYING GNAT!

ALL I'VE GOT TO DO IS TICKLE HIS EAR LONG ENOUGH TO MAKE HIM DROP THAT **TREE** HE'S HOLDING!

THAT'S **IT!** OKAY, BIG BUDDY -- IT'S ALL UP TO **YOU** NOW!

THERE! I'VE RETURNED TO MY FIGHTING TWELVE-FOOT SIZE! SO IT'S **NOW** -- OR **NEVER!**

13

IF YOU COULDN'T FIGHT ME WHEN YOU WERE *THIRTY-FEET* TALL, WHAT CAN YOU DO *NOW??*

JUST WAIT AND *SEE*, HIGH POCKETS!! HAVE *YOU* GOT A SURPRISE COMING!!

OOOOFF!!

I WEAR OUT MORE PAIRS OF *BOOTS* THIS WAY-- BUT I GUESS IT'S WORTH IT!

HANK! HANK OL' BOY, TAKE IT *EASY!* DON'T FORGET COLOSSUS HAS A PRETTY LITTLE *PASSENGER!*

SORRY, JAN! YOU'D BETTER SHOVE OFF NOW! THE PARTY'S LIABLE TO BECOME KINDA *ROUGH!*

OKAY! I'LL--*OHH!* I FORGOT!! I CAN'T *FLY* IN THIS ATMOS- PHERE! I'M *FALLING!*

AM I GOING *MAD??* I KEEP HEARING STRANGE *VOICES* IN MY HEAD!!

I'VE *GOT* TO REACH HER IN TIME! IF ANYTHING HAPPENS TO *JAN*, THEN NOTHING ELSE MATTERS!

THERE, HONEY! YOU'RE *SAFE!*

BUT *YOU'RE* NOT, HANK! *LOOK OUT!* COLOSSUS IS CHARGING RIGHT *AT* YOU!

HAH!! SO IT IS *COLOSSUS* WHO WINS, AFTER ALL!! YOU PUT UP A *VALIANT* FIGHT, MASKED MAN-- BUT IT *HAD* TO END LIKE THIS!

14

HANK--IF-- IF THIS IS IT... REMEMBER --I LOVE YOU! I'VE ALWAYS--

JAN! WAIT, DARLING! LOOK! HE'S NOT TRYING TO THROW US OVER THE PRECIPICE! DON'T STRUGGLE YET--

HE'S APPROACHING THAT GIANT MUSHROOM! OR-- IS IT A GIANT MUSHROOM???

WHAT ARE YOU GETTING AT, HANK?

NO TIME TO EXPLAIN! LISTEN-- WHEN I AIM MY FIST AT HIS CHEST-- FIRE ANOTHER AIR BLAST--FULL INTENSITY!

WILL DO, BOSS-MAN! MY WASP'S STING SHOULD BE FULLY RECHARGED BY NOW!

NOW, JAN!! NOW!!

PERFECT!! HE DIDN'T EXPECT IT--IT CAUGHT HIM OFF-BALANCE! AND NOW, BEFORE HE CAN GATHER HIS WITS--

AS GIANT-MAN, RELEASED FROM THE ASTONISHED COLOSSUS' GRIP, TUMBLES TO THE GROUND, HE QUICKLY WILLS HIMSELF TO ONCE AGAIN TURN INTO --ANT-MAN!

AND THE DAZED, UNCOMPREHENDING COLOSSUS, SEEING HIS ADVERSARY SEEMINGLY VANISH BEFORE HIS EYES, IS TOTALLY AT A LOSS TO EXPLAIN THE MIND-STAGGERING EVENTS HE HAS OBSERVED!!

IT ISN'T POSSIBLE!! HE'S BEWITCHED!! THIS ENTIRE PLACE IS BEWITCHED!!

15

I'VE GOT TO *FLEE!* I'VE GOT TO *ESCAPE* BEFORE I TOO FALL UNDER SOME MYSTIC SPELL *!!!*

I ASKED THE NATIVES TO SEND ME A SACRIFICE -- SO I COULD HAVE AN EARTHLY SPECIMAN TO BRING TO MY OWN GALAXY FOR STUDY --

-- BUT I NEVER SUSPECTED THAT EARTHLINGS ARE *MAGICIANS!!* IF I STAY ANY LONGER, THEY MAY MAKE A PRISONER OF *ME!!* THIS ENTIRE *PLANET* IS ENCHANTED *!!*

MY HUNCH WAS *RIGHT,* JAN! IT *WASN'T* A GIANT MUSHROOM -- IT WAS SOME SORT OF *SPACE CRAFT,* FROM ANOTHER GALAXY!

GOSH! IT LOOKS LIKE THE *GRAN-DADDY* OF ALL FLYING SAUCERS!

AGENT 7M CALLING VEGA SUPERIOR! REMOVE PLANET EARTH FROM LIST OF PRIMITIVE WORLDS! NEW EVIDENCE INDICATES EARTHLINGS ARE SUPERIOR TO US!

EARTH CREATURES CAN CHANGE SIZE -- AND VANISH COMPLETELY, AT WILL! ALSO HAVE POWER TO KNOCK A FOE OFF HIS FEET MERELY BY POINTING AT HIM! MUST BE CONSIDERED TOO DANGEROUS TO VISIT AGAIN! THAT IS ALL!

I GUESS THAT WRAPS IT UP, JAN! MIGHT AS WELL START DESCENDING THE WAY WE ARRIVED!

RIGHT, HANK! AND -- WHAT I SAID TO YOU BEFORE -- WHEN I THOUGHT WE WERE FINISHED -- I HOPE YOU DON'T THINK --

FORGET IT! PEOPLE SAY THINGS THEY DON'T MEAN IN MOMENTS OF STRESS! I UNDERSTAND!

16

A SHORT TIME LATER --

THE BIG *LUNK!* I WAS TRYING TO TELL HIM I *DID* MEAN IT! HOW AM I *EVER* GOING TO CON-VINCE HIM HOW I FEEL ??

IF YOU EVER HAPPEN TO GO TO EQUATORIAL AFRICA, BE SURE TO VISIT THE BORA-BURU REGION, WHERE YOU WILL SEE THE TALLEST IDOL ON THE CONTINENT --FASHIONED IN THE IMAGE OF THE ONE WHO CAME FROM NOWHERE AND VAN-QUISHED THE DREADED COLOSSUS!

The END

*B*IG NEWS!! NEXT ISSUE WILL FEATURE A SPECIAL TREAT FOR YOU MARVEL FANS -- AND THAT INCLUDES JUST ABOUT EVERYONE! GIANT-MAN AND THE WASP WILL MEET -- *THE INCREDIBLE HULK!* IT'S AS GREAT AS YOU EXPECT IT TO BE! 'NUFF SAID!

STARRING The Wonderful WASP!

"The MAGICIAN AND The MAIDEN!"

MOST BIG GAME HUNTERS HAVE TROPHY ROOMS...AND OUR BEAUTIFUL ADVENTURESS IS NO EXCEPTION, FOR SHE HUNTS THE MOST DANGEROUS GAME OF ALL... *EVIL-DOERS!!*

WHAT A BIZARRE COLLECTION OF COLORFUL CRIMINALS! THE *PORCUPINE, THE HUMAN TOP* AND ALL THOSE *OTHER* RUTHLESS MENACES WERE THE STUFF HEADACHE PILLS ARE MADE FOR! BUT NOW, THANKS TO *GIANT-MAN* AND HIS WONDERFUL, ENCHANTING, GLAMOROUS LITTLE PARTNER, THOSE OBNOXIOUS VILLAINS WILL MENACE SOCIETY NO LONGER... *I HOPE!!*

STORY PLOT: STAN LEE
SCRIPT and ART: LARRY LIEBER
LETTERING S. ROSEN

WE INTERRUPT THIS PROGRAM TO BRING YOU A SPECIAL BULLETIN!

X-698

THIS MORNING THE MASTER CRIMINAL KNOWN AS *THE MAGICIAN* ESCAPED FROM THE STATE PRISON! ROADBLOCKS HAVE BEEN SET UP AND AN *"ALL POINTS ALARM"* HAS GONE OUT!

NOW, WHY DID OL' "TRICKY FINGERS" BREAK OUT? DOESN'T HE KNOW THAT HANK AND I WILL SIMPLY CAPTURE HIM AGAIN AND SEND HIM BACK TO JAIL?!

BUT UNTIL WE *DO* CAPTURE HIM, I'LL TAKE HIS PICTURE DOWN! I'VE NO RIGHT TO HANG A TROPHY WHILE THE QUARRY IS FREE AND LOOSE!

LIKE MOST OF US, JAN LISTENS TO COMMERCIALS WITH ONLY HALF AN EAR! THAT IS, UNTIL...

YES, LADIES! THIS WEEK BENSON'S DEPARTMENT STORE IS FEATURING *WASP-INSPIRED* FASHIONS FOR WOMEN! THEY HAVE SCORES OF STUNNING OUTFITS INSPIRED BY THE CHIC COSTUME OF THAT FAMOUS HEROINE!

SAY! I CAN HARDLY WAIT TO *SEE* THOSE CLOTHES! IMAGINE DESIGNING THEM LIKE MY COSTUME! GOOD THING I'M AS MODEST AS I AM WONDERFUL, OR THIS MIGHT GIVE ME A SWELLED HEAD!

BUT LET US LEAVE OUR "MODEST" HEROINE FOR A MOMENT AND TURN OUR ATTENTION TO HENRY PYM! ON THE WAY TO HIS LAB, HE HAS JUST HEARD THE RADIO ANNOUNCEMENT OF HIS FORMIDABLE FOE'S PRISON BREAK!

NOW THAT HE'S AT LARGE, IT'S A GOOD BET THE MAGICIAN WILL SEEK *REVENGE* AGAINST JAN AND MYSELF!

I MUST CONTACT HER AT ONCE...TO TELL HER TO GO TO MY LAB AND LIE LOW THERE TILL THE MAGICIAN IS CAUGHT! BUT I'M FORTY MILES FROM THE NEAREST TOWN AND TELEPHONE! THERE'S ONLY ONE THING TO DO!

STOPPING HIS CAR, THE WORRIED SCIENTIST QUICKLY WRITES A NOTE! THEN HE REMOVES A SMALL INSTRUMENT FROM THE GLOVE COMPARTMENT!

GOOD THING I CARRY A SPARE CYBERNETIC TRANSMITTER! I'LL CONTACT THOSE WINGED ANTS AND USE THEM AS FLYING POSTMEN!

AND, MINUTES LATER, AS JANET VAN DYNE IS LEAVING HER APARTMENT...

I'LL JUST SCURRY OVER TO BENSON'S TO SEE THEIR WASP-INSPIRED FASHIONS!

SAY! LEAVE A WINDOW OPEN IN THIS TOWN AND THERE'S NO TELLING *WHAT* WILL FLOAT IN! WAIT...THAT SCRAP OF PAPER *ISN'T* FLOATING! IT'S BEING CARRIED BY FLYING ANTS! IT MUST BE A MESSAGE FROM THE BIG MAN!

"JAN...THE MAGICIAN IS AT LARGE AGAIN! GO TO MY LAB AND REMAIN THERE FOR YOUR SAFETY! I'LL SEE YOU SOON! HANK"

I LOVE HANK FOR CARING, BUT SOMETIMES HE'S A WORRY WART! HE DOES NOT REALIZE THAT I CAN HANDLE MYSELF! I'M NOT THE LEAST BIT SCARED OF THE MAGICIAN! I'M *GOING* TO BENSON'S DEPARTMENT STORE!

2.

I *LIKE* BEING A FAMOUS CELEBRITY, BUT I *DON'T* ENJOY BEING GRABBED, PAWED, AND SCREAMED AT BY MY OVER-ZEALOUS FANS! HOWEVER, WITH THIS CIVILIAN DISGUISE OVER MY COSTUME, NO ONE IS APT TO RECOGNIZE ME!

AND A MOMENT LATER, JAN BEAMS WITH FEMALE PRIDE AS SHE VIEWS A STUNNING TRIBUTE TO HER NATION-WIDE FAME...

LOOK AT ALL THE GOWNS, COATS, SPORT CLOTHES... ALL INSPIRED BY MY WASP COSTUME! GOLLY! I'VE BEEN IMMORTALIZED BY THE FASHION INDUSTRY... AND TO A *GAL* THAT ALMOST EQUALS BEING CARVED ON MOUNT RUSHMORE!

BUT, UNKNOWN TO OUR ELATED HEROINE, AN OMINOUS FIGURE IS LURKING IN THE SHADOWS, FURTIVELY WATCHING THE NEARBY SCENE!

BY NOW *THE WASP* MUST BE AMONG THOSE WOMEN! ONE SO *VAIN* COULD *NEVER RESIST* THE TEMPTATION TO COME AND SEE FASHIONS THAT SHE'S INSPIRED! I NEED WAIT NO LONGER! I SHALL STRIKE *NOW!*

I MERELY WAVE MY MAGIC WAND! *ABRA KADABRA, ALLA KAZAM!*

AND, THE NEXT, INCREDIBLE INSTANT...

I CAN'T GET *OUT!* THIS DOOR WON'T OPEN!!

NEITHER WILL *THIS* ONE!

WE'RE LOCKED IN THE STORE!

AND THEN, TO TOP THE UNBELIEVABLE WITH THE SEEMINGLY IMPOSSIBLE...

GO, MY ENCHANTED WAND! FLOAT THROUGH THE AIR! SEARCH AMONG THE CUSTOMERS! FIND THE ONE YOUR MASTER SEEKS!

3.

LIKE A DIVINING ROD, THE FANTASTIC STICK FLOATS OVER THE BEWILDERED WOMEN, FINALLY COMING TO REST ABOVE JAN.

THAT FLOATING WAND IS *POINTING* AT ME! THERE IS ONLY ONE MAGICIAN WHO COULD PULL THIS *STUNT!*

I WAS RIGHT! IT'S *HIM!* HE'S FOUND ME OUT!

HE'S THAT ESCAPED CONVICT! ...*THE MAGICIAN!*

HELP! I'M GOING TO FAINT!

SILENCE, FEMALES. I WON'T HARM YOU. I'M ONLY AFTER THAT ONE MEDDLESOME CREATURE WHO CALLS HERSELF *THE WASP!*

THE WASP!!

YES! SHE AND HER OVERSIZED PARTNER DEALT ME A CRUSHING DEFEAT DURING OUR LAST ENCOUNTER! BUT NOW VENGEANCE SHALL BE *MINE!* IT WAS *I* WHO CONCEIVED THIS IDEA OF *"WASP" FASHIONS* AND THROUGH OUTSIDE SOURCES ARRANGED FOR THIS SALE! ALL OF IT FOR THE PURPOSE OF TRAPPING MY CHARMING FOE... AS I HAVE SO NEATLY *DONE!*

I'M NOT TRAPPED *YET,* CHUM! JUST ONE CAPSULE, AND *AWAYYYY WE GO!*

A FUTILE GESTURE WASP...FOR NO MATTER HOW TINY YOU BECOME, I'LL BE ABLE TO SEE YOU THROUGH THESE OPTO-RAY MAGNIFYING GLASSES! YOU'LL *NEVER* BE OUT OF MY SIGHT!

"NEVER OUT OF YOUR SIGHT, HUH? HOW ROMANTIC! BUT THAT'S NOT WHY I SHRANK! THIS IS MY *BATTLE SIZE,* AS YOU'LL KNOW WHEN YOU FEEL MY *STING!*

BUT, JUST AS THE TINY COSTUMED FIGURE FIRES A STUNNING BURST OF COMPRESSED AIR, THE MAGICIAN PRODUCES A SILK CLOTH FROM HIS SLEEVE!

BEHOLD HOW THE HAND IS *QUICKER* THAN THE EYE!

YOUR CLOTH ABSORBED THE FULL FORCE OF THE AIR BURST! ROUND ONE GOES TO *YOU!*

ROUND TWO WILL BE MINE ALSO AS SOON AS I GET MY *HANDS* ON YOU!

EVER TRY CATCHING A FLYING GAL *BEFORE!* BELIEVE ME, IT'S EASIER *SAID* THAN *DONE!*

4

DON'T WORRY! YOU'RE *ONE* FLY GIRL WHO'S ABOUT TO BE *GROUNDED!*

JUST AN OLD FAMILY FORMULA FOR PUTTING SMART ALECK MEDDLERS IN THEIR PLACE... AS YOU'LL SOON SEE!

HIS POWDER IS ALL OVER MY WINGS! IT MAKES THEM FEEL SO *HEAVY* I CAN HARDLY *LIFT* THEM! I CAN'T STAY ALOFT!

NO LONGER ABLE TO FLY, THE QUICK-THINKING WASP GLIDES AS SHE DESCENDS... GLIDES TO THE TOY DEPARTMENT, AND LANDS IN A TINY ELECTRIC-POWERED CAR!

YOU CAN'T FLY! YOU'RE HELPLESS! THIS IS MY MOMENT OF TRIUMPH!

MUSTN'T LET HIM GET HIS GRUBBY HANDS ON ME! I HAVE TO KEEP MOVING FAST... EVEN IF IT'S ONLY IN CIRCLES!

THIS TOY CAR BETTER START WORKING AS SOON AS I THROW THE SWITCH!

IT *DID!!*

IT WILL TAKE MORE THAN A CHILD'S PLAYTHING TO SAVE YOU! I'LL SWAT YOU AS I WOULD... WHA...?? I *MISSED!!*

AGAIN AND AGAIN THE MAGICIAN STRIKES AT HIS TINY FOE, BUT EACH TIME...

I KEEP MISSING! IT'S THESE BLASTED *GLASSES!* THEIR MAGNIFICATION THROWS MY SENSE OF TIMING OFF!!

MAYBE YOU NEED AN EYE EXAM! WHY DON'T YOU SEE A DOCTOR? ...LIKE RIGHT *NOW!!*

I'VE HAD *ENOUGH* OF YOUR WISECRACKS! I'M THROUGH PLAYING GAMES! YOUR FREE RIDE IS *OVER,* AND IT'S THE LAST YOU'LL EVER *TAKE!*

HE SMASHED THE MOTOR! THE CAR HAS *STOPPED!* I'D BETTER THINK OF SOMETHING FAST OR I'M A *GONER!*

I CAN'T FLY WITH ALL THIS POWDER STILL STUCK TO MY WINGS... BUT I *CAN* GLIDE AGAIN, DOWN OVER TO THE ESCALATOR!

THAT'S RIGHT, WASP... *FLEE!* YOUR SITUATION IS *HOPELESS!* BUT YOU'RE TOO BRAINLESS TO *REALIZE* IT!

A CLEVER MOVE, WASP! BUT IT WON'T WORK! HIDING BETWEEN THE RIDGES OF AN ESCALATOR STEP WON'T SAVE YOU FROM THE MAGICIAN!

THIS TIME IT'S NOT SAFETY I'M AFTER, CHUM! I NEED A BATTLE-SITE THAT'S MORE ADVANTAGEOUS TO ME, AND I'VE FOUND IT!

IT'S NOT EASY, WHILE POISED ON A MOVING ESCALATOR, TO REACH DOWN AND SEIZE A TINY OBJECT, BUT THE MAGICIAN CAN DO ANYTHING! I JUST HAVE TO REACH SLOWLY, CAREFULLY...

AND, JUST AS THE RELENTLESS HUNTER STRIKES AT HIS TINY PREY...

I MADE IT! NOW FROM THIS HEIGHT, I CAN FIRE MY AIR STING AT THE CORRECT ANGLE...

...AND I CAN JAM HIS CLOAK DOWN BETWEEN THE ESCALATOR STEPS AND THE SIDE RAILING!

WHA...??!

THE ESCALATOR HAS STOPPED! THE CLOAK MUST HAVE GOTTEN ENTANGLED IN SOME GEARS UNDERNEATH AND JAMMED THEM!

BLASTED CLOAK! I CAN'T GET LOOSE!!

RUSHING OVER TO A TOY ROBOT ON DISPLAY, THE WASP OPERATES IT THROUGH ITS REMOTE CONTROL PANEL...MAKING THE AUTOMATON WALK TO A NEARBY COUNTER...

IT'S RESPONDING PERFECTLY TO MY CONTROL...EXTENDING ITS ARM AND OPENING ITS HAND TO PICK UP THOSE JUMP ROPES!

AND, A FEW MOMENTS LATER, OUR TINY HEROINE PUTS THE AUTOMATON THROUGH A MORE SOPHISTICATED MANEUVER...

NO TIN TOY IS GOING TO TIE ME UP! I'LL SMASH IT TO BITS! BUT I CAN'T REACH IT!!

THAT'S A CRYING SHAME, BIG BAD BUDDY! I'LL SEND YOU A LETTER OF CONDOLENCE!

6

Having bound her foe securely, the Wasp then stings the store's electric release button, *unlocking* all the doors!

PING!

Hey, what *happened* in the store? Why was it *locked?*

I don't know *what* was going on in there, but... *look!!*

Well, if this doesn't *beat all...?!*

The great *magician* himself! Bound and helpless as a baby!

...and delivered into the waiting arms of the law by the friendly Wasp Carting Company!

It's ironic! The magician's vanity demanded revenge for the defeat he suffered from Giant-Man and me... but instead, he's now received an even *more* humiliating defeat than last time! His self-esteem may *never* recover! Well, I guess that's one loss the world can bear!

Later, at Henry Pym's laboratory, Jan is warmly greeted by the man she loves!

I was worried, honey! But at last you're *here*, where I know you'll be safe until the magician is captured!

That means he hasn't heard the *news* yet!

I was worried, too! But now that *you're* here, Hank...

That's it, darling...hold me tight! I love being in your arms! They're so strong, so capable... and I'll always need them to protect weak little me!

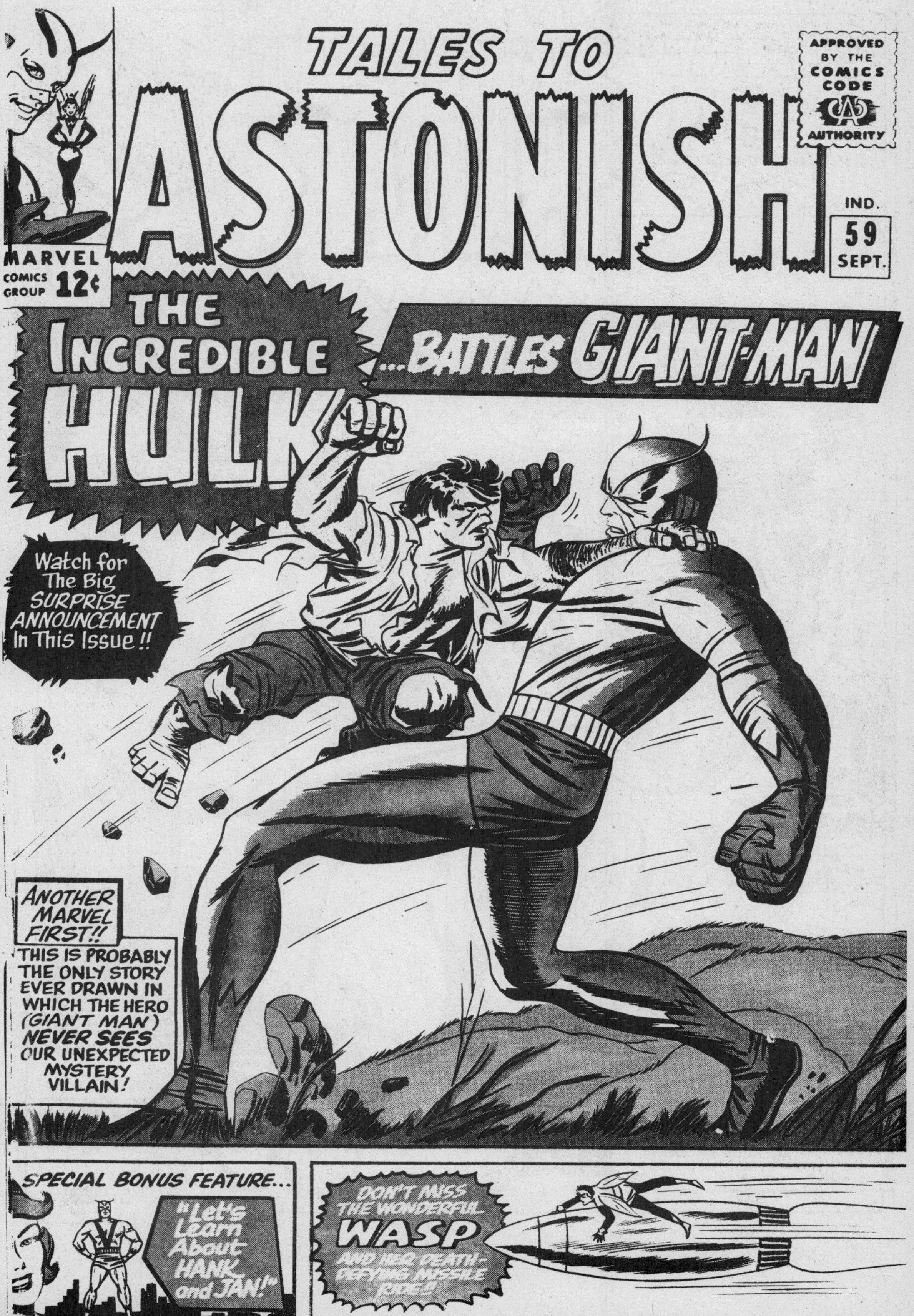
TALES TO ASTONISH
APPROVED BY THE COMICS CODE AUTHORITY
IND. 59 SEPT.
MARVEL COMICS GROUP 12¢
THE INCREDIBLE HULK ...BATTLES GIANT-MAN
Watch for The Big SURPRISE ANNOUNCEMENT In This Issue!!
ANOTHER MARVEL FIRST!!
THIS IS PROBABLY THE ONLY STORY EVER DRAWN IN WHICH THE HERO (GIANT MAN) NEVER SEES OUR UNEXPECTED MYSTERY VILLAIN!
SPECIAL BONUS FEATURE...
"Let's Learn About HANK and JAN!"
DON'T MISS THE WONDERFUL WASP AND HER DEATH-DEFYING MISSILE RIDE!!

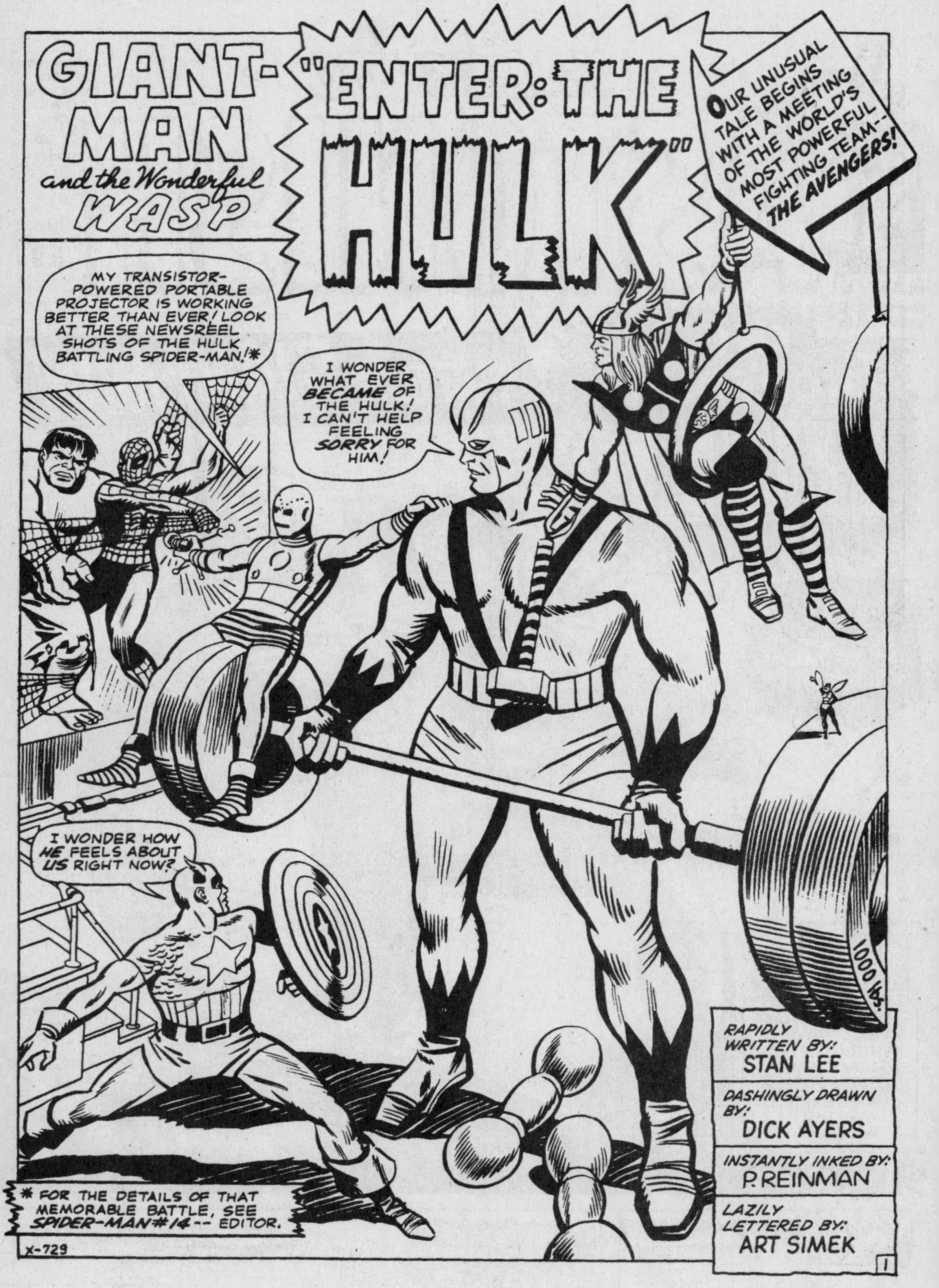
GIANT-MAN and the Wonderful WASP
"ENTER: THE HULK"
OUR UNUSUAL TALE BEGINS WITH A MEETING OF THE WORLD'S MOST POWERFUL FIGHTING TEAM-- THE AVENGERS!
MY TRANSISTOR-POWERED PORTABLE PROJECTOR IS WORKING BETTER THAN EVER! LOOK AT THESE NEWSREEL SHOTS OF THE HULK BATTLING SPIDER-MAN!*
I WONDER WHAT EVER BECAME OF THE HULK! I CAN'T HELP FEELING SORRY FOR HIM!
I WONDER HOW HE FEELS ABOUT US RIGHT NOW?
1000 LBS.
* FOR THE DETAILS OF THAT MEMORABLE BATTLE, SEE SPIDER-MAN #14 -- EDITOR.
RAPIDLY WRITTEN BY: STAN LEE
DASHINGLY DRAWN BY: DICK AYERS
INSTANTLY INKED BY: P. REINMAN
LAZILY LETTERED BY: ART SIMEK
X-729
1

NOT VERY FAR AWAY, ON THE WEST SIDE OF TOWN, A BITTER MAN NAMED *DAVY CANNON* READS A NEWSPAPER ACCOUNT OF GIANT-MAN'S RECENT VICTORY OVER *COLOSSUS!* *

WELL, WELL, SO MY OLD "PAL" GIANT-MAN IS HOGGIN' THE HEADLINES AGAIN, IS HE? I WONDER IF HE'S FORGOTTEN ABOUT *ME*?

HE PROBABLY DOESN'T EVEN KNOW THAT *THE HUMAN TOP* WAS FREED ON PAROLE LAST WEEK!

DAILY NEWS

EXCLUSIVE!! NEW GIANT-MAN ADVENTURE!

THE REPORTER DISPATCH

GIANT-MAN DOES IT AGAIN! *

COLOSSUS DEFEATED BY GIANT-MAN!

* REFER TO *TALES TO ASTONISH #55* -- EDITOR.

I REMEMBER OUR *LAST* BATTLE! I MADE HIM LOOK *SICK* ON THE ROOFTOPS! *

TALES TO ASTONISH #55 -- EDITOR.

I'D HAVE LICKED HIM WITH MY "TORNADO FUNNEL" IF HE HADN'T LANDED ON SOME HIGH WIRES!

"MY BIGGEST MISTAKE WAS THINKING HE WAS *CLUMSY!* BOY, HOW WRONG I WAS! BUT I'LL NEVER UNDERESTIMATE HIM AGAIN!"

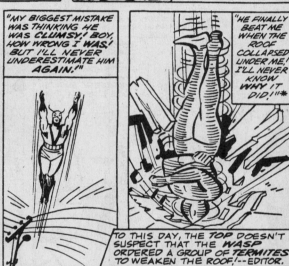

"HE FINALLY *BEAT* ME WHEN THE *ROOF* COLLAPSED UNDER ME! I'LL NEVER KNOW WHY IT DID!" *

TO THIS DAY, THE *TOP* DOESN'T SUSPECT THAT THE *WASP* ORDERED A GROUP OF *TERMITES* TO WEAKEN THE ROOF! --EDITOR.

GIANT-MAN IS THE *ONLY* ONE EVER TO BEAT ME--AND I'LL NEVER REST TILL I PAY HIM *BACK* FOR IT! HE CAN'T IMAGINE HOW MUCH *MORE* DANGEROUS I AM *NOW* THAN I WAS!

"WITH MY SUPERHUMAN SPINNING POWER, I'VE LEARNED TO FOCUS THE FORCE OF THE AIR PRESSURE I GENERATE INTO A STREAM POWERFUL ENOUGH TO BLAST A HOLE IN A BRICK WALL," AND I'VE LEARNED NOT TO WEAR THAT OLD STUPID COSTUME WHICH MADE ME TOO EASY TO RECOGNIZE!"

WHOOOSH!

2

BUT LEAVE US LEAVE THE *TOP* WITH HIS *BITTER* THOUGHTS, AND TURN BACK TO THE *AVENGERS*, WHOSE MEETING HAS JUST ENDED...

YOU MEN GO AHEAD! I'M GOING TO STAY HERE A WHILE LONGER!

ALONE WITH THE WASP AT AVENGERS' HEADQUARTERS, THE GIANT-SIZED ADVENTURER ONCE MORE STUDIES THE FILMED ACCOUNT OF THE *HULK'S* LAST RECORDED BATTLE...

COME ON, BIG *BOYFRIEND*-- LET'S GO OUT TO DINNER! WE'VE SEEN THIS FILM A DOZEN TIMES!

I *KNOW*, JAN! I JUST CAN'T GET THE *HULK* OUT OF MY MIND! WELL, WE'LL TALK ABOUT HIM WHILE WE LEAVE!

DON'T BOTHER TAKING A GROWTH CAPSULE, HONEY! I'LL *"THINK"* YOU BACK TO NORMAL SIZE, JUST AS I DO FOR MYSELF!

HENRY J. PYM!! I *ASKED* YOU NOT TO *DO* THAT! YOU'RE JUST SHOWING OFF WITH YOUR NEW CYBERNETIC MENTAL SIZE CONTROL, THAT'S ALL!

JUST IGNORE THOSE STREET CORNER WOLVES, HANK! THEY'RE NOT BOTHERING ME ONE BIT!

MAYBE *NOT*, JAN-- BUT THEY'RE SURE RUBBING *ME* THE WRONG WAY! OH WELL--I'LL PRETEND I DIDN'T HEAR THEM!

HEY, BOYS!! LOOK AT THE LIVIN' *DOLL* WALKIN' WITH THAT SQUARE!

HEY, SISTER! WHY DON'T YOU DITCH THAT ITCH AND DATE A *REAL* MAN?? NAMELY *ME*!

MMMM--COULD THAT TOMATO AND *ME* MAKE BEAUTIFUL MUSIC?!!

WHAT ARE YOU TWO *WEARIN'*? LONG UNDERWEAR??

C'MON, LET'S *FOLLOW* 'EM AND SEE WHA --WHA--*HOLY HANNAH!!* LOOK!!

IT'S G-GIANT MAN!!

OKAY, LOUD-MOUTHS!! IF YOU'RE LOOKIN' FOR A LITTLE *ACTION*, I'LL SEE IF I CAN *OBLIGE* YOU!

I NEVER SAW HANK DOUBLE HIS SIZE SO *FAST* BEFORE!

3

EXACTLY TWO MINUTES LATER--

AWW, COME BACK! DON'T LEAVE US LIKE THIS!

MILLIONS OF PEOPLE IN THIS TOWN, AND WE HADDA PICK ON GIANT-MAN!

BUT, AS LUCK WOULD HAVE IT, ANOTHER PAIR OF EYES HAVE ALSO WITNESSED THE INCIDENT IN THE STREET BELOW! THE EYES OF-- THE HUMAN TOP!

BOY! WHAT A BREAK! THE TWO PEOPLE I MOST WANTED TO FIND! NOW, I'VE GOT TO MAKE SURE THEY DON'T GET AWAY FROM ME!

I'LL FOLLOW THEM, AND KEEP THEM IN SIGHT UNTIL THE TIME IS RIGHT FOR ME TO GET MY REVENGE ON THAT OVERGROWN CLOWN!

AND SO, SPINNING SO RAPIDLY THAT THE HUMAN EYE CANNOT POSSIBLY SEE HIM, THE TOP RACES FROM HIS APARTMENT AND BEGINS HIS PURSUIT OF GIANT-MAN AND THE WASP!

IF I FOLLOW THEM LONG ENOUGH, SOONER OR LATER I'LL GET THE OPPORTUNITY I WANT!

GOSH, HANK --IT'S SO WINDY ALL OF A SUDDEN! LET'S GET TO THE RESTAURANT FAST!

SORRY, JAN! FORGET ABOUT DINNER FOR NOW! WE'RE TAKING A TRIP INSTEAD! WE'LL EAT ON THE PLANE!

WHY? WHERE ARE WE GOING?

TO NEW MEXICO! THE HULK WAS LAST SEEN THERE--AND I WON'T BE ABLE TO REST TILL I'VE FOUND HIM, AND TRIED TO TALK HIM INTO REJOINING THE AVENGERS!

WELL, WELL! THAT SOUNDS REAL INTERESTING! I THINK THE HUMAN TOP WILL JUST JOIN THEM!

4

A FEW HOURS LATER...

FASTEN YOUR SAFETY BELTS, PLEASE! WE'RE ABOUT TO LAND!

THE HULK IS *SOMEWHERE* DOWN THERE! I'VE *GOT* TO FIND HIM!

THERE THEY GO! IT'LL BE A *CINCH* TO KEEP 'EM IN SIGHT! THIS IS ALMOST *TOO* EASY FOR THE HUMAN TOP!

IT'S A GOOD THING I'M SO *AVERAGE* LOOKING! I DON'T EVEN HAVE TO *DISGUISE* MYSELF!

HANK, NEW MEXICO IS A MIGHTY BIG STATE! WHERE WILL YOU START SEARCHING?

THE AIR FORCE MISSILE BASE, JAN! THE HULK WAS LAST REPORTED IN THAT VICINITY! I THINK GENERAL "*THUNDERBOLT*" ROSS WILL REMEMBER ME!

LATER, A RENTED HELICOPTER LANDS AT THE BASE...

EASY ON THE TRIGGER, JOE! HE *SEES* US! HE'S LANDING!

LOS DIABLOS MISSILE BASE

GIANT-MAN! WE DIDN'T *KNOW*, SIR!

TAKE ME TO GENERAL ROSS, SOLDIER!

AND SO...

THEN YOU HAVEN'T SEEN ANY TRACE OF THE HULK FOR WEEKS, GENERAL? BUT I THOUGHT...

LOOK, MISTER--I'VE HAD ENOUGH OF THAT RAMPAGING MENACE TO LAST ME A *LIFETIME!* I'VE GOT A FEW *OTHER* LITTLE THINGS TO DO, LIKE RUN THIS MISSILE BASE! BUT I'LL ASK ONE OF MY CIVILIAN SCIENTISTS TO HELP YOU!

SOMEONE GET *BRUCE BANNER* HERE--ON THE DOUBLE!

THERE HE IS *NOW!* DR. BANNER, I'D LIKE TO SPEAK TO YOU ABOUT THE *HULK!* I'M TRYING TO *FIND* HIM, AND GENERAL ROSS THOUGHT YOU MIGHT HELP! I RECOGNIZE YOU FROM YOUR NEWSPAPER PHOTOS!

WASP! GET THAT WHIRLYBIRD OFF THE FIELD! THIS ISN'T A BLAMED *PARKING LOT!*

SORRY, GIANT-MAN! I CAN'T HELP YOU! I KNOW *NOTHING* ABOUT THE HULK-- AND I CARE *LESS!*

OKAY THEN-- WE'LL SEARCH FOR HIM IN OUR OWN WAY! BUT IF YOU *DO* HEAR OF HIM--CONTACT ME VIA MY SPECIAL AVENGERS' BAND SHORT WAVE!

SO! THE AVENGERS ARE STILL SEEKING THE *HULK*, EH? WILL THEY *NEVER* LEAVE HIM IN PEACE??

BRUCE! WHAT'S *WRONG!* I SAW GIANT-MAN SPEAK TO YOU AND THEN YOU LOOKED SO *ANGRY!*

5

"NOTHING'S WRONG, BETTY! EVERYTHING'S WRONG! WHAT DIFFERENCE DOES IT MAKE! YOU'RE THE GENERAL'S DAUGHTER, AND I'M A HUMBLE ATOMIC SCIENTIST-- WITH A SECRET I CAN NEVER REVEAL TO A LIVING SOUL!"

"BRUCE--WAIT! COME BACK, BRUCE, MY DARLING! I'VE NEVER SEEN YOU THIS WAY BEFORE! WAIT!"

"POOR BETTY! I LOVE HER FAR TOO MUCH TO INVOLVE HER IN MY PROBLEM! HOW COULD SHE KNOW-- HOW COULD SHE EVEN SUSPECT-- THAT THE MAN SHE KNOWS AS DR. ROBERT BRUCE BANNER IS, IN REALITY, THE INCREDIBLE HULK??!"

"SOMETHING IS TERRIBLY WRONG-- I KNOW IT! I CAN'T LET HIM DRIVE OFF LIKE THAT! I'LL GET MY CAR AND FOLLOW-- HE MAY NEED ME!"

HIS MIND IN A TURMOIL, NEVER DREAMING THAT GIANT-MAN HAS COME TO HELP THE HULK, BRUCE BANNER DRIVES INTO THE HILLS, A BURNING RAGE IN HIS HEART!

"I'VE TRIED TO FORGET THE HULK-- TO PRETEND HE NEVER EXISTED! BUT THEY WON'T LET ME--!!"

"NO! I MUSTN'T GET EXCITED! I MUSTN'T LET MY BLOOD PRESSURE RISE! WHEN IT DOES, I CAN'T CONTROL MYSELF! I-- BEGIN TO CHANGE--"

"-- INTO-- THE HULK!!"

AND THUS, THE INCREDIBLE HULK APPEARS ONCE MORE!! THE STRONGEST LIVING MORTAL ON THE FACE OF THE EARTH! A RAGING HUMAN ENGINE OF DESTRUCTION AND WRATH!

"SO!! GIANT-MAN SEEKS THE HULK, DOES HE??"

WITH A BELLOW OF SHEER ANIMAL RAGE, THE MOST POWERFUL LEGS IN THE WORLD PROPEL THE HULK SKYWARD, IN THE FIRST OF HIS MANY PRODIGIOUS LEAPS-- SO HIGH, AND SO FAST THAT HE SEEMS TO BE FLYING!

"WELL, HE'LL FIND THE HULK-- TO HIS EVER-LASTING REGRET!!"

6

NOT LONG AFTERWARDS, PANIC SEIZES A NEARBY TOWN...

LOOK! IT'S THE *HULK*!

RUN! RUN! THE HULK IS HERE!

SOMEONE SEND FOR THE *ARMY*!! ONLY *THEY* CAN STOP HIM!

BUT, AMONG THE FEARFUL TOWNSPEOPLE, THERE IS ONE WHO SMILES WITH GLEE...

ALL THE BREAKS ARE FALLIN' MY WAY! THE *HULK* IS WHAT I NEED TO FINISH OFF GIANT-MAN!!

MEANWHILE, GENERAL *"THUNDERBOLT"* ROSS'S LOVELY DAUGHTER, BETTY, COMES UPON BRUCE BANNER'S OVERTURNED VEHICLE ALONG THE LONELY MOUNTAIN ROAD...

BRUCE'S *JEEP*! IT'S BEEN IN AN *ACCIDENT*!! THAT MUST MEAN-- OH NO--*NO*!!!

BUT, THERE'S NO SIGN OF BRUCE!! *WAIT!* THESE GLASSES-- HIS TORN COAT!! AND THOSE *FOOTPRINTS*!! THEY CAN ONLY BELONG TO-- THE *HULK*!

IT CAN ONLY MEAN-- THE HULK HAS *TAKEN* HIM-- THERE'S NO *CHANCE* FOR HIM!

LOOKS LIKE HANK AND I ARRIVED JUST IN TIME!

SEARCHING THE AREA ATOP A FLY-ING ANT, IN HIS ORIGINAL IDENTITY AS *ANT-MAN*, THE ASTONISHING ADVENTURER CRIES OUT...

THERE *IS* A CHANCE, MISS ROSS!

GIANT-MAN! BUT WHERE DID YOU *COME* FROM?? HOW--??

EXPLANATIONS ARE TOO BORING! BUT I *KNOW* THE HULK-- HE WON'T HARM YOUR BOY FRIEND WITHOUT

CAUSE, NO MATTER *WHAT* PEOPLE SAY ABOUT HIM!

I'LL FIND HIM AND *PROVE* IT!

7

MEANTIME, THE *HUMAN TOP* SPINS JUST OUTSIDE OF TOWN -- WAITING FOR THE *HULK* TO APPEAR!

HE'S *GOT* TO COME THIS WAY SOON --AND WHEN HE *DOES*--!

I'LL *STOP* HIM AND MAKE HIM AN OFFER! WITH HIS STRENGTH AND *MY* BRAINS, WE'LL BOTH FINISH OFF GIANT-MAN *EASY!*

AND, IF THE HULK *REFUSES* ME, I'LL HURL MY SPEED BLAST AT HIM! IF IT CAN SHATTER A *BOULDER,* IT OUGHT TO BE ABLE TO TAKE CARE OF ANYONE THAT LIVES!

BUT, EVEN THE HUMAN TOP DOESN'T SUSPECT HOW *FAST* THE HULK CAN LEAP! AND, THE RAMPAGING CREATURE APPEARS BEFORE THE TOP HAS TIME TO EVEN STOP HIS SPIN!

I'VE GOT TO FIND *GIANT-MAN!* I'LL FINISH HIM *FOREVER!*

NOTHING WILL STAND IN MY WAY!! *NOTHING! NOTHING!!*

IT'S *HIM!!* BUT-- HE'S CRASHING INTO THAT *PEAK!* HE'S *TOPPLING* IT! I NEVER DREAMT HIS STRENGTH WAS *SO GREAT!*

ONLY BY SPINNING AT MAXIMUM SPEED CAN THE TOP CREATE A WIND SCREEN DENSE ENOUGH TO PROTECT HIM FROM THE FALLING BOULDERS!

AND, BY THE TIME THE HULK HAS GONE...

I *MISSED* MY *CHANCE!* BUT I'LL CATCH UP WITH HIM *YET!*

THEN, THE VERY MAN THE HULK IS SEEKING SEES *HIM* FIRST!

THERE HE *GOES!*

8

I'VE BEEN CARRYING THIS TINY CARBON-DIOXIDE POWER ROCKET FOR JUST SUCH AN OCCASION!

BY TRANSFORMING MYSELF TO *ANT-MAN*, I'LL BE ABLE TO *RIDE* IN IT--AND DESPITE ITS SIZE, IT HAS SUPER-SONIC SPEED!

IT'S GOOD FOR ONLY *ONE* BRIEF USE BEFORE ITS POWER IS GONE, BUT THAT'LL BE ENOUGH FOR *ME!*

THE HULK IS HEADING FOR THE NEXT TOWN! I'VE GOT TO REACH THERE BEFORE *HE* DOES!

SOONER OR LATER I'LL FIND GIANT-MAN! HE'S TOO BIG TO HIDE FROM ME MUCH LONGER! I'LL SEARCH EVERY TOWN TILL I'VE *GOT* HIM!

MY MINIATURE MISSILE IS SO SWIFT, AND SILENT, THAT HE DOESN'T EVEN *NOTICE* IT ROCKETING PAST HIM!

MADE IT! NOW, I'VE GOT TO FIND A WAY TO MAKE THE HULK *LISTEN* TO ME WHEN HE GETS HERE!

FIRST THING TO DO IS *EVACUATE* THE TOWN! THIS *BILLBOARD* WILL HELP DO IT!

STANDICK MOTOR OIL
BEST FOR YOUR CAR!

9

ROLLING THE BILLBOARD UP LIKE PAPER IN HIS MASSIVE, DOUBLE-SIZED HANDS, GIANT-MAN USES IT AS A *MEGAPHONE*.....

ATTENTION! ATTENTION!! THE *HULK* IS COMING! *EVACUATE* THE TOWN!! *EMERGENCY!*

THE *HULK* AT LARGE AGAIN?? CAN WE *BELIEVE* HIM?

BELIEVE HIM?? MISTER, THAT'S *GIANT-MAN!* HE DIDN'T COME HERE TO PLAY *GAMES!*

WITHIN SECONDS, A MASS EXODUS BEGINS OUT OF THE SMALL TOWN...

ANOTHER FEW SECONDS AND THE TOWN WILL BE EMPTY! AND NOT AN INSTANT TOO SOON!

NOW I WON'T HAVE TO WORRY ABOUT ANY INNOCENT PEOPLE BEING HURT WHEN HE AP-PEARS!

I'VE GOT TO FIND A WAY TO CONVINCE HIM THAT MAN-KIND *ISN'T* HIS ENEMY! IF ONLY HE'LL GIVE ME THE *CHANCE!*

AND, JUST AT THE OUTSKIRTS OF THE LITTLE TOWN, AS THE HULK PREPARES TO MAKE THE FINAL LEAP WHICH WILL BRING HIM TO THE MAIN STREET--

HULK! WAIT--! I'VE SOMETHING TO *TELL* YOU!

THE HULK WAITS FOR *NOBODY!!*

BUT THIS IS *IMPORTANT!!*

10

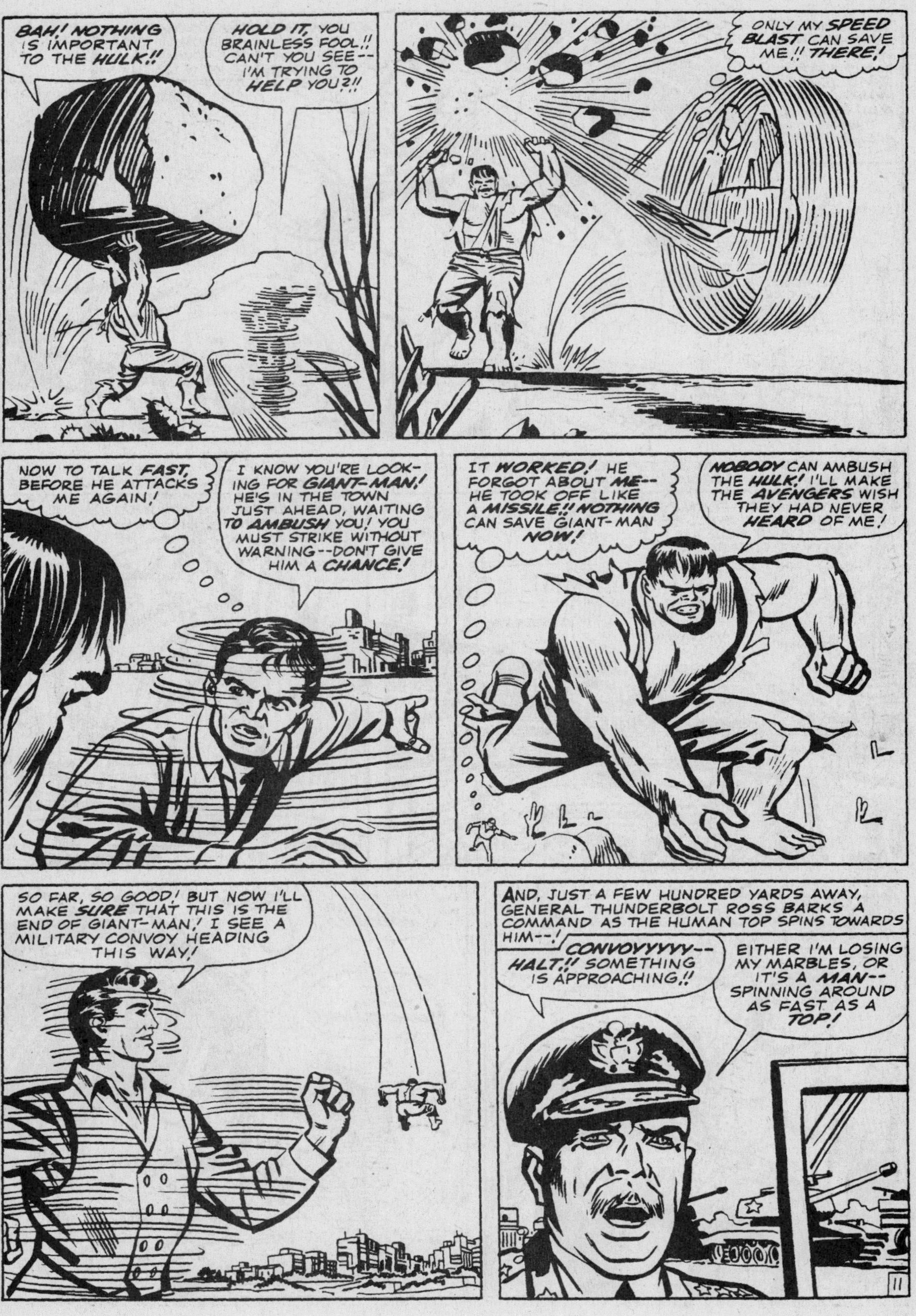
BAH! NOTHING IS IMPORTANT TO THE HULK!!
HOLD IT, YOU BRAINLESS FOOL!! CAN'T YOU SEE-- I'M TRYING TO HELP YOU?!!
ONLY MY SPEED BLAST CAN SAVE ME!! THERE!
NOW TO TALK FAST, BEFORE HE ATTACKS ME AGAIN!
I KNOW YOU'RE LOOKING FOR GIANT-MAN! HE'S IN THE TOWN JUST AHEAD, WAITING TO AMBUSH YOU! YOU MUST STRIKE WITHOUT WARNING--DON'T GIVE HIM A CHANCE!
IT WORKED! HE FORGOT ABOUT ME-- HE TOOK OFF LIKE A MISSILE!! NOTHING CAN SAVE GIANT-MAN NOW!
NOBODY CAN AMBUSH THE HULK! I'LL MAKE THE AVENGERS WISH THEY HAD NEVER HEARD OF ME!
SO FAR, SO GOOD! BUT NOW I'LL MAKE SURE THAT THIS IS THE END OF GIANT-MAN! I SEE A MILITARY CONVOY HEADING THIS WAY!
AND, JUST A FEW HUNDRED YARDS AWAY, GENERAL THUNDERBOLT ROSS BARKS A COMMAND AS THE HUMAN TOP SPINS TOWARDS HIM--!
CONVOYYYYY-- HALT!! SOMETHING IS APPROACHING!!
EITHER I'M LOSING MY MARBLES, OR IT'S A MAN-- SPINNING AROUND AS FAST AS A TOP!
11

NEVER HAVING HEARD OF "THE HUMAN TOP", THE GENERAL WATCHES INCREDULOUSLY UNTIL...

I'VE COME TO **WARN** YOU! THE **HULK** IS IN THE TOWN AHEAD OF YOU!

THE **HULK??!** ARE YOU **CERTAIN**, MAN??

YES SIR! THE ENTIRE TOWN HAS BEEN **EVACUATED!** IT'S **EMPTY**--EXCEPT FOR THE **HULK!**

IF WHAT YOU SAY IS **TRUE,** THIS IS MY ONE CHANCE TO STOP THAT RAMPAGING MENACE FOR **GOOD!**

WITHIN SECONDS, THE BATTLE-WISE MILITARY LEADER SENDS OUT SCOUTS, AND WHEN THEY RETURN...

THE REPORT IS **CORRECT,** SIR! THE TOWN HAS BEEN EVACUATED! ALL THE INHABITANTS HAVE FLED TO SANDY POINT, IN THE NEXT DISTRICT!

BUT THIS IS THE CHANCE I'VE BEEN **WAITING** FOR--TO RID THE WORLD OF THE **HULK!**

EXACTLY TWO MINUTES LATER, THUNDERBOLT ROSS'S COMMAND CAR RACES TO THE LEAD TANK...

I HEARD FROM COMMAND HEADQUARTERS! THEY AUTHORIZE USING A NUCLEAR WARHEAD SHELL!

THAT MEANS **PLAN B!** TAKE YOUR STATIONS, MEN!

MEANWHILE, IN THE CENTER OF TOWN, THE **HULK** AND **GIANT-MAN** FINALLY MEET FACE TO FACE!

THE HULK! AT **LAST** I'VE FOUND YOU!

WRONG, MISTER! I FOUND **YOU**-- AND NOW I'M GONNA SHOW YOU WHAT I DO TO MY ENEMIES --NO MATTER **HOW** BIG THEY ARE!

WAIT!! DON'T BE A **FOOL!** I CAME HERE TO **HELP** YOU--TO OFFER YOU--

IT WON'T **WORK!** YOU CAN'T TRICK ME! YOU'RE MY **ENEMY--ALL MEN** ARE MY **ENEMIES!!**

THEN, WITHOUT WARNING, WITH THE FORCE OF A THUNDERBOLT, THE IN-CREDIBLE HULK STRIKES!

IT WON'T TAKE ME LONG TO CHOP YOU DOWN TO **MY SIZE**--SO I'LL BEGIN **NOW!**

12

BUT, GIANT-MAN NIMBLY PARRIES THE BLOW, DUCKING QUICKLY TO ONE SIDE...

-- WHEW! -- EVEN THOUGH HE ONLY *GRAZED* ME, IT FEELS LIKE I'VE BEEN HIT BY A *BULL-DOZER!* WHAT *POWER* HE HAS!!

AND THEN, UNEXPECTEDLY, THE TOWERING AVENGER PERFORMS A FEAT NO LIVING BEING HAS EVER DARED ATTEMPT--OR *COULD* EVER ATTEMPT--

MY ONLY HOPE IS TO KEEP HIM OFF-- BALANCE LONG ENOUGH FOR ME TO *REASON* WITH HIM!

AND THE MOST *IMPORTANT* THING IS TO WIN HIS *RESPECT*-- TO SHOW HIM HE'S UP AGAINST SOMEONE AS POWERFUL AS *HE* IS!

OKAY, HULK-- *NOW* ARE YOU READY TO TALK SENSE??

EVEN THOUGH I *KNOW* HOW STRONG HE IS, IT'S HARD TO BELIEVE HE CAN GET RIGHT UP AS THOUGH NOTHING HAS HAPPENED! HE JUST *CAN'T* BE HURT!

YOU THINK YOU CAN WEAR ME OUT? SLOW ME DOWN? YOU'RE A *FOOL*, GIANT-MAN!

YOU DON'T *KNOW* THE HULK! THE ANGRIER I GET, THE *STRONGER* I GET! AND I'VE NEVER BEEN *ANGRIER!*

SO! YOU SIDE-STEPPED MY BLOW! WELL, YOU CAN'T KEEP SIDE-STEPPING *FOREVER!*

13

AND THEN, BEFORE GIANT-MAN CAN MAKE ANOTHER MOVE, THE HULK MAKES ONE OF HIS LIGHTNING-FAST *LEAPS*--!

I'VE GOT YOU *NOW!*

NOTHING THAT *LIVES* CAN BREAK THE HULK'S GRIP!!

DON'T *KID YOURSELF*, HULK!

WHAT GOOD IS YOUR GRIP IF I SUDDENLY SHRINK DOWN TO THE SIZE OF AN *ANT??*

NO MATTER *HOW* STRONG YOU ARE, IT'S NOT TOO EASY TO KEEP A TIGHT GRIP ON A TINY *ANT*, IS IT??

AND THEN, IN THE VERY NEXT SPLIT-SECOND...

BUT HERE, I'LL MAKE *EASIER* FOR YOU-- I'LL BECOME *GIANT-MAN* AGAIN!

NOW WILL YOU STOP FIGHTING AND LISTEN TO REASON??

AND GIVE YOU A CHANCE TO *TRICK* ME?? *NEVER!* NO MATTER *HOW* YOU CHANGE YOUR SIZE, I'LL SMASH YOU *YET!!* MY STRENGTH *HAS* TO WIN IN THE END!

THEN, GRASPING THE LEDGE OF A NEARBY BUILDING, THE *HULK* BRINGS A SECTION OF THE WALL DOWN ON HIS HUGE ADVERSARY BEFORE GIANT-MAN CAN MAKE ANOTHER MOVE!

-*UGH!* MY *SHOULDER!!*

14

WHERE IS YOUR CONFIDENCE *NOW??* WHERE ARE YOUR BOASTS, YOUR SMART REMARKS? IN THE END, *NOTHING* CAN BEAT THE RAW POWER OF THE *HULK!!*

HE'S LEAPING AT ME! IF HE CONNECTS, I'M A *GONER!*

WITH PERFECT TIMING, THE TWELVE-FOOT TITAN ROLLS OUT OF HARM'S WAY AT THE LAST SECOND!!

CRASH!

AT THAT MOMENT, JUST OUTSIDE OF TOWN, THE WASP OVER-HEARS A STARTLING COMMAND....!

WE'RE ZEROED IN ON THE CENTER OF TOWN, SIR!

THEN FIRE THE SMALL BORE ATOMIC SHELL! IT WILL DAMAGE A MINIMUM OF PROPERTY, BUT IT'S SURE TO PUT THE *HULK* OUT OF ACTION!

OH *NO!!* THEY THINK THE HULK IS *ALONE!* THEY DON'T KNOW *GIANT-MAN* IS THERE!

NO TIME TO *STOP* THEM!! THEY'VE *FIRED* IT! IT'LL BE THE END OF HANK, UNLESS--

IT'S A CHANCE IN A MILLION-- BUT I'VE *GOT* TO TAKE IT!!

MADE IT! NOW, IF ONLY I CAN REACH THE DETONATING DEVICE BEFORE IT STRIKES ITS TARGET!!

I'LL KEEP TRYING TILL THE LAST SECOND-- AND, IF I'M TOO LATE-- THEN AT LEAST HANK AND I WILL GO *TOGETHER!* I'LL BE WITH THE MAN I LOVE TILL THE VERY END!!

15

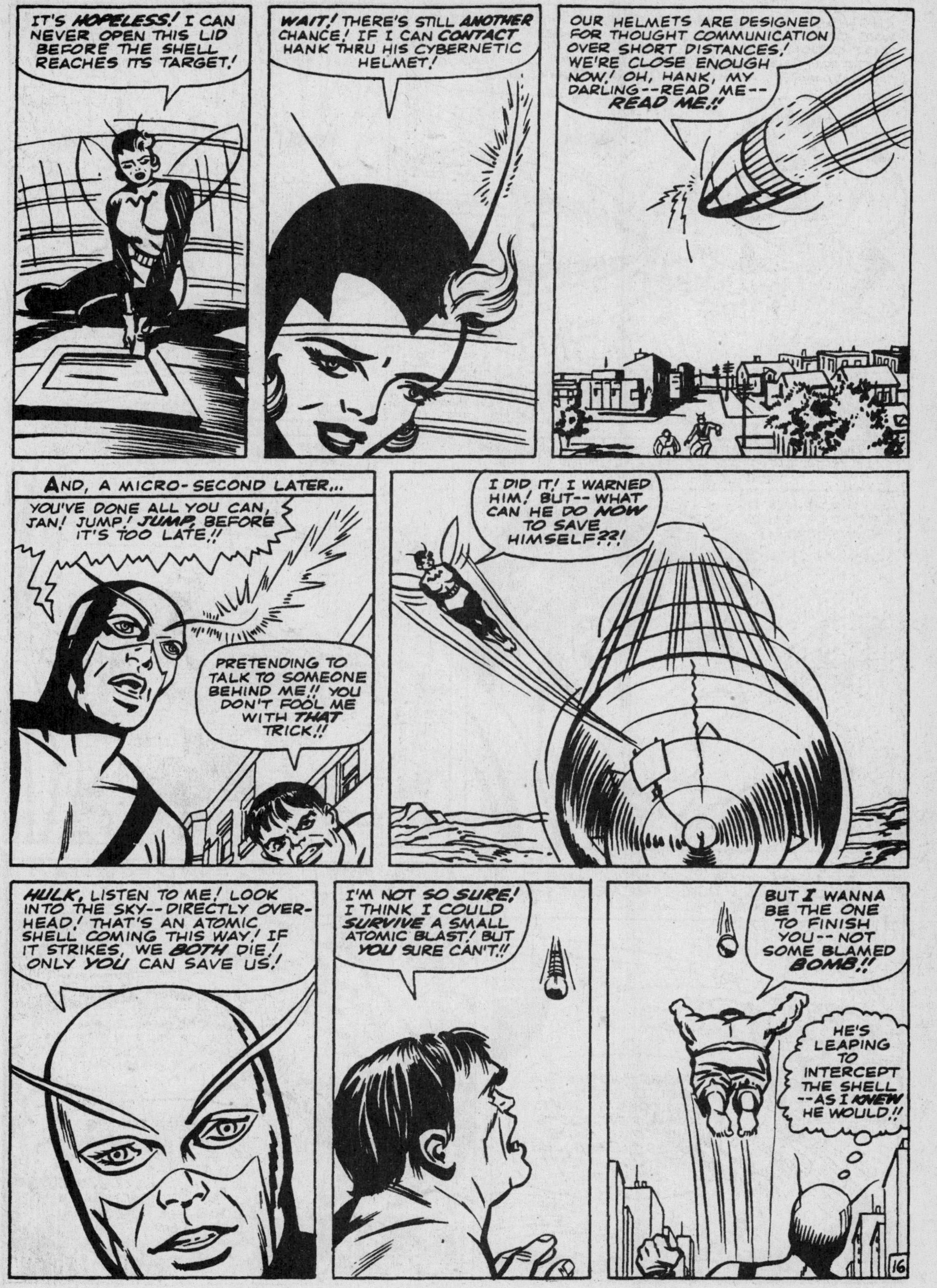
IT'S HOPELESS! I CAN NEVER OPEN THIS LID BEFORE THE SHELL REACHES ITS TARGET!
WAIT! THERE'S STILL ANOTHER CHANCE! IF I CAN CONTACT HANK THRU HIS CYBERNETIC HELMET!
OUR HELMETS ARE DESIGNED FOR THOUGHT COMMUNICATION OVER SHORT DISTANCES! WE'RE CLOSE ENOUGH NOW! OH, HANK, MY DARLING--READ ME--READ ME!!
AND, A MICRO-SECOND LATER...
YOU'VE DONE ALL YOU CAN, JAN! JUMP! JUMP, BEFORE IT'S TOO LATE!!
PRETENDING TO TALK TO SOMEONE BEHIND ME!! YOU DON'T FOOL ME WITH THAT TRICK!!
I DID IT! I WARNED HIM! BUT--WHAT CAN HE DO NOW TO SAVE HIMSELF??!
HULK, LISTEN TO ME! LOOK INTO THE SKY--DIRECTLY OVER-HEAD! THAT'S AN ATOMIC SHELL COMING THIS WAY! IF IT STRIKES, WE BOTH DIE! ONLY YOU CAN SAVE US!
I'M NOT SO SURE! I THINK I COULD SURVIVE A SMALL ATOMIC BLAST! BUT YOU SURE CAN'T!!
BUT I WANNA BE THE ONE TO FINISH YOU--NOT SOME BLAMED BOMB!!
HE'S LEAPING TO INTERCEPT THE SHELL--AS I KNEW HE WOULD!!
16

IF THIS IS GONNA BE THE END OF THE HULK, THEN WHO *CARES??* MAYBE IT'LL BE THE BEST THING THAT COULD HAPPEN!! I'M NO GOOD TO MYSELF-- OR TO ANYONE ELSE!! THE WHOLE WORLD HATES ME ALMOST AS MUCH AS I HATE *MYSELF!*

WHOOM!

WATCHING FROM A SAFE DISTANCE, THE *HUMAN TOP* SEES HIS SINISTER SCHEME RUINED BY THE POWER OF THE HULK!

WHY DID HE *DO* IT?? WHY DID HE SAVE GIANT-MAN???

THERE'S NO TELLING *WHERE* HE'LL LAND WITH THAT THING! I'D BETTER GET *OUT* OF HERE!

BUT, AS A CAPRICIOUS FATE WOULD HAVE IT, THE HULK FINALLY HURLS THE ATOMIC SHELL UP INTO THE HILLS...

THERE!! NOTHING'LL FEEL IT WHEN IT EXPLODES EXCEPT FOR A FEW ROCKS AND SOME SAND DUNES!! LOOKS LIKE *MY* TIME HASN'T COME YET!

...AND THE POTENT SHELL FINALLY EXPLODES IN THE SAME HILLS WHERE THE HUMAN TOP HAD TAKEN REFUGE...!

HE SAVED *ME*-- BUT WHAT ABOUT THE *HULK??* WAS HE HIM- SELF CAUGHT IN THE SHOCK WAVE OF THE EXPLOSION??

17

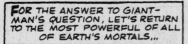

FOR THE ANSWER TO GIANT-MAN'S QUESTION, LET'S RETURN TO THE MOST POWERFUL OF ALL OF EARTH'S MORTALS...

BEIN' TOSSED LIKE A FEATHER IN THE BREEZE! EVERYTHING SPINNIN' ROUND -- BLACKING OUT--!

LATER, AFTER THE SMOKE HAS CLEARED FROM THE MODERN, LOW-YIELD ATOMIC SHELL, A FORM BEGINS TO STIR ON THE SPOT WHERE THE HULK HAD FALLEN...

BUT, IT IS NOT THE MASSIVE FORM OF THE RAMPAGING MAN-BRUTE! IT IS THE SLIM, GAUNT FIGURE OF DR. ROBERT BRUCE BANNER!

I'M ALIVE! I I'VE CHANGED BACK TO MYSELF AGAIN! THE FORCE OF THE EXPLOSION MUST HAVE DONE IT!

AND, A SHORT TIME LATER...

DAD! OH, DAD-- LOOK! GIANT-MAN WAS RIGHT! IT'S BRUCE-- THE HULK DIDN'T HARM HIM!

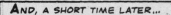

HUNDREDS OF RUGGED, HUSKY MILITARY MEN IN MY COMMAND -- BUT THAT SCATTER-BRAINED DAUGHTER OF MINE HAS TO FALL FOR A SKINNY, WEAKLING PENCIL PUSHER! BAH!

WELL, JAN, IT LOOKS LIKE I FAILED! I COULDN'T CONVINCE THE HULK TO JOIN US AGAIN!

BUT YOU SAW HIM SAVE YOUR LIFE AT THE END! PERHAPS, IN A WAY, YOU SUCCEEDED MORE THAN YOU KNOW!

THE NEXT DAY, GIANT-MAN AND THE WASP ARE BACK IN NEW YORK FOR A REGULARLY-SCHEDULED MEETING OF THE AVENGERS...

ALL MEMBERS PRESENT AND ACCOUNTED FOR, SO THE MEETING WILL COME TO ORDER!

18

WE'VE NO URGENT BUSINESS TODAY! THINGS HAVE BEEN QUIET IN TOWN SINCE LAST MEETING!

INDEED! THEN NOBODY HAS ANYTHING TO REPORT!

OH WELL, THAT'S THE WAY THE MOP FLOPS! I GUESS WE CAN'T EXPECT TO HAVE A RIP-SNORTING ADVENTURE EVERY TIME WE STEP OUT OF THE DOOR!

BLUE EYES, YOU'RE A CAUTION!

the END

NEXT ISH: MORE THRILLS AND SURPRISES WITH THE BIGGEST MAN AND THE TINIEST GAL IN ADVENTUREDOM! DON'T MISS IT!

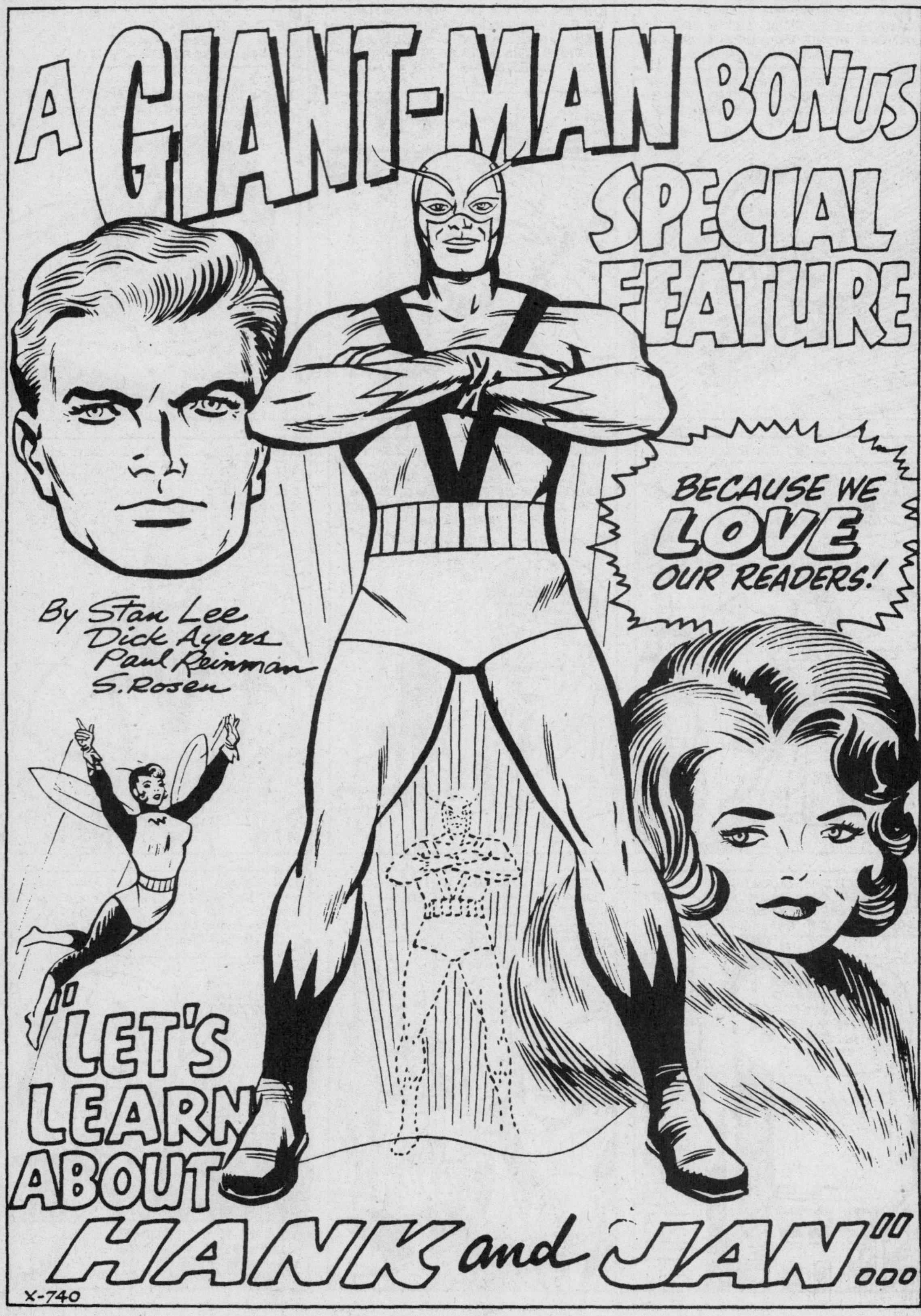
A GIANT-MAN BONUS
SPECIAL FEATURE
BECAUSE WE LOVE OUR READERS!
By Stan Lee
Dick Ayers
Paul Reinman
S. Rosen
"LET'S LEARN ABOUT HANK and JAN"...
X-740

YOU ARE LOOKING AT ONE OF THE MOST ASTONISHING MEN ON EARTH --- THE RENOWNED BIOCHEMIST, HENRY PYM! SOFT-SPOKEN, THOUGHTFUL, HE IS A MAN OF MANY MOODS!

WHEN HE TAKES ON THE IDENTITY OF THE WORLD-FAMOUS GIANT-MAN, THE CYBERNETIC HELMET HE WEARS IS FAR MORE THAN JUST ORNAMENTATION!

BENEATH IT'S COLORFUL EXTERIOR IS AN INGENIOUS CYBERNETIC "NERVE CENTER..."

BY MERELY USING MENTAL IMPULSES, GIANT-MAN CAN ACTIVATE HIS ANTENNAE...

...SENDING OUT CYBERNETIC FORCE WAVES WHICH CAN INSTANTLY ALTER THE SIZE OF HIS GORGEOUS PARTNER-IN-PERIL --- THE WASP!

AND HIS OWN SIZE ALSO CAN BE CHANGED IN A SPLIT-SECOND, BY MERELY USING THE NORMALLY UNTAPPED POWER OF HIS BRAIN...

SO QUICKLY CAN GIANT-MAN SHRINK TO ANT-MAN THAT MANY OF HIS FOES THINK HE HAS BECOME INVISIBLE!

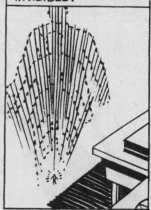

THE ASTONISHING ANT-MAN CAN ALSO GROW FROM ANT-SIZE TO GIANT-SIZE WITH EQUAL SPEED AND EASE...

...AND ONLY HIS OWN MENTAL CONTROL CAN LIMIT THE EXTENT OF HIS GROWTH...

HE MUST BE CAREFUL NOT TO EXCEED A HEIGHT OF TWELVE FEET, FOR AS HE GROWS BEYOND THAT HEIGHT, HE BECOMES PROPORTIONATELY WEAKER!

2.

ONE OF GIANT-MAN'S NEWEST AND CLEVEREST GADGETS IS THIS REVOLUTIONARY CLIMBING-AID DEVICE...FOR USE WHILE HE'S ANT-SIZE!

SHOOTING IT UP TO ANY OBJECT, ITS SUCTION PADS ADHERE FIRMLY...AS ANT-MAN HOLDS THE SPOOLED-OUT WIRE BELOW...

THEN, AT THE PRESS OF AN ELECTRONIC BUTTON, THE WIRE RETRACTS, PULLING THE DIMINUTIVE ADVENTURER UP WITH IT!

ANOTHER BRILLIANT AID IS THE "AIR-GUN" WHICH HENRY PYM DESIGNED FOR THE WONDERFUL WASP! WORN ON HER WRIST, IT IS A TRULY UNIQUE WEAPON!

BY MEANS OF A CABLE RELEASE ATTACHED TO HER FINGER, THE WASP FIRES HER "GUN" BY MERELY BENDING HER WRIST!

ONE HIGH-POWERED BLAST EXERTS ENOUGH FORCE TO TOPPLE ALMOST ANY FOE!

ANOTHER OF ANT-MAN'S ASSETS IS HIS ABILITY TO RIDE HIS FLYING ANTS, OR TO BE PULLED BY THEM IN HIS INSECT-SIZED CHARIOT!

HOWEVER, HE NEEDS ALMOST NO WEAPONS OR GADGETS WHEN HE HAS GROWN TO HIS 12-FOOT GIANT-SIZE!

HIS TREMENDOUSLY-INCREASED STRENGTH IS USUALLY ALL HE NEEDS TO HELP HIM OVERCOME ANY FOES OR OBSTACLES!

3.

THIS IS A MEDICINE-BALL SHOOTER HANK HAS RECENTLY DEVELOPED...

FIRING A HEAVY MEDICINE BALL FROM WALL TO WALL, IT AIDS HIM IN DEVELOPING HIS SPEED...

...TODAY, AFTER MANY LONG HOURS OF PRACTICE, GIANT-MAN'S SPEED, AGILITY, AND COORDINATION ARE MANY TIMES WHAT THEY WERE A YEAR AGO!

WHEN HE ATTAINS HIS FULL FIGHTING SIZE, GIANT-MAN CAN EASILY PRESS UPWARDS OF 2,000 POUNDS! WITH SUCH AWESOME STRENGTH, HE HAS LITTLE NEED FOR WEAPONS!

HIS AMAZING DEXTERITY, COUPLED WITH HIS OVER-DEVELOPED MUSCLES, ARE LIVING PROOF OF WHAT CONSTANT EXERCISE AND PRACTICE CAN DO!

HIS POWERFUL HANDS, TRAINED IN KARATE BY HIS FELLOW AVENGER, CAPTAIN AMERICA, ARE CAPABLE OF SPLITTING THE STRONGEST TELEPHONE POLE IN TWO!

4.

ONE OF THE MOST SPECTACULAR OF HIS INVENTIONS IS THIS INCREDIBLE "SKY-HOOK" OUTSIDE THE WALL OF HIS HEAD-QUARTERS BUILDING...

ACTIVATED BY A MENTAL IMPULSE FROM HIS TWIN ANTENNAE, THE SKY-HOOK COMES DOWN TO HIM, AND THEN ---

...ITS TENSION SPRING RELEASE ENABLES HIM TO REACH HIS QUARTERS IN A SPLIT-SECOND!

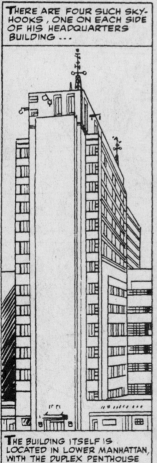

THERE ARE FOUR SUCH SKY-HOOKS, ONE ON EACH SIDE OF HIS HEADQUARTERS BUILDING...

THE BUILDING ITSELF IS LOCATED IN LOWER MANHATTAN, WITH THE DUPLEX PENTHOUSE SUITE OCCUPIED BY GIANT-MAN ON LONG-TERM LEASE!

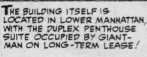
5.

LAB SECTION AND WORK-SHOP OF GIANT-MAN'S DUPLEX PENT-HOUSE... PAID FOR WITH ROYALTIES RECEIVED BY HENRY PYM FOR PATENTED BIO-CHEMICAL DISCOVERIES!

NOTE OVERSIZED GYM AND TRAINING AREA, WHERE GIANT-MAN CAN GET THE EXERCISE HIS ENORMOUS MUSCLES REQUIRE DAILY...

LOWER FLOOR CONTAINS REFERENCE ROOMS, COMMUNICATIONS SECTION, AND LIVING QUARTERS... ALL SOUND-PROOFED AND FITTED WITH COMPLEX BURGLAR ALARMS!

WOULD YOU LIKE TO SEE MORE OF THESE SPECIAL BONUS FEATURES? BE SURE TO WRITE AND TELL US, HEAR?

WATCH FOR OUR NEXT SPECIAL FEATURE! I HAVE A SNEAKY SUS-PICION IT'LL STAR MY FAVORITE HEROINE... NAMELY ME!

The End.

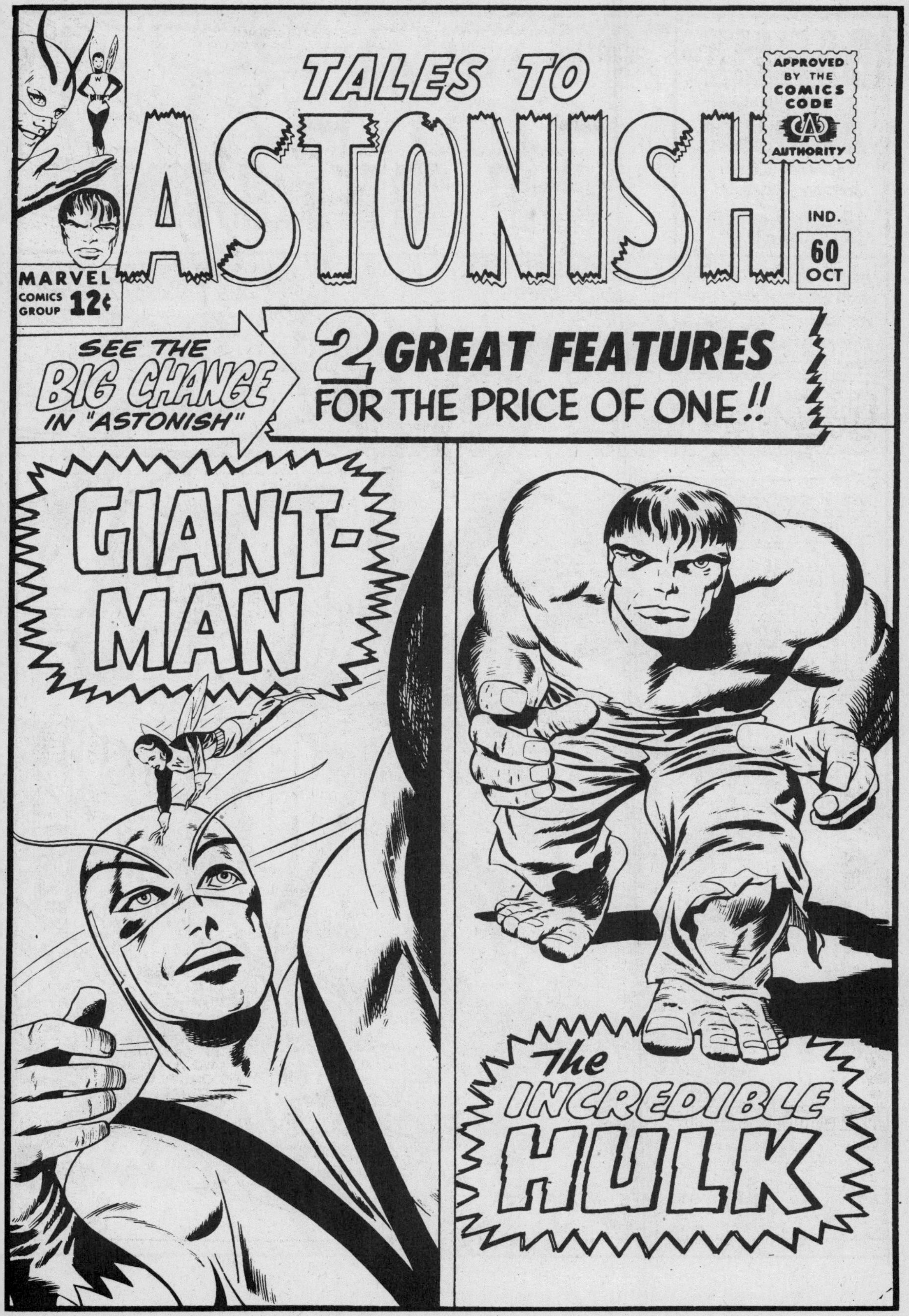

TALES TO ASTONISH
APPROVED BY THE COMICS CODE AUTHORITY
MARVEL COMICS GROUP 12¢
IND. 60 OCT
SEE THE BIG CHANGE IN "ASTONISH"
2 GREAT FEATURES FOR THE PRICE OF ONE!!
GIANT-MAN
The INCREDIBLE HULK

GIANT-MAN and the wonderful WASP

"THE BEASTS OF BERLIN!"

EXCITINGLY WRITTEN BY..... STAN LEE
EXQUISITELY DRAWN BY....... DICK AYERS
EXTRAVAGANTLY INKED BY..... PAUL REINMAN
EMOTIONALLY LETTERED BY... ART SIMEK

X-765

1

YOU'D ALL BETTER *LEAVE* NOW! I'VE NEVER *SEEN* GIANT-MAN SO UPSET BEFORE! I'M SURE HE DOESN'T *MEAN* WHAT HE SAID--!!

DON'T WORRY, MA'AM! WE UNDERSTAND! WE SHOULDN'T HAVE BARGED IN THE WAY WE DID!

TELL GIANT-MAN IF THERE'S ANYTHING WE CAN DO TO *HELP*--

GO! GO! GO!

GM

OUR LEADER G.M.

GIANT-MAN BOOSTERS

DID YOU *HEAR* THEM?? AFTER THE DISGRACEFUL WAY YOU *YELLED* AT THEM, ALL THEY WANT TO DO IS *HELP* YOU! I HOPE YOU'RE *PROUD* OF YOURSELF, HENRY PYM!!

KNOCK IT OFF, JAN! I'M IN NO MOOD FOR A *LECTURE!* I JUST READ SOME *BAD NEWS!!* AN OLD FRIEND OF MINE IS IN *BIG TROUBLE* --AND I'VE GOT TO HELP HIM-- SOMEHOW!!

WHO *IS* IT, HANK?

HIS NAME'S *LEE KEARNS!* HE'S AN EX-F.B.I. MAN,* AND ONE OF THE BRAVEST, MOST PATRIOTIC MEN YOU'LL EVER *KNOW!*

I SEEM TO REMEMBER YOU MENTIONING HIM! WHAT *HAPPENED* TO HIM?

*SEE *TALES TO ASTONISH #44* --EDITOR.

ACCORDING TO THIS NEWSPAPER REPORT, THE REDS CAUGHT HIM IN EAST BERLIN--BEHIND THE WALL--AND THEY ACCUSE HIM OF SPYING ON THEM! THERE'S NOTHING OUR GOVERNMENT CAN DO OFFICIALLY TO HELP HIM!

DAILY GLOBE

EXTRA

AMERICAN CAPTURED BEHIND IRON CURTAIN!

REDS CLAIM LEE KEARNS WAS ON SPYING MISSION...SENTENCED TO DIE IN EAST BERLIN! (PHOTOS ON PG. TWO)

IF HE ISN'T *RESCUED* BEFORE FRIDAY, HE'LL BE *EXECUTED!!*

BUT HOW CAN THE *AVENGERS* HOPE TO FREE SOMEONE FROM THE HEART OF EAST BERLIN??

THIS ISN'T A CASE FOR THE *AVENGERS!* THERE'S NO TIME TO GET THEM TOGETHER! I'VE GOT TO DO IT *ALONE!*

BUT-- IT'S *IMPOSSIBLE!*

SO *WHAT??* LEE KEARNS IS MY *FRIEND!!*

WELL, IF YOUR MIND'S MADE UP, I'LL GET PACKED RIGHT AWAY--!!

NO! THE REDS KILLED MY WIFE YEARS AGO!! I CAN'T LET *YOU* ENDANGER YOURSELF THE SAME WAY!!

YOU PROMISED THAT YOU'D TELL ME HOW IT HAPPENED SOME DAY, HANK--

ALRIGHT-- SINCE THE YEARS HAVE PASSED, IT ISN'T AS PAINFUL NOW.! I THINK I CAN TALK ABOUT IT--AT LAST--!

2

MARIA HAD BEEN A HUNGARIAN FREEDOM FIGHTER WHO CAME TO AMERICA AND MARRIED ME!

BUT, SHE MISSED HER HOMELAND, AND HER FAMILY! AND SO-- THINKING IT WAS SAFE, WE RETURNED TO HUNGARY FOR OUR HONEYMOON...

"BUT, WE WERE SOON TO LEARN IT *WASN'T* SAFE! THE REDS RECOGNIZED HER-- AND, ONE DAY, IN BROAD DAYLIGHT--"

YOU WILL NOT MAKE A SOUND, MARIA TROVAYA, OR YOUR AMERICAN HUSBAND WILL BE SHOT!

WHAT *IS* THIS??

SILENCE, AMERICAN!

"THEN, BY THE TIME I REALIZED WHAT WAS HAPPENING--IT WAS TOO LATE!!"

WAIT!! YOU CAN'T-- --UGH!--

AND THAT WAS THE LAST I EVER SAW OF HER!! I WAS LATER TOLD THAT SHE WAS-- DEAD! THE NEWS ALMOST DROVE ME OUT OF MY MIND! I LOST TRACK OF TIME -- OF PEOPLE -- OF EVERYTHING! BUT THEN, WHEN I RECOVERED, I PLEDGED MY LIFE TO FIGHTING EVIL -- TO AVENGE MARIA'S DEATH!

BUT-- ARE YOU *POSITIVE* THAT SHE REALLY DIED? DO YOU HAVE ABSOLUTE *PROOF??*

YES-- UNFORTUNATELY I DO -- SO I DON'T EVEN HAVE A SLIM HOPE TO HANG ON TO -- BUT -- I'D RATHER NOT TALK ABOUT IT ANY MORE--!

WHAT A FOOL I'VE BEEN! I SHOULD HAVE GUESSED-- *THAT* MUST BE WHY HE SOMETIMES SEEMS SO UNROMANTIC --SO DISTANT! HE STILL CAN'T FORGET MARIA, HIS FIRST WIFE!

HER WOMAN'S INTUITION TELLS HER NOT TO INSIST--AND SO, THE WASP TELLS GIANT-MAN SHE UNDERSTANDS--TELLS HIM SHE'LL REMAIN BEHIND WHILE HE ATTEMPTS TO BREACH THE RED WALL ALONE! THEN, A FEW HOURS LATER, A SPECIALLY-ASSIGNED AIR FORCE JET SPEEDS THRU THE STRATOSPHERE AT BETTER THAN TWO-THOUSAND MILES PER HOUR...

I DIDN'T TELL JAN THE *WHOLE* STORY! LEE KEARNS HAD WRITTEN TO ME LAST WEEK--TELLING ME THAT THE REDS HAD CREATED A POWERFUL SECRET WEAPON--

THAT'S WHY HE DARED TO CROSS THE WALL! HE WANTED TO LEARN MORE ABOUT IT! AND THAT'S WHY *I* MUST CROSS THE WALL-- THIS MISSION CAN *NOT* BE ALLOWED TO FAIL!!

3

LATER, IN THE VERY SHADOW OF THE BERLIN WALL, GIANT-MAN IS BRIEFED BY A NEUTRAL CORRESPONDANT...

LEE KEARNS CROSSED THE WALL AS A PRIVATE CITIZEN, AND WAS CAPTURED AND CONVICTED OF SPYING! THERE'S NOTHING THAT ANYONE CAN DO TO HELP!

THAT'S *YOUR* OPINION, FRIEND! I'VE GOT MY *OWN*!

REMEMBER, THIS WALL IS ONE OF THE MOST-HEAVILY-GUARDED PLACES ON EARTH!

I'LL BE SURE TO KEEP IT IN MIND! AND NOW, I'VE GOT *THINGS* TO DO!

VERBOTEN!

I WISH YOU LUCK, AMERICAN! YOU SHALL *NEED* IT!

I'LL WAIT TILL HE'S OUT OF SIGHT, AND THEN GO INTO ACTION!

THEN, AS SOON AS HE IS ALONE, IN THE SHADOWS OF THE GRIM WALL-- ONE SHARP *THOUGHT* ACTIVATES GIANT-MAN'S CYBERNETIC ANTENNAE, AND...

DESPITE THE GREAT POWER OF GIANT-MAN...

...THIS IS ONE JOB THAT *ANT-MAN* CAN DO BETTER!

ALL I'LL NEED IS MY SUCTION-TIPPED SPRING-POWERED CLIMBING DEVICE!

AND SO, SECONDS LATER, ONE OF HENRY PYM'S NEWEST AND MOST USEFUL CREATIONS IS BROUGHT INTO PLAY--

ONCE IT STICKS TO A SURFACE, THE UNBREAKABLE CORD ROLLS UP LIKE A WINDOW SHADE, TAKING ANT-MAN *WITH* IT!

THEN, REACHING THE TOP OF THE WALL...

SO FAR, SO GOOD! BUT, THIS IS ONLY THE *BEGINNING*!!

4

WHAT GOES UP, MUST COME DOWN! AND ANYONE SEEING ME, WILL TAKE ME FOR SOME SORT OF *INSECT!*

I *MADE* IT! NOW, I'LL USE MY CYBERNETIC ANTENNAE TO SUMMON SOME *ANTS!*

LUCKY THAT CYBERNETIC THOUGHT COMMANDS ARE THE SAME ANY-WHERE! LANGUAGE IS NO BARRIER TO ANTS!

I AM *ANT-MAN!* I COMMAND YOU TO FLY ME TO MY DESTINATION! I AM YOUR LEADER!

AND SO...

THE REDS HAVE A RADAR WATCHDOG SYSTEM SECOND TO NONE IN THIS AREA! BUT THEY'RE ABOUT TO LEARN THAT YOU CAN'T GUARD YOURSELF AGAINST *EVERYTHING!*

I'D LOVE TO SEE THEIR FACES IF THEY EVER LEARNED THEY'RE BEING INVADED BY A MAN ASTRIDE A FLYING ANT!!

NOW I'D BETTER SEND SOME CYBERNETIC COMMANDS TO THE ANTS WHICH ARE SURE TO BE WITHIN THE EAST BERLIN PRISON!

LATER, IN RESPONSE TO *ANT-MAN'S* MENTAL COMMAND, TWO SMALL ANTS RIDE ATOP A VOPO'S* BOOT...

*VOPO: RED POLICE GUARD. —EDITOR.

EVENTUALLY, THEY ARE BROUGHT TO THE CELL OF HENRY PYM'S IMPRISONED FRIEND, FROM WHERE THEY BROADCAST A CYBERNETIC SIGNAL....

...WHICH, WHEN PICKED UP BY ANT-MAN'S SUPER-SENSITIVE ANTENNAE, GUIDES HIM UNERRINGLY TO THE CORRECT CELL!

THIS IS THE PLACE! BUT, A RED AGENT JUST ENTERED! I'D BETTER WAIT AND SEE WHAT HAPPENS...

5

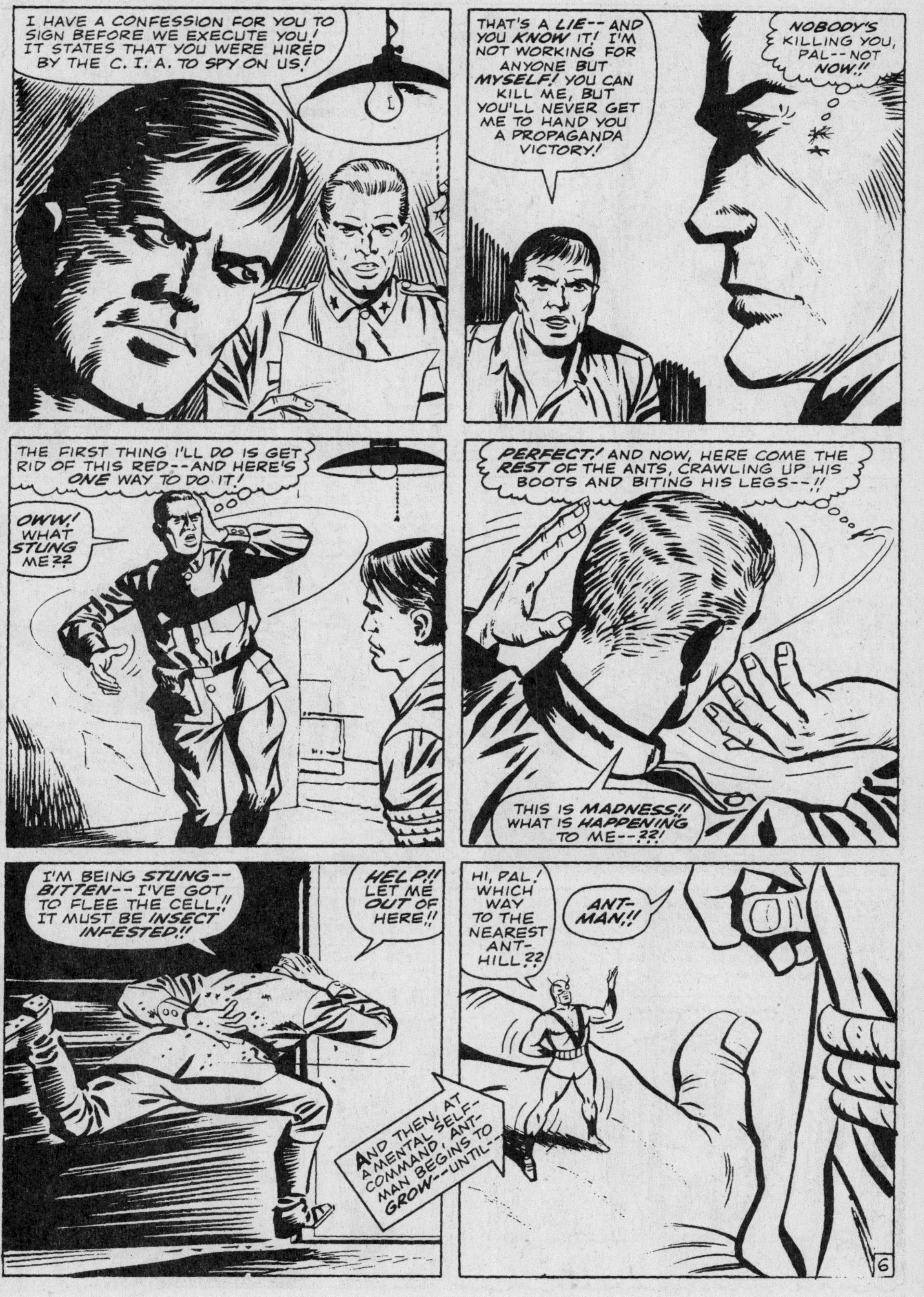
I HAVE A CONFESSION FOR YOU TO SIGN BEFORE WE EXECUTE YOU! IT STATES THAT YOU WERE HIRED BY THE C. I. A. TO SPY ON US!
THAT'S A LIE-- AND YOU KNOW IT! I'M NOT WORKING FOR ANYONE BUT MYSELF! YOU CAN KILL ME, BUT YOU'LL NEVER GET ME TO HAND YOU A PROPAGANDA VICTORY!
NOBODY'S KILLING YOU, PAL--NOT NOW!!
THE FIRST THING I'LL DO IS GET RID OF THIS RED--AND HERE'S ONE WAY TO DO IT!
OWW! WHAT STUNG ME??
PERFECT! AND NOW, HERE COME THE REST OF THE ANTS, CRAWLING UP HIS BOOTS AND BITING HIS LEGS--!!
THIS IS MADNESS!! WHAT IS HAPPENING TO ME--??!
I'M BEING STUNG-- BITTEN-- I'VE GOT TO FLEE THE CELL!! IT MUST BE INSECT INFESTED!!
HELP!! LET ME OUT OF HERE!!
AND THEN, AT A MENTAL SELF-COMMAND, ANT-MAN BEGINS TO GROW--UNTIL--
HI, PAL! WHICH WAY TO THE NEAREST ANT-HILL??
ANT-MAN!!
6

UH UH--THAT WAS A FEW SECONDS AGO! RIGHT NOW, I'M A HALF-SIZE VERSION OF *GIANT-MAN!* NOW, WHAT'S THIS ABOUT A NEW RED WEAPON?

IT'S THEIR MOST CLOSELY GUARDED SECRET! WE'VE GOT TO *DESTROY* IT, NO MATTER *WHAT* THE COST! LET ME TELL YOU--

IT'S NOT A WEAPON IN THE USUAL SENSE OF THE WORD! IT'S A STRANGE *RAY* WHICH CAN INCREASE THE INTELLIGENCE OF BEASTS! THE REDS DISCOVERED IT ACCIDENTALLY--THERE'S ONLY *ONE* IN EXISTENCE! BUT, THEY'RE TRYING TO MAKE OTHERS!

"THEY'VE BEEN USING IT ON *GORILLAS*--MAKING THEM SMART ENOUGH TO *READ*--TO OBEY ANY COMMANDS! I'VE SEEN IT WITH MY OWN EYES!!"

"THEY'RE SECRETLY TRYING TO CREATE AN ARMY OF *BEASTS!* IMAGINE WHAT IT WOULD *MEAN*-- THE STRENGTH OF A GORILLA, AND THE INTELLIGENCE OF A HUMAN!!"

"BUT THEY HAVEN'T BEEN ABLE TO *DUPLICATE* THE RAY MACHINE YET--WHICH IS WHY IT'S SO CAREFULLY GUARDED! IF WE CAN SMASH IT, WE'LL DEFEAT THEIR PLAN!"

"EVEN WHILE WE SPEAK, THEY'RE CREATING MORE AND MORE BESTIAL GUARDS--STATIONING THEM AT EVERY ENTRANCE AND EXIT TO GUARD THE RAY MACHINE UNTIL THEY THEMSELVES CAN LEARN HOW AND WHY IT WORKS!"

I GET THE PICTURE, FELLA! I'LL TURN INTO *GIANT-MAN*, AND WE'LL TEAR THIS PLACE APART!!

IT WON'T BE THAT EASY --NOT EVEN FOR *YOU!* THEY'RE STRONGER THAN YOU SUSPECT!!

7

THERE'S ONE OF THEM *NOW!* HE'S ACTING AS A *GUARD!*

LOOK AT THE *SIZE* OF HIM!!

UH OH--THIS IS NO JOKING MATTER! I FORGOT HOW *KEEN* A BEAST'S SENSE OF SMELL IS--HE KNOWS WE'RE *HERE!*

ARGHHHH!

WE HAVEN'T A *CHANCE!* HE'S *GOT* US!

STEADY, LEE! DON'T LET HIS *SIZE* THROW YOU! I'VE GOT A TRICK OR TWO UP MY SLEEVE! WATCH--!

FIRST, BY DUCKING UNDER THE ASSAULT AND ROLLING WITH THE BLOW, I TURN HIS WEIGHT ADVANTAGE *AGAINST* HIM, IN THE BEST JUDO FASHION!!

I HOPE YOU'RE TAKING NOTES, LEE--THERE MAY BE A *TEST* LATER!

AND NOW, MANEUVER #2--A QUICK CHANGE IN SIZE!!

THERE'S NOTHING LIKE HAVING *SURPRISE* ON YOUR SIDE--

WHAM!

AND, THE IMPORTANT THING IS-- TO TAKE *ADVANTAGE* OF IT! --LIKE *THIS!*

8

THIS IS *INCREDIBLE!* I NEVER DREAMED THAT *ANT-MAN* WAS ALSO *GIANT-MAN!!* AND YET-- I SHOULD HAVE *GUESSED!*

TO THINK-- YOU DEFEATED A GIGANTIC GORILLA WITH YOUR *BARE HANDS!*-- PERHAPS WE *DO* HAVE A CHANCE!!

THAT'S THE WAY TO TALK, LEE! NOW, I'LL BECOME NORMAL SIZE WHILE WE PLAN OUR NEXT MOVE--!

REMEMBER, WE CAN'T LEAVE HERE TILL WE'VE DESTROYED THE *INTELLIGENCE RAY* BEFORE THEY CAN DUPLICATE IT!

THAT MAKES SENSE TO *ME!* BUT, WHERE *IS* THE RAY?

I BELIEVE IT'S IN THE LAB-- IN THIS BUILDING! WE CAN *REACH* IT!

BUT, REACHING IT AND *DESTROYING* IT ARE TWO DIFFERENT THINGS! IT'S GUARDED BY HALF A DOZEN MORE GORILLAS!

AND, THOUGH YOU MANAGED TO BEAT *ONE* BEFORE-- THESE SIX ARE THE BIGGEST AND STRONGEST OF ALL!

IN *THAT* CASE, WE'D BETTER GET STARTED! I HATE TO FIGHT PAST MY BEDTIME!

GIANT-MAN, I WONDER IF ANY-ONE KNOWS HOW MUCH *COURAGE* IS MASKED BEHIND THOSE FLIPPANT REMARKS OF YOURS?

LISTEN! THE ALARM!! THEY KNOW WE'VE ESCAPED!

AND, IN A COMMAND ROOM, NOT FAR AWAY...

WE HAVE JUST RECEIVED WORD FROM COMRADE LEADER! WE ARE TO WORK AT TOP SPEED, PRODUCING AN ARMY OF INTELLIGENT BEASTS AS SOON AS POSSIBLE!

DA, COMRADE GENERAL!

9

AND, IN THE CLOSELY-GUARDED RED LAB...

ACTIVATE THE RAY MACHINE! BRING IN MORE GORILLAS! WE MUST HURRY!

GOOD! GOOD! PLACE THEM IN FRONT OF THE RAY, AND THEN TURN THEM INTO INTELLIGENT, OBEDIENT SERVANTS OF THE FATHERLAND!

NOTICE THE ONE GORILLA WHOSE INTELLIGENCE HAS BEEN INCREASED BY THE RAY! SEE HOW EASILY HE CAN COMMAND THE OTHERS!

BUT, BEFORE THE GRIM RAY CAN BE SWITCHED ON, THERE IS A SUDDEN INTERRUPTION--!

DON'T GO 'WAY, BOYS! THE PARTY'S JUST BEGINNING--!

WHO WANTS TO BE FIRST FOR FUN AND GAMES!

HE FIGHTS LIKE A DEMON POSSESSED! STOP HIM, MY OBEDIENT SLAVE! STOP HIM!

IT LOOKS BAD! ONE I CAN LICK-- BUT SIX--?!

10

WELL, THIS IS A TIME FOR *BRAINS*, NOT *BRAWN*.!!

SO IT'S *BACK DOWN* TO *ANT-SIZE* FOR ME!

AND, AS THE STAGGERINGLY-POWERFUL BEASTS CRASH INTO EACH OTHER IN THEIR FRANTIC SEARCH FOR THEIR MISSING PREY, THEY DON'T NOTICE THE INSECT-SIZED FORM WHO QUICKLY DARTS AWAY.!!

—WHEW— THAT WAS A *CLOSE* ONE!

NOW, MY NEXT STEP IS TO *QUICKLY* CONTACT A *FLYING ANT*.!! I HOPE THERE'S ONE NEARBY!

AH, SO FAR MY LUCK'S HOLDING OUT! NOW, *LITTLE FRIEND*, SUPPOSE YOU CARRY ME TO THE *LAB*—LIKE *FAST*.!!

AND, A FEW SECONDS LATER...

WELL, YOU MAY NEVER WIN THE KENTUCKY DERBY, BUT YOU'RE OKAY IN *MY* LEAGUE! THAT MUST BE THE RAY—RIGHT AHEAD OF US!

SUDDENLY, THE STARTLED REDS SEE—

LOOK.! THE *RAY.!!* IT'S TURNING TOWARDS *US*.!!

IT *CAN'T* BE MOVING BY *ITSELF.!!* AND YET, I DON'T *SEE* ANYONE—.!!

I'VE GOT A *THEORY*.!! AND, IF IT WORKS, WE'LL *BEAT* THESE REDS, *YET!*

AND, IF IT *DOESN'T* WORK, KEARNS AND I BETTER RESERVE A COMFORTABLE CELL FOR OURSELVES IN EAST BERLIN—BECAUSE WE WON'T BE LEAVING!

11

THE RAY IS *HITTING* US!! IT--IT MAKES ME FEEL *STRANGE*--*BESTIAL*--I--I LONG FOR THE *JUNGLE!*

YOU ARE GOING *MAD,* COMRADE!! BUT--WAIT--NOW *I* FEEL STRANGE, TOO--!

WITHIN MINUTES, THE POWER OF THE MYSTERIOUS RAY BEGIN TO ASSUME THE MANNERISMS AND MENTALITY OF ANTHROPOID *APES!!*

IT *WORKED!!* I *SUSPECTED* THAT THE RAY WOULD AFFECT HUMANS THE SAME AS IT AFFECTED *BEASTS*--ONLY IN *REVERSE!*

AND NOW, THIS IS MY CHANCE TO *WRECK* THEIR DIABOLICAL WEAPON, ONCE AND FOR ALL--!

BUT THEN...

ANT-MAN-- LOOK OUT!! THE GORILLAS!!

OH! I SHOULDN'T HAVE SHOUTED!! THEY'RE TURNING--!!

I'M *DONE FOR!* SAVE YOURSELF, ANT-MAN-- SMASH THEIR RAY--!!

DON'T WORRY, LEE--WE'LL SMASH IT, ALRIGHT--BUT I'M NOT DESERTING *YOU!!* HOLD ON--HERE I COME--!!

GOOD! THE GORILLAS ARE TURNING! THEY HEAR MY VOICE BUT CAN'T *SEE* ME! IT'S *MADDENING* TO THEM!

NOW, I'LL JUST SHOOT OUT MY "CLIMBING WIRE" WITH ENOUGH FORCE FOR IT TO ENCIRCLE *ALL* THE GORILLAS AT ONCE!

12

HMMM, NOT A BAD SHOT FOR A STUFFY OL' BIOCHEMIST!!

SAY, I JUST REALIZED SOMETHING! THE GORILLA GUARDS ARE ACTING LIKE ORDINARY BEASTS NOW--IT'S AS THOUGH THEIR INTELLIGENCE HAS RETURNED TO NORMAL AGAIN!

THAT MEANS THE RAY'S EFFECTS AREN'T PERMANENT! IT MUST BE RENEWED EVERY SO OFTEN! EVEN THE RED OFFICERS WHOM I CAUGHT WITH THE RAY WILL RETURN TO NORMAL SOON!

BUT, I'M GOING TO TAKE NO CHANCES...

I'LL BECOME GIANT-MAN AGAIN, AND MAKE SURE THIS RAY NEVER DOES ANY MORE HARM!!

YOU DID IT!

I HEAR MORE RED TROOPS COMING! THE COMMOTION MUST HAVE ALERTED THE VOPOS--BUT IT DOESN'T MATTER NOW!

EVEN THOUGH ESCAPE IS IMPOSSIBLE, NO MATTER WHAT HAPPENS TO US NOW, IT WILL BE WORTH IT! FOR, WE HAVE KEPT THE REDS FROM DISCOVERING THE SECRET OF A POTENT WEAPON!!

I AGREE WITH YOU, LEE--EXCEPT FOR ONE THING--

--WHO SAYS ESCAPE IS IMPOSSIBLE?! FOLLOW ME!!

AFTER THEM!!

THEY'RE HEADING FOR THE WALL!

13

GIANT-MAN!! YOU'LL NEVER MAKE IT OVER THE WALL!! YOU HAVEN'T ENOUGH *ROOM* TO GET A GOOD START FOR YOUR *JUMP!!*

JUMP?? JUMPING IS FOR *NORMAL*-SIZED MEN! JUST PUT YOUR HEAD DOWN, SHUT YOUR EYES, AND HANG ON!! WE'RE GOING *THRU!!*

WHOOM!

SAY! HOW ABOUT THIS RECEPTION COMMITTEE, LEE? PRETTY TERRIFIC, I'D SAY!

YOU CAN SLOW DOWN NOW, GENTS! SOMEHOW, I DON'T THINK THE COMRADES WILL CHASE YOU ANY FURTHER!

THEN, A SHORT TIME LATER...

BIG FELLA, ALL I CAN SAY IS-- YOU MAKE ME PROUD TO BE AN AMERICAN! I KNOW YOU DON'T WANT ANY THANKS, BUT IF EVER I CAN--

FORGET IT, FRIEND! IT'S ALL IN A DAY'S WORK!

AND, WITHIN THE HOUR, HENRY PYM IS WINGING HIS WAY BACK ACROSS THE ATLANTIC--

CHALK UP ANOTHER BLOW FOR LIBERTY! PERHAPS, IN SOME SMALL WAY, I'VE AVENGED MARIA'S DEATH! AT ANY RATE, WHEREVER SHE IS, I PRAY SHE KNOWS--AND UNDERSTANDS!

THEN, AFTER REACHING THE STATES, HANK GIVES JAN A BRIEF REPORT...

IT WASN'T MUCH, JAN-- I FOUGHT A FEW MONKEYS AND MANAGED TO SLIP A FRIEND OUT FROM BEHIND THE IRON CURTAIN!

IS *THAT* SO?! WELL, MR. PYM, FOR *YOUR* INFORMATION, THE LATE TV NEWS HAS A REPORT OF SOMEONE, WHO ALMOST TOOK E. BERLIN *APART!* NOW, WHO DO YOU SUPPOSE THAT CAN BE??

CAN YOU GIVE ME A *HINT*, JAN?? I HAVEN'T THE SLIGHTEST IDEA!

GOOD NEWS, FRIENDS!! YOUR ENJOYMENT IS ONLY *HALF* THRU! DON'T WASTE A MINUTE! TURN THE PAGE RIGHT AWAY AND START READING THE FIRST IN A CONTINUING SERIES OF THE INCREDIBLE *HULK!* BE SURE TO TELL US HOW YOU *LIKE* (OR--ULP--*DISLIKE*) THE IDEA OF THE *HULK* SHARING *TALES TO ASTONISH* WITH OL' HIGH POCKETS! AND, UNTIL NEXT ISH, DON'T TAKE MORE THAN A COUPLE OF GROWTH PILLS A DAY-- CEILINGS ARE *SO* EXPENSIVE TO REPAIR!

the END

14

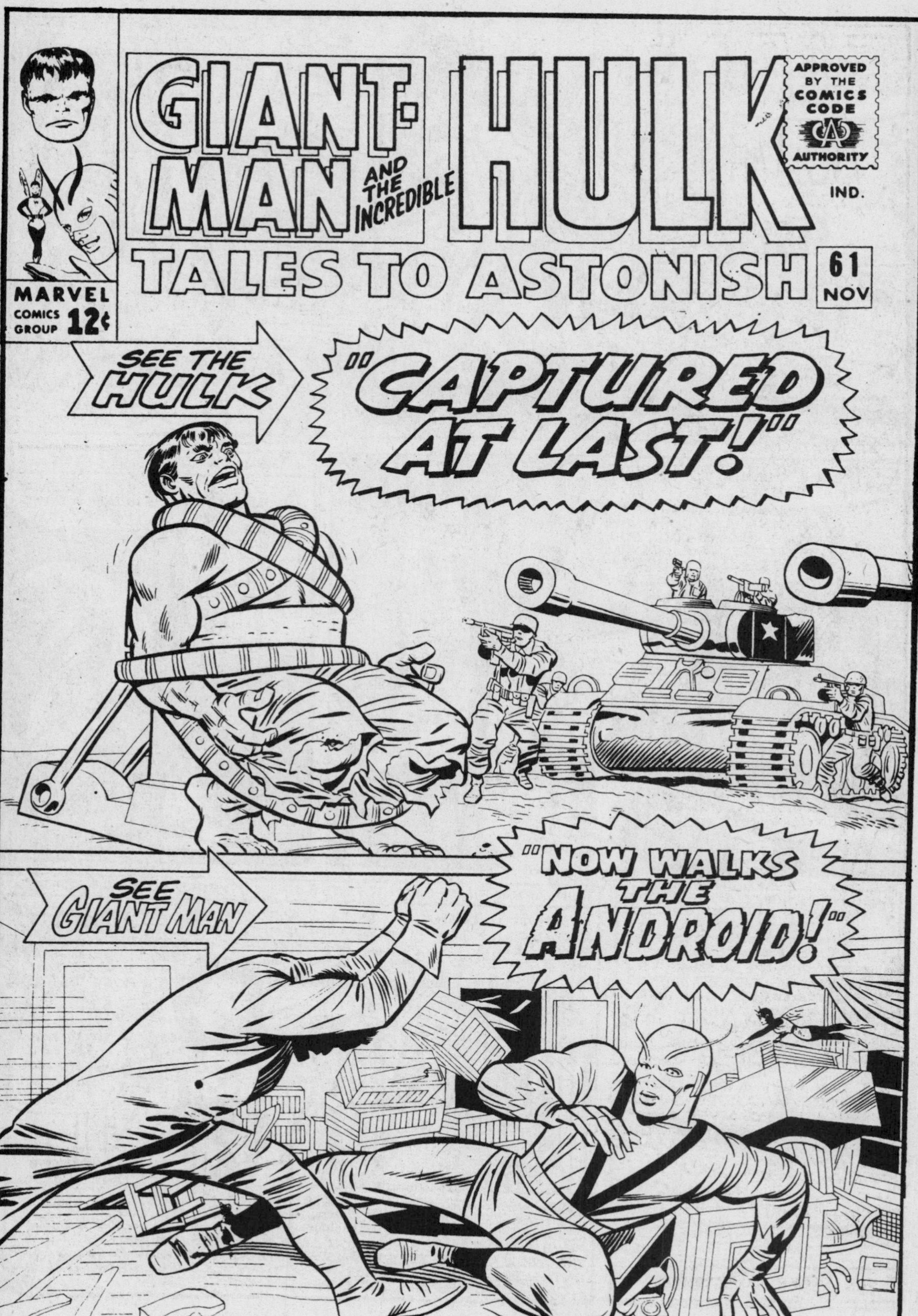

GIANT-MAN AND THE INCREDIBLE HULK
APPROVED BY THE COMICS CODE AUTHORITY
IND.
TALES TO ASTONISH
61 NOV
MARVEL COMICS GROUP 12¢
SEE THE HULK
"CAPTURED AT LAST!"
SEE GIANT MAN
"NOW WALKS THE ANDROID!"

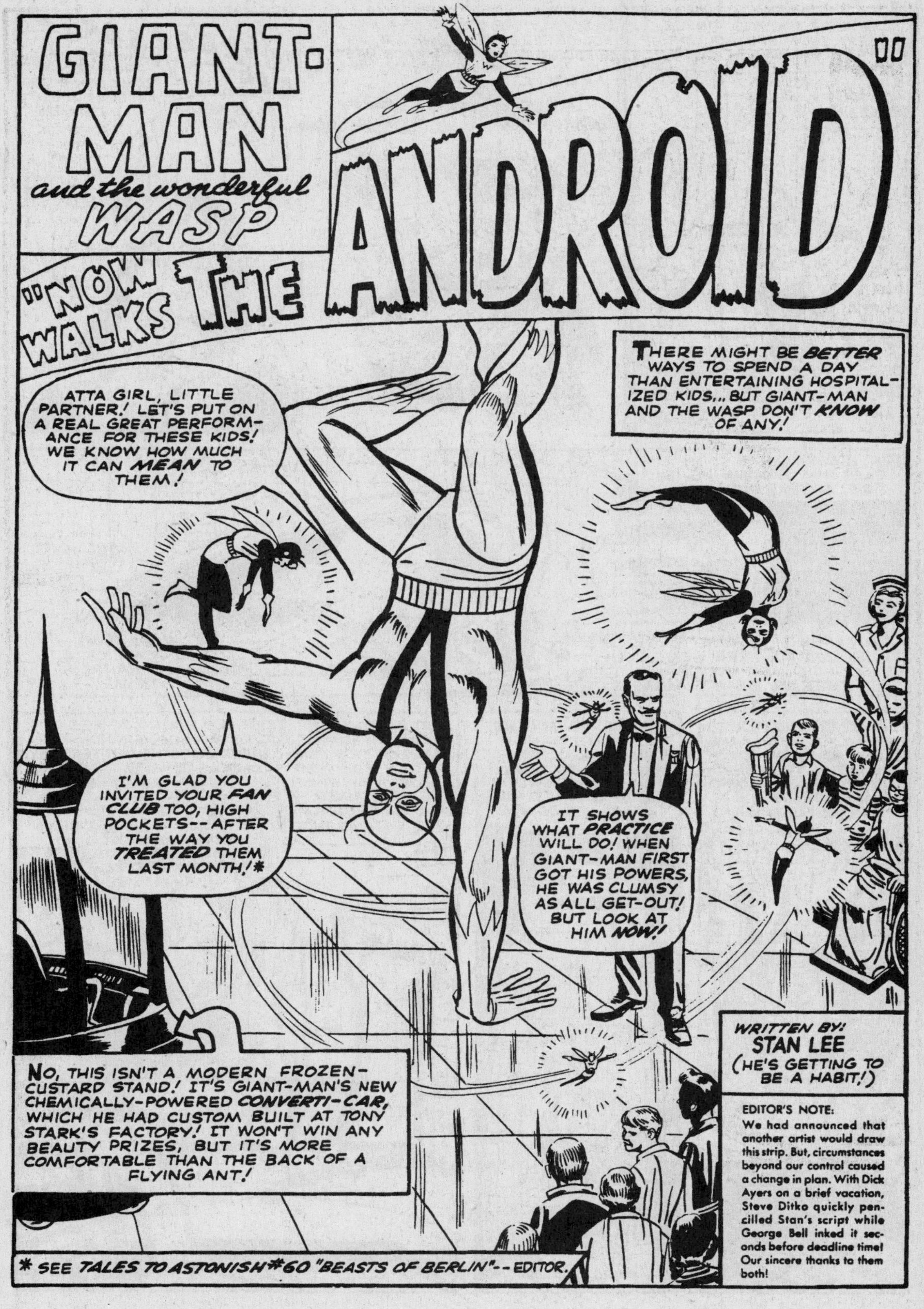
GIANT-MAN and the wonderful WASP
"NOW WALKS THE ANDROID"
THERE MIGHT BE BETTER WAYS TO SPEND A DAY THAN ENTERTAINING HOSPITALIZED KIDS... BUT GIANT-MAN AND THE WASP DON'T KNOW OF ANY!
ATTA GIRL, LITTLE PARTNER! LET'S PUT ON A REAL GREAT PERFORMANCE FOR THESE KIDS! WE KNOW HOW MUCH IT CAN MEAN TO THEM!
I'M GLAD YOU INVITED YOUR FAN CLUB TOO, HIGH POCKETS--AFTER THE WAY YOU TREATED THEM LAST MONTH!*
IT SHOWS WHAT PRACTICE WILL DO! WHEN GIANT-MAN FIRST GOT HIS POWERS, HE WAS CLUMSY AS ALL GET-OUT! BUT LOOK AT HIM NOW!
NO, THIS ISN'T A MODERN FROZEN-CUSTARD STAND! IT'S GIANT-MAN'S NEW CHEMICALLY-POWERED CONVERTI-CAR, WHICH HE HAD CUSTOM BUILT AT TONY STARK'S FACTORY! IT WON'T WIN ANY BEAUTY PRIZES, BUT IT'S MORE COMFORTABLE THAN THE BACK OF A FLYING ANT!
WRITTEN BY: STAN LEE (HE'S GETTING TO BE A HABIT!)
* SEE TALES TO ASTONISH #60 "BEASTS OF BERLIN"--EDITOR.
EDITOR'S NOTE: We had announced that another artist would draw this strip. But, circumstances beyond our control caused a change in plan. With Dick Ayers on a brief vacation, Steve Ditko quickly pencilled Stan's script while George Bell inked it seconds before deadline time! Our sincere thanks to them both!

NOW FOR A ROUSING FINALE, HONEY! SHOW HOW YOU ZIP UP TO NORMAL SIZE IN A WINK!

ANYTHING TO MAKE YOU HAPPY, BLUE EYES! HOW'S *THIS?*

YAY!

WOW-EE! LOOK AT *THAT!*

SUDDENLY, THE SOUND OF A WAILING POLICE SIREN FILLS THE AIR, AS SPEEDING SQUAD CARS RACE PAST THE HOSPITAL...

WHEEEEEEEEEEE

EEEEEEEEEE

LISTEN-- SIRENS!

PROBABLY A ROUTINE POLICE CASE! IT DOESN'T CONCERN *US!*

BUT, GIANT-MAN IS SOON TO LEARN HOW *WRONG* HE IS! FOR, AT THAT MOMENT...

I'M SAFE--FOR *NOW!* BUT I MUST REMAIN FREE LONG ENOUGH TO GET MY FINAL REVENGE ON *GIANT-MAN!*

AFTER *THAT*, I DON'T CARE WHAT HAPPENS TO ME!

I *HAD* TO BREAK OUT OF JAIL! I MUST MAKE GIANT-MAN *PAY* FOR THE INDIGNITY OF BEATING *ME*--A MAN WHO IS MANY TIMES HIS MENTAL SUPERIOR!

BUT I'VE HAD MONTHS TO DREAM UP A NEW PLAN--A PLAN SO BRILLIANT, SO FOOL-PROOF, THAT ONLY *EGGHEAD* COULD HAVE CONCEIVED OF IT!

FORTUNATELY, THE POLICE DO NOT YET KNOW OF THIS COMPLETELY-EQUIPPED LABORATORY WHICH I'VE MAINTAINED FOR EMERGENCY USE SUCH AS THIS!

THEY'RE BOUND TO RECAPTURE ME SOONER OR LATER--BUT IT DOESN'T MATTER--SO LONG AS I HAVE TIME TO DESTROY *GIANT-MAN!*

AND NOW--I MUST BEGIN WORK IMMEDIATELY! MY *BRAIN* AGAINST HIS *MIGHT!* WHAT A *BATTLE* THIS SHALL BE!

2

THE LONG HOURS DRAG ON AS EGGHEAD WORKS, OBLIVIOUS TO TIME, IMPERVIOUS TO FATIGUE, BURNING WITH AN UNQUENCHABLE DESIRE FOR *REVENGE!*

NOW FOR THE FINAL TEST!

IT *WORKS!* ACTIVATED BY MY LIVING-CELL BEAM, A LIFELESS DOLL CAN BE MADE TO MOVE-- TO REACT TO MY MENTAL COMMANDS!

BUT, IT WILL TAKE *MORE* THAN A MINIATURE DOLL TO DEFEAT THE POWERFUL *GIANT-MAN!* SO, IT IS TIME FOR *PHASE TWO* OF MY PLAN!

I MUST BE *CAUTIOUS!* I'VE COME TOO FAR-- PLANNED TOO LONG-- TO LET ANYTHING STOP ME *NOW!*

REACHING A DARKENED, DESERTED CLOTHING STORE, THE BRILLIANT BUT EVIL EGGHEAD USES ANOTHER OF HIS MANY SPECIALLY DESIGNED DEVICES...

NO SIMPLE DOOR LOCK CAN WITHSTAND MY VIBRATION RAY!

THERE! IT'S UNLOCKED!

AHH-- *THIS* IS WHAT I SEEK!

NOW, BY JUST MERELY SWITCHING MY VIBRATION RAY TO *WEIGHT REDUCTION,* I NEED NOT TIRE MYSELF OUT!

AND THERE, IN THE DARKENED STREET, NO HUMAN EYES BEHOLD THE STARTLING SIGHT OF A MASTER CRIMINAL TRANSPORTING A LIFELESS MANIKIN BY MEANS OF A STRANGELY POWERFUL RAY!

ONCE INSIDE MY LAB AGAIN, *NOTHING* WILL STOP ME!

MINUTES LATER, ONE OF THE MOST INCREDIBLE EXPERIMENTS EVER RECORDED IS BEGUN!

THERE YOU STAND --A WAX FIGURE,! LIFELESS! BRAINLESS! WITH NO OTHER PURPOSE THAN TO BE USED AS A CLOTHING DUMMY!

WHO COULD EVER EXPECT THAT I AM ABOUT TO TRANSFORM YOU INTO ONE OF THE MOST POWERFUL BEINGS TO WALK THE EARTH?!!

POWERFUL ENOUGH TO TOTALLY DEFEAT AND *DESTROY* MY ACCURSED ENEMY, *GIANT-MAN!*

13

FIRST, TO GIVE YOU ALMOST LIMITLESS STRENGTH, I'LL APPLY THIS SPECIAL COMPOUND TO YOUR WAXEN SKIN!

THEN, ONCE YOU ARE COMPLETELY COATED WITH IT, IT WILL BE TIME FOR PHASE *TWO*!

HAH! IT'S WORKING-- AS I *KNEW* IT WOULD! BY BATHING YOU WITH THIS ULTRA-BETA BEAM, MY COMPOUND FEEDS UPON ITSELF, INCREASING YOUR SIZE--BIGGER--BIGGER--

--UNTIL YOU STAND AS TALL AS *GIANT-MAN*!

THEN, AS THE BETA BEAM REACHES ITS FULL INTENSITY, EGGHEAD STEPS IN FRONT OF THE MOTIONLESS FIGURE, BATHING *HIMSELF* IN THE SHIMMERING RAYS!

NOW FOR THE MOST *IMPORTANT* PHASE! UPON THE SUCCESS OF *THIS* ACTION MY ENTIRE PLAN DEPENDS!

OHH-- I-I DIDN'T *DREAM* IT WOULD-- BE SO--PAINFUL--!

CAN'T *BEAR* ANY MORE--! IT'S *OVER*! BUT --DID IT WORK??

SUDDENLY, THE EXHAUSTED SCIENTIST HEARS A SHUFFLING SOUND ABOVE HIM! BREATHLESSLY HE LOOKS UP, AND SEES--

HE'S *MOVING*! MY ANDROID IS *MOVING*! BUT-- HE'LL *TRAMPLE* ME, UNLESS I CAN *STOP* HIM!

HALT! COME NO FURTHER, MY ANDROID! I AM YOUR *MASTER*!

4

I'VE **DONE** IT! HE **OBEYED** ME! HE'S MINE TO COMMAND!

AND THE POWER I'VE GIVEN HIM IS MORE THAN A MATCH FOR GIANT-MAN'S! **THIS** TIME I CANNOT FAIL! THIS IS THE MOMENT I'VE DREAMED OF! THIS WILL BE EGGHEAD'S SUPREME TRIUMPH!

THE NEXT DAY, TWO OF THE WORLD'S MOST GLAMOROUS ADVENTURERS SPEED THRU THE SKY IN THEIR SPECTACULAR CONVERTI-CAR...

LIKE THE WAY SHE RIDES, JAN?

SURE, HANK! BUT I'D FEEL PRETTY SILLY SMOOCHING IN A DRIVE-IN THEATRE INSIDE OF THIS OVERGROWN FISHBOWL!

I DIDN'T HAVE **SMOOCHING** IN MIND WHEN I DESIGNED IT, YOUNG LADY!

THAT'S THE **TROUBLE**, HANDSOME! YOU NEVER THINK OF THOSE IMPORTANT THINGS!

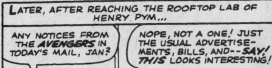

LATER, AFTER REACHING THE ROOFTOP LAB OF HENRY PYM...

ANY NOTICES FROM THE **AVENGERS** IN TODAY'S MAIL, JAN?

NOPE, NOT A ONE! JUST THE USUAL ADVERTISEMENTS, BILLS, AND--**SAY!** **THIS** LOOKS INTERESTING!

GOSH! IT'S FROM A **TV PRODUCER!** HE WANTS TO DO A FILM SERIES BASED ON OUR ADVENTURES! **IMAGINE!**

COUNT ME **OUT**, GORGEOUS! I'M A BIO-CHEMIST BY TRADE--AN ADVENTURER BY ACCIDENT--AND AN **AVENGER** BY CHOICE! BUT AN **ACTOR**??? UH UH!

HENRY PYM, I'M **ASHAMED** OF YOU! HAVEN'T YOU ANY **AMBITION?** DON'T YOU EVER WANT TO **GET** ANYWHERE?

YOU **BET!** I WANT TO GET BACK TO MY **WORK**-- SO, I'LL SEE YOU AROUND, LITTLE FRIEND!

5

BUT, HANK--EVEN IF YOU DON'T WANT TO ACT, THINK WHAT AN INSPIRATION SUCH A TV SERIES WOULD BE TO THE YOUTH OF THE NATION! HOW CAN YOU LET OUR YOUNG PEOPLE DOWN??

HOW COME YOU NEVER BECAME A LAWYER, KID?!

THINK OF IT! INSTEAD OF WATCHING PHONY ACTORS, THEY COULD SEE THE REAL THING! YOU'D BE ENDORSED BY THE P.T.A.-- THE BOY SCOUTS--

OKAY! OKAY! I KNOW WHEN I'M BEATEN! GET YOUR COAT, AND LET'S GET IT OVER WITH!

HIGH POCKETS--YOU'RE THE GREATEST!

BOY! I HIRE A PARTNER-IN-PERIL--AND I END UP WITH A TUESDAY WELD!

A SHORT TIME LATER, OUR TWO TEMPESTUOUS TROUBLE-SHOOTERS REACH THE ADDRESS ON THE LETTER, ONLY TO FIND...

I DON'T LIKE IT, JAN! IT'S A DARK, WINDOW-LESS, DEPRESSING-LOOKING BUILDING!

HONESTLY, HANK--HOW FOOLISH CAN YOU BE?? DON'T YOU KNOW ANYTHING ABOUT SHOW BIZ??

THEY NEED BUILDINGS LIKE THAT TO DO THEIR FILMING --WHERE NO LIGHT OR SOUND FROM THE STREET WILL INTERFERE!

OKAY, HONEY--IF YOU SAY SO! I GUESS THIS IS THE ENTRANCE!

IT MUST BE-- IT'S THE ONLY DOOR!

NOW THERE'S A BRILLIANT PIECE OF DEDUCTION!

-WHEW- I'LL BET THE LAST SHOW THEY FILMED HERE WAS "THE SON-IN-LAW OF FRANKENSTEIN"!

NOW DON'T TELL ME GIANT-MAN IS DISTURBED BY A CREAKY DOOR!

CREAK!

6

I HATE TO SOUND LIKE A PARTY POOP -- BUT IF *THIS* IS A TV STUDIO, I'M DOCTOR DOOM!

THE TROUBLE WITH *YOU* IS YOU'RE ALWAYS SO SUSPICIOUS OF EVERY-- HANK! LOOK *BEHIND* US!

WE ENTER THRU A CREAKY WOODEN DOOR, AND THEN A TEN-TON *STEEL* DOOR SLAMS SHUT BEHIND US, TRAPPING US INSIDE!

STILL THINK I'M JUST AN OLD WORRY WART, LITTLE ONE?

I- I DON'T KNOW *WHAT* TO THINK!

BANG!

BUT, IF SHE COULD SEE WHAT WAS TRANSPIRING IN EGGHEAD'S LAB AT THAT VERY MOMENT, JANET VAN DYNE WOULD HAVE A FAR *BETTER* IDEA OF WHAT TO THINK!

THE WARNING LIGHT! IT MEANS THEY'VE WALKED INTO MY LITTLE TRAP! AND NOW--

BY WEARING MY BETA-RAY MENTAL ENERGY TRANSMITTER, I'LL BE ABLE TO TAKE CHARGE OF THE SITUATION!

I SHALL SEE EVERYTHING MY ANDROID SEES-- FEEL EVERYTHING HE FEELS-- AND DIRECT HIS EVERY MOVEMENT BY MY OWN MENTAL PROCESSES!

THE MOMENT IS *NOW*, MY MIGHTY SERVANT! *SHOW YOURSELF!*

QUIET, JAN! THERE'S SOMETHING MOVING IN THE SHADOWS!

WHO-WHAT IS IT??

7

I don't *KNOW*, honey--but stay back! We seem to have blundered into something far more fateful than a screen test!

LISTEN! That *VOICE!*

How right you *ARE*, you two pathetic doomed fools!

I *KNEW* your own *VANITY* would make you enter my little trap! You couldn't resist the lure of your names in lights, could you??

It sounds so triumphant--so gloating--and yet--not quite *HUMAN!*

It's all my fault! If only I hadn't insisted--!

Look! *THERE'S* the one who spoke! But--he's a *GIANT!* Hank--that face--what can he *BE?*

QUICKLY--become wasp-size! Leave him to *ME!* I'll tackle him as an *EQUAL!*

I *EXPECTED* you to try that GIANT-MAN! But you are his equal in *SIZE* only--you will find that his *POWERS* far exceed your own puny ones!

NOW GO, my android! Fulfil the mission for which you have been created! *DEATH TO GIANT-MAN!*

The *VOICE* comes from his lips--but they don't *MOVE!* He's so expressionless--so inhuman!

He's an *ANDROID*--an artificial man--devised for only *ONE* purpose--to defeat *ME!*

But you must give *CREDIT* where credit is *DUE!* The guiding brain who accomplished this is --*EGGHEAD'S!*

8

EGGHEAD! I SHOULD HAVE GUESSED!

ONE FINAL WORD, MY SOON-TO-PERISH FOE! YOU HAVE BUT ONE HOUR'S TIME TO FIND A WAY TO DEFEAT MY INVULNERABLE ANDROID -- FOR THE AIR WITHIN THAT BUILDING WILL LAST NO LONGER!

WHAT DO WE DO NOW, BLUE EYES??

YOU JUST GET YOURSELF A GOOD SEAT, HONEY! YOU'RE ABOUT TO SEE ME PULVERIZE ONE LIFELESS ANDROID!

I MISJUDGED HIS WEIGHT!! HE'S LIGHT AS A FEATHER! I SWUNG TOO HARD -- THREW MYSELF OFF-BALANCE!

THEN, WITH ALL THE FORCE BEHIND HIS POWER-PACKED, DOUBLE-SIZED MUSCLES, GIANT-MAN SWINGS -- ONLY TO FIND --

NOT MEETING THE RESISTANCE OF A HEAVY BODY WHICH HE HAD EXPECTED, THE SMASHING BLOW HURLS GIANT-MAN TO THE FLOOR WITH SHATTERING IMPACT!

ARE -- ARE YOU ALRIGHT??

WELL, I WOULDN'T WANT TO MAKE A CAREER OF THIS!

AS CLUMSY AS EVER, EH, MY BUMBLING ADVERSARY?? HOW I'VE DREAMED OF THIS MOMENT! HOW I RELISH IT NOW!

EGGHEAD, I'VE BEATEN YOU THREE TIMES BEFORE! WON'T YOU EVER LEARN NOT TO UNDERESTIMATE ME??

9

DID YOU THINK AN ALMOST WEIGHTLESS ANDROID COULD BEAT ME??

CAREFUL! YOU KNOW HOW TRICKY EGGHEAD IS!

JUST WAIT! YOU HAVE ANOTHER SURPRISE IN STORE FOR YOU!

WELL, WHILE I'M WAITING, I'LL POLISH OFF YOUR TOWERING FRIEND!

JUST YOU STAY THERE FOR A SEC, PAL-- THIS WON'T TAKE VERY LONG!

AND, ONCE HE'S OUT OF THE WAY, EGGHEAD-- I'LL FIND YOU-- NO MATTER WHERE YOU ARE!

YOU CAN COUNT ON THAT, MISTER!

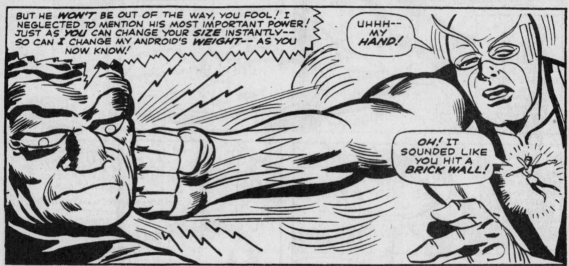

BUT HE WON'T BE OUT OF THE WAY, YOU FOOL! I NEGLECTED TO MENTION HIS MOST IMPORTANT POWER! JUST AS YOU CAN CHANGE YOUR SIZE INSTANTLY-- SO CAN I CHANGE MY ANDROID'S WEIGHT-- AS YOU NOW KNOW!

UHHH-- MY HAND!

OH! IT SOUNDED LIKE YOU HIT A BRICK WALL!

QUICK! TURN ANT-SIZE! PERHAPS WE CAN ESCAPE THAT WAY! IT'S YOUR ONLY CHANCE!

NO! NEVER! I WON'T GIVE UP! I'LL BEAT HIM SOMEHOW!

AND, SAFELY ENSCONCED IN HIS HIDDEN LAB, THE DEMONIAC EGGHEAD SAVORS EVERY WORD, EVERY ACTION WHICH TAKES PLACE WITHIN HIS SINISTER TRAP!

GOOD! GOOD! KEEP FIGHTING! DON'T GIVE UP! DON'T TRY TO ESCAPE! I WANT TO SEE YOU BATTLE HELPLESSLY-- HOPELESSLY! I WANT TO ENJOY THE FRUITS OF MY TRIUMPH TILL THE LAST POSSIBLE SECOND!

10

AND *NOW*, GIANT-MAN, YOU ARE ABOUT TO RECEIVE THE BEATING OF YOUR LIFE! IN FACT, THE *FINAL* BEATING OF YOUR LIFE!

UHH! WHAT WAS *THAT.?!!*

SOMETHING YOU *FORGOT* ABOUT, FATSO! MY *WASP'S STING!*

I'VE GOT TO GAIN *TIME* FOR HANK-- TILL HE CAN PULL HIMSELF TOGETHER!

WASP! LOOK, *OUT!*

THERE! IT THREW HIM OFF-BALANCE JUST LONG ENOUGH FOR YOU TO BE ABLE TO DODGE HIS ATTACK!

MIGHTY HANDY LITTLE WEAPON YOU INVENTED FOR ME, BIG BOY!

YOU'RE A MIGHTY HANDY LITTLE GAL TO HAVE AROUND, BEAUTI-FUL!

NOW THAT THE MUTUAL ADMIRA-TION SOCIETY HAS COME TO ORDER 'SCUSE ME WHILE I PLAY TAG WITH ANDY ANDROID!

WHUP.!

THWUP.!

NYAH! NYAH! CAN'T CATCH ME!

HOLD IT.! NO MORE! IT'S TOO DANGEROUS! LET *ME* BATTLE HIM NOW!

WHOOM!

OKAY, KILLJOY-- HE'S ALL YOURS!

BUT WHATEVER YOU DO, IT BETTER BE DONE *FAST*-- THAT HOUR OF AIR IS ALMOST *UP!*

I *KNOW*, HONEY! DON'T WORRY-- I WON'T FAIL YOU!

11

YOU *LIE*, GIANT-MAN! YOU'VE *ALREADY* FAILED!

HANK'S STILL GROGGY! HOW MUCH MORE CAN HE *TAKE*??

HE'S BECOME FEATHER-LIGHT AGAIN-- FLOATING INTO THE AIR! *LOOK OUT*, WASP--!

IN A SPLIT-SECOND, BEFORE THE BRUISED CRIME-FIGHTER CAN MAKE ANOTHER MOVE, THE GIANT ANDROID CHANGES WEIGHT AGAIN-- PLUMMETING DOWN WITH THE FORCE OF A PILE DRIVER!

HANK GUESSED WHAT WAS COMING, AND TENSED HIS OWN HUGE MUSCLES! BUT-- EVEN SO-- IT WAS A PUNISHING BLOW!

NO! YOU MUST HAVE MORE FAITH IN ME THAN *THAT*-- RUNNING AND HIDING WON'T HELP-- THERE ISN'T *TIME*! I'VE GOT TO DESTROY THAT ANDROID!

PLEASE-- YOU'VE *GOT* TO BECOME ANT-SIZE! ANOTHER SUCH ATTACK WILL *FINISH* YOU! *PLEASE--* MY DARLING--

WHY DON'T YOU *PLEAD*, GIANT-MAN! LET ME HEAR YOU BEG FOR MERCY! NOT THAT IT WILL *HELP*!

HERE COMES OUR NEXT ATTACK! BUT, HOW WILL YOU *MEET* IT? WILL MY ANDROID BE HEAVY AS LEAD-- OR LIGHT AS A CLOUD??

KEEP TALKING, EGGHEAD! GLOAT WHILE YOU MAY! YOUR TIME IS RUNNING OUT!

BAH! EMPTY WORDS! MEANINGLESS THREATS! IT'S *YOUR* TIME WHICH IS RUNNING OUT! *ALREADY* I CAN TELL THAT THE WASP IS GASPING FOR BREATH! YOU'VE ONLY MINUTES LEFT! I'VE WON! DON'T YOU UNDERSTAND? *I'VE WON!*

12

HAVE YOU? THEN HOW COME I'M STILL FIGHTING?

TO WHAT AVAIL? I OUTFOXED YOU AGAIN! I'M LIGHTER THAN AIR NOW!

THAT'S JUST WHAT I WANTED, BRIGHT EYES! NOW I'VE GOTCHA!

SUDDENLY, GIANT-MAN MOVES WITH STAGGERING SPEED, GRASPING THE ANDROID'S LEGS BEFORE EGGHEAD CAN REACT....!

I WON'T WASTE TIME TRYING TO HIT YOU--

IT WOULD BE LIKE SWINGING AT A SMOKE RING!

THIS WILL BE FAR MORE EFFECTIVE--WON'T IT, EGGHEAD?

WHAT'S WRONG, EGGHEAD? I DON'T HEAR YOU TAUNTING ME ANY MORE! HAVE YOU SUDDENLY GROWN SHY?

OR, HAS WHAT I WANTED TO HAPPEN TAKEN PLACE? SOMEHOW, I SUSPECT IT HAS!

YOU ADMITTED THAT YOU COULD SEE AND HEAR WHAT THE ANDROID SAW AND HEARD! SO, IT'S ONLY NATURAL THAT YOU CAN FEEL WHAT HE FEELS, ALSO!

WHICH MEANS THAT I'M MAKING YOU TOO DIZZY TO THINK-- TOO DIZZY TO CONTROL HIS WEIGHT AGAIN--TOO DIZZY TO DO ANYTHING --EXCEPT WATCH YOUR PLAN GO UP IN SMOKE!

HE'S RIGHT! I CAN'T TAKE IT! IT'S UNBEARABLE!

13

STOP IT! STOP IT! EVERYTHING IS SPINNING AROUND! EVERYTHING IS GETTING HAZY! I'M BLACKING OUT! STOP IT!

ONLY IF YOU RAISE THAT STEEL DOOR, FREEING US! THE CHOICE IS YOURS! THERE'S ENOUGH AIR HERE FOR ME TO HOLD OUT FOR AT LEAST ANOTHER FIVE MINUTES!

I-I COULDN'T STAND FIVE MINUTES MORE -- NOT FIVE SECONDS MORE! I'LL DO ANY-THING -- ANYTHING!

THERE! I'VE DONE IT! I'VE RAISED THE DOOR! YOU CAN GO FREE! THE CONTACT IS BROKEN -- THE ANDROID IS HARMLESS!

AND, AS THE LIFE-GIVING AIR RUSHES IN, GIANT-MAN HURLS THE ANDROID FROM THE BUILDING, IN ONE FINAL TRIUMPHANT GESTURE!

WE'VE WON! WE'VE BEATEN EGGHEAD AGAIN!

AND YOU DID IT THE WAY YOU WANTED -- MATCHING POWER FOR POWER!

THERE'S NO NEED FOR ME TO REMAIN AS GIANT-MAN NOW -- IT'S OVER! EGGHEAD WON'T DARE USE THE ANDROID AGAIN!

...NOT SINCE WE'VE FOUND ITS WEAKNESS -- FOR EGG-HEAD FEARS PHYSICAL PAIN MORE THAN ANYTHING ELSE!

BUT, WHAT WILL HAPPEN TO THE ANDROID NOW?

HAVE YOU FORGOTTEN? IT HAS NO LIFE OF ITS OWN -- NO BRAIN -- NO WILL! IT WILL KEEP MOVING BLINDLY IN THAT DIRECTION FOR ANOTHER MINUTE OR TWO, AND THEN...

-- IT WILL FALL TO ITS FINAL RESTING PLACE!

YOU BIG, WONDERFUL HUNK OF MAN -- I'VE NEVER BEEN PROUDER OF YOU THAN NOW!

I'LL BET YOU TELL THAT TO ALL THE GIANT-MEN, LITTLE GIRL!

AND, SOMEWHERE IN THE CITY A MAN WAITS -- WAITS FOR THE INEVITABLE KNOCK ON THE DOOR -- THE INEVITABLE RETURN TO PRISON -- THE INEVITABLE PRICE HE MUST PAY FOR -- HIS FINAL FAILURE!

THE END

GIANT-MAN AND THE INCREDIBLE HULK

TALES TO ASTONISH

MARVEL COMICS GROUP 12¢

APPROVED BY THE COMICS CODE AUTHORITY

IND.

62 DEC

THE HULK BREAKS LOOSE and ATTACKS THE CHAMELEON!

GIANT-MAN FIGHTS FOR HIS LIFE AGAINST THE WASP! WHY? HOW DID IT HAPPEN??

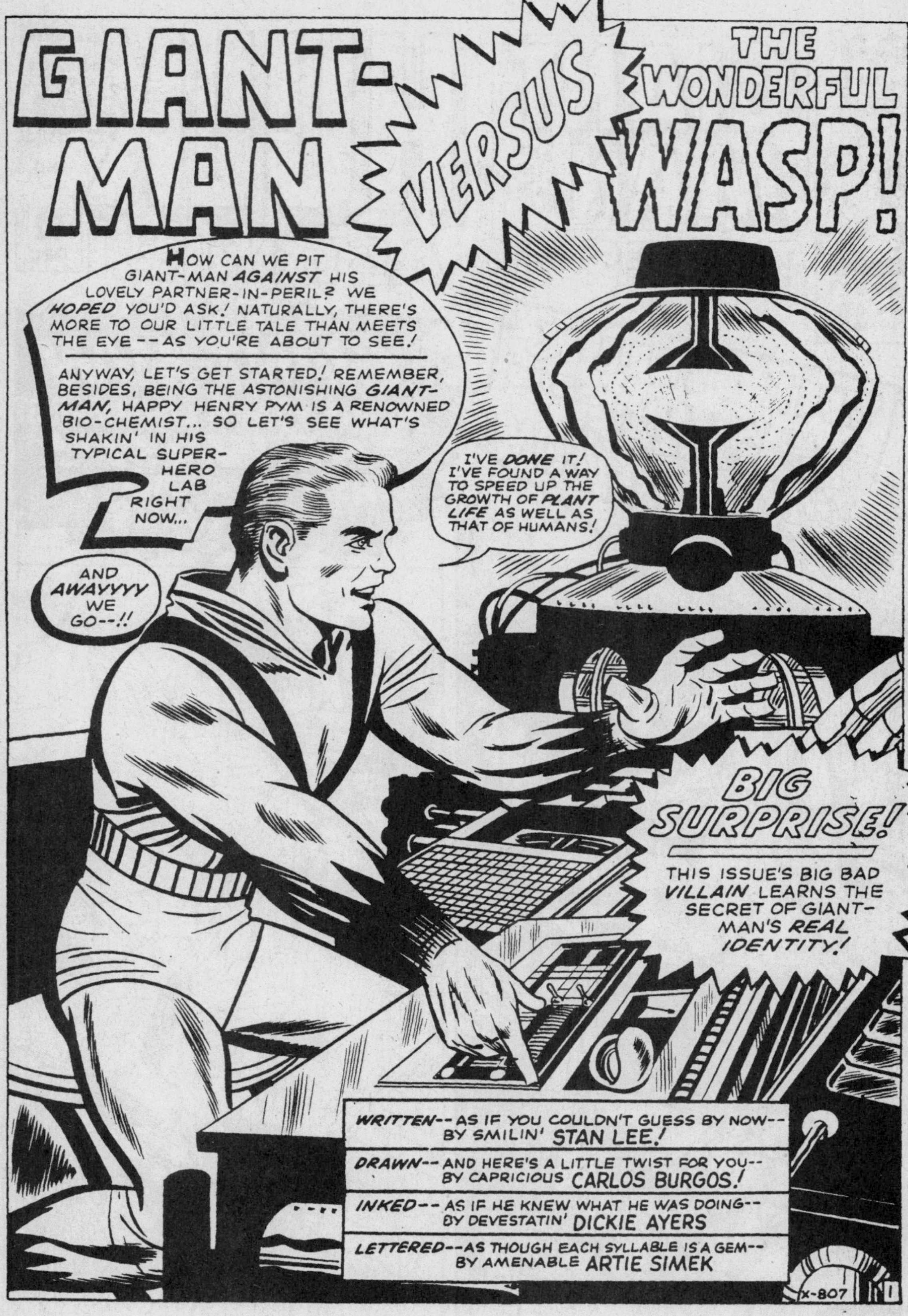
GIANT-MAN VERSUS THE WONDERFUL WASP!
HOW CAN WE PIT GIANT-MAN AGAINST HIS LOVELY PARTNER-IN-PERIL? WE HOPED YOU'D ASK! NATURALLY, THERE'S MORE TO OUR LITTLE TALE THAN MEETS THE EYE -- AS YOU'RE ABOUT TO SEE!
ANYWAY, LET'S GET STARTED! REMEMBER, BESIDES, BEING THE ASTONISHING GIANT-MAN, HAPPY HENRY PYM IS A RENOWNED BIO-CHEMIST... SO LET'S SEE WHAT'S SHAKIN' IN HIS TYPICAL SUPER-HERO LAB RIGHT NOW...
AND AWAYYYY WE GO--!!
I'VE DONE IT! I'VE FOUND A WAY TO SPEED UP THE GROWTH OF PLANT LIFE AS WELL AS THAT OF HUMANS!
BIG SURPRISE!
THIS ISSUE'S BIG BAD VILLAIN LEARNS THE SECRET OF GIANT-MAN'S REAL IDENTITY!
WRITTEN-- AS IF YOU COULDN'T GUESS BY NOW-- BY SMILIN' STAN LEE!
DRAWN-- AND HERE'S A LITTLE TWIST FOR YOU-- BY CAPRICIOUS CARLOS BURGOS!
INKED-- AS IF HE KNEW WHAT HE WAS DOING-- BY DEVESTATIN' DICKIE AYERS
LETTERED-- AS THOUGH EACH SYLLABLE IS A GEM-- BY AMENABLE ARTIE SIMEK
X-807
1

WHAT A GREAT BOON THIS COULD BE FOR THE HAVE-NOT NATIONS OF THE WORLD! IT'LL ENABLE THEM TO MORE THAN *DOUBLE* THEIR FOOD SUPPLY!

NOW TO CHECK THE RATE OF GROWTH! I'VE STARTED MY SPLIT-SECOND ELECTRONIC TIMER! I'LL GIVE IT A MINUTE, AND THEN--

BUT, AFTER LESS THAN TWENTY SECONDS...

I'VE MADE IT *TOO* EFFECTIVE! IT'S GROWING *TOO FAST!* IT'S *OUT OF CONTROL!*

THAT'S THE *TROUBLE* WITH SCIENTIFIC MIRACLES! SOMETIMES THEY GET OUT OF HAND! ANYWAY, BEFORE A FULL MINUTE HAS PASSED, HAPPY HENRY FINDS HIMSELF BEHIND THE BIO-CHEMICAL EIGHT-BALL!

IT *DOUBLES* ITS RATE OF GROWTH WITH EACH PASSING MICRO-SECOND! IF I DON'T *STOP* IT, IT'LL OVER-RUN THE ENTIRE *CITY* WITHIN AN HOUR! BUT-- I'VE NO TIME TO CREATE AN *ANTIDOTE!*

THEN, UTILIZING HIS ASTONISHING POWER OF CYBERNETIC MENTAL SIZE CONTROL...

I'VE GOT TO SHRINK DOWN, *FAST!* IF I CAN REACH THE *TAP ROOT* IN TIME, THERE'S STILL A CHANCE!

THUS, LOCATING THE EXACT PORTION OF THE MINDLESS PLANT WHICH CONTROLS ITS GROWTH, THE MASTER OF MANY SIZES DELIVERS A SKILLFUL, AVENGERS-TYPE KARATE BLOW... SEVERING THE VITAL *TAP ROOT!*

THIS SHOULD DO THE TRICK!

WHIPPP

2

BUT NOW, LET'S SHIFT OUR SIGHTS FOR A MOMENT, AND LOOK INTO THE TOP-FLOOR APARTMENT OF A NEARBY BUILDING! UNAWARE OF THE GIGANTIC PLANT WHICH IS STILL WRITHING IN ITS DEATH THROES, A FURTIVE BURGLAR IS RANSACKING THE PREMISES...

NOT A BAD HAUL FOR SECOND-STORY SAMMY! LOOKS LIKE I MAY GET *AWAY* WITH IT FOR ONCE!

HEY, *WAIT!* I'D BETTER TAKE A CLOSER *LOOK* AT THIS STUFF...!

RATS! OF ALL THE CRUMMY LUCK! IT'S NOTHIN' BUT WORTHLESS *COSTUME JEWELRY!* JUST CHEAP IMITATIONS!

AND, AS IF *THAT* AIN'T BAD ENOUGH, I HEAR SOMEONE STARTIN' TO OPEN THE *DOOR!* I'VE GOTTA *LAM!*

WHAT A PLEASANT VISIT WITH OUR NEXT-DOOR NEIGHB-- *HONEY!* LOOK!

OUR APARTMENT'S BEEN *BURGLED!*

WHEW! JUST IN TIME!

LOOK OUT, SAMMY! THAT LEDGE *ISN'T SAFE!*

SUDDENLY...

I'M FALLIN'! WHERE'D THESE GIANT *LEAVES* COME FROM?? IF--IF I CAN JUST *GRAB* ONE...

LUCKILY FOR THE UNSUCCESSFUL BURGLAR, HE FALLS ONTO A LONG, QUIVERING LEAF WHICH IS STRONG ENOUGH TO SUPPORT HIS WEIGHT AS HE FEARFULLY SLIDES DOWN, AND AROUND-- CRAZILY FOLLOWING THE TWISTING LENGTH OF THE WEAVING, SHAKING, SLOWLY-DYING PLANT...

I MUST BE *DREAMIN'!* THIS IS *NUTTY!* IT'S *IMPOSSIBLE!*

UNTIL... THE NIGHTMARISH TOBOGGAN SLIDE SAFELY DEPOSITS HIM DIRECTLY ONTO THE LEDGE OF THE APARTMENT WHERE HENRY PYM HAS JUST CHANGED BACK TO NORMAL SIZE,...!

I-I'M SAFE! BUT--WHAT *HAPPENED??* WHAT'S GOIN' ON??!

3

STEALTHILY ENTERING THE TOP FLOOR LAB OF THE HARD-WORKING BIO-CHEMIST, THE UNBELIEVING BURGLAR PEERS THRU A PARTIALLY-OPENED DOOR, AND SEES...

BY SUCCEEDING *TOO WELL*, I'VE ACTUALLY *FAILED!* MY PLANT GROWTH SERUM IS USELESS UNTIL I CAN LEARN TO *CONTROL* IT!

I'M SURE GLAD THE *WASP* IS AT A *MOVIE!* IF JAN WERE *HERE* NOW, THAT PERKY LITTLE PIXIE WOULD NEVER STOP *RIBBING* ME!

BUT, EVEN THE BEST OF US -- EVEN THE WISEST AND MOST CAREFUL SCIENTISTS CAN GET CARELESS SOMETIMES! SO WRAPPED UP IN HIS THOUGHTS IS HAPPY HANK, THAT HE COMBINES TOO POTENT AN ADDITIVE TO HIS MIXTURE, AND...

I WONDER IF JAN EVER -- *WHA* --??!!

WHOOM

HURLED CLEAR ACROSS THE ROOM BY THE FORCE OF THE EXPLOSION, THE COSTUMED CRUSADER STRIKES HIS HEAD AGAINST A PIECE OF IRON APPARATUS...

THUD!

THEN, AS THE INJURED SCIENTIST LOSES CONSCIOUSNESS...

I'D RECOGNIZE THAT MONKEY SUIT ANYWHERE! IT'S *GIANT-MAN* HIMSELF!

HE'S OUT LIKE A LIGHT! WHAT A BREAK FOR ME! IF I CAN FIND OUT WHO HE REALLY *IS* --!

THERE'S A *CARD* ON THE FLOOR! DROPPED FROM THE TABLE!

WELL, WHATTAYA *KNOW*?!! LOOKS LIKE THIS IS MY LUCKY DAY! THE SECRET OF GIANT-MAN'S IDENTITY OUGHTTA BE WORTH A *FORTUNE!*

HENRY PYM
BIO-CHEMIST

RB 4 6 3 2 5

4

AND I THOUGHT I WAS A *FAILURE!* WHAT A *LAUGH!* I DID SOMETHIN' NO CROOK IN THE *WORLD* HAS BEEN ABLE TO PULL OFF TILL NOW!

BUT *WAIT* A MINUTE--- JUST SELLIN' THE SECRET OF HIS IDENTITY TO THE MOBS MAY BE SMALL POTATOES! I'M GONNA START TO THINK *BIG!*

WHY SHOULDN'T I GRAB HIS COSTUME?? WHY CAN'T I BECOME GIANT-MAN??!

I *FIGURED* THIS OUTFIT MUST BE MADE OUTTA SOME SORT OF STRETCH MATERIAL, SO THAT IT CAN GET BIG AND SMALL ON 'IM! IT FITS ME LIKE A *GLOVE!* BUT-- HOW DOES HE CHANGE HIS SIZE??

THERE MUST BE MORE TO IT THAN JUST *WANTIN'* TO GROW BIG!

BUT, THE MINUTE SECOND-STORY SAMMY *THINKS* OF GROWING BIG, PYM'S ASTONISHING CYBERNETIC HELMET GOES INTO IMMEDIATE OPERATION, AND...

I'M BECOMIN' A *GIANT!!!*

HOWEVER, THE INCREDULOUS CRIMINAL HAS THE SAME PROBLEM THAT HANK HAD WITH HIS GROWTH SERUM! HE DOESN'T KNOW HOW TO *STOP* THE RUNAWAY PROCESS!

I'M GETTIN' *TOO* BIG! REACHIN' FOR THE SKY! I'LL *SUFFOCATE* IN THE ATMOSPHERE-- GOTTA *STOP*-- SHRINK DOWN-- BUT HOW??

IF I COULD ONLY GET *SMALL* AGAIN!

AND AGAIN, NO SOONER DOES THE THOUGHT CROSS HIS MIND, THEN...

WOW! SO *THAT'S* HOW IT WORKS! ALL YOU GOTTA DO IS *THINK* ABOUT IT!

MAN! I'VE GOT IT *MADE!* I CAN REALLY *BE* GIANT-MAN!

THEN, THE TRIUMPHANT IMPOSTER QUICKLY PUTS THE *REAL* GIANT-MAN INTO A CLOSET--BUT, BEFORE HE CAN LOCK THE CLOSET DOOR...

SOMEONE AT THE DOOR!

I BETTER CUT *OUT* OF HERE TILL I CAN PLAN MY NEXT MOVE!

CLICK

5

SO QUICKLY DOES THE FLEEING MAN DASH PAST THE GIRL AT THE DOOR, THAT JANET VAN DYNE BELIEVES HIM TO BE--

HENRY PYM! WHERE ON EARTH--!!?

HE DIDN'T EVEN ANSWER ME!

LEAVING THE PUZZLED GIRL BEHIND, SECOND-STORY SAM RACES THRU THE DARK, NEARLY DESERTED STREETS, UNTIL...

A JEWELRY STORE! THAT OUGHTTA BE A BREEZE FOR GIANT-MAN TO BUST INTO!

YES SIREE! NOBODY KNOWS IT YET, BUT THE GUY CALLED GIANT-MAN IS ABOUT TO BEGIN A BRAND NEW CAREER-- WHICH MEANS THAT LITTLE SAMMY WILL SOON BE THE MOST SUCCESSFUL CROOK IN THE WORLD!

THE 'K' DIAMOND VALUE $350,000

ALL A GUY WITH THE POWER TO CHANGE HIS SIZE HAS TO DO IS BECOME SMALL AS AN ANT AND SNOOP AROUND TILL HE CAN FIND A SMALL OPENING-- LIKE THAT TINY SPACE BETWEEN THE STORE FRONT AND THE WALL--

--AND HERE I AM--INSIDE!

NOW, I'LL JUST THINK MYSELF BIG ENOUGH TO GRAB A WHOLE MESS OF SPARKLERS, AND... HEY!

BLAST IT! I STILL CAN'T HANDLE THIS SIZE-CHANGING BUSINESS RIGHT! I GOT TOO BIG -- SET OFF THE BLAMED BURGLAR ALARM!!

ALARM

SCREEEE

SUDDENLY PANICKING AS HE HEARS THE SOUND OF APPROACHING POLICE SIRENS, THE ERSTWHILE JEWEL THIEF AGAIN SHRINKS TO ANT SIZE, HIDING AMONG THE DISPLAY OF GEMS...

NOT MUCH CHANCE OF ANYONE FINDIN' ME DOWN HERE!

MEANWHILE, AS THE POLICE SQUAD CARS CONVERGE IN FRONT OF THE JEWELRY STORE, ONE ADDITIONAL STALK HAS TAKEN ROOT, STILL SATURATED WITH PYM'S POTION, AND IT NOW BEGINS ITS PHENOMENAL GROWTH, CAUSING A NEW MENACE TO SPREAD OVER THE CITY!

GET THESE CROWDS OFF THE STREET! WE'LL HAVE TO DECLARE MARTIAL LAW!

WHEEEE

6

SECONDS LATER...

I DON'T UNDERSTAND! NOTHING SEEMS TO BE MISSING!

THE THIEF WAS PROBABLY SCARED AWAY BY THE GROWING PLANT! YOU'D BETTER GET HOME NOW! THE STREETS ARE DANGEROUS TILL WE FIND A WAY TO *STOP* THOSE GIANT VINES!

MY CYBERNETIC HELMET IS TINGLING!

GIANT-MAN'S HELMET MUST BE NEARBY, CAUSING THIS REACTION!

HAVING FOLLOWED THE SPEEDING SQUAD CARS IN HER BEWILDERED SEARCH FOR GIANT-MAN, THE NOW-TINY *WASP* SENSES THE PRESENCE OF THE ONE SHE *THINKS* IS HER EVASIVE PARTNER-IN-PERIL....!

THERE HE IS--IN HIS IDENTITY AS *ANT-MAN!* BUT, WHY IS HE HIDING AMONG THESE GEMS?? HE'S NEVER BEEN *BASHFUL* BEFORE!

SAY THERE, BLUE EYES! THIS IS NO TIME FOR *WINDOW SHOPPING!* OR ARE YOU PLAYING HIDE AND SEEK WITH ME?

IT'S PYM'S FLYIN' *PARTNER*--THE PESTY WASP!

I'VE GOT TO GET *RID* OF HER!

BEAT IT, BABY! I'M WORKIN' ON A PRIVATE CAPER HERE! SO TAKE A POWDER!

NOW LOOK *HERE*, HANDSOME HANK! YOU DON'T GET RID OF *ME* BY TALKING LIKE A REFUGEE FROM *"THE UNTOUCHABLES"!*

BESIDES, YOU HAVEN'T EVEN TOLD ME HOW YOU LIKE THE NEW STYLE I DESIGNED FOR MY HELMET, AND-- *WAIT A MINUTE!* YOU'RE NOT MY PARTNER!!

TOO BAD YOU REALIZED THAT, LADY! TOO BAD FOR *YOU!* NOW *CLAM UP!* I DON'T WANT TO BE SPOTTED HERE!

≥MMFFF≤

WHOEVER THIS IS--IF *HE* HAS HANK'S COSTUME--AND THE POWER TO SHRINK TO ANT-SIZE, HOW DID HE GET IT?? HANK WOULD NEVER HAVE GIVEN IT UP--NOT WHILE HE *LIVED!!* OH *NO* --IT *CAN'T* MEAN--!!!

7

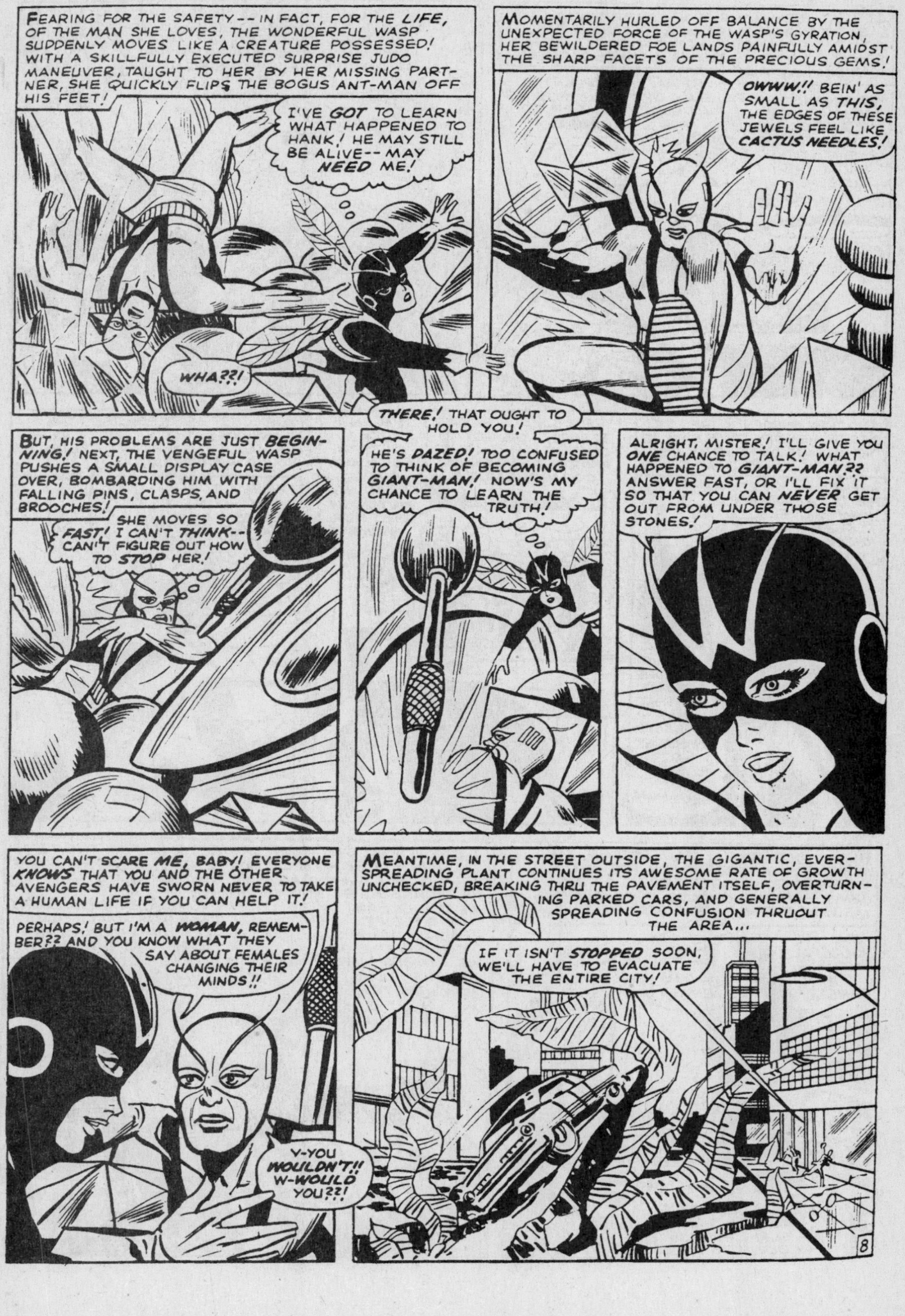
FEARING FOR THE SAFETY -- IN FACT, FOR THE LIFE, OF THE MAN SHE LOVES, THE WONDERFUL WASP SUDDENLY MOVES LIKE A CREATURE POSSESSED! WITH A SKILLFULLY EXECUTED SURPRISE JUDO MANEUVER, TAUGHT TO HER BY HER MISSING PARTNER, SHE QUICKLY FLIPS THE BOGUS ANT-MAN OFF HIS FEET!
I'VE GOT TO LEARN WHAT HAPPENED TO HANK! HE MAY STILL BE ALIVE -- MAY NEED ME!
WHA??!
MOMENTARILY HURLED OFF BALANCE BY THE UNEXPECTED FORCE OF THE WASP'S GYRATION, HER BEWILDERED FOE LANDS PAINFULLY AMIDST THE SHARP FACETS OF THE PRECIOUS GEMS!
OWWW!! BEIN' AS SMALL AS THIS, THE EDGES OF THESE JEWELS FEEL LIKE CACTUS NEEDLES!
BUT, HIS PROBLEMS ARE JUST BEGINNING! NEXT, THE VENGEFUL WASP PUSHES A SMALL DISPLAY CASE OVER, BOMBARDING HIM WITH FALLING PINS, CLASPS, AND BROOCHES!
SHE MOVES SO FAST! I CAN'T THINK -- CAN'T FIGURE OUT HOW TO STOP HER!
THERE! THAT OUGHT TO HOLD YOU!
HE'S DAZED! TOO CONFUSED TO THINK OF BECOMING GIANT-MAN! NOW'S MY CHANCE TO LEARN THE TRUTH!
ALRIGHT, MISTER! I'LL GIVE YOU ONE CHANCE TO TALK! WHAT HAPPENED TO GIANT-MAN?? ANSWER FAST, OR I'LL FIX IT SO THAT YOU CAN NEVER GET OUT FROM UNDER THOSE STONES!
YOU CAN'T SCARE ME, BABY! EVERYONE KNOWS THAT YOU AND THE OTHER AVENGERS HAVE SWORN NEVER TO TAKE A HUMAN LIFE IF YOU CAN HELP IT!
PERHAPS! BUT I'M A WOMAN, REMEMBER?? AND YOU KNOW WHAT THEY SAY ABOUT FEMALES CHANGING THEIR MINDS!!
V-YOU WOULDN'T!! W-WOULD YOU??!
MEANTIME, IN THE STREET OUTSIDE, THE GIGANTIC, EVER-SPREADING PLANT CONTINUES ITS AWESOME RATE OF GROWTH UNCHECKED, BREAKING THRU THE PAVEMENT ITSELF, OVERTURNING PARKED CARS, AND GENERALLY SPREADING CONFUSION THRUOUT THE AREA...
IF IT ISN'T STOPPED SOON, WE'LL HAVE TO EVACUATE THE ENTIRE CITY!
8

AT THAT VERY MOMENT, IN HENRY PYM'S SILENT LAB, THE SHRILL BLARE OF A TELEPHONE BELL CUTS THE STILLNESS, AS THE MAYOR'S EMERGENCY COUNCIL SUMMONS ALL BIO-CHEMISTS TO SEEK THEIR AID!

THE RINGING PHONE BROUGHT ME BACK TO CONSCIOUSNESS! LUCKY THE CLOSET WASN'T LOCKED FROM THE OUTSIDE!

WHAT?? THE PLANT IS STILL GROWING--POSING A DEADLY DANGER TO THE ENTIRE CITY?!!

QUICKLY HANGING UP, THE STARTLED CHEMIST RUSHES TO THE WINDOW, AND SEES--

I THOUGHT I HAD DESTROYED THE MAIN TAP ROOT--BUT THERE MUST HAVE BEEN ANOTHER ONE! BUT-- HOW CAN I FIND IT NOW?? THE GROWTH PROCESS HAS SPREAD TOO FAR!

AND THEN, SUDDENLY, THE LAST BITS OF MEMORY COME BACK TO THE VALIANT AVENGER AS HIS MIND NOW CLEARS COMPLETELY...

WHERE'S MY COSTUME?? WAIT! I REMEMBER NOW! THAT EXPLOSION--IT KNOCKED ME OUT!!

WHAT IF SOMEONE FOUND ME THAT WAY-- GUESSED MY SECRET --AND TRIED TO USURP MY IDENTITY??

THERE'S NOT A SECOND TO LOSE! I'VE GOT TO CONTACT JAN ON THE PROTOTYPE CYBERNETIC COMMUNICATOR!

I'M IN LUCK! SHE'S IN COSTUME! SHE'LL READ ME INSTANTLY THRU HER HELMET!

AND, JUST AS PREDICTED, THE WASP DOES RECEIVE HANK'S URGENT SIGNAL AS HER HEART BEGINS TO POUND WITH RELIEF!

HANK! IT'S YOU! YOU'RE ALIVE! YOU'RE ALIVE!

BUT, IN THAT JOYFUL SPLIT-SECOND, JAN MOMENTARILY FORGETS HER FOE WHO HAS MANAGED TO WRIGGLE FREE OF THE GEMS--AND WHO ALSO RECEIVES THE MESSAGE THRU HIS CYBERNETIC HELMET!

JAN! BE CAREFUL! YOU'RE IN DANGER!

HMMM? WHAT?

I'VE STILL GOT A CHANCE! IF I CAN SLAM THIS LID DOWN IN TIME!

I DID IT! BY THE TIME SHE GETS OUT OF THERE I'LL HAVE LOST MYSELF IN THE CITY BEFORE PYM CAN FIND ME!

HE THINKS HE'S IN THE CLEAR! HE DOESN'T REALIZE HANK IS ORDERING ONE OF HIS WINGED ANTS TO THE SCENE IMMEDIATLY!

I'VE BEATEN THEM BOTH! I'M NOT A SMALL TIME FLOP OF A CROOK ANY MORE! I'M THE MOST POWERFUL CRIMINAL OF THEM ALL!

CLACK!

9

AND, SURE ENOUGH, NO SOONER DOES "THE MOST POWERFUL CRIMINAL OF THEM ALL" REACH THE STREET, STILL ANT-SIZED, THEN HE HEARS THE SWISH OF SWOOPING WINGS, AND FINDS HIMSELF WHISKED HIGH INTO THE AIR BY A SEEMINGLY-GIGANTIC FLYING ANT!

I-- I CAN'T SAVE MYSELF! IF I THINK MYSELF ANY TALLER, I'M LIABLE TO BE TOO HEAVY FOR HIM TO HOLD -- HE'LL DROP ME TO MY DEATH!!

THEN, MINUTES LATER...

WELL DONE, LITTLE FRIEND! YOU MAY FLY OFF NOW!

SO! YOU THOUGHT YOU'D IMPERSONATE ME, EH? BECOME NORMAL SIZE SO I CAN GET A LOOK AT YOU!

I'LL DO BETTER'N THAT, SMART GUY! I'LL THINK MYSELF BIGGER THAN NORMAL SIZE -- AND I'LL PULVERIZE YA ON THE WAY UP!!

BUT, SECOND-STORY SAM SOON LEARNS THAT IT TAKES MORE THAN A COSTUME TO MAKE A SUCCESSFUL SUPER-POWERED FIGHTER! HANDSOME HENRY'S YEARS OF TRAINING PAY OFF IN SPADES!

WHAP!

DIDN'T IT OCCUR TO YOU THAT I'D NAIL YOU BEFORE YOU COULD GROW PAST ME??!

THEN, WITH HIS ERSTWHILE FOE BLISSFULLY COUNTING SHEEP, HANK PUTS THE WORLD-FAMOUS COSTUME UPON ITS RIGHTFUL OWNER ONCE MORE, AND PREPARES TO TACKLE THE MENACE OF THE GROWING PLANT....!

ATTENTION, ALL ANTS! ASSEMBLE YOUR NUMBERS! TOP PRIORITY! YOU MUST FIND THE MAIN ROOT OF THE PLANT WHICH IS THREATENING THE CITY! THAT IS ALL!

THE CYBERNETIC COMMUNICATOR WILL TRANSFORM MY MESSAGE INTO THOUGHT IMPULSES WHICH THE ANTS CAN UNDERSTAND! AND NOW I'VE GOT TO SHRINK DOWN FAST AND BE READY FOR ACTION!

WHAT LUCK! THEY'VE FOUND IT ALREADY! IT'S NOT FAR FROM HERE! PERHAPS I'M STILL NOT TOO LATE!

10

WITHIN MINUTES, THE MIRACULOUS MITE-SIZED AVENGER HAS ENTERED ONE OF THE MANY COUNTLESS ANT HILLS WHICH EXIST VIRTUALLY UNNOTICED BENEATH THE FEET OF THE POPULACE! GUIDED BY HIS LOYAL ANTS, HE RACES THRU THE TWISTING TUNNELS AND PASSAGEWAYS BENEATH THE SURFACE, UNTIL...

YOU *FOUND* IT!! GOOD WORK, LITTLE PARTNERS! NOW, IT'S UP TO *ME!*

HOWEVER, AS YOU CAN WELL IMAGINE, THERE IS A VAST DIFFERENCE BETWEEN *LOCATING* THE DANGEROUS, EVER-SWELLING TAP ROOT, AND FINDING A MEANS OF *DESTROYING* IT! BUT, WE PAUSE FOR A MOMENT NOW, TO BRING ALL YOU ANT-LOVERS A SPECIAL DIAGRAM WHICH WILL BETTER ACQUAINT YOU WITH THE INTRICACIES OF AN AVERAGE ANT CITY...

CROSS SECTION OF ANT CITY

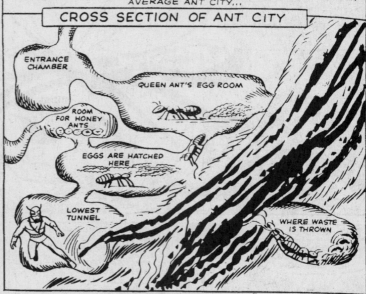

ENTRANCE CHAMBER

QUEEN ANT'S EGG ROOM

ROOM FOR HONEY ANTS

EGGS ARE HATCHED HERE

LOWEST TUNNEL

WHERE WASTE IS THROWN

AND NOW, WE RETURN AGAIN TO THE ASTONISHING ANTICS OF PEERLESS MR. PYM! WITHOUT WASTING A SECOND, HE ORDERS EVERY ANT TO EVACUATE THE ENTIRE ANT HILL-- AS WELL AS ALL THE SURROUNDING ANT HILLS! THEN, ONCE HE IS ASSURED THAT HIS NEXT MOVE WILL CAUSE NO HARM, HE GRASPS PART OF THE ENORMOUS ROOT IN AN IRON GRIP, AND INSTANTLY THINKS HIMSELF INTO *GIANT SIZE!*

SO QUICKLY DOES HE DO IT--EXERTING EVERY BIT OF MENTAL POWER AT HIS COMMAND, THAT THE VERY FORCE OF THE LIGHTNING-LIKE CHANGE HURLS HIM HIGH INTO THE AIR, AND WITH HIM, STILL GRASPED TIGHTLY FOR DEAR LIFE, THE MONSTEROUS PLANT, RIPPED BODILY FROM THE GROUND BY THE AWESOME STRENGTH OF *GIANT-MAN!*

JUST IN *TIME!* ANOTHER FEW MINUTES, AND IT WOULD HAVE BEEN TOO SECURELY ROOTED FOR ANY POWER ON EARTH TO DISLODGE!

11

THEN, AS THE DOUBLE-SIZED DAZZLER MAKES A GRACEFUL DIVE INTO THE CENTRAL PARK LAKE, A SWARM OF *TERMITES* RETURN TO THE ANT HILL BELOW AND QUICKLY DESTROY EVERY LAST VESTAGE OF THE TAP ROOT WHICH MIGHT REMAIN!

MEANWHILE, HAVING FINALLY FREED HERSELF FROM THE TRANSPARENT JEWEL BOX, THE *WASP* FLIES BACK TO HQ. AS FAST AS HER LITTLE WINGS WILL CARRY HER...

THERE ARE NO TRACES LEFT OF THE GIGANTIC PLANT! MY BLUE-EYED DREAMBOAT MUST HAVE SOMEHOW POLISHED IT OFF!

THERE HE *IS!* BUT-- *WAIT* A MINUTE! WHAT IF IT *ISN'T* HANK?? WHAT IF IT'S THAT EVIL *IMPOSTER?* I-I'D BETTER TAKE NO CHANCES!

YOU SAY YOU WANT THE WHOLE STORY? SURE, BOYS --COME ON UP! I'LL BE GLAD TO GIVE YOU AN INTERVIEW!

MY *WASP'S STING* WILL KEEP HIM QUIET LONG ENOUGH FOR ME TO MAKE CERTAIN!

THWIP!

WHA--??!

YOU NUTTY LITTLE FEATHER-BRAIN! IS *THAT* THE WAY YOU GREET THE EVER-LOVIN' PRINCE CHARMING WHO SPENDS ALL HIS TIME KEEPING YOU SAFE FROM HARM!

OH, HANK HONEY-- IT *IS* YOU! I'M SO GLAD!

SO AM I! IF THAT'S THE WAY YOU GREET YOUR *BOY FRIEND,* I'D HATE TO BE ONE OF YOUR *ENEMIES!*

AND THEN, THE *NEWSMEN* BURST IN...

GIANT-MAN! YOU PROMISED US THE STORY OF HOW YOU DESTROYED THAT FANTASTIC GROWING PLANT!

I'M FROM J. J. JAMESON'S DAILY BUGLE--WE WANT TO DO A *FEATURE* ON YOU!

THIS IS FRONT PAGE STUFF! LET'S GET A SHOT OF GIANT-MAN AND THE *WASP* TOGETHER!

SAY! WHO'S THAT FELLA *WITH* YOU? A NEW ASSISTANT?

NOT EXACTLY, BOYS! YOU MIGHT SAY HE'S A *FRIEND--* HE WAS JUST PASSING BY AND SO HE DROPPED IN!

HENRY J. PYM! YOU *KNOW* HE'S THE ONE WHO *FOUGHT* ME BEFORE! WHAT'S GOING *ON* HERE?

WAIT TILL WE'RE ALONE, PRETTY GAL, AND I'LL *TELL* YOU!

OKAY--GRAB ALL THE PIX YOU CAN, BOYS, WHILE I ASK THE QUESTIONS!

FINALLY, AFTER THE INTERVIEW, WHEN EVERY-ONE HAS LEFT...

HOW COULD YOU LET HIM GO, HANK?? HE KNEW YOUR TRUE IDENTITY....

NOT *QUITE,* JAN! WE BIO-CHEMISTS KNOW A FEW LITTLE TRICKS, TOO! I JUST HAPPENED TO HAVE SOME *MEMORY-LOSS* SERUM LYING AROUND! HE DOESN'T EVEN REMEMBER HE HAD BEEN A *CROOK!* HE'LL GO *STRAIGHT* FROM NOW ON!

THE END

AND SO WILL *WE--* STRAIGHT TO THE *HULK* THRILLER THAT FOLLOWS! LET'S GO--!

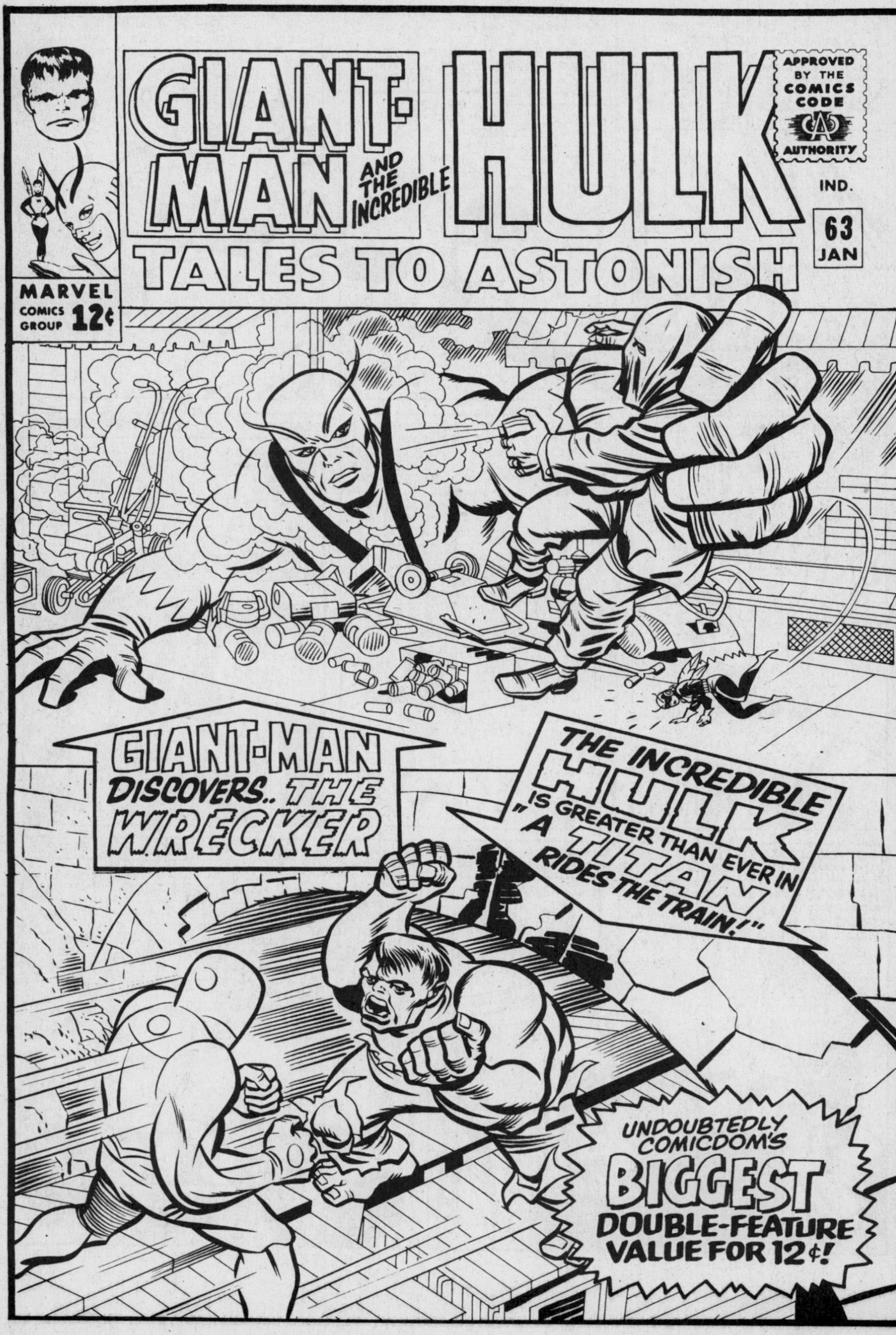

MARVEL COMICS GROUP 12¢
GIANT-MAN AND THE INCREDIBLE HULK
TALES TO ASTONISH
APPROVED BY THE COMICS CODE AUTHORITY
IND.
63 JAN
GIANT-MAN DISCOVERS.. THE WRECKER
THE INCREDIBLE HULK IS GREATER THAN EVER IN "A TITAN RIDES THE TRAIN!"
UNDOUBTEDLY COMICDOM'S BIGGEST DOUBLE-FEATURE VALUE FOR 12¢!

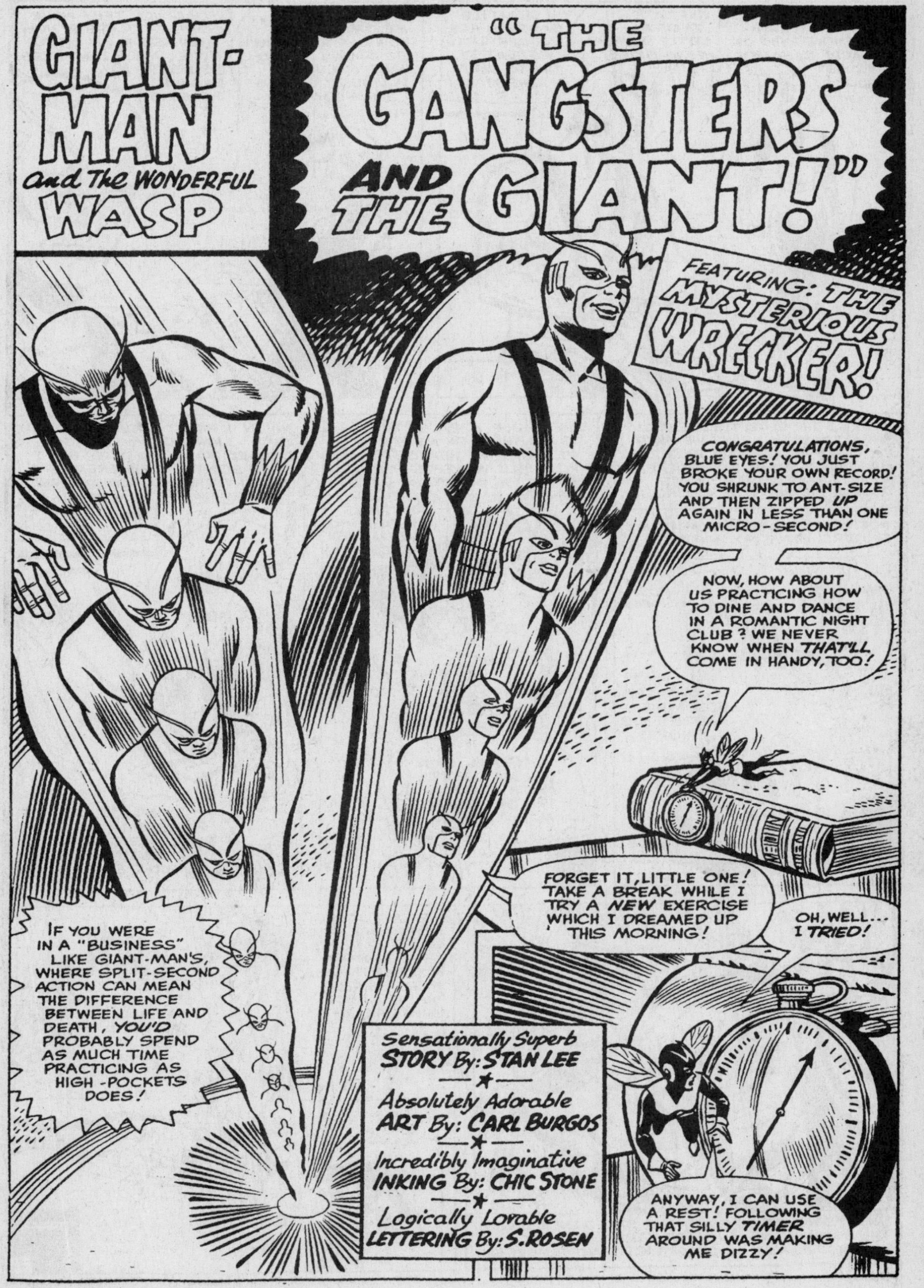
GIANT-MAN and The WONDERFUL WASP
"THE GANGSTERS AND THE GIANT!"
FEATURING: THE MYSTERIOUS WRECKER!
CONGRATULATIONS, BLUE EYES! YOU JUST BROKE YOUR OWN RECORD! YOU SHRUNK TO ANT-SIZE AND THEN ZIPPED UP AGAIN IN LESS THAN ONE MICRO-SECOND!
NOW, HOW ABOUT US PRACTICING HOW TO DINE AND DANCE IN A ROMANTIC NIGHT CLUB? WE NEVER KNOW WHEN THAT'LL COME IN HANDY, TOO!
IF YOU WERE IN A "BUSINESS" LIKE GIANT-MAN'S, WHERE SPLIT-SECOND ACTION CAN MEAN THE DIFFERENCE BETWEEN LIFE AND DEATH, YOU'D PROBABLY SPEND AS MUCH TIME PRACTICING AS HIGH-POCKETS DOES!
FORGET IT, LITTLE ONE! TAKE A BREAK WHILE I TRY A NEW EXERCISE WHICH I DREAMED UP THIS MORNING!
OH, WELL... I TRIED!
Sensationally Superb STORY By: STAN LEE
Absolutely Adorable ART By: CARL BURGOS
Incredibly Imaginative INKING By: CHIC STONE
Logically Lovable LETTERING By: S. ROSEN
ANYWAY, I CAN USE A REST! FOLLOWING THAT SILLY TIMER AROUND WAS MAKING ME DIZZY!

I'LL GROW TO NORMAL SIZE SO YOU CAN FEAST YOUR EYES ON ME MORE *CLEARLY*, YOU LUCKY DEVIL!

WHAT ARE *THOSE* LITTLE WHATCHA-MAWHOZIES, HANK?

THESE LITTLE GADGETS ARE CONCENTRATED *WEIGHTS*! TRY TO *LIFT* ONE, JAN...!

YOU'RE PUTTING ME *ON*, BIG BOY! HOW CAN ANYTHING SO *SMALL* BE SO HARD TO LIFT?? I'LL JUST... JUST... 〈, *UNNGGHH*!! 〈

I *TOLD* YOU THEY WERE *CONCENTRATED*! NOW STEP ASIDE, MY LITTLE PIXIE, WHILE I IMPRESS YOU WITH MY *DASHING DERRING-DO*!

HOOKING THE DECEPTIVELY SMALL, BUT EXTREMELY HEAVY WEIGHTS ONTO HIS ACCESSORY BELT, THE MASTER OF MANY SIZES LEAPS TO THE TRAPEZE BAR ON HIS DOUBLE-HEIGHT GYM CEILING...

NOTICE, JAN... AT NO TIME DO MY FINGERS LEAVE MY HANDS!!

WELL, WELL! MY PARTNER'S BECOMING ANOTHER BOB HOPE!

THE WHOLE *IDEA* OF THIS IS TO GO THROUGH MY PACES WEARING THE HEAVIEST POSSIBLE WEIGHTS! THEN, WHEN I'M IN ACTION *WITH-OUT* THEM, ANYTHING I DO WILL SEEM *EASY* TO ME!

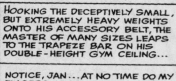

CAREFUL, HANK! YOU MAY NOT BE MUCH, BUT YOU'RE THE ONLY GIANT-MAN I *HAVE*!

WHEN I FIRST BECAME GIANT-MAN, I WAS CLUMSY AND UNUSED TO MY POWERS! BUT I WISH SOME OF THE ENEMIES I FOUGHT THEN COULD SEE ME *NOW*!

THE WEIGHTS ARE PREVENTING ME FROM REACHING THE SECOND TRAPEZE! THAT MEANS A SPLIT-SECOND SIZE CHANGE!

MADE IT!!

INCREASING HIS SIZE WITH THE SPEED OF THOUGHT, THE ASTONISHING AVENGER STRETCHES OUT ENOUGH TO BE ABLE TO GRASP THE DISTANT TRAPEZE BAR!

THEN, RETURNING TO NORMAL SIZE AGAIN...

NOT BAD,-- FOR A MERE-MALE, THAT IS! AND, *NOW* CAN WE...?

HOLD IT, HON! THERE'S THE DOOR-BELL!

RRR INN GG!

2.

I'LL GET IT WHILE YOU REMOVE THOSE SILLY WEIGHTS!

OH! AN OFFICER!

I'D LIKE TO SPEAK TO GIANT-MAN, MA'AM!

HE WAS HERE JUST A MINUTE AGO! OH, WHAT'S THAT?!

SOUNDED LIKE SOMETHING FALLING! FROM THE NEXT ROOM!

SLAM!

WHO WAS AT THE DOOR, WASP?

AN OFFICER TO SEE YOU! BUT, WHAT WAS THAT NOISE??

LET'S GO IN AND HAVE A LOOK....!

WELL!! I SHOULD HAVE GUESSED! DON'T YOU EVER STOP PRACTICING?

GOT A MINUTE, BIG FELLA?

THUMP!

SURE! I'LL SHRINK DOWN AND BE RIGHT WITH YOU!

I GUESS THIS MEANS NO DINNER DATE FOR YOUR LITTLE FLYING FEMALE FRIEND!

THUD!

I HATE TO DISTURB YOU IF YOU HAD A DATE PLANNED, GIANT-MAN... BUT THE CHIEF WANTS TO SEE YOU AT HEADQUARTERS AS SOON AS POSSIBLE!

THEN IT MUST BE MIGHTY IMPORTANT! OKAY, I'LL BE THERE IN TWO SHAKES!

I HAVE A SQUAD CAR DOWNSTAIRS!

FINE! THEN YOU CAN GIVE THE WASP A LIFT! I'LL MEET YOU THERE!

WAIT! WHAT ARE YOU DOING??!

STOP!! YOU'RE ON THE TOP FLOOR!!

3.

OH! I FORGOT ABOUT THE TENSION SPRING ESCAPE CABLE WHICH HANGS OUTSIDE OUR WINDOW! CAREFUL, YOU BIG SHOW-OFF!!

OH, NO!! I CAN'T BELIEVE IT!! HE..HE LET GO!! HE'LL BE KILLED!

DON'T WORRY, GORGEOUS! I KNOW WHAT I'M DOING!!

I HATE TO WORRY HER, BUT I DIDN'T HAVE TIME TO EXPLAIN! I'VE BEEN WANTING TO TRY THIS FOR DAYS!!

FIRST, I'LL SEND OUT A MENTAL SIGNAL, CYBERNETICALLY...

...AND THEN, I'LL MAKE A SPLIT-SECOND REDUCTION TO ANT-SIZE...!!

LOOK! IT'S GIANT-MAN!!

HE'S SHRINKING... TRYING TO BREAK HIS FALL!!

AND IN THE STREET BELOW, A STARTLED, STUNNED CROWD WATCHES THE AWESOME SIGHT...

SHRINKING WON'T HELP HIM! HE CAN'T FLY!

CAN'T SEE HIM ANY MORE! HE GOT TOO SMALL! HE'S GONE!! BUT... WHERE???

BUT EVEN AS THE ONLOOKERS WONDER, A SPEEDY FLYING ANT, SUMMONED BY HENRY PYM'S CYBERNETIC COMMAND, HAS FLOWN TO THE FALLING FIGURE AND CARRIED HIM SAFELY TO EARTH, FASTER AND SMALLER THAN ANYONE CAN SEE!

4.

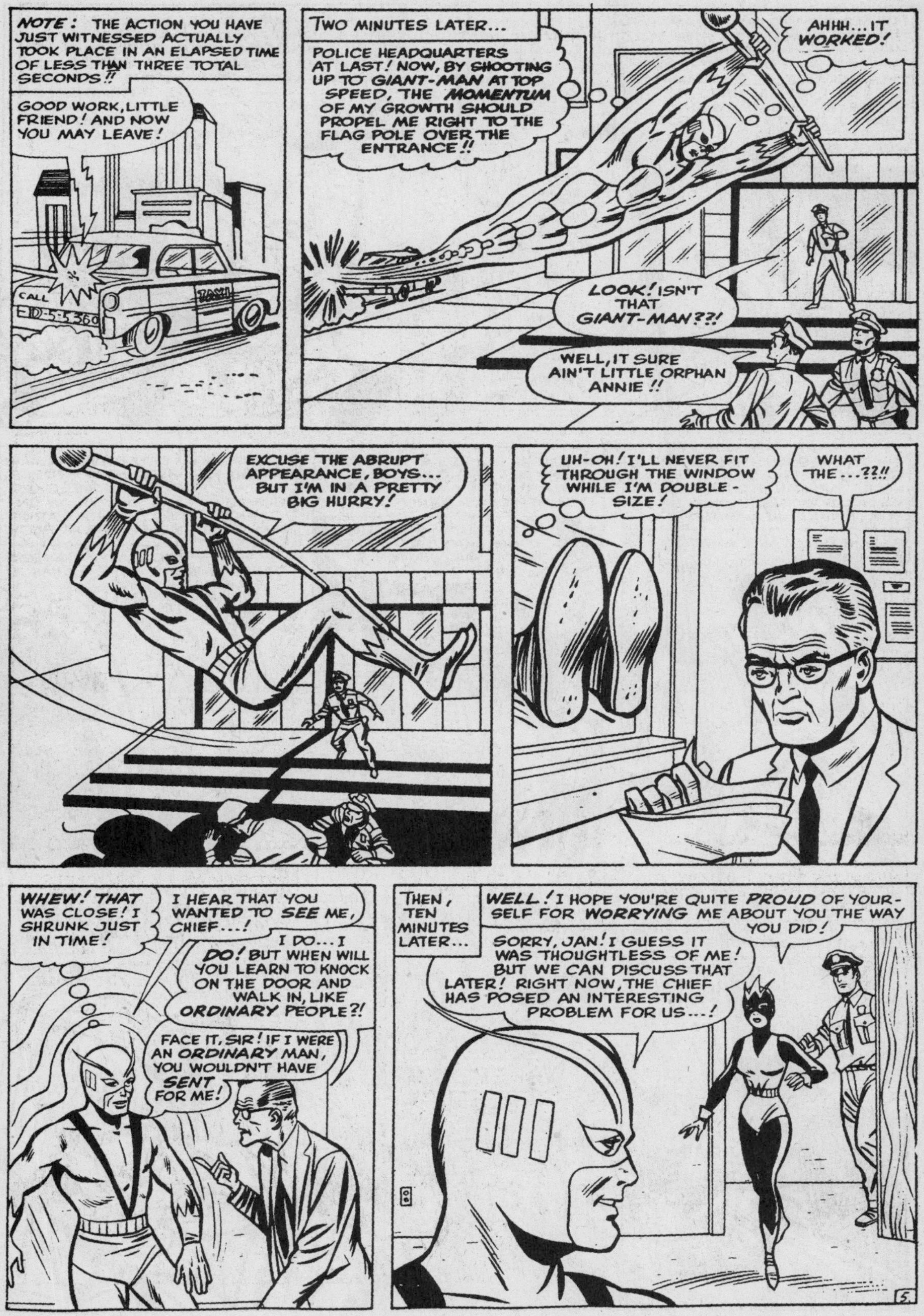
NOTE: THE ACTION YOU HAVE JUST WITNESSED ACTUALLY TOOK PLACE IN AN ELAPSED TIME OF LESS THAN THREE TOTAL SECONDS!!
GOOD WORK, LITTLE FRIEND! AND NOW YOU MAY LEAVE!
CALL
ED-5-5360
TAXI
TWO MINUTES LATER...
POLICE HEADQUARTERS AT LAST! NOW, BY SHOOTING UP TO GIANT-MAN AT TOP SPEED, THE MOMENTUM OF MY GROWTH SHOULD PROPEL ME RIGHT TO THE FLAG POLE OVER THE ENTRANCE!!
AHHH... IT WORKED!
LOOK! ISN'T THAT GIANT-MAN??!
WELL, IT SURE AIN'T LITTLE ORPHAN ANNIE!!
EXCUSE THE ABRUPT APPEARANCE, BOYS... BUT I'M IN A PRETTY BIG HURRY!
UH-OH! I'LL NEVER FIT THROUGH THE WINDOW WHILE I'M DOUBLE-SIZE!
WHAT THE...??!!
WHEW! THAT WAS CLOSE! I SHRUNK JUST IN TIME!
I HEAR THAT YOU WANTED TO SEE ME, CHIEF...!
I DO... I DO! BUT WHEN WILL YOU LEARN TO KNOCK ON THE DOOR AND WALK IN, LIKE ORDINARY PEOPLE?!
FACE IT, SIR! IF I WERE AN ORDINARY MAN, YOU WOULDN'T HAVE SENT FOR ME!
THEN, TEN MINUTES LATER...
WELL! I HOPE YOU'RE QUITE PROUD OF YOURSELF FOR WORRYING ME ABOUT YOU THE WAY YOU DID!
SORRY, JAN! I GUESS IT WAS THOUGHTLESS OF ME! BUT WE CAN DISCUSS THAT LATER! RIGHT NOW, THE CHIEF HAS POSED AN INTERESTING PROBLEM FOR US...!
5.

I'VE ALREADY BRIEFED *GIANT-MAN*, BUT I'LL RUN THROUGH IT AGAIN TO GIVE *YOU* THE PICTURE, WASP!

THIS IS A MAP OF THE BROWNS-VILLE SECTION OF BROOKLYN! EACH DOT REPRESENTS A *STORE* WHICH HAS BEEN FORCED TO PAY PROTECTION MONEY TO THE *WRECKER*!

THE WRECKER?? WHO'S HE??

NO ONE KNOWS HIS *REAL* IDENTITY... BUT HE'S HEAD OF A MERCILESS GANG WHICH MAKES INNOCENT STOREKEEPERS PAY LARGE SUMS OF MONEY IN ORDER FOR THE WRECKER NOT TO INJURE THEM OR DAMAGE THEIR STORES!

TELL HER WHAT YOU'VE TOLD *ME* ABOUT HIM, CHIEF! THE WASP WILL WORK *WITH* ME ON THIS!

"NO ONE HAS EVER *SEEN* THE WRECKER'S REAL FACE! HE NEVER APPEARS ANYWHERE WITHOUT AN ALL-CONCEALING *HOOD* WHICH HE WEARS!"

IF THEY CAN'T *FIND* US, THEY CAN'T *CATCH* US! ALWAYS REMEMBER THAT!

"AFTER HE STRIKES AT A STORE, HE AND HIS MEN FLEE LIKE THE COWARDS THEY ARE BEFORE OUR OFFICERS ARRIVE!"

THE YELLOW PUNKS! LOOK WHAT THEY DID TO POOR MR. MARVIN'S SHOP!

"I'VE POSTED DETECTIVES IN MANY OF THE NEIGHBORHOOD STORES, HOPING TO TRAP THE WRECKER, BUT HE SEEMS TO HAVE AN UN-CANNY INSTINCT WHICH WARNS HIM TO STAY AWAY FROM SUCH SHOPS!"

TOO MANY STRANGERS THERE! I WON'T TAKE A CHANCE!

HAIRCUT $2.00
SHAVE $1.00

"WE'RE CERTAIN TO GET HIM SOONER OR LATER, BUT WE FELT THAT WITH *YOUR* HELP IT MIGHT BE SOONER! AND EVERY DAY HE'S AT LARGE, HE'S CAPABLE OF CAUSING STILL MORE INJURIES AND DAMAGE!"

WHEN THE *OTHER* WAREHOUSE OWNERS FIND OUT I PUT A MINIATURE PROTON BOMB IN THIS EMPTY OLD CONDEMNED BUILDING, THEY'LL ALL FALL INTO LINE WITH THEIR PROTECTION PAYMENTS TO ME!!

WAREHOUSE

AND THAT'S THE STORY! YOU TWO HAVE HELPED US IN THE PAST, AND I THOUGHT YOU MIGHT BE ABLE TO HELP US AGAIN, BY ENABLING US TO BRING THE WRECKER TO JUSTICE AS QUICKLY AS POSSIBLE!

YOUR MEN HAVE BEEN DOING A FINE JOB, CHIEF... BUT PERHAPS *WE* CAN THINK OF A DIFFERENT, MORE UN-ORTHODOX APPROACH!

6.

IS THERE ANYTHING YOU'LL NEED, SON? ANY SPECIAL WEAPONS, OR...?

NO, THANKS, CHIEF! THE WASP IS MY ONLY LITTLE SECRET WEAPON!

I'D RATHER YOU THOUGHT OF ME AS YOUR DREAM-BOAT, BUT I GUESS A GAL CAN'T HAVE EVERYTHING!

WE'LL CHECK WITH YOU LATER, CHIEF!

LATER... IT FEELS STRANGE TO BE STARTING ON A CASE WITHOUT WEARING OUR COSTUMES, JAN!

BUT I LIKE THE CHANGE! A GAL BEGINS TO FEEL FOOLISH WEARING THOSE WHACKY ANTENNAE ON TOP OF HER HEAD ALL THE TIME!

LOOK, HANK! ISN'T THIS WHAT WE'RE AFTER? A STORE FOR SALE!

STORE FOR SALE

WE'RE INTERESTED IN BUYING A HARD-WARE STORE, AND THIS LOOKS LIKE THE TYPE WE WANT! HOW MUCH IS IT?

MISTER, IF I HAD MY WAY, I'D PAY YOU TO TAKE IT!

REALLY? WHY?

BECAUSE OF THE WRECKER, THAT'S WHY!!! ALL THE OTHER MERCHANTS IN THE NEIGHBORHOOD PAY HIM PROTECTION MONEY BECAUSE THEY'RE AFRAID OF HIM! BUT I WON'T DO IT! AND NOW HE'S EVEN GOT MY CUSTOMERS SCARED! THEY'VE STOPPED SHOPPING IN MY STORE!

WELL, THAT DOESN'T BOTHER ME! I'M WILLING TO PAY A LITTLE MONEY TO THE WRECKER EACH WEEK IF IT MEANS I WON'T BE BOTHERED BY HIM OR HIS MEN!

THEN YOU'RE A COWARD, TOO... JUST LIKE ALL THE OTHERS! WELL, I DON'T CARE! I'LL SELL YOU THE STORE.. AND HE CAN ROB YOU, ALSO! AT LEAST I WON'T HAVE TO BE CONNECTED WITH A BUNCH OF COWARDS!

THEN A FEW DAYS LATER... I HEAR THAT SMITH'S HARDWARE STORE RE-OPENED AT THE CORNER OF 15TH STREET! YOU BOYS KNOW WHAT TA DO! GET GOING!

SURE THING, BOSS! WE DON'T WANT TA GET STALE JUST HANGIN' AROUND!

AND SO... I HAD A HUNCH THE WRECKER'S MEN WOULD GET HERE SOON! THEY DON'T SUSPECT A THING! AS FAR AS THEY KNOW, WE'RE AN AVERAGE YOUNG COUPLE WHO JUST BOUGHT A STORE!

WE'LL MAKE IT SHORT AND SWEET, MAC! YOU SIGN THIS PROTECTION CONTRACT, OR ELSE YOUR STORE GETS WRECKED BY THE WRECKER! DIG?

CONTRACT

HERE'S JUST A LITTLE SAMPLE OF WHAT CAN HAPPEN IF YOU DON'T COUGH UP THE WEEKLY PAYMENTS!

OH! OUR GLASS DISPLAY CASE!

CRACK!

7.

I GUESS WE **SHOULD** PAY YOU... FOR IF WE **DON'T**, YOU'RE LIABLE TO GET ROUGH... LIKE **THIS!**

WHULP!

AND THEN, THE CHANCES ARE THAT YOU'D RETURN AGAIN, AND TRY TO BEAT ME UP A **SECOND** TIME, LIKE **THIS!** AND I CERTAINLY WOULDN'T WANT **THAT** TO HAPPEN, WOULD I??

WHOP!

HEY! YOU CAN'T DO THAT TO ROCKY! I'LL... I'LL... AYYYY

I'M REALLY DOING YOU A **FAVOR** STOPPING YOU WITH THIS JUDO HOLD! BECAUSE IF MY ANGRY **PARTNER** EVER GETS HIS HANDS ON YOU... YOU'LL **KNOW** IT!

THANK YOU, GENTLEMEN! ..CALL AGAIN!

DID YOU TAKE ENOUGH MONEY FROM THEM TO PAY FOR THE DAMAGE THEY DID, LITTLE ONE?

YES, HANDSOME! IT'S ALL HERE! BUT MAYBE I SHOULD HAVE ASKED IF THEY'D RATHER CHARGE IT TO THE DINER'S CLUB?

MINUTES LATER, AFTER THE STARTLING NEWS HAS SPREAD...

THAT WAS A VERY **BRAVE** THING YOU DID, YOUNG MAN! BUT I'M AFRAID YOU'VE PUT YOURSELF IN GRAVE DANGER!

YOU MEAN BECAUSE THE **WRECKER** WILL RETURN WITH **MORE** OF HIS MEN? DON'T WORRY... WE'LL BE **READY** FOR THEM!

IN FACT, WE'LL BE VERY DISAPPOINTED IF HE **DOESN'T** SHOW UP!

MEANWHILE, BACK AT THE WRECKER'S HEADQUARTERS...

YOU LET ONE ORDINARY, WEAK COUPLE THROW YOU OUT OF THEIR STORE?!! I OUGHT TO HAVE YOUR **HIDES** FOR THAT! **NEXT** TIME I WON'T BE SO LENIENT WITH YOU!

AND NOW, I'LL ATTEND TO THEM **PERSONALLY!**

SECONDS LATER, THE **WRECKER** CONTACTS HIS ENTIRE NETWORK OF CRIMINALS VIA A SPECIAL COMMUNICATIONS SYSTEM ...

ATTENTION! ATTENTION! THIS IS THE **WRECKER!** ALL UNITS ABANDON YOUR TASKS AND EXECUTE PLAN "W" IMMEDIATELY! THAT IS ALL!

8.

AND SO, *PLAN "W"* IS PROMPTLY PUT INTO OPERATION! NORMALLY, THE POLICE ARE ON HAND TO AID THE OTHER MUNICIPAL AGENCIES, SUCH AS THE FIRE DEPARTMENT, IN THEIR VITAL WORK!... BUT *NOW*...

EVERYTHING'S FINALLY GETTING UNDER CONTROL!

IT'S STRANGE... THERE WERE NO *POLICE* ON THE SCENE! I WONDER WHY!?

WHY INDEED? THE WRECKER'S *PLAN "W"* IS PARTLY TO BLAME! FOR AT THAT MOMENT, HIS FAR-FLUNG BAND OF LAWBREAKERS ARE DOING ALL THEY CAN TO KEEP THE LAW ENFORCEMENT OFFICERS BUSY!

GRAB THAT MAN RUNNING PAST YOU, JOHN! HE'S THE LAST OF 'EM!

HOLD IT, MISTER! YOU'RE NOT GOING ANY-WHERE NOW!

WE'VE GOT HIM, CAP-TAIN! BUT I DON'T UNDERSTAND! THERE DOESN'T SEEM TO BE ANY *REASON* FOR THIS SUDDEN RIOT!

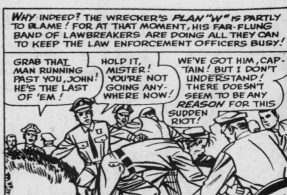

IN EVERY NEIGHBORHOOD BORDERING THE ONE IN WHICH GIANT-MAN'S STORE IS LOCATED, RUFFIANS AND HOODLUMS KEEP THE POLICE CONSTANTLY ON THE GO...!

EVERYONE STAND WHERE YOU ARE! YOU'RE ALL SUR-ROUNDED! NOBODY MOVE!

OUR INFORMATION WAS RIGHT! LOOKS LIKE WE ARRIVED JUST IN TIME TO PREVENT A RUMBLE! BUT WHO *ARE* THESE CHARACTERS? I'VE NEVER SEEN THEM HERE BEFORE!

CALLING CAR SEVEN! CALLING CAR SEVEN!

SNAP IT UP, BOYS! *ANOTHER* CALL'S COMING IN!

MEANWHILE...

SO! THIS IS THE PLACE, EH?

NOW, IF MY MEN HAVE DONE THEIR JOBS WELL, I SHOULD BE ABLE TO DEAL WITH THE COUPLE INSIDE BEFORE THE POLICE CAN REACH THE SPOT TO HELP THEM!

STOP THE CAR AND FOLLOW ME!

HARDWARE

BUT A DOUBLE-SIZED SURPRISE IS AWAITING THE BRUTAL MOB LEADER...

HERE THEY COME, DOLL FACE! READY?

THEN, LET'S *GO*!!

YOU *BET*!

WE'RE A LITTLE SHORT OF HELP TODAY, GENTS... SO I HOPE YOU WON'T MIND IF I WAIT ON YOU ALL AT *ONCE*!

WHAM!

IT'S GIANT-MAN!

9.

I DON'T KNOW WHERE *YOU* CAME FROM, BUT THIS TEAR GAS BOMB WILL AFFECT *YOU* JUST LIKE ANYONE ELSE!

HE'S *RIGHT!* HIS HOOD PROTECTED *HIM* FROM THE EFFECTS... BUT I'LL NEED SOME FRESH AIR IF I'M TO BE ABLE TO RETURN TO THE FIGHT!

WE'LL TAKE CARE OF GIANT-MAN, BOSS! HE CAN'T DO MUCH WHILE HE'S GASPIN' FOR AIR!

SEE 'THAT YOU DON'T SLIP UP! IN THE MEANTIME, WE'LL PUT THE *WASP* OUT OF ACTION!

HARDW

BUT SKILLFULLY USING THE *STUN GUN* WHICH HANDSOME HANK HAD DESIGNED FOR HER, THE FAST-FLYING WASP PROVES TO BE NO EASY FOE FOR HER SLOWER-MOVING ANTAGONISTS!

HOW DOES SHE *DO* IT? THOSE AIR BLASTS SHE'S SHOOTIN' AT US HAVE THE KICK OF A *MULE!*

UGH! YOU'RE TELLIN' *ME!*

DON'T CROWD, BOYS! I WON'T OVERLOOK ANY OF YOU!!

HOWEVER, THE DIABOLICAL *WRECKER* ONCE AGAIN SAVES HIMSELF AND HIS MEN WITH AN UNEXPECTED MANEUVER!

YOU *FORGOT* THAT EVERY HARDWARE STORE CARRIES CANS OF DDT BUG KILLER! LET'S SEE HOW SUCH A SPRAY WOULD REACT ON A FLYING *WASP!*

OHHH!... GIANT-MAN! ---HELP ME!

AT THAT INSTANT, HIS LUNGS ONCE MORE FILLED WITH LIFE-GIVING AIR, THE ASTONISHING AVENGER HEARS THE CRY FOR HELP FROM HIS BELOVED! WITH AN ANGRY BELLOW, LIKE SOME GIGANTIC JUNGLE BEAST, HE SHAKES HIS NORMAL-SIZED ATTACKERS FROM HIM AS THOUGH THEY'RE MERELY TOYS...!

OFF, YOU PUNY VERMIN! I'LL ATTEND TO YOU LATER! I'VE GOT TO REACH THE *WASP!*

THESE TEAR GAS AND DDT VAPORS DON'T AFFECT ME NOW BECAUSE I CAN LIFT MY HEAD *ABOVE* THEM...

BUT *SHE* IS SOMEWHERE BELOW! I'VE GOT TO CLEAR THE *AIR* FOR HER!

10.

AN *EXHAUST* FAN! I HAVEN'T TIME TO FIND THE SWITCH! I'LL JUST RIP AWAY PART OF THE CEILING AND FIND THE RIGHT WIRES... *THERE!* IT'S *ON!*

HE'LL BE COMING AFTER *ME* NEXT! I'VE GOT TO *STOP* HIM!

THE *WRECKER!* QUICK... WHERE'S THE *WASP? TELL ME*, OR I'LL MAKE YOU REGRET THE DAY YOU EVER *SAW* HER!

THIS IS MY LAST CHANCE! HE'S SO ANGRY... COMING SO FAST ...THAT HE DOESN'T YET NOTICE THIS *BEAR TRAP* WHICH I GRABBED FROM THE SPORTING GOODS SHELF! IT'S STRONG ENOUGH TO STOP EVEN *HIM!*

BUT, THE INSTANT HE HEARS THE SOUND OF THE IRON JAWS SNAPPING CLOSED, THE TRIGGER-FAST BRAIN OF BRILLIANT HENRY PYM BEGINS TO PLAN FOR A LIGHTNING-SWIFT *ESCAPE!*

A *BEAR TRAP!!*

ONLY ONE POSSIBLE WAY TO *ELUDE* IT... IF I CAN MOVE *FAST* ENOUGH!

SNAP!

THEN, IN LESS THAN ONE MICRO-SECOND... BEFORE THE TEETH OF THE TRAP CAN MANAGE TO SERIOUSLY CUT THROUGH HIS PROTECTIVE FOOT COVERING, THE ASTONISHING MAN OF MANY SIZES SHRINKS TO *ANT SIZE*, SLIPPING THROUGH THE LOOSENED TRAP, AND THEN, WITHOUT PAUSE, HURTLES UP TO *GIANT SIZE* ONCE MORE!

IT..IT'S... *IMPOSSIBLE!!* IT *CAN'T* BE !!! *NOBODY* CAN MOVE LIKE THAT!

GIANT-MAN *CAN!* NOW *TALK*, YOU SPINELESS HEEL... THIS IS YOUR *LAST* CHANCE... *WHERE IS THE WASP?!!*

CAN'T DEFY HIM ANY MORE...HE'S TOO ANGRY...TOO POWERFUL!!

SHE'S ON THE DISPLAY TABLE...NEAR THE PAINTS AND TILES SECTION!

I'D *BETTER* FIND HER THERE... AND SHE'D BETTER BE ALL RIGHT! MEANTIME, YOU'LL KEEP UNTIL LATER!

THE *WRECKER!* WE'LL TAKE CARE OF HIM!!

WHEEEE!

LISTEN... SIRENS! THE POLICE ARE ALREADY ON THE WAY!

11.

ONCE AGAIN, WITH BLINDING SPEED, THE ASTONISHING HENRY PYM SHRINKS TO ANT-SIZE...

AND WITHIN SECONDS...

SHE MUST BE HERE SOMEWHERE! I..I HEAR BREATHING!

THIS SIDE UP

PLASTIC TILE

DIRECTIONS FOR USE:

THERE SHE IS! BUT..SHE'S UNCONSCIOUS!! WASP! WAKE UP... SPEAK TO ME!

SHE'S COMING TO!! OH, JAN, MY DARLING! IF YOU ONLY KNEW WHAT YOU MEAN TO ME!

IF ANYTHING EVER HAPPENED TO YOU....I..I COULDN'T GO ON ANY LONGER! JAN...

HANK.. IS THAT YOU..?

OF COURSE IT IS, DEAREST! DON'T WORRY...EVERY-THING IS ALL RIGHT NOW! YOU'RE SAFE...!

MMMM!

WHY, BLUE EYES! I NEVER KNEW YOU WERE SO ROMANTIC!

ME? OH, I..EH..I WAS JUST TRYING TO REVIVE YOU BY MOUTH-TO-MOUTH RESUSCITATION!

WHATEVER YOU WANT TO CALL IT, DREAM-BOAT, I HOPE IT BECOMES HABIT-FORMING!

I SEE THE POLICE HAVE UNMASKED THE WRECKER! IT'S THE ONE WHO SOLD US THE STORE! I WONDERED WHY HIS STORE HADN'T BEEN WRECKED TILL WE BOUGHT IT!

DON'T WORRY, WRECKER...YOU WON'T BE LONELY IN JAIL! WE CAP-TURED ALL YOUR HOODS AFTER GIANT-MAN BOOTED THEM OUT OF THE STORE!

AND SO...

NOW I KNOW HOW TO MAKE HIM KISS ME MORE OFTEN ...I'LL PRETEND TO BE UNCONSCIOUS!

A PENNY FOR YOUR THOUGHTS, JAN!

THEY WOULDN'T INTEREST YOU, HANK! I WAS JUST WONDERING WHO'LL WIN THE ELECTION!

AND SO WE TAKE OUR LEAVE OF HIGH-POCKETS AND HIS WONDERFUL WENCH FOR NOW! BUT, BE SURE TO BE WITH US AGAIN NEXT ISH WHEN WE HAVE A SPECIAL TREAT FOR YOU! REMEMBER ATTUMA, THE FANTAST-IC UNDERSEA VILLAIN OF FANTASTIC FOUR #33? YEP, YOU GUESSED IT! GIANT-MAN AND THE WASP -BATTLE HIM IN ASTONISH #64!! IT'S THE GREATEST! — — — 'NUFF SAID!

12.

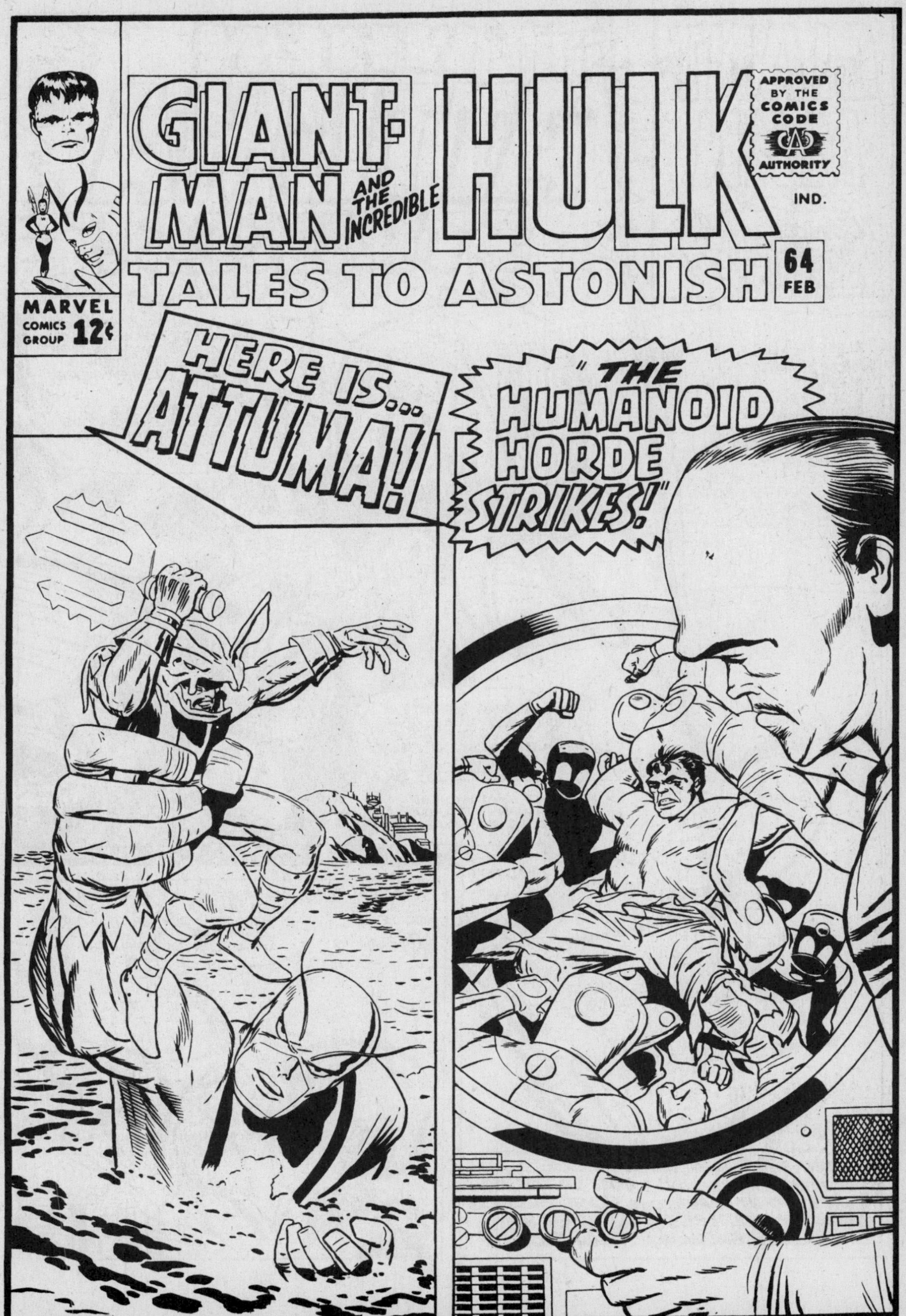

APPROVED BY THE COMICS CODE AUTHORITY
GIANT-MAN AND THE INCREDIBLE HULK
IND.
TALES TO ASTONISH
64 FEB
MARVEL COMICS GROUP 12¢
HERE IS... ATTUMA!
"THE HUMANOID HORDE STRIKES!"

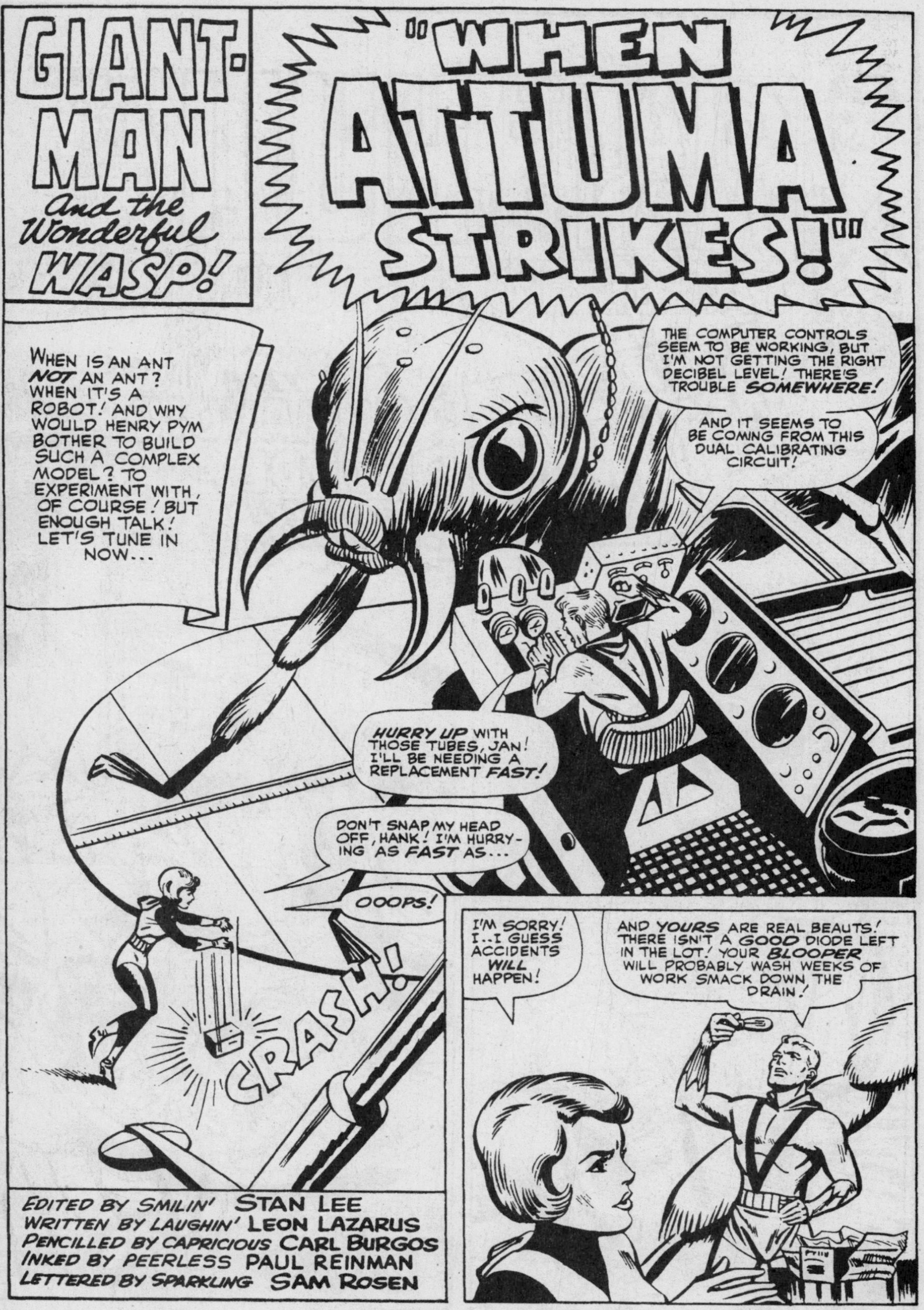
GIANT-MAN and the Wonderful WASP!
"WHEN ATTUMA STRIKES!"
WHEN IS AN ANT NOT AN ANT? WHEN IT'S A ROBOT! AND WHY WOULD HENRY PYM BOTHER TO BUILD SUCH A COMPLEX MODEL? TO EXPERIMENT WITH, OF COURSE! BUT ENOUGH TALK! LET'S TUNE IN NOW...
THE COMPUTER CONTROLS SEEM TO BE WORKING, BUT I'M NOT GETTING THE RIGHT DECIBEL LEVEL! THERE'S TROUBLE SOMEWHERE!
AND IT SEEMS TO BE COMING FROM THIS DUAL CALIBRATING CIRCUIT!
HURRY UP WITH THOSE TUBES, JAN! I'LL BE NEEDING A REPLACEMENT FAST!
DON'T SNAP MY HEAD OFF, HANK! I'M HURRYING AS FAST AS...
OOOPS!
CRASH!
EDITED BY SMILIN' STAN LEE
WRITTEN BY LAUGHIN' LEON LAZARUS
PENCILLED BY CAPRICIOUS CARL BURGOS
INKED BY PEERLESS PAUL REINMAN
LETTERED BY SPARKLING SAM ROSEN
I'M SORRY! I..I GUESS ACCIDENTS WILL HAPPEN!
AND YOURS ARE REAL BEAUTS! THERE ISN'T A GOOD DIODE LEFT IN THE LOT! YOUR BLOOPER WILL PROBABLY WASH WEEKS OF WORK SMACK DOWN THE DRAIN!

HE'S NEVER SPOKEN TO ME THAT WAY BEFORE! AS THOUGH I...I MEAN *NOTHING* TO HIM!! HOW *COULD* HE... WHEN I *LOVE* HIM SO?

MAYBE I CAN DO *WITHOUT* THE TUBE...

I'LL JUST *BYPASS* THE CIRCUIT, STEP UP THE VOLTAGE AND... LET'S SEE...

MOMENTS LATER, IN THE PRIVACY OF HER ROOM JAN PROVES THAT A GIRL IS A GIRL, EVEN IN AN ADVENTURESS' UNIFORM!

I KNOW I'M ACTING *FOOLISH*, BUT I CAN'T HELP LOVING THE GUY! ... DESPITE THE WAY HE TREATS ME!

BUT WHAT'S THE POINT IN WASTING MY TIME? HE'LL NEVER *RETURN* MY LOVE!

I'VE GOT TO LEAVE... FIND TIME TO THINK THIS OUT!

I KNOW HE'S OVER-WORKED, STRAINED TO THE SNAPPING POINT, BUT I CAN'T GO ON THIS WAY! I'VE GOT TO MAKE A CLEAN BREAK!

I'LL FORCE MYSELF TO PUT HIM OUT OF MY MIND... AND OUT OF MY HEART! I'LL TRY CONVINCING MYSELF I DON'T LOVE HIM!

I'LL GET A PLANE TICKET, GO *SOMEWHERE! ANYWHERE!* MAKE IT A *COMPLETE* CHANGE OF SCENE!

AND I'LL JUST PACK SOME CLOTHES! I DON'T WANT MY *WASP* UNIFORM, OR GUN... ANYTHING THAT WILL REMIND ME OF *HIM!*

MAINTAINANCE *MUSTS*

OIL EVERY 3 DAYS

"WASP STING"

USE LEATHER OIL ON THONGS

CHECK FELT ON BOTTOM OF MOUNT

SHORTLY AFTERWARDS, AS THE ENGINES OF A HUGE JET PIERCE THE SILENCE OF NIGHT, A HEART-BROKEN JAN BOARDS THE AIRCRAFT ALONG WITH THE OTHER PASSENGERS...

I HOPE IT ISN'T AN OMEN, BUT I'VE GOT A FEELING THAT SOMETHING *AWFUL* IS ABOUT TO HAPPEN!

AND, AT THAT MOMENT, BACK IN THE LAB...

IT *WORKS!* THE ROBOT ANT RESPONDS PERFECTLY TO THE DATA FED INTO ITS MEMORY DISCS! IN A MONTH'S TIME I'LL ACCUMULATE MORE INFORMATION ABOUT MY LITTLE FRIENDS THAN I COULD GET FROM *YEARS* OF RESEARCH WITH LIVE ANTS!

I'VE GOT TO TELL JAN THE *GOOD NEWS!* WE'LL *CELEBRATE!* HAVE DINNER TOGETHER! POOR KID, GUESS I'VE BEEN A LITTLE *ROUGH* ON HER LATELY!

2.

BUT, WHEN JAN FAILS TO ANSWER, AND GIANT-MAN'S SEARCH PROVES FRUITLESS...

SHE ISN'T IN THE GYM, THE LAB, OR ANYWHERE ELSE! BUT SHE WOULDN'T LEAVE WITHOUT...? WAIT! THERE'S A NOTE ON THE DESK!

To Hank

QUICKLY, GIANT-MAN SCANS THE PAPER, SCARCELY BELIEVING WHAT HE READS...

...AND SO, RATHER THAN COMPLICATE YOUR LIFE ANY FURTHER, I THINK A CLEAN BREAK WOULD SOLVE EVERYTHING!

SHE'S GONE! AND I'M TO BLAME! I'VE DRIVEN HER AWAY! THE ONE AND ONLY PRECIOUS THING I HOLD DEAR IN LIFE!

BLANKED OUT BY THE SOUL-SHOCKING NEWS, GIANT-MAN'S BODY, IN AN INVOLUNTARY ACTION, BREAKS LOOSE IN WILD, RUN-AWAY GROWTH... SHATTERING DOORS AND WALLS BEFORE IT...

SMASHING THROUGH INTO THE ADJOINING LAB, THE MASSIVE BODY IS ENSNARED IN A SKEIN OF HIGH VOLTAGE LINES, AND STAGGERED REPEATEDLY BY THE SEARING CURRENT...

THEN, A KINDER FATE STEPS IN! ALREADY EXHAUSTED BY MONTHS OF INTENSIVE RESEARCH ON HIS ROBOT, THE HERCULEAN FIGURE, SHRINKING OF ITS OWN ACCORD, SAGS FORWARD, COLLAPSING TO THE FLOOR...

MEANWHILE, AS JAN'S PLANE WINGS SOUTHWARD OFF COASTAL WATERS, THE PASSENGERS ARE SHOCKED BY TWO STRANGE SIGHTS...

LOOK, TIM! UP AHEAD! ISN'T THAT A FOUNTAIN OF BUBBLES COMING RIGHT OUT OF THE SEA!?

AND THAT ISLAND BELOW! I'VE MADE THIS FLIGHT DOZENS OF TIMES, BUT NEVER SAW IT BEFORE!

3

BUT, AS THE PLANE APPROACHES THE STRANGE, BUBBLING ERUPTION, ITS PASSAGE DOES NOT GO UNNOTICED! UNSEEN, BUT LURKING JUST BELOW THE MURKY SURFACE, A MONSTROUS UNDERSEA SHIP THAT ACTUALLY *SUPPORTS* THE ARTIFICIAL ISLAND, NOW GIRDS FOR *ACTION*...

AND, OF ALL THE PASSENGERS ON THE SPEEDING JET, ONLY ONE HEART-SICK GIRL IS SO WRAPPED IN HER OWN THOUGHTS, THAT SHE IS COMPLETELY UNAWARE OF THE STRANGE EVENTS TRANSPIRING BELOW!

A WINGED CRAFT OF SOME SORT APPEARS ON OUR AQUA-SCOPE SCREEN! WOULD THAT SUIT YOUR PURPOSE, MY *LORD*?

TO *PERFECTION!* ACCELERATE THE *APOXY* GENERATORS TO FULL INTAKE *STRENGTH!*

AS THE ORDER RINGS OUT, THE BUBBLY MIXTURE ERUPTING FROM THE SHIP'S GIANT STACK BECOMES DENSER, THICKER, AND MORE *MENACING*...

SECONDS LATER... *LOOK!* THE WINGED CRAFT IS BEING DRAWN INTO THE GENERATOR'S FLOW! ITS PUNY EFFORT TO RESIST IS *USELESS!*

THE MOMENT IS AT HAND! NOW I, THE CONQUERING *ATTUMA*, RULER OF THE MURKY DEPTHS, SHALL ACHIEVE MY CHERISHED GOAL! THE FIRST STEP IN MY CONQUEST OF THE WORLD'S SURFACE CREATURES, HAS BEGUN!

OUR MIGHTY WAR LORD THRIVES ON CONQUEST! SINCE HIS DEFEAT AT THE HANDS OF SUB-MARINER * HE MUST HAVE A VICTORY TO REDEEM HIS *HONOR!*

IT IS FORTUNATE HE LEARNED OF A SURFACE WORLD WE CAN ATTACK!

* SEE FANTASTIC FOUR # 33

4.

AND ABOVE, THE AIRCRAFT, TRAPPED IN THE STRANGE BUBBLY FLOW, CONTINUES ITS FUTILE ATTEMPT TO ESCAPE FROM THE INESCAPABLE!

WHAT'S *HAPPENING* TO US??

WE'RE TRAPPED INSIDE OF SOME STRANGE, FANTASTIC *CLOUD!!*

THE PLANE IS OUT OF *CONTROL!!* WE'RE LOSING ALTITUDE! WE'RE GOING TO *CRASH!*

AND FINALLY, EVEN THE HOMESICK GIRL COMES TO REALIZE...

SOMETHING INCREDIBLE HAS HAPPENED TO THE SHIP... BUT *WHAT?*

STEADILY, THE PLANE CONTINUES ITS DESCENT AS THE UNCANNY BUBBLES UNRELENTINGLY SUCK IT DOWN TOWARDS THE ISLAND BELOW...

THE PILOTS ARE HELP-LESS! NOTHING CAN SAVE US!

THIS IS NO NATURAL OCCURRENCE! IF GIANT-MAN WERE ONLY HERE NOW!

WHILE, INSIDE THE FLIGHT CABIN...

I'VE FLOWN THROUGH ALL SORTS OF WEATHER, BUT NOTHING LIKE *THIS!* IT FEELS LIKE *GLUE!* I CAN'T KEEP HER NOSE UP! YOU'D BETTER MAKE RADIO CONTACT, *PRONTO!*

CAN'T, SKIPPER! THE RADIO'S *OUT!* IT SUDDENLY WENT *DEAD!*

AND INSIDE THE UNDERSEA SHIP, THE MYSTERIOUS *ATTUMA,* RULER OF THE MURKY DEPTHS, BELLOWS HIS COMMANDS...

LET THE APOXY GENERATORS OPERATE AT PEAK POWER! MAKE READY ALL LANDING STATIONS! FROM THIS POINT ON, *I* WILL HANDLE ALL CONTROLS!

AT ONCE, *SIRE!*

THE APOXY MIST IS STRONGER THAN THE *TOUGHEST* STEEL, MORE POWERFUL THAN THE GREATEST *MAGNETIC* FIELD! THE WINGED CRAFT *CANNOT ESCAPE!*

SOON, I WILL HAVE THE SPECIMENS I NEED... A GROUP OF SURFACE CREATURES THAT I CAN STUDY! ONCE I KNOW THEIR WEAKNESSES AND STRENGTHS, THE *CONQUEST* OF THEIR SPECIES WILL FOLLOW EASILY!

AND HERE THEY COME! THE MIST EMBRACES THEM IN ITS RIGID GRIP! BUT, IT WILL ALSO *CUSHION* THEIR LANDING, PREVENTING ANY *DAMAGE* OR *INJURIES* FROM TAKING PLACE!

5.

THEY ARE *DOWN!* SAFE AND UNHURT, AS I PLANNED! TRULY A PRIZED CATCH! AHH! THAT ONE ALIGHTING AT THIS MOMENT IS A *FEMALE* OF THE SPECIES! WE SHALL BEGIN OUR STUDIES WITH *HER!* DESPATCH A *ROBOTRON* AT ONCE!

AS YOU *COMMAND,* GREAT ONE!

MEANWHILE, AS THE DAZED PASSENGERS AND CREW GATHER OUTSIDE THE PLANE...

IT'S A *MIRACLE* WE DIDN'T CRASH! SOMEHOW, THIS SOAPY STUFF FORCED US DOWN WITHOUT SO MUCH AS A BUMP! BUT *HOW??*

NEVER MIND *THAT!* LOOK WHAT'S *COMING!*

CLINK-CLANK!

I AM A *ROBOTRON,* A CREATION OF THE MIGHTY *ATTUMA!* I BID YOU ALL WELCOME, AND BRING WORDS OF ASSURANCE! BE NOT ALARMED BY THE STRANGE MANNER IN WHICH YOU ARRIVED! *OBEY* THE COMMANDS AS GIVEN, AND NO *HARM* SHALL COME TO YOU!

OBEY WHOM? *WHAT??*

CLINK

CLANK!

THE FEMALE ONE SHALL COME ABOARD *FIRST!* ALL OTHERS STAND *ASIDE!*

IT...IT MEANS *ME!*

As the announcement causes fear and confusion to sweep through the group, the huge aircraft is suddenly drawn by the robotron's magnetic discs! Simultaneously, a metal ramp slides forward...

THEY'RE TAKING THE PLANE! OUR *LAST* HOPE! NOW WE'LL *NEVER* GET OFF THIS ISLAND!

I REPEAT THE ORDER! THE FEMALE ONE I HAVE CHOSEN WILL MOUNT THE RAMP *FIRST!* ALL OTHERS STAND *ASIDE!*

6.

BUT, WHEN THE PLANE'S PILOT INTERCEDES IN JAN'S BEHALF...

HALT! I HAVE GIVEN A FINAL *WARNING!* THE FEMALE WILL COME ABOARD ALONE!

WE'D BETTER DO AS HE SAYS, CAPTAIN! HIS TONE SOUNDS NASTY! I THINK HE'LL USE *FORCE* IF HE DOESN'T HAVE HIS WAY!

ALL THE SAME, MISS, AS CAPTAIN I HAVE A RESPONSIBILITY TOWARD THE SAFETY OF ALL PASSENGERS ABOARD MY AIRCRAFT!

NOW, LOOK HERE! NO ONE WILL BOARD THIS VEHICLE UNTIL I'VE SPOKEN WITH WHOEVER IS IN CHARGE!

SO YOU REMAIN *DEFIANT!*

EASY, SKIPPER! THAT GADGET HE'S LUGGING LOOKS *UGLY!*

SUDDENLY, TWIN BOLTS OF DAZZLING LIGHT STAB FORWARD, ENVELOPING THE ADVANCING PAIR...

I CAN'T *MOVE!*

NEITHER CAN I! IT'S SOME KIND OF PARALYZING RAY!

SPOTTING A NEARBY ANT-HILL, A SUDDEN THOUGHT FLASHES THROUGH JAN'S MIND! HOPEFULLY, SHE SCANS THE SCATTERED CONTENTS OF HER PURSE...

I'M REALLY IN THE SOUP! I KNOW I DIDN'T BRING ANY OF MY WASP EQUIPMENT, AND I DON'T EVEN HAVE A SINGLE REDUCING CAPSULE! *WAIT!* THESE LOOK LIKE THE CRUMBS FROM A PREVIOUS CAPSULE! IT'S ALMOST NOTHING, AND YET IT MAY BE ENOUGH TO HELP IF I SWALLOW THEM QUICKLY!

BUT, THOUGH THE FEW LEFTOVER CRUMBS ARE NOT SUFFICIENT TO REDUCE JAN'S SIZE, THEY DO GIVE HER ONE ADVANTAGE...

I SEEM ABLE TO GET OFF A *WEAK* CYBERNETIC MESSAGE! IF I CAN ONLY GET *THROUGH* TO THEM...

SUDDENLY...

THERE GOES ONE OF THE *WINGED-ANTS* NOW! I PRAY IT GOT MY *MESSAGE!* THE POTENCY OF THOSE FEW CRUMBS HAS JUST ABOUT WORN OFF!

NO SOONER HAS THE FATEFUL FLYING ANT DISAPPEARED, THAN...

YOU HAVE NOW SEEN THE *POWER* OF OUR WEAPONS! DO YOU COME ABOARD, OR DO YOU CHOOSE TO *RESIST?*

LEAD! I WILL FOLLOW!

THANK HEAVENS! HE DIDN'T NOTICE THE ANT!

7.

THE HOURS PASS, AND AS *GIANT-MAN* RECOVERS FROM HIS GRUELING ELECTRICAL BARRAGE, A BUZZING SOUND BRINGS HIM TO A QUICK ALERT...

A FLYING ANT!! BRINGING A CYBERNETIC MESSAGE FROM JAN! SHE'S ALIVE! BUT IN GRAVE *DANGER!*

I HAVEN'T A *SECOND* TO SPARE! THIS CALLS FOR A QUICK CHANGE...

...TO ANT SIZE AND MY WAITING *CONVERTI-CAR!*

A SPLIT-SECOND LATER, AS THE MESSENGER-ANT CYBERNETICALLY GUIDES HIS HUMAN MASTER...

WE'RE PASSING OVER THE HARBOR AND MOVING OUT TO *SEA!* THE WHOLE THING IS VERY CONFUSING BUT THE ANTS HAVE NEVER GIVEN ME A CYBERNETIC *FALSE ALARM* BEFORE!

FINALLY, WHEN THE TINY CRAFT APPROACHES THE ISLAND...

I'M RECEIVING A STRONG, URGENT, CYBERNETIC MESSAGE FROM BELOW! JAN *IS* DOWN THERE! BUT WHAT'S *THAT?* SOME KIND OF HUGE MACHINE WITH STRANGE GUARDS POSTED ALL AROUND! JUDGING BY JAN'S ALARM, THEY MUST BE HOSTILE!

THIS CALLS FOR A QUICK LANDING AND SOME KIND OF *SHOCK* TACTIC!

TOUCHING DOWN UNSEEN, THE MAN OF MANY SIZES BECOMES 50-FEET HIGH, CONTENT TO SACRIFICE MAXIMUM STRENGTH FOR MAXIMUM SURPRISE...

BY NEPTUNE! WHAT *MONSTROUS* THING IS *THIS?*

HE IS AS LARGE AS ANY CREATURE FROM THE OCEAN'S DEPTHS!

EVEN THOUGH I'M NOT NOW AS STRONG AS AT MY 12-FOOT HEIGHT, I'M STRONG ENOUGH TO HANDLE THESE TWO!

I'LL PUT YOU TWO OUT OF THE WAY, WHILE I TRY TO LEARN WHAT A GROUP OF BLUE-SKINNED STRANGERS ARE DOING ON AN ISLE THAT WASN'T HERE A FEW DAYS AGO!

THEN, AS GIANT MAN STRIDES FORWARD, FOLLOWING THE CYBERNETIC BEAM, ATTUMA'S SHOCKED GUARDS SCATTER BEFORE THE HERCULEAN FORM LIKE LEAVES BEFORE A GALE...

A WALKING COLOSSUS! FLEE!

NOTHING LIKE A FIFTY-FOOT HEIGHT TO MAKE A FELLA FEEL IMPORTANT!

8

INFORMED CYBERNETICALLY BY THE ISLAND'S ANTS THAT JAN IS HELD PRISONER WITHIN *ATTUMA'S* MACHINE, GIANT-MAN SWINGS INTO ACTION WITH A VENGEANCE...!!

WHAM!

THE STEEL DOOR CRUMPLES BENEATH A SINGLE *BLOW!*

AND THEN, AT LAST, THE TWO PARTNERS-IN-PERIL MEET!!!

JAN!! THANK HEAVENS YOU'RE SAFE!! *QUICK!!* GET INTO YOUR FIGHTING GEAR!

SHE'S NOT MOVING! SOMETHING'S *WRONG!*

JAN!! *DARLING!!* WHAT *IS* IT??

I'M TRAPPED WITHIN THIS *PARALYZING* BEAM, HANK! I CAN'T *MOVE!* I CAN BARELY SPEAK!

NO BLUE-SKINNED REFUGEES FROM A MONSTER MOVIE ARE GONNA TREAT *MY* GAL THAT WAY! HOLD ON, HONEY...A COUPLE OF *KARATE CHOPS* OUGHT TO FIX THINGS!

CRASH!

WHAM!

THEN, AS ATTUMA'S TROOPS SWIM TO ATTACK...

HOLD! THIS FANTASTIC CREATURE INTERESTS ME! NEVER IN OUR OWN WORLD WITHIN THE WATERY DEPTHS HAVE I SEEN SUCH A *COLOSSUS!* I WILL PROPOSE A *BARGAIN!*

JOIN ME, TITANIC ONE, IN THE *CONQUEST* OF YOUR SURFACE WORLD, AND I WILL MAKE YOU A *WAR LORD* OF MY REALM!

YOU'VE GOT THE *WRONG BOY!* I DON'T MAKE DEALS WITH *PETTY TYRANTS!*

AND AS FOR YOU AND YOUR *FISHY* CROWD, YOU'LL SOON BE HEADING BACK TO YOUR WATERY WORLD BELOW... AND BE *GLAD* OF IT!

EMPTY WORDS! YOU CAN'T MAKE GOOD YOUR *BOAST!*

HE COULD BE RIGHT! I'VE BEEN AT THIS 50-FOOT HEIGHT TOO LONG! I'M ALREADY STARTING TO FEEL RUBBERY IN THE KNEES!

THE TOWERING CREATURE'S BACK IS TURNED! IT PROVIDES A GOOD MOMENT TO APPROACH...SHOULD *ATTUMA* NEED HELP!

9.

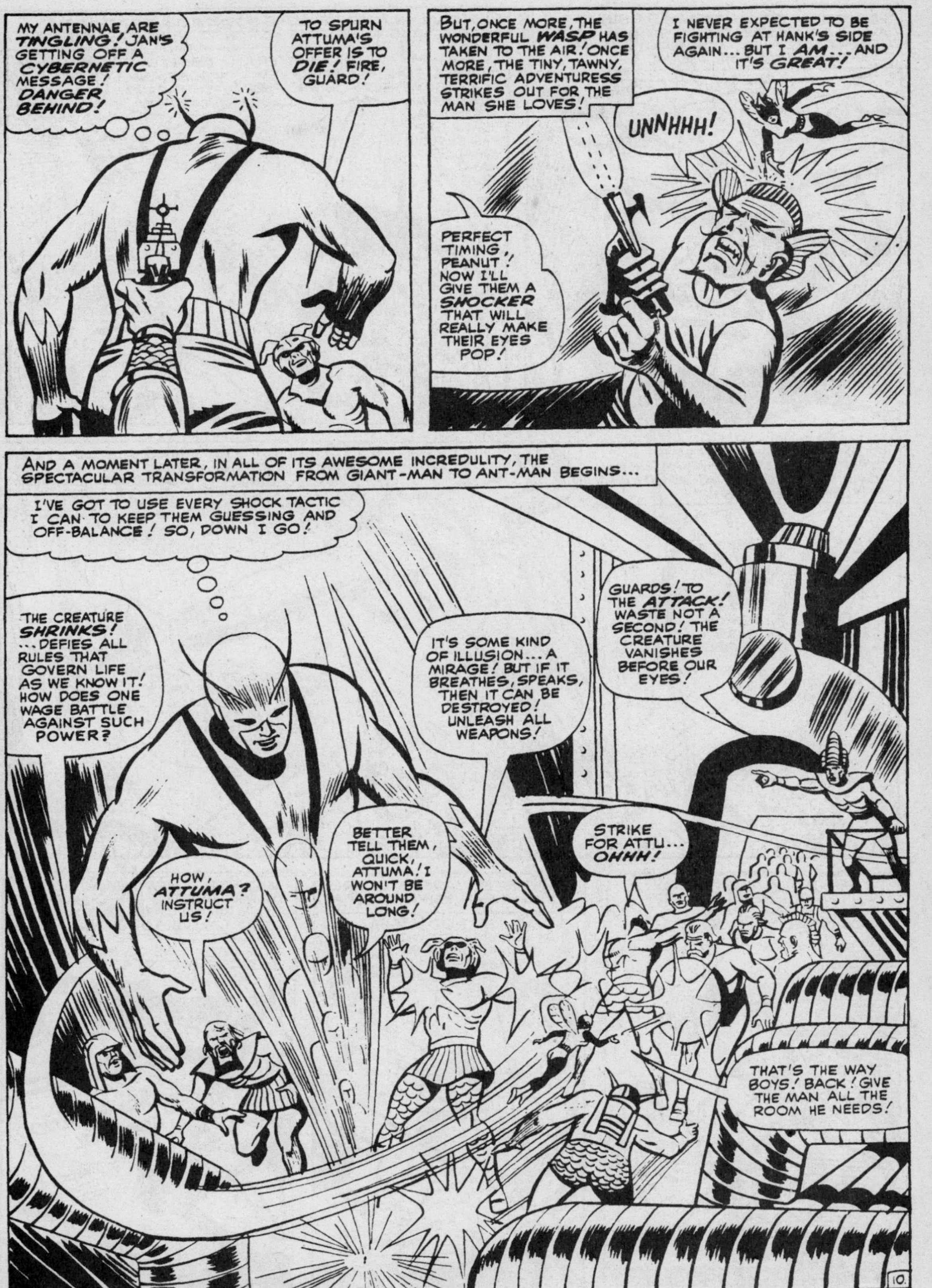
MY ANTENNAE ARE TINGLING! JAN'S GETTING OFF A CYBERNETIC MESSAGE! DANGER BEHIND!
TO SPURN ATTUMA'S OFFER IS TO DIE! FIRE, GUARD!
BUT, ONCE MORE, THE WONDERFUL WASP HAS TAKEN TO THE AIR! ONCE MORE, THE TINY, TAWNY, TERRIFIC ADVENTURESS STRIKES OUT FOR THE MAN SHE LOVES!
I NEVER EXPECTED TO BE FIGHTING AT HANK'S SIDE AGAIN... BUT I AM... AND IT'S GREAT!
UNNHHH!
PERFECT TIMING, PEANUT! NOW I'LL GIVE THEM A SHOCKER THAT WILL REALLY MAKE THEIR EYES POP!
AND A MOMENT LATER, IN ALL OF ITS AWESOME INCREDULITY, THE SPECTACULAR TRANSFORMATION FROM GIANT-MAN TO ANT-MAN BEGINS...
I'VE GOT TO USE EVERY SHOCK TACTIC I CAN TO KEEP THEM GUESSING AND OFF-BALANCE! SO, DOWN I GO!
THE CREATURE SHRINKS! ...DEFIES ALL RULES THAT GOVERN LIFE AS WE KNOW IT! HOW DOES ONE WAGE BATTLE AGAINST SUCH POWER?
IT'S SOME KIND OF ILLUSION... A MIRAGE! BUT IF IT BREATHES, SPEAKS, THEN IT CAN BE DESTROYED! UNLEASH ALL WEAPONS!
GUARDS! TO THE ATTACK! WASTE NOT A SECOND! THE CREATURE VANISHES BEFORE OUR EYES!
HOW, ATTUMA? INSTRUCT US!
BETTER TELL THEM, QUICK, ATTUMA! I WON'T BE AROUND LONG!
STRIKE FOR ATTU... OHHH!
THAT'S THE WAY BOYS! BACK! GIVE THE MAN ALL THE ROOM HE NEEDS!
10

HE'S GONE! *DISAPPEARED!* BUT IT'S ALL A *LIE,* A *TRICK* OF SORTS...AN ATTEMPT TO TWIST OUR SANITY, GIVE US CAUSE FOR *PANIC!*

SUDDENLY, AN ANGRY BUZZING SOUND FILLS THE AIR AS THE WASP SPARKS A DIVERTING ACTION TO INSURE HER PARTNER'S SAFETY...

IT IS THE SAME FEMALE WE HELD PRISONER, *ATTUMA!* ONLY SHE HAS BECOME SMALLER...AND *FLIES!*

NO MATTER! BRING HER DOWN! *FIRE!*

I'M HIT... SOME KIND OF PARALYZING RAY!

I'M FALLING! CAN'T FLY! H...HELP, HANK!

UPON RECEIVING THE WASP'S CYBERNETIC MESSAGE, GIANT-MAN AGAIN USES HIS ENLARGING POWER WITH IMPRESSIVE SKILL!

WE ARE NO MATCH FOR *HIM!* ALL IS *LOST!*

HE VANISHES AND RE-APPEARS AT WILL! WE ARE PITTED AGAINST A *DEMON!* WE ARE *DOOMED!*

GOT YOU, *LITTLE ONE!*

THANKS, *BLUE EYES!* JUST LOOKING AT YOU MAKES ME FEEL MUCH BETTER ALREADY!

ATTUMA BEATEN BY *ONE* PAIR OF SURFACE CREATURES? *NEVER!!* ALL IS NOT LOST! I HAVE A PLAN! EVERY-ONE CLEAR THIS CHAMBER!

HURRY! HE IS STILL TOO BIG TO FOLLOW US THROUGH THE DOOR! WE SHALL *DESTROY* HIM YET!

AND, AS THE MASSIVE DOOR CLANGS SHUT BEHIND ATTUMA...

GOOD! BIG OR SMALL, THEY ARE SEALED WITHIN... AS SECURELY AS IN A *TOMB!*

AND NOW... *VENGEANCE!* IN A FEW MINUTES THE CHAMBER WILL BE FLOODED *THROUGH-OUT!* THERE CAN BE NO ESCAPE! NO MATTER WHAT HIS SIZE...HE CANNOT BREATHE WATER, AS *WE* CAN!

EMERGENCY FLOOD CONTROL TANK

HATCH 4

11.

AND, AS THE WATER GUSHES INTO THE SEALED CHAMBER...

ESCAPE, HANK! IT'S ALL OVER THIS TIME!

THERE'S NO ESCAPE, HANK! IT'S ALL OVER THIS TIME! BUT I LOVE YOU, DARLING! GOOD-BYE, MY DEAREST!

NO, HONEY! DON'T GIVE UP NOW! I'M ZOOMING DOWN TO ANT-SIZE! REDUCE AND STICK CLOSE!

REDUCING WITH SPLIT-SECOND SPEED, THE DIMINUTIVE PAIR ARE SWEPT, SWIRLED, THEN BLOWN INTO ONE OF THE AIR BUBBLES SET UP BY THE TURBULENT FLOW...

CONSERVE YOUR ENERGY, JAN! OUR TINY BODIES NEED ONLY A MINIMUM OF AIR, AND THERE MAY BE ENOUGH INSIDE THIS BUBBLE TO LAST US AWHILE... IF IT DOESN'T BURST!

I THINK IT WILL HOLD, HANK! IT HAS A SOAPY TEXTURE! I'M ALMOST CERTAIN THE FLOOD CONTROL TANK CONTAINED SOME OF THE POWERFUL STUFF ATTUMA USED TO TRAP THE PLANE I WAS ON!

BUT, CRUCIAL MOMENTS LATER, WHEN ATTUMA HAS THE CHAMBER CLEARED OF WATER AND ORDERS THE HATCH REOPENED...

GO TO IT, JAN... WHILE I TAKE CARE OF ATTUMA! THIS TIME FOR GOOD!

BY NEPTUNE'S BEARD! THEY STILL LIVE! I HAVE SEEN ENOUGH! THEY ARE TRULY INVINCIBLE!

HOLD!! IF SURFACE CREATURES CAN CHANGE SIZE AT WILL, FLY, SURVIVE A FLOODING... THEN ATTUMA HAS ERRED! SPARE ME YOUR WRATH AND I VOW TO RETURN TO MY OWN REALM... NEVER TO RETURN!

THE BARGAIN STRUCK, ATTUMA CUTS LOOSE FROM THE ISLE, PLUNGING DOWNWARD TOWARDS HIS MURKY KINGDOM IN THE ABYSMAL DEPTHS!

AND THAT'S THE WHOLE OF IT, HANK! LUCKILY, ATTUMA LET THE PLANE AND THE OTHERS RESUME THEIR FLIGHT BEFORE YOU ARRIVED... BUT HE HELD ON TO ME FOR FURTHER STUDY!

AND, AS THE STRANGE UNDERSEA CRAFT CONTINUES ITS DOWNWARD PLUNGE INTO THE UNFATHOMABLE DEPTHS, THE REMARKABLE PAIR BOARD THEIR OWN UNUSUAL VEHICLE FOR THE JOURNEY HOME! IN THE DARKNESS, THEIR HANDS REACH OUT... MEET...

I HAVE NO RIGHT TO ASK THIS, JAN, NOT AFTER THE SHABBY WAY I'VE TREATED YOU IN THE PAST! BUT, COULD YOU FIND IT IN YOUR HEART TO FORGIVE ME AND COME BACK!?

IT TOOK GOING AWAY TO KNOW I COULDN'T EVER REALLY LEAVE YOU! AND WHAT WOULD GIANT-MAN BE WITHOUT THE WASP? IT WOULD BE LIKE BRINKLEY WITHOUT HUNTLEY... ONLY WORSE!

AND SO, AS THE SILENT MOON SHINES DOWN ON A PLACID SEA, ALL SEEMS WELL! BUT, AS ALL TRUE MARVEL FANS KNOW, ANY PEACEFUL INTERLUDE IS MERELY THE LULL BEFORE OUR NEXT STORM! BE WITH US NEXT ISH FOR A BIG SURPRISE WHEN WE PRESENT THE NEW GIANT-MAN!

12.

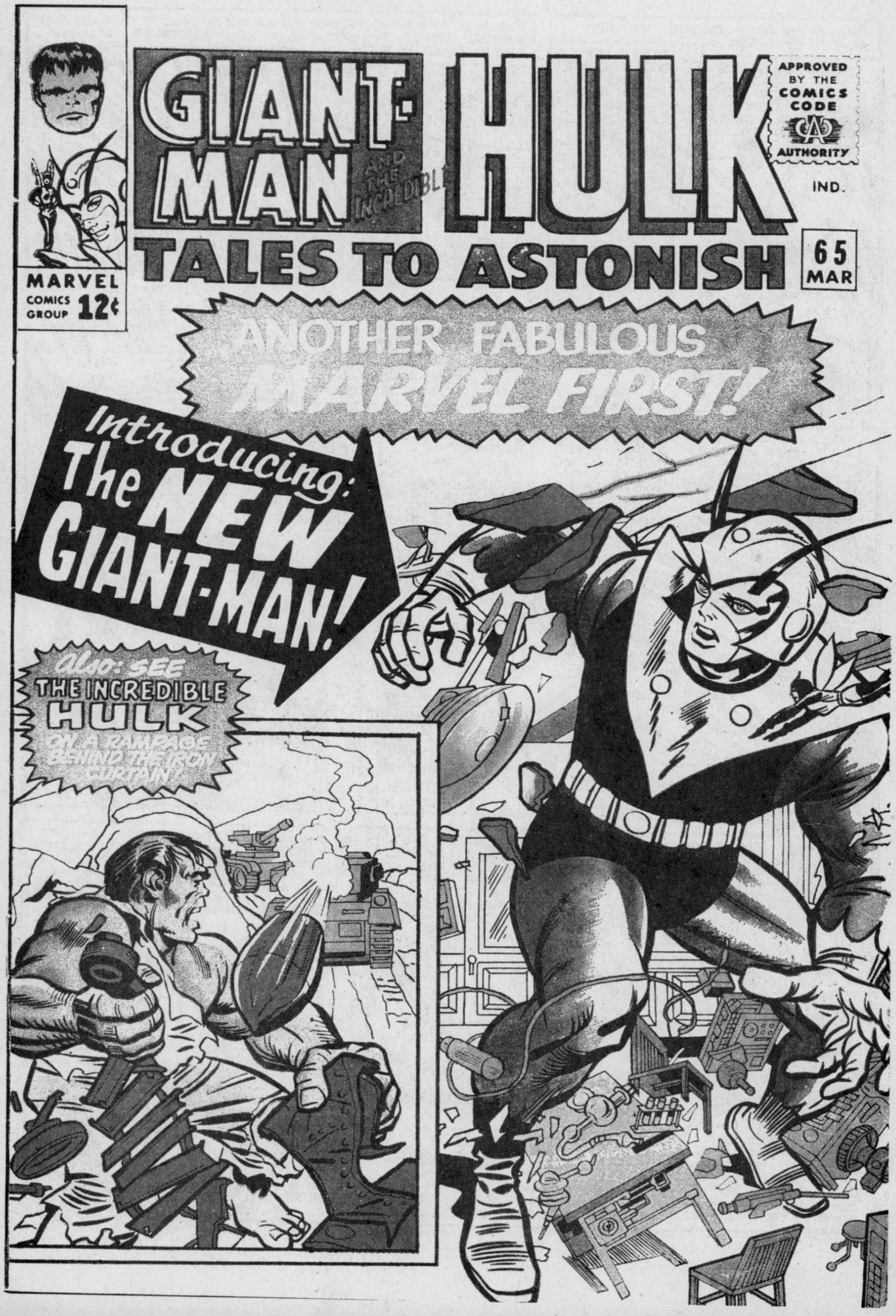
MARVEL COMICS GROUP 12¢
GIANT-MAN AND THE INCREDIBLE HULK
TALES TO ASTONISH
APPROVED BY THE COMICS CODE AUTHORITY
IND.
65 MAR
ANOTHER FABULOUS MARVEL FIRST!
Introducing: The NEW GIANT-MAN!
ALSO: SEE THE INCREDIBLE HULK ON A RAMPAGE BEHIND THE IRON CURTAIN!

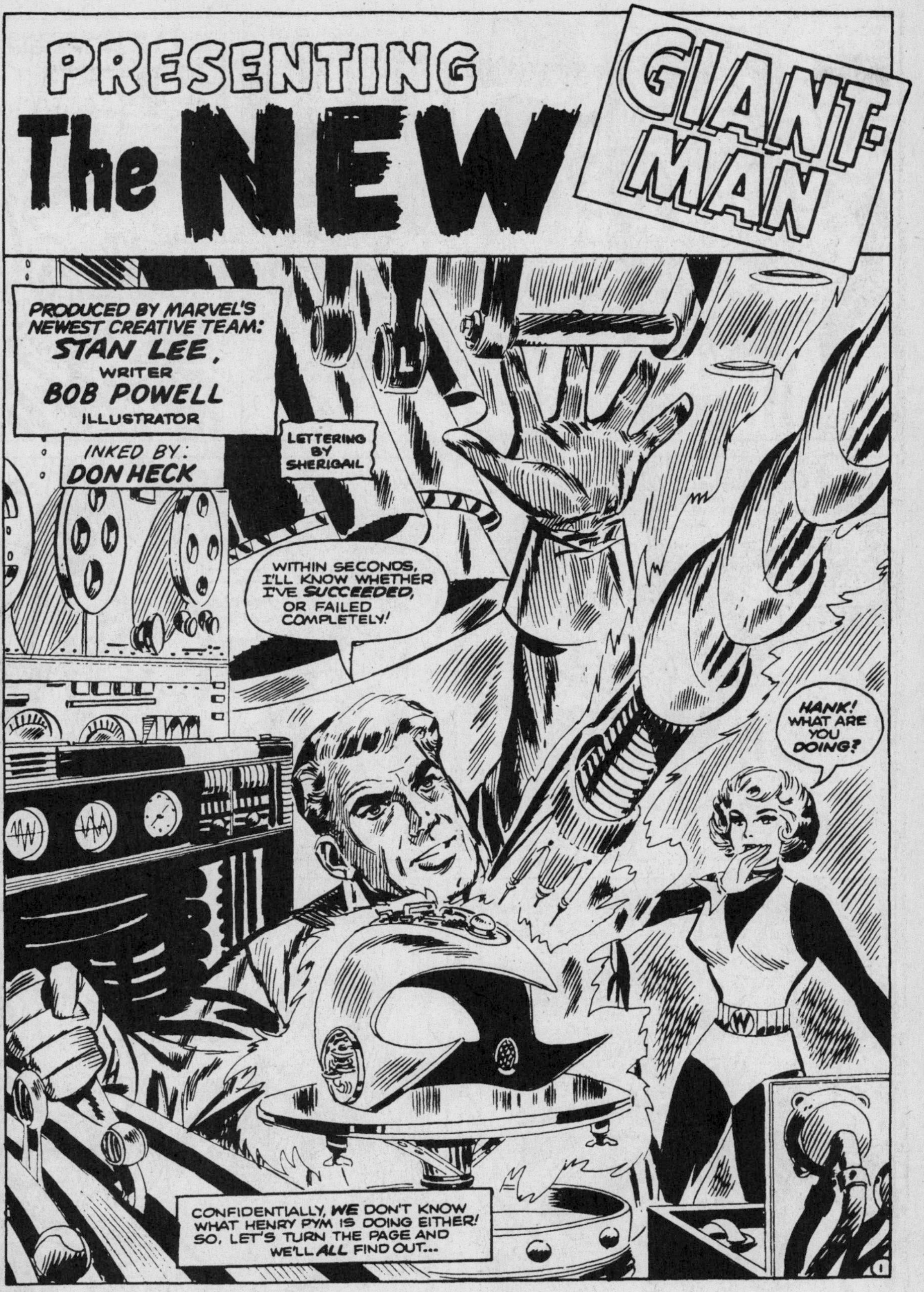

PRESENTING The NEW
GIANT-MAN
PRODUCED BY MARVEL'S NEWEST CREATIVE TEAM: STAN LEE, WRITER BOB POWELL ILLUSTRATOR
INKED BY: DON HECK
LETTERING BY SHERIGAIL
WITHIN SECONDS, I'LL KNOW WHETHER I'VE SUCCEEDED, OR FAILED COMPLETELY!
HANK! WHAT ARE YOU DOING?
CONFIDENTIALLY, WE DON'T KNOW WHAT HENRY PYM IS DOING EITHER! SO, LET'S TURN THE PAGE AND WE'LL ALL FIND OUT...
1

DON'T YOU EVEN SAY **HELLO** TO A GIRL, BLUE EYES?

IT WORKS! THAT MEANS I CAN BEGIN THE FINAL TESTING PROCEDURE RIGHT AWAY!

MISTER PYM! IN CASE YOU'VE FORGOTTEN, I'M JANET VAN DYNE!

HE'S IN A WORLD OF HIS OWN! BUT AS THE **WASP**, I'LL **MAKE** HIM NOTICE ME!

WHAT'S BUZZING AROUND ME? OH, JAN...IT'S **YOU!**

HOW **NICE!** YOU REMEMBERED MY NAME!

FORGIVE ME, PRETTY GIRL! I WAS CONCENTRATING SO HARD I DIDN'T HEAR YOU! C'MON, MAKE YOURSELF LARGE ENOUGH FOR ME TO PUT MY ARM AROUND YOU!

MMMMM! NOW YOU'RE TALKING **MY** LANGUAGE, HANDSOME!

BUT YOU **STILL** HAVEN'T TOLD ME WHAT YOU'RE **WORKING ON**, HANK?

I'VE DECIDED I NEED A **WEAPON**...SOMETHING **MORE** THAN JUST THE ABILITY TO SHRINK OR GROW TO GIANT SIZE! AND I'VE FINALLY **FOUND** IT!

THAT'S A WEAPON?!!

IT SURE IS, HONEY! SEE HOW THIS NEW DEVICE FITS RIGHT OVER MY OLD HELMET? IT GIVES ME A POWER BEFITTING MY POSITION IN THE **AVENGERS!**

AND I WISH YOU'D **MISS** A FEW MEETINGS! YOU'RE BEGINNING TO SOUND LIKE THAT STUFFY **THOR**

OH, STOP FROWNING! I WAS ONLY FOOLING! NOW WHAT **IS** THIS BIG POWER OF YOURS?

IT'S BUILT INTO THIS NEW ULTRA-CYBER-NETIC SECTION OF MY HEADGEAR!

THAT TELLS ME A **LOT!**

2

WELL, LET'S SEE HOW I CAN EXPLAIN IT SO THAT YOU CAN UNDERSTAND IT!

LOOK, I'VE GOT A BETTER IDEA, HANK! WHY DON'T YOU LET ME WATCH A DEMONSTRATION WHEN YOU'RE READY? TABBY AND I HATE LONG EXPLANATIONS!

OKAY! IN FACT, I WAS PLANNING TO USE TABBY TO TEST MY POWER ON!

HENRY PYM! YOU WEREN'T GOING TO INJURE YOUR PUSSYCAT PET, WERE YOU?

OF COURSE NOT, BUTTON NOSE! MY POWER DOESN'T INJURE ANYONE!

THEN, HOW CAN IT BE A WEAPON FOR YOU?

THAT'S WHAT I'M GOING TO SHOW YOU!

BUT, IF YOU'RE GETTING A NEW POWER, THERE'S SOMETHING ELSE I'D LIKE YOU TO CHANGE, TOO!

NOW, JAN, YOU'RE NOT GOING TO START THAT AGAIN, ARE YOU?

I CERTAINLY AM! YOUR COSTUME IS THE MOST ATROCIOUS THING SINCE CASTRO'S BEARD!

I KNOW YOU NEED IT TO HOLD ALL YOUR DARLING LITTLE CYBERNETIC DOOHICKEYS, BUT IT DOESN'T HAVE TO BE SO UGLY!

JAN, I'M A SCIENTIST... NOT A FASHION MODEL!

TO ME, BLUE EYES, YOU'RE PRINCE CHARMING, ROBIN HOOD, AND BEN CASEY ALL ROLLED INTO ONE! AND YOU'RE NOT GOING TO WEAR THIS SILLY LOOKING GET-UP ANY LONGER!

BUT JAN HONEY, ONE COSTUME'S AS GOOD AS ANOTHER!

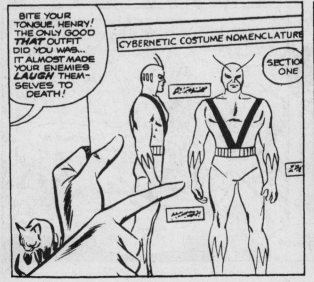

BITE YOUR TONGUE, HENRY! THE ONLY GOOD THAT OUTFIT DID YOU WAS... IT ALMOST MADE YOUR ENEMIES LAUGH THEMSELVES TO DEATH!

CYBERNETIC COSTUME NOMENCLATURE

SECTION ONE

OKAY, OKAY! IF YOU WANT TO GET YOUR LITTLE SEWING BOX AND MAKE ME A NEW COSTUME, BE MY GUEST! MEANTIME, I'LL GET BACK TO WORK!

ALL RIGHT! BUT DON'T YOU DARE HURT TABBY WHILE I'M GONE!

I'VE LOST HIM AGAIN! HE'S BACK IN HIS PRIVATE DREAM WORLD!

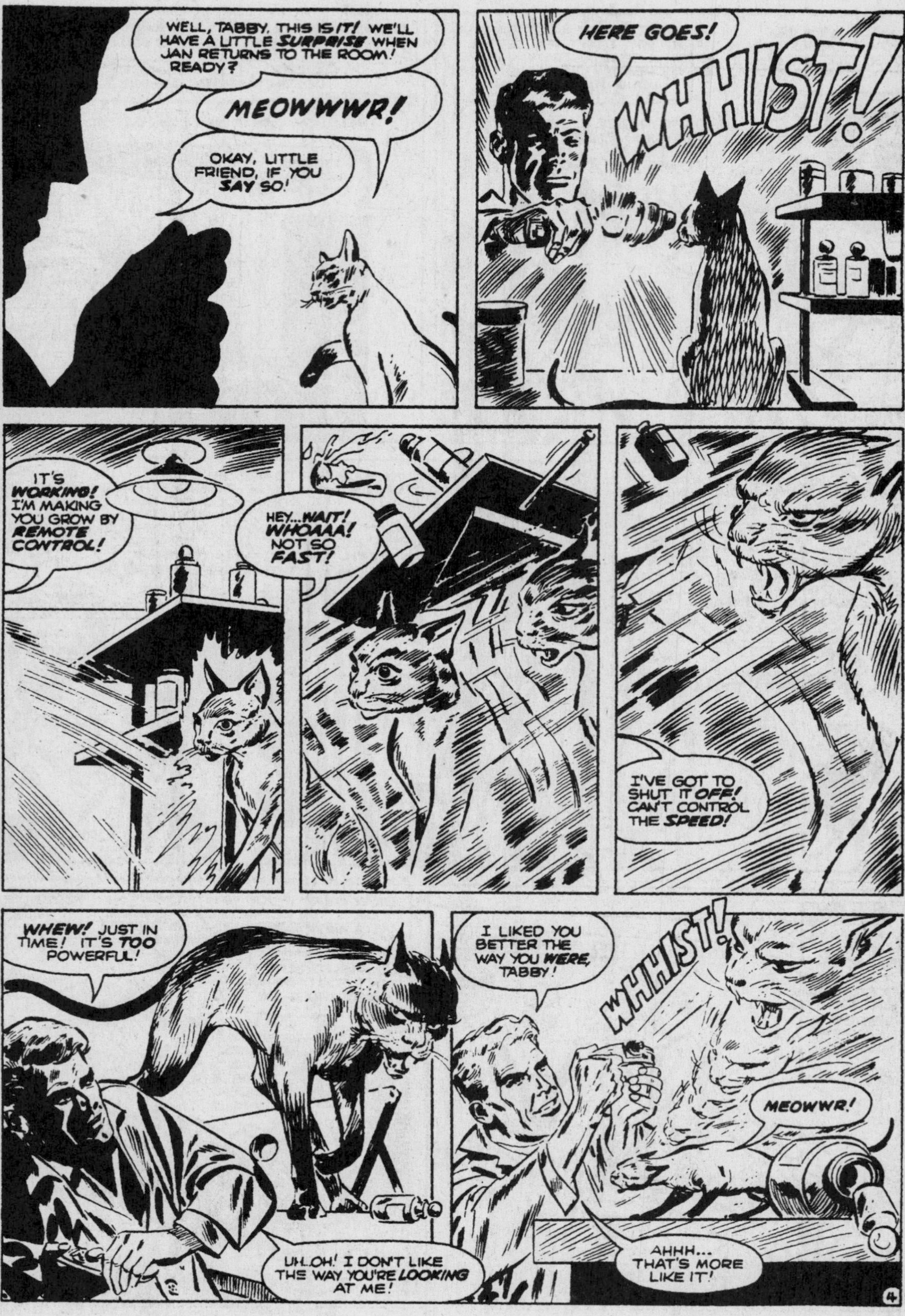

WELL, TABBY, THIS IS IT! WE'LL HAVE A LITTLE SURPRISE WHEN JAN RETURNS TO THE ROOM! READY?
MEOWWWR!
OKAY, LITTLE FRIEND, IF YOU SAY SO!
HERE GOES!
WHHIST!
IT'S WORKING! I'M MAKING YOU GROW BY REMOTE CONTROL!
HEY...WAIT! WHOAAA! NOT SO FAST!
I'VE GOT TO SHUT IT OFF! CAN'T CONTROL THE SPEED!
WHEW! JUST IN TIME! IT'S TOO POWERFUL!
UH-OH! I DON'T LIKE THE WAY YOU'RE LOOKING AT ME!
I LIKED YOU BETTER THE WAY YOU WERE, TABBY!
WHHIST!
MEOWWR!
AHHH... THAT'S MORE LIKE IT!
4

BEFORE JAN RETURNS, I'VE GOT TO SEE IF I CAN CONTROL THE RATE OF GROWTH BETTER! SO, I'LL MAKE *MYSELF* GIANT-SIZED FIRST, THEN I CAN *HANDLE* YOU IF YOU GET TOO DANGER-OUS, TABBY!

NOW, YOU JUST *SIT* THERE, NICE AND QUIET...

THIS IS ONLY GOING TO TAKE...

...A SECOND OR TWO!

HOLD IT, TABBY! DON'T BE SCARED!

OKAY! NOW, LET'S SEE IF I CAN MAKE YOU GROW A LITTLE *SLOWER!* HERE GOES...

WHHIST!

BLAST IT! I DIDN'T *COUNT* ON THIS!

THERE'S A *FEEDBACK* THAT MAKES *ME* SHRINK WHILE *YOU* GROW!

LUCKY I CLICKED IT *OFF* BEFORE YOU GOT AS LARGE AS LAST TIME, AND...

MEOWR!

HEY! DON'T! IF I LOSE *THAT*, WE'LL *ALL* BE IN A MESS!

5

HE'S GONNA *LEAP!*

JUST *MADE* IT!

BRO...*THER!* I WAS NEVER SO GLAD TO SEE A NORMAL-SIZED PUSSYCAT BEFORE!

MEOWWR!

I'VE GOT THE WEAPON I WANTED, TABBY...BUT I'VE GOT TO DEVELOP A BETTER *CONTROL* FOR IT BEFORE IT'LL BE SAFE ENOUGH TO USE!

BUT, AT THAT MOMENT, HENRY PYM DOESN'T NOTICE A DROP OF HIS SPECIAL SIZE-CHANGE ACTIVATOR FLUID SPILLING OUT OF THE OVERTURNED BOTTLE WHICH HAS BEEN LYING AT THE TABLE'S EDGE...

OH, WELL, I GUESS IT'S BACK TO THE DRAWING BOARD FOR A WHILE...

---AND, AS A CAPRICIOUS FATE WOULD HAVE IT, A CRAWLING *SPIDER* HAPPENS TO BE DIRECTLY BELOW AT THAT VERY SECOND...

PLINK

AND THEN...

HOW CARELESS CAN YOU *BE?* LOOK WHAT I LEFT LYING AT THE TABLE'S EDGE!

AND IT'S *UNCORKED* TO BOOT!

I'D BE DRUMMED OUT OF THE MAD SCIENTISTS' UNION IF THEY EVER HEAR ABOUT THIS!

I'D BETTER MAKE SURE NO DROPS SPILLED ON THE FLOOR! IF AN *INSECT* COMES INTO CONTACT WITH IT...WE'LL BE IN *REAL* TROUBLE!

6

MEANTIME, IN THE NEXT ROOM...

I MAY NOT BE THE WORLD'S GREATEST SEAMSTRESS...

BUT, IF I COULDN'T DESIGN SOMETHING BETTER THAN THAT RIDICULOUS GETUP HANK'S BEEN WEARING...

FIRST OF ALL, IF HE'S GOING TO SPORT A NEW HELMET, THE REST OF HIS COSTUME SHOULD TIE IN WITH IT! AND, IT SHOULD BE PRACTICAL AS WELL AS COLORFUL!

SO, THIS SHOULDER ASSEMBLY IS JUST WHAT HE NEEDS! WELL, LOOKY HERE! IT'S A PERFECT FIT!

MAYBE I OUGHT TO GIVE UP "WASPING" AND GET A JOB WITH CHRISTIAN DIOR!

WELL, ANYWAY... ALL OF HANK'S KOOKIE LITTLE CONTROL BUTTONS CAN FIT VERY NICELY UNDER THE NEW SHOULDER

THERE! IF I DO SAY SO MYSELF, I'M A GENIUS!

NOW, I'LL SLIP INTO MY OWN DUDS AND SEE HOW WE LOOK TOGETHER!

I'M ALL READY, HANDSOME! HERE'S YOUR...

SAY! YOU LOOK LIKE YOU'RE PRACTICING FOR THE 100-YARD DASH!

I, EH... JUST DROPPED SOMETHING!

WELL, LET IT GO FOR NOW, BUTTER-FINGERS! HERE, SLIP INTO THIS, WHILE I WAIT IN THE NEXT ROOM!

OKAY, HONEY!

THAT GAL WON'T BE SATISFIED TILL I TOP THE LIST OF BEST DRESSED COSTUMED CHAR...? WHAT'S THAT??!

EEEEEEK!

7

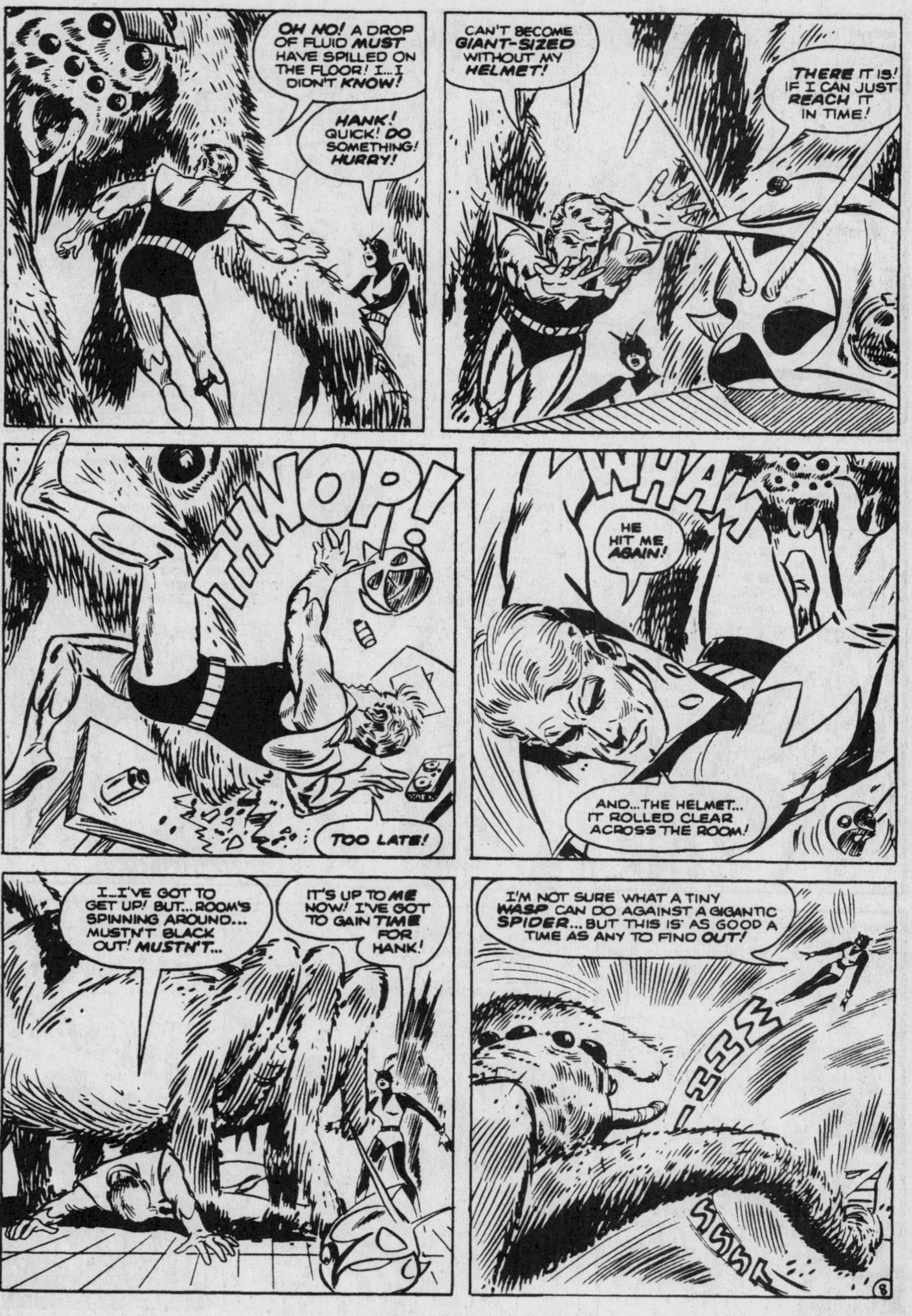

OH NO! A DROP OF FLUID MUST HAVE SPILLED ON THE FLOOR! I...I DIDN'T KNOW!
HANK! QUICK! DO SOMETHING! HURRY!
CAN'T BECOME GIANT-SIZED WITHOUT MY HELMET!
THERE IT IS! IF I CAN JUST REACH IT IN TIME!
THWOP!
TOO LATE!
WHAM
HE HIT ME AGAIN!
AND...THE HELMET... IT ROLLED CLEAR ACROSS THE ROOM!
I...I'VE GOT TO GET UP! BUT...ROOM'S SPINNING AROUND... MUSTN'T BLACK OUT! MUSTN'T...
IT'S UP TO ME NOW! I'VE GOT TO GAIN TIME FOR HANK!
I'M NOT SURE WHAT A TINY WASP CAN DO AGAINST A GIGANTIC SPIDER... BUT THIS IS AS GOOD A TIME AS ANY TO FIND OUT!
8

NOW, HANK! TRY FOR YOUR HELMET! I'LL DISTRACT THE SPIDER!

OH! CAREFUL! HE...HE SEES YOU!

HE'S TOO BIG! MY WASP STING WON'T STOP HIM!

JAN! LEAVE ME! SAVE YOURSELF! HE'S TOO DANGEROUS! NOTHING YOU CAN DO!

NO! NEVER! DON'T GIVE UP! IT CAN'T END...LIKE THIS!

HE'S GOT ME! YOU MUST FLEE, JAN! HE MUSTN'T GET YOU, TOO!

HANK, MY DARLING! I'LL NEVER LEAVE YOU!

BUT THEN, SUDDENLY...

HE DROPPED ME! IT CAN ONLY MEAN...HE SEIZED JAN!

NO! I HEAR HER VOICE!

I DID IT, HANK! THIS TIME THE WASP'S STING YOU GAVE ME WORKED!

EVEN THOUGH IT ISN'T STRONG ENOUGH TO HURT HIM...I CAN BLIND HIM BY USING IT IN FRONT OF HIS EYES!

AND I JUST REMEMBERED...YOU DON'T NEED YOUR HELMET! REACH UNDER THE SHOULDER PADS OF YOUR NEW COSTUME...HURRY!

CAN'T UNLATCH THE BLAMED THING! WHERE'D YOU PUT THE TAB? OH...HERE IT IS! NOW...IF ONLY THERE'S TIME...

THERE! I DID...OH NO!!!

JAN, HONEY...YOU LEFT OUT THE ISO-DIODE! IT ISN'T STRONG ENOUGH!

WHHIST!

HANK, MY DARLING! I'VE FAILED YOU!

DON'T SAY THAT, JAN! THERE'S STILL A CHANCE!

ALTHOUGH I CAN'T AFFECT THE SPIDER, I CAN STILL ALTER MY OWN SIZE!

STAY OUT OF MY WAY, JAN! KEEP OUT OF REACH WHILE I GO INTO ACTION! I'VE GOT A PLAN! IF I CAN SHRINK FAST ENOUGH...

FAST ENOUGH TO DUCK UNDER HIM BEFORE HE CAN GRAB ME... I MIGHT BE ABLE TO MAKE IT TO WHERE MY HELMET IS! HERE GOES...!

UNNGHH! I DID IT TOO FAST! I SHRUNK BEFORE I HAD TIME TO DROP TO THE FLOOR...HIT HIS UNDERSIDE...LOST ALL MY MOMEMTUM!

THUD!

BUT, PERHAPS BY GRABBING THIS PENCIL... AND USING IT AS A VAULTING POLE...

NO! HE'S RELEASING HIS WEB! I...I'M HEADING RIGHT INTO IT! TOO LATE TO CHANGE DIRECTION!

HE CAUGHT ME... LIKE A FLY IN A TRAP!

HOLD ON, HANK! I'VE ANOTHER IDEA!

DON'T COME WITHIN REACH OF HIM! DON'T...

10

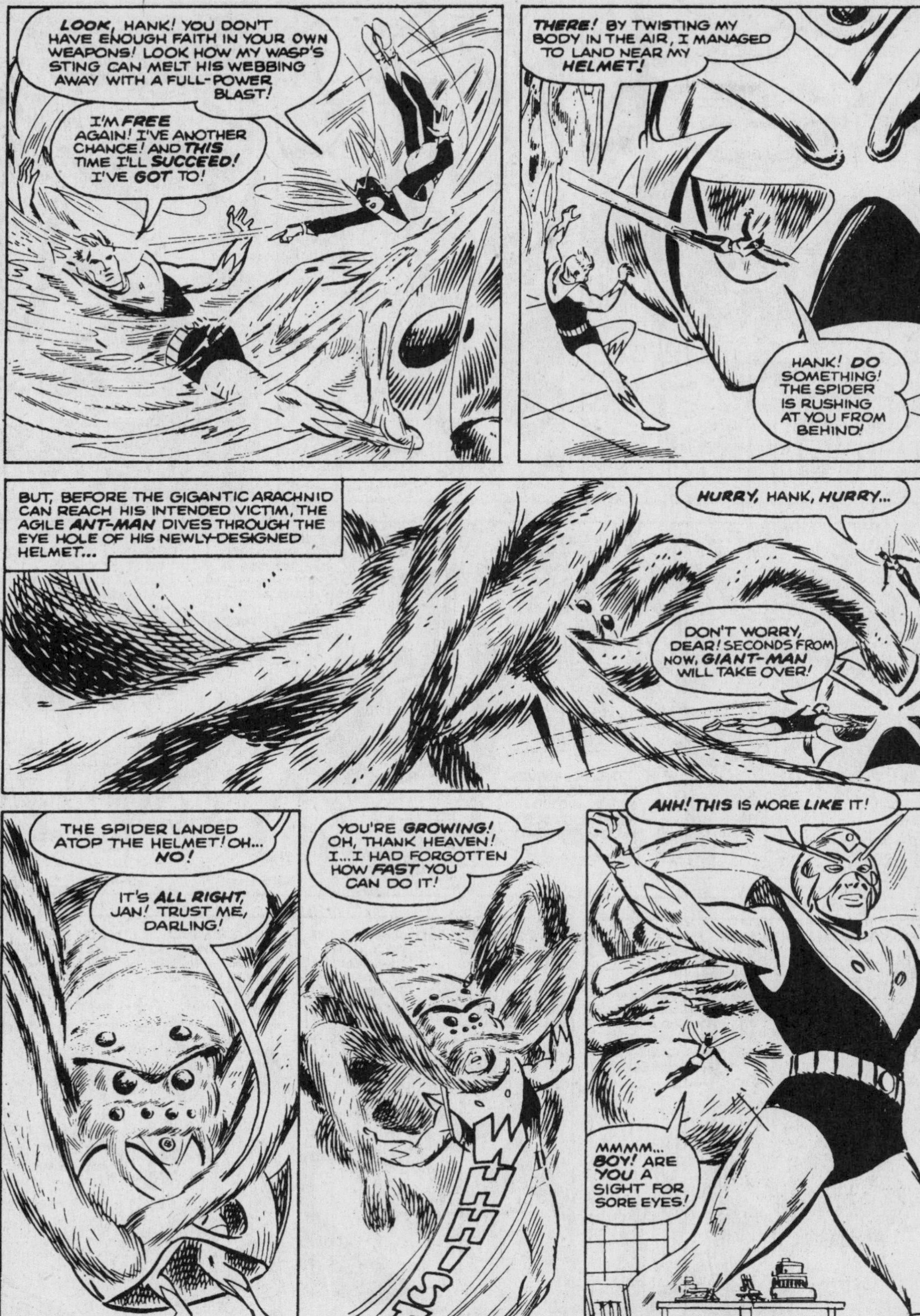
LOOK, HANK! YOU DON'T HAVE ENOUGH FAITH IN YOUR OWN WEAPONS! LOOK HOW MY WASP'S STING CAN MELT HIS WEBBING AWAY WITH A FULL-POWER BLAST!
I'M FREE AGAIN! I'VE ANOTHER CHANCE! AND THIS TIME I'LL SUCCEED! I'VE GOT TO!
THERE! BY TWISTING MY BODY IN THE AIR, I MANAGED TO LAND NEAR MY HELMET!
HANK! DO SOMETHING! THE SPIDER IS RUSHING AT YOU FROM BEHIND!
BUT, BEFORE THE GIGANTIC ARACHNID CAN REACH HIS INTENDED VICTIM, THE AGILE ANT-MAN DIVES THROUGH THE EYE HOLE OF HIS NEWLY-DESIGNED HELMET...
HURRY, HANK, HURRY...
DON'T WORRY, DEAR! SECONDS FROM NOW, GIANT-MAN WILL TAKE OVER!
THE SPIDER LANDED ATOP THE HELMET! OH... NO!
IT'S ALL RIGHT, JAN! TRUST ME, DARLING!
YOU'RE GROWING! OH, THANK HEAVEN! I...I HAD FORGOTTEN HOW FAST YOU CAN DO IT!
WHHH-ISST
AHH! THIS IS MORE LIKE IT!
MMMM... BOY! ARE YOU A SIGHT FOR SORE EYES!
11

AND *THAT* TAKES CARE OF THAT!

BUT, HANK... WHAT IF HE *HITS* SOMEONE ON THE STREET BELOW!

DON'T WORRY, HONEY! NOW THAT I'VE GOT MY HELMET AND ALL MY CYBERNETIC POWERS, I CAN HANDLE THIS WITH *EASE!* WATCH...

THAT'S MY NEW WEAPON, JAN! THE ABILITY TO CONTROL THE SIZE OF *OTHERS!*

THANK HEAVEN THE SPIDER WAS STILL WITHIN MENTAL CYBER-NETIC *RANGE!*

WHISSSST

MINUTES LATER...

IN CASE NOBODY EVER *TOLD* YOU, LADY...YOU'RE A MIGHTY HANDY GAL TO HAVE AROUND IN A PINCH!

WHY, HENRY PYM! COMING FROM *YOU*, THAT SOUNDS PRACTICALLY LIKE A *LOVE SONNET!*

KNOW SOMETHING, JAN? I'M BEGINNING TO SUSPECT THAT YOU DON'T THINK I'M VERY ROMANTIC!

YOU *KNOW* IT, BLUE EYES! YOU'RE ABOUT AS ROMANTIC AS A CASE OF THE MEASLES!

BUT, I GUESS I'VE GOTTEN *USED* TO YOU THE WAY YOU ARE! AND, YOU LOOK SO *OOMPHY* IN YOUR NEW COSTUME!

I WISH YOU'D CALL IT A *UNIFORM*, JAN! *COSTUME* SOUNDS TOO THEATRICAL!

NEVER MIND ABOUT THAT! HOW ABOUT TAKING YOUR LITTLE WASP OUT DANCING?

SO WHO NEEDS TO BE ROMANTIC? I'M *DOING FINE* THE WAY I AM!

THE EVER LOVIN' *END!*

12

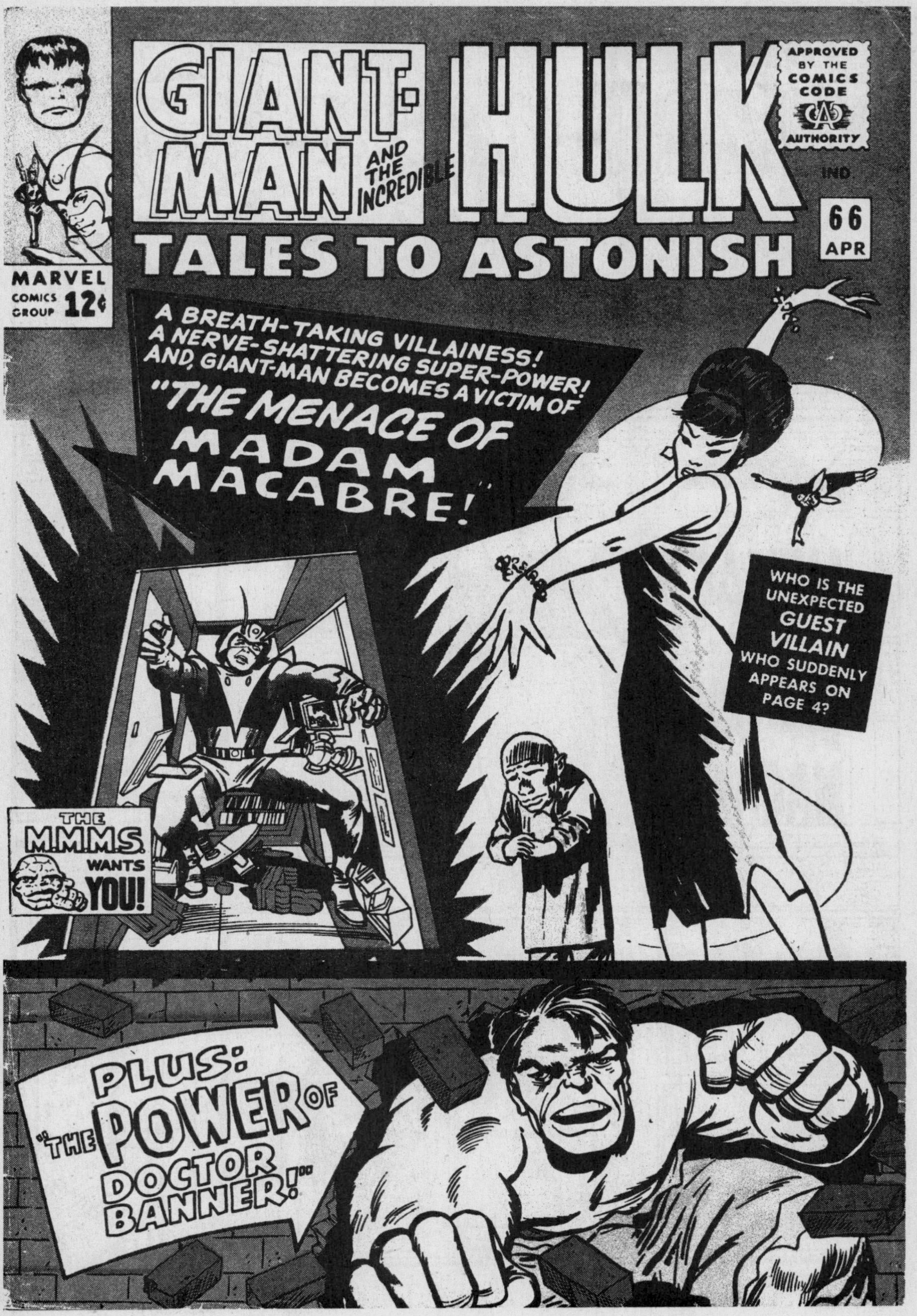

GIANT-MAN AND THE INCREDIBLE HULK
TALES TO ASTONISH
APPROVED BY THE COMICS CODE AUTHORITY
IND.
66 APR
MARVEL COMICS GROUP 12¢
A BREATH-TAKING VILLAINESS! A NERVE-SHATTERING SUPER-POWER! AND, GIANT-MAN BECOMES A VICTIM OF
"THE MENACE OF MADAM MACABRE!"
WHO IS THE UNEXPECTED GUEST VILLAIN WHO SUDDENLY APPEARS ON PAGE 4?
THE M.M.M.S. WANTS YOU!
PLUS: "THE POWER OF DOCTOR BANNER!"

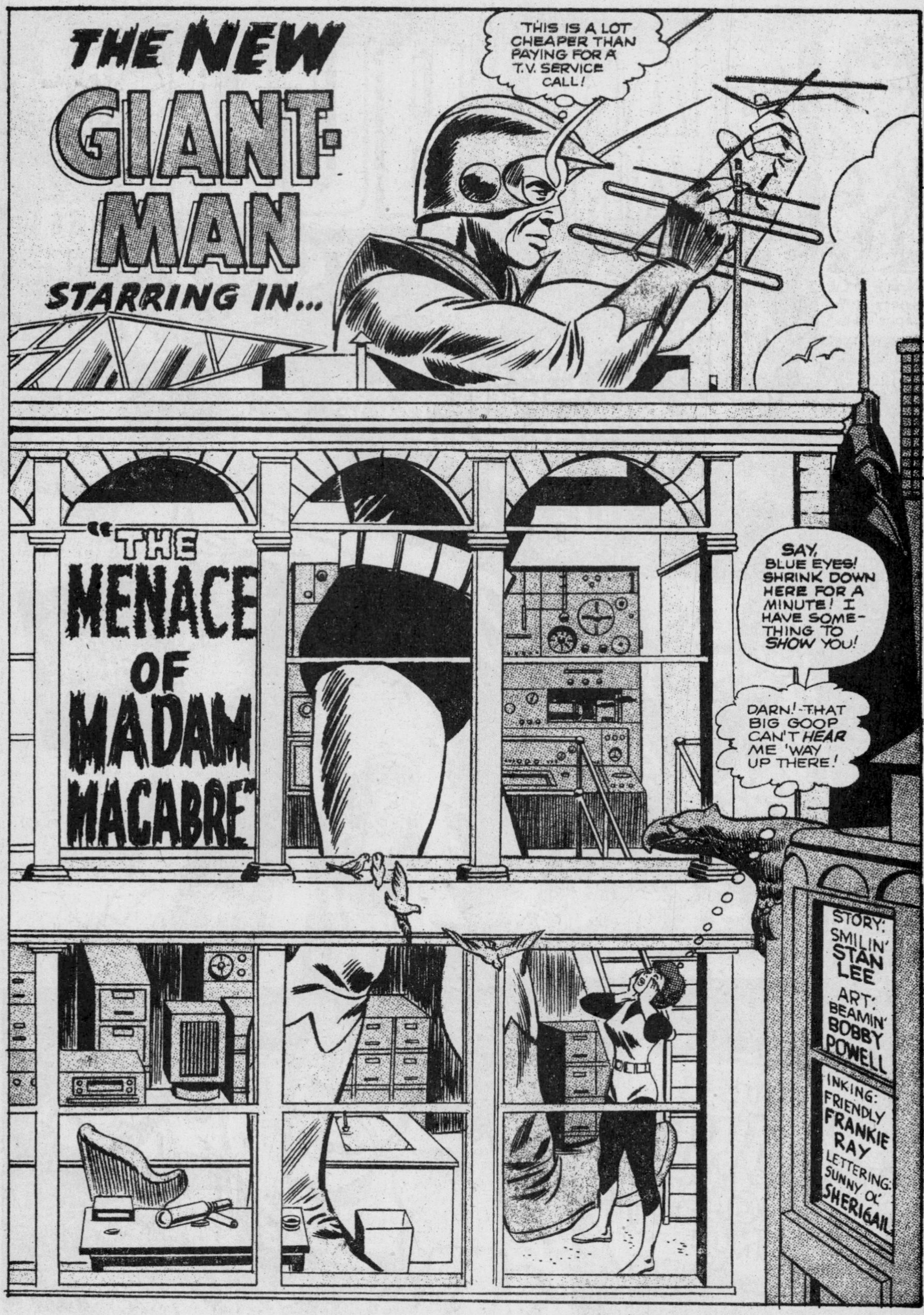
THE NEW
GIANT-MAN
STARRING IN...
THIS IS A LOT CHEAPER THAN PAYING FOR A T.V. SERVICE CALL!
"THE MENACE OF MADAM MACABRE"
SAY, BLUE EYES! SHRINK DOWN HERE FOR A MINUTE! I HAVE SOME-THING TO SHOW YOU!
DARN! -THAT BIG GOOP CAN'T HEAR ME 'WAY UP THERE!
STORY: SMILIN' STAN LEE
ART: BEAMIN' BOBBY POWELL
INKING: FRIENDLY FRANKIE RAY
LETTERING: SUNNY OL' SHERIGAIL

HENRY PYM! OH, THIS IS *HOPELESS*! I'M GETTING *HOARSE* FOR NOTHING!

WELL, IF JANET VAN DYNE CAN'T ATTRACT HIS ATTENTION...

...THE WASP CAN!

HENRY PYM! IF YOU AREN'T THE MOST *INFURIATING* MALE I'VE BEEN WANTING TO *SHOW* YOU SOMETHING!

HUH? OH, WHY DIDN'T YOU *CALL* ME?

WHAT DO YOU *THINK* I'VE BEEN DOING?

YOU'VE GOT TO SEE THIS! THE PAPERS ARE ALL WRITING ABOUT *MADAM MACABRE*!

WHO?

SHE'S AN ORIENTAL SCIENTIST WHO CLAIMS TO BE ABLE TO MAKE ANY OBJECTS *GROW AND SHRINK* AT WILL!

SHE MIGHT BE COMPETITION FOR *YOU*!

I WOULDN'T WORRY ABOUT IT, PRETTY GIRL! IT PROBABLY IS JUST A PUBLICITY STUNT! BUT, IF SHE *DOES* HAVE A POWER SIMILAR TO MINE, THEN PERHAPS WE CAN MAKE HER PART OF OUR TEAM! THINK HOW *USEFUL* A GIRL LIKE THAT WOULD BE!

I'M JUST THINKING OF WHAT *COMPETITION* SHE'D BE...FOR *ME*! AND I DON'T LIKE IT!

BUT, THE SPIRITED *WASP* MIGHT LIKE IT EVEN *LESS*, IF SHE COULD SEE WHAT IS TRANSPIRING AT THE STRANGE LABORATORY OF THE MYSTERIOUS FEMALE KNOWN AS *MADAM MACABRE*...

PUT MY LATEST CREATION ON THE ENLARGING AREA, GOGO! I WISH TO TEST MY POWER ONCE AGAIN!

YES, MADAM! I HAVE CARVED THIS ONE WITH GREAT CARE! IT SHALL WORK *PERFECTLY*!

2

NOW *STAND ASIDE*, FAITHFUL GOGO, WHILE I MAKE THE NECESSARY GESTURE!

AS YOU COMMAND, MADAM! I LIVE ONLY FOR THE PURPOSE OF SERVING YOU!

IT *WORKS!* SEE HOW THE TINY TRACTOR EXPANDS! SEE IT GROW BIGGER... BIGGER...

ALTHOUGH THE POWER IS *MINE*, GOGO, THE CRAFTS-MANSHIP IS YOURS! I COMMEND YOUR SKILL, MY LOYAL ONE!

THANK YOU, MADAM! THANK YOU!

BUT, MY POWER ONLY WORKS WITH *TOYS* SUCH AS THESE! ONLY WITH OBJECTS FASHIONED BY *YOUR* HANDS OUT OF THE UNCANNY PLASTIC MATERIAL YOU HAVE DEVELOPED! IT IS NOT *ENOUGH!*

I COMMAND IT TO *SHRINK!* BECOME THE SIZE OF THE *TOY* ONCE AGAIN!

I WANT TO HAVE POWER OVER *LIVING THINGS!* THE SAME POWER THAT THE WORLD-FAMOUS *GIANT-MAN* POSSESSES!

NO! YOU MUSTN'T! IT IS *IMPOSSIBLE!*

NOTHING IS IMPOSSIBLE FOR MADAM MACABRE!

GIANT-MAN WILL NEVER TELL ME HIS SECRETS *VOLUNTARILY!* *BUT,* WITH THE AID OF MY LITTLE *TOYS*, I SHALL *FORCE* HIM TO GIVE ME THE POWER HE HIMSELF POSSESSES!

BUT *NONE* HAVE EVER BEATEN THE TITANIC AVENGER! YOU KNOW NOT WHAT...

SOME ONE AT THE DOOR! IT IS *KALYA!*

OUT OF THE WAY, GOGO! I HAVE BUSINESS WITH YOUR MISTRESS!

HAVE A *CARE,* KALYA! ONE DAY YOU WILL PUSH ME TOO FAR! THEN, *NOTHING* WILL SAVE YOU!

DO NOT TOUCH GOGO, KALYA!

I HAVE A NEW JOB FOR YOU! TAKE THIS SMALL TOY *WALL* TO THE CENTRAL PARK ART GALLERY! YOU WILL KNOW WHAT TO DO THERE!

MEANWHILE, I SHALL VISIT THE LABORATORY OF *GIANT-MAN!*

NO, MADAM YOU MUST *NOT!*

SILENCE, GOGO! FETCH MY CAR!

3

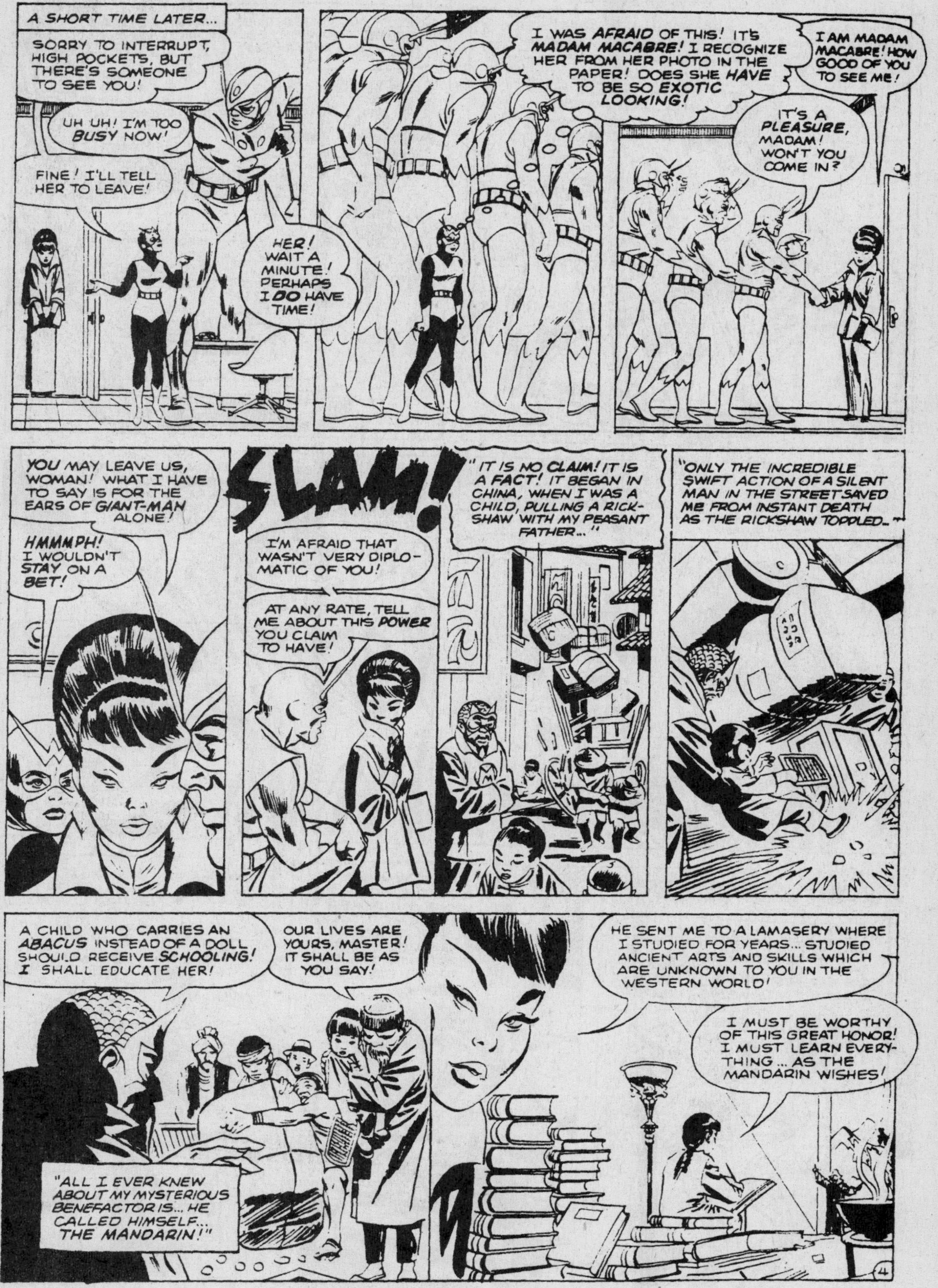
A SHORT TIME LATER...
SORRY TO INTERRUPT, HIGH POCKETS, BUT THERE'S SOMEONE TO SEE YOU!
UH UH! I'M TOO BUSY NOW!
FINE! I'LL TELL HER TO LEAVE!
HER! WAIT A MINUTE! PERHAPS I DO HAVE TIME!
I WAS AFRAID OF THIS! IT'S MADAM MACABRE! I RECOGNIZE HER FROM HER PHOTO IN THE PAPER! DOES SHE HAVE TO BE SO EXOTIC LOOKING!
I AM MADAM MACABRE! HOW GOOD OF YOU TO SEE ME!
IT'S A PLEASURE, MADAM! WON'T YOU COME IN?
YOU MAY LEAVE US, WOMAN! WHAT I HAVE TO SAY IS FOR THE EARS OF GIANT-MAN ALONE!
HMMMPH! I WOULDN'T STAY ON A BET!
SLAM!
I'M AFRAID THAT WASN'T VERY DIPLOMATIC OF YOU!
AT ANY RATE, TELL ME ABOUT THIS POWER YOU CLAIM TO HAVE!
"IT IS NO CLAIM! IT IS A FACT! IT BEGAN IN CHINA, WHEN I WAS A CHILD, PULLING A RICKSHAW WITH MY PEASANT FATHER..."
"ONLY THE INCREDIBLE SWIFT ACTION OF A SILENT MAN IN THE STREET SAVED ME FROM INSTANT DEATH AS THE RICKSHAW TOPPLED..."
A CHILD WHO CARRIES AN ABACUS INSTEAD OF A DOLL SHOULD RECEIVE SCHOOLING! I SHALL EDUCATE HER!
OUR LIVES ARE YOURS, MASTER! IT SHALL BE AS YOU SAY!
"ALL I EVER KNEW ABOUT MY MYSTERIOUS BENEFACTOR IS... HE CALLED HIMSELF... THE MANDARIN!"
HE SENT ME TO A LAMASERY WHERE I STUDIED FOR YEARS... STUDIED ANCIENT ARTS AND SKILLS WHICH ARE UNKNOWN TO YOU IN THE WESTERN WORLD!
I MUST BE WORTHY OF THIS GREAT HONOR! I MUST LEARN EVERYTHING ... AS THE MANDARIN WISHES!
4

BUT, THE MOST *IMPORTANT* THING I LEARNED WAS THE POWER OF SHRINKING CERTAIN OBJECTS AND MAKING THEM GROW! HERE...LOOK AT MY LITTLE *TOYS!*

HMMM...MINIATURE CARS! VERY SKILLFULLY MADE! BUT WHAT...?

THEY ARE *MORE* THAN MINIATURE CARS! STEP BACK...AND *WATCH!*

SEE ??! ALL I NEED TO DO IS MAKE A CERTAIN *GESTURE*, AND MY LITTLE *TOY* BECOMES ANY SIZE I WISH... *INSTANTLY!*

THIS IS THE GREAT POWER I GAINED AFTER A LIFETIME OF STUDY!

IT'S *UNCANNY!* I CAN DO IT WITH *LIVING THINGS!* BUT YOU...!

YES, *I* CAN ONLY DO IT WITH MY *TOYS!* BUT, THINK OF THE *POWER* WE WOULD HAVE IF WE *JOINED FORCES!* WE COULD CONTROL *EVERY THING!* WE WOULD BE *INVINCIBLE!*

WHY SHOULD YOU DEVOTE YOUR SKILL TO THE *AVENGERS,* WHEN WITH ME, YOU COULD BE *SUPREME!*

THEY SAID I'D BE WASTING MY TIME SEEING YOU! BUT I *KNEW* YOU'D UNDERSTAND!

HOLD ON, LADY! I THOUGHT YOU WERE *KIDDING!* YOU'RE NOT SERIOUS ABOUT THAT CORNY "WE CAN RULE THE WORLD" JAZZ, ARE YOU?

YOU MEAN...YOU DO NOT ACCEPT MY OFFER OF PARTNERSHIP?

THEN *TAKE WARNING!* IF YOU ARE NOT *WITH* ME, WE MUST BE *ENEMIES!*

I NEED ANOTHER PARTNER LIKE THE HUMAN TORCH NEEDS A *MATCH!*

ONLY *YOU* MIGHT HAVE THE KNOW-LEDGE...THE *POWER* TO STOP MY FUTURE PLANS! THEREFORE, I SHALL DEFEAT *YOU* FIRST...WITH THE AID OF MY LITTLE *TOYS!*

WHEW! SHE OPENED THE DOOR BY MERELY *WAVING* AT IT!

WHEN NEXT WE MEET... BE ON *GUARD!* I SHALL LET *NO ONE* STAND IN MY WAY!

5

YOU, LITTLE *IMP!* WILL YOU EVER STOP *EAVESDROPPING?*

I'M *PROUD* OF YOU, HIGH POCKETS! YOU HAD ME *WORRIED* THERE FOR A MINUTE!

THAT'S A RELIEF! IT WAS *JAN* WHO OPENED THE DOOR!

I KNOW I'VE NO RIGHT TO ACT JEALOUS, HANK! BUT, WHEN I SEE OTHER GIRLS MAKING A PLAY FOR YOU... I... I JUST CAN'T *BEAR* IT!

JAN, HONEY...DON'T! I CAN'T *BEAR* TO SEE YOU UNHAPPY! I WOULDN'T HURT YOU FOR THE *WORLD!* YOU *MUST* KNOW THAT! YOU *MUST!*

BESIDES, BLUE EYES, HOW DO YOU THINK *I* FEEL? YOU DIDN'T SAY A WORD ABOUT MY BRAND NEW *CREW CUT* ALL DAY!

CHANGING THE SUBJECT WILL *NOT* CHEER ME UP, AVENGER! BUT A *KISS* MIGHT!

YOUNG LADY...YOU'RE *IMPOSSIBLE!* --- AND I *LOVE* IT!

BUT NOW, LET US RETURN TO THE LUXURIOUS QUARTERS OF MADAM MACABRE...

YOU NEVER FAIL ME, GOGO! TELL ME, WHAT IS THE BEST WAY TO DEFEAT *GIANT-MAN?*

JUST AS A CHAIN HAS ITS WEAKEST LINK... SO DOES HE! YOU MUST STRIKE AT HIM THRU THE *WASP*...IT IS THE SAFEST WAY, MADAM!

OF *COURSE!* YOU ARE *RIGHT*, AS USUAL!

AND I KNOW JUST HOW TO DO IT! KALYA IS ALREADY ON HIS WAY TO THE CENTRAL PARK ART GALLERY! *THAT* WILL BE THE PLACE TO TRAP HER! NOW, HERE IS WHAT *YOU* WILL DO...

I CAN ALREADY *GUESS* WHAT YOU HAVE IN MIND!

THEN, NOT LONG AFTERWARDS...

SOMEONE SENT ME AN INVITATION TO THE ART EXHIBIT AT THE CENTRAL PARK GALLERY!

...F.E. DEAR! RUN ALONG! MAYBE I CAN JOIN YOU LATER!

AND SO...

I'VE *WANTED* TO SEE THIS EXHIBIT FOR DAYS!

I WONDER WHY THEY ASKED ME TO WEAR MY WASP COSTUME UNDER MY COAT? PERHAPS THEY WANT TO TAKE SOME PUBLICITY PHOTOS?

THAT'S STRANGE! NOBODY ELSE SEEMS TO *BE* HERE! I *KNOW* IT'S PAST CLOSING TIME, BUT MY TICKET SAID THERE WAS A SPECIAL SHOWING AT THIS HOUR!

WELL, PERHAPS EVERYONE IS ALREADY INSIDE...

TO EXHIBIT

NO...IT'S TOO *DARK* IN HERE!

WAIT! I... I... *HEARD* SOMETHING!

EXHIBIT

QUICK! GET HER!

6

SO FAR, SO GOOD! THAT CHLOROFORM NEVER FAILS! SHE'LL SLEEP FOR AT LEAST TEN MINUTES!

THIS IS OUR CHANCE TO UNMASK HER, MADAM!

NO! IT IS NOT WORTH THE TROUBLE! SHE WILL CONCERN US NO LONGER!

TIE HER SECURELY AND PLACE HER NEAR THE WINDOW, WHERE GIANT-MAN WILL BE SURE TO SEE HER!

...AND THUS DO WE BAIT OUR LITTLE TRAP!

A SHORT TIME LATER, AT THE LAB, HENRY PYM BEGINS TO WONDER ABOUT HIS LOVELY PARTNER-IN-PERIL...

I THOUGHT SHE'D HAVE CALLED BY NOW...TO TELL ME EXACTLY WHERE TO MEET HER!

THE SIGNAL LIGHT! CAN THAT BE HER?

OH, IT'S YOU, TABBY!

I REALLY AM GETTING JUMPY!

HMMM! IT'S LATER THAN I THOUGHT! I'D BETTER GO AND SEE IF JAN'S ALL RIGHT! IT ISN'T LIKE HER NOT TO CALL!

AND SO...

THAT'S ODD! THE PLACE SEEMS DESERTED... CLOSED!

BUT, IF THAT'S THE CASE...THEN WHERE'S JAN?

I'D BETTER DO A LITTLE INVESTIGATING... AND I CAN DO IT BEST AS...

GIANT-MAN!

THUS, IT'S ONLY A MATTER OF SECONDS BEFORE THE TOWERING TITAN SEES THE "BAIT" WHICH MADAM MACABRE HAS INTENDED FOR HIM TO SEE...

SHE'S BEEN CAPTURED!

7

TENDERLY, WITH SURPRISING GENTLENESS FOR ONE SO HUGE, GIANT-MAN LIFTS THE UNCONSCIOUS GIRL AND UNTIES HER BONDS...
THEN, REALIZING SHE HAS BEEN CHLOROFORMED, HE PLACES HER ON A NEARBY ROOFTOP UNTIL SHE REGAINS CONSCIOUSNESS, AS HE AGAIN TURNS TO THE ART GALLERY WINDOW... A DARK RAGE FILLING HIS HEART...
WHOEVER IS RESPONSIBLE MAY STILL BE INSIDE! AND, IF THEY ARE...
TWO MEN... STEALING ART TREASURES! THEY'RE USING FALSE WALLS TO HIDE THEIR OPERATION FROM ANY WATCHMAN WHO MIGHT PASS BY!
HE IS AT THE WINDOW OUTSIDE, WATCHING US, GOGO!
GOOD, KALYA! WE MUST CONTINUE AS THOUGH WE SUSPECT NOTHING! WE MUST BE SURE HE COMES IN AFTER US!
THEY MUST BE ONES WHO CAUGHT THE WASP! THAT'LL MAKE TACKLING THEM A DOUBLE PLEASURE FOR ME!
I'LL SHRINK DOWN JUST ENOUGH TO FIT IN THRU THE WINDOW...
THEY SEE ME! THEY'RE TRYING TO ESCAPE!
MIGHT AS WELL SAVE YOURSELVES THE TROUBLE, BOYS! YOU'RE NOT GOING ANYWHERE!
HE'S ALMOST ON TOP OF US!
IT'S ALL UP TO MADAM MACABRE NOW!
THEN, SUDDENLY...
THE ENTIRE ROOM IS SHRINKING AROUND ME! I'VE STUMBLED INTO SOME SORT OF A TRAP! IT CAN ONLY BE MADAM MACABRE'S DOING!
8

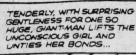

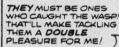

THE WALLS ARE SOME SORT OF REINFORCED PLASTICIZED STEEL! I CAN'T SHATTER THEM!

ONLY WAY TO SAVE MYSELF FROM BEING CRUSHED IS TO BECOME *ANT-SIZED!*

THE ROOM STOPPED SHRINKING! BUT I'M TRAPPED AS EFFECTIVELY AS IF I WERE IN A SEALED DUNGEON!

A WOMAN'S SHOE! IT LOOKS LIKE... IT *MUST* BE... MADAM MACABRE!

YOU'VE *DONE* IT, MADAM! YOU'VE *DEFEATED* GIANT-MAN!

NOT *QUITE*, GOGO! HE STILL *LIVES!* WE MUST TAKE HIM TO MY *LABORATORY* NOW!

MY ONLY HOPE IS TO SIGNAL THE WASP!

MEANWHILE, ON THE ROOF OF THE BUILDING ACROSS THE STREET, THE WONDERFUL *WASP* RECOVERS CONSCIOUSNESS AGAIN...

I'M *FREE* AGAIN! SOMEONE MUST HAVE FOUND ME, AND... IT COULD ONLY HAVE BEEN *HANK!*

HE MUST HAVE GONE INTO THE GALLERY *HIMSELF* NOW!

THAT MEANS HE MAY NEED *HELP!*

I... I FEEL A *CYBERNETIC* TINGLING!

IT'S *HANK!*

HE'S *SIGNALLING!* HE WANTS ME TO *FOLLOW* HIM!

IT WILL BE *EASY!* ALL I NEED TO DO IS ZERO IN ON THE CYBERNETIC IMPULSES... LIKE A HOMING PIGEON!

AND, IN AN INNER CHAMBER OF MADAM MACABRE'S HIDEAWAY...

THIS IS YOUR *LAST CHANCE*, GIANT-MAN! PROMISE TO GIVE ME ALL YOUR SECRETS OF LIVING SIZE CONTROL... OR YOU'LL NEVER LEAVE THAT BOX ALIVE!

I *CAN'T* TELL YOU! THEY'D KICK ME OUT OF THE SUPER-HEROES UNION!

YOU DARE TO BE FLIPPANT WITH ME AT A TIME LIKE *THIS?*

WHY *NOT?* IT'S AS GOOD A TIME AS *ANY*, ISN'T IT?

9

VERY WELL, THEN! IF *I* CAN'T HAVE YOUR SECRETS, *NO ONE* WILL...INCLUDING *YOU!* YOU WILL PERISH *WITH* THEM!

SHE *MEANS* IT! MY ONLY CHANCE IS TO HOPE THAT JAN CAUGHT MY MESSAGE AND CAN REACH HERE IN TIME!

AND NOW, I SHALL SHRINK THAT CUBICLE INTO *NOTHINGNESS*... WITH YOU INSIDE!

OH, NO YOU *DON'T!*

I WAS *HOPING* I'D GET A CHANCE TO USE MY *WASP'S STING* ON YOU!

HAVE NO FEAR, HANDSOME... WASPIE IS HERE!

SHE THINKS HER LITTLE TINY SIZE WILL KEEP HER SAFE FROM ME! BUT, SHE IS *WRONG!*

HAH! I WAS TOO *FAST* FOR YOU! YOU'LL *NEVER* ESCAPE FROM THIS BOTTLE!

I CAN'T FIND THE REGULAR CAP, BUT THIS TIGHT *CORK* WILL DO!

THIS SHOULD QUALIFY ME FOR THE BOOBY PRIZE OF THE YEAR!

NOW, I SHALL SHRINK THE BOX, THE BOTTLE, THE ROOM...*EVERYTHING!* YOU AND YOUR LOVED ONE CAN SHARE EACH OTHER'S FATE...*FOREVER!*

10

SHE'S *DOING* IT! THE ENTIRE ROOM AND EVERYTHING IN IT IS SHRINKING! THE BOTTLE IS GETTING SMALLER... NO MORE ROOM...

WHY IS THE *CORK* REMAINING THE SAME SIZE?

OH! I SHOULD HAVE GUESSED IT! EVERYTHING IS *PLASTICIZED METAL* EXCEPT THE *CORK!* THE CORK IS A NATURAL SUBSTANCE!

I'M FREE! THE *CORK* SAVED ME! BY NOT SHRINKING ITSELF, IT CAUSED THE GLASS TO SHATTER WHEN IT WOULD NO LONGER *FIT!*

CRACK

I'VE ONLY SECONDS BEFORE THE ROOM SHRINKS IN ON BOTH OF US! I'VE GOT TO CARRY HIM THRU THAT HOLE WHILE THERE'S STILL *TIME!*

I *DID* IT. BUT... UH OH! SHE *SEES* ME!

YOU'VE *ESCAPED!*

HANK IS TOO HEAVY! CAN'T HOLD HIM ANY LONGER!

YOU INSECT SIZED *FOOL!* I'LL ENLARGE THIS TOY TANK TO ATTACK YOU BEFORE YOU CAN POSSIBLY GET YOUR TRAPPED PARTNER TO SAFETY!

OH *NO!*

WELL, TWO CAN PLAY AT THAT GAME!

IF THE *TRACTOR* CAN ENLARGE ITS SIZE, SO CAN THE *WASP...*

AND THINGS WILL BE DIFFERENT WITH *ME* IN THE DRIVER'S SEAT!

I'VE GOT TO *SWERVE* IT BEFORE IT CAN HIT HANK!

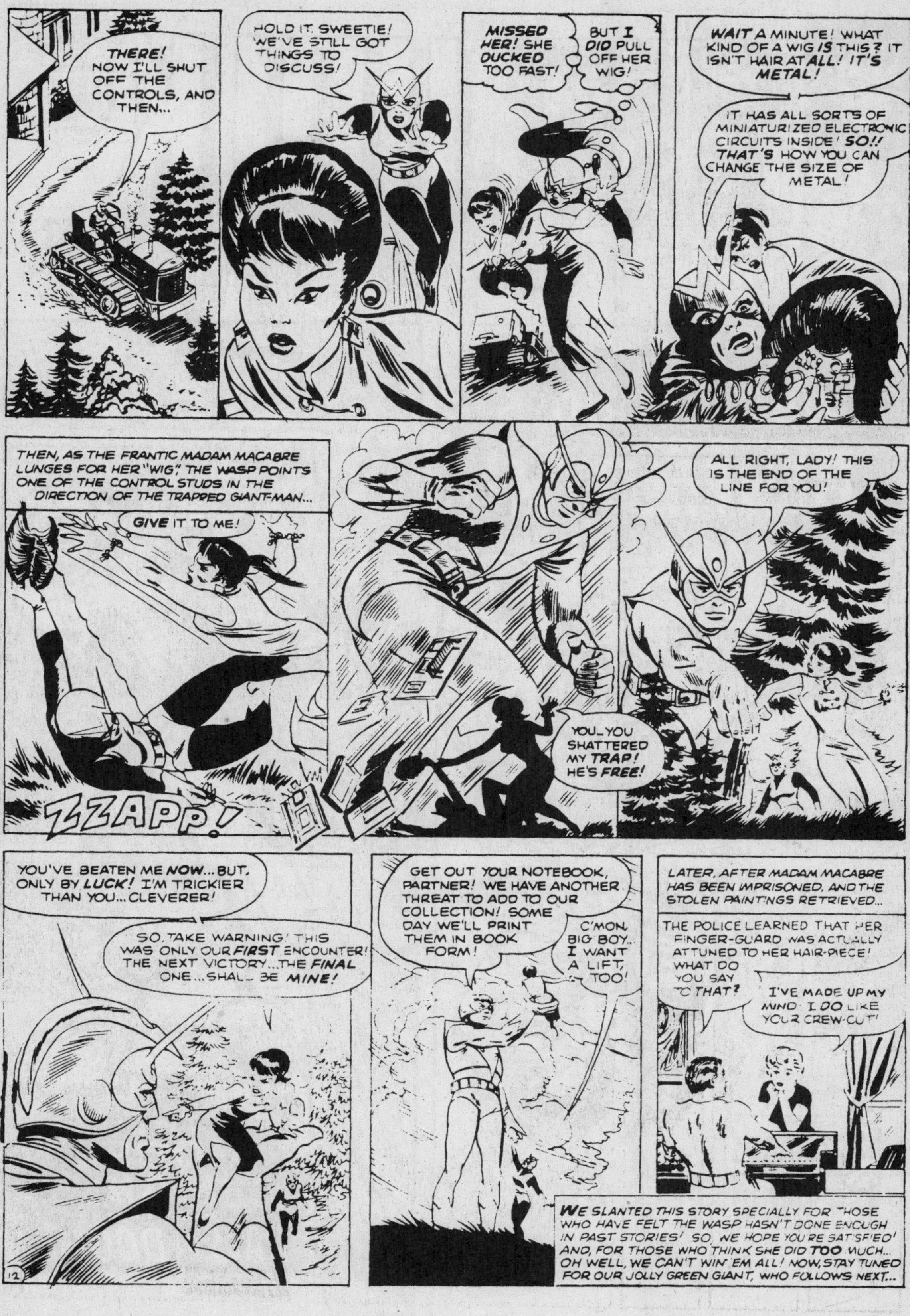
THERE! NOW I'LL SHUT OFF THE CONTROLS, AND THEN...
HOLD IT, SWEETIE! WE'VE STILL GOT THINGS TO DISCUSS!
MISSED HER! SHE DUCKED TOO FAST!
BUT I DID PULL OFF HER WIG!
WAIT A MINUTE! WHAT KIND OF A WIG IS THIS? IT ISN'T HAIR AT ALL! IT'S METAL!
IT HAS ALL SORTS OF MINIATURIZED ELECTRONIC CIRCUITS INSIDE! SO!! THAT'S HOW YOU CAN CHANGE THE SIZE OF METAL!
THEN, AS THE FRANTIC MADAM MACABRE LUNGES FOR HER "WIG", THE WASP POINTS ONE OF THE CONTROL STUDS IN THE DIRECTION OF THE TRAPPED GIANT-MAN...
GIVE IT TO ME!
ZZAPP!
YOU—YOU SHATTERED MY TRAP! HE'S FREE!
ALL RIGHT, LADY! THIS IS THE END OF THE LINE FOR YOU!
YOU'VE BEATEN ME NOW... BUT, ONLY BY LUCK! I'M TRICKIER THAN YOU... CLEVERER!
SO, TAKE WARNING! THIS WAS ONLY OUR FIRST ENCOUNTER! THE NEXT VICTORY... THE FINAL ONE... SHALL BE MINE!
12
GET OUT YOUR NOTEBOOK, PARTNER! WE HAVE ANOTHER THREAT TO ADD TO OUR COLLECTION! SOME DAY WE'LL PRINT THEM IN BOOK FORM!
C'MON, BIG BOY... I WANT A LIFT, TOO!
LATER, AFTER MADAM MACABRE HAS BEEN IMPRISONED, AND THE STOLEN PAINTINGS RETRIEVED...
THE POLICE LEARNED THAT HER FINGER-GUARD WAS ACTUALLY ATTUNED TO HER HAIR-PIECE! WHAT DO YOU SAY TO THAT?
I'VE MADE UP MY MIND: I DO LIKE YOUR CREW-CUT!
WE SLANTED THIS STORY SPECIALLY FOR THOSE WHO HAVE FELT THE WASP HASN'T DONE ENOUGH IN PAST STORIES! SO, WE HOPE YOU'RE SATISFIED! AND, FOR THOSE WHO THINK SHE DID TOO MUCH... OH WELL, WE CAN'T WIN 'EM ALL! NOW, STAY TUNED FOR OUR JOLLY GREEN GIANT, WHO FOLLOWS NEXT...

GIANT-MAN AND THE INCREDIBLE HULK

APPROVED BY THE COMICS CODE AUTHORITY

IND.

MARVEL COMICS GROUP 12¢

TALES TO ASTONISH

67 MAY

"WHERE STRIDES THE BEHEMOTH!"

THE M.M.M.S. WANTS YOU!

"THE HIDDEN MAN AND HIS RAYS OF DOOM!"

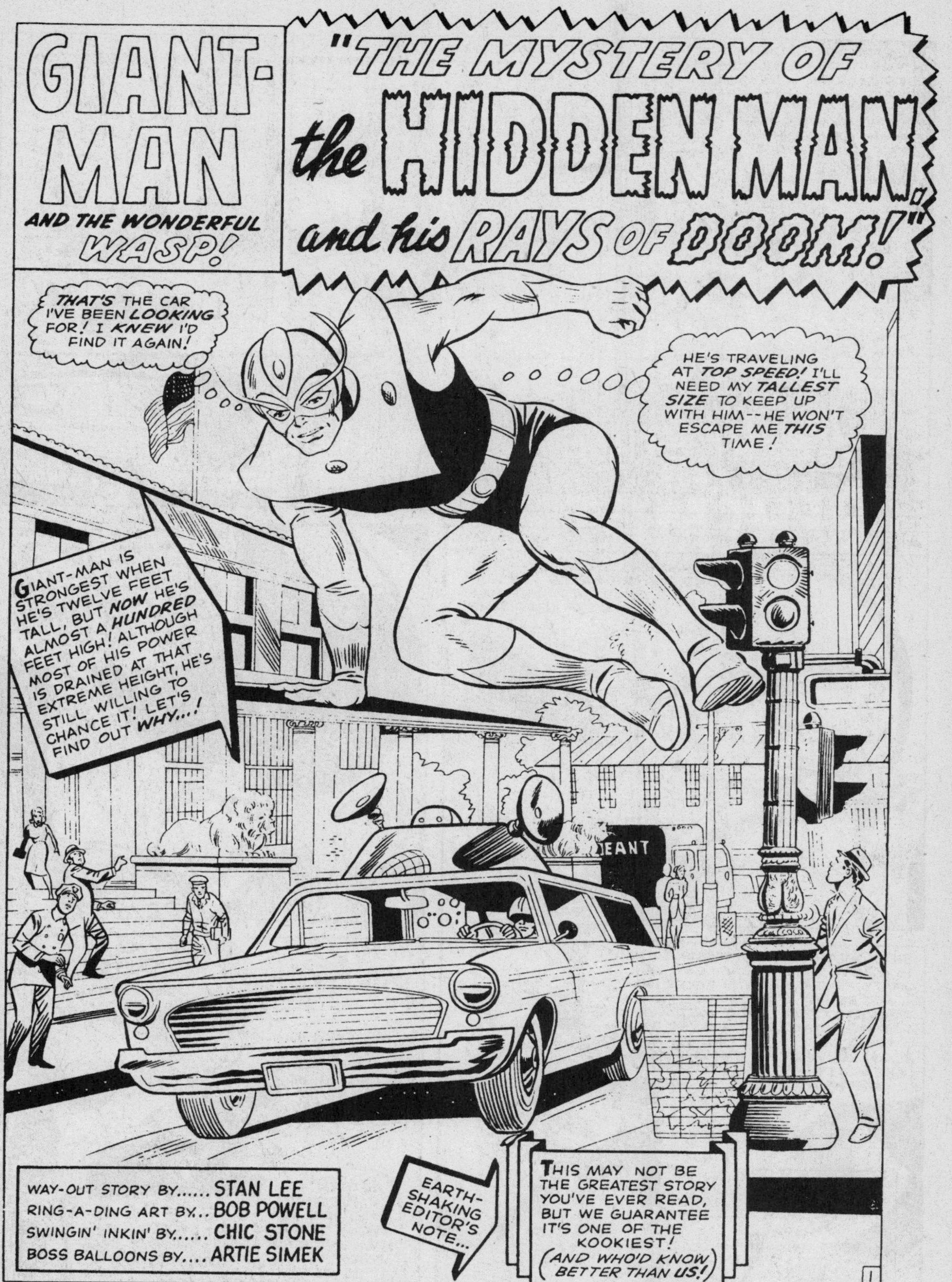

GIANT-MAN AND THE WONDERFUL WASP!
"THE MYSTERY OF the HIDDEN MAN, and his RAYS OF DOOM!"
THAT'S THE CAR I'VE BEEN LOOKING FOR! I KNEW I'D FIND IT AGAIN!
HE'S TRAVELING AT TOP SPEED! I'LL NEED MY TALLEST SIZE TO KEEP UP WITH HIM--HE WON'T ESCAPE ME THIS TIME!
GIANT-MAN IS STRONGEST WHEN HE'S TWELVE FEET TALL, BUT NOW HE'S ALMOST A HUNDRED FEET HIGH! ALTHOUGH MOST OF HIS POWER IS DRAINED AT THAT EXTREME HEIGHT, HE'S STILL WILLING TO CHANCE IT! LET'S FIND OUT WHY...!
WAY-OUT STORY BY...... STAN LEE
RING-A-DING ART BY.. BOB POWELL
SWINGIN' INKIN' BY...... CHIC STONE
BOSS BALLOONS BY.... ARTIE SIMEK
EARTH-SHAKING EDITOR'S NOTE...
THIS MAY NOT BE THE GREATEST STORY YOU'VE EVER READ, BUT WE GUARANTEE IT'S ONE OF THE KOOKIEST! (AND WHO'D KNOW BETTER THAN US!)
1

TO LEARN WHY HIGH-POCKETS IS INTERESTED IN THAT SPEEDING CAR, LET'S GO BACK A FEW HOURS, WHERE WE FIND...

LUCKY I WAS PASSING BY! THIS HIGH-TENSION CONNECTION IS LOOSE! I'D BETTER ENLARGE MYSELF ENOUGH TO REACH AND TIGHTEN IT!

BUT, SECONDS LATER...

A GIANT! I MUST BATHE MY GREEN RAY ON HIM BEFORE HE CAN SAVE HIMSELF!

WHA-- WHAT'S HAPPENING TO ME!

MY GLOVES ARE COMPLETELY INSULATED! IT CAN'T BE AN ELECTRIC SHOCK!

NO! IT'S THAT TRUCK-- EMITTING A GREEN RAY-- BATHING ME IN IT!

IT'S MAKING ME WEAK! I CAN HARDLY STAND! MUST--HOLD ON-- KNEES BUCKLING--!

AND, IN A HIDDEN LABORATORY, SOME DISTANCE AWAY...

GOOD WORK, LOKO! YOU HAVE FOUND A RARE PRIZE FOR ME! KEEP THE GREEN RAY ON HIM! I MUST HAVE ALL OF HIS POWER!

IF I CAN GAIN THE GREAT GIFT OF BEING ABLE TO CHANGE MY SIZE-- IN ADDITION TO ALL MY OTHER SPECIAL "TALENTS," I SHALL BE ABLE TO GAIN MASTERY OF THE HUMAN RACE FAR SOONER THAN I HAD DARED TO HOPE!

BUT, SOMETHING IS WRONG! THE GIANT'S POWER IS NOT BEING TRANSMITTED TO ME! LOKO, YOU CLUMSY BUMBLER, WHAT ARE YOU DOING WRONG?

NOTHING, SUPREME ONE! I SWEAR IT! THE RAY IS TURNED TO FULL POWER-- THE VICTIM GROWS WEAKER BY THE MINUTE--EVERY-THING IS PERFECT!

THEN WHY AM I NOT RECEIVING HIS POWER?

PHFFFISSSST!

OH, NO! SUPREME ONE--THE GIANT'S WILL TO RESIST HAS CAUSED THE GREEN RAY TO BLOW A FUSE!

RETURN FOR EMERGENCY REPAIRS AT ONCE! THEN YOU SHALL FIND HIM AGAIN! THAT IS ALL!

MUST HOLD ON-- MUSTN'T BLACK OUT --MUST FIGHT THE RAY--FIGHT-- FIGHT--!

IP-772

2

BUT, HOURS LATER, WHEN THE MYSTERIOUS VEHICLE AGAIN APPEARS, THE TITANIC AVENGER IS *READY* FOR IT... AND, AFTER A HECTIC CHASE...

GOTCHA!

I HAD A *FEELING* YOU'D BE BACK! YOU DIDN'T EXPECT ME TO GIVE YOU A CHANCE TO BATHE ME IN THAT GREEN GLOW A *SECOND* TIME, DID YOU?

HEY, *HOLD IT!* I'VE BEEN PRACTICING THIS LITTLE SPEECH FOR AN *HOUR!*

I MUST *ESCAPE!* HE MUST NOT *GET* ME!

MY VERY *LIFE* WILL BE FORFEIT IF I SHOULD FAIL THE SUPREME ONE!

HE LEAPED INTO THE DRINK AS THOUGH A *DEMON* WAS AFTER HIM! I NEVER SAW A FELLA LOOK SO SCARED-- AND I DON'T THINK IT WAS BECAUSE OF *ME!*

WELL, I'VE A FEELING *HE* WAS JUST SOMEBODY'S MESSENGER BOY! I'M MORE INTERESTED IN WHAT'S INSIDE THIS *STATION WAGON!* MMMM ...IT'S SOME SORT OF PORTABLE ELECTRONIC LAB!

AND, AS GIANT-MAN PROCEEDS TO BRING THE STRANGE TRUCK TO HIS LAB FOR DETAILED STUDY, WE SWITCH SCENES ONCE AGAIN...

I *ESCAPED* HIM, SUPREME ONE! HE LEARNED *NOTHING* FROM ME! I DID NOT FAIL YOU!

YOU *FOOL!* *YOU* ARE OF NO IMPORTANCE! BUT THE *CAR!* HE HAS THE *CAR* BY NOW!

NO! NO! DO NOT KILL ME! I HAVE SERVED YOU FAITHFULLY! PLEASE! I BEG YOU--!

SILENCE, LOKO! YOU ARE NOT EVEN DESERVING OF MY *WRATH!* YOU ARE LIKE THE *DUST* BENEATH MY FEET! YOU SHALL LIVE-- TO SERVE ME *AGAIN!*

THANK YOU-- *THANK YOU,* MASTER--!

3

I **MUST** HAVE THE POWER WHICH THE GIANT ONE POSSESSES! I, **TOO**, MUST BE ABLE TO CHANGE MY SIZE AT WILL! IT IS ONLY FITTING THAT THE FUTURE MASTER OF EARTH ALSO BE THE MASTER OF **SIZE!**

OF **COURSE** --YOU ARE **RIGHT**--YES, YES, SUPREME ONE!

MEANWHILE, BACK AT THE LAB, THE MAN IN QUESTION IS DOING SOME HEAVY THINKING--OR **TRYING** TO, WHILE THE LOVELY **WASP** KEEPS INTERFERING...

SOME OF THESE CIRCUITS ARE DIFFERENT FROM ANY I'VE EVER SEEN BEFORE! IT'S AS THOUGH THEY'RE BASED ON AN ENTIRELY **DIFFERENT** TYPE OF MATHEMATICAL PROGRESSION!

C'MON, BLUE EYES, FOR-GET ABOUT THAT SILLY OU CAR, AND LET ME TELL YOU ABOUT A **REAL** PROBLEM!

WHAT'S WRONG, HONEY? DID YOU LOSE AN EYEBROW PENCIL? OR IS IT SOMETHING EVEN **WORSE?**

HMMPH! IT'S A GOOD THING YOU DON'T HAVE TO TELL **JOKES** FOR A LIVING!

NOW, WHILE YOU'VE GOT YOUR THINKING CAP ON, I'D LIKE YOU TO INVENT A WAY FOR ME TO KEEP **UP** WITH YOU WHEN YOU'RE RACING ALONG AS A GIANT!

WHAT'S THE MATTER WITH YOUR **WASP'S** WINGS, HONEY?

THEY'RE OKAY FOR SHORT DISTANCES, BUT WHEN YOU'RE REALLY CLIPPING ALONG WITH THOSE FIFTY-FOOT STRIDES, I GET **EXHAUSTED** TRYING TO FLY AFTER YOU! DON'T FORGET HOW **TINY** MY WINGS ARE!

OKAY--BECOME **WASP**-SIZE AND I'LL SHOW YOU A SURPRISE! I'LL RACE YOU DOWN!

NO FAIR! YOU HAD A HEAD START! WHAT'S THE **SURPRISE??**

HANK! LOOK OUT FOR THAT **BEE!**

DON'T WORRY, JAN! HE'S THE **SURPRISE** I WAS TELLING YOU ABOUT!

I'VE BEEN TRAINING HIM TO CARRY ME, AS MY FLYING ANTS DO! HE'S STRONGER-- AND MUCH **FASTER!**

HOP ON! HE'S JUST WHAT YOU **NEED!**

BUT WHY A **BEE?** WHY NOT A **WASP,** FOR GOODNESS SAKE?!!

BECAUSE BEES ARE GENTLER, SMARTER, AND EASIER TO TRAIN THAN WASPS!

HENRY PYM, I **RESENT** THAT! WELL, ANYWAY-- WASPS ARE **PRETTIER!**

I AGREE, HONEY-- ALTHOUGH ANOTHER **BEE** MIGHT BEG TO DIFFER WITH YOU!

WHEEE! THIS IS **GROOVY!** HE'S MUCH FASTER THAN I--AND **STRONGER!** GIDDIYAP, OL' PAINT!

DON'T FLAP YOUR WINGS, JAN! LET **HIM** DO THE WORK! GUIDE HIM BY HIS ANTENNAE!

THAT SHOULD KEEP HER BUSY LONG ENOUGH FOR ME TO GET BACK TO THAT **CAR!**

AND, BACK TO THE SUPREME ONE'S LAB... LITTLE DO THEY DREAM THAT EVERYTHING THEY SAY AND DO IS BEING TRANS-MITTED TO ME BY THE CIRCUITS IN MY CAR WHICH ARE **STILL** OPERATING!

4

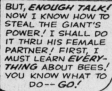

Panel 1:
BUT, *ENOUGH TALK!* NOW I KNOW HOW TO STEAL THE GIANT'S POWER! I SHALL DO IT THRU HIS *FEMALE* PARTNER! FIRST, I MUST LEARN *EVERYTHING* ABOUT BEES! YOU KNOW WHAT TO DO-- *GO!*

YES, YES, OF *COURSE,* SUPREME ONE! OUR *OTHER* CAR HAS A NEW RAY, ALL READY FOR OPERATION!

Panel 2:

MINUTES LATER, OUTSIDE THE HOME OF FENTON FARNUM, WORLD'S GREATEST AUTHORITY ON BEES...

I HAVE *FOUND* HIM, MASTER! I AM NOW ACTIVATING THE GREEN RAY...

Panel 3:
WHAT IS *HAPPENING* TO ME?? I'M BEGINNING TO FEEL *WEAK--* MY HEAD-- IT'S *THROBBING* SO -- THROBBING--

Panel 4:
GOOD! *GOOD!* IT WORKS *PERFECTLY!* I FEEL HIS KNOWLEDGE ENTERING MY BRAIN!

Panel 5:
CONTINUE THE PROCESS, LOKO! DO NOT STOP TILL I KNOW EVERYTHING ABOUT BEES WHICH *HE* HAS KNOWN!

Panel 6:
ENOUGH! HIS MIND IS SATURATED! HIS KNOWLEDGE IS NOW *MINE!* ONCE AGAIN MY GREEN RAY HAS SERVED ME WELL!

Panel 7:
AND, AT THAT MOMENT, BACK AT HENRY PYM'S LAB AGAIN...

WHY DID YOU SEND FOR ME, PYM? WHAT'S WRONG?

THAT'S WHAT I WANT *YOU* TO TELL *ME,* DOCTOR! I'M A BIO-CHEMIST, BUT I'VE BEEN WRESTLING WITH A PROBLEM IN *PHYSICS!* AND *YOU'RE* THE TOP MAN IN THAT FIELD!

NOT ANY *MORE,* HENRY! LATELY, I SEEM TO HAVE LOST MY ABILITY...!

YOU WON'T MIND IF *I* GO FOR A RIDE WHILE YOU'RE IN CONFERENCE, HANK?

NO, JAN! I'LL SEE YOU LATER!

Panel 8:
I CAN'T FIGURE OUT THE THEORY BEHIND THIS ELECTRONIC APPARATUS, DOC! YOU SEE--

WAIT A MINUTE! WHAT DID YOU *MEAN* YOU SEEM TO HAVE LOST YOUR ABILITY??

Panel 9:
EXACTLY THAT! A FEW DAYS AGO, WHILE I WAS IN MY LAB, A STRANGE *GREEN RAY* SEEMED TO ENVELOP ME -- MAKING ME LOSE CONSCIOUSNESS! WHEN I RECOVERED, I HAD FORGOTTEN *EVERYTHING* I EVER KNEW ABOUT PHYSICS!

5

I'M PERFECTLY NORMAL IN EVERY *OTHER* RESPECT-- BUT, WHEN IT COMES TO MY *SCIENCE*, IT'S AS THOUGH SOMEONE, OR SOMETHING, HAS STOLEN ALL THE KNOWLEDGE FROM ME WHICH I ONCE POSSESSED!

A GREEN RAY TOOK ALL YOUR KNOWLEDGE OF PHYSICS FROM YOU?! IT'S *INCREDIBLE!*

COULD IT BE THE SAME GREEN RAY WHICH WEAKENED *ME* RECENTLY??

AND I'M NOT THE *ONLY* ONE IT'S HAPPENED TO! *OTHER* SCIENTISTS HAVE BEEN REPORTING THE SAME STRANGE OCCURRENCE! IT'S AS THOUGH SOME POWERFUL FORCE IS TRYING TO ROB US OF ALL OUR SCIENTIFIC KNOWLEDGE!

WELL, SORRY I CAN'T HELP YOU, MY FRIEND!

YES, SO AM *I!* I APPRECIATE YOUR COMING OVER, DOCTOR! THANKS VERY MUCH!

AND, THOUGH YOU DON'T *KNOW* IT, YOU'VE HELPED ME FAR MORE THAN YOU SUSPECT!

THEN, NO SOONER HAS THE PHYSICIST LEFT HIS LAB, WHEN...

WHOEVER BATHED ME IN THAT GREEN RAY WAS TRYING TO GET MY KNOWLEDGE OF *SIZE-CHANGING* FROM ME! BUT, WHILE I WAS GIANT-SIZED, THE RAY WAS TOO WEAK TO WORK AGAINST ME!

HOWEVER, HE'S SURE TO TRY AGAIN WITH A *STRONGER* RAY -- SO I MUST BE *READY* FOR HIM!

I'VE GOT TO FIND *JAN!* WHERE CAN SHE *BE?*

THEN, AS IF IN ANSWER TO GIANT-MAN'S UNSPOKEN THOUGHT...

LOOK, HANK! I'VE GOT THIS BEE SO WELL-TRAINED AS A *BABY!* I MAY ENTER HIM IN THE NEXT KENTUCKY DERBY!

GLAD YOU'RE HAPPY WITH HIM, PRETTY GIRL-- BUT, WE'VE GOT A *JOB* TO DO!

OH, DON'T BE AN OLD KILL-JOY, HANK! LET ME RIDE HIM JUST A LITTLE BIT MORE!

BUT SUDDENLY, AN EERIE, *GREEN GLOW* ENVELOPS BOTH THE BEE AND ITS RIDER, AND THEN...

HANK! WHAT'S *HAPPENING*?? IS THIS A TRICK OF *YOURS*??

THE *GREEN RAY!* I DIDN'T THINK HE'D STRIKE SO *SOON!* FLY AWAY FROM THE BEE, JAN! *QUICKLY!*

BUT, THE DESPERATE WARNING COMES TOO *LATE*...!

OWWW! H-HE STUNG ME!

THE GREEN RAY STOLE THE *BEE'S* KNOWLEDGE! HE FORGOT MY TRAINING-- FORGOT THAT JAN WAS HIS MISTRESS! NOW, IT'S ALL UP TO *ME!*

6

MOVING WITH SKILLFUL PRECISION, COUPLED WITH BLINDING SPEED, THE MASTER OF MANY SIZES STRIKES AS ONLY HE CAN....!

WHIT!

MY *FIRST* TASK IS TO *SEPARATE* JAN FROM THE BEE! *THERE!* I *DID* IT!

NEXT, I'VE GOT TO *CATCH* HER! THE STING MADE THE POOR KID BLACK OUT!

I'VE GOT TO REMOVE THE BARB *INSTANTLY!* IT COULD BE *FATAL* TO HER WHILE SHE'S WASP-SIZED! NO TIME TO GET HER TO A DOCTOR!

BUT, I'M TOO BIG AND CLUMSY THIS SIZE! I'LL HAVE TO SHRINK DOWN TO *HER* SIZE, IN ORDER TO SAVE HER!

WHOEVER STRUCK WITH THE GREEN RAY MUST STILL BE IN A POSITION TO STRIKE *AGAIN!* BUT I CAN'T WORRY ABOUT THAT NOW-- I'VE GOT TO LOOK AFTER JAN WHILE THERE STILL IS TIME!

THAT *TWEEZERS* --WHICH I USE FOR MY STAMP COLLECTION! IT'S JUST WHAT I NEED!

BUT, EVEN AS THE MIGHTY AVENGER BEGINS TO REMOVE THE DEADLY BARB, HE HEARS A SOUND BEHIND HIM, AND TURNS TO SEE...

THE *GREEN RAY!* I COULD SAVE MYSELF BY BECOMING *GIANT-SIZED* AGAIN-- BUT I CAN'T FORSAKE JAN NOW!

I'VE JUST GOT TO PRAY THAT I CAN HOLD OUT TILL I'VE REMOVED THE BARB! AFTER THAT-- IT DOESN'T MATTER *WHAT* HAPPENS TO ME! JUST SECONDS LONGER-- NOW-- NOW--

I *DID* IT! SHE'S *SAFE!* I--I-- OHHHH...

7

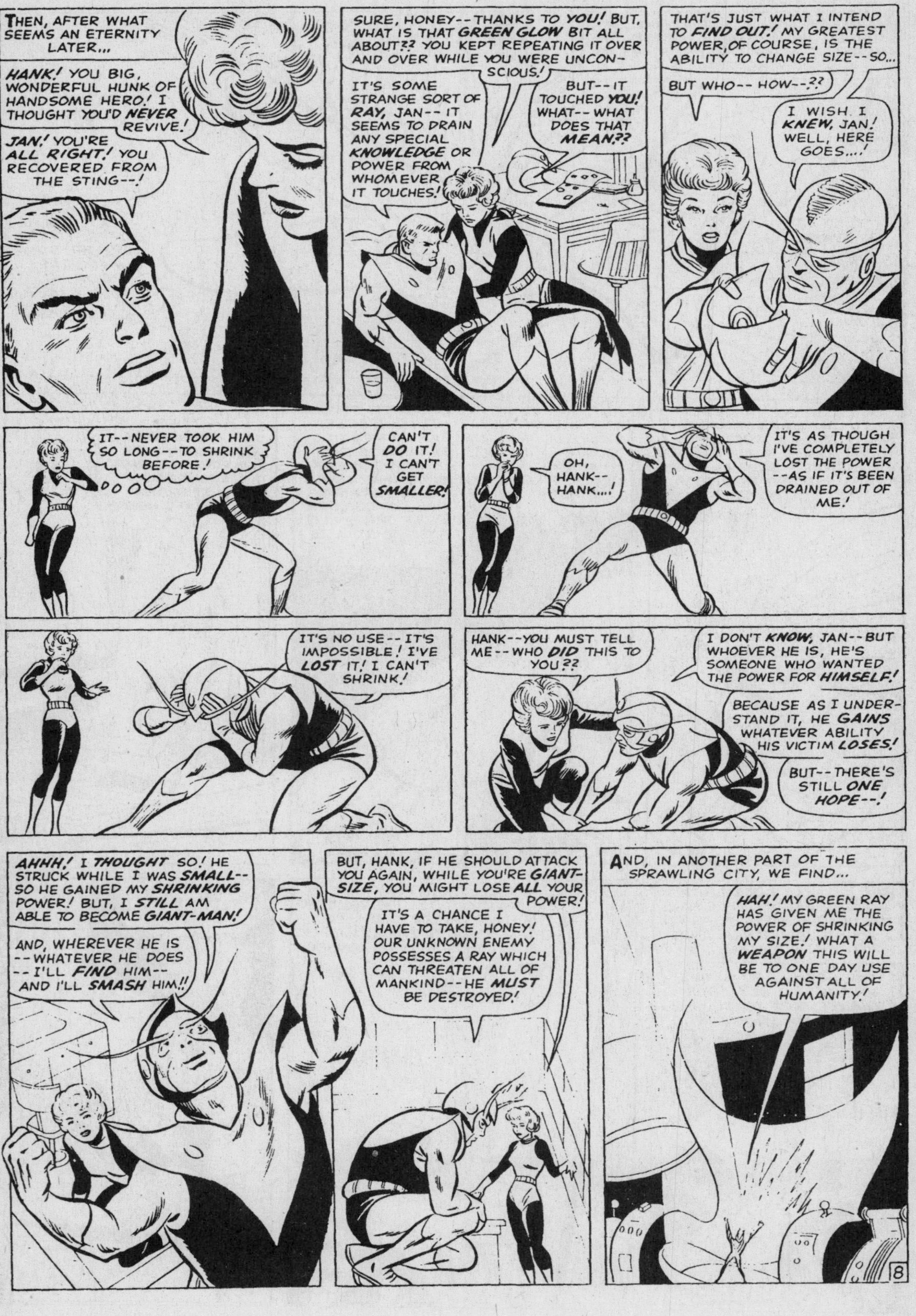

THEN, AFTER WHAT SEEMS AN ETERNITY LATER...
HANK! YOU BIG, WONDERFUL HUNK OF HANDSOME HERO! I THOUGHT YOU'D NEVER REVIVE!
JAN! YOU'RE ALL RIGHT! YOU RECOVERED FROM THE STING--!
SURE, HONEY--THANKS TO YOU! BUT, WHAT IS THAT GREEN GLOW BIT ALL ABOUT?? YOU KEPT REPEATING IT OVER AND OVER WHILE YOU WERE UNCONSCIOUS!
IT'S SOME STRANGE SORT OF RAY, JAN-- IT SEEMS TO DRAIN ANY SPECIAL KNOWLEDGE OR POWER FROM WHOMEVER IT TOUCHES!
BUT--IT TOUCHED YOU! WHAT--WHAT DOES THAT MEAN??
THAT'S JUST WHAT I INTEND TO FIND OUT! MY GREATEST POWER, OF COURSE, IS THE ABILITY TO CHANGE SIZE--SO...
BUT WHO-- HOW--??
I WISH. I KNEW, JAN! WELL, HERE GOES....!
IT--NEVER TOOK HIM SO LONG--TO SHRINK BEFORE!
CAN'T DO IT! I CAN'T GET SMALLER!
OH, HANK-- HANK....!
IT'S AS THOUGH I'VE COMPLETELY LOST THE POWER --AS IF IT'S BEEN DRAINED OUT OF ME!
IT'S NO USE--IT'S IMPOSSIBLE! I'VE LOST IT! I CAN'T SHRINK!
HANK--YOU MUST TELL ME--WHO DID THIS TO YOU??
I DON'T KNOW, JAN--BUT WHOEVER HE IS, HE'S SOMEONE WHO WANTED THE POWER FOR HIMSELF!
BECAUSE AS I UNDERSTAND IT, HE GAINS WHATEVER ABILITY HIS VICTIM LOSES!
BUT--THERE'S STILL ONE HOPE--!
AHHH! I THOUGHT SO! HE STRUCK WHILE I WAS SMALL-- SO HE GAINED MY SHRINKING POWER! BUT, I STILL AM ABLE TO BECOME GIANT-MAN!
AND, WHEREVER HE IS --WHATEVER HE DOES --I'LL FIND HIM-- AND I'LL SMASH HIM!!
BUT, HANK, IF HE SHOULD ATTACK YOU AGAIN, WHILE YOU'RE GIANT-SIZE, YOU MIGHT LOSE ALL YOUR POWER!
IT'S A CHANCE I HAVE TO TAKE, HONEY! OUR UNKNOWN ENEMY POSSESSES A RAY WHICH CAN THREATEN ALL OF MANKIND--HE MUST BE DESTROYED!
AND, IN ANOTHER PART OF THE SPRAWLING CITY, WE FIND...
HAH! MY GREEN RAY HAS GIVEN ME THE POWER OF SHRINKING MY SIZE! WHAT A WEAPON THIS WILL BE TO ONE DAY USE AGAINST ALL OF HUMANITY!

BUT, EVEN THE "SUPREME ONE" IS CAPABLE OF MAKING A MISTAKE...

JAN--LISTEN!! SOME OF THE CIRCUITS IN THIS CAR ARE STILL OPERATING! I SUSPECT THEY'RE FEEDING ELECTRONIC INFORMATION BACK TO OUR UNKNOWN FOE!

AND THAT GIVES ME AN IDEA HOW TO FIND HIM!

ALL I HAVE TO DO IS ADJUST MY CYBERNETIC HELMET, TO ZERO IN ON HIS OWN WAVELENGTH...!

MINUTES LATER... YOU WAIT HERE, JAN! I'LL CALL YOU IF I NEED YOU!

DON'T BE LONG, HIGH-POCKETS! I HATE TO COMPLAIN, BUT THOSE BEES AREN'T THE GREATEST COMPANY FOR A SWINGIN' SWEETIE LIKE ME!

THEN, USING HIS CYBERNETIC HELMET LIKE A MINIATURE RADAR DEVICE, THE TOWERING AVENGER BEGINS HIS QUEST...

THE SIGNAL IS COMING IN STRONG AND CLEAR! I SHOULD HAVE HIM SOON!

DRAT! WHY SHOULD HE HAVE ALL THE FUN, WHILE I STAY BEHIND TO BECOME A GLORIFIED BABY-BEE-SITTER!

THEY SAY IF YOU'RE THROWN OFF A HORSE, YOU SHOULD GET RIGHT BACK ON AND RIDE HIM AGAIN, TO CONQUER YOUR FEAR! WELL, THE SAME THING PROBABLY APPLIES TO BEES!

SO, HERE GOES NOTHING!

MEANWHILE... SUPREME ONE! THE ALARM!! WE ARE IN DANGER! SOMEONE IS COMING!

OF COURSE! IT IS THE GIANT! I HAVE BEEN EXPECTING HIM! HE SHALL NOT FIND ME UNPREPARED!

INTO OUR SPECIAL VEHICLE, LOKO! REMAIN THERE UNTIL YOU RECEIVE A COMMAND FROM ME! NOW GO!

I SHALL DEAL WITH OUR TOWERING VICTIM IN MY OWN WAY!

9

THERE HE *IS!* HE IS *LARGER* THAN I THOUGHT HE WOULD BE! HOW *CAREFULLY* HE WALKS, TO AVOID INJURING ANYBODY!

HE DOESN'T *SEE* ME YET! AND, WHEN HE *DOES*-- IT WILL BE *TOO LATE!*

THERE!! ONE BLAST SHOULD BE ENOUGH TO TOPPLE HIM --*FOREVER!*

ZAPP!

UNNHHH--

IT'S NO *GOOD!!* HE WAS *TOO BIG!!* MY ATTACK ONLY *STUNNED* HIM! BUT I CAN'T RECHARGE FOR FIVE MINUTES!

MUSTN'T *FALL*--MIGHT *CRUSH* SOMEONE --MUST *HOLD ON*--!!

BUT, AS GIANT-MAN BRACES HIMSELF *WEAKLY, LOKO* RECEIVES HIS MASTER'S COMMAND...

NOW, LOKO.!! THIS IS YOUR *CHANCE!* HIT HIM! HIT HIM!

THAT *TRUCK!!* IT'S ABOUT TO RUN DOWN THE OLD MAN CROSSING IN FRONT OF IT--!!

I'VE *GOT* TO STOP IT-- NO MATTER *WHAT!!*

WHUMM!

THEN, BEFORE THE SLIPPERY *LOKO* CAN ESCAPE...

NO! DON'T HURT ME! IT'S NOT *MY* FAULT! I ONLY OBEYED THE *SUPREME ONE!* I *HAD* TO.!! HE'S TOO POWERFUL! *NOBODY* CAN DEFY HIM!

WE'LL *SEE* ABOUT THAT, MISTER!

HE'S ALL *YOURS,* OFFICER! I'M GOING AFTER HIS *BOSS!*

NICE WORK, BIG MAN! YOU SAVED THAT OLD GENT'S LIFE!

10

GIANT-MAN--- WAIT! YOUR ARM IS INJURED!! YOU CAN'T--!!

I'VE GOT TO!! I'M THE ONLY ONE WHO CAN REACH HIM IN TIME!

I'LL SHRINK TO MY TWELVE-FOOT SIZE-- I'M STRONGEST THIS WAY!

AND I'LL NEED EVERY BIT OF STRENGTH I POSSESS!

HAH! THE FIVE MINUTES ARE UP! I CAN FIRE ANOTHER BLAST NOW!

WHA--?! ALTHOUGH HE'S NOW SMALLER, HE'S STRONGER THAN EVER! HE SURVIVED IT AGAIN!

WHOOOOSH!

HIS COURAGE MATCHES HIS STRENGTH! I DARE NOT FACE HIM AGAIN! I'VE GOT TO RUN!

HE'S COMING!! MY ONLY HOPE IS TO SHRINK-- TO USE THE POWER I STOLE FROM HIM!

MY LEFT ARM IS USELESS! BUT, I CAN'T STOP NOW! HE'S MAKING HIMSELF SMALL-- TRYING TO GET AWAY--!

GOT TO REACH HIM BEFORE HE GETS DOWN THAT DRAIN PIPE-- -UHHH- CAN'T-- LEFT ARM HOLDING ME BACK-- PAIN-- UNBEARABLE--!!

HE MADE IT TO THE LEDGE BELOW, BUT THAT WON'T HELP HIM! NOTHING WILL KEEP ME FROM GETTING HIM NOW!

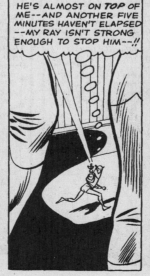

HE'S ALMOST ON TOP OF ME--AND ANOTHER FIVE MINUTES HAVEN'T ELAPSED --MY RAY ISN'T STRONG ENOUGH TO STOP HIM--!!

IT'S FINISHED!! I'VE GOT YOU!

11

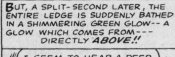

BUT, A SPLIT-SECOND LATER, THE ENTIRE LEDGE IS SUDDENLY BATHED IN A SHIMMERING GREEN GLOW -- A GLOW WHICH COMES FROM --- DIRECTLY *ABOVE*!!

I SEEM TO HEAR A DEEP, MUFFLED SOUND -- LIKE THE THROATY ROAR OF UNLIMITED *POWER*!

DO NOT TRY TO OBSERVE US -- DO NOT TRY TO PENETRATE THE GREEN GLOW! OUR BUSINESS IS NOT WITH *YOU*, GIGANTIC ONE!! FOR YOU, THERE SHALL BE MERELY A BRIEF *SLUMBER*--

I'M SUDDENLY TIRED -- CAN'T KEEP MY EYES OPEN -- MUST SLEEP -- SLEEP--!

THEN, THE EERIE GREEN GLOW SEEMS TO NARROW -- TO SINGLE OUT THE ONE WHOM GIANT-MAN HAD CAPTURED -- AND, BATHED IN ITS UNEARTHLY BRILLIANCE, HE FLOATS UPWARD -- HELPLESSLY...

YOU KNOW THE PENALTY FOR TRYING TO CONQUER PRIMITIVE PLANETS, SUPRAMOR! YOUR CRIME IS UNFORGIVEABLE!

BUT, WE SHALL UNDO WHATEVER HARM YOU HAVE DONE!

THEN, THE LAST THING GIANT-MAN REMEMBERS BEFORE CONSCIOUSNESS LEAVES HIM, IS THE SOUND OF A MIGHTY ROCKET ENGINE, ROARING INTO SPACE...

A *STAR SHIP*!! IT *HAS* TO BE -- IT CAN ONLY BE -- IT CAN -- OHHH...

RRRRRRRR

FINALLY, AFTER WHAT SEEMS TO BE AN ETERNITY LATER...

HANK! DARLING -- WAKE UP! WHAT HAPPENED?? ARE YOU ALL *RIGHT*?? IF -- IF I DIDN'T KNOW BETTER, I'D SAY YOU FELL *ASLEEP*!

HUH? WHA-- OH, JAN! YOU CAME *AFTER* ME! BUT -- EVERYTHING IS *OVER* NOW! THE DANGER HAS PASSED!

WHAT DANGER, FOR GOODNESS SAKE?? WHAT'S IT ALL *ABOUT*, HANK??

HOW CAN I TELL HER? SHE'D NEVER *BELIEVE* ME!

NOTHING, HONEY -- I GUESS I *DID* FALL ASLEEP! BY THE WAY, HOW DID YOU *GET* HERE?

MY NOBLE WINGED STEED BROUGHT ME, KIND SIR! WE'RE GOOD FRIENDS, WE TWO! HE'S TAME AS A KITTEN!

GOOD! I *KNEW* IT WOULD WORK OUT!

AND, IF YOU SAY OUR LITTLE ADVENTURE IS OVER, I WON'T ASK ANY MORE QUESTIONS! I WAS *AFRAID* YOU'D TELL ME THE GREEN RAY WAS SOMETHING FROM OUTER SPACE, OR SOMETHING EQUALLY RIDICULOUS!

OH! YOU HURT YOUR ARM! HERE, LET ME HAVE A *LOOK* AT IT, YOU POOR, DEAR THING!

I COULD ALMOST BELIEVE IT *WAS* JUST A DREAM -- EXCEPT FOR THAT TINY, UNEARTHLY *RAY GUN*, LYING JUST WHERE MY EX-CAPTIVE DROPPED IT!

12

FOR LONG, SILENT MOMENTS, THE MASTER OF MANY SIZES STARES THOUGHTFULLY AT THE EVENING SKY -- AND AT THE SOFT, GREEN GLOW WHICH SLOWLY SEEMS TO FADE INTO THE NOTHINGNESS OF SPACE...

FOR ONE BRIEF, FLEETING MOMENT IN ETERNITY, TWO LIVING BEINGS MET, FOUGHT, THEN PARTED -- NOW, IT'S OVER! AND -- NO ONE WILL EVER KNOW!

THE END

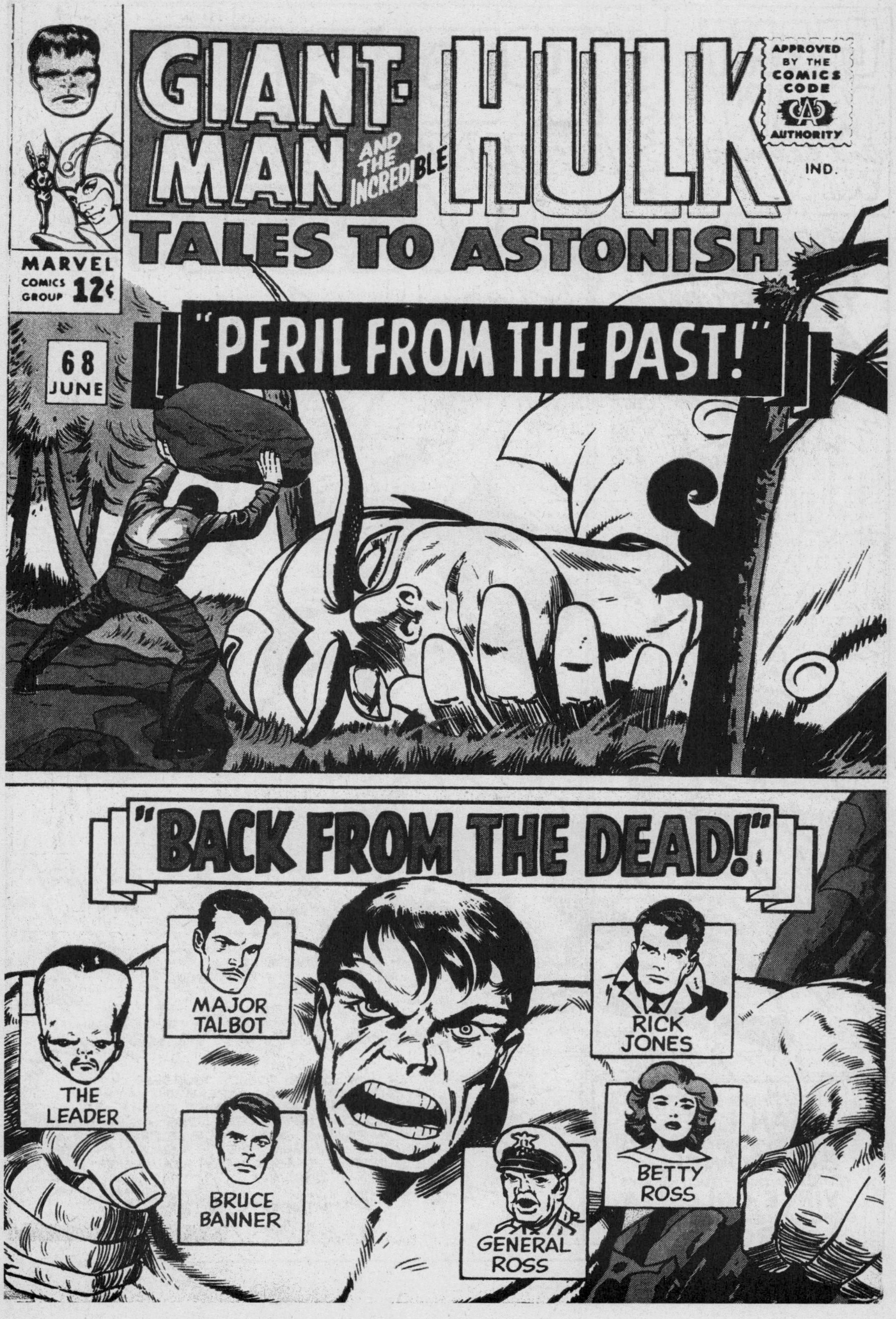

GIANT-MAN AND THE INCREDIBLE HULK
TALES TO ASTONISH
MARVEL COMICS GROUP 12¢
APPROVED BY THE COMICS CODE AUTHORITY
IND.
68 JUNE
"PERIL FROM THE PAST!"
"BACK FROM THE DEAD!"
MAJOR TALBOT
RICK JONES
THE LEADER
BRUCE BANNER
GENERAL ROSS
BETTY ROSS

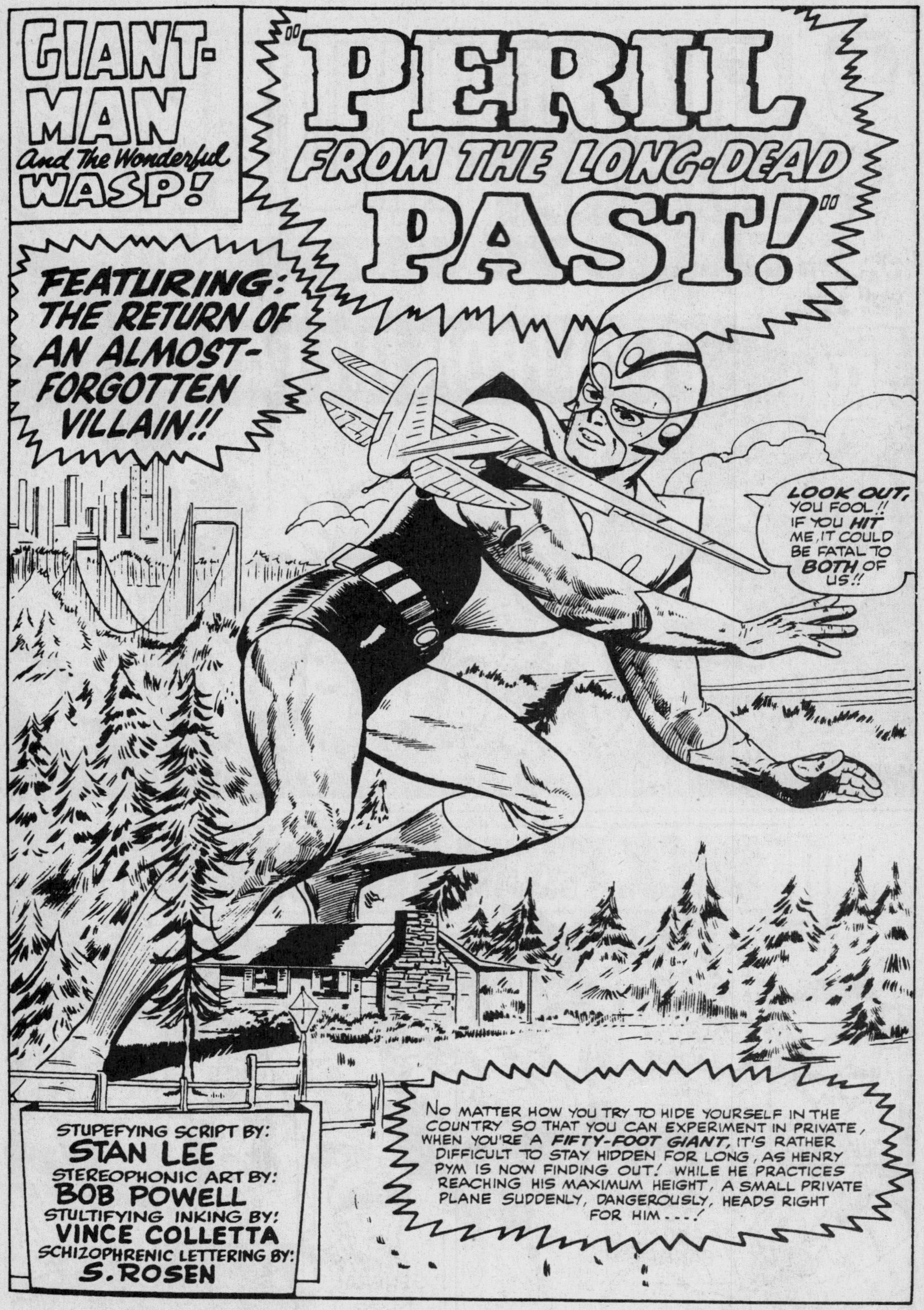
GIANT-MAN And The Wonderful WASP!
"PERIL FROM THE LONG-DEAD PAST!"
FEATURING: THE RETURN OF AN ALMOST-FORGOTTEN VILLAIN!!
LOOK OUT, YOU FOOL!! IF YOU HIT ME, IT COULD BE FATAL TO BOTH OF US!!
STUPEFYING SCRIPT BY: STAN LEE
STEREOPHONIC ART BY: BOB POWELL
STULTIFYING INKING BY: VINCE COLLETTA
SCHIZOPHRENIC LETTERING BY: S. ROSEN
NO MATTER HOW YOU TRY TO HIDE YOURSELF IN THE COUNTRY SO THAT YOU CAN EXPERIMENT IN PRIVATE, WHEN YOU'RE A FIFTY-FOOT GIANT, IT'S RATHER DIFFICULT TO STAY HIDDEN FOR LONG, AS HENRY PYM IS NOW FINDING OUT! WHILE HE PRACTICES REACHING HIS MAXIMUM HEIGHT, A SMALL PRIVATE PLANE SUDDENLY, DANGEROUSLY, HEADS RIGHT FOR HIM...!

HE'S NOT TURNING! HE **WANTS** TO HIT ME!

ALL I CAN DO IS SHIELD MYSELF BY LETTING MY **ARM** TAKE THE IMPACT!

CRACK!

STUNNED AND INJURED, THE HEROIC TITAN STILL MANAGES TO MISS THE COTTAGE BENEATH HIM AS HE FALLS....!

MUSTN'T FALL ON THAT HOUSE BELOW ME... SOME-ONE MIGHT BE HURT!

THEN, SUDDENLY, THE GIGANTIC AVENGER NOTICES...

THE PILOT JUMPED OUT... HE'LL BE **KILLED!**

HE **KNEW** THE PLANE WOULD CRASH... THOUGHT HE'D SAVE HIMSELF BY LANDING IN THE TREES!

BUT HE WAS TOO **HIGH**... THE FALL WILL BE **FATAL**... UNLESS...

UNLESS I CAN **CATCH** HIM!!

I'M OFF-BALANCE... FALLING!! BUT... I'VE GOT TO REACH... JUST A LITTLE FURTHER... FURTHER...!!

DISREGARDING HIS OWN SAFETY, GIANT-MAN HURLS HIMSELF FORWARD, STRETCHING... REACHING.. GRASPING... PITCHING HEADLONG AGAINST A TOWERING PINE TREE... BUT, SAVING THE MAN WHO HAD ALMOST KILLED HIM AS HE FALLS!!

I **GOT** HIM... UNNNHH...!

THUD!

2.

HE'S *UNCONSCIOUS*!! THE FOOL! I TRIED TO *DESTROY* HIM, AND YET HE KNOCKED HIMSELF OUT TO *SAVE* ME! BUT IF HE EXPECTS *GRATITUDE* FROM ME, HE'LL BE SORELY DISAPPOINTED!

I'D FINISH HIM OFF *NOW*... WITH THIS ROCK... BUT, IT'S TOO *SMALL*! IT MIGHT ONLY SERVE TO STING HIM SO THAT HE'D *REVIVE*!

IF ONLY HE HADN'T MOVED HIS ARM UP SO QUICKLY BEFORE! MY SPEEDING *PLANE* WOULD HAVE DONE THE JOB FOR ME! NOW, I'LL HAVE TO PLAN A NEW ATTACK... WAIT FOR ANOTHER OPPORTUNITY!

THE LAST TIME I FOUGHT HIM, I HAD THE *HULK* DO MY DIRTY WORK FOR ME... AND GIANT-MAN NEVER EVEN KNEW I HAD ARRANGED THE WHOLE THING!*

IT TOOK AN *ATOMIC EXPLOSION* TO SAVE HIM... AND IT ALMOST FINISHED *ME*!

*AS DESCRIBED IN ASTONISH #59... STAN.

BUT I SAVED MYSELF BY TAKING SHELTER INSIDE A DEEP CAVE! I REMAINED THERE IN SAFETY TILL THE LOW-YIELD FALLOUT HAD PASSED!

IT TAKES MORE THAN AN ACCIDENTAL EXPLOSION TO DESTROY ANYONE AS TALENTED... AS SUPER-POWERED AS...

...THE *HUMAN TOP*!!

HE'S COMING TO! I'LL LEAVE HIM NOW... BEFORE HE FINDS ME! BUT, OUR *NEXT* MEETING WILL BE THE *LAST*... FOR *HIM*!!

MINUTES LATER...

THAT'S STRANGE! I WAS *SURE* I HAD CAUGHT HIM, AND YET... THERE'S NO *TRACE* OF HIM! I COULDN'T HAVE BEEN *IMAGINING* IT... THE WRECKAGE OF THE PLANE IS RIGHT THERE!

WHO COULD HE HAVE *BEEN*? WHY DID HE TRY TO FLY *INTO* ME?

WELL, NOTHING MORE I CAN DO *HERE*! I'D BETTER RETURN TO THE LAB...!

3

AND SO, A SHORT TIME LATER, WE FIND...

THAT'S THE STORY, JAN! OF COURSE, IT MIGHT HAVE JUST BEEN AN *ACCIDENT*! HIS PLANE COULD HAVE BEEN OUT OF CONTROL! BUT YET, I WONDER...?

THAT'S ONE BAD THING ABOUT BEING A HUMAN SKYSCRAPER, HANK! IF ANY ENEMIES ARE WITHIN *MILES* OF YOU, YOU SURE MAKE A TEMPTING TARGET AS YOU GO SKIPPING THROUGH THE COUNTRYSIDE!

MAYBE YOU OUGHT TO STICK TO BEING *ANT-MAN*! IT'S NOT AS GLAMOROUS, BUT IT'S A LOT *SAFER*!

THAT'S JUST *IT*, HONEY... I *CAN'T*! SINCE I LOST MY ANT-SIZE SHRINKING POWERS TO THE MAN WITH THAT GREEN RAY LAST MONTH *, I'VE BEEN UNABLE TO GET THEM *BACK* AGAIN! THAT'S WHY I WAS IN THE COUNTRY PRACTICING TODAY!

YOU MEAN YOU *CAN'T* BECOME ANT-MAN ANY MORE?? GOSH, THE FLAGS WILL BE AT HALF-MAST IN EVERY ANT-HILL FROM COAST TO COAST!

* AS RECENTLY SHOWN IN ASTONISH #67..STAN.

IT'S NO LAUGHING MATTER, JAN! IT MEANS I HAVE TO DEPEND ON MY *GIANT SIZE* FROM NOW ON!

BUT YOU *CAN* GET BACK TO *NORMAL-SIZE* WHEN YOU WANT TO, CAN'T YOU?

SURE! BUT IF I TRY TO GO *SMALLER*, I GET DIZZY SPELLS AND BLACK OUT!

ALL I CAN DO IS HOPE IT'S JUST *TEMPORARY*, AND KEEP TRYING FROM TIME TO TIME!

ANYWAY, NOW THAT MY *GIANT POWER* IS ALL I HAVE, I'VE BEEN WORKING ON *STRENGTHENING* IT!

REMEMBER HOW I USED TO BE MY STRONGEST AT *TWELVE FEET*?

YEP! AND YOU *STILL* LOOK MIGHTY STRONG TO ME!

BUT, IF I COULD ONLY FIND A WAY TO MAKE MY STRENGTH *INCREASE* WHEN I GROW TO *100 FEET*... INSTEAD OF DECREASING!

IT'S NO USE! I *CAN'T*! THE STRAIN OF MY MUSCLES AND MOLECULES STRETCHING IS TOO GREAT!

A *FIFTY-FOOT* HEIGHT IS BETTER... BUT STILL SHORT OF GIVING ME MY TOP STRENGTH!

THIS IS IT... 35 FEET! PERFECT!

OHHH...GETTING *GROGGY* AGAIN!

HANK! WHAT *IS* IT? WHAT'S *WRONG*??

THE STRAIN...OF ALL THAT CHANGING... LOOK OUT, JAN...!

4

HAVE TO HOLD ON... CAN'T TOPPLE NOW...!

HANK! HANK!!

I'M TOO SMALL!! EVEN MY AIR BLAST... MY WASP'S STING... ISN'T STRONG ENOUGH TO PUSH HIM BACK ONTO THE LEDGE!!

HANK!! MY DARLING! ...DON'T FALL!!

QUICK... MAKE YOURSELF NORMAL SIZE...!!

THAT'S IT! NOW YOU CAN HOLD ON EASIER... YOU'VE LESS WEIGHT TO SUPPORT!

THEN FINALLY...

HOOO BOY! IF YOU EVER FRIGHTEN ME LIKE THAT AGAIN, HENRY PYM...!!

SORRY, HONEY! IT WASN'T MY IDEA OF A BALL, EITHER!

THANKS FOR THE ASSIST, LITTLE PARTNER!

THEN, BACK IN THE LAB, A SHORT TIME LATER...

THAT SETTLES IT! IT'S WHAT I'VE BEEN AFRAID OF...! I CAN'T KEEP CHANGING TO DIFFERENT SIZES AS OFTEN AS I USED TO! THE STRAIN IS TOO GREAT FOR ANY HUMAN BODY!

I'VE GOT TO USE ONLY ONE SIZE WHEN I BECOME GIANT-MAN... AND STICK TO THAT ONE SIZE!

AND I'VE DECIDED THAT MY THIRTY-FIVE FOOT HEIGHT IS THE BEST NOW! I'LL BE MUCH BIGGER THAN BEFORE... BUT NOT BIG ENOUGH TO WEAKEN ME ANY FURTHER!

BUT, HANK...YOU'LL NEVER BE ABLE TO HIDE FROM ANYONE AT THAT SIZE! AND THERE'LL BE SO MANY PLACES YOU CAN'T GO, BECAUSE YOU'LL BE TOO LARGE! AN ENEMY COULD ESCAPE YOU BY JUST LOCKING HIMSELF IN A ROOM!

IT'S A CHANCE I'LL HAVE TO TAKE, JAN! IT'LL STILL BE BETTER THAN GETTING ANY MORE DIZZY SPELLS!

OKAY, BOSS MAN! ANYWAY, IF YOU HAVE TO FALL HEAD OVER HEELS, I WISH IT WOULD BE OVER ME!

YOU LITTLE FAKER! YOU KNOW I LOST MY HEART TO YOU MONTHS AGO... YOU JUST WANT TO HEAR ME KEEP REPEATING IT!

AND WHAT GIRL WOULDN'T, PRAY TELL?!!

NEVERTHELESS, WE HAVE OTHER MATTERS TO ATTEND TO FIRST! THE FIRST THING I MUST DO IS ADJUST MY CYBERNETIC HELMET SO THAT I'LL AUTO-MATICALLY REACH A 35 FOOT HEIGHT WHENEVER I WILL MYSELF TO GROW! SO, IF YOU'LL EXCUSE ME FOR A MOMENT!..!

I'LL GET TO WORK NOW WHILE I HAVE THE OPPORTUNITY!

WHY MUST YOU ALWAYS MAKE WITH THE "MAD SCIENTIST" BIT EVERYTIME I FEEL LIKE TALKING MOON-JUNE TALK?

I'VE GOT NEWS FOR YOU! YOU JUST ANSWERED YOUR OWN QUESTION!

5.

THUS, FOR THE NEXT FEW HOURS ...

I'VE GOT TO ALTER THE TIMING-CIRCUIT IN MY HELMET TO SLOW DOWN ITS SPEED....!

THE SLOWER I ALTER MY SIZE, THE LESS CHANCE THERE IS OF THE SHOCK TO MY NERVOUS SYSTEM *WEAKENING* ME!

NOW, IN ORDER TO MAKE THE CYBERNETIC ADJUSTMENT *PERMANENT*, I'VE GOT TO SUBJECT THE HEART OF THE SENSITIZED UNIT TO A NUCLEAR BOMBARDMENT! IF I MISCALCULATE BY AS LITTLE AS ONE THOUSANDTH OF A DEGREE, I'LL RUIN THE ENTIRE PROCESS!

BUT, THE MOST FAMED BIO-CHEMIST OF HIS TIME IS NOT THE TYPE OF MAN TO MAKE SO SERIOUS A MISCALCULATION... AND WITHIN A MATTER OF MINUTES ...

IT'S *DONE!* FROM NOW ON, I'LL *REALLY* BE A *GIANT-MAN* REACHING *THIRTY-FIVE FEET* EACH TIME I GROW!

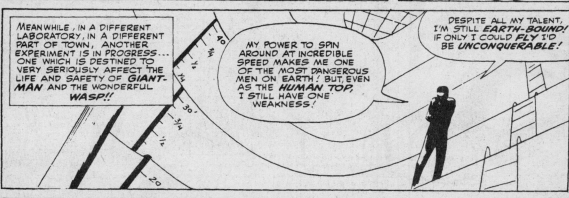

MEANWHILE, IN A DIFFERENT LABORATORY, IN A DIFFERENT PART OF TOWN, ANOTHER EXPERIMENT IS IN PROGRESS... ONE WHICH IS DESTINED TO VERY SERIOUSLY AFFECT THE LIFE AND SAFETY OF *GIANT-MAN* AND THE WONDERFUL *WASP!!*

MY POWER TO SPIN AROUND AT INCREDIBLE SPEED MAKES ME ONE OF THE MOST DANGEROUS MEN ON EARTH! BUT, EVEN AS THE *HUMAN TOP*, I STILL HAVE ONE WEAKNESS!

DESPITE ALL MY TALENT, I'M STILL *EARTH-BOUND!* IF ONLY I COULD *FLY* I'D BE *UNCONQUERABLE!*

THERE *MUST* BE A WAY! AND, IF THERE *IS*, I'LL FIND IT SOMEHOW!!

FIRST, I'LL SLIP INTO THE COSTUME I USED TO WEAR... IT'S PERFECT FOR REDUCING AIR DRAG AND ALLOWING ME TO SPIN AT TOP SPEED!

NOW, I'LL TRY LEAPING FROM THIS HEIGHT! PERHAPS I CAN SPIN FAST ENOUGH TO REMAIN ALOFT LIKE THE WHIRLING BLADE OF A HELICOPTER!

I NEVER AGAIN WANT TO SUFFER THE HUMILIATION OF BEING RESCUED FROM A FALL BY MY MOST HATED ENEMY!!

HERE I GO!!

UHHH...IT'S NOT WORKING!! I'M LOSING MOMENTUM...CAN'T MAINTAIN THE PROPER SPEED!! I'M *FALLING!*

6.

IF I COULD ONLY SPIN FASTER... FASTER... I MUST!

IT'S HOPELESS! I'M JUST LIKE A HUMAN TURNIP IN THIS BLASTED COSTUME!!

THUMP!

I'LL NEVER WEAR IT AGAIN! IT'S USELESS TO ME! I'M THROUGH WITH IT!

I'VE GOT TO DESIGN A NEW ONE... BASED ON AERO-DYNAMIC PRINCIPLES! A COSTUME WHICH WILL HELP TO MAKE ME BUOYANT... WHICH WILL GIVE ME LIFT WHEN I'M IN THE AIR!

MY FIRST MISTAKE WAS TRYING TO DESIGN AN OUTFIT BASED ON THE SHAPE OF A TOP! I DIDN'T STOP TO THINK THAT A TOP CAN'T FLY!

BUT NOW, I'LL CHANGE IT COMPLETELY... AND I KNOW JUST HOW TO DO IT!

I'LL CUT OUT A NEW PATTERN OF CLOTH... ONE WHICH WILL TAKE EVERY ADVANTAGE OF AIR CURRENTS AND BREEZES! AND THEN, WHEN I'M DONE...

I'LL WEAVE HUNDREDS OF LITTLE CELLS INTO IT... CELLS WHICH CAN BE FILLED WITH A SPECIAL TYPE OF GAS...!

HELIUM GAS... THE TYPE THAT RISES INTO THE AIR! IT WILL GIVE ME JUST THE LIFT I NEED BY LIGHTENING MY OWN BODY WEIGHT!

THERE! THE HELIUM IS SEALED WITHIN MY SUIT NOW!

SO, ALL THAT REMAINS IS TO TRY IT! AND, THIS TIME, I KNOW IT CANNOT FAIL!

THE NEXT TIME WE MEET, GIANT-MAN WON'T HAVE A CHANCE AGAINST ME, NO MATTER WHAT HIS SIZE!

BUT, EVEN AS THE HUMAN TOP PREPARES TO TEST HIS NEW COSTUME, HIS ARCH-FOE'S ALSO MAKING PREPARATIONS...!

THAT'S RIGHT, BOYS! EVERYTHING MUST BE REMODELLED SO THAT A THIRTY-FIVE FOOT FORM CAN EASILY PASS IN AND OUT!

WE'LL HAVE TO INSTALL A SPECIAL CRANE TO LIFT THE APPARATUS, MR. PYM!

NO, DON'T BOTHER! SINCE WE'RE DOING THIS FOR MY FRIEND, GIANT-MAN... I'LL CALL HIM AND SEE IF HE CAN COME OVER. HE CAN DO THE JOB MUCH FASTER THAN ANY CRANE.

OKAY BY ME!

OH, HANK, DARLING! I'VE SOMETHING TO *SHOW* YOU!

CAN IT *WAIT*, HONEY? I'VE GOT TO GO NEXT DOOR AND CHANGE! IT'LL JUST TAKE A *SEC*! LOOK AT THIS FOR A MINUTE!

A LITTLE BOX! WHAT'S *IN* IT?

THE CUTEST LITTLE *WASP*! I NEVER *DID* LIKE THAT *BEE* YOU GOT FOR ME LAST MONTH!*

SORRY, PRETTY GIRL! I CAN'T DELAY THOSE WORKMEN TO LOOK AT A *WASP*... ESPECIALLY IF IT'S ONLY A *REAL* ONE! I'LL BE RIGHT BACK!

*ASTONISH #67, 'NATCH! ...STAN.

SLAM!

SECONDS LATER...

DID THAT NAUGHTY OL' GIANT-MAN HURT OO'S LITTY BITTY FEELINGS, WASPIE? SHAME ON MEAN OL' GIANTIE!

FOR PETE'S SAKE! BABY-TALK TO A *WASP*! THAT'S *ENDSVILLE*!

MIND IF I COME IN? HENRY PYM ASKED ME IF I'D GIVE YOU FELLOWS A HAND!

GIANT-MAN!!

A *HAND*?? ONE *FINGER* OUGHTA BE ENOUGH!

LOOK AT THE *SIZE* OF 'IM!

NO WONDER WE'RE MAKIN' THE WINDOWS AND DOORS SO MUCH BIGGER!!

JUST HOLD THAT GLASS PANE IN PLACE WHILE WE ATTACH IT!

HOW'S IT FEEL TO BE ORDERIN' *GIANT-MAN* AROUND, SAM??

BOY! TWO MORE LIKE *YOU*, AND WE COULD SCRAP EVERY DERRICK IN TOWN!

IF HE EVER PLAYS BASKETBALL, *LOOK OUT*!

IF HE *SNEEZES*, I'M LEAVIN' TOWN!

FINALLY...

IT'S PERFECT! JUST THE RIGHT SIZE FOR ME! YOU CAN GO NOW, MEN!

WE'LL COME BY TOMORROW TO CLEAN UP THE MESS!

SAY GOOD-BYE TO MR. PYM FOR US, WILL YOU?

I SURE WILL! SO LONG, BOYS!

OH, JAN... ARE *YOU* STILL HERE?

NATURALLY!

I'VE BEEN WAITING TO *TALK* TO YOU, YOU BIG LUG!

B

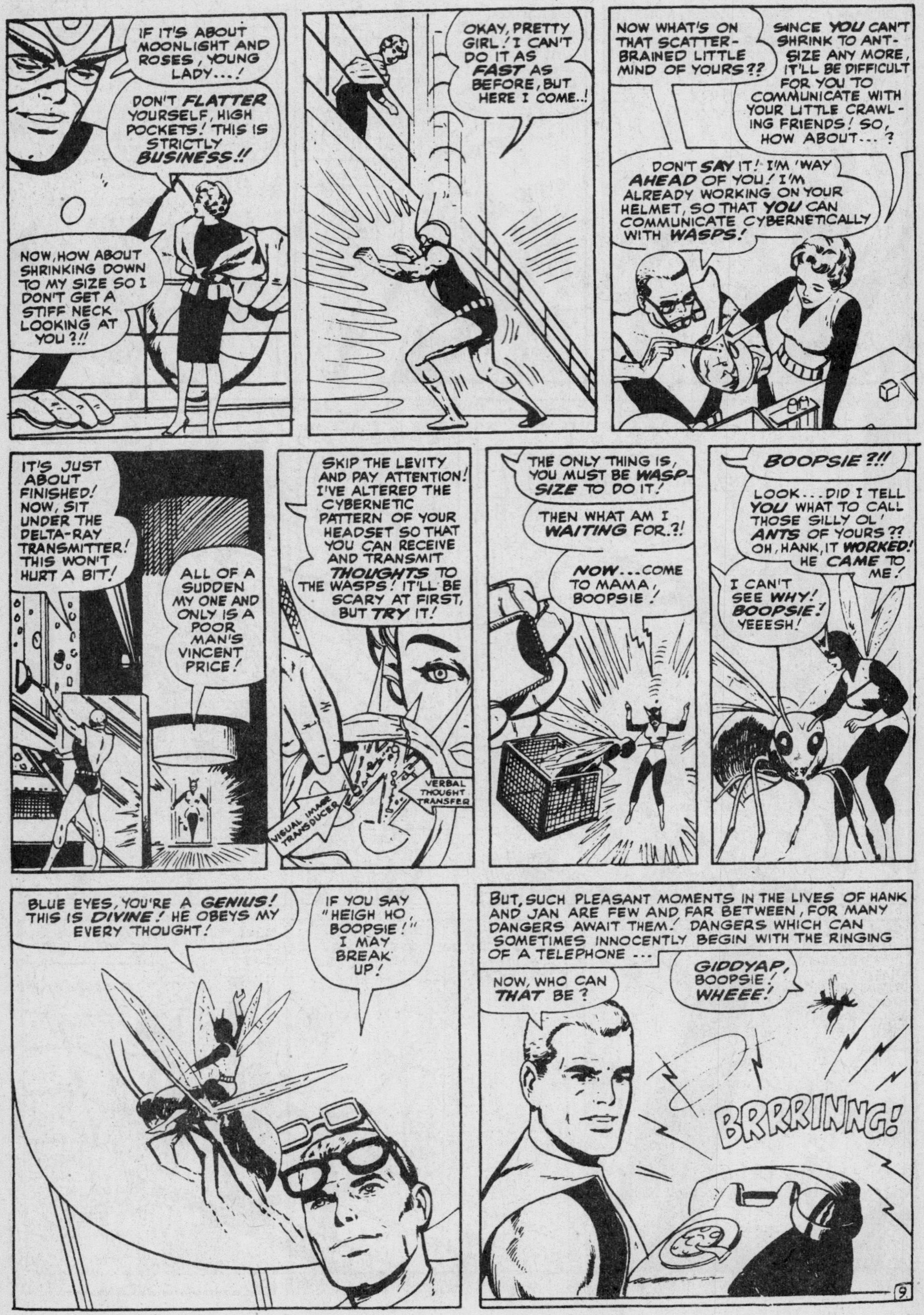
IF IT'S ABOUT MOONLIGHT AND ROSES, YOUNG LADY...!
DON'T FLATTER YOURSELF, HIGH POCKETS! THIS IS STRICTLY BUSINESS.!!
NOW, HOW ABOUT SHRINKING DOWN TO MY SIZE SO I DON'T GET A STIFF NECK LOOKING AT YOU?!!
OKAY, PRETTY GIRL! I CAN'T DO IT AS FAST AS BEFORE, BUT HERE I COME..!
NOW WHAT'S ON THAT SCATTER-BRAINED LITTLE MIND OF YOURS??
SINCE YOU CAN'T SHRINK TO ANT-SIZE ANY MORE, IT'LL BE DIFFICULT FOR YOU TO COMMUNICATE WITH YOUR LITTLE CRAWLING FRIENDS! SO, HOW ABOUT...?
DON'T SAY IT! I'M 'WAY AHEAD OF YOU! I'M ALREADY WORKING ON YOUR HELMET, SO THAT YOU CAN COMMUNICATE CYBERNETICALLY WITH WASPS!
IT'S JUST ABOUT FINISHED! NOW, SIT UNDER THE DELTA-RAY TRANSMITTER! THIS WON'T HURT A BIT!
ALL OF A SUDDEN MY ONE AND ONLY IS A POOR MAN'S VINCENT PRICE!
SKIP THE LEVITY AND PAY ATTENTION! I'VE ALTERED THE CYBERNETIC PATTERN OF YOUR HEADSET SO THAT YOU CAN RECEIVE AND TRANSMIT THOUGHTS TO THE WASPS! IT'LL BE SCARY AT FIRST, BUT TRY IT!
VISUAL IMAGE TRANSDUCER
VERBAL THOUGHT TRANSFER
THE ONLY THING IS, YOU MUST BE WASP-SIZE TO DO IT!
THEN WHAT AM I WAITING FOR.?!
NOW...COME TO MAMA, BOOPSIE!
BOOPSIE?!!
LOOK...DID I TELL YOU WHAT TO CALL THOSE SILLY OL' ANTS OF YOURS?? OH, HANK, IT WORKED! HE CAME TO ME!
I CAN'T SEE WHY! BOOPSIE! YEEESH!
BLUE EYES, YOU'RE A GENIUS! THIS IS DIVINE! HE OBEYS MY EVERY THOUGHT!
IF YOU SAY "HEIGH HO, BOOPSIE!" I MAY BREAK UP!
BUT, SUCH PLEASANT MOMENTS IN THE LIVES OF HANK AND JAN ARE FEW AND FAR BETWEEN, FOR MANY DANGERS AWAIT THEM! DANGERS WHICH CAN SOMETIMES INNOCENTLY BEGIN WITH THE RINGING OF A TELEPHONE...
NOW, WHO CAN THAT BE?
GIDDYAP, BOOPSIE! WHEEE!
BRRRINNG!
9

IT'S OUR PRIVATE GUARD, DOWN-STAIRS! WE HAVE A CALLER!

YOU CAN SEE HIM *ALONE*, DREAMBOAT! I WANT TO STAY ON BOOPSIE, SO I'LL *LEAVE* FOR A WHILE!

IT'S A *REPORTER*, FROM THE *GLOBE*, SIR!

OKAY! *SHOW* HIM UP, FRANK!

HOLD IT, MEN! THAT'S A PRIVATE ELEVATOR! YOU CAN'T USE IT WITHOUT SIGNING THIS REGISTER!

IT LEADS TO *GIANT-MAN'S* LAB! I HAVE TO CALL FOR PERMISSION BEFORE ANYONE CAN GO UP THERE!

WITH ALL THE *ENEMIES* HE MUST HAVE, IT'S A GOOD THING YOU *TAKE* THOSE *PRECAUTIONS*, MISTER!

ALTHOUGH IT'S TOO BAD YOU DIDN'T THINK TO ASK ME FOR MY *CREDENTIALS* BEFORE YOU BELIEVED THAT I'M A REPORTER FOR THE *GLOBE!*

THEN, AFTER THE "REPORTER" HAS SIGNED THE LEDGER...

TELL ME... GUARD... DOES ANY-ONE KNOW GIANT-MAN'S *REAL* IDENTITY?

LOOK, SIR... I'M JUST PAID TO WATCH THAT ELEVATOR.. NOT TO GO SHOOTIN' MY MOUTH OFF ABOUT MY BOSS!

HE'S PROBABLY A *MIDGET* IN REAL LIFE! C'MON, LET'S GO BACK TO WORK!

AND *SECONDS* LATER ...

I DON'T *USUALLY* GIVE INTERVIEWS WITHOUT AN APPOINTMENT, BUT I'VE GOT A FEW MINUTES TO SPARE NOW!

I GUESS THIS IS MY LUCKY DAY!

HAVE WE *MET* BEFORE? YOU SEEM SORT OF FAMILIAR...

MAYBE! I MEET A *LOT* OF PEOPLE IN MY WORK! HOW ABOUT SHOWING ME AROUND YOUR LAB?

AS A MATTER OF FACT, YOU'RE THE FIRST ONE TO SEE IT SINCE I'VE HAD IT REMODELLED! IT'S ALL BEEN ENLARGED TO GIVE ME MORE ROOM!

SO I SEE! WHAT ARE THOSE THINGS WITH THE BURLAP *COVERS* OVER THEM?

SORRY! THEY'RE PRIVATE COMPUTERS AND CYBERNETIC INSTRUMENTS! THEIR FUNCTIONS AND OPERATION ARE NOT TO BE MADE PUBLIC!

MEANTIME, HAVING FINISHED HER *WASP-RIDE*, JANET VAN DYNE RETURNS TO THE LAB, AND...

BY THE WAY, THIS IS JUST ROUTINE, OF COURSE... BUT I'D BETTER HAVE A LOOK AT YOUR *CREDENTIALS!*

YOU CAN'T BE WORRIED ABOUT A LITTLE FELLA LIKE *ME*, CAN YOU?

I'VE HEARD THAT VOICE *BEFORE!*

10

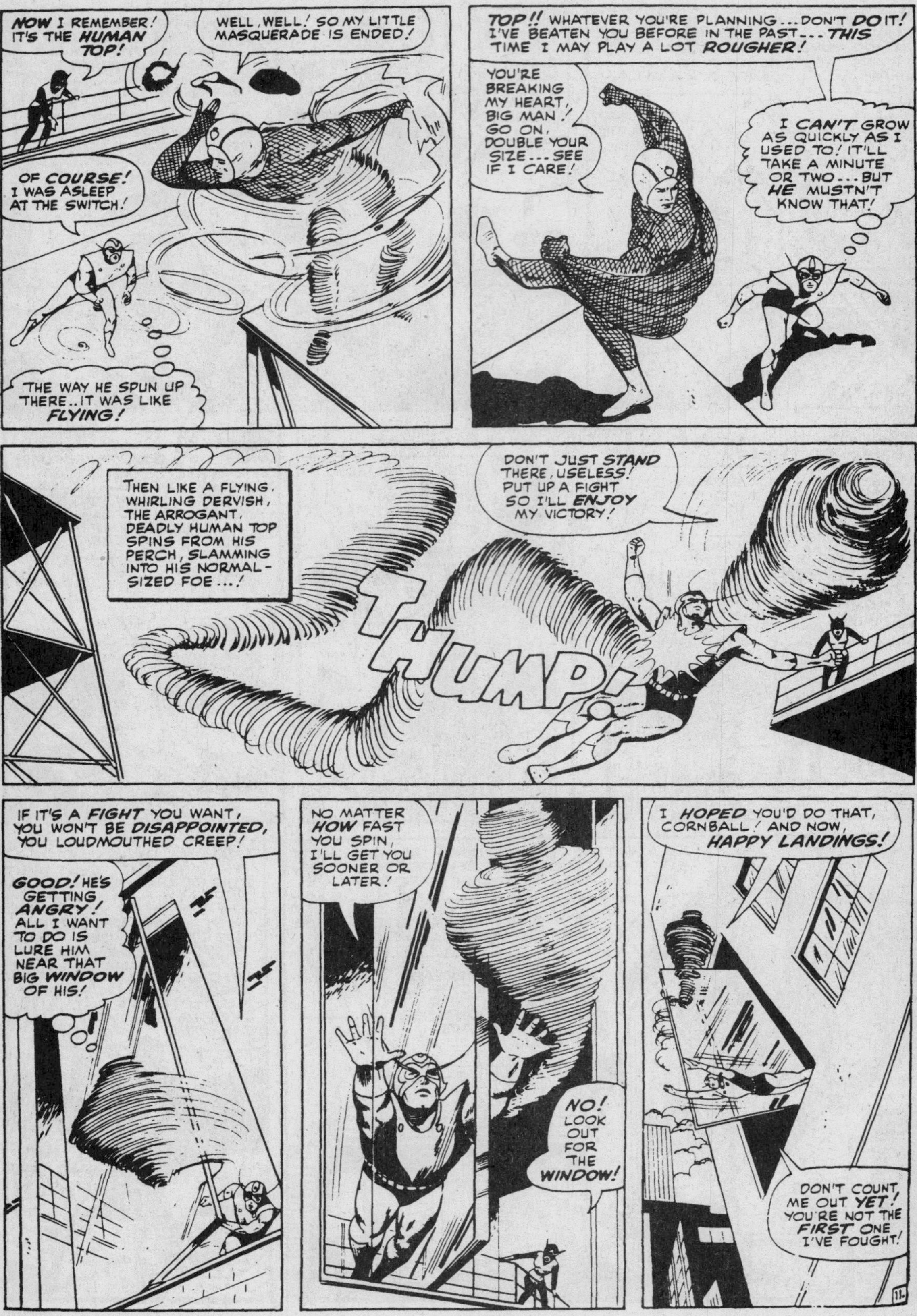
NOW I REMEMBER! IT'S THE HUMAN TOP!
WELL, WELL! SO MY LITTLE MASQUERADE IS ENDED!
OF COURSE! I WAS ASLEEP AT THE SWITCH!
THE WAY HE SPUN UP THERE..IT WAS LIKE FLYING!
TOP!! WHATEVER YOU'RE PLANNING... DON'T DO IT! I'VE BEATEN YOU BEFORE IN THE PAST--- THIS TIME I MAY PLAY A LOT ROUGHER!
YOU'RE BREAKING MY HEART, BIG MAN! GO ON, DOUBLE YOUR SIZE--- SEE IF I CARE!
I CAN'T GROW AS QUICKLY AS I USED TO! IT'LL TAKE A MINUTE OR TWO... BUT HE MUSTN'T KNOW THAT!
THEN LIKE A FLYING, WHIRLING DERVISH, THE ARROGANT, DEADLY HUMAN TOP SPINS FROM HIS PERCH, SLAMMING INTO HIS NORMAL-SIZED FOE...!
DON'T JUST STAND THERE, USELESS! PUT UP A FIGHT SO I'LL ENJOY MY VICTORY!
THUMP!
IF IT'S A FIGHT YOU WANT, YOU WON'T BE DISAPPOINTED, YOU LOUDMOUTHED CREEP!
GOOD! HE'S GETTING ANGRY! ALL I WANT TO DO IS LURE HIM NEAR THAT BIG WINDOW OF HIS!
NO MATTER HOW FAST YOU SPIN, I'LL GET YOU SOONER OR LATER!
NO! LOOK OUT FOR THE WINDOW!
I HOPED YOU'D DO THAT, CORNBALL! AND NOW, HAPPY LANDINGS!
DON'T COUNT ME OUT YET! YOU'RE NOT THE FIRST ONE I'VE FOUGHT!
11.

--AND YOU WON'T BE THE *LAST!*

OH *NO!* NO!

HANG ON, MY DARLING! ...*HANG ON!!!*

EASY, HONEY! YOU KNOW I'M HARDER TO LOSE THAN DANDRUFF! JUST KEEP YOUR EYE ON THE *TOP!*

GET *BACK,* WASP! I'M STARTING TO *GROW* NOW! I CAN SAVE MYSELF! BUT *YOU'RE* IN DANGER!!

NO! I'VE GOT TO HELP YOU IN! IF YOU FALL...IT'LL BE THE *END!*

YOU STUBBORN NUT! I *WON'T* FALL! BUT THE *TOP* IS STILL AROUND HERE!

WHO CARES ABOUT *HIM* WHEN *YOU'RE* IN DANGER?! GIVE ME YOUR HAND!

OH! THAT NOISE.. ABOVE ME....!

DIDN'T REALIZE I COULD *FLY,* DID YOU ?? AND NOW... IT'S *TOO LATE!*

HE.. HE'S *GOT* ME!

CAN'T *REACH* HER IN TIME!

YOU CAN *STAY* THERE, GIANT-MAN! I'VE *GOT* WHAT I WANT!

BUT NOT FOR *LONG!*

THIS TIME THE *TOP* HAS GONE *TOO FAR!!*

THIS TIME HE'S PASSED THE POINT OF *NO RETURN!*

THIS TIME HE'LL FEEL THE FULL POWER...THE FULL VENGEANCE OF *GIANT-MAN...* AND NOTHING THAT LIVES WILL SAVE HIM!!

IDLE BOAST... OR DIRE PRE- DICTION ? WE'LL FIND OUT IN THE MOST SPECTACULAR BATTLE OF ALL NEXT ISH! TILL THEN, STAY ONE SIZE AND FACE FRONT!

12.

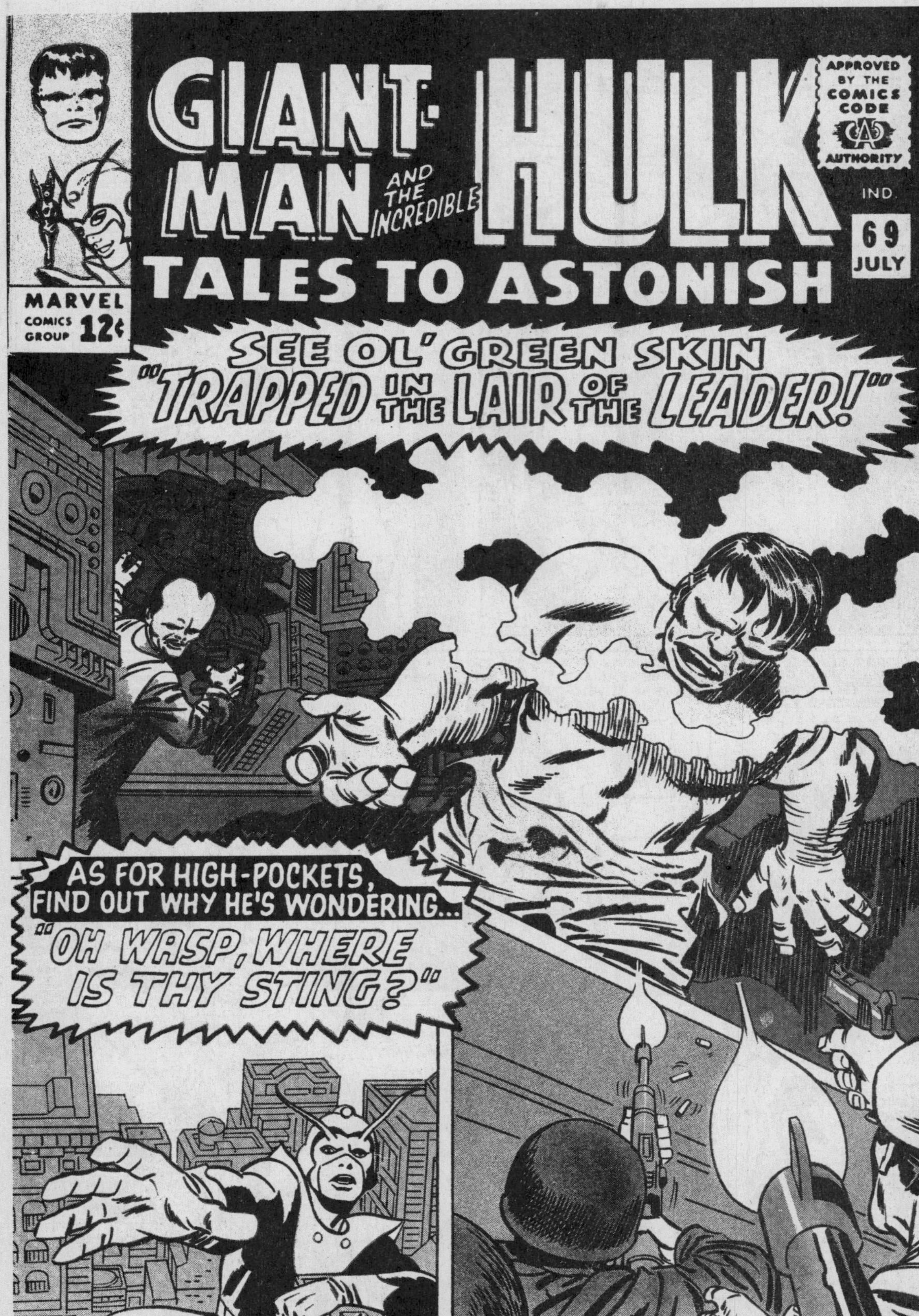
MARVEL COMICS GROUP 12¢
GIANT-MAN AND THE INCREDIBLE HULK
APPROVED BY THE COMICS CODE AUTHORITY
IND.
69 JULY
TALES TO ASTONISH
SEE OL' GREEN SKIN "TRAPPED IN THE LAIR OF THE LEADER!"
AS FOR HIGH-POCKETS, FIND OUT WHY HE'S WONDERING...
"OH WASP, WHERE IS THY STING?"

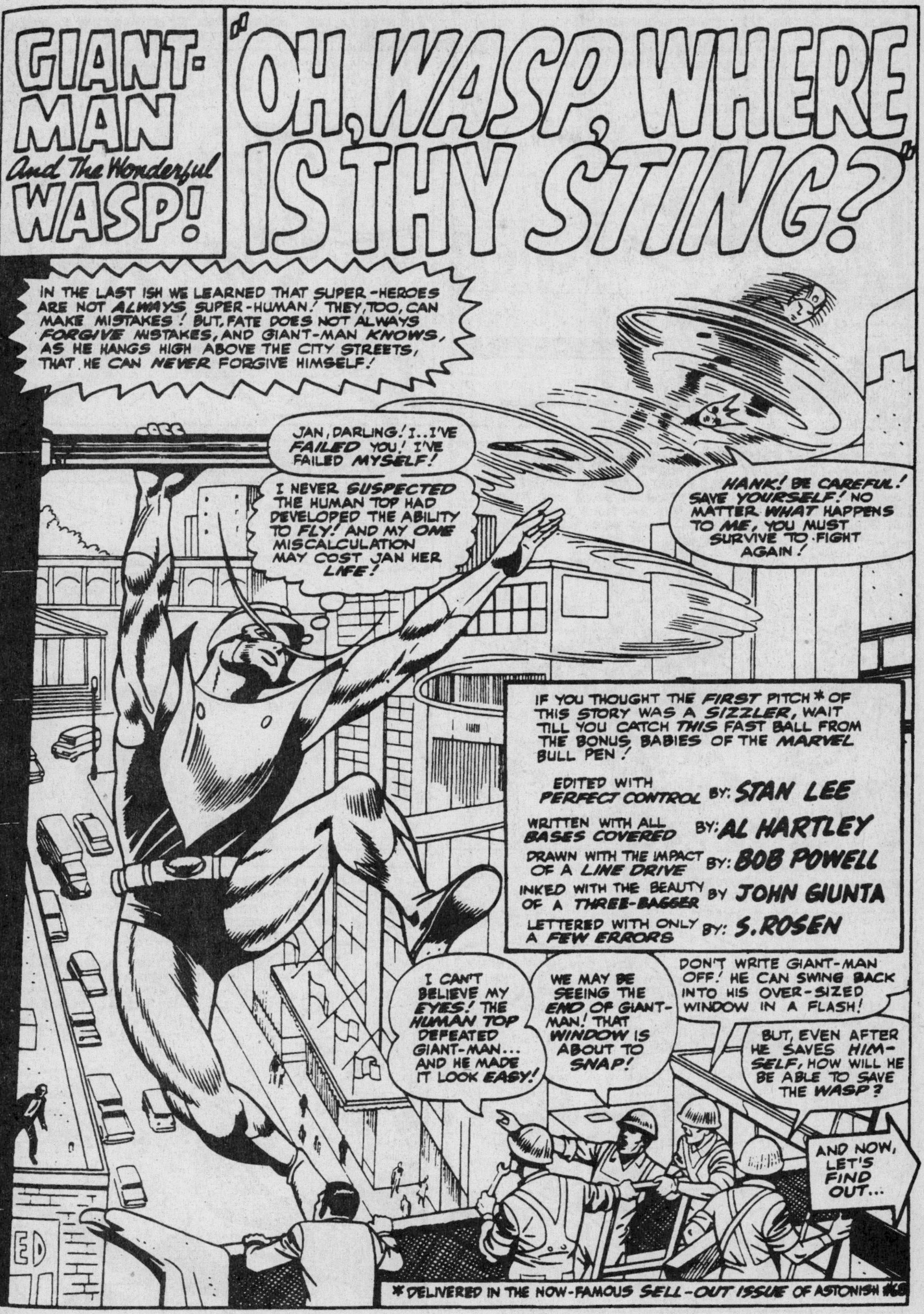
GIANT-MAN And The Wonderful WASP!
"OH, WASP, WHERE IS THY STING?"
IN THE LAST ISH WE LEARNED THAT SUPER-HEROES ARE NOT ALWAYS SUPER-HUMAN! THEY, TOO, CAN MAKE MISTAKES! BUT, FATE DOES NOT ALWAYS FORGIVE MISTAKES, AND GIANT-MAN KNOWS, AS HE HANGS HIGH ABOVE THE CITY STREETS, THAT HE CAN NEVER FORGIVE HIMSELF!
JAN, DARLING! I..I'VE FAILED YOU! I'VE FAILED MYSELF!
I NEVER SUSPECTED THE HUMAN TOP HAD DEVELOPED THE ABILITY TO FLY! AND MY ONE MISCALCULATION MAY COST JAN HER LIFE!
HANK! BE CAREFUL! SAVE YOURSELF! NO MATTER WHAT HAPPENS TO ME, YOU MUST SURVIVE TO FIGHT AGAIN!
IF YOU THOUGHT THE FIRST PITCH* OF THIS STORY WAS A SIZZLER, WAIT TILL YOU CATCH THIS FAST BALL FROM THE BONUS BABIES OF THE MARVEL BULL PEN!
EDITED WITH PERFECT CONTROL BY: STAN LEE
WRITTEN WITH ALL BASES COVERED BY: AL HARTLEY
DRAWN WITH THE IMPACT OF A LINE DRIVE BY: BOB POWELL
INKED WITH THE BEAUTY OF A THREE-BAGGER BY JOHN GIUNTA
LETTERED WITH ONLY A FEW ERRORS BY: S. ROSEN
I CAN'T BELIEVE MY EYES! THE HUMAN TOP DEFEATED GIANT-MAN... AND HE MADE IT LOOK EASY!
WE MAY BE SEEING THE END OF GIANT-MAN! THAT WINDOW IS ABOUT TO SNAP!
DON'T WRITE GIANT-MAN OFF! HE CAN SWING BACK INTO HIS OVER-SIZED WINDOW IN A FLASH!
BUT, EVEN AFTER HE SAVES HIMSELF, HOW WILL HE BE ABLE TO SAVE THE WASP?
AND NOW, LET'S FIND OUT...
*DELIVERED IN THE NOW-FAMOUS SELL-OUT ISSUE OF ASTONISH #68

AS PREDICTED, THE TITANIC AVENGER SMOOTHLY SWINGS INSIDE THE BUILDING BEFORE HIS TREMENDOUS WEIGHT CAN SNAP THE WINDOW, AND, WITHOUT WAITING AN INSTANT, SETS OUT IN PURSUIT OF THE HUMAN TOP!

I MUST FIND HIM QUICKLY! HE'S THE MOST INSIDIOUS MENACE I'VE EVER FOUGHT!

AND JAN IS COMPLETELY AT HIS MERCY!

BUT, THE TALLEST ADVENTURER TO STRIDE THE EARTH CAN FIND NO TRAIL TO FOLLOW!

BUT, HE'S VANISHED WITHOUT A TRACE!

...NOW THAT HE CAN FLY, HE LEFT NO TRACKS BEHIND HIM!

MY SEARCH IS FUTILE THIS WAY! I'M JUST WASTING PRECIOUS TIME! AND EACH PASSING MOMENT PLACES JAN IN STILL GREATER DANGER!

I MUST FIND HER! SHE MUST LIVE! IF THE SIZE AND MIGHT OF GIANT-MAN CANNOT SAVE HER, THEN ALL THE BATTLES I HAVE FOUGHT AND WON WILL HAVE BEEN A HOLLOW MOCKERY!

AT THAT VERY MOMENT, THE HUMAN TOP ARRIVES AT HIS LABORATORY WITH HIS STILL-STRUGGLING HOSTAGE!

WHAT A SWEET VICTORY THIS HAS BEEN! AND WHAT A PRECIOUS PRIZE I HAVE WON!

GIANT-MAN HAS PROBABLY ALREADY FALLEN TO HIS DOOM!

BUT EVEN IF HE SURVIVED, I AM PREPARED FOR HIM!

NOW I MUST TURN MY ATTENTION TO THE WASP!

SHE SUFFERS VORTEX VERTIGO...AND LITTLE WONDER! I HAD TO REACH 6500 RPM'S IN ORDER TO CARRY HER ALOFT! HER DELICATE BODY IS HARDLY ACCUSTOMED TO SUCH FORCES!

BUT THEN, WHO HAS THE STAMINA OF BODY OR BRILLIANCE OF MIND TO EQUAL MINE?

AH! SHE'S COMING TO...

2.

AWAKEN TO YOUR *MASTER*, LOVELY ONE, AND DO NOT DECEIVE YOURSELF BY FALSE HOPES! YOU HAVE SEEN THE *LAST* OF GIANT-MAN!

FROM THIS MOMENT ON, YOU WILL SERVE *ME* AS FAITHFULLY AS YOU SERVED YOUR FALLEN HERO!

YOU ARROGANT *FIEND!* THE ONLY WAY I'LL SERVE *YOU* IS ON A PLATTER...TO GIANT-MAN!

WHEN HE GETS HERE, HE'LL *UNWIND* YOU...FOR KEEPS!

IF ONLY I *FELT* AS CONFIDENT AS I'M TRYING TO *SOUND!*

AHA! I ADMIRE YOUR SPIRIT, WASP! BUT LISTEN CAREFULLY...

DO YOU REALLY *BELIEVE* THE MIND THAT OUT-WITTED YOUR BELOVED GIANT-MAN CANNOT OUTWIT HIM *AGAIN...* AND *AGAIN*, IF NECESSARY!

IT MUST NOT *HAPPEN* AGAIN! BUT THE HUMAN TOP *DID* BEAT HANK BEFORE... *COULD* HE BEAT *HIM* AGAIN?

EVEN IF HE SUCCEEDS IN *FINDING* ME, HE WILL *NEVER* FIND THE MEANS TO OVERCOME ME... I *PROMISE* YOU THAT!

I'VE WAITED TOO LONG, PLANNED TOO CAREFULLY! HE WILL BE AS HELPLESS WHEN HE ARRIVES AS HE WAS WHEN I LEFT HIM DANGLING FROM HIS WINDOW!

OBSERVE THE HUGE DIMENSIONS OF THE *EXCAVATION* I'VE PREPARED! REGARDLESS OF HOW *BIG* YOUR GIANT-MAN MAY BECOME, THAT PIT WILL BE SUFFICIENT TO *TRAP* HIM AND *ELIMINATE* HIM FOR ALL TIME!

NOTICE THE LIGHT-WEIGHT BUILDINGS THAT WILL PROVIDE A *CAMOUFLAGE* COVER FOR THE PIT IN WHICH HE WILL MEET HIS *DOOM!*

HE'S *MAD!* AND FAR MORE *DANGEROUS*... FAR MORE *POWERFUL*... THAN HANK OR I HAD REALIZED!

CAN'T YOU JUST *SEE* THE PRETTY PICTURE? THE WEIGHT OF YOUR PONDEROUS PARTNER WILL SEND HIM *PLUNGING* THROUGH THE IMITATION VILLAGE, INTO THE *TOMB* BELOW!

HE *WANTS* HANK TO FIND US! IT'S ALL PART OF THE MOST FOOLPROOF TRAP I'VE EVER SEEN! HANK WON'T HAVE A *CHANCE*... AND THERE'S NO WAY FOR ME TO *WARN* HIM!

AND THERE, WHILE HE IS THUS HELPLESS, I HAVE ONE *FINAL*, FATAL SURPRISE... WHICH YOU WILL BOTH LEARN WHEN THE TIME COMES!

3.

SOON THE *FINAL* VICTORY...THE *GREATEST* VICTORY, WILL BE *MINE!* LET GIANT-MAN COME! I AM READY! DO YOU HEAR...*READY!!*

WAIT! THERE *IS* A CHANCE! IF I CAN CONTACT MY TRAINED *WASP*, PERHAPS *SHE* CAN SOMEHOW WARN HANK!

...AND SURELY, WHEN YOU HAVE SEEN THE *EASE* WITH WHICH I *DISPOSE* OF HIM, YOU WILL NOT QUESTION THAT *I*, THE HUMAN TOP, AM *INVINCIBLE* AMONG MEN!

ONLY *I* AM DESERVING OF YOUR LOYALTY... AND PERHAPS, ONE DAY, EVEN OF YOUR *LOVE!*

BUT AS THE HUMAN TOP SPINS WITH FIENDISH GLEE, GIANT-MAN SITS MOTIONLESS, ALL ENERGIES DEVOTED TO SOLVING THE MOST DESPERATE CRISIS OF HIS CAREER!

I DARE NOT *FAIL* HER! SHE MUST BE *FOUND*... AND *SAVED!*

BUT EVEN MY TOWERING SIZE...MY ALMOST LIMITLESS STRENGTH...ARE USELESS, UNLESS I CAN *FIND* HER! BUT *WHERE* DO I *START?*

OH, WASP, DEAR WASP, WHERE *IS* THY STING?*

*AND, FROM THESE MOST *POIGNANT* LINES IN COMIC-DOM, WE TAKE OUR STORY TITLE!

EVEN JAN'S FLYING *WASP* SEEMS TO SENSE THE SITUATION!

CAN SOME INTUITION BE TELLING HER SOMETHING IS WRONG?

WAIT! SHE'S DISPLAYING *MORE* THAN MERE INSECT INTUITION! SHE'S TRYING TO *TELL* ME SOMETHING!

OF *COURSE!* SHE CAN *LEAD* ME TO WHERE JAN IS!

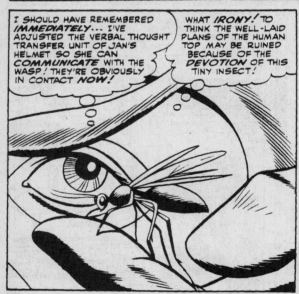

I SHOULD HAVE REMEMBERED *IMMEDIATELY*... I'VE ADJUSTED THE VERBAL THOUGHT TRANSFER UNIT OF JAN'S HELMET SO SHE CAN *COMMUNICATE* WITH THE WASP! THEY'RE OBVIOUSLY IN CONTACT *NOW!*

WHAT *IRONY!* TO THINK THE WELL-LAID PLANS OF THE HUMAN TOP MAY BE RUINED BECAUSE OF THE *DEVOTION* OF THIS TINY INSECT!

THE TOP SURPRISED ME BY *FLYING* AWAY! NOW I'LL SURPRISE *HIM* BY FLYING TO HIS LAIR...ON THE BACK OF JAN'S LOYAL PET!

ALL I NEED DO IS REDUCE MYSELF TO NORMAL SIZE...

4.

...AND THEN TRANSFER MY *GROWTH* POWER TO OUR LITTLE WINGED ALLY!

SHE'S *GROWING,* BUT SHE MUST GROW STILL *MORE!*

AND THERE'S A DREADFUL *RISK* IN THIS---

UNLESS THE WASP IS ABLE TO REALIZE WHAT I AM DOING, AND *WHY,* SHE MAY BECOME CONFUSED!

AND, IF HER SIMPLE BRAIN CANNOT UNDERSTAND THE URGENT *NEED* FOR THE SEVERE STRAIN I'M PUTTING UPON HER, SHE MAY *TURN* UPON ME WITH HER NOW-FATAL STING!

BUT, I HAVE TO *TAKE* THAT RISK, OR *ANY* RISK, IN ORDER TO SAVE JAN!

WITHOUT *HER,* MY LIFE IS *MEANINGLESS!*

NOTE: (FOR NATURE LOVERS)

THE STRESS OF GROWING MANY TIMES HER NORMAL SIZE, HAS INDEED CONFUSED THE INSECT'S BRAIN! UNABLE TO UNDERSTAND JAN'S WARNING MESSAGE, THE WASP CAN ONLY FOLLOW THE THOUGHT SIGNALS TO THEIR SOURCE!

ANDREW, *LOOK!* THAT HENRY PYM HAS GONE TOO *FAR!* EVER SINCE HE MOVED INTO THAT LAB, WE'VE SEEN NOTHING BUT ANTS AND WASPS! BUT, THIS IS *TOO* MUCH!

YOU'RE *RIGHT,* MILDRED! HOW CAN A MAN RELAX WITH GIANT FLYING *INSECTS* BUZZING BACK AND FORTH OUTSIDE HIS WINDOW?!

HONESTLY! YOU'D THINK A MAN HIS AGE WOULD HAVE *OUTGROWN* SUCH NONSENSE!

5

MEANWHILE, WITH JAN'S CYBERNETIC SIGNALS TO GUIDE HER, THE WASP MAKES A BEE LINE TO THE HUMAN TOP'S IMITATION VILLAGE! AND THEN...

THIS IS THE SECOND TIME WE'VE CIRCLED THIS SPOT!

JAN MUST BE HELD CAPTIVE *DIRECTLY* BELOW!

THIS IS THE *CRITICAL* MOMENT! THE GIANT INSECT IS CONFUSED-- BEWILDERED--!

AND *THAT* COULD LEAD TO BLIND RAGE...

--- I DON'T DARE DELAY ANY LONGER!

YOU'VE DONE YOUR JOB *WELL*, MY LOYAL PET!

BUT NOW, I MUST REDUCE YOU TO *NORMAL* SIZE!

AND ONCE AGAIN ASSUME THE SIZE AND THE *POWER* OF GIANT-MAN!

I MUST CONCENTRATE ON EXTENDING MY GROWTH *DOWNWARD* THIS TIME!

AND THEREBY BREAK MY FALL!

GOOD!

NOW TO APPROACH THAT VILLAGE WITH *CAUTION!* IF I MAKE *ONE* MISTAKE, IT COULD MEAN THE END FOR *JAN!*

6

I CAN'T ANTICIPATE WHAT *DANGER* AWAITS ME! I ONLY KNOW I'VE *GOT* TO SAVE JAN ...EVEN IF IT COSTS MY OWN *LIFE!*

AND, IF I DO *SUCCEED* IN RESCUING HER FROM THE TOP, I *VOW* I'LL *NEVER* PLACE HER IN SUCH JEOPARDY AGAIN!

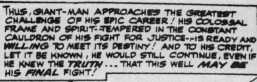

THUS, GIANT-MAN APPROACHES THE GREATEST CHALLENGE OF HIS EPIC CAREER! HIS COLOSSAL FRAME AND SPIRIT-TEMPERED IN THE CONSTANT CAULDRON OF HIS FIGHT FOR JUSTICE--IS READY AND WILLING TO MEET ITS DESTINY! AND TO HIS CREDIT, LET IT BE KNOWN, HE WOULD STILL CONTINUE, EVEN IF HE KNEW THE *TRUTH* ...THAT THIS WELL *MAY BE* HIS *FINAL* FIGHT!

I'M COMING, JAN ...MY DARLING!

I PRAY I'M NOT TOO LATE!

HOWEVER, GIANT-MAN WOULD BE DISMAYED TO LEARN THAT NOT ONLY THE *WASP* (AND OUR FEW MILLION READERS) KNOW HE'S COMING, BUT THE *HUMAN TOP* IS IN ON THE SECRET, TOO!

AHA! HE'S CROSSED MY LASER IMPULSE BEAM! IN FORTY SECONDS HE'LL START TO FEEL ITS EFFECT!

IF ONLY I COULD *WARN* HANK OF THE DANGER..! BUT ...HOW?

NOW I WILL ACTIVATE THE EQUIPMENT THAT HAS *ALREADY* BEEN PROGRAMMED TO GIVE ME *TOTAL MASTERY* OVER GIANT-MAN!

AND, WITH HIS *DEATH*, YOU AND THE ENTIRE *WORLD* WILL BE MY PAWNS!

I'VE GOT TO *STOP* HIM!

WATCH CLOSELY, MY HELPLESS BEAUTY! GIANT-MAN WILL SOON BE HOPELESSLY TRAPPED WITHIN MY PIT! THEN, THE *REAL FUN* WILL BEGIN!

NO! NO! YOU *CAN'T!* YOU *MUSTN'T!!*

GET *BACK*, YOU *FOOL!*

I'VE PLANNED EVERY DETAIL OF THIS MOMENT DOWN TO THE *SPLIT-SECOND!* IT CANNOT BE UPSET BY YOUR SILLY DISPLAY OF EMOTION!

BULLPEN NOTE: IF THE HUMAN TOP HAD *ANY* ADMIRERS AT ALL, HE HAS CERTAINLY *LOST* THEM BY THIS UNGALLANT BEHAVIOR!

7.

THEN, AS GIANT-MAN SURVEYS THE SITUATION, A SLOWLY DAWNING SUSPICION FILLS HIS MIND..AS HE REALIZES...

THERE'S SOMETHING *STRANGE* HERE...

I'M BEING SUBJECTED TO A *SUBTLE* ATTACK! I..I'M NOT AS *ALERT* AS I SHOULD BE... I FEEL *GROGGY*...

WAIT! I HEAR SOMETHING! LIKE A SPEEDING, SPINNING FORM.. COMING CLOSER.. CLOSER...

AHA! MY LASER IMPULSE BEAM SLOWED YOUR *REFLEXES!* YOU COULDN'T *DUCK* IN TIME!

AND NOW, IT'S *TOO LATE* FOR YOU! TOO LATE FOR *ANYTHING!*

THE AIR IS *SHATTERED* BY AN AWFUL SOUND OF LANDSLIDE PROPORTIONS, AS GIANT-MAN CRASHES THROUGH THE SHAM VILLAGE AND FALLS *HELPLESSLY* INTO THE ENORMOUS PIT BELOW!

HE'S DONE IT *AGAIN!* HE CAUGHT ME OFF GUARD!

AND YET...I'VE FALLEN INTO A *DOZEN* TRAPS LIKE THIS... AND SURVIVED THEM ALL!

WHY SHOULD *THIS* TIME BE ANY DIFFERENT?

I WAS *AFRAID* OF THIS! HERE COMES A HEAVY LID THAT'S DESIGNED TO ENCASE ME HERE *PERMANENTLY!* CAN'T BUDGE IT...IT'S HYDRAULICALLY ACTIVATED!

WELCOME, MY JOLLY GREENHORN GIANT! YOU ARE ABOUT TO BE *QUICK-FROZEN* INTO ETERNITY!

IT'S THE TOP! HE'S BEEN *WATCHING* ME! AND *JAN* IS WITH HIM!

NOW I'VE GOT TO BREAK OUT OF HERE!

8

TAKE A GOOD LOOK, WASP! IT'S A WIDE. SCREEN -- IN *LIVING COLOR*! WATCH WHILE I *FREEZE* YOUR BOY-FRIEND INTO A MASSIVE MONUMENT TO MY *SUPERIORITY*!

OH, NO! THIS CAN'T BE THE END! NOT LIKE *THIS*!

DON'T GIVE UP, DARLING! IT'S NOT OVER *YET*!

AWW, GIANT-MAN! WHAT AN EXIT LINE! CAN'T YOU FIND SOMETHING MORE *PROFOUND* THAN *THAT* TO SAY!?

JUST WAIT'LL I GET MY HANDS ON YOU..-YOU'LL *FIND OUT*!

WASP! OPEN THAT DOOR WHILE YOU CAN!

I'LL NOT ONLY *OPEN* IT, I'LL *USE* IT! WHATEVER THE *OUTCOME*, WE'LL SHARE IT TOGETHER!

COME *BACK*! IF YOU JOIN HIM, IT MEANS *YOUR* DOOM, TOO!

HOLD IT, FELLA! ONLY ONE CUSTOMER AT A TIME!

-OOF!!

NOW! IF I CAN REACH THAT CONTROL PANEL, I CAN GAIN *TIME*, AND PERHAPS EVEN UP THE ODDS!

CAREFUL, DARLING! HE HAS A WEAPON!

YOUR CLUMSY OVERSIZED HANDS ARE NO MATCH FOR THE *HUMAN TOP*!

≡ WHEW! ≡ I SNAPPED BACK MY FINGERS JUST IN TIME!

WHIRRRR!

AND, AS FOR *YOU*, WASP, YOU HAD YOUR CHANCE TO LIVE IN *GLORY* AS MY PARTNER! NOW, YOU SHALL DIE IN *IGNOMINY*... WITH HIM!

I'VE GOT LESS THAN *TWO* MINUTES TO THWART THE PLANS HE MUST HAVE BEEN MAKING FOR *MONTHS*!

THERE! I'VE THROWN THE SWITCH! WHAT A *PITY* THE REFRIGERATION UNIT WILL MAKE YOUR END COME SO *FAST*! I'D PREFER TO LINGER OVER THIS TRIUMPHANT MOMENT!

THAT SUDDEN *COLD*!! I'M *FREEZING*!

GO OUT LIKE A *REAL* SUPER-HERO, GIANT-MAN! KEEP CALM AND *COOL*!

QUICK, HONEY! REDUCE YOUR-SELF TO *WASP* SIZE!

9

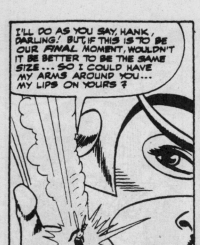

I'LL DO AS YOU SAY, HANK, DARLING! BUT, IF THIS IS TO BE OUR *FINAL* MOMENT, WOULDN'T IT BE BETTER TO BE THE SAME *SIZE*... SO I COULD HAVE MY ARMS AROUND YOU... MY LIPS ON YOURS?

THIS *WOULDN'T* BE THE END... IT *CAN'T* BE! HAVE FAITH, DARLING! *QUICK!* SLIP BENEATH MY COSTUME AND *TRUST* IN ME!

NOW, GIANT-MAN, I WILL SPRAY YOU WITH *WATER*, TO HASTEN THE FREEZING PROCESS!

HE HASN'T MISSED A TRICK!

I'LL BE FROZEN IN *SECONDS!*

WITHIN EVEN *LESS* TIME THAN GIANT-MAN THOUGHT, THE WATER AND FRIGID TEMPERATURES COMBINE TO TRANSFORM HIM INTO A GIGANTIC CAKE OF *ICE*, STANDING MOTIONLESS AND SILENT IN THE COLD, CRUEL CRYPT!

IT IS *DONE!*

NOW I'LL ENCASE THE FROZEN REMAINS IN *EPOXY* SO THAT THEY WILL STAND AS A SYMBOLIC STATUE TO THE BRILLIANCE AND THE *POWER* OF THE HUMAN TOP!

THUS, THE HEROIC FRAME OF GIANT-MAN IS HOISTED AND PLACED ABOVE THE GROUND AS A WARNING TO ALL WHO WOULD DEFY THE HUMAN TOP!

IF EVER ANY *OTHER* MISGUIDED CHAMPIONS OF JUSTICE ATTEMPT TO CURB MY AMBITIONS, THEY WILL SEE THEIR *OWN* FATE BEFORE THEM!

OH, C'MON NOW! YOU DON'T REALLY *BELIEVE* ALL THAT JAZZ, DO YOU?

GIANT-MAN!!

WELL, I'M NOT *PATSY WALKER!* NOW THAT I'M IN THE SMALL ECONOMY SIZE, LET'S FIGHT THIS OUT ON EQUAL *TERMS!* NO HIGH POCKETS FOR *ME*, NO ICE CUBES FOR *YOU!*

KA-RACK!

NOW? HOW DID YOU SURVIVE..? ≷UNNH!≶

10

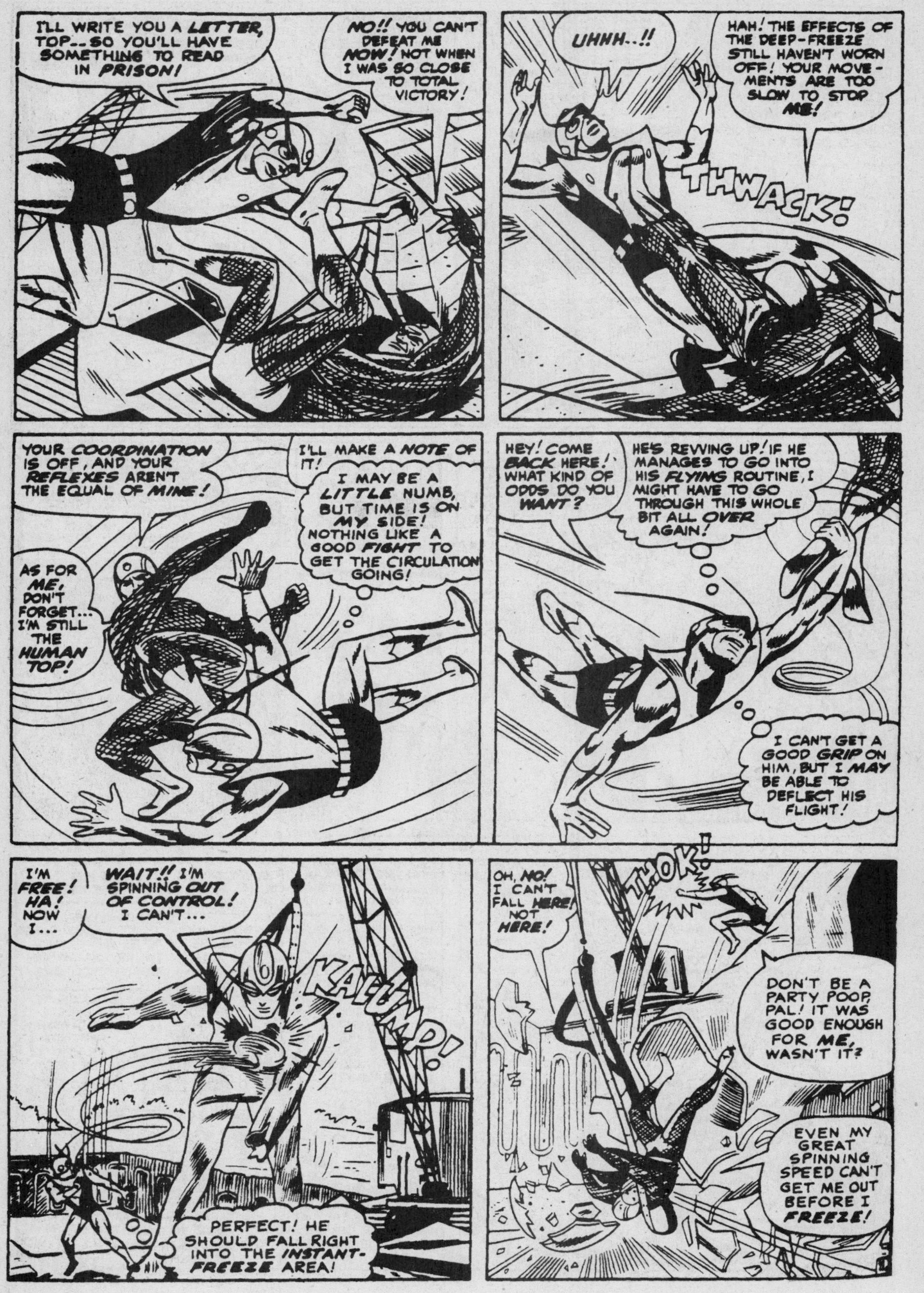
I'LL WRITE YOU A LETTER, TOP-- SO YOU'LL HAVE SOMETHING TO READ IN PRISON!
NO!! YOU CAN'T DEFEAT ME NOW! NOT WHEN I WAS SO CLOSE TO TOTAL VICTORY!
UHHH..!!
HAH! THE EFFECTS OF THE DEEP-FREEZE STILL HAVEN'T WORN OFF! YOUR MOVEMENTS ARE TOO SLOW TO STOP ME!
THWACK!
YOUR COORDINATION IS OFF, AND YOUR REFLEXES AREN'T THE EQUAL OF MINE!
AS FOR ME, DON'T FORGET... I'M STILL THE HUMAN TOP!
I'LL MAKE A NOTE OF IT!
I MAY BE A LITTLE NUMB, BUT TIME IS ON MY SIDE! NOTHING LIKE A GOOD FIGHT TO GET THE CIRCULATION GOING!
HEY! COME BACK HERE! WHAT KIND OF ODDS DO YOU WANT?
HE'S REVVING UP! IF HE MANAGES TO GO INTO HIS FLYING ROUTINE, I MIGHT HAVE TO GO THROUGH THIS WHOLE BIT ALL OVER AGAIN!
I CAN'T GET A GOOD GRIP ON HIM, BUT I MAY BE ABLE TO DEFLECT HIS FLIGHT!
I'M FREE! HA! NOW I...
WAIT!! I'M SPINNING OUT OF CONTROL! I CAN'T...
KA-LUMP!
PERFECT! HE SHOULD FALL RIGHT INTO THE INSTANT-FREEZE AREA!
OH, NO! I CAN'T FALL HERE! NOT HERE!
THOK!
DON'T BE A PARTY POOP, PAL! IT WAS GOOD ENOUGH FOR ME, WASN'T IT?
EVEN MY GREAT SPINNING SPEED CAN'T GET ME OUT BEFORE I FREEZE!

I WAS ONLY IN THE COLD CHAMBER FOR A SPLIT-SECOND, BUT I'M FROZEN STIFF! HOW COULD GIANT-MAN POSSIBLY SURVIVE DOWN THERE FOR SO MUCH LONGER WITH THE LID CLOSED?

LUCKY FOR THE HUMAN TOP HE GOT TANGLED IN THAT SLING! IF HE HAD BEEN DOWN THERE ANY LONGER, WE WOULD HAVE BROUGHT HIM OUT TOO LATE!

THERE YOU ARE, OFFICERS! HAVE YOU EVER SEEN A VILLAIN PUT ON ICE MORE NEATLY THAN THAT?

I CAN'T MOVE! THERE'S NO CHANCE TO SPIN AWAY!

CONGRATULATIONS, TOP! YOUR DEEP-FREEZE WORKS PERFECTLY... WHEN YOU REALLY GET INTO IT!

IF YOU'LL EXCUSE MY CHOICE OF WORDS... WELL, PUT HIM IN THE COOLER!

DARLING, YOU WERE WONDERFUL.... JUST WONDERFUL!

JUST A MINUTE, GIANT-MAN! I'D LIKE TO TALK TO YOU!

TELL ME, HOW WERE YOU ABLE TO ESCAPE BEING FROZEN DOWN THERE?

WELL, IT WAS REALLY VERY SIMPLE! I USED MY POWER OF MANY SIZES TO COMBAT THE TOP... HERE'S HOW!

"AS SOON AS THE ICE LAYER AROUND ME FROZE SOLID ENOUGH TO SUPPORT ITS OWN WEIGHT, I REDUCED DOWN TO INSECT SIZE AND SIMPLY CLIMBED INTO THE CAVITY OF ONE OF THE ICE HANDS!"

"THE WASP WAS ALSO INSECT-SIZE, AND TOGETHER WE HUDDLED WITHIN THE INSULATION OF THE ICE! SO, THE WEAPON THE HUMAN TOP DESIGNED SO CAREFULLY WAS ACTUALLY OUR PROTECTION!"

OH, HANK! SOMEHOW IT'S GOING TO BE VERY HARD FOR ME TO HATE THE HUMAN TOP AFTER THIS!

AND, AS THE MAN OF MANY SIZES RE-LIVES HIS AWESOME EXPERIENCE, HE RECALLS THE VOW HE MADE.. TO THE WASP... AND TO HIMSELF!

ANY MAN OF COURAGE IS WILLING TO FIGHT FOR RIGHT AND FOR THE WOMAN HE LOVES! BUT NO MAN HAS THE RIGHT TO LIVE SO DANGEROUSLY THAT THE WOMAN AT HIS SIDE IS CONSTANTLY IN PERIL! FROM THIS MOMENT ON, HONEY, I PROMISE YOU, THINGS WILL BE DIFFERENT!

DARLING, I DON'T WANT THINGS TO BE DIFFERENT! I'M PROUD OF YOU JUST AS YOU ARE!

SOUNDS TO ME LIKE GIANT-MAN IS GETTING READY TO RETIRE!

IS THIS REALLY HENRY PYM'S LAST ADVENTURE AS GIANT-MAN? ONLY HANK HIMSELF KNOWS THE MEANING OF HIS WORDS! BUT WE MIGHT JUST HAVE A LITTLE SURPRISE FOR YOU NEXT ISH! TRY US AND SEE!

THE END